"Chris Morgan is one of this generation's most trusted theologians. His work at California Baptist is known to many and is deeply respected throughout the evangelical world. This new work, *Christian Theology: The Biblical Story and Our Faith*, is a welcomed addition to the field of Systematic Theology. This work will well serve seminary students, Christian college students, ministers of the gospel, and even lay persons desiring to dig into their faith more deeply. I highly recommend this book."

—**Jason K. Allen**, president and professor of preaching and pastoral ministry, Midwestern Baptist Theological Seminary

"*Christian Theology* is a stunning accomplishment, unrivaled in many ways by other systematic theologies. It is a biblically faithful, lucidly written systematic theology expounded with consistent reference to the Bible's dramatic narrative. A brilliant piece of work that will be used in classrooms and studies for years to come. Highly recommended."

—**Bruce Riley Ashford**, dean of faculty, provost, and professor of theology and culture, Southeastern Baptist Theological Seminary

"How can I understand, explain, and live out my Christian faith? *Christian Theology*, by Christopher Morgan with Robert Peterson, wonderfully equips us to answer this question. This succinct and yet highly informed textbook is precise, practical, and a delight to read. No matter which is your denomination, tradition, or preferred school of thought—you will find unity, clarity, and perspective in this book."

—**Sam Chan**, cultural analyst, author, and public speaker, City Bible Forum, Australia

"Christopher Morgan knows theology both past and present, and how to express it in engaging accessible ways. He is a master teacher as this volume of Christian theology shows. He covers the traditional topics and does so in ways that are biblically grounded, informed by the flow of redemptive history, aware of the Christian past, and with a sharp eye on the relevance of the Word of God to life today and life together. Indeed, the last chapter is on the Christian life. Would that all works of theology show his faithfulness, deftness, carefulness, and concern for connection with real life. Outstanding!"

—**Graham A. Cole**, dean and professor of biblical and systematic theology, Trinity Evangelical Divinity School

"This important new work by Chris Morgan, written with Robert Peterson, is a splendid introductory theology textbook. Thoroughly biblical and orthodox, eminently readable, thoughtfully designed, and pastoral in its tone and approach, this volume will serve as a remarkable resource for college and seminary students. Each chapter seeks to bring clarity to areas that have often brought division to Christians. Readers will discover much in Christian Theology worthy of praise, including careful biblical exegesis, helpful biographical portraits, introductions to global thinkers, and thoughtful engagement at key points with the Christian tradition, always with an eye on the church. I gladly and heartily commend this excellent volume to Christian leaders, professors, students, and interested laypersons."

—**David S. Dockery**, theologian-in-residence,
Southwestern Baptist Theological Seminary, and president,
International Alliance for Christian Education

"*Christian Theology* is a rare jewel among one volume systematic theologies— doctrinally coherent, biblically grounded, historically aware, and shaped by the grand narrative of Scripture. Add to that its accessibility to lay readers and college and seminary students, and this is a text that should be not only on every pastor's and professor's shelf but their first recommendation to students and congregants alike. Evangelical Christians, and particularly Baptists, will find this volume to be a one-stop shop for learning and training in systematic theology."

—**Matthew Y. Emerson**, associate professor of religion and director, Master of Arts, Hobbs College of Theology and Ministry, Oklahoma Baptist University

"There has long been the need for a mid-sized systematic theology written with both undergraduate and graduate students in mind, and *Christian Theology: The Biblical Story and Our Faith* fills that need and more. Morgan is a seasoned theologian and devoted churchman, which is reflected in the way he frames theology as an edifying discipline that is meant to aid the believer in spiritual maturity. The strong emphasis on biblical theology is very helpful, and the inclusion of quotes from Christian history and theologians from the global church is a welcome contribution. This book will not only be widely adopted in undergraduate and graduate courses, but it will be the go-to theology resource for pastors and other ministry leaders."

—**Nathan Finn**, provost and dean of the university
faculty, North Greenville University

"This book tells a story—not just any story, but the true story of the one eternal God of holiness and love, his saving mission in Jesus Christ, and his still ongoing redemptive purpose. This is a primer of theology written with clarity, insight, and depth. I recommend it highly."

—**Timothy George**, founding dean and research professor
of divinity, Beeson Divinity School, Samford University

"*Christian Theology* provides a straightforward introduction to the major doctrines of the Christian faith. Morgan does a masterful job of introducing basic theology in a robust way that manages to remain warm, personal, and accessible from start to finish. The book shows how each doctrine flows out of the biblical story line, explains its significance, and demonstrates its practical value for the Christian life. I highly recommend it as a textbook for general theology courses and an excellent resource for the church."

—**Jason S. Hiles**, dean, College of Theology, Grand Canyon University

"This volume excels in explaining salvation in Christ as the heart of Christian doctrine. It rightly stresses the international scope of Christian confession by presenting global theological voices. College and seminary teachers will find it biblically orthodox and accessible to students."

—**Paul House**, professor of divinity, Beeson
Divinity School, Samford University

"The best systematic theologies grow in the rich soil of God's authoritative Word, keep the glorious gospel of the blessed triune God at the center, take shape in conversation with the Christian tradition, listen to voices of the past and (global) present, and clarify how theology is to be lived. Morgan has provided a wonderful work that both flows from decades of teaching students and possesses a humble and charitable tone that models Christian scholarship at its best. What a great gift this book is to the church—read and use it!"

—**Oren R. Martin**, assistant professor of Christian
theology and program coordinator for the Seminary track,
The Southern Baptist Theological Seminary

"Chris Morgan's systematic theology is concise, easy to understand, and edifying. He models how to do theology by rooting his conclusions in exegesis and biblical theology while considering historical theology and culminating in practical theology."

—**Andy Naselli**, associate professor of systematic theology
and New Testament, Bethlehem College & Seminary

"As an introductory text, *Christian Theology: The Biblical Story and Our Faith* is a remarkable achievement. Morgan gives students of theology a concise, readable survey of the major doctrinal themes of Scripture, but the brevity of the material never takes away from its substance. The close attention given to the biblical narrative is a welcome departure from some works in this genre that never seem to find their hermeneutical footing. Students, professors, and pastors will be greatly pleased with this resource."

—**Rhyne Putman**, associate professor of theology and
culture, New Orleans Baptist Theological Seminary

"Morgan has composed a theology text that wonderfully captures the biblical narrative. This insightful theological guide is accessible, refreshingly even-handed, and useful in a variety of learning environments. This text is truly a gift to the church."

—**Walter R. Strickland II**, assistant professor of systematic
and contextual theology and associate vice president for
diversity, Southeastern Baptist Theological Seminary

"In *Christian Theology*, Chris Morgan draws from decades of study, teaching, and life as a disciple of Jesus, and offers a rich exploration of biblically grounded, historically informed, and practically helpful Christian doctrine. This book is refreshingly accessible yet edifyingly deep and would be helpful in undergraduate, graduate, or local church training. I hope that this book is widely read and highly influential because it will provide much needed theological ballast for the church in our day."

—**Erik Thoennes**, professor and chair of theology, Talbot School of Theology, Biola University, and pastor, Grace Evangelical Free Church of La Mirada

"Systematic theology often gets a bad rap for being speculative and divisive ('doctrine divides!'). *Christian Theology* dispels that caricature by grounding the system in the story of Scripture and by focusing on doctrines that unite Christians everywhere and at all times: 'one Lord, one faith, one baptism' (Eph 4:5). Chris Morgan is an experienced teacher, logging hundreds of hours in college and seminary classrooms. It shows: the biblical storyline from creation to consummation frames his treatment of each doctrine, even as he shows how each doctrine facilitates readers' understanding of the biblical story. Each chapter includes practical objectives and other helps that contribute to the book's aim: to help believers grow in the knowledge and love of God and to live lives that serve God and others for their good and his glory."

—**Kevin J. Vanhoozer**, research professor of systematic theology, Trinity Evangelical Divinity School

"In a day when the church desperately needs sound and faithful biblical and theological thinking that impacts our lives, there is no better place to start than *Christian Theology*. Written as a clear, accessible, and basic introduction to Christian theology this book admirably succeeds in its aim. Helping Christians think through the Bible's story line, working from biblical texts to theological conclusions, and always with the goal of knowing our glorious triune God in the face of our Lord Jesus Christ, this work will feed both mind and heart, and greatly help the church recover her calling to know and love God. I highly recommend this work for pastors, church leaders, and all Christians who want to think faithfully and deeply about God's Word and its application to their lives."

—**Stephen J. Wellum**, professor of Christian theology, The Southern Baptist Theological Seminary

"*Wonderful* describes this book—wonderful in clarity, comprehensiveness, conciseness, and charity toward a full range of valid Christian views. It models an expositional theological method which highlights Scripture's teaching as it unfolds through the Bible's story line. This will become a go-to textbook for learning and living out true Christian faith."

—**Robert W. Yarbrough**, professor of New Testament, Covenant Theological Seminary

CHRISTIAN
THEOLOGY

CHRISTIAN THEOLOGY

THE BIBLICAL STORY AND OUR FAITH

CHRISTOPHER W. MORGAN

WITH ROBERT A. PETERSON

ACADEMIC
NASHVILLE, TENNESSEE

To Shelley and Chelsey:
I am blessed beyond measure to be your husband and daddy.
—Chris

To Mary Pat, my faithful wife and the love of my life.
To Rob, Matt, Curtis, and David, four caring sons,
and Julie, a great daughter-in-law.
Also, to Noble and Blake, two awesome grandsons.
—Robert

CONTENTS

ACKNOWLEDGMENTS

Many of God's richest blessings are the people he has placed in our lives. There are too many to mention all of them by name, but I (Chris) want to express gratitude to those who have impacted this project:

Dr. Robert Peterson, for your collaboration, theological insight, and terrific research and writing assistance.

Dr. Tony Chute and Dr. Greg Cochran, for sharing life, ministry, leadership, administration, and theology together, and for offering helpful comments on this volume.

Dr. Ron Ellis, Dr. Chuck Sands, Kent Dacus, the trustees, and the administration at California Baptist University, for your vision and support.

Gary McDonald, for joyfully participating in life together and excelling in grace and generosity.

SoCal Baptist Ministries and the Baptist Foundation of California, for your wonderful generosity and support.

Dr. Milton Higgins, for your friendship, warm love, consistent prayers, and faithful generosity.

CBU's School of Christian Ministries' faculty, for your friendship and your resolve to exalt the Lord, serve churches, and invest in students.

Maigen Turner, for your positive attitude, skillful work, and eagerness to help.

Students at California Baptist University, for your desire to grow in God's Word to serve Christ's church.

Elliott Pinegar, for your quality editorial help.

Jim Baird, Chris Thompson, Sarah Landers, Audrey Greeson, Jessi Wallace, and the whole B&H team, for your creativity, encouragement, service, and commitment to serve the church.

INTRODUCTION

This volume seeks to serve as an accessible textbook for general theology courses. Chris, an experienced university professor (who has taught related courses more than sixty times for more than twenty years), worked in conjunction with Robert, who served as a seminary theology professor for thirty-five years. As a theology textbook, this work treats the major doctrines of the Christian faith: knowing God, revelation, the Trinity, God's attributes and works, humanity, sin, Christ, the work of Christ, salvation, the Holy Spirit, the church, and last things.

This volume also shows how the standard topics and their order flow from the biblical story line of creation, fall, redemption, and new creation. It frames doctrines in light of the biblical story, substantial biblical exegesis, and biblical theology.

The book is geared for believers and focuses on application throughout. It relates the doctrines to Christians' identity and mission, and underlines how the biblical story and all of us exist for the glory of God. It concludes with a chapter on how the Christian faith drives the Christian life.

This work is evangelical, written with a high view of Scripture and consistent with historic confessions of faith. It focuses on what is clear and agreed upon, longing to unite believers around our common beliefs and to avoid the temptation to highlight and defend individual particularities. The structure is personal. For example, instead of the heading

"Regeneration," it uses "We Are Alive in Christ," then treats regeneration in the paragraphs that follow.

Each chapter unfolds this way: introduction, objectives, outline, the doctrine in the biblical story, the doctrine in selected passages, and the overall theological treatment of the doctrine, concluding with key terms and suggestions for further reading. One special feature deserves mention. We, the writers, include "voices" in our systematic theology, both voices from church history and voices from the global church, to highlight our desire to study theology in community with the whole people of God.

We invite readers to join us as we explore the rich teachings of God's Word. We pray that God will change us as he teaches us his story, character, deeds, and will. "For from him and through him and to him are all things. To him be the glory forever. Amen" (Rom 11:36).

1

KNOWING
GOD

"This wondrous knowledge is beyond me. It is
lofty; I am unable to reach it." (Ps 139:6)

"God, how precious your thoughts are to
me; how vast their sum is!" (v. 17)

In Psalm 139, David contemplates the infinity of God. God's infinity
somehow does not result in his being distant from us, but intimately
close. God searches us and knows us completely. He knows us when we
wake up, when we go to sleep, and every place in between. He understands our very thoughts. He watches all our steps and knows what we
are about to say before we say it. God is beyond us, yet around us, with
us. God is present with us, no matter where we are. He is present with
us in heaven, and he is present in the grave/Sheol. He is with us when we
live in the West and when we live in the East. He is there when it is light
and when it is dark. God intricately creates us, paying attention to every
feature. God knows us while we are in our mother's womb and plans our
days "before a single one of them [begins]" (v. 16).

Interestingly, David's knowledge of God's infinity leads David not to despair but to humility and hope. God's thoughts are beyond our ability to track, and his ways are above ours. So David humbly cries out to God for wisdom. David knows that he will never know God completely. But God knows him, and he knows God. So even when his enemies oppose him, David finds hope in God as his ever-present covenant Lord.

Further, recognizing his limited ability to grasp God's infinity does not keep David from singing about what he does know. Indeed, what he *does* know about God is foundational to his emphasis on what he does *not* know. It is his genuine knowledge of the truth about God that drives David to confess that he cannot fully comprehend God. David knows God truly but cannot know him exhaustively. And this leads to faith. God is the infinite Creator, and we are his finite creatures. God is holy, and we are sinners. Yet God graciously stoops to communicate with us; and, even more graciously, God loves us and sends his Son to save us. Through faith in Christ, we are saved and become his people. As with David, God knows us, and we know God. So, like David, we rightly feel the burden of our finiteness and realize that we will never plumb the depths of God. And like David, we simultaneously strive to know as much as we possibly can about our covenant Lord.

That is what this book is about: knowing God through the biblical story and recognizing the key teachings of the Christian faith that flow from that story. Our title is *Christian Theology: The Biblical Story and Our Faith*; it reflects that this volume is a *systematic theology*, a study of God that strives to summarize and synthesize the doctrines (teachings) of the Christian faith. As we will develop later, this means that we study biblical passages and themes, church history, and insights from general revelation to work toward theological syntheses. We view the various doctrines in light of the biblical story line: creation, fall, redemption, and new creation. We introduce key truths of the Christian faith: God, his revelation of himself, humanity, sin, Jesus, Jesus's saving work, salvation, the Holy Spirit, the church, and the future. Along the way, we will increasingly know more about God, ourselves, and how God shapes our identity and mission—all for our good and his glory.

▨ OBJECTIVES

- To study theology with a biblical approach
- To study theology to know God better
- To articulate the biblical story
- To understand how the biblical story shapes the topics of theology
- To understand how the biblical story shapes the content of theology
- To use sound theological methodology

▨ OUTLINE

Knowing God and Our Posture in Theology
Knowing God and the Biblical Story
    Creation
    Fall
    Redemption
    Consummation
Knowing God, the Biblical Story, and Our Theology
    God, His Revelation, and Our Theology
    Creation and Our Theology
    Humanity and Our Theology
    Sin and Our Theology
    Christ and Our Theology
    Salvation and Our Theology
    The Holy Spirit and Our Theology
    The Church and Our Theology
    The Future and Our Theology
Knowing God and Our Sources in Theology
    Scripture
    Tradition
    Reason
    Experience
Knowing God and Our Process in Theology
    Biblical Exegesis

Knowing God and Our Posture in Theology

Voices from Church History: Augustine of Hippo

Augustine (354–430) was the prominent theologian of the early church, famous for his personal *Confessions* and magisterial *The City of God.* Luther and Calvin looked to him as a father of the Reformation because of his teachings on salvation and grace. He wrote of God in the opening of the *Confessions*, "You give us delight in praising you, because you have made us for yourself and our hearts are restless until they find their rest in you."[1]

How do we as Christians approach the study of God and his Word?

Psalm 119 is a helpful guide. This psalm is a prayer addressed to God and is Scripture's most focused meditation on itself.[2] It is an acrostic, with units of eight verses all beginning with successive letters of the Hebrew alphabet, from *aleph* to *taw* (like *A* to *Z*). Throughout, the psalm uses eight major terms to refer to Scripture, each teaching us much about its nature, authority, and effects: *instruction* (or *law*), *word, decrees, precepts, statutes, promises, commands,* and *judgments.*

The psalm ascribes many attributes to God's Word: it is "righteous" (v. 7), "good" (v. 39), "just" (v. 75), "true" (v. 86), and "pure" (v. 140). Verses

---

[1] Philip Schaff, ed., *The Confessions and Letters of St. Augustin with a Sketch of His Life and Work*, vol. 1, A Select Library of the Nicene and Post-Nicene Fathers of the Christian Church (Buffalo, NY: Christian Literature Company, 1886), 1.

[2] In this section we were helped by Derek Kidner, *Psalms 73–150*, Tyndale Old Testament Commentaries (Downers Grove, IL: InterVarsity, 1973), 416–29.

137–38 ascribe the same attribute to God's Word that they do to God: "You are *righteous*, LORD. . . . The decrees you issue are *righteous*." The psalm assigns other attributes to God's Word as well: it is enduring (v. 89), reliable (v. 91), "wondrous" (v. 129), and "trustworthy" (v. 138).

God's Word has numerous powerful effects on us as we read it in faith. God uses his Word to produce reverence for him (v. 38), to purify (vv. 9–11), to strengthen (v. 28), to comfort (v. 52), and to give life (vv. 93), hope (v. 49), discernment (v. 66), wisdom (vv. 98–100), understanding (v. 104), and guidance (v. 105).

God's Word also stimulates many healthy responses in us. The Word engenders attitudes in us toward itself: longing (vv. 40, 131), delight (vv. 16, 24), love (vv. 47, 97), and fear (vv. 120, 161). It also elicits our meditation (vv. 15, 48), obedience (vv. 4–5), joy (vv. 1–2) and rejoicing (vv. 14, 162), hope (vv. 43, 74), and gratitude to God (v. 62).

As the psalm teaches us much about God's Word, it simultaneously offers us guidance in studying God and his Word. We study as *humble listeners* who receive God's instruction: "LORD, . . . teach me your statues" (v. 12). We study theology as *diligent seekers*, seeking the Lord and his commands with all our hearts (vv. 2, 10). We study as *faithful servants* who accept his authority, follow his will, and heed his counsel (vv. 17, 23–24). We study theology as *tested travelers* facing opposition as sojourners in a hostile world who desperately need wisdom from the Word (vv. 19–24). We study theology as *joyful worshippers*: "My lips pour out praise, for you teach me your statutes. My tongue sings about your promise, for all your commands are righteous" (vv. 171–72). Psalm 119 thus compels us to study theology as *whole persons*, integrating our minds with our hearts, our ways, our lips, and our feet.

For the psalmist, this means that the study of God and his Word is linked to our lives.[3] We study theology with *love*: love for the Lord, his Word, and his ways (vv. 41–48, 97). We study theology with *holiness*,

---

[3] In this section, we were helped by Martin Luther, "Preface to the Wittenberg Edition of Luther's German Writings," in *Martin Luther's Basic Theological Writings*, ed. Timothy F. Lull (Minneapolis: Fortress, 1989), 63–68; and Wayne Grudem, *Systematic Theology* (Grand Rapids: Zondervan, 1994), 32–37.

walking according to God's Word, keeping his commands (vv. 1–8). We study theology with *prayer*, knowing we need God to help us understand his Word: "Open my eyes so that I may contemplate wondrous things from your instruction" (v. 18); "Give me understanding according to your word" (v. 169). We study theology with *meditation*, giving careful thought to God and his ways: "I will meditate on your precepts and think about your ways" (v. 15). We study theology amid *trials*, which, as Martin Luther observes, "teach [us] not only to know and understand, but also to experience how right, how true, how sweet, how lovely, how mighty, how comforting God's Word is, wisdom beyond all wisdoms."[4]

We study theology with *conviction*, knowing that God's Word and teachings are true, even when governments, teachers, or societies try to shame us (vv. 22–24, 41–46, 99–100). We study theology with *diligence*, reading, searching, and thinking hard about the Word (vv. 94–95). We study theology with *delight*: "Your statutes are the theme of my song" (v. 54); "Your instruction is my delight" (v. 77). We study theology with *reverence*, reading, thinking, and analyzing as we stand in awe of God (v. 120). We study theology with *tears*, grieved that we and others do not fully prize God or his Word: "My eyes pour out streams of tears because people do not follow your instruction" (v. 136).

We study theology with *humility*, acknowledging our insufficiency for the task and relying on God's ability to help us: "Teach me, LORD" (v. 33); "Help me understand" (v. 34); "Help me stay on the path of your commands" (v. 35).[5] We study theology with *hope*, knowing that God has spoken in his Word, that he loves to give us understanding through his Word, and that he has already taught us much truth through his abiding Word: "LORD, your word is forever; it is firmly fixed in heaven" (v. 89). We study theology *in community*, knowing that we learn directly from God's Word and indirectly through one another (vv. 63, 74, 79).

---

[4] Luther, "Preface," in *Martin Luther's Basic Theological Writings*, 66–67. Luther focuses on prayer, meditation, and trials in his essay.

[5] Luther adds, "The longer you write and teach the less you will be pleased with yourself. When you have reached this point, then do not be afraid to hope that you have begun to become a real theologian." Luther, "Preface," 67.

Knowing God and the Biblical Story[6]

Creation

"In the beginning God created the heavens and the earth" (Gen 1:1). Already in existence before matter, space, or time, the eternal, self-existent God creates the universe and all that exists. Bruce Waltke introduces Gen 1:1–2:3: "The creation account is a highly sophisticated presentation, designed to emphasize the sublimity (power, majesty, and wisdom) of the Creator God and to lay the foundation for the worldview of the covenant community."[7]

As the chief character in Genesis 1, God "creates, says, sees, separates, names, makes, appoints, blesses, finishes, makes holy, and rests."[8] God is not the sky, sun, moon, water, trees, animals, or anything else created; God creates them, and they are subject to him. The creation is neither God nor a part of God; he is absolute and has independent existence, whereas creation has derived existence from him and continually depends on him as its sustainer (see Acts 17:25–28).

The Creator, who is above and beyond everything (transcendent), is sovereign and has amazing authority and power. Like a king, he effects his will by his very word, bringing things into being out of nothing (Gen 1:3; Heb 11:3). He further displays his authority over all creation by calling and naming the elements (Gen 1:5).

The transcendent, sovereign Creator is also personal. On each day of creation God is personally involved in every detail, crafting his world in a way that pleases him and benefits his creatures. In dramatic fashion, on the sixth day he personally creates man in his own image, breathing life into him. The personal God has made humans personal as well, with the

---

[6] For a thorough treatment of how the biblical story frames theology, see D. A. Carson, *The Gagging of God: Christianity Confronts Pluralism* (Grand Rapids: Zondervan, 1996), 193–345.

[7] Bruce K. Waltke, *Genesis: A Commentary* (Grand Rapids: Zondervan, 2001), 56.

[8] C. John Collins, *Genesis 1–4: A Linguistic, Literary, and Theological Commentary* (Phillipsburg, NJ: P&R, 2006), 71.

ability to relate to him, live in community, and have dominion over creation. As D. A. Carson reminds us, "We are accorded an astonishing dignity," and "there is implanted within us a profound capacity for knowing God intimately."[9] By making us in his image, God distinguishes us from the rest of creation and establishes that he is distinct from us—we are not gods, but creatures made in the Creator's image.

God is also good, which is reflected in the goodness of his creation and reinforced in the steady refrain, "And God saw that it was good" (Gen 1:10, 12, 18, 21, 25; see also v. 4). On the sixth day creation is even described as "very good" (v. 31). The inherent goodness of creation leaves no room for a fundamental dualism between spirit and matter, such that spirit is good and matter is bad. Indeed, material creation reflects God's goodness, which is also evident in his generous provision of light, land, vegetation, animals, and creeping, crawling things. These are blessings given for humanity's benefit, as are the ability to relate to God, fertility to procreate, and authority to use the earth's abundant provisions for humanity's good. Although creation reaches its summit in God's creating man in his image, Gen 1:1–2:3 culminates in the rest of God. By the seventh day God finishes his creative work, rests, and blesses and sanctifies the day as holy, as a Sabbath to be kept. In doing so, God displays his joy and satisfaction in his creation and his celebration of completion, and he commemorates this special event.[10]

God provides the garden of Eden as a place in which man and woman may live and work.[11] God "forms the man, plants the garden, transports man there, sets up the terms of a relationship with man, and searches for a helper fit for the man, which culminates in the woman."[12] Man is formed from the dust of the ground but is more than dust; his life comes directly from the very breath of God (2:7). In planting the garden and moving man there, the Creator and covenant Lord provides a delightful and sacred

---

[9] Carson, *The Gagging of God*, 205.

[10] Allen P. Ross, *Creation and Blessing: A Guide to the Study and Exposition of Genesis* (Grand Rapids: Baker, 1996), 114.

[11] Collins, *Genesis 1–4*, 39, 101.

[12] Collins, 132.

space in which humans can enjoy a harmonious relationship with him, each other, the animals, and the land. Waltke observes, "The Garden of Eden is a temple-garden, represented later in the tabernacle."[13] As such, the garden highlights God's presence with humans.

So, God creates Adam and Eve in his image as good and with wonderful privileges and significant responsibilities in the garden of Eden. They experience an unhindered relationship with God, intimate enjoyment of each other, and delegated authority over creation. God establishes the terms for living in his presence and graciously puts forward only one prohibition: they must not eat of the tree of the knowledge of good and evil.

Fall

Sadly, Adam and Eve do not obey God's command but fall (Genesis 3). This account begins with a tempter who calls into question God's truthfulness, sovereignty, and goodness. The tempter is "cunning" and deflects the woman's attention from the covenantal relationship God has established. In verses 6–8, the central scene in the story of the fall reaches its climax. The fatal sequence is described rapidly in 3:6: she saw, she took, she ate, and she gave, culminating in "he ate." Wenham observes that the midpoint of verses 6–8, "and he ate," employs the key verb of the narrative—"eat"— and is placed between the woman's inflated expectations in eating (the fruit is good to eat, is a delight to the eyes, and gives insight) and its actual effects: the man's and woman's eyes are opened, they know they are nude, and they hide among the trees.[14] The contrast is striking: the forbidden fruit does not deliver what the tempter has promised but brings dark new realities warned about by the good and truthful covenant Lord.

This initial act of human rebellion brings divine justice: "They sinned by eating, and so would suffer to eat; she led her husband to sin, and so would be mastered by him; they brought pain into the world by their

---

[13] Waltke, *Genesis*, 85.

[14] Gordon J. Wenham, *Genesis 1–15*, Word Biblical Commentary (Waco, TX: Word, 1987), 75.

disobedience, and so would have painful toil in their respective lives."[15] The consequences of their sin are fitting and devastating. The couple immediately feels shame, realizing they are naked (3:7). They sense their estrangement from God, even foolishly trying to hide from him (vv. 8–10). They are afraid of God and how he might respond (vv. 9–10). Their alienation from each other also emerges as the woman blames the serpent, while the man blames the woman and, by intimation, even God (vv. 10–13). Pain and sorrow also ensue. The woman experiences greater pain in childbirth; the man toils in trying to grow food in a land with pests and weeds; and both discover dissonance in their relationship (vv. 15–19). Even worse, the couple is banished from Eden and from God's glorious presence (vv. 22–24).

How they wish they had listened to God's warning: if you eat of the tree of the knowledge of good and evil, "you will certainly die" (2:17). Upon eating the forbidden fruit, they do not immediately fall over and die from something like cardiac arrest. But they do die. They die spiritually, and their bodies also begin to experience the gradual decay that leads ultimately to their physical deaths (3:19).

Most devastating is that these consequences do not only befall Adam and Eve but extend to their descendants as well. Sin enters the picture and brings disruption and alienation in each human relationship—with God, oneself, one another, and creation. The immediate context and story line of Genesis 4–11 underline this gloomy new reality. In 4:7, God warns Cain that sin is "crouching at the door" and that its "desire is for [him], but [he] must rule over it." Sadly, Cain refuses to heed the advice and kills his brother Abel. Cain is consequently cursed by God, alienated from the ground, and banished from God's presence (vv. 10–16).

Genesis 5 reminds us that God creates humans in his image and blesses them; the chapter offers hope through mention of Enoch and Noah but soberly underlines the domain of death with the refrain "then he died" eight times. Genesis 6 clarifies the extension and intensification of sin, which is portrayed as massive, pervasive, continual, and characteristic (vv. 5–11). God graciously establishes a covenant with Noah and

---

[15] Ross, *Creation and Blessing*, 148.

appropriately judges humanity with the flood (Genesis 6–9). After the flood God reemphasizes the creational blessing and mandate and offers a covenant promise (9:1–17). Genesis then recounts the history of the Tower of Babel, at which God judges proud, self-seeking humans who attempt to make a name for themselves and to multiply their influence rather than serving as God's image bearers and advancing his name (11:1–9).

Redemption

Thankfully, God does not completely eradicate humanity for such cosmic treason but graciously begins a restoration project instead. He starts the process of restoring humanity and the cosmos, particularly restoring humans as full image bearers so that we can participate in and reflect the glory, identity, and mission that we long for the whole time.

God calls Abraham from a family of idol worshippers and enters into a covenant with him, promising to be God to him and his descendants (Gen 12:1–3; 17:7). God promises to give Abraham a land, to make him into a great nation, and through him to bless all peoples (12:3). From Abraham come Isaac and later Jacob, whose name God changes to Israel and from whom God brings twelve tribes of his people. The rest of the Old Testament concerns God's dealings with the twelve tribes of Israel.

Through Moses, great plagues, and a dramatic exodus, God calls Israel out of Egyptian bondage to be his people. He gives them the Ten Commandments, promises to be their God, and claims them as his people. He promises to be with them and gives them the Promised Land, which they occupy under Joshua's leadership after defeating the Canaanites.

After Joshua dies, judges such as Gideon, Deborah, and Samson become leaders of the people.[16] History repeats itself as generation after generation experiences peace, then rebels, then receives God's judgment, then cries out to God, and then experiences peace once again.

God gives his people a human king—first Saul, then David, then Solomon. Under David, a man after God's own heart, the kingdom grows

---

[16] Preben Vang and Terry G. Carter, *Telling God's Story: The Biblical Narrative from Beginning to End*, 2nd ed. (Nashville: B&H Academic, 2013), 1–9.

significantly, Jerusalem becomes the capital, and God renews his covenant promise with his people. God promises to make David's descendants into a dynasty and to establish the throne of one of them forever.
God uses David's son Solomon to build a temple, where God's covenant
presence is manifest. Solomon does much right but also disobeys God
in major ways, and this leads to the kingdom splitting into northern and
southern kingdoms (Israel and Judah).

God sends many prophets to call the people to covenant faithfulness.
They warn his people of the judgment that will come if they do not repent
of their sins and turn to the Lord. Nevertheless, the people repeatedly
rebel against him and his prophets. In response he sends the northern
kingdom of ten tribes into captivity in Assyria in 722 BC and the southern
kingdom of two tribes, Judah and Benjamin, into captivity in Babylon in
586 BC. Through the prophets God also promises to send a Deliverer (Isa
9:6–7; 52:13–53:12).

God promises to restore his people to their land from Babylonian captivity after seventy years (Jer 25:11–12), and he brings this about under
Ezra and Nehemiah. The people rebuild the walls of Jerusalem and build a
second temple. Yet the Old Testament ends with God's people continuing
to turn away from him (Malachi).

After four hundred years God sends his Son as the promised Messiah,
Suffering Servant, King of Israel, and Savior of the world. The Son of God
is conceived of a virgin and becomes fully human while remaining fully
divine. In time, Jesus is baptized, successfully defeats Satan's temptation
in the wilderness, and is declared to be the Messiah. Jesus chooses and
invests in twelve disciples as new leaders of his messianic community. He
teaches about the kingdom of God, that God's rule has come in Jesus the
Messiah. Jesus displays this by casting out demons, performing miracles,
and preaching the good news to the poor. Jesus completely follows the
will and plan of God, remaining without sin. He is loved by many but is
opposed by Jewish religious and political leaders. Not only does he not
fit their conception of a messiah, he also undercuts their pride, beliefs,
and traditions. The opposition increases as the Jewish Sanhedrin condemns Jesus in an illegal trial. Since the nation is occupied by the Roman
Empire, the leaders must send Jesus to their staunch enemy, Pontius

Pilate, who finds Jesus innocent. Under pressure from the Jewish leaders and crowds, however, Pilate crucifies Jesus anyway. Jesus the innocent One, the righteous One, dies on a cross. From a human vantage point, Jesus dies as a victim in this despicably evil act. Yet the biblical story highlights that this death is part of God's eternal plan to save sinners. Jesus's mission is to seek and save the lost, and he does not fail to do so. Jesus saves sinners as their substitute, victor, sacrifice, new Adam, Redeemer, and peacemaker.

Incredibly, Jesus not only bears the sin of the world on the cross but also is raised from the dead three days later. In a variety of places, situations, and group settings, more than 500 people witness the resurrected Jesus. Through his resurrection he confirms his identity, defeats sin and death, gives new life to his people, and provides a foretaste of his people's future resurrection.

Jesus directs his disciples to take the gospel to all nations to fulfill God's promise to Abraham to bless all peoples through him. His disciples are to make disciples of others, who will then make disciples of still others. On the day of Pentecost, Jesus sends his Spirit, who forms the church as the New Testament people of God. The Spirit empowers the church to bear witness to Christ among the nations.

The early church "devote[s] [itself] to the apostles' teaching, to the fellowship, to the breaking of bread, and to prayer" (Acts 2:42). The early church is involved in evangelism (vv. 38–41), sharing the gospel with those who do not know Christ as the means of salvation. The church is committed to discipleship, instructing believers in how to follow Jesus as a way of life. The church is devoted to fellowship (vv. 42–47), sharing life together, knowing one another, loving one another. The church is also involved in ministry (vv. 42–46), praying for one another, giving to one another, meeting each other's needs. The church is active in worship (v. 46), praising God, publicly meeting together, and privately teaching, praying, giving, and partaking of food together. The church grows and faces persecution, but the gospel keeps spreading. Some Jews and many Gentiles trust Christ, churches are planted, and the cycle continues. Along the way, the churches teach sound doctrine, correct error, and call believers to live in love, unity, holiness, and truth.

Apostles such as Paul and Peter also teach about salvation. God the Father plans salvation; the Son accomplishes it; and the Spirit applies it to all who believe in Christ. God chooses, calls, and gives new life in Christ to believers. God forgives, declares righteous, and adopts into his family all who have faith in Christ. God is making his people holy in Christ and will finally glorify all who know him. God saves out of his generous love and for his glory.

Consummation

Jesus will finish what he has started. He will return to reign as King, bringing justice, peace, delight, and victory. The kingdom is God's reign over his people through King Jesus. The kingdom is both a present reality and a future promise tied to Christ's second coming. Jesus brings it in phases. It is inaugurated in his public ministry as he teaches, performs miracles, and casts out demons (Matt 12:28; 13:1–50). When Jesus ascends to God's right hand, the place of greatest power, the kingdom expands (Eph 1:20–21) and thousands enter it through the apostles' preaching (Acts 2:41, 47). The fullness of the kingdom awaits Christ's return, when he will sit on his glorious throne (Matt 25:31). Jesus will judge the world, inviting believers into the final stage of the kingdom while banishing unbelievers to hell (25:34, 41).

The classic passage depicting the consummation and these related truths is Revelation 20–22. Just as Genesis 1–2 reveals that the biblical story begins with God's creation of the heavens and the earth, Revelation 20–22 shows that it ends with God's creation of a new heaven and a new earth. The story begins with the goodness of creation and ends with the goodness of the new creation. The story begins with God dwelling with his people in a garden-temple and ends with God dwelling with his covenant people in heaven, a new earth-city-garden-temple.

Once and for all, God's victory is consummated. God's judgment is final, sin is vanquished, justice prevails, holiness dominates, God's glory is unobstructed, and the kingdom is realized. God's eternal plan of cosmic reconciliation in Christ is actualized, and God is "all in all."

As a part of his victory, God casts the devil and his demons into the lake of fire, where they are not consumed but "tormented day and night forever and ever" (20:10). Satan and the demons are not restored but go to hell to receive their due punishment, and they remain there to suffer forever. Then God judges everyone: those whom the world deems important, those whom the world never notices, and everyone in between. "Anyone whose name [is] not found written in the book of life [is] thrown into the lake of fire" (v. 15). God does not send only the ruthless Roman emperors to hell (which we might expect); he consigns to hell all who are not the people of Jesus (see Dan 12:1; Rev 14:10–11; 21:8, 27).

Magnificently, the new heavens and new earth arrive and God dwells with his covenant people (Rev 21:3, 7), brings comfort to them (no more pain, death, etc., in v. 4), makes all things new (v. 5), and proclaims, "It is done!" (v. 6). Heaven is then depicted as a perfect temple, glorious, multinational, and holy (vv. 9–27). The people of God rightly bear God's image: serving him, reigning with him, encountering him directly, and worshipping him (22:1–5). God receives the worship he is due, and humans are blessed beyond description, finally living to the fullest the realities of being created in his image.[17]

Knowing God, the Biblical Story, and Our Theology

The biblical story shapes and frames our topics in theology.[18] Creation, fall, redemption, and consummation frame the order and topics of theology, which are essentially extensions of those themes: God, creation and humanity, sin, Jesus and his saving work, the Holy Spirit's application of Christ's work to our salvation and the church, and the future.

The biblical story also shapes and frames the content of our theology. Thus, we strive to interpret the Bible and develop our theology in

---

[17] For a more thorough overview of the biblical story, framed with the doctrine of God, see D. A. Carson, *The God Who Is There: Finding Your Place in God's Story* (Grand Rapids: Baker, 2010).

[18] For more on studying God and related issues of epistemology, philosophy, method, language, and culture, see Millard J. Erickson, *Christian Theology*, 2nd ed. (Grand Rapids: Baker, 1998), 17–174.

accordance with and under the guidance of the biblical story and world-view.[19] We want to read Scripture as humble listeners, under God and thus under his Word. Therefore, our chapters address these topics and follow the biblical story line, to which we add a chapter to introduce and another to apply these truths:

- Knowing God
- God's Revelation
- God the Trinity
- God's Attributes and Works
- Humanity and Sin
- Jesus
- Jesus's Saving Work
- Salvation
- The Holy Spirit
- The Church
- The Future
- The Christian Life

Before we look at the particulars in each chapter, it is helpful to see how these truths from the biblical story foster and clarify our approach to theology. We will look broadly at the contours of the biblical story and see how each guides us in pursuing theology.[20]

God, His Revelation, and Our Theology

The nature of God is the foundation of all truth and provides a compass for our theology. God's infinity underlines the fact that he alone possesses full knowledge: past, present, and future. We are limited; he is not. God's graciousness initiates our theology, for all knowledge of God flows from

---

[19] Vern S. Poythress, *Symphonic Theology: The Validity of Multiple Perspectives in Theology* (Phillipsburg, NJ: P&R, 2001), 21.

[20] These sections build on Christopher W. Morgan, "How to Do Theology: Worldview and Process," in *Systematic Theology Study Bible* (Wheaton: IL: Crossway, 2017): 1623–27.

his generous self-revelation. We would know nothing about God apart from his grace, but we can and do know him by his grace. God's truthfulness shows that his self-disclosure communicates truth, and does so coherently. God's personal nature reminds us that knowledge of him is also relational, pointing us to a covenant relationship with him. God's holiness clarifies that theology is holistic, leading us to fear the Lord and walk in holiness. God's love clarifies that Christian theology must not be self-absorbed but directed outwardly—toward God and the good of others. God's glory underlines that all true knowledge of God is from God, through God, and to God (Rom 11:33–36).

God's self-revelation reflects him and also guides our theology. God's self-revelation is gracious: he freely initiates it and blesses us through it. It is truthful, representing faithfully who God is, what he does, and how he relates to us. It is a unity: although transmitted in a variety of forms (see below), God's communication about himself, humanity, and life coheres. It is personal, communicating God and his ways to us. It is propositional (making a statement or assertion), disclosing truth about God, humanity, life, history, and salvation. Since we are the recipients of God's self-revelation, it is analogical, as he uses human contexts, cultures, and languages to communicate. It is partial, since the infinite God can reveal only limited information to us as finite humans. It is historical, as God communicates with us in space and time. It is progressive within Scripture, as he relates to multiple generations and gradually expands his self-disclosure over time.

As such, theology is possible only through divine initiative, rests on the content and unity of revealed truth, has objective and subjective components, requires insight into human culture, cannot be exhaustive, is linked to all of life, and its study is a perennial process.

Further, God's gracious self-disclosure is given in a variety of ways and in a variety of contexts, yet with striking unity. God reveals himself to all people at all times in all places through creation, which witnesses to him as its Creator and Lord (Ps 19:1–6; Rom 1:18–32). He also does so through creating humans in his image (which will be addressed below); the moral law is written on the human heart (2:12–16). Our theology, therefore, engages a variety of intellectual, cultural, and vocational worlds.

General revelation and common grace remind us that even explicitly non-Christian work and culture will inevitably include some witness to God's truth. Theology can "recognize and celebrate the glimpses of justice, wisdom, truth, and beauty we find around us in all aspects of life. Ultimately, a grasp of the gospel and of biblical teaching on cultural engagement should lead Christians to be the most appreciative of the hands of God behind the work of our colleagues and neighbors."[21]

God also reveals himself to particular people at particular times and places, gradually and more clearly communicating himself and his covenant relations. He displays himself through historical actions (e.g., the exodus), divine speech (e.g., the Ten Commandments), and his covenant people, whose holiness, love, and justice are to reflect his own character (Exod 19:5–6; Lev 19:1–18). God reveals himself most fully in Jesus and his incarnation, sinless life, teaching, proclamation of the kingdom, miracles, crucifixion, resurrection, ascension, reign, and promised return (John 1:1–18; Heb 1:1–4). God reveals himself also through the inspired prophets, apostles, and Holy Scripture, which accurately records and interprets God's self-revelation. Moreover, the Scriptures are called God's Word and are themselves the most accessible form of God's self-revelation (Ps 19:7–14; Matt 5:17–20; John 10:35; 2 Tim 3:15–4:5; 1 Pet 1:22–25).

Because of this, theology begins with the fear of the Lord (Prov 1:1–7). It requires us to see ourselves as creatures seeking to know the Creator and his world through dependence on his self-revelation, communicated most clearly in the truthful and authoritative Scriptures.

Creation and Our Theology

God's creation also functions as a compass for our theology. The infinite, self-existent, personal, sovereign, holy, and good Lord spoke powerfully and created a good cosmos, evidenced by the steady refrain, "And God saw that it was good" (Gen 1:10, 12, 18, 21, 25; see also 1:4), a goodness

---

[21] Timothy Keller, with Katherine Leary Alsdorf, *Every Good Endeavor: Connecting Your Work to God's Work* (New York: Dutton/Penguin, 2014), 201.

highlighted on the sixth day of creation: "it was very good" (v. 31). God's generous provisions of light, land, vegetation, and animals are blessings given for our benefit, as are our abilities to know God, marry, procreate, and work.

Thus, the good God creates a good world for believers' good and the good of others. Creation testifies to God and his goodness and power. Truth, goodness, beauty, and peace abound. As a result, it is fitting that we seek to understand all of creation, all of life, in light of God's revelation.

Humanity and Our Theology

Who we are as humans also guides our theology. As creatures, we naturally bear all the marks of finitude. All our knowledge as humans is limited, reflective of the Creator-creature distinction. Even more, we are created by God in his image to love him, reflect his character, and serve his mission.

As such, knowledge is not merely a nice additive to pursue but relates to God's original and fundamental purposes for us: to love and serve God, others, and the creation (Gen 1:26–28). Such love and service require our knowledge of God, self, culture, and creation. Knowing God, and therefore knowing theology as part of knowing God, is thus significant for fulfilling our purpose. As we increasingly know God and these truths, we can appropriately pursue truth, goodness, beauty, and peace as noble ends in themselves and as ways of glorifying God by knowing, reflecting, and serving him.

Sin and Our Theology

Unfortunately, the reality of our sin distorts our knowledge of God, and thus our theology. Humans rebel against God, disrupting our relationship to him, ourselves, others, and creation (Genesis 3; Rom 5:12–21). We are now characterized both by the image of God and by sin. We appropriately long for justice, peace, and beauty, but we tend to distort these things or seek them for self-interest alone rather than for God's glory and the good of others. Indeed, sin infects and affects our minds, affections, attitudes, will, and actions. Scripture explains this corruption in various ways, using such images as spiritual death, darkness, hardness, bondage, and blindness (Mark 7:20–23; Rom 1:18–32; 3:9–20; 2 Cor 4:3–4; Eph 2:1–3; 4:17–19).

As such, our theology is too often marked by finitude, bias, and cultural myopia and may be driven by selfishness, pride, prestige, greed, or thirst for power. Even our Christian scholarship reflects these problems.

Christ and Our Theology

Thankfully, Christ is greater than our sin, and he sheds light on how we are to grow in theology. Jesus is the Word, the fullest and clearest revelation of God (John 1:1–18; Heb 1:1–4). Jesus is the truth and the Light to the world, darkened as it is by sin (John 1:4–18; 8:12; 14:6). Jesus is the Lord, the preeminent authority who deserves and demands our allegiance and submission in all of life, including our thinking (Phil 2:5–11). He is also a teacher who molds us as his disciples and invests in us, teaching us about the kingdom of God and building his church, his community.

Further, Jesus proclaims that true worship is in Spirit and in truth, urges us to search the Scriptures, which testify of him, and expects us to examine his identity, miracles, teachings, and works to see that he is from God. Jesus links himself to the truth, corrects error, and sends the Holy Spirit as one who will guide us in the truth. Jesus also defines eternal life as knowing God and prays that God would make us holy by the Word, which he characterizes as truth (Matthew 5–7; John 1:15–18; 14:6; 17:3–17).

In Christ, the apostle asserts, "are hidden all the treasures of wisdom and knowledge" (Col 2:3). As a result, all truth, and thus all theology, finds its source and focus in Jesus himself. Indeed, all of creation—including all of our knowledge, teaching, and vocations—is by Christ, held together in Christ, and for Christ (1:15–20).

Salvation and Our Theology

Wonderfully, our theology is not an abstract attempt to dissect or probe God. Theology is covenantal; that is, God creates us in his image, patiently endures our rebellion, and sends his Son to save us that we might know him and be in a covenant relationship with him. Theology is intensely personal because it is about God and about us in relationship with God. And the doctrine of salvation in the biblical story highlights this truth and defines Christians' identity in light of it. We are joined spiritually to Christ and are recipients of new life. We are believers in Christ and accepted as righteous in him. We are God's children and are being transformed into holy people, into the image of Christ. We are in Christ. We have nothing to fear, nothing to prove, nothing to hide. So the task of theology enables and fosters our pursuit of our identity, our growth, and our security. Theology offers us wisdom to walk in God's ways, according to God's Word, and by God's power.

The Holy Spirit and Our Theology

Jesus's work for us is applied to us through the Spirit's uniting us to Christ. The Holy Spirit has inspired the Scripture and enables us now to understand it. He indwells us, empowers us, and produces fruit in us. He guides our church leaders and enables our worship. He grants us spiritual gifts in order to bless the church through us. As a result, our theology is dependent on the Spirit for its content: he inspired the Bible. Our theology is dependent on the Spirit for its insight: we study hard, but he enables us to interpret the Word rightly. Our theology is dependent on the Spirit for its church context: he inaugurated and indwells the church. Our theology is dependent on the Spirit for its fruitfulness: he empowers our church teachers and catapults us and our theology into service of God and others.

The Church and Our Theology

Through his sinless life, substitutionary death, and bodily resurrection, Jesus redeems us as a people for himself. As the church, we are marked by truth. We are shaped by the apostles' teaching, we oppose error, and we share life together as a community of the Word. Through our union with Christ, we even display the goodness of God, particularly his oneness, holiness, love, and truth (Acts 2:41–47; Eph 2:4–10; 4:1–24). As the people of God, we worship God by yielding ourselves to him as living, holy, and acceptable sacrifices, in part through being transformed by the renewing of our minds and the discernment of God's will (Rom 12:1–2; Eph 4:17–24).

As such, our theology is not merely our own individualistic endeavor but is integrated into the whole of life and pursued in community as the people of God under the authoritative Word of God. It requires things of us too, calling for humility, faith, dependence on grace, respect for others, diligence, patience, carefulness, and persistence. As Christians we need each other and learn theology together, in community, under the Word, as we share life together.

The Future and Our Theology

God's ultimate purposes for history also guide our approach to theology. Jesus's return, triumph, and judgment declare his lordship, vindicate us as his people, and permanently establish cosmic justice and peace (2 Thess 1:5–10; Rev 20:10–15). All falsehood will be overthrown, and all who practice falsehood will be banished into an eternal hell (Revelation 20–22). The new heaven and the new earth will be characterized by God's personal presence with us. And because we have new life in Christ, the new earth will be characterized by his glory and ours, his holiness and ours, his love and ours, his goodness and ours.

So history is linear, purposeful, eschatological, for our good, and preeminently for God's glory (Rom 8:18–39; Eph 1:3–14). As such, theology is a worthy process in which we seek to understand God and his goodness, love, justice, and peace in order to serve one another and to glorify God. Even more, our theological pursuit accepts that we "know in part," grow in our knowledge of God over time, and long for the day when faith will be sight (1 Cor 13:9–12).

As Christians, we rightly value theology: it glorifies God and naturally grows out of the biblical story. God, his self-revelation, creation, our identity as humans created in his image, Jesus, Jesus's work, salvation, the Holy Spirit, the church, and the future all guide how we study theology. Wonderfully, each part of the biblical story and each truth in the Christian faith shapes our faith, hope, and love—indeed, every aspect of our daily lives.

Knowing God and Our Sources in Theology

The biblical story and a Christian worldview compel us to grow in our theology and clarify how we understand it and go about it. But what sources do we have that help us develop our theology?

In studying theology, we learn from four sources:

- Scripture
- Tradition
- Reason
- Experience

Scripture

As is obvious from what we outlined above from the biblical story, Scripture is the chief source of all theology. As we will see later, Scripture is uniquely inspired by God, is the Word of God, and is the supreme authority for all faith and practice. All other sources are under Scripture. These other sources are important, but only serve in interpreting Scripture and must be judged by Scripture, the highest standard (this is the doctrine of *sola Scriptura*).

Tradition

Tradition is important because it shows us what other Christians have said about perennial topics. We are not the first to pick up the Bible and study it. Others have gone before us and have much insight for us. Tradition conveys historical interpretations of Scripture. It relates the church's teachings (creeds, confessions, etc.), corrects false teachings, and offers historic perspectives on doctrinal issues.

Reason

Reason is important because it helps us reflect on revelation. Reason clarifies concepts, questions, relationships, and arguments. Knowing God is beyond our abilities and requires our faith as well as all of our mental faculties. We need to think hard and clearly, reject false dichotomies, see truths in relationships, and analyze systems. Reason is key to these tasks.

Experience

Experience is also important to us. Our theology not only shapes who we are but is shaped by who we are. As we do theology as whole people who perceive through the lens of our particular faith experiences, church contexts, family backgrounds, ethnicities, cultures, genders, and life situations, experience plays a role in helping us interpret the Scripture.

Tradition, reason, and experience are good and meaningful sources. They are good guides and teachers but not infallible ones. Tradition can err (see Gal 1:6–9; 2:11–21). Reason can forget mystery and submission to God (see 2 Cor 11:3). Experience can be left unchecked (see Jude vv. 3–4). Each should be valued, and each should be used, for each helps us in interpreting Scripture. But each must always be judged by Scripture, whose authority comes from God, not the church, reason, or experience. The church stands under the Word, trusting its affirmations, embracing its judgments, and obeying its commands.

Knowing God and Our Process in Theology

The process of studying theology is called *theological method*. As we study, we desire to follow a sound theological method. This incorporates a process that includes

- Biblical Exegesis
- Biblical Theology
- The Church/Historical Theology
- Various Disciplines
- Systematic Theology
- Practical Theology/Application

Though there is a basic order to these elements, each is inevitably interwoven with the others and should not be conducted in isolation from them. The process of developing our theology includes a concern for each, and we work through each of these approaches—but not in the sequence of a math problem. Much like the members of an orchestra, each of these areas has a part to play in forming our theology. And while each area may have a featured part at some stage, none should be allowed to play a purely solo act. For example, systematic theology should follow biblical exegesis, but a basic theology already precedes such exegesis. Why? Because we all study the Bible with previously existing, even if undeveloped, beliefs, including theological ones.[22]

This has led some skeptics to consider all interpretation to be hopelessly circular, as if our current beliefs completely control our study. We agree that all biblical interpretation and theology are done by interpreters, people who read biblical texts with and sometimes toward an already-existing theology. None of us comes to passages with a clean slate. To our reading of the Bible and our theology we all bring perspectives of God, ourselves, the Bible, Jesus, salvation, the church, history, the meaning of life, and how things work.

These perspectives can offer us much insight as vantage points from which to understand theology. For example, Christians under persecution will often see more clearly and integrate more fully the biblical themes of God's presence with his people, God's ultimate victory over evil, and God's justice that prevails. Our trials often improve our theology. As it's tested by struggles in our travels, our theology matures.

But if we allow our perspectives to become our interpretive keys, mistakes will follow. Some interpret Scripture from perspectives other than those shaped by the biblical story and worldview. This is flawed from the start. Such critical, outsider approaches to interpretation are often imperialistic and intend to critique biblical texts from their presumed ideology or

---

[22] The ideas in this section are developed further in Matthew Y. Emerson and Christopher W. Morgan, "Toward Holistic Hermeneutics: Exegesis, Narrative, Doctrine, the Church, and Application in Concert," *Journal of Mid-America Baptist Theological Seminary* 1 (2014). http://www.mabts.edu/sites/all/themes /midamerica/uploads/pdf/emerson_morgan.pdf.

conform those texts to that ideology. This is the opposite of the approach of Psalm 119 to read Scripture as *humble listeners* who receive God's instruction; as *diligent seekers*, seeking the Lord and his commands with all of our hearts; as *faithful servants* who accept his authority, follow his will, and heed his counsel; as *tested travelers* who face opposition as sojourners in a hostile world and desperately need wisdom from the Word; as *God's people* in community, finding encouragement from one another, walking in God's ways together; and as *joyful worshippers* who declare, "Your statutes are the theme of my song" (v. 54).

Allowing our perspectives to serve as interpretive keys also leads to another potential mistake: presumptuously equating our interpretation of God's Word with God's Word itself. We are still works in progress, and this means that our theology is always under construction. It is grounded in what we currently know of God's Word and is *always being reformed* according to God's Word.

So, we bring ourselves and our views to our biblical interpretation. But this does not lead to skepticism. Our starting point does shape our path, but it does not ultimately have to dictate our destination. A better approach is to acknowledge and discern our already-existing theological assumptions, pray for the illumination of the Spirit, learn from the wisdom of the church (discussed below), and trust the Scripture as the supreme authority over tradition, reason, and experience (and this includes our initial perspectives). If we follow this approach, there is a very real sense in which every time we study the Bible, our interpretive and theological lenses are tweaked, even if ever so slightly. Given enough time, this can lead to improved theological perspectives and increased interpretive accuracy, which can lead to even better theological perspectives and to increasingly developed and sound interpretations. Thus, the assumption of a hermeneutical circle is unnecessary. In a sound approach to biblical interpretation and theology, there is a hermeneutical spiral,[23] even a

---

[23] See Grant R. Osborne, *The Hermeneutical Spiral: A Comprehensive Introduction to Biblical Interpretation*, 2nd ed. (Downers Grove, IL: IVP Academic, 2006); Anthony C. Thiselton, *The Two Horizons: New Testament Hermeneutics and Philosophical Description* (Grand Rapids: Eerdmans, 1980), 104–110, 143–69.

theological spiral. Or, in our symphonic metaphor, no matter how out of tune our instruments are, we can tune them according to a standard. Such tuning may take a while, but it can happen. Similarly, as we embrace God and his self-revelation in Scripture as the standard, increasingly recognize our own assumptions and biases, consistently read and carefully study God's Word, and listen to the wisdom of the church, our theology matures, spiraling gradually toward the truth.

Biblical Exegesis

Voices from Church History: William Tyndale

Tyndale (c.1494–c.1536) was an English scholar and key Reformation figure who translated the Bible into English from Hebrew and Greek. He famously said, "I will cause a boy who drives the plow to know more of the Scripture than the pope." In 1536, he was condemned for translating the Bible into English and executed. The Tyndale Bible played an ongoing role in spreading Reformation ideas and significantly influenced the King James Bible of 1611.

Tyndale's motive in translating the New Testament into English? "Because I had perceived by experience how that it was impossible to establish the lay people in any truth, except the Scripture were plainly laid before their eyes in their mother tongue, that they might see the process, order, and meaning of the text."[24]

The foundation of all good theology is understanding the meaning of biblical passages, beginning with the biblical author's intention through the text. There are many helpful tools that can assist us in understanding the meaning of such passages, including good study Bibles, Bible dictionaries, and commentaries.[25] When studying a passage, we must note the par-

---

[24] David Daniell, ed., *Tyndale's Old Testament* (New Haven, CT: Yale University Press, 1992), 4.

[25] See, for example, *ESV Systematic Theology Study Bible* (Wheaton, IL: Crossway, 2017); *CSB Christian Worldview Study Bible* (Nashville: B&H, 2018); *NIV Zondervan Study Bible* (Grand Rapids: Zondervan, 2015); *Holman Bible Dictionary* (Nashville: B&H, 2003); *A Concise Dictionary of Theological Terms* (Nashville: B&H, 2020); and the New American Commentary series (B&H).

ticular literary genre (narrative, proverb, parable, Gospel, letter, etc.) and consider literary strategies appropriate to that genre. Literary context is also critical, as the placement of any given passage assists us in interpreting what a biblical author means. The meaning of a word often emerges through studying it in its surrounding phrases, clauses, and sentences; the meaning of a sentence appears in its paragraphs or scenes; and the meaning of a scene surfaces in the surrounding episodes, sections, or overall book. The historical setting is also formative because knowing the text's occasion, recipients, author, and church context fosters good interpretation.

Two mistakes related to theological exegesis occur at this stage. First, sometimes readers are so focused on finding a particular theme or doctrine in the Bible that they may read into a passage what is not there. The key to guarding against this temptation is to read passages first for what they are intending to communicate, and only then to consider how any one doctrine relates to those passages. Second, readers may mistakenly give attention only to passages in which the author explicitly instructs about a theological issue. But remember that the biblical authors write from theological convictions and with theological intentions. And while particular doctrines are not always the primary goal of a given passage, the writers are teaching theology so that God's people can follow God appropriately, even if the emphasis is ethical and the theology is the substructure of the ethics. So, first and foremost, good theology is grounded on biblical exegesis.

Biblical Theology

Ultimately, the context of every biblical passage is not only its particular book, but also the entire canon, which places the biblical texts into God's unfolding plan that moves from creation and the fall to redemption and new creation. This biblical story line frames, orders, and connects the doctrines. Furthermore, it culminates in the person and work of Christ, which distinguishes what comes before and after the Gospels (Heb 1:1–4). It is wise, therefore, for us both to locate passages within the biblical story line and also to relate them to other passages on the subject. We look for how the Bible's story develops through the biblical covenants in the Old Testament, particularly in the Law, Prophets, and Writings, as well as in the New Testament in the dawning of the new covenant, particularly in the Gospels, Acts, Epistles, and Revelation. Our attention should be given not only to the specific doctrines we are studying but also to the central themes of each book of the Bible and the central themes throughout the Bible (covenant, kingdom, atonement, glory, love, holiness, etc.). This will enable us to see the connections of the doctrine being studied to these other major themes, which will enable us to understand and synthesize the doctrine in its relationships, in proportion, and in light of Christ. Thus, good theology is grounded on biblical exegesis and rooted in biblical theology.

The Church/Historical Theology

Our tendency might be to read the Bible individualistically, reading it privately to learn about God and how to follow him better personally. While this is helpful and significant, we should also consider the centrality of the church and of church history to the interpretive process. The church has been the historical interpreter of Scripture. While historical church teachings and creeds are not authoritative over believers in the same way that Scripture alone is (*sola Scriptura*), modern and postmodern approaches to interpretation have sometimes highlighted the individual interpreter (modern) or contemporary communities of readers (postmodern) at the expense of historic church teachings. We are not the first ones to read the Bible, but stand in the stream of God's people throughout the centuries and can learn much from church history's leading thinkers (e.g., Athanasius, Augustine, Thomas Aquinas, Martin Luther, John Calvin, John Owen, Jonathan Edwards, John Wesley, etc.).[26] We should diverge

---

[26] Due to space constraints and the purpose of this volume, we only interact with historical theology at key points and with key voices. For an excellent treatment of historical theology on the topics of theology, see Gregg R. Allison,

from the church's historic stream of thought with great hesitancy and only when thoroughly convinced by sacred Scripture or evident reason. We should also read the Scripture in the context of our present church community, realizing that Scripture guides our life together with other believers. Thus good theology is done by, with, and for the church; with respect for historic church teachings; and in life together.

Various Disciplines

As previously noted, God's general revelation witnesses truthfully to God, creation, and humanity. Although our perception of general revelation is distorted by sin, we do gain some knowledge from such revelation, and we are expected to learn from it (Ps 19:1–6; John 1:4–9; Acts 14:17; Rom 1:18–32). As a result, a wide array of disciplines (e.g., arts, sciences, education, etc.) may be useful to theology. For example, philosophy assists theology by examining clarifying questions, terms, categories, concepts, interrelationships, cultural issues, and arguments. To be sure, these disciplines are not themselves identical to general revelation. But most are warranted studies of it. They are also not to be considered entirely reliable, as they are too often rooted in non-Christian assumptions. But insofar as they are reasoned assessments consistent with Scripture, they can be helpful. In sum, following good theological method means trusting the unity of God's revelation, building our theology on special revelation, and valuing insights from other disciplines.[27]

Systematic Theology

Based on our work in biblical exegesis, biblical theology, church history, and general revelation, we push forward toward a theological synthesis.

Historical Theology: An Introduction to Christian Doctrine (Grand Rapids: Zondervan, 2011).

[27] For helpful interactions with various disciplines along the topics of theology, see Gordon R. Lewis and Bruce A. Demarest, *Integrative Theology* (Grand Rapids: Zondervan, 1996).

We seek to incorporate primary biblical themes, address central theological topics, and show priorities and interrelationships among the doctrines. Such theology is best organized and communicated in light of the biblical story line (creation, fall, redemption, new creation; or, more particularly, God, revelation, creation, humanity, fall, Israel, person of Christ, saving work of Christ, the Holy Spirit, salvation, the church, and the future). We also desire to express our theology in a way that is contextual, clear, and beneficial to others.

Practical Theology/Application

Theology is incomplete until it is lived out in the church. God uses theology to improve our beliefs and the entirety of our lives. Accordingly, we seek to apply biblical truth to the contemporary church in light of its original purpose. So our approach to love, faith, prayer, evangelism, discipleship, fellowship, ministry, worship, marriage, parenting, friendship, hospitality, forgiveness, finances, preaching, teaching, missions, church planting, and so on, flows from such application.

Theology thus calls each of us and the church as a whole to appropriate ways of being, loving, thinking, believing, and following. The biblical story is our story; indeed, it is every Christian's story. As God's people, we are derived from it, defined by it, and extensions of it as we live, love, and serve God and others for their good and for his glory.

KEY TERMS

authority	revelation
biblical theology	Scripture
doctrine	*sola Scriptura*
exegesis	sources in theology
experience (as source)	systematic theology
historical theology	theology
practical theology	tradition
reason	truth

◼ RESOURCES FOR FURTHER STUDY

Blomberg, Craig L. *Can We Still Believe the Bible? An Evangelical Engagement with Contemporary Questions*. Grand Rapids: Brazos, 2014.

Carson, D. A. *The Gagging of God: Christianity Confronts Pluralism*. Grand Rapids: Zondervan, 1996.

———. *The God Who Is There: Finding Your Place in God's Story*. Grand Rapids: Baker, 2010.

Chicago Statement on Biblical Inerrancy. https://library.dts.edu/Pages/TL/Special/ICBI_1.pdf.

Doriani, Daniel. *Putting the Truth to Work*. Phillipsburg, NJ: P&R, 2001.

Jensen, Peter. *The Revelation of God*. Contours of Christian Theology. Downers Grove, IL: InterVarsity, 2002.

Kapic, Kelly M. *A Little Book for New Theologians*. Downers Grove, IL: InterVarsity, 2012.

Larkin, William J., Jr. *Culture and Biblical Hermeneutics: Interpreting and Applying the Authoritative Word in a Relativistic Age*. Grand Rapids: Baker, 1988.

Lints, Richard. *The Fabric of Theology: A Prolegomenon to Evangelical Theology*. Grand Rapids: Eerdmans, 1993.

Vanhoozer, Kevin J. *The Drama of Doctrine: A Canonical Linguistic Approach to Christian Theology*. Louisville: Westminster John Knox, 2005.

Wenham, John. *Christ and the Bible*, 3rd ed. Eugene, OR: Wipf and Stock, 2009.

2

GOD'S REVELATION

We are all familiar with the idea of revelation. We know people who are easy to get to know and those who are not so easy to get to know. Amazingly, God is easy to get to know, for he takes the initiative and reveals himself to us. In fact, he is the revealing God, who delights to make himself known. He reveals himself to all people, both outside and inside of them. He makes himself known outside of us in the world he has made. All God's creatures bear witness to their Creator, for they are his creations. He also reveals himself in his caring for and guiding events in his world. In addition, he makes himself known within every human being, writing his law on our hearts and giving each of us a conscience.

God not only reveals himself to all humans but also personally makes himself known to many. He does this in several ways. He sometimes performs miracles in his world to teach his people. He inspires Scripture through his prophets, who bring his word to his people—Israel in the Old Testament and the church in the New. Best of all, God himself becomes a human being to make himself known as never before. Who could reveal God better than God? And who could reveal God to humans better than a human? The Son of God becomes a human while continuing to be God. He is the perfect revealer of God. Jesus makes God known in word and deed. His deeds glorify God and reveal Jesus's identity as the promised

One and Savior. He speaks God's words like no other. He so perfectly reveals God that God calls him the Word, the communication of God.

OBJECTIVES

- To lay a biblical foundation for understanding God's revelation
- To experience the goal of God's revelation—to know, love, and serve him
- To articulate the significance and limitations of general revelation
- To recognize our need for special revelation
- To foster a high view of Scripture, as God's very words in human language
- To encourage us to believe, read, meditate on, and obey Holy Scripture
- To establish our identity as people to whom God has revealed himself

OUTLINE

God's Revelation in the Biblical Story
God's Revelation in Selected Passages
       Exodus 7–15
       Matthew 11:25–27
       Hebrews 1:1–2
       James 1:18–25
Knowing God through His Revelation
       The Meaning of "Revelation"
       Our Need for Revelation
Knowing God through General Revelation
       God Reveals Himself in Creation
       God Reveals Himself in Humanity
       God Reveals Himself in Providence
       A Theology of General Revelation
Knowing God through Special Revelation
       Old Testament Revelation

God's Revelation in the Biblical Story

God's self-revelation begins at creation, particularly in the garden of Eden. God reveals his power, wisdom, beauty, and more in the world and in the beautiful garden that he makes. He manifests his holiness and justice within Adam and Eve's hearts, and they obey their Maker. God reveals his generosity and faithfulness in providence as he gives our first parents fruits, vegetables, and grains in abundance. God makes himself known before the fall, not only in general revelation but in special revelation too. Adam and Eve receive the word of God verbally. They also know his presence in the garden.

What effects does the fall have on God's revelation? Two things are noteworthy. First, God's original revelation is relational. He makes himself known in numerous ways to Adam and Eve, who know, love, and obey him. The fall breaks that relationship, illustrated by our first parents' hiding themselves from God's presence. Second, as a result of the broken relationship, God's unified revelation now appears fragmented. God still bombards the first pair with knowledge of him from outside and within them, in history, and in word and presence, but because of the effects of sin on their minds, such revelation now appears disjointed to their cloudy vision.[1]

In Christ we enter into a personal relationship with God and recover some of revelation's original unity. Seeing the world as God's handiwork, rather than as all that there is, leads us to perceive the grass as greener green and the sky as bluer blue. We heed the warnings of conscience as it works with the law "written" on our hearts (Rom 2:15). We view life and the future in light of God's providence. We love God's presence in worship and esteem Christ as the "one priceless pearl" (Matt 13:46). We cherish his written Word and treasure it in our hearts (Ps 119:11).

In our future resurrection and life on the new earth, our appreciation for God's unified revelation will be fully restored. In fact, things will be better than they were before the fall, for as God's people, we will no longer be able to sin, and God will dwell in our midst as never before. We will rejoice in God's making himself known in a renewed creation, to perfected consciences, and in the history of eternity future. We will love the Word and will worship the Father, Spirit, and incarnate Son, who says, "I am . . . the Living One. I was dead, but look—I am alive forever and ever, and I hold the keys of death and Hades" (Rev 1:17–18).

God's Revelation in Selected Passages

God reveals himself in general revelation, given to everyone everywhere, and in special revelation, given to particular people at particular places. In passages below, we will see that special revelation includes historical events, such as the plagues and exodus, in which God displays himself as Warrior and Redeemer, who judges false gods and delivers his people.

Jesus orients us to special revelation, teaching that humans cannot acquire it on their own but that God sovereignly gives it. It is trinitarian in character and received by the humility of faith. It is both propositional and personal, reflecting its Giver, who is both the truth and a person.

---

[1] We thank Richard Gaffin Jr. for his unpublished systematic theology notes that contributed to many of these ideas.

God especially reveals himself in the Scriptures. Whereas God gives Old Testament revelation by the prophets, he gives New Testament revelation by his incarnate Son, who pours out the Holy Spirit on the apostles. God uses his Word to communicate his will, to bring about new birth into a new creation, and to promote freedom, life, and flourishing. Believers must be quick to obey the Scriptures and be blessed.

Exodus 7–15

The Bible teaches that God's revelation comes in historical events, such as the exodus. God reveals himself to Moses and calls him to lead his people out of Egyptian oppression into a land that God prepares for them (Exod 3:1–4:26). Moses obeys God, urging Pharaoh to let God's people go so that they can worship him. Pharaoh stubbornly refuses, pretentiously asking, "Who is the Lord that I should obey him?" (5:2). Pharaoh arrogantly increases his oppression of Israel (5:4–20). God responds, planning both to deliver his people and to remedy Pharaoh's ignorance. He promises to redeem Israel from Egyptian bondage "with an outstretched arm and great acts of judgment" (6:6). God sends ten dreadful plagues upon Egypt (7:14–12:32) and declares that the plagues reveal that "[he is] the Lord" (7:5, 17; 10:2).

Specifically, these historical events display God's power, his possession of the world, and his covenant-keeping love. In at least half of the plagues, the Lord distinguishes between Egypt and Israel, sparing his people (see 11:4–7). Pharaoh's stubborn defiance results in the tenth plague, the death of all firstborn males in Egypt, including Pharaoh's son (12:29). God graciously protects the Israelites, who obediently put a sacrificed lamb's blood on their doorposts and lintels. Because the Lord passes over Israel's homes when he comes to judge the firstborn, Israel is to celebrate the Passover as an annual feast to the Lord.

Pharaoh relents and lets the Israelites go, but he quickly changes his mind and furiously chases after them. God powerfully opens the Red Sea for his people to cross. When the Egyptians follow, God closes the water over their chariots and destroys their horsemen (14:28). The exodus is a major historical event and a major means by which God reveals himself, as Moses's and Miriam's songs acclaim. In the exodus, God judges his enemies and delivers his people. In the exodus, God also communicates who he is: Yahweh, the covenant Lord (6:7; 10:2). He loves, protects, and remains faithful to his covenant people (3–4). He is powerful over nations, leaders, false gods, and even the sea (9:16; 11:9). He is Lord over life and death (12:29–32). The exodus is special revelation, celebrating that there is no one like Yahweh, who is highly exalted, glorious, powerful, majestic, holy, and loving. God is a warrior, the Redeemer, the eternal King, mighty to save (15:1–18).

Matthew 11:25–27

Jesus also orients us to the topic of revelation. He denounces for lack of repentance the Galilean cities in which he has performed many miracles. Then he bursts forth in worship and depth of insight:

> I praise you, Father, Lord of heaven and earth, because you have hidden these things from the wise and intelligent and revealed them to infants. Yes, Father, because this was your good pleasure. All things have been entrusted to me by my Father. No one knows the Son except the Father, and no one knows the Father except the Son and anyone to whom the Son desires to reveal him. (Matt 11:25–27)

Praise belongs to the Trinity for its work of revelation. God the Father is the Author of revelation; he is the revealer (v. 25). The Son is also involved, for he reveals the Father (v. 27) and is even the great subject of revelation (Luke 24:27). The Holy Spirit, too, is involved (Luke 10:21). This all points to the trinitarian character of revelation.

Jesus shows that revelation is also personal, for its content is knowledge of the Father and the Son (Matt 11:27). Revelation is necessary: we need to know God (v. 25). Furthermore, revelation is sovereignly given: God the Father is sovereign in revelation (vv. 25–26), and so is the Son (v. 27). God takes the initiative and makes revelation effective.

"Hidden" means to be beyond human ability or reason; humans cannot acquire revelation on their own. Instead we need the humility of faith. We must humble ourselves, become like little children, and trust God (Mark 10:15). In addition, joy is a proper response to revelation (Luke 10:21).[2]

Hebrews 1:1–2

This passage informs us about how revelation relates to salvation history. In particular, God's revelation through the Old Testament and his revelation in Jesus are set side by side: "Long ago God spoke to the fathers by the prophets at different times and in different ways. In these last days, he has spoken to us by his Son" (Heb 1:1–2).

As the writer of Hebrews compares Old and New Testament revelation, he sets forth four distinctions. He distinguishes timing, audience, mediators, and manner. With regard to timing, he contrasts "long ago" with "in these last days." The Old Testament uses the expression "the last days" to point to the future. Fulfilling Old Testament expectation, Christ's coming causes the addition of the word "these"—"in *these* last days."

The author contrasts audiences. Old Testament revelation came to the "fathers," the patriarchs and their descendants. New Testament revelation comes to "us," those living after the coming of the Messiah.

With regard to the mediators of revelation, God's previous Word came "by the prophets," but now God has spoken "by his Son." Jesus is the Mediator of New Testament revelation.

The fourth contrast is implied. God manifested himself to his Old Testament people "in different ways." Corresponding to this, New Testament revelation has come "by his Son." All such revelation is "Son-revelation." The eternal Son is the great prophet who "became flesh" (John 1:14) to reveal God as never before. After Christ's death, resurrection, and ascension, he fulfills his promises to send the Spirit of truth to his disciples to remind them of, and to teach them, many truths (John 14:25–26; 15:26; 16:13–15; Acts 1:1). From heaven Jesus has revealed the New Testament by the Holy Spirit though his apostles.

---

[2] We acknowledge Richard Gaffin Jr.'s unpublished systematic theology notes for many of these ideas.

James 1:18–25

In this brief section, James speaks of revelation as "the word of truth" (Jas 1:18), "the implanted word" (v. 21), "the word" (vv. 22–23), "the perfect law" (v. 25), and "the . . . law of freedom" (v. 25; see also 2:12). Later in the letter, James also refers to "the royal law" (2:8), the "law" (2:9–11; 4:11), and "the Scripture" (2:8, 23; 4:5). Along the way, James stresses that the law is a unity, communicates the will of the Lawgiver, and serves as a basis of judgment (2:8–13; 4:11–12). He does so by incorporating Old Testament material, such as that relating to Abraham, Rahab, Elijah, the prophets, Job, Exodus 20, Leviticus 19, and Deuteronomy, as well as the teachings of Jesus.[3]

In this passage, James writes of "the word of truth," associating the Word with truth, which connects the Word to the God who is characterized by and communicates truth (Jas 1:18). God uses the Word of truth to bring about the new birth into a new creation (v. 18; see also 1 Pet 1:23). James contrasts the Word of truth as an instrument that leads to life, with sin as an instrument that results in death (Jas 1:13–18). In contrast with the desire that births sin, the Word of truth births believers as a new creation. The Word functions as God's seed to bring the new birth (vv. 16–18), and it is God's agent by which he shapes believers (v. 21). This Word, like every good and perfect gift, comes down from God and is to be received.

James uses "word" and "law" somewhat interchangeably, and both terms appear to depict broadly the Old Testament, key ethical teachings in the Old Testament, and the new covenant promises revealed in the gospel and the teachings of Jesus. James treats "word" and "law" synonymously in 1:19–25, which begins by emphasizing the importance of doing the Word and ends with a blessing on those who do the law.

The Word/law is also the "perfect law of freedom" (v. 25; see also 2:12). In continuity with Psalm 19, James highlights not only the idea of the law's perfection but also interrelated themes of life, wisdom, joy, purity,

---

[3] For more on the Word in James, see Christopher W. Morgan, *A Theology of James: Wisdom for God's People*, Explorations in Biblical Theology (Phillipsburg, NJ: P&R, 2010), 115–26.

cleanness, righteousness, and reward. The perfect law is the means to freedom, promoting life, flourishing, holiness, and service.

The Word also bears the authority of the God who gives it. Because of this, believers are to be quick to "listen" to the Word (see also Deut 6:1–9), to lay aside sin in preparation to receive it, to receive it with meekness, and to hear and do it (Jas 1:19–25). Believers who do the Word will be blessed in their doing (v. 25). God uses the Word at the beginning, middle, and end of the Christian life (vv. 18–25). And at each step of the journey, God's people are to submit their thinking and lives to God's authoritative Word.[4]

Knowing God through His Revelation

The Meaning of "Revelation"

A standard dictionary defines *revelation* as "the disclosure or communication of knowledge, instructions, etc., by divine or supernatural means" (*Oxford English Dictionary*). The English word *revelation* derives from the Latin *revelationem*, which means to "unveil, uncover, lay bare." The Vulgate uses this Latin word to translate the Greek *apocalypsis*, which means "revelation, disclosure." The New Testament commonly uses *apocalypsis* to point to the uncovering of previously hidden truths, especially about God and his plan. The widespread Old Testament view that God has made known himself and his will to Israel stands behind this usage. This idea of revelation runs so steadily through the Old and New Testaments that we are able to speak of a biblical concept of revelation.

God communicates himself in a variety of ways, often categorized as general and special revelation. *General revelation* refers to God's self-disclosure to all people at all times and places, showing who he is and making all people accountable. *Special revelation* refers to God's self-disclosure to particular people at specific times and places, enabling them to enter into a redemptive relationship with him.[5]

---

[4] For more on this passage, see Morgan, *A Theology of James*, 81–84, 116–23.

[5] Erickson, *Christian Theology*, 177–245 (see chap. 1, n. 18).

Our Need for Revelation

GOD IS INFINITE AND WE ARE FINITE

God is the infinite Creator, and we are his finite creatures. By *infinite* we mean that God is unlimited. Scripture points to this reality, specifically mentioning his power and understanding: "Our Lord is great, vast in power; his understanding is infinite" (Ps 147:5). Isaiah says, "The LORD is the everlasting God, the Creator of the whole earth. He never becomes faint or weary; there is no limit to his understanding" (Isa 40:28). This infinite God is great beyond comparison. He alone is "the High and Exalted One" (57:15), and there is no one like him.

Compared to this great, infinite God, we are very limited. We would never learn knowledge of God or know him apart from his taking the initiative to communicate who he is to us. Thankfully, our infinite God generously reveals himself to us, his weak, finite creatures.

GOD IS HOLY AND WE ARE SINFUL

In addition to being limited by finitude, we humans are sinful. Angels proclaim "Holy, holy, holy is the LORD of Armies; his glory fills the whole earth" (Isa 6:3). To this Isaiah cries, "Woe is me for I am ruined because I am a man of unclean lips . . . because my eyes have seen the King, the LORD of Armies" (v. 5). God reveals his wrath "against all godlessness and unrighteousness of people" (Rom 1:18). Indeed, fallen human beings' "thinking became worthless, and their senseless hearts were darkened. Claiming to be wise, they became fools" (vv. 21–22).

Limited by our finiteness and blinded by our sin, we would never succeed in knowing God or truth about him. Apart from God's revelation, all human beings have misconceptions of him. But, amazingly, he graciously makes himself known to Adam and Eve and to every human being since. Although we are lost and have distorted knowledge of him, God in grace reveals himself. Revelation is therefore gracious.[6]

---

[6] We thank David G. Dunbar for help in this section.

Knowing God through General Revelation

As already stated, God discloses himself in both general and special revelation. In the latter he makes himself known to particular people in particular times and places. In the former he makes himself known to all people in all times and places. There are three main forms of general revelation, which we will examine in turn:

1. Creation
2. Humanity
3. Providence

God Reveals Himself in Creation

PSALM 19:1–6

God reveals himself outside of us in creation, as Psalm 19 proclaims: "The heavens declare the glory of God, and the expanse proclaims the work of his hands" (v. 1). This is called external general revelation. The mode of this revelation is God's creation, which reveals some knowledge of the Creator. The content of this revelation is God's glory and handiwork, which implies that God exists and reveals that he is awesome, powerful, and brilliant. The timing of this revelation is continuous: "Day after day they pour out speech; night after night they communicate knowledge" (v. 2). The extent of this revelation is universal: "Their message has gone out to the whole earth, and their words to the ends of the world" (v. 4). This revelation's universality is epitomized by the sun, which "rises from one end of the heavens and circles to their other end" (v. 6). External general revelation thus occurs everywhere, all the time, revealing God's existence and glory and the fact that he is Creator. This is communicated regardless of human appropriation of this revelation.

ROMANS 1:18–25

Paul likewise speaks of external general revelation in Romans 1, where he tells of the world's need for the gospel. God is angry against the rebellion of those "who by their unrighteousness suppress the truth" (v. 18). "The truth" of which Paul speaks is God's revelation in creation: "his invisible attributes, that is, his eternal power and divine nature, have been clearly seen . . . being understood through what he has made" (v. 20). Paul speaks of God's invisible qualities as "clearly seen." He explains that God's character, specifically his "eternal power and divine nature," is manifested through his creation. Moreover, these attributes have been revealed "since the creation of the world" (v. 20).

Putting this together for our doctrine of general revelation, we learn (a) the mode of revelation is God's creation; (b) the content is God's "eternal power and divine nature," connoting that God is the Creator and is awesome, powerful, and God (1:20); (c) the timing of the revelation is constant, occurring ever since creation; and (d) the extent is universal, spreading as far as creation does. Paul's teaching on general revelation here is strikingly similar to that in Psalm 19.

The major difference is that Psalm 19 speaks of general revelation in the context of the covenant people of God, who have also received special revelation, the Word of God. Psalm 19 is a Davidic psalm praising God and relishing in his witness through his creation and his Word. The response of God's people to God's revelation includes worship, joy, reverence, wisdom, delight, confession, and prayer.

The context is quite different in Romans 1, where Paul's teaching on general revelation shows that all people "are without excuse" and in need of the message of salvation (v. 20). How does this work? Paul explains that this revelation gets through to people so that they know that God is the powerful Deity. Paul goes to great lengths to highlight this: "the truth" about God is "known," "evident," "shown," "clearly seen," and "understood" (vv. 18–21). But man's response to it is to "suppress the truth" actively (v. 18). For although God makes this revelation known to them,

> they did not glorify him as God or show gratitude. Instead, their thinking became worthless, and their senseless hearts were darkened. Claiming to be wise, they became fools and exchanged the glory of the immortal God for images. . . . They exchanged the truth of God for a lie, and worshiped and served what has

been created instead of the Creator, who is praised forever. (vv. 21–23, 25)

Since the fall, humans on their own do not respond positively to God's external general revelation.[7] Although such revelation has been offered everywhere ever since the time of creation, and although God makes it clear to all, sinners do not value this knowledge of God in creation as they ought. They continually suppress it. They do not give thanks to God or glorify him. Instead, their thoughts become foolish and their hearts darkened. They claim to be wise but in reality are foolish and practice sin (vv. 21–25). As a result, God justly judges sinners (v. 18), regarding them as "without excuse" (v. 20). He abandons humankind to idolatry (v. 23), moral depravity (vv. 24–27), and a depraved mind (v. 28).

Thus Romans 1 reiterates much of Psalm 19's teaching on general revelation, while adding two truths. First, general revelation is sufficiently clear to make us accountable to God. Second, general revelation on its own does not lead sinners to faith in God. Sadly, ever since the fall, when blessed with clear truth about God, sinners resolutely suppress him and his truth.

JOHN 1:3–9

The Word, who was with the Father before creation, is the Creator of everything. He is God, and eternal life within him is the source of all created life. This life in the Word that issued in creation is "the light of men" (John 1:4), God's revelation to people. This external general revelation continues to reveal God ever since the creation (v. 5). Since the fall (presupposed with the mention of "darkness"), people fight God's revelation in creation, but they are not able to extinguish it. The Son of God is the true light, "who gives light to everyone" (v. 9). Although he creates everyone and gives truth to everyone, the world does not know him or receive him (vv. 10–11).

In brief, John adds to our understanding about general revelation: the Son of God is the agent of God's self-revelation; revelation is continual;

---

[7] For more on the fall and our guilt, see chapter 5, "Humanity and Sin."

revelation is opposed by the world; revelation cannot be extinguished by its opponents.

God Reveals Himself in Humanity

God makes himself known in his creation; he also makes himself known inside of us in our very nature. This is called internal general revelation.

ROMANS 1:32; 2:12–16

Paul teaches here that all of us have the requirements of the law written on our hearts. God reveals his moral demands within us. This is internal general revelation (Rom 2:14–15). These legal requirements affect our behavior. Even before we know Christ or his Word, we do by nature the things of the law. Even though the Gentiles do not have the Ten Commandments, God's requirements written on their hearts cause them to be a law to themselves. They themselves are a sort of moral revelation from God. The law *works*; it expresses itself by passing judgment on our actions (vv. 14–15).

Our consciences work sometimes to accuse and sometimes to defend our actions. Presumably, our consciences work in accordance with our internal moral principles to pass judgment on our behavior (v. 15). We all know God's moral requirements very well. We know that our sinful actions are wrong and worthy of God's judgment (1:32).

This internal general revelation reveals God's attributes of holiness and justice and his work of judgment (v. 32). This internal general revelation is known by all people (an implication from the passage). It is suppressed and perverted so that people have a tendency to apply moral requirements in judgment of others while excusing themselves for the same sins (2:1–3).

ECCLESIASTES 3:11

"He has made everything appropriate in its time. He has also put eternity in their hearts, but no one can discover the work God has done from beginning to end" (Eccl 3:11). Something inside of us reaches out for eternal things. However, as the end of this verse bears out, we are frustrated in our desire for the eternal because we cannot understand God's plan in its entirety.[8] A note in the *NIV Study Bible* bears quotation: "God's beautiful but tantalizing world is too big for us, yet its satisfactions are too small. Since we were made for eternity, the things of time cannot fully and permanently satisfy."[9]

God Reveals Himself in Providence

God's general revelation is made known in creation, conscience, and also providence. God communicates many of his qualities by working providentially in history.

ACTS 14:14–18

In Acts 14, Paul and Barnabas go to Lystra on the first missionary journey. At Paul's word, a man lame from birth jumps up and begins to walk (vv. 8–10). The people proclaim Paul and Barnabas to be the gods Hermes and Zeus, respectively. The apostles do not understand the Lycaonian language the people are speaking. But the body language of the priest of Zeus is unmistakable when he approaches to sacrifice oxen to them (v. 13). In response, Paul and Barnabas tear their robes in revulsion and shout:

> People! Why are you doing these things? We are people also, just like you, and we are proclaiming good news to you, that you turn from these worthless things to the living God, who made the heaven, the earth, the sea, and everything in them. In past generations he allowed all the nations to go their own way, although he did not leave himself without a witness, since he did what is good by giving you rain from heaven and fruitful seasons and filling you with food and your hearts with joy. (vv. 15–17)

God the Creator bears witness of himself in providence. There is general revelation of God in his ordering of life and history (v. 17). Specifically,

---

[8] We acknowledge help from Michael A. Eaton, *Ecclesiastes*, Tyndale Old Testament Commentaries (Downers Grove, IL: InterVarsity, 2009).

[9] Derek Kidner, *NIV Study Bible*, ed. Kenneth Barker (Grand Rapids: Zondervan, 1995), note on Eccl 3:11, 988.

he testifies of himself in his providential acts of giving rain to grow crops and fruit to satisfy our physical and emotional needs (v. 17). This reveals God's existence, his role as Creator, and his generosity (goodness) to all people. The time of this revelation is continual: season after season (implied). And the extent of this revelation is worldwide: wherever there is rain, food, and happiness (implied).

Acts 17:22–29

In Acts 17, Paul addresses the Athenians and notes that among their countless idols is an altar "To an Unknown God." Paul declares to them the one living and true God of whom they are ignorant (v. 23): "The God who made the world and everything in it—he is Lord of heaven and earth" and therefore cannot be confined to a temple. His creatures cannot control or manipulate him, for "he himself gives everyone life and breath and all things" (vv. 24–25). God is not only Creator of all; he also sustains his creation, including humanity. His common grace, his benevolence and kindness to saved and unsaved alike, blesses us with life, breath, and all good gifts (see also Jas 1:16–18).

Following the pattern of Genesis 1, Paul moves from the creation of the heavens and earth to that of men and women. Humanity is one because all are descended from God's first man, Adam. God plans for human beings in general to subdue and care for the earth. He also has particular plans for each nation, appointing the "times and the boundaries of where they live" (Acts 17:26). Note God's purpose in doing this: "that they might seek God, and perhaps they might reach out and find him" (v. 27). God makes human beings to know him, and he is close to all of us. In fact, we depend on him for life, whether or not we realize it (vv. 27–28). God reveals himself in his providential ordering of nations' times and locations so that they might seek and find him.

A Theology of General Revelation

We affirm the objective reality of God's general revelation. God reveals himself to all people, always and everywhere. He discloses himself in creation (Ps 19:1–2; Rom 1:20–21; John 1:4–5), in human beings' moral nature (Rom 1:32; 2:14–15; Eccl 3:11), and in his providence (Acts 14:15–17; 17:26–27). He thus bombards all men and women with knowledge of him. The world around us testifies to its Maker. Our moral makeup bears witness to God. The benefits he confers on humanity in providing rain testify to him.

What does general revelation reveal about God? It manifests his existence, glory (Ps 19:1), divine nature, power, role as Creator (Rom 1:20), holiness, justice, work of judgment (Rom 2:4–15), and goodness (Acts 14:17; 17:26–27). Other divine attributes are inferred: wisdom, beauty, and majesty come quickly to mind.

God's general revelation is universal, occurs at all times, and extends to all people. We thus cannot get away from his revelation. We pass judgments every day that reveal the reality of God's law engraved in our nature (Rom 2:14–15). When we look at the sky or any creature, we see his handiwork. We cannot eat fruits or vegetables without being exposed to his providential goodness (Acts 14:15–17). He arranges nations' times and boundaries so that people might seek him (17:27–28). God does not hide the knowledge of himself!

There are also subjective aspects of general revelation. What gets through to human beings? How do they respond to it? Paul teaches that God makes his external general revelation clear to all people (Rom 1:20). They perceive God's qualities when they look at the things he has made. In this sense, all know God. It is the same with internal general revelation: people show a knowledge of God's holiness whenever they pass judgment on their actions and either excuse or accuse themselves (2:15). In this sense they are a revelation to themselves and others of God's holiness and justice.

However, although God objectively reveals himself to all of us, and although he sees to it that this revelation reaches us, we do not fully profit from God's revelation in creation, conscience, or providence as we ought.[10] Until we come to know Christ, we actively suppress, distort, and misuse God's good disclosure of himself. We oppose his external general

---

[10] For historical and contemporary perspectives on general revelation, see Daniel Strange, "General Revelation," in *Faith Comes by Hearing: A Response to*

revelation, and in pride and rebellion exchange the knowledge of the living God for idols. We misuse his internal general revelation by exercising our sense of morality in hypocrisy (Rom 2:2–3) or by indulging in what we know to be wrong and urging others to do the same (1:32). We enjoy God's providential goodness but fail to give him the glory and instead worship idols, even those we create in our minds (Acts 14:14–17; 17:26–28).

God is patient, but he will not fail to respond to such human rebellion and ingratitude. In the preaching of the gospel, he offers salvation in Christ for all who believe. But he also shows his wrath against all who persistently oppose general revelation (Rom 1:16–18). He gives up such people to their sinful desires and allows them to pursue idolatry, practice sin, and suffer darkened thinking (vv. 21–28). He will justly condemn those who know what is right yet do what is wrong (v. 32). Those hypocritical in their moral judgments are "storing up wrath" for themselves "in the day of wrath, when God's righteous judgment is revealed" (2:5). In sum, due to these people's sinful responses to general revelation, God holds them "without excuse" (1:20).

Other questions emerge. *Is a natural theology (one based on general revelation, not Scripture) possible for unsaved people?* As we have seen, some truths about God shine through general revelation: God's existence, glory (Ps 19:1), divine nature, power, role as Creator (Rom 1:20), holiness, justice, work of judgment (Rom 2:4–15), and goodness (Acts 14:17; 17:26–27). Other truths are surely implied: we are sinners; the wicked will be punished; we need forgiveness; people matter; God is the reason for life, and so forth. But many key truths and concepts would never be known: the Trinity, Jesus, his substitutionary death, his bodily resurrection, justification by faith, the Holy Spirit, and others. Even more, apart from Christ and special revelation, we distort the knowledge and truth we are given. Unfortunately, without Christ we run not to the light but away from it. We exchange God's truth for idolatry, and we avoid God's path and choose obvious sin instead.

Inclusivism, ed. Christopher W. Morgan and Robert A. Peterson (Downers Grove, IL: InterVarsity Press, 2008), 40–77.

Will unsaved people be saved by heeding the light of general revelation?[11] The answer to the question is sadly, no.

Voices from the Global Church: Lausanne Covenant

"We, members of the Church of Jesus Christ, from more than 150 nations . . . praise God for his great salvation. . . . We believe the gospel is God's good news for the whole world, and we are determined by his grace to obey Christ's commission to proclaim it to all mankind and to make disciples of every nation. . . . We affirm that there is only one Saviour and only one gospel. . . . We recognize that everyone has some knowledge of God through his general revelation in nature. But we deny that this can save, for people suppress the truth by their unrighteousness. We also reject as derogatory to Christ and the gospel every kind of syncretism and dialogue which implies that Christ speaks equally through all religions and ideologies. . . . Rather it [to proclaim Jesus as the 'Saviour of the world'] is to proclaim God's love for a world of sinners and to invite everyone to respond to him as Saviour and Lord in the wholehearted personal commitment of repentance and faith."[12]

The Bible is filled with straightforward teaching that Jesus alone is Savior and that faith in Christ is the only means of receiving his salvation. For example, John 3:18 states, "Anyone who believes in [the Son] is not condemned, but anyone who does not believe is already condemned, because he has not believed in the name of the one and only Son of God." John 14:6 states, "Jesus told him, 'I am the way, the truth, and the life. No one comes to the Father except through me'" (see also Acts 4:12; Rom 10:13–17; 1 John 5:11–12).

But we should note that nothing is wrong with general revelation, for it is genuine and clear, effectively communicating many truths about God. The problem is neither general revelation nor its Giver. Rather, the problem is its recipients: fallen people. While Romans 1 shows that people

---

[11] We address this question at length in Morgan and Peterson, *Faith Comes by Hearing.*

[12] https://www.lausanne.org/content/covenant/lausanne-covenant.

should respond positively to God through general revelation, Romans 1 and 3 teach that all are guilty because no one responds in that way on their own. God demands that all humans be righteous (1:18), but "there is no one righteous, not even one" (3:10). Through creation all know God and his truth (1:19–21), but "there is no one who understands" (3:11). God gives a witness so that humans would seek after him (Acts 17:27; Rom 1:18–21), but apart from grace no one does (Rom 3:11). Humans should fear, love, thank, and worship the Creator (1:21–25), but they trade him for idols resembling the creation and have "no fear of God before their eyes" (1:23–25; 3:18). This rebellion and its ensuing guilt are universal. Paul stresses that the problem lies not in God or his general revelation but in universal human rejection of both.

How does general revelation relate to missions? What prompts this question is Paul's practice in evangelism of appealing to general revelation. When preaching Jesus to fellow Jews, Paul points to him as fulfilling the Law and Prophets, citing the Old Testament (see Acts 13:13–52). But when preaching to people from other religions, Paul places the gospel in a larger framework. In Acts 14:8–18 Paul points first to God as Creator and to his witness in general revelation. In Acts 17:16–31 he likewise highlights God as Creator and his true nature and witness through creation and providence. For Paul, then, general revelation is insufficient for salvation but is an important starting point for the gospel. Before missionaries arrive, God is at work, communicating to unbelievers his existence, glory (Ps 19:1), divine nature, power, role as Creator (Rom 1:20), holiness, justice, work of judgment (Rom 2:4–15), and goodness (Acts 14:17; 17:26–27). Missionaries repeat, clarify, and expand this previous communication by sharing the gospel. Missionaries do not start from scratch but build on the point of contact God has made with unbelievers in his general revelation as they urge unbelievers to turn to Christ in faith.[13]

---

[13] See "Answers to Notable Questions" in Morgan and Peterson, eds., *Faith Comes by Hearing*, 247–48.

Knowing God through Special Revelation

As noted from Heb 1:1–2, there are distinctions between revelation in the Old and New Testaments, but we dare not miss the underlying *unity of God's revelation*: "Long ago God spoke to the fathers by the prophets at different times and in different ways. In these last days, he has spoken to us by his Son." *God* reveals himself in the Old and New Testaments. He is the author of biblical revelation. He is the revealer, the speaking God. Old and New Testament revelation is unified because it is all God's speech.[14]

It is also clear from Heb 1:1–2 that *God's revelation is progressive*; that is, he gradually reveals himself to his people over time. God spoke by the prophets and has spoken by his Son. The progressive nature of revelation is inevitably tied to God's providing it to humans gradually in history.

Both the unity and the progressive nature of God's revelation stand out in Jesus's familiar words: "Don't think that I came to abolish the Law or the Prophets. I did not come to abolish but to fulfill. For truly I tell you, until heaven and earth pass away, not the smallest letter or one stroke of a letter will pass away from the law until all things are accomplished" (Matt 5:17–18). We see the unity of revelation in three ways: Jesus's teaching that he does not abolish but fulfills the Law and Prophets (i.e., Old Testament revelation); his graphic assertion about the permanence of the Law and Prophets; and his emphasis that it will all be accomplished. Such revelation's progressive nature is also clear: the Law and the Prophets are moving forward toward fulfillment in Jesus.

Old Testament Revelation

VARIETIES

God reveals himself in the Old Testament "in different ways" (Heb 1:1). These include theophanies, visions and dreams, the Urim and Thummim,

---

[14] Carl F. H. Henry, *God, Revelation, and Authority* (Waco, TX: Word Books, 1976–1983; repr., Wheaton, IL: Crossway, 1999), 2:7–76.

casting of lots, miracles, audible speech, and prophetic declaration.[15] We will examine these in turn.

Theophanies are manifestations of God to human senses, especially sight. The invisible God makes himself visible by appearing to Moses in the burning bush (Exod 3:1–6), to Israel in a pillar of cloud by day and a pillar of fire by night (13:21), and to Isaiah as a King on his throne (Isa 6:1–5), to cite just three examples.

Visions and dreams are means by which God makes known his will to Old Testament saints, including Daniel (in a vision in Dan 10:4–9) and Jacob (in a dream in Gen 28:10–17).

The Urim and Thummim are "a means by which the high priest, when wearing the ephod (a kind of linen waistcoat or jacket) and the breastplate of judgment, learned the will of God concerning the nation of Israel, in cases in which the will of God was not clear (Exod 28:30; Num 27:21; 1 Sam 28:6; Ezra 2:63; Neh 7:65)."[16]

The casting of lots is a means for God to announce his decision between two alternatives or to assign tasks (Lev 16:8–10; 1 Chr 24:1–19; Esth 3:7; 9:24–26; Prov 16:33).

Miracles are supernatural acts of God that reveal his character and will (Deut 4:32–35). They tend to cluster in five critical periods in biblical history: the exodus and conquest of the Promised Land, Elijah and Elisha's ministries, the exile (Daniel), Christ and the apostles' ministries, and the Second Coming.

God's audible speech makes him known to his people, both to the nation of Israel (Exod 19:3–7) and to individuals, such as Samuel (1 Sam 3:1–19).

Prophetic declaration is a common means of God's speaking forth to his people (Isaiah 1) as well as foretelling the future (9:6–7). This includes writing (Ps 19:7–14; Jer 36:2–3, 27–30).

---

[15] We credit the late Robert J. Dunzweiler, former professor of systematic theology at Biblical Theological Seminary, Hatfield, PA, for this material.

[16] Dunzweiler's theology notes.

CHARACTERISTICS

The first characteristic of revelation is its variety: "The complex of Old Testament revelation includes personal encounter, the giving of information and interpretation of events, and God's mighty works."[17]

Revelation is personal. God manifests *himself* to lead people into a saving relationship with him. That is, revelation is primarily redemptive and covenantal in purpose (Gen 17:7; Exod 20:2, 6). Revelation is gracious. God takes the initiative in making himself known (Gen 12:1–3; 15:1; Exod 3:1–6).

Biblical revelation is historical, for God makes himself known in historical events. It is linear, for these events begin with creation and move toward the new heavens and new earth. It is progressive, for God reveals himself not all at once but gradually over time. Revelation thus builds upon itself. Each subsequent revelation complements and supplements preceding revelation. No contradictions are involved, but only clarifications and completions.

Revelation is propositional. It includes the inspired interpretation of God's acts. This interpretation comes through statements of truth (i.e., Scripture). Revelation calls for a response. Faith, repentance, confession, obedience, missions work, prayer, and worship are but a few examples.

New Testament Revelation

VARIETIES

New Testament revelation includes all the varieties noted from the Old Testament except for the Urim and Thummim (as we might expect, since Jesus has fulfilled the role of high priest; Heb 4:14–5:10). These consist of theophanies (Acts 9:1–6), visions (10:9–16), dreams (Matt 1:20–21), casting of lots (Acts 1:23–26), miracles (John 9:1–7), audible speech (12:27–29), and prophetic declaration (Acts 2:14–36) including Scripture and the

---

[17] William A. Dyrness, *Themes in Old Testament Theology* (Downers Grove, IL: InterVarsity, 1980), 37.

witness of the Holy Spirit (John 14:25–26; 15:26; 16:13–15). In addition, New Testament revelation centers on the person and work of Christ.

THE INCARNATION

The incarnation of the Son of God is God's fullest revelation to date (Heb 1:1–2), and we learn of it in Holy Scripture. The invisible God makes himself visible in the incarnation: "No one has ever seen God. The one and only Son, who is himself God and is at the Father's side—he has revealed him" (John 1:18). The God-man is uniquely qualified to be both Revealer and revelation. Erickson's insight is helpful: Christ's humanity "was the means that conveyed the revelation of deity."[18] The apostles have sensory experience of "the Word of life" become flesh: he is, in John's explanation, "what we have heard, what we have seen with our eyes, what we have observed and have touched with our hands" (1 John 1:1).

Jesus makes God known in his character, words, and actions. His character reveals God as never before. The incarnate Son is "the image of the invisible God" (Col 1:15), "the radiance of God's glory and the exact expression of his nature" (Heb 1:3). The apostles testify that in Christ they see God's glory, grace, and truth (John 1:14). Jesus is exasperated when one of his disciples asks for a theophany: "Have I been among you all this time and you do not know me, Philip? The one who has seen me has seen the Father. How can you say, 'Show us the Father'?" (14:9). Jesus's character reveals God as holy, just, generous, merciful, compassionate, faithful, truthful, powerful, sovereign, and wise.

Jesus's words reveal God as never before. Although God manifests himself in Old Testament times "by the prophets," supremely "in these last days, he has spoken to us by his Son" (Heb 1:1–2). The temple police, sent to arrest Jesus, come back empty-handed. Why? They answer: "No man ever spoke like this!" (John 7:46). Jesus himself declares, "The words that I have spoken to you are spirit and are life" (6:63). His words so powerfully reveal God that to reject Jesus is to reject biblical revelation (5:38–47).

Jesus's actions reveal God as never before. His miracles testify mightily to God's presence (Matt 12:28), power (8:23–27), justice (11:20–24),

---

[18] Erickson, *Christian Theology*, 215.

and compassion (9:18–25; 14:14). Moreover, his healings, exorcisms, and nature miracles anticipate the resurrection of the dead and the new earth, as Bavinck asserts: "The anticipation of final glory can be seen especially in Jesus's powerful acts of healing and restoring creation."[19] Jesus's greatest revelatory actions are his death and resurrection, which disclose God's wisdom (Eph 1:7–8), love (Rom 5:6–8), righteousness (3:25–26), power (Heb 2:14–15), and more.

Knowing God through Scripture

Key Passages

An indispensable form of special revelation is Holy Scripture. It is the source of our knowledge of the other forms of revelation, records the history of special revelation, and—most importantly—tells us of Jesus's love, life, death, resurrection, and return. We begin our study of Scripture as revelation with a survey of five key passages.[20]

Mark 12:35–37

On Tuesday of Passion Week, Jesus debates the Pharisees and Herodians over paying a poll tax to Caesar, the Sadducees over the resurrection, and a scribe over the greatest commandment (Mark 12:13–34). Then he confronts the Jews:

> How can the scribes say that the Messiah is the son of David? David himself says by the Holy Spirit: "The Lord declared to my Lord, 'Sit at my right hand until I put your enemies under your feet.'" David himself calls him "Lord"; how then can he be his son? (vv. 35–37)

---

[19] Herman Bavinck, *Reformed Dogmatics*, abridged in one volume, ed. John Bolt (Grand Rapids: Baker Academic, 2011), 78.

[20] For more on this, see our previous treatment of Psalm 119 and Matt 5:17–18, as well as upcoming comments on Psalm 19.

Jesus confounds his enemies. The scribes acknowledge that the Messiah will be a descendant of David, that is, a man. Jesus does not deny the Messiah's humanity but makes his foes deal with an additional truth: the Messiah is also divine. David writes Psalm 110. He relates how God ("the Lord") told David's Lord, the Messiah ("my Lord"), to sit at God's right hand until he defeated the Messiah's enemies. Inspired by the Holy Spirit, King David acknowledges two individuals as Lord: God and the Messiah. As king, David regards no mere man as lord; after all, he was human lord (king) over Israel. Jesus clinches the argument (in v. 37): David calls the Messiah "Lord." But then how is he David's son? How can he be man and God simultaneously? The great crowd enjoys hearing Jesus perplex the Jewish leaders and teachers.

Jesus acknowledges the human authorship of Holy Scripture, for David wrote Psalm 110. Jesus also teaches the divine authorship of Scripture, for David speaks Ps 110:1 "by the Holy Spirit" (Mark 12:36). The Spirit is the agent by which David writes. The Christian Standard Bible's rendering of a parallel passage in Matt 22:43 captures the sense: "How is it then that David, inspired by the Spirit, calls him 'Lord?'" Psalm 110:1 is not merely the product of King David; the Holy Spirit is also guiding the writing process. There is a divine as well as a human aspect to the Bible.

John 10:35

Jesus concludes his Good Shepherd Discourse by claiming that he and the Father are one in keeping God's people safe (John 10:30). The Jews respond by picking up stones to stone him (v. 31). Jesus asks them for which of his many good works from the Father they want to stone him (v. 32). They reply that they are going to stone him not for good works but for blasphemy, because he, a mere man, is making himself equal with God (v. 33). Jesus then uses an Old Testament argument to show that he is not guilty of blasphemy. He appeals to Psalm 82, where the Lord rebukes wicked Israelite magistrates for dealing dishonestly by favoring the wicked and taking advantage of the poor and needy. The Lord reminds them that he is their Judge in heaven, and they will pass away.

Nevertheless, God calls them "gods" because they stand in his place on earth and administer justice to fellow human beings.[21]

Jesus uses a Jewish argument from the harder to the easier. If the more difficult thing is true, that God would call mere human beings "gods," then the less difficult thing is also true, that Jesus could be called God's Son. At first glance, Jesus does not appear to claim deity. Yet on closer inspection, we see that he speaks of his preexistence and incarnation when he mentions "the one the Father set apart and sent into the world" (John 10:36).

Jesus mentions the authoritative Old Testament when he declares, "The Scripture cannot be broken" (v. 35). He provides a clue to the interpretation of the word "broken" by referring to the Jewish law (in v. 34) and quoting from Psalm 82 (in John 10:35). Jesus does not quote from the Law proper, the five books of Moses; he cites a psalm to demonstrate his right to be called Son of God. Jesus regards the whole Old Testament as law, and as such, none of it "can be broken," annulled, or lightly set aside as if it had little authority. He thus teaches that all of the Old Testament is law in the sense of being authoritative.

Jesus also treats the Old Testament as inspired by God. He regards it as God's authority that is able to settle theological disputes. Jesus's affirming the Old Testament's authority implies its inspiration, for the only reason it is authoritative for theology is because it is God's inspired Word.

Jesus does not often speak specifically of the Old Testament's inspiration, but in many passages he demonstrates that he regards it as God's very Word. John Wenham has studied Jesus's own view of Scripture and concluded that he treats it as historically accurate, authoritative for theology and ethics, and verbally inspired revelation from God. Jesus submits himself to it and obeys it throughout his earthly life. Wenham's summary bears repeating.

> To Christ the Old Testament was true, authoritative, inspired. To him the God of the Old Testament was the living God and the

---

[21] For details, see Allen P. Ross, *A Commentary on the Psalms*, vol. 2 *(42–89)* (Grand Rapids: Kregel, 2013), 5–26.

teaching of the Old Testament was the teaching of the living God. To him what Scripture said, God said.

[Moreover, t]o Christ his own teaching and the teaching of his Spirit-taught apostles was true, authoritative, inspired. To him, what he and they said under the direction of the Spirit, God said. To him the God of the New Testament was the living God, and in principle the teaching of the New Testament was the teaching of the living God.[22]

1 Corinthians 14:37–38

Paul writes to correct abuses in the Corinthian congregation concerning the use of the gifts of prophecy and tongues. Apparently some of the Corinthians are being disorderly. Paul urges them to do everything "decently and in order" (1 Cor 14:40). He uses rhetorical questions with sarcasm to confront the Corinthians with the fact that they insist on their own ways and ignore God's (v. 36). He is forced to insist on the apostolic authority of his words: "If anyone thinks he is a prophet or spiritual, he should recognize that what I write to you is the Lord's command. If anyone ignores this, he will be ignored" (vv. 37–38).

Paul desires the spiritual health of the Corinthian church. He appeals to that church, which has an abundance of spiritual gifts, to recognize that he is an apostle and prophet of God. As such, what he writes to them "is the Lord's command" (v. 37). If anyone ignores Paul's words, then he and other believers will ignore that person. This is tantamount to rejection by God. Paul thus exercises his apostolic authority to bring order into the Corinthian church. However, he does not want to squelch their use of spiritual gifts but wants them to regulate and order their use of such gifts under the Word of God (vv. 39–40).

Paul teaches that his writings are the very commandments of God and are to be received and obeyed as possessing divine authority. These are weighty claims for a Jewish man of the first century AD. He puts

---

[22] John Wenham, *Christ and the Bible*, 3rd ed. (Eugene, OR: Wipf and Stock, 2009), 17, 127.

his writings on the same level as God's Old Testament commandments. He thus claims inspiration and divine authority for this section of 1 Corinthians, and by extension, for all of his letters.[23]

2 Timothy 3:14–17

The best-known passage on the inspiration of Scripture is 2 Tim 3:14–17. Paul predicts that the last days will be "hard times" (v. 1). He describes the sinful lifestyle of the people of the last days (vv. 2–9): they will hold to "the form of godliness" (they will be religious), although they will deny "its power" (v. 5). They will "resist the truth" as "men who are corrupt in mind and worthless in regard to the faith" (v. 8). Over against all such wickedness and apostasy, Timothy follows Paul's example in both teaching and life (vv. 10–11). Paul warns Timothy that "evil people and impostors will become worse, deceiving [others] and being deceived [themselves]" (v. 13). Paul predicts doctrinal error and moral decay in the last days.

In contrast to evil men and impostors (v. 13), Timothy is to follow a different path. Paul urges him to continue in the good teachings of the Word of God. Timothy's grandmother, Lois, and mother, Eunice (1:5), have instructed him in proper doctrine and conduct. He has received this instruction and developed convictions concerning it (3:14–15).

Timothy has known the sacred writings of the Old Testament from childhood. Paul describes the Old Testament "sacred Scriptures" as able to make Timothy wise for salvation (v. 15). These holy writings bear the message of saving faith in Jesus Christ.

Paul tells why the Scriptures can rescue sinners: every Scripture passage is "breathed out by God" (v. 16 ESV). Paul pictures God as breathing out or speaking his Word (see Ps 33:6). That is to say, Scripture is God's Word; God is the source of Holy Scripture. Paul further describes

---

[23] Note especially 2 Pet 3:15–16, where the apostle Peter equates Paul's letters with Scripture: "Also, regard the patience of our Lord as salvation, just as our dear brother Paul has written to you according to the wisdom given to him. He speaks about these things in all his letters. There are some matters that are hard to understand. The untaught and unstable will twist them to their own destruction, as they also do with the rest of the Scriptures."

the Bible as useful or beneficial. He gives four areas in which the Bible is useful: for "teaching" (instructing), "rebuking" (convicting), "correcting" (improving), and "training in righteousness" (2 Tim 3:16). The purpose of the Scripture's utility is to make the "man of God" (the pastor or elder; see 1 Tim 6:11) "complete," that is, "equipped for every good work" (2 Tim 3:17). The Scriptures are able to make the pastor proficient and to fit him for service to God and people. And the pastor is to preach Scripture, which Paul simply calls "the word," so that the same effect comes to the church (4:1–5).

In this incredible passage, we learn much about biblical inspiration: (1) Scripture is inspired by God. (2) Scripture is equated with the Word of God. (3) The writings themselves (composed of words), not just the writers, are inspired. (4) Scripture is authoritative for what to believe and how to live. (5) Scripture is effective, a powerful tool that God uses to change us.

2 Peter 1:16–21

In context, Peter tells how God gives the promises of his Word to believers so that they may avoid sin (2 Pet 1:4). He spurs on his readers to godly virtues (vv. 5–7). Peter encourages Christians to pursue godliness in order to strengthen their assurance of salvation (v. 10). Nearing death (v. 14), the apostle writes to remind readers to live for Christ and gives them a written record of these important matters (vv. 12–15). He says,

> We did not follow cleverly contrived myths when we made known to you the power and coming of our Lord Jesus Christ; instead, we were eyewitnesses of his majesty. For he received honor and glory from God the Father when the voice came to him from the Majestic Glory, saying "This is my beloved Son, with whom I am well-pleased!" We ourselves heard this voice when it came from heaven while we were with him on the holy mountain. We also have the prophetic word strongly confirmed, and you will do well to pay attention to it, as to a lamp shining in a dark place, until the day dawns and the morning star rises in your hearts. Above all,

you know this: No prophecy of Scripture comes from the prophet's own interpretation, because no prophecy ever came by the will of man; instead, men spoke from God as they were carried along by the Holy Spirit. (vv. 16–21)

Peter affirms that he and the other apostles did not cleverly concoct myths when they bore witness of Jesus. Peter, James, and John were eyewitnesses of Christ's divine majesty at his transfiguration. The Majestic Glory, God the Father, gave glory and honor to the Lord Jesus Christ. That happened when the Father declared, "This is my beloved Son, with whom I am well-pleased!" (v. 17). Peter and his two fellow disciples heard that utterance when they were with Christ on the Mount of Transfiguration (v. 18).

Next, Peter speaks of the reliable Old Testament prophetic word.[24] Peter, a first-century Jewish Christian, regards the Old Testament as an authority higher than his own experience. He regards the Old Testament prophetic word as very reliable. He exhorts his readers to pay careful attention to Scripture. He uses a simile of a lamp shining in a dark room to show the great reliability of the Bible as a guide. We will need the Word of God in that guiding capacity until the eschatological day breaks and the sun, here a symbol for the returning Jesus, rises in believers' hearts.

Peter next says, "Above all, you know this," stressing the importance of what is to follow: "no prophecy of Scripture comes from the prophet's own interpretation" (v. 20). The prophets do not explain God's Word on their own; they are spokesmen for God.

"No prophecy ever came by the will of man; instead, men spoke from God as they were carried along by the Holy Spirit" (v. 21). Peter explains the previous verse: the prophets do not invent their messages. God is

---

[24] There are three primary views of Peter's meaning in v. 19. View 1: the prophetic word is "strongly confirmed" by the experience of Christ's transfiguration. View 2: believers have something even more reliable than the transfiguration experience: the Old Testament Scriptures—"we also have a more sure word of prophecy" (KJV, Calvin). View 3: the adjective "confirmed" (or "reliable" NIV) is a comparative used as a superlative, hence the Old Testament is "something completely reliable" (NIV).

the source of revelation for the words that they spoke. This was because "they were carried along by the Holy Spirit." The Old Testament writers are the Holy Spirit's instruments when they write Scripture.

There is a human side to Scripture. Human beings speak when they write God's Word (v. 21). This passage emphasizes not the human side, however, but the divine. When the writers write, "they spoke from God" (v. 21). The source of their writing lays outside of themselves, in God. He speaks through them.

Specifically, God the Holy Spirit moves the writers of Scripture as they speak from God. The Spirit so directs the writers that they speak for God. The words of Scripture are not the products of human will alone. They are also the very words of God, for by his Spirit he guides the writers so that they write his Word. The source of the Bible, then, is ultimately God himself. Peter's words pertain first of all to the autographs. The *autographs* are the original texts of the books of the Bible, rather than copies. God inspires the autographs through human authors.

Because of this divine-human character, the Word of God has great authority and reliability. We are to base our faith on it. It confirms the apostles' experiences with Christ. It is an essential guide as we live in a dark world until Jesus returns. By implication from the following context, Scripture is also the antidote to false teaching (2 Peter 2). Scripture has a trinitarian character: the Father spoke concerning the Son through Spirit-directed writers.

Scripture Is Inspired

VIEWS OF INSPIRATION

We begin with five views set forth by Millard Erickson.[25]

The *intuition theory* holds that inspiration is a matter of insight exercised by religious geniuses. Some people are naturally endowed with great spiritual awareness. The Bible's inspiration is similar to that of other

---

[25] Erickson, *Christian Theology*, 231–33.

thinkers, such as Plato. The Bible is grand religious literature reflecting the religious genius of the Hebrew people.

The *illumination theory* holds that the Holy Spirit influences the Scripture writers by heightening their normal powers. The Spirit works in all believers in the same way; he works in the Scripture writers to a greater degree. The Spirit does not specially communicate truth or guide the writers of the Bible. He increases their sensitivity to spiritual matters when they write.

The *dynamic theory* holds that God works in combination with human writers to produce the Scriptures. Specifically, the Spirit guides the writers to have the thoughts or concepts that he desires. God permits the writers to express his thoughts in their own words.

The *verbal theory* holds that the Holy Spirit not only gives the writers the thoughts that God wants them to have, but also guides their use of words. The result is that the Bible contains the very words God wants written. This differs from the dictation theory. In the verbal theory, God actively guides the thoughts and words, but the human author is active too.

The *dictation theory* holds that God dictates the very words of the Bible to the Scripture writers. The writers are largely passive in the process. The emphasis here is on the divine side of Scripture; the human is greatly minimized.

To these we would add two more views.

The *neoorthodox view* critiques both conservative and liberal views of revelation. One proponent censures orthodoxy for identifying revelation as biblical propositions, for defining faith as acceptance of facts instead of as trust in God, and for holding that God dictated the Bible.[26] That same proponent censures liberalism for overemphasizing reason and for attempting to separate the kernel and husk of Scripture. He holds that revelation consists of God himself, not propositions about him, but in acts. These revelatory acts occur in Israel's history and climax in Jesus Christ, God's supreme revelation. The interpretation of these acts varies

---

[26] John Baillie, *The Idea of Revelation in Recent Thought* (New York: Columbia University Press, 1956).

based on the critical leanings of the theologian. Revelation is subjective, so that without appropriation, no revelation occurs.

Limited inerrancy is set forth in contrast to full inerrancy. Some scholars make a distinction between full and limited inerrancy, with the latter holding that Scripture is inerrant in what pertains to faith and life but need not be inerrant in matters of history, science, and so on. Some advocates of limited inerrancy hold that Scripture is not inerrant but infallible, defined as Scripture's unfailingly accomplishing God's intended purpose of salvation. Those adopting full inerrancy hold to the complete truthfulness of the Bible without denying its infallibility.

EVALUATING THE VIEWS OF INSPIRATION

Contrary to the *intuition theory*, inspiration is not a matter of religious geniuses exercising spiritual insight. Inspiration is a special work of God, speaking his Word through the Scripture writers. God is the author of Scripture in a much more immediate sense than this theory allows. It is correct to think of inspiration as involving God's providential preparing of the writers before writing. It is incorrect to say that God is the source of Scripture only in the sense of endowing those writers with great religious awareness. God is the source of his Word in that he is its ultimate author. The Spirit directed the writers so that they spoke *for God* (2 Pet 1:21).

Contrary to the *illumination theory*, the inspiration of Scripture is different in kind, not only in degree, from other types of "inspiration." Every Scripture passage is the result of God's speaking forth his Word (2 Tim 3:16).

The *dynamic theory* is correct in seeing both God and humans as actively working together in the production of Scripture. God works in the writers of Scripture and uses their styles, vocabularies, and personalities to express his Word. Real humans speak when they write God's Word. However, this theory errs when it limits God's influence to the thoughts of Scripture. God also breathes out the words (2 Tim 3:16).

The *verbal theory* of inspiration is correct in what it affirms but is incomplete. It is not enough to affirm that God inspires the words of Scripture and to deny dictation. The Bible gives information that leads us to say more about Scripture's production. The divine-human working together of the dynamic theory is also an important aspect of a biblical theory of inspiration.

The dictation theory rightly affirms that the words of Scripture are the words of God. But it incorrectly posits dictation as the mode of inspiration. Parts of the Bible are dictated, for example, the Ten Commandments. Nevertheless, the different styles and vocabularies of the writers, the statement of Luke 1:1–4, and other scriptural data will not allow for dictation of the whole. God authors the Bible through human writers. The result is God's words in human language. This is an expression of God's grace, as he reveals himself *through* human beings *to* human beings.

The *neoorthodox view* rightly affirms the importance of God's personal revelation. But it errs in four ways. First, it denies that personal revelation occurs in words and posits a false dichotomy between personal and verbal inspiration.[27] Scripture's narratives, psalms, and parables are not ends in themselves. Rather, they are God's means to draw people into fellowship with him (1 John 1:3). Second, this view caricatures the verbal theory. Though God dictates parts of Scripture, mostly he uses the authors' experiences, vocabularies, and so on to produce his holy Word. Evangelicals consistently reject the dictation theory, adopting instead an organic view of inspiration in which God and human authors play roles. In ways we do not understand, God directs their writing, as "men spoke from God as they were carried along by the Holy Spirit" (2 Pet 1:21). Third, God reveals himself in deed *and* word. He acts in history, but deeds are not self-interpreting. So God acts and speaks to interpret his acts. Fourth, though people do not benefit spiritually from God's truth without faith, revelation occurs whether or not they appropriate it.[28]

Limited inerrancy rightly denies that the Bible is a history or science text. Its advocates err, however, when they teach that Scripture stumbles

---

[27] This dichotomy appears in Jack Rogers and Donald McKim, *The Authority and Interpretation of the Bible: An Historical Approach* (Eugene, OR: Wipf and Stock, 1999).

[28] We thank David G. Dunbar for help in this section. See also Henry, *God, Revelation, and Authority*; David S. Dockery, "Special Revelation," in *A Theology for the Church*, ed. Daniel L. Akin, 2nd ed. (Nashville: B&H, 2011), 103–53.

in matters of history, science, and other subjects. God speaks truth in
his Word. Its purposes are to save and sanctify his people. In writing to
accomplish those goals, God speaks truthfully of other matters as well.
The Bible may not speak with modern scientific precision, but it speaks
truth. Some holding to limited inerrancy deny inerrancy but hold to infallibility, which they define as Scripture unfailingly accomplishing God's
purposes. This misuses the word "infallibility" to teach errancy. Scripture
uses various literary genres to accomplish God's many purposes, but it
does so inerrantly. The biblical concept of truth involves not only faithfulness but also factualness and completeness.[29]

A THEOLOGY OF INSPIRATION

It is time to draw together a theology of the inspiration of Scripture. We
hold to an organic view of inspiration in which both God and the human
writers play roles. This view has also been called *concursus*, underlining
the coauthorship of Scripture, and *confluence*, as in two rivers running
together to become one. Scripture originates with God, who speaks forth
his Word. Thus, it will not do to speak of God's inspiring the authors
but not the words: "All *Scripture* is inspired by God" (2 Tim 3:16). God
is Scripture's ultimate author; this is our starting place. God directly
inspires the autographs of Scripture. The *autographs* are the original
texts of the biblical books, not copies. In his providence, he also preserves Scripture through the centuries so that the Bibles we have today
are reliable copies.

God uses human authors to produce his Word: "men spoke from God
as they were carried along by the Holy Spirit" (2 Pet 1:21). The Spirit
guides the writers so that they speak his words. Scripture is human and
divine. Its humanity is evident. The writers have different vocabularies, styles, and emphases. They study (Luke 1:1–4) and write of their

---

[29] See the language of "truth," "word," "gospel, and "sound doctrine" in the
Pastoral Epistles. See also Roger Nicole, "The Biblical Concept of Truth," in
Scripture and Truth, ed. D. A. Carson and John D. Woodbridge (Grand Rapids:
Baker Academic, 1992), 287–98; John D. Woodbridge, *Biblical Authority: A
Critique of the Rogers/McKim Proposal* (Grand Rapids: Zondervan, 1982).

experiences (1 John 1:1–3; 2 Cor 11:21–33). God graciously uses humans to communicate to humans.

We reject the idea that the writers get their ideas from their own minds, apart from God. God uses their minds, but they never get their information merely from themselves, since "no prophecy of Scripture comes from the prophet's own interpretation" (2 Pet 1:20). Likewise, we affirm that God providentially guides in giving Scripture. He uses Moses's education and background as he writes the Pentateuch; he uses Paul's rabbinical training as he writes his letters. But we affirm that God does more than exercise his providence in preparing the writers. He not only guides; he speaks. He works in a special way when the writers write. Our inability to understand fully how God does this is not surprising, for divine/human interaction is beyond our grasp. We believe Christ is God and man, although we cannot fully explain the incarnation. Likewise, we believe that the Bible is God's Word without fully understanding inspiration.

We know that God works through people to give us his Word. The result is the very Word of God written, "the sacred Scriptures" (2 Tim 3:15). The ways that God uses to do this largely remain a mystery. Organic inspiration affirms a divine-human working together, a concursus or confluence. This is in keeping with the message of Scripture, which tells us the result of inspiration but little about the means God employed.

We affirm the plenary and verbal inspiration of Scripture on the basis of 2 Tim 3:16: "*All* Scripture is inspired by God." *Plenary* means that not only the parts but also the whole of Scripture is God's Word. *Verbal* means that not only the ideas but also the words are God's Word. *Inspiration* pertains to the writers and the writings, the process and the product of Scripture.

Jesus and his apostles affirm verbal inspiration. Jesus assures, "Until heaven and earth pass away, not the smallest letter or one stroke of a letter will pass away from the law until all things are accomplished" (Matt 5:18). His point in Matt 22:32 rests on the tense of a verb in Exod 3:6. Similarly, Paul's point in Gal 3:16 rests on a singular noun in Gen 12:7.

Moreover, God directs the writing of the words of Scripture to convey the thoughts he wants. Words convey thoughts. Thus, we cannot talk about the inspiration of the words apart from thoughts or the giving of thoughts apart from words.

THE RESULTS OF INSPIRATION

Vital results follow from the fact that God is the ultimate Author of the Bible. Because this is so, Scripture is God's Word, authoritative, inerrant, sufficient, clear, and beneficial. The rest of this chapter addresses these themes.

Scripture Is God's Word

Voices from Church History: Carl F. H. Henry

Henry (1913–2003) was an American evangelical Baptist theologian who helped lead evangelicalism in the mid-to-late twentieth century. He helped create the Evangelical Theological Society to encourage academic dialogue among evangelicals. He was the founding editor of *Christianity Today* as a scholarly voice for evangelical Christianity and a challenger to the liberal *Christian Century*. In 1978 he signed the Chicago Statement on Biblical Inerrancy. Henry finished his most famous work, the six-volume *God, Revelation, and Authority*, in 1983.

> God's revelation is rational communication conveyed in intelligible ideas and meaningful words, that is, in conceptual-verbal form. The mediating agent in all divine revelation is the Eternal Logos (Jesus)—preexistent, incarnate, and now glorified. God's revelation is uniquely personal both in content and form. God reveals himself not only universally in the history of the cosmos and of the nations, but also redemptively within this external history in unique saving acts (e.g., the Exodus, . . . the Church, etc.). The climax of God's special revelation is Jesus of Nazareth, the personal incarnation of God in the flesh; in Jesus Christ, the source and content of revelation converge and coincide. . . . Jesus of Nazareth is not simply the bearer of an inner divine authority, but is himself the Word enfleshed.[30]

---

[30] Henry, "Fifteen Theses on Revelation," *God, Revelation, and Authority*, 2:10–12.

We affirm that Scripture is the Word of God for four reasons. First, it is routinely called (and equated with) the Word of God. It is the "sacred" writings (2 Tim 3:15), "breathed out by God" (v. 16 ESV), "the word" (4:2), "the truth" (v. 4). Paul does not break new ground in saying this but reminds Timothy of what he already knows from the Old Testament. Indeed, texts such as Ps 19:7–11 underline that the Scripture is the Word "of the LORD," using repetition for effect:

> The instruction of the LORD is perfect, renewing one's life;
> the testimony of the LORD is trustworthy, making the inexperienced
>   wise.
> The precepts of the LORD are right, making the heart glad;
> the command of the LORD is radiant, making the eyes light up.
> The fear of the LORD is pure, enduring forever;
> the ordinances of the LORD are reliable and altogether righteous.
> They are more desirable than gold—than an abundance of pure
>   gold;
> and sweeter than honey, dripping from a honeycomb.
> In addition, your servant is warned by them; and in keeping them
>   there is an abundant reward.

Second, as we saw, God directs the writers so that Scripture is inspired by him (2 Pet 1:20–21; 2 Tim 3:16). This is dynamic and verbal inspiration: the supernatural work of the Holy Spirit upon Scripture's human authors so that they write what God intends to communicate—his truth.[31] This definition speaks both of God's action by his Spirit in the human authors and of the nature of the resulting text.

Third, Scripture bears characteristics of God and performs key functions for him. In Psalm 19, quoted above, the Word of the Lord, like its author, is described as perfect, trustworthy, right, radiant, pure, enduring forever, reliable, and altogether righteous. And because God's Word bears these marks, it is effective to accomplish God's purposes: it renews life,

---

[31] D. A. Carson, "Approaching the Bible," in *Collected Writings on Scripture*, compiled by Andrew David Naselli (Wheaton, IL: Crossway, 2010), 31.

brings wisdom, fosters joy, teaches truth, warns, and leads to blessing (vv. 7–11).

Fourth, Jesus and the apostles attribute to God many Old Testament statements not originally attributed to him: Matt 19:4–5 of Gen 2:24, Acts 4:25–26 of Ps 2:1–2, Acts 13:35 of Ps 16:10, and Heb 1:7 of Ps 104:4. New Testament writers also sometimes say that God "said" or "the Holy Spirit . . . says" when citing Old Testament passages in which God does not directly address the writer (e.g., Heb 7:21; 10:15–17). Carson notes, "The words of Scripture and the words of God are so equated that Paul can personify Scripture (Rom 9:17; Gal 3:8, 22)."[32] Paul thus presupposes that what Scripture says, God says.

We believe that Scripture is God's Word, and we believe that the Bible is simultaneously a human book. God gives us Scripture through human authors, in human language, to human beings, so that people would come to know and love him. It is one book composed of sixty-six books, grounded in history and written over 1,600 years on three continents (Asia, Africa, and Europe). It is written by forty authors from all walks of life with various gifts, styles, and personalities.

Written in human languages (Hebrew, Greek, and a little Aramaic), in ordinary speech, with loose quotations and approximations, Scripture uses varied literary genres, as Carson lists:

> Poetry and prose, narrative and discourse, oracle and lament, parable and fable, history and theology, genealogy and apocalyptic, proverb and psalm, Gospel and letter, law and Wisdom Literature, missive and sermon, couplet and epic—the Bible is made up of all of these, and more. Covenantal patterns emerge with some likeness to Hittite treaties; tables of household duties are found with startling resemblances to codes of conduct in the Hellenistic world. And these realities, a by-product of the humanness of the Bible, necessarily affect how we must approach the Bible to interpret it aright.[33]

---

[32] Carson, "Approaching the Bible," 31.

[33] Carson, 26. We found much help in this section from this insightful volume. See also Carson, *The Gagging of God*, 193–345 (see chap. 1, n. 6).

The Bible addresses a wide range of subjects: history, psychology, child rearing, poetry, music, moral law, political law, military strategy, philosophy, science, and primarily salvation.

Over time it progressively tells the story of God and his relationship with people. It bears human witness to God through stories of love and joy, pain and persecution, fear and hope.

Scripture is collected from its beginning to the first century AD, and the church progressively recognizes it. It is written for us to know God, love him, love others, and live according to his purposes. Despite its diversity in authors, times, genres, and topics, it has an amazing unity of message. This is because Scripture is the very Word of God in human words.[34]

Scripture Is Authoritative

Voices from the Global Church: Conrad Mbewe

Mbewe from Zambia wrote, "The Bible is God's Word to humankind, revealing heaven's great plan of salvation. Scripture therefore comes to us from above, calling for reverence. . . . As we read, then, we are to sit under the Word of God, not stand over it. We must 'receive with meekness the implanted word' (James 1:21; compare John 12:48). When the commands of God contradict our own desires, we must submit to what God has revealed to us. This requires a deliberate humility to receive the Bible in its entirety, whatever it says. Such is the reverence called for by the sacred nature of Scripture."[35]

Because God gives Scripture, it possesses his authority. By *authority* we mean the right to teach God's truth and command obedience. Scripture has supreme authority because it is the Word of God—to us and for us.

---

[34] See Christopher W. Morgan, "New Testament Theology," in *Theology, Church, and Ministry: A Handbook for Theological Education*, ed. David S. Dockery (Nashville: B&H, 2017), 217–32.

[35] Conrad Mbewe, "How to Read and Understand the Bible," in *ESV Global Study Bible* (Wheaton, IL: Crossway, 2012), 1866.

In Psalm 19, quoted above, the psalmist likens the Word of God to God's instruction, his witness, his precepts, his command, his fear, and his ordinances, and it carries his authority.

In 2 Timothy 3, treated previously, Paul teaches that God gives Scripture for four purposes: teaching, rebuke, correction, and training in righteousness (v. 16). The Bible is given to teach us what to believe, what not to believe, what not to do, and what to do. It is authoritative over our beliefs and behavior, which is also why Paul urges Timothy to preach the Word (4:1–5).

In 2 Peter 1, also treated previously, Peter teaches concerning Scripture and warns the churches accordingly: "You will do well to pay attention to it" (v. 19). God inspires Scripture, so naturally we should listen to it and follow its teachings.

Christ and the apostles regard Scripture as our authority for theology and ethics.[36] The degree to which we refuse to submit to biblical authority is the degree to which we create our own beliefs and rules for living. And the degree to which we do not study Scripture is the degree to which we may inadvertently follow our culture's theologies and ethics.

That Scripture bears God's authority also means that we do not get to pick and choose what we like or do not like in it. The Word of God is over us: we respect it, believe it, and obey it even if we initially do not prefer it. We remain humble listeners, not the Word's critics, editors, or redactors. If we pick and choose what we want to believe from Scripture, we assert ourselves as the chief authorities rather than God.

Scripture Is Inerrant

Scripture is inspired by God and is his Word. As we have seen, God inspires the biblical *writers*, as Peter explains: "No prophecy of Scripture comes from the prophet's own interpretation, because no prophecy ever came by the will of man; instead, men spoke from God as they were carried along by the Holy Spirit" (2 Pet 1:20–21).

---

[36] See also Mark 12:35–37; John 10:35; 1 Cor 14:37–38.

And God inspires the biblical *writings* (2 Tim 3:16). He uses the experiences, personalities, and thoughts of the prophets and apostles, yet he directs what they speak and write. Thus, inspiration is *dynamic*; God actively works through the active human authors. This inspiration is also *verbal*, referring to the actual writings (v. 16) and words (not only the ideas) that the prophets spoke (2 Pet 1:20–21). And it is *plenary* (full), as God inspires all Scripture (not merely its parts; Ps 119:160; 2 Tim 3:15–17).

The result is that Scripture is *inerrant*, truthful in all that it affirms. Carson summarizes: inspiration is the "supernatural work of God's Holy Spirit upon the human authors of Scripture such that what they wrote was precisely what God intended them to write in order to communicate his truth." He adds, "The definition speaks both of God's action, by his Spirit, in the human author and of the nature of the resulting text."[37] Thus, inspiration includes God's verbal revelation and historical human witness, "words of human beings and words of God, the truth that God chose to communicate and the particular forms of individual human authors."[38] Inspired by God, Scripture is truthful, authoritative over our beliefs and lives, and one way God acts in the world to accomplish his mission (2 Tim 3:15–4:5) so that people glorify God through faith in Jesus, the Lord and Savior (John 20:28–31; 1 John 5:12–13).

CLARIFICATIONS OF INERRANCY[39]

Regarding Scripture as fully truthful brings confidence but also demands clarification.

Inerrancy is ascribed to the autographs (the original texts), not to copies of the Bible. We respect historical process and value textual criticism because textual variants are undergirded by an inerrant original text.[40]

---

[37] Carson, "Approaching the Bible," 31.

[38] Carson, 32.

[39] We credit David G. Dunbar for many of the ideas in this section. For a more thorough treatment of these issues, see the Chicago Statement on Biblical Inerrancy (1978, https://library.dts.edu/Pages/TL/Special/ICBI_1.pdf).

[40] We were helped by David G. Dunbar, "The Biblical Canon," in *Hermeneutics, Authority, and Canon* (Eugene, OR: Wipf and Stock, 2005), 299–326. Dunbar suggests concerning the canon (the authoritative books of the Bible) that

Inerrancy is rooted in the belief that the Bible is simultaneously a human book and the Word of God. Therefore, we prize the human aspects of the Bible. These aspects do not diminish the Bible's truthfulness but show that God uses real people in historical contexts to write to real people with real needs. The biblical authors write in ordinary form and style, and as such, there are certain things not required for inerrancy:

> Inerrancy does not expect Scripture's adherence to modern rules of grammar or spelling.

> Inerrancy is compatible with figurative language of various literary genres.

> Inerrancy does not expect historical precision or completeness.

> Inerrancy does not expect the technical language of modern science.

> Inerrancy does not expect that the Gospel writers give the exact words of Jesus, only the exact voice. They give the correct sense of Jesus's words but do not always quote in contemporary forms. This is the same for the speeches and sermons in Acts.

Inerrancy informs exegesis. Since the Word of God comes in the language of human authors, we must pay attention to the words, sentences, context, genres, arguments, and themes of any passage. The Bible's meaning is related to its authors' intentions.

Inerrancy relates to *hermeneutics* (approach to interpretation). A commitment to inerrancy involves not only appreciating the Bible's diversity but also recognizing its unity and doctrinal consistency. This also leads us to the hermeneutical *analogy (rule) of faith*, whereby we compare Scripture with Scripture and interpret it in harmony with its overall message.

---

the church recognized rather than established the canon, as the church father Irenaeus already taught; that the canon is not only apostolic but fundamentally Christological or redemptive-historical; that the words and deeds of Jesus interpreted to the community of apostles form the standard for the early church; that the church regarded apostolicity as the qualifying factor for canonical recognition—not strictly authorship, but content and chronology; and that we acknowledge God's providential control of history in this process.

Scripture is not only authoritative and *inerrant* (truthful) but also infallible. Until the mid-twentieth century, the term *infallible* was used synonymously with "inerrant." In light of recent developments, Kevin Vanhoozer proposes a broader definition: inerrancy is a subset of infallibility. Infallibility means that God's Word, by means of its different genres, accomplishes many things unfailingly.[41] Scripture aims at more than communicating truth. It does so inerrantly but also gives wisdom, warns, encourages, offers hope, energizes, and so on. God uses many types of biblical literature to achieve his many purposes (Isa 55:10–11; Rom 1:16; 10:17; Heb 4:12–13).

Scripture Is Sufficient

God's Word provides all that his people need to gain eternal life and to live godly lives. This is called *the sufficiency of Scripture*. Referring to God, Peter explains:

> His divine power has given us everything required for life and godliness through the knowledge of him who called us by his own glory and goodness. By these he has given us very great and precious promises, so that through them you may share in the divine nature, escaping the corruption that is in the world because of evil desire. (2 Pet 1:3–4; see also v. 19; 2 Tim 3:15–17)

Peter extols God's power because it supplies us with "everything required for life and godliness"—all we need to know God and pursue holiness (2 Pet 1:3). God's "glory and goodness," his beauty and moral perfection, give us his Word with its "very great and precious promises" (v. 4). In turn, Scripture's promises enable us to partake of God's nature and escape the world's corruption (v. 4). Peter does not mean that we will become divine but that by God's grace we will share his moral excellence at Christ's return. Even now God uses his Word to promote his

---

[41] Kevin J. Vanhoozer, "The Semantics of Biblical Literature," in *Hermeneutics, Authority, and Canon*, ed. D. A. Carson and John D. Woodbridge (Eugene, OR: Wipf and Stock, 2005), 94.

people's godliness. Scripture is sufficient to save and sanctify those who believe it.

The Word of God is also sufficient to guide us. Peter likens the Word to a lamp that provides light in a dark room: "We also have the prophetic word . . . and you will do well to pay attention to it, as to a lamp shining in a dark place, until the day dawns and the morning star rises in your hearts" (v. 19). Although the world is dark, devoid of the knowledge of God, we have the "word" and follow it as "a lamp" for our feet and "a light" for our path (Ps 119:105) until the Second Coming.

Reason, experience, and tradition all have a place in theological study, but they are subordinate to Holy Scripture, which alone is sufficient. In Jesus's parable, when a rich man in hell asks father Abraham (who speaks for God) to send someone from the dead to warn his unrepentant broth-ers, "Abraham [says], 'They have Moses and the prophets; they should listen to them.' 'No, father Abraham,' he said. 'But if someone from the dead goes to them, they will repent.' But he told him, 'If they don't listen to Moses and the prophets, they will not be persuaded if someone rises from the dead'" (Luke 16:29–31).

The sufficiency of Scripture does not mean, however, that we do not need each other or anything else. Obviously, and as we discussed in the process of theology, God gives us church leaders and teachers to help us learn and apply his Word. We need others to teach us, and they need us too.

Scripture Is Clear

God so reveals himself in Scripture that, as God's people, we are able to understand its basic message. This is called the *clarity* or *perspicuity of Scripture*. The Word makes wise the "inexperienced" (or, "simple"; Ps 19:7 ESV, NIV). Parents are to teach the Word to their children (Deut 6:1–9). Believers are expected to understand it. Scripture's clarity, though, does not mean that all things in it are equally easy to understand (Rom 11:33–36; 2 Pet 3:16). It means instead that the gospel and the basic teach-ings of the Bible, including those pertaining to the Christian life, can be understood. God inspires his Word to teach us, help us, and change us, and he does so effectively.

Voices from the Global Church: Whan Kim

Kim from South Korea wrote, "[The Bible] is not accessible only to an elite and specially favored few. That the books of the Bible were written by many human writers from diverse places over many centuries does not undermine its clarity, for the singularity of the divine authorship guarantees the continuity and organic unity of its contents and message. . . . Yet while the Bible is in places hard to understand, this is not because of any elitism on the part of the biblical authors. The Bible is written for ordinary people, not using some kind of heavenly language or mysterious code words but ordinary, plain language, which the Bible's first readers could readily interpret. Consequently, those who today earnestly seek to understand the Bible can be confident of success in their endeavor."[42]

However, believers read the Bible with God's help, for the Holy Spirit is their teacher. This is God's illumination of his Word. *Illumination* is the work of the Holy Spirit to enable people to understand, believe, and apply Scripture. The same Spirit who inspires the Word of God works in us so that we embrace its message.

There is a famine of the Word of God among the exiles taken to Babylon under King Nebuchadnezzar and who returned to Jerusalem with Nehemiah and others (Neh 7:4–7). The people ask Ezra the scribe to read the Scriptures to them (8:1). He does so from "daybreak until noon" for adults and children old enough to understand. "All the people listened attentively to the book of the law" (v. 3). The Word is clear to them, and they understand it, for "all the people were weeping as they heard" it (v. 9). After they are encouraged, the people had "a great celebration, because they had understood the words that were explained to them" (v. 12).

After jealous Jews caused a riot in Thessalonica, believers send Paul and Silas to Berea (Acts 17:10). As is their custom, they go to the synagogue and preach Christ. Luke, the author of Acts, commends the Bereans: "The people here were of more noble character than those in Thessalonica, since they received the word with eagerness and examined

---

[42] Whan Kim, "The Reliability and Authority of the Bible," in *ESV Global Study Bible*, 1872–73.

the Scriptures daily to see if these things were so" (v. 11). The Bereans
eagerly and diligently study the Old Testament to see if Paul's message
about Christ is true. Assumed here is the clarity of the Scriptures. The
Bereans are able to understand the Old Testament's message concerning
the Messiah. They compare that message with Paul's words and find his
words true. The Word of God is clear and powerful, for "consequently,
many of them believed, including a number of the prominent Greek
women as well as men" (v. 12).[43]

Scripture Is Beneficial

God's holy Word is useful and beneficial to believers in many ways. First,
it alone brings the message of salvation, as Timothy learned at a young
age. Paul reminds him, "You know that from infancy you have known
the sacred Scriptures, which are able to give you wisdom for salvation
through faith in Christ Jesus" (2 Tim 3:15).

Second, God uses Scripture to equip pastors for their ministries: God
inspired his Word "so that the man of God may be complete, equipped for
every good work" (v. 17). Moreover, the pastor's main task is to minister
God's Word to God's people: "Preach the word; be ready in season and
out of season; rebuke, correct, and encourage with great patience and
teaching" (4:2).

Third, Scripture is God's antidote to the poison of false teaching.
The two great New Testament passages on Scripture (2 Tim 3:16–17 and
2 Pet 1:20–21) are embedded in contexts that warn of false teaching in
the last days (2 Tim 4:3–4; 2 Pet 2:1–2). God gives his Word to protect his
people from the false teaching that characterizes the last days.

Fourth, the Bible is God's main tool to help his people grow in grace
and in the knowledge of Christ. Paul gives a powerful general statement
to this effect: God gives Scripture, and it "is profitable for teaching, for
rebuking, for correcting, for training in righteousness" (2 Tim 3:16). When

---

[43] We affirm Scripture's clarity, and we value the importance of the Holy Spirit
working with the Word. The Spirit takes the Word and makes it effective in hearers' lives.

it comes to particulars, God uses his Word to minister to his people in numerous ways. From Psalm 19 we find that God's Word renews life, brings wisdom, fosters joy, teaches truth, warns, and leads to blessing (vv. 7–11).

Psalm 119, the Bible's longest chapter, is filled with ways that God uses his Word to benefit us. Scripture produces reverence for God (vv. 38, 79), purifies (vv. 9, 11), strengthens (vv. 28, 175), comforts (vv. 50, 52), and gives life (vv. 93, 156), hope (vv. 49, 116), discernment (v. 66), wisdom (vv. 98–100), understanding (vv. 104, 130, 169), and guidance (vv. 105, 130).

God's Word is beneficial in that it prompts in us such attitudes toward the Word as longing (vv. 40, 131), delight (vv. 16, 174), love (vv. 97, 167), and fear (vv. 120, 161). In addition, it elicits meditation (vv. 15, 148), obedience (vv. 5, 112), joy (vv. 2, 111), rejoicing (vv. 14, 162), hope (vv. 43, 147), and gratitude to God (v. 62). The priceless value of God's Word compels us to echo the words of the psalmist:

> Open my eyes so that I may contemplate wondrous things from your instruction. (v. 18)

> Instruction from your lips is better for me than thousands of gold and silver pieces. (v. 72)

> LORD, your word is forever; it is firmly fixed in heaven. (v. 89)

> How sweet your word is to my taste—sweeter than honey in my mouth. (v. 103)

> I rejoice over your promise like one who finds vast treasure. (v. 162)

▓ KEY TERMS

apostle	limited inerrancy
authority	natural revelation
canon	necessity
clarity	prophet
dictation theory	providence
dynamic theory	revelation
general revelation	Scripture
illumination	*sola Scriptura*
illumination theory	sufficiency
inerrancy	tradition
infallibility	truth
inspiration	verbal inspiration
intuition theory	

▓ RESOURCES FOR FURTHER STUDY

Allison, Gregg R. *Historical Theology: An Introduction to Christian Doctrine.* Grand Rapids: Zondervan, 2011, 59–184.

Carson, D. A., ed. *The Enduring Authority of the Christian Scriptures.* Grand Rapids: Eerdmans, 2016.

Chicago Statement on Biblical Inerrancy. https://library.dts.edu/Pages/TL /Special/ICBI_1.pdf.

Demarest, Bruce. *General Revelation: Historical Views and Contemporary Issues.* Grand Rapids: Zondervan, 1982.

Dockery, David S. *Christian Scripture.* Nashville: B&H, 1995.

Geisler, Norman L., ed. *Inerrancy.* Grand Rapids: Zondervan, 1980.

Helm, Paul. *The Divine Revelation: The Basic Issues.* Westchester, IL: Crossway, 1982.

Henry, Carl F. H. *God, Revelation and Authority.* 1976–83. Reprint, Wheaton: Crossway, 1999.

Jensen, Peter. *The Revelation of God.* Contours of Christian Theology. Downers Grove, IL: InterVarsity, 2002.

Kruger, Michael. *Canon Revisited: Establishing the Origins and Authority of the New Testament Books.* Wheaton, IL: Crossway, 2012.

Morris, Leon. *I Believe in Revelation.* London: Hodder and Stoughton, 1976.

Packer, J. I. *"Fundamentalism" and the Word of God.* London: InterVarsity, 1958.

Stott, John R. W. *The Authority of the Bible.* Downers Grove, IL: InterVarsity, 1974.

Ward, Timothy. *Words of Life: Scripture as the Living and Active Word of God.* Downers Grove, IL: InterVarsity, 2009.

Wenham, John. *Christ and the Bible.* 3rd ed. Eugene, OR: Wipf and Stock, 2009.

3

GOD THE TRINITY

This whole book is about *theology*, the study of God. Although every chapter in this book concerns the study of God, the next two chapters focus on God in a special way. In this chapter we view God in light of the biblical story, examine select passages about God, and focus on the Trinity: God as Father, Son, and Holy Spirit. In the next chapter we will study God's attributes, both unique ones and those he shares with humans, as well as his works of creation and providence.

OBJECTIVES

- To lay a biblical foundation for understanding the doctrine of God
- To motivate us to love, worship, and serve the Holy Trinity
- To establish our identity as individuals who belong to God

OUTLINE

Our God in the Biblical Story
Our God in Selected Passages
    Genesis 1
    Exodus 3:14–15

Our God in the Biblical Story

The Bible is the grand story of creation, fall, redemption, and new creation. God is the Author of the story, as he plans it from eternity past (Eph 1:11). God is also the main character, as the story line focuses on God and how he relates to us. As Creator, God makes us; as the covenant Lord, God is the offended party when we rebel; as Redeemer, God saves us in Jesus; and as victor, God ensures that justice will prevail and that he will bring about the new creation.

God is the Creator, who makes the heavens and earth and everything in them (Gen 1:31; 2:1). Before space, time, or matter exist, the eternal God already exists. Without the use of preexisting materials, God freely, graciously, and powerfully brings into being all that is. He does so by his word (Genesis 1; Ps 33:6, 9). God not only creates by his word, but he also preserves by his word (Col 1:16; Heb 1:3). He likewise governs his world, directing it mysteriously toward his goals (Eph 1:9–10). Therefore, it all belongs to him, and he is worthy of our worship (Rev 4:11).

The crown of God's creative work is making Adam and Eve in his image. He makes them holy and blesses them that they might love and serve him with their minds, bodies, and lives. He is their Lord, and they are to function as little lords—stewards of his good creation. He makes them in proper relation to himself, one another, and his world. They are to praise the magnificence of their Creator's name forever (Ps 8:1, 9).

Sadly, Adam and Eve rebel against him. They reject God's word and are unfaithful to him. Their rebellion disrupts their relationship with him, one another, and the world. Their mutiny brings disorder and pain into God's good creation. They need a Redeemer. And God in his mercy immediately promises one. Before expelling Adam and Eve from the garden, God makes the first promise of redemption (Gen 3:15).

God alone is Creator, sustainer, and Savior. There is no other. He makes promises to Abraham and enters into a saving relationship with him and his offspring (Gen 17:7). He promises that the seed of Abraham will be the Redeemer (Gal 3:16). God changes the name of Abraham's grandson Jacob to Israel, and from him brings twelve tribes, from one of which he will bring the Redeemer (Judah, Mic 5:2). In the fullness of time, he does just that.

God sends his Son to become a man, live a sinless life, and die in the place of sinners. God raises him on the third day, promising eternal life to all who trust him. After ascending to the Father, Jesus pours out the Spirit on the church, empowering it to take the gospel to the ends of the earth. God triumphs over sin, death, demons, the devil, and hell in the death and resurrection of his Son (Col 2:15; Heb 2:15). In the return of Christ, God will raise the dead, judge human beings and angels at the last judgment, send people to their eternal destinies, and put all things under his subjugation (1 Cor 15:28; Phil 3:21). He will dwell in the midst of his people on the new earth for eternity, banishing grief, pain, and death (Rev 21:3–4).

Our God in Selected Passages

The doctrine of God is so important that we devote two chapters to it: this one, on the Trinity, and the next one, on God's attributes and works. Therefore, this section treats biblical passages that pertain to both chapters. These passages portray God as almighty Creator, the "I AM," marked by freedom and faithfulness; he is the loving, just, and jealous Lawgiver. He is of unsearchable greatness and has a glorious and gracious name. He is all-knowing and everywhere present for his people; the great and awe-inspiring God, who keeps covenant with them despite their obstinacy. He is Yahweh, the covenant Lord, who punishes sin and abounds in love; our forgiving and firm Father. Indeed, he is the Trinity: Father, Son, and Holy Spirit.

Genesis 1

Genesis 1 forcefully declares that God is the Creator of all things. As it does, it highlights the nature of God. God is the King who sovereignly decrees, "Let there be . . ." and creation obeys (1:3, 6, 14; see also vv. 9, 11, 20, 24, 26). God is unique, distinct from his creation. He creates the sun, moon, stars, animals, and humans; he is not them. This sovereign and independent King is also good; he sees that what he creates is "good," even "very good" (1:4, 10, 12, 18, 21, 25, 31). God is personal, personally and intricately making humans in his image (1:26–31). God is active, not only creating the world but interacting with it before and after the fall. God is on a mission, creating humans to love and serve him, as well as to lead the creation to fulfill its intended purposes (1:26–31). Such truths about God show us that he is the sole Creator of all (against naturalism and atheism); moreover, he is the true God as opposed to the gods of Egypt, the ancient Near East, and numerous ones today. He is separate from his creation (against animism and pantheism), infinite (against panentheism), personal and active (against deism), and good (against dualism). God and his nature set the contours of our Christian faith.

Exodus 3:14–15

When God appoints Moses to deliver his people, he asks God for his name. God replies:

"I AM WHO I AM. This is what you are to say to the Israelites: I
AM has sent me to you." God also said to Moses . . . "The LORD, the
God of your fathers, the God of Abraham, the God of Isaac, and
the God of Jacob . . . This is my name forever; this is how I am to
be remembered in every generation." (Exod 3:14–15)

This revelation to Moses, the mediator of the Sinai covenant, is
weighty because with it, God proclaims his identity "forever." First, God
declares that he is "I AM." He uses the same verb contained in his promise to be with his people (in v. 12), stressing his covenant faithfulness to
them. Second, "I AM," from the verb "to be," also reveals God's sovereign
freedom. He does not depend on the Israelites, but they depend on him.
Third, God replaces "I AM" with "Yahweh" (translated "the LORD" in v. 15)
and says he is the God of Abraham, Isaac, and Jacob. He is the Lord, who
keeps covenant with his people.

Exodus 19–20

God also reveals his nature in the Ten Commandments. These famous
truths underline God's covenant faithfulness and love, as his words to
Moses show: "You have seen what I did to the Egyptians and how I carried
you on eagles' wings and brought you to myself" (Exod 19:4). God routs
Israel's oppressors, delivers his people, and enters into relationship with
them. Indeed, he identifies himself as their Redeemer: "I am the LORD your
God, who brought you out of the land of Egypt, out of the place of slavery"
(20:2). God's will to bless outshines his desire to punish, as he may punish
a few generations but shows "faithful love to a thousand generations of
those who love [him] and keep [his] commands" (v. 6).

God declares his uniqueness and primacy in prohibiting the worship
of other gods (v. 3). God's nature as Spirit is clear, for physical representa-
tions of him are forbidden (v. 4). God is the only one worthy of worship,
is suitably jealous for our affection, and judges those committing idolatry (vv. 5–6). God is holy and requires that his name be treated as such

(v. 7). He is the Creator who rested, and he requires that his people rest in honor of his provision and lordship (vv. 8–11). God is good, blesses his people with family, and expects them to honor their parents (v. 12). He is the Creator who gives life and is Lord over life, not allowing anyone to murder (v. 13). God is good, providing marriage and forbidding adultery (v. 14). God is truthful and opposes false testimony (v. 16). He is generous, providing us with enough and requiring that we neither steal nor covet what he has given others (vv. 15, 17).

Exodus 19–20 make clear that God calls us to live according to his nature. His holiness is to be reflected in our holiness (19:5–6). His universal lordship shapes our universal mission (vv. 5–6). His nature shapes our worship (20:3–11). His goodness, generosity, truth, and love are to be reflected in ours (vv. 4–17).

Exodus 34:5–8

Exodus 34 contains a foundational revelation of God's character. After Moses boldly asks to see God's glory, God graciously gives him a partial revelation of it (33:21–23) and then proclaims his name, his identity, to him:

> The LORD—the LORD is a compassionate and gracious God, slow to anger and abounding in faithful love and truth, maintaining faithful love to a thousand generations, forgiving iniquity, rebellion, and sin. But he will not leave the guilty unpunished, bringing the fathers' iniquity on the children and grandchildren to the third and fourth generation. (34:6–7)

God reveals himself as Yahweh, the covenant Lord who is full of mercy and grace. He explains that he is angry toward sin and sinners, but he is patient, slow to wrath. He is holy and must punish sin, but he abounds in love and faithfulness. He forgives iniquity, rebellion, and sin. God punishes the next few generations descended from those who hate him, but he shows his covenant faithfulness and love to his people for a thousand generations. God's love is overflowing toward us, and he is tenacious to keep his covenant promise to us.

Psalm 139

Astoundingly, Scripture tells his people to call the Creator of the heavens and the earth "our God" and "our Lord" (see Ps 99:5; 147:1–5). God enters into covenant with us, promises to be our God, and claims us as his people. In Psalm 139, David simultaneously expresses vital truths about God in both universal and personal terms. As God's people sing his greatness, they proclaim that they belong to him and he belongs to them. God, who knows everything, knows his people intimately (vv. 1–5). He knows their daily routines, their comings and goings, and their words before they speak them. As his knowledge surrounds them, he compassionately puts his hand on them, as a loving parent on a child.

The psalm continues by declaring that God is everywhere in the world and is everywhere with those who love him (vv. 7–12). David imagines that he wants to get away from God, but finds it impossible. If he ascends high into the clouds or descends to the depths of the grave, God is there. Whether he travels east or west, God is there. If he tries to hide in the dark, he finds it impossible, as God is present everywhere. Anywhere we believers might go, God is there with us to guide and lovingly hold us with his hand (v. 10).

The psalmist continues, rejoicing that God, the Creator of the heavens and the earth (Gen 1:1), is also the Creator of every human being. He sees us when we are formless and knits us together in our mothers' wombs (Ps 139:13, 16). God wonderfully makes us and plans each of our days before birth (vv. 14–16).

This marvelous psalm, then, teaches universal truths about God. He is all-knowing, everywhere present, Creator of all, and holy. At the same time, David personalizes these truths. Not only is God all-knowing, but he knows all about us. Not only is he everywhere present, but he is present with us. Not only is he Creator of the heavens and earth, but he shaped us in our mothers' wombs. Not only is he the Holy One, who will judge his enemies, but he loves us enough to convict us of evil within that we may confess it and walk with him. Not only is God the true and living God; he is our God, and we are his people. For this reason, when describing God's attributes, we will not say merely that "God is holy" or

"God is loving" but that "our God is holy" and "our God is loving." These expressions mean both that he is holy and loving and that he is ours and we are his.

Psalm 145

This psalm begins and ends the same way—praising God:

> I exalt you, my God the King, and bless your name forever and ever. I will bless you every day; I will praise your name forever and ever. (vv. 1–2)

> My mouth will declare the LORD's praise; let every living thing bless his holy name forever and ever. (v. 21)

What's more, it overflows with praise throughout. This is fitting because "the LORD is great and is highly praised; his greatness is unsearchable" (v. 3).

David extols God's many perfections, including greatness (vv. 3, 6), righteousness (vv. 7, 17), compassion (v. 9), power (vv. 4, 6, 11–12), and faithfulness (vv. 13, 17). He acclaims God's loving-kindness in a manner reminiscent of Exod 34:6–7: "The LORD is gracious and compassionate, slow to anger and great in faithful love" (Ps 145:8). He expands on God's goodness, his generosity, to all his creatures:

> The LORD helps all who fall; he raises up all who are oppressed. All eyes look to you, and you give them their food at the proper time. You open your hand and satisfy the desire of every living thing. (vv. 14–16)

God is the divine King (v. 1), adorned with "splendor and glorious majesty" (v. 5). He is mighty to accomplish awesome deeds (v. 6) and abounds in goodness (v. 7). He is good to all, and generous to all of his creatures, including animals, whom he blesses with nourishment as they eat from his open hand (vv. 8, 15–16). His kingdom, full of glory and splendor (vv. 11–12), will never end (v. 13). He responds differently to the godly and the ungodly. He is near to, hears the cries of, guards, delivers, and preserves all who love and fear him (vv. 17–20), but judges all the wicked (v. 20).

Nehemiah 9

After the people rebuild the walls of Jerusalem and the exiles return from captivity, the scribe Ezra reads the Law, and the people respond with weeping, confession, and worship. The Levites then lead the people in a remarkable prayer that focuses on God's history with his people and their ongoing rebellion.

The Levites' praise is exuberant: "Blessed be the LORD your God from everlasting to everlasting" (Neh 9:5). They praise him for his glorious name and for being the only God and Creator of all (vv. 5–6). They praise him for his gracious dealings with his people, from his choice of Abraham to his returning them to their land from captivity in Persia. The Levites recount many events in between, including God's deliverance of his people from Egypt, giving the Law, miraculous provision and guidance in the wilderness, enabling them to possess the Promised Land, warning them through the prophets, and not forsaking them in captivity.

Alongside the litany of God's compassionate deeds is a list of his people's wayward behaviors. They are evil, arrogant, stiff-necked, disobedient, rebellious, idolatrous, blasphemous, and murderous (vv. 16–18, 26, 29, 33–35). By contrast, God is righteous (vv. 8, 33), faithful (vv. 8–15, 33), "forgiving . . . gracious and compassionate, slow to anger and abounding in faithful love" (v. 17; see also v. 31), and patient (v. 30). In light of God's grace and the people's confession of sin, they enter into a binding agreement in writing (v. 38; 10:29) and make a vow of faithfulness to "the great, mighty, and awe-inspiring God who keeps his gracious covenant" (9:32).

Daniel 9

Daniel understands from Jeremiah's writings "that the number of years for the desolation of Jerusalem would be seventy" (Dan 9:2). Consequently, he seeks the Lord in prayer and confession. He pours out his heart in admission of his people's sins. They have acted wickedly (v. 15) and are guilty of disobedience (vv. 10–11, 14), disloyalty, and rebellion toward God (vv. 7, 9). Furthermore, they reject God's prophets (v. 6) and remain unrepentant (v. 13). As a result, God gives them over to public shame (vv. 7–8), making them an object of ridicule to surrounding peoples (v. 16).

Daniel entreats the "Lord—the great and awe-inspiring God," who, in spite of his people's obstinacy, is faithful to "his gracious covenant" (v. 4). He is righteous (vv. 7, 14, 16) and full of compassion and forgiveness (vv. 9, 18), evidenced by his delivering his people "out of the land of Egypt with a strong hand" (v. 15). Though Israel deserves only God's anger and wrath (v. 16), Daniel pleads with him to hear his petitions on behalf of them and their ruined temple "for the Lord's sake" (v. 17). Daniel urgently appeals to God's glory: "We are not presenting our petitions before you based on our righteous acts, but based on your abundant compassion. Lord, hear! Lord, forgive! Lord, listen and act! My God, for your own sake, do not delay, because your city and your people bear your name" (vv. 18–19).

Matthew 6:9–13

Jesus treats six areas in his famous model prayer in Matthew 6. First, we are to pray that God's name (his person) would be honored as holy (v. 9). Second, Jesus tells us to pray for the coming of God's kingdom. Third, closely related to praying that the kingdom would come is asking that the Father's "will be done on earth as it is in heaven" (v. 10). Fourth, Jesus instructs us to request daily bread from our Father's hand (v. 11). Fifth, we are to pray, "And forgive us our debts, as we also have forgiven our debt-ors" (v. 12). Sixth, Jesus tells us to ask our Father not to lead us into those places where we would stumble and fall. Instead, we are to seek God's deliverance from the devil and the evil with which he tempts us (v. 13). This simple prayer covers the most important areas of life—glorifying God, his kingdom coming, doing his will, our daily food, ongoing forgiveness, and victory over evil. These are aspects of our Father's love for us and ways we can honor him as we live on earth, with the knowledge that he is our heavenly Father.

Through this classic prayer, Jesus teaches us much about God. He is "our Father," the covenant Lord of his people and the personal, loving, authoritative Father who has a relationship with his children. He is transcendent ("in heaven") and immanent ("on earth"). He is holy yet relates to this sinful world. He is a King with a kingdom. He is personal with a will, and sovereign in that he plans to accomplish it. He is good and provides for our physical needs. He is gracious and forgives our sins. He is with us every step of the way, leading us into holiness and delivering us from evil.

Jude vv. 20–21

Jude urges his readers to "contend for the faith that was delivered to the saints once for all" (v. 3) because ungodly teachers are turning God's grace into sensuality and thereby denying Christ. He blasts these false teachers and points to their sure condemnation (vv. 5–19). Then he urges his readers to persist in faith, prayer, and God's love as they live in light of the Second Coming (vv. 20–21).

When Jude exhorts his readers to steadfastness, he includes the Trinity. They are to pray "in the Holy Spirit," to remain in "the love of God" the Father, and to wait "expectantly for the mercy of our Lord Jesus Christ" (vv. 20–21).

Jude teaches that each of the three persons of the Trinity is God. He does this by putting each of their names in a role that only God can fulfill. We are to pray only "in God"; in this case, "in the Holy Spirit." We must keep ourselves only in God's love; in this case, the Father's. We are to wait expectantly for the mercy of God alone for eternal life; in this case, "of our Lord Jesus Christ." Jude thus teaches the deity of the Father, Son, and Spirit.

Our Triune God

The Trinity in Church History[1]

The doctrine of the Trinity highlights the importance of the church taking its time to understand Christian theology in the light of the message of

---

[1] We gratefully acknowledge much help from Robert Letham, *The Holy Trinity: In Scripture, History, Theology, and Worship* (Phillipsburg, NJ: P&R, 2004).

Scripture while rejecting the errors of false teachers. The Bible teaches but does not systematize the doctrine of the Trinity. The church fathers follow the biblical trajectory and rightly teach that the one God eternally exists as the three persons of Father, Son, and Holy Spirit.

The Old and New Testaments consistently affirm that there is only one living and true God (Deut 4:35; 6:4; 1 Tim 2:5; Jas 2:19). Although the tree of the doctrine of the Trinity grows in the New Testament, its roots are in the Old Testament. An important biblical development is the New Testament's threefold (triadic) understanding of God. This triadic pattern played an important part in the church's developing understanding that God is the Holy Trinity. Here is a list of seven passages displaying this pattern from six different New Testament writers:

> "Go, therefore, and make disciples of all nations, baptizing them in the name of the Father and of the Son and of the Holy Spirit." (Matt 28:19)

> God sent his Son, born of a woman, born under the law, to redeem those under the law, so that we might receive adoption as sons. And because you are sons, God sent the Spirit of his Son into our hearts, crying, "*Abba*, Father!" (Gal 4:4–6)

> . . . how much more will the blood of Christ, who through the eternal Spirit offered himself without blemish to God, cleanse our consciences from dead works so that we can serve the living God? (Heb 9:14)

> To those chosen . . . according to the foreknowledge of God the Father, through the sanctifying work of the Spirit, to be obedient and to be sprinkled with the blood of Jesus Christ. (1 Pet 1:1–2)

> He has given us of his Spirit. And we have seen and we testify that the Father has sent his Son as the world's Savior. (1 John 4:13–14)

> But you, dear friends, as you build yourselves up in your most holy faith, praying in the Holy Spirit, keep yourselves in the love of God, waiting expectantly for the mercy of our Lord Jesus Christ for eternal life. (Jude vv. 20–21)

Grace and peace to you from the one who is, who was, and who is to come, and from the seven spirits before his throne, and from Jesus Christ, the faithful witness, the firstborn from the dead and the ruler of the kings of the earth. (Rev 1:4–5)

The early Christians never wavered from the biblical understanding that God is one. Their theological challenge was combining that truth with something new—the worship of Jesus. Worshipping Christ as Lord implied his deity. How could they worship Jesus while simultaneously holding to their settled belief in God's unity? This task was complicated, and ironically helped, by false teaching concerning the person of Christ to which the church responded. Therefore, it took a few centuries for the church to crystallize the doctrine of the Trinity.

Early Christian apologists (the most famous of which was Justin Martyr [c.100–c.165]) defended the Christian faith against pagan attacks. They followed the lead of John 1 and called Jesus "the Word." They clearly taught the unity of God and three truths concerning Jesus: the Word existed before he became a man, the Word was one with God the Father, and the Word appeared in history as a man. But they did not yet put these facts into a coherent whole. And they did not as yet understand that the Word was a person. This suggests that an important principle when studying historical theology is to avoid anachronism, the error of attributing something to a historical period to which it does not belong. In this case, it is unfair of us to expect earlier writers to use definitions that the church made later. And it is unfair of us to judge earlier writers by the later language of the church's trinitarian creeds.

Irenaeus (c.120/140–c.202/203), the first noteworthy theologian of the early church, taught the unity of God. In addition, he taught that the Father, the Word (the Son), and the Wisdom (the Spirit) are God. Famously, Irenaeus told how all three persons were involved in creation. He depicted the Father as having two "hands," the Word and Wisdom, who were eternal like the Father, and through whom he made all things. It was to them he spoke when he said, "Let us make man in our image" (Gen 1:26). Irenaeus presented a threefold pattern of salvation as well as creation, for the Father gives incorruption and eternal life, the Spirit sanctifies, and the Son recovers what we lost in Adam. Irenaeus's recapitulation theory said the Word became incarnate so Jesus might obey through every age of human life for everyone, reversing Adam's disobedience. Irenaeus thus advanced the church's thinking about the Trinity, but did not develop the relations of the three persons to one another.

Tertullian (c.160–220) was a major early Christian theologian who coined key theological terms, opposed false teaching, and defended the faith in theological and practical treatises. He combated modalism, which denied the distinctions between the Father, Son, and Holy Spirit, regarding them instead as identical. Sabellius, the most famous modalist, held that the one God did not exist *simultaneously* as three "persons" (a term Tertullian introduced). Rather, God revealed himself *successively* in three modes—first, as Father, then as Son, and finally as Spirit. Tertullian attacked this error and maintained that there were genuine personal distinctions between the persons of the "Trinity" (another term that he coined). The one God exists in three eternal persons. The Father, Son, and Holy Spirit are distinct persons in the one substance of God. Tertullian introduced an order of first, second, and third to characterize the Father, Son, and Spirit, respectively. Unintentionally, he opened the door for the error of subordinationism, in which the second and third persons are regarded as less than the Father.

Athanasius (c.296–373) was a Christian theologian, church father, and the chief defender of trinitarianism against a powerful attack on the deity of Christ called Arianism. His unwavering commitment to Christ's deity resulted in his being exiled five times. He taught that the Father, Son, and Holy Spirit are equal. He defined the oneness of God not in terms of the Father but in terms of the whole Godhead. Therefore, he taught the full deity of the Son and the Holy Spirit in the one being of God. God is one indivisible being who exists eternally in three persons related to each other. Athanasius grounded the Trinity in the doctrines of creation and redemption. In creation he emphasized that the Word was God's agent in making all things. In redemption his chief argument for Christ's deity was that Jesus must be God to be able to save sinners. Following the Gospel of John (e.g., 14:9–11), Athanasius taught that the trinitarian persons mutually indwell one another. His allowance for variance in terminology to express the same concepts helped the church fathers East and West eventually to come to an agreement on a historic statement of the Trinity—the Niceno-Constantinopolitan Creed.

The three church fathers credited with helping the church to reach a resolution concerning the doctrine of the Trinity were the Cappadocians (so called because they lived in the province of Cappadocia in Asia Minor): Basil the Great (329–379); Gregory of Nyssa, Basil's brother (335–395); and Gregory Nazianzus (329–390). While holding that God was one indivisible person, they explicitly taught that the Spirit and the Son are God along with the Father. This ruled out the error of subordinationism, which denied the other two persons' equality to the Father. The Cappadocians clearly taught that the Father, Son, and Holy Spirit were eternally distinct from one another. This shut the door on modalism, which held that the persons were distinct only successively and not simultaneously. The three persons also eternally indwelled one another and related to each other in love and fellowship. The Cappadocians refused to consider God's essence by itself, for God *is* the Father, Son, and Holy Spirit. They followed Athanasius in showing linguistic flexibility in their definitions pertaining to the Trinity. Their adoption of a more flexible vocabulary paved the way for the great settlement between East and West at Constantinople in 381.

The Council of Constantinople produced the famous Niceno-Constantinopolitan Creed, often called the Nicene Creed. It summarizes much of the fathers' progress in understanding the Trinity.[2] Here is the Creed:[3]

> We believe in one God the Father Almighty, maker of heaven and earth and of all things visible and invisible;
>
> And in one Lord Jesus Christ, the Son of God, the Only-begotten, begotten by his Father before all ages, Light from Light,

---

[2] In this section we rely much on Letham's award-winning volume *The Holy Trinity*.

[3] This translation appears in Letham, 171–72, which credits R. P. C. Hanson, *The Search for the Christian Doctrine of God: The Arian Controversy 318–381* (Edinburgh: T&T Clark, 1988), 815–16.

true God from true God, begotten not made, consubstantial with the Father, through whom all things came into existence, who for us men and for our salvation came down from the heavens and became incarnate by the Holy Spirit and the Virgin Mary and became a man, and was crucified for us under Pontius Pilate and suffered and was buried and rose again on the third day in accordance with the Scriptures and ascended into the heavens and is seated at the right hand of the Father and will come again with glory to judge the living and the dead, and there will be no end to his kingdom;

And in the Holy Spirit, the Lord and life-giver, who proceeds from the Father, who is worshipped and glorified together with the Father and the Son, who spoke by the prophets;

And in one holy, catholic and apostolic church;

We confess one baptism for the forgiveness of sins;

We wait for the resurrection of the dead and the life of the coming age. Amen.

God is one being who has always existed as three persons: the Father, the Son, and the Holy Spirit. God cannot be divided, which is one aspect of divine simplicity. Therefore, each person is entirely God, and the entire God is in each person. The Father, Son, and Holy Spirit are of the same divine essence ("consubstantial"). When the church fathers use the language of origin—the Father "begets" the Son, who is "the Only-begotten," the Spirit "proceeds" (is sent) from the Father (and the Son)—they do not teach that the persons of the Trinity are created beings. Instead, this language refers to the eternal relationships between the persons. God has always been the Father. The Son has always been the Son of the Father. The Spirit has always proceeded from the Father and the Son. The relationships between the persons are eternal. God has always been the Father, Son, and Holy Spirit; there is no other God.

Significantly, the creed clarifies the church's teaching on the Holy Spirit. It teaches the Spirit's personality when it says that he "spoke by the prophets." Only a person, not an impersonal force, could "speak," and that is what the Spirit has done. The creed also teaches the deity of the

Holy Spirit. First, it calls him by the divine name "Lord." Second, when it says, "The Holy Spirit . . . is worshipped and glorified together with the Father and the Son," it accords him the worship due God alone. Third, it ascribes to the Spirit the divine works of creation and redemption when it says that he is "life-giver," the One who gives physical life in creation and spiritual life in redemption.

Augustine (354–430), the foremost theologian of the early church, shaped the development of Western Christianity. He is best known for *Confessions, The City of God,* and *On the Trinity.* In the last of these, he distinguishes between "use" and "enjoyment." We are to "use," or utilize, the things God gives us as means to the end of glorifying him. But "enjoyment" pertains to God alone. We are not to "use" him as a means to another end, for he is the highest end. Instead, we are to "enjoy" him and find fulfillment in him by loving and serving him, even in our "use" of other good things. Augustine's quotation from *On Christian Doctrine* forms a fitting conclusion to our survey of church history:

Voices from Church History: Augustine of Hippo

The true objects of enjoyment, then, are the Father and the Son and the Holy Spirit, who are at the same time the Trinity, one Being, supreme above all, and common to all who enjoy Him. . . . The Trinity, one God, of whom are all things, through whom are all things, in whom are all things. Thus the Father and the Son and the Holy Spirit, and each of these by Himself, is God, and at the same time they are all one God; and each of them by Himself is a complete substance, and yet they are all one substance. The Father is not the Son nor the Holy Spirit; the Son is not the Father nor the Holy Spirit; the Holy Spirit is not the Father nor the Son: but the Father is only Father, the Son is only Son, and the Holy Spirit is only Holy Spirit. To all three belong the same eternity, the same unchangeableness, the same majesty, the same power.[4]

---

[4] Augustine, *On Christian Doctrine,* bk. 1, chap. 5.5, in P. Schaff, ed., J. F. Shaw, trans., *St. Augustin's City of God and Christian Doctrine* (Buffalo, NY: Christian Literature Company, n.d.), 2:524.

The Bible teaches that the living and true God is triune.[5] As we explore what this means, we will unpack seven statements:

1. There is one God.
2. The Father is God.
3. The Son is God.
4. The Spirit is God.
5. The Father, Son, and Spirit are inseparable but distinct.
6. The Father, Son, and Spirit indwell one another.
7. The Father, Son, and Spirit exist in unity and equality.

There Is One God

Both Testaments uniformly confess monotheism, the belief that there is only one God.

DEUTERONOMY 6:4–5

Passages such as this one lay the foundation for the New Testament doctrine of the Trinity: "Listen, Israel: The LORD our God, the LORD is one" (Deut 6:4). Although this passage concentrates on God's exclusivity, it implies his unity too. The Lord had confronted and defeated the so-called gods of Egypt in the plagues and exodus. Now, through Moses, he calls upon the Israelites to acknowledge publicly that he (that is, God) belongs to them. Earlier Moses had proclaimed God's uniqueness: "To you it was shown, that you might know that the LORD is God; there is no other besides him" (4:35). In the midst of rampant ancient Near Eastern polytheism, Moses powerfully confesses the unity of God. Despite the claims of Canaanites, who worship Baal; Egyptians, who revere Amon-Re; and Babylonians, who are devoted to Marduk, Israel's God alone is God. There is no other.

---

[5] For an accessible presentation of the Trinity, see Fred Sanders, *The Deep Things of God: How the Trinity Changes Everything* (Wheaton, IL: Crossway, 2017). For a more detailed treatment, see Letham, *The Holy Trinity.*

Israel professes faith in the Lord alone (Deut 6:4–5). Israel is not only to profess monotheism but to truly believe and practice it: "Love the Lord your God with all your heart, with all your soul, and with all your strength" (v. 5). God's people must love him with all they are and all they have. And they must cherish God's words and impart them to their children in daily life (vv. 6–7).

James 2:14–26

James writes to Jewish Christians who realize that the unity of God is a basic tenet of Judaism. The book of James underlines that God is one, but also points out that simply confessing this vital truth is insufficient. James notes that even demons know there is only one God, and they certainly do not trust Jesus for salvation (2:19).

1 Timothy 2:5–6

Paul affirms, "For there is one God and one mediator between God and humanity, the man Christ Jesus, who gave himself as a ransom for all" (1 Tim 2:5–6). Paul declares the unity of God, in concert with Old Testament teaching (Deut 4:35). He then adds to it, presenting Jesus as the only Mediator between God and people. The living and true God makes himself known in his Son, who rescues all believers: he "gave himself as a ransom for all."

While affirming God's unity, the church holds that there are three persons in the Godhead: the Father, the Son, and the Holy Spirit. Against modalism, the church teaches that these are not just three manifestations of his being but that the Father, the Son, and the Holy Spirit are God simultaneously, not successively.[6]

---

[6] Despite Jewish and Muslim objections, Christianity has never denied the unity of God. It has always affirmed monotheism and rejected tritheism. This fact is highlighted by two errors in early church history, both called Monarchianism, that held to monotheism. Some individuals struggled to understand God's oneness in light of the incarnation. Dynamic Monarchianism, seeking to preserve monotheism, held that the one God endowed the man Jesus with the Spirit, enabling him to perform miracles. Advocates believed that to think of Jesus as divine was to threaten God's unity. Modalistic Monarchianism, or modalism, was equally

Below we summarize biblical material pointing to the deity of each person: Father, Son, and Spirit.

The Father Is God

God the Father's deity is so evident in Scripture that many people assume it. It shows up from many angles:

DIVINE TITLES

The ways Scripture refers to the Father reveal that he is God. He is . . .

> Father, Lord of heaven and earth (Matt 11:25)
>
> Holy Father (John 17:11)
>
> the God of all comfort (2 Cor 1:3)
>
> the God of our Lord Jesus Christ, the glorious Father (Eph 1:17)
>
> one God and Father of all, who is above all and through all and in all (4:6)
>
> our Lord and Father (Jas 3:9)
>
> the God and Father of our Lord Jesus Christ (1 Pet 1:3)

HIS RELATION TO CHRIST

Scripture shows the Father's deity by how it relates him and Christ to one another. At Jesus's baptism, the Father announces from heaven that Jesus is his Son (Matt 3:16–17). He and Jesus share unique reciprocal knowledge (11:27). The Father sends Jesus into the world (John 3:17; 10:36; 17:4) and gives him authority (17:2; Rev 2:27), words (John 8:28; 12:49–50), and

---

committed to the fact that there is only one God. Proponents granted that the Father, Son, and Holy Spirit were divine successively, but not simultaneously. The one God revealed himself in three temporal ways, disclosing himself first as Father, later as Son, and still later as Spirit. But the three were not God at the same time. Ironically, both Monarchian errors underscored commitment to God's unity.

work (5:36; 17:4). Jesus does nothing on his own (5:30), obeys the Father (6:38; 8:29; 14:31), and prays to him (14:16; 17).

DIVINE ATTRIBUTES

The Father possesses divine qualities in himself.[7] These include self-existence (John 5:26), infinite understanding (Ps 147:5), omnipresence (Jer 23:23–24), omnipotence (Eph 1:18–19), omniscience (Isa 40:28), eternity (Ps 90:2), immutability (Mal 3:6), glory (Matt 16:27), holiness (6:9), justice (18:35), righteousness (John 17:25), sovereignty (Matt 11:25), knowledge (6:8), generosity (5:45), mercy (Luke 6:36), faithfulness (Jas 1:17), and love (John 3:16).

WORSHIP

The Father receives worship that belongs only to God. His people give him praise (Jas 3:9), glory (Phil 4:20), and thanksgiving (Eph 5:20) due to God alone. He is the object of religious devotion (Jas 1:27). Baptism is performed in the name of the Trinity, beginning with his name (Matt 28:19). Christians live for him (1 Cor 8:6), have fellowship with him (1 John 1:3), and pray to him (Eph 3:14–17), for he is God.

DIVINE DEEDS

The Father occupies the roles and performs the deeds of God. He is Creator of all (1 Cor 8:6). He sends his Son to be Savior of the lost (1 John 4:14) and the Holy Spirit to apply salvation (John 14:26). He gives believers new birth (1 Pet 1:3), grace, and peace (Rom 1:7; 2 John 3). He commands obedience (2 John 4) and comforts us in affliction (2 Cor 1:3). He will raise the dead (John 5:21) and judges impartially (1 Pet 1:17).

The biblical material is plentiful and clear: the Father is God.

The Son Is God

Because we extensively unpack the Son's deity in chapter 6, we only list significant indicators here.

---

[7] For more on these attributes, see chapter 4, "God's Attributes and Works."

Jesus is identified with God.

Jesus performs the works of God.

Jesus saves us in union with him.

Jesus brings the age to come.

Jesus receives devotion due to God.

The Holy Spirit Is God

Because we extensively unpack the Spirit's deity in chapter 9, we only summarize significant indicators here.

The Holy Spirit has divine attributes.

The Holy Spirit does divine works.

The Holy Spirit's name is interchangeable with God.

The Father, Son, and Spirit Are Inseparable but Distinct

The one living God eternally exists in three persons. The Father, Son, and Spirit are inseparable.

All three persons take part in creation:

The Father: "In the beginning God created the heavens and the earth" (Gen 1:1).

The Son: "All things were created through him, and apart from him not one thing was created that has been created" (John 1:3).

The Holy Spirit: "The Spirit of God was hovering over the surface of the waters" (Gen 1:2). "The Spirit of God has made me, and the breath of the Almighty gives me life" (Job 33:4). "When you send forth your Spirit, they are created, and you renew the face of the ground" (Ps 104:30 ESV).

All three persons also take part in redemption:

Peter, an apostle of Jesus Christ:

To those chosen, living as exiles dispersed abroad in Pontus, Galatia, Cappadocia, Asia, and Bithynia, chosen according to the foreknowledge of God the Father, through the sanctifying work of the Spirit, to be obedient and to be sprinkled with the blood of Jesus Christ. (1 Pet 1:1–2)

The Father foreknows the people of God; the Spirit sets them apart from sin to obey the gospel; and as a result, the Son cleanses them with his blood, his violent death.

People sometimes cite Jesus's loud cry of abandonment on the cross as an exception: "My God, my God, why have you abandoned me?" (Matt 27:46). This cry does indeed point to a separation between the Father and the Son, but it does not occur on the order of being (ontologically); it is a temporary separation of fellowship, when the Son bore the world's sins.

In fact, though only Jesus is crucified, even then the three persons are not separated but work together. For "in Christ, God was reconciling the world to himself" (2 Cor 5:19), and Christ "through the eternal Spirit offered himself without blemish to God" (Heb 9:14).

Although we do not separate the three persons, we distinguish and do not confuse them. The Son becomes incarnate, not the Father or the Spirit. The Son dies on the cross, not either of the other two persons. All three persons are at Jesus's baptism. When he comes out of the water, the Spirit descends on him, and the Father speaks from heaven (Matt 3:16–17).

When the Trinity does the work of salvation from beginning to end, Scripture does not confuse the persons. The Father plans salvation (Eph 1:4, 11), the Son dies to accomplish it (v. 7), and the Spirit is God's seal, protecting believers until the day of redemption (vv. 13–14; 4:30).

The Father, Son, and Spirit Indwell One Another

A biblical theme stresses the oneness of the three trinitarian persons. They are in one another or mutually indwell one another. In John's Gospel, Jesus says that the Father and the Son indwell or live in one another. He says the Father is in him and indwells him: "Don't you believe that I am in the Father and the Father is in me? The words I speak to you I do not speak on my own. The Father who lives in me does his works" (14:10).

Jesus prays to the Father: "I have given them the glory you have given me, so that they may be one as we are one. I am in them and you are in me, so that they may be made completely one, that the world may know you have sent me and have loved them as you have loved me" (17:22–23).

Not only is the Father in Jesus. Jesus also teaches that he is in the Father, and furthermore, that he and the Father are in one another:

> Don't you believe that I am in the Father and the Father is in me? The words I speak to you I do not speak on my own. The Father who lives in me does his works. Believe me that I am in the Father and the Father is in me. Otherwise, believe because of the works themselves. (14:10–11; see also 10:37–38; 14:20)

> I pray not only for these, but also for those who believe in me through their word. May they all be one, as you, Father, are in me and I am in you. May they also be one in us, so that the world may believe you sent me. (17:20–21)[8]

The Father, Son, and Spirit live in one another, or said differently, they are in one another. They mutually exist in one another. They share the divine life. Each person of the Trinity, then—Father, Son, and Holy Spirit—is wholly God. That is why Jesus says seeing him means seeing the invisible Father (14:9). The fact that God eternally exists in three persons is a mystery that surpasses human understanding. The mutual indwelling of the divine persons is a mystery of the Holy Trinity.[9] The Father, Son, and Holy Spirit coinhere in the divine essence and in one another. They mutually indwell each other.

The Father, Son, and Spirit Exist in Unity and Equality

Passages that join the three trinitarian persons in unity and equality confirm our conclusions. Texts joining the three persons in unity and equality

---

[8] For discussion of believers' being in the Father and the Son, see chapter 8, pages 335–36. Scripture does not speak of believers' being in the Holy Spirit. But the Spirit's indwelling believers is ongoing union with Christ, which involves our being in God.

[9] Theologians call it *perichoresis* (Greek), *circumincession*, or *coinherence* (both Latin).

are plentiful, but we will sample from the Gospels, just three authors of New Testament Epistles, and Revelation.

In his Great Commission, Jesus tells his disciples to make disciples of all nations, baptizing them "in the name of the Father and of the Son and of the Holy Spirit" (Matt 28:19). The word "name" is singular, yet the names of the three persons follow, suggesting their three-in-oneness. Moreover, baptism is done only in God's name, implying the deity of all three persons. The three exist as one God, but they are distinct and not to be confused.

Paul portrays the three persons as the source of divine blessings in his benediction: "The grace of the Lord Jesus Christ and the love of God and the fellowship of the Holy Spirit be with you all" (2 Cor 13:13). Only God bestows grace, love, and fellowship, and that is exactly what the three persons do!

Salvation is the work of God alone. Paul presents the Father's kindness, love, and mercy as the source of salvation, the Spirit's regeneration and renewal as its application, and Christ as the channel of the Spirit (Titus 3:4–6). The persons are distinct and not mistaken for one another, and each plays a role in salvation.

John teaches how to distinguish the Holy Spirit from false spirits: "Every spirit who confesses that Jesus Christ has come in the flesh is from God" (1 John 4:2). Each is "from God"; each conveys his truth. The Father sends teachers who testify to the incarnation of his Son and are prompted by the Holy Spirit. "But every spirit that does not confess Jesus is not from God" (v. 3). Spirits, and the teachers they inspire, that deny the incarnation are from the Antichrist, not God the Father.

After warning of false teachers, Jude counsels his readers, "But you, dear friends, as you build yourselves up in your most holy faith, praying in the Holy Spirit, keep yourselves in the love of God, waiting expectantly for the mercy of our Lord Jesus Christ for eternal life" (vv. 20–21). They must edify the church on the foundation of the "most holy faith," the gospel. They are to pray relying on the Spirit. Returning to themes of the Father loving and the Son keeping them (v. 1), Jude tells his readers to abide in the Father's love (by obeying him). They are also to look for mercy and eternal life from Christ at his return. Scripture again distinguishes the three persons, telling of the Father's love, prayer in the Spirit, and anticipation of Christ's return.

John prays that God would grant grace and peace "to the seven churches in Asia" to which he writes (Rev 1:4). But instead of writing "God," he writes, "the one who is, who was, and who is to come," "the seven spirits before his throne," and "Jesus Christ," referring to the Father, Spirit, and Son, respectively (vv. 4–5). John distinguishes the three persons and portrays them as giving divine blessings, thereby implying their divine status.

Conclusion

There is one God, who eternally exists as Father, Son, and Holy Spirit. The persons are inseparable but must be distinguished. Mysteriously, the three are in one another—they live in one another—as three persons within the one divine essence. The fact that texts joining the three persons in unity and equality come from the Gospels, three different Epistle authors, and Revelation reminds us of the breadth of the New Testament's witness to the Trinity.

At times Scripture combines expressions of God's greatness with other attributes. The following passages do this for his sovereignty, faithfulness, and power, respectively:

> For I know that the LORD is great; our Lord is greater than all gods. The LORD does whatever he pleases in heaven and on earth, in the seas and all the depths. (Ps 135:5–6)

> LORD, the God of the heavens, the great and awe-inspiring God who keeps his gracious covenant with those who love him and keep his commands . . . (Neh 1:5)

> LORD, there is no one like you. You are great; your name is great in power. Who should not fear you, King of the nations? It is what you deserve. For among all the wise people of the nations and among all their kingdoms, there is no one like you. (Jer 10:6–7)

The Psalms praise God for the greatness of his name, his person (8:1, 9; 148:13). They also praise him for the greatness of his works:

The LORD is great and is highly praised; his greatness is unsearchable. One generation will declare your works to the next and will proclaim your mighty acts. I will speak of your splendor and glorious majesty and your wondrous works. They will proclaim the power of your awe-inspiring acts, and I will declare your greatness. (145:3–6)

God's greatness leads us to worship him and him only (Ps 86:8–10; 96:3–5; Luke 1:46–48). It leads us to fear him (Ps 96:3–5; Jer 10:6–7), submit to his sovereign hand (Ps 135:5–6), and trust in his covenant faithfulness (Neh 1:5). God's greatness also inspires us to bear witness of him to others (Ps 145:3–6).

4

GOD'S ATTRIBUTES AND WORKS

In the last chapter we focused on God as the Trinity. Here we will consider God's attributes and works. He has unique (incommunicable) attributes, those he does not share with us: God is self-existent, infinite, everywhere, all-powerful, all-knowing, eternal, and unchanging. He also has attributes that he shares with his people (communicable attributes): God is sovereign, wise, truthful, faithful, holy, righteous (just), loving, gracious, merciful, generous (good), patient (long-suffering), great, and glorious.

We will also consider God's works of creation and providence. Finally, we will examine God's creatures known as angels, including those that rebelled.

OBJECTIVES

- To convince readers of the attributes of God
- To encourage us to live in light of God's creation and providence
- To confirm our identity as people who belong to God

▨ OUTLINE

Our God's Attributes: Introduction
Our God's Unique Attributes (Incommunicable)
    Our God Is Living (Aseity)
    Our God Is One (Unity)
    Our God Is Spirit
    Our God Is Infinite
    Our God Is Present (Omnipresent)
    Our God Is All-Powerful (Omnipotent)
    Our God Is All-Knowing (Omniscient)
    Our God Is Eternal
    Our God Is Unchanging (Immutable)
    Our God Is Great
Our God's Shared Attributes (Communicable)
    Our God Is Personal
    Our God Is Sovereign
    Our God Is Wise
    Our God Is Truthful
    Our God Is Faithful
    Our God Is Holy
    Our God Is Righteous (Just)
    Our God Is Loving
    Our God Is Gracious
    Our God Is Merciful
    Our God Is Good (Generous)
    Our God Is Patient (Long-Suffering)
    Our God Is Glorious
Our God's Works
    Our God Creates Everything (Creation)
    Our God Guides History (Providence)
    Our God Creates Angels, and Some Rebel
Key Terms
Resources for Further Study

Our God's Attributes: Introduction

Having explored the doctrine of the Trinity, we move to God's attributes, which are "those qualities of God that constitute what he is, the very characteristics of his nature."[1] They are intrinsic, eternal, permanent, objective, and inseparable, and they express what God is like. Before we begin, we suggest some cautions and clarifications.

First, because God is infinite, we will never plumb the depths of his character. Even as resurrected saints on the new earth, we will never cease learning of him.

Second, because God is eternal, we should view all his attributes as eternal. God has been, is, and always will be each and all of these attributes. Since his attributes are eternal and thus permanent, God has been, is, and will be infinite, loving, holy, good, and so forth.

Third, because God is one, we should be wary of overly differentiating his attributes. Though the Bible describes God with various adjectives and images, it also explains that he is one. He is unified, not divisible into separate parts. So his attributes may be distinguishable, but they are also inseparable. Below we list more than twenty attributes of God, but he is not one-twentieth holy, loving, faithful, and so on. God is altogether holy, loving, faithful, and so forth.

Fourth, because God is a person, we should not focus on an attribute itself but on our one God, who is truthfully characterized by the attribute. In other words, we are not studying love per se, but God, who is loving. We are not primarily studying sovereignty, but God, who is sovereign. And according to Scripture, the God who is love is also sovereign, simultaneously. His love is a sovereign love, and his sovereignty is a loving sovereignty. Likewise, God is all-powerful and holy. So, if being all-powerful

---

[1] Erickson, *Christian Theology*, 291 (see chap. 1, n. 18). See also his helpful discussion of God's attributes, 289–345. For more detailed treatments, see John M. Frame, *The Doctrine of God* (Phillipsburg, NJ: P&R, 2002); and John S. Feinberg, *No One Like Him: The Doctrine of God*, Foundations of Evangelical Theology (Wheaton, IL: Crossway, 2001).

means he can do anything that power can do, his holiness reminds us that all his powerful actions are also holy.

Fifth, because God reveals himself, we can know him truthfully. God graciously communicates who he is to us, and we can know him and his attributes truly, even if never exhaustively. Our God really is one, personal, loving, gracious, truthful, and so on. Of course, these are human descriptions, human categories, and human images. How else could God communicate with humans but in human forms? God uses our cultures, thought forms, words, and images as analogies to reveal himself and truths about himself to us. We can have confidence in their validity to truthfully communicate what he is like.

Sixth, because God is one, all attempts to categorize his attributes are flawed from the start. We admit that. So, why do we discuss these attributes as incommunicable (unique) and communicable (shared)?

Voices from the Global Church: Matthew Ebenezer

Ebenezer from India wrote, "No absolute distinction should be drawn between God's incommunicable and communicable attributes. While even God's incommunicable attributes are to some degree shared by humans, and even God's communicable attributes are only imperfectly shared by people, the distinction is a useful one. For the distinction reminds us of the great distance and difference between God the Creator and creaturely humanity, as well as of the unique likeness between God and humanity by virtue of humans being created in his image and glory."[2]

A few reasons. One long list of twenty or more profound attributes without some organization is too much for us to synthesize.

Even more, though calling God's attributes "incommunicable" and "communicable" is not perfect and the categories overlap,[3] the categorization itself reminds us of how we relate to God. Many times, the Bible stresses

---

[2] Matthew Ebenezer, "The Great Truths of the Bible," in *ESV Global Study Bible*, 1876 (see chap. 2, n. 35).

[3] Note, for example, how God's holiness is both incommunicable (holiness as incomparable uniqueness) and communicable (holiness as moral purity, consecration to the good).

that we are not like God. The *incommunicable attributes* highlight this distinction. He is the self-existent Creator; we are creatures, totally dependent on him for existence. He is infinite; we are finite. He is omnipresent; we are spatially located. He is all-powerful; we have limited strength. He is eternal; we are time-bound. He is unchanging; we are always in process.

At other times, the Bible stresses that we are to reflect God in our character, and the *communicable attributes* highlight this. We are created in the image of God; saved by Christ, the true image of God; and being conformed to that image. This means that God is actually transforming us into people who reflect him. But how? We certainly cannot reflect his incommunicable attributes, as we will never be self-existent or infinite. By his grace and through our union with Christ, however, we can and do reflect his communicable attributes to the extent that redeemed creatures can. God is completely sovereign, and we are given dominion over his creation as stewards. God is infinitely wise, and we grow in wisdom. God is truthful, and we are increasingly so. God is faithful, and so should we be. God is loving, and we love too. And so on. Categorizing the attributes of God in this way underlines this important truth: the virtues of the Christian life (e.g., fruit of the Spirit, Beatitudes, etc.) and the marks of the church are essentially the communicable attributes of God.[4]

Our God's Unique Attributes (Incommunicable)

As we previously discussed, the incommunicable attributes refer to those qualities or characteristics of God that are unique to God. He does not share these with his people.

Our God Is Living (Aseity)

By *living* we mean that God relies on nothing else for his existence. This is also called God's *aseity*. God is the source of his own being, as Jesus

---

[4] For more on how the church reflects God's communicable attributes, see Christopher W. Morgan, "The Church and God's Glory," in *The Community of Jesus: A Theology of the Church*, ed. Kendell H. Easley and Christopher W. Morgan (Nashville: B&H, 2013), 213–36.

implies when he says, "The Father has life in himself" (John 5:26). The Creator and Lord of all gives life to all and needs nothing. He who "gives everyone life and breath" (Acts 17:24–25) does not need to be given life. Images of God that pertain to this attribute include the fountain of living water (Jer 2:13).

No one made God; no one gave him life, for he is the living God, who has always existed. Isaiah portrays the Babylonian idols as cowering and unable to save those who trust in them (Isa 46:1–2). The prophet questions the logic of someone who fashions his god with his hands from wood.

> He kindles a fire and bakes bread; he even makes it into a god and worships it; he makes an idol from it and bows down to it. He burns half of it in a fire, and he roasts meat on that half. He eats the roast and is satisfied. He warms himself and says, "Ah! I am warm, I see the blaze." He makes a god or his idol with the rest of it. He bows down to it and worships; he prays to it, "Save me, for you are my god." (44:15–17)

In contrast to lifeless idols, the living God "gives life to all" (1 Tim 6:13).

Although God does not need us, he is personal and even commits himself to his people and claims their allegiance. It is our great privilege to realize our utter dependence on the living God, who has pledged, "I will be their God, and they will be my people" (Jer 31:33).

Our God Is One (Unity)

There is only one living and true God, and he is a unity. He is not composed of parts, and he should not be mentally divided into separate parts. For more on this, see our previous discussions on the Trinity in chapter 3 and the unity of the attributes on pages 117–18.

Our God Is Spirit

God is a person who is a wholly spiritual being and does not have a body as we do. This attribute is called the spirituality of God. Jesus tells the Samaritan woman, "God is spirit, and those who worship him must worship in Spirit and in truth" (John 4:24). Though God in the old covenant manifests his name on Mount Zion in Israel and not Mount Gerizim in Samaria, God is a spiritual being, whose new covenant worship is not tied to one geographical place.[5] Rather, his worship is "in Spirit" (spiritual) and "in truth," based on his revelation of himself in Jesus.

How do we understand God's revealing his presence physically: to Moses in the burning bush (Exod 3:2–6), to Isaiah in a temple vision (Isa 6:1–4), in fire and wind at Pentecost (Acts 2:1–3)? These are occasions when God, an invisible spirit, makes himself known physically to strengthen his people. They do not indicate that God is a physical being any more than when Scripture speaks of him as if he had a face (Num 6:25; Ps 34:16), eyes and ears (Ps 34:15), a hand (Exod 6:1), and so on. We call these *anthropomorphisms*, for they speak of God as if he were a human. Because God is a spirit, he is invisible (1 Tim 1:17), and idolatry is folly (Deut 4:15–19).[6]

Our God Is Infinite

By *infinite* we mean that God is unlimited in his person and perfections. Images of God that pertain to his infinity include the High and Exalted One (Isa 57:15). Scripture teaches that God is unlimited, specifically mentioning his power and understanding:

> Our Lord is great, vast in power; his understanding is infinite. (Ps 147:5)

> The LORD is the everlasting God, the Creator of the whole earth. He never becomes faint or weary; there is no limit to his understanding. (Isa 40:28)

> I pray that the eyes of your heart may be enlightened so that you may know . . . what is the immeasurable greatness of his power

---

[5] One could argue that God as spirit is better viewed as a communicable attribute since man, too, has a spirit. We place it here to stress that God is not physical and to underline how this relates to God's presence (omnipresence).

[6] However, the Son of God became human and thus physical in his incarnation.

toward us who believe, according to the mighty working of his strength. (Eph 1:18–19)

God's infinity is not his only attribute but is in harmony with the rest of his attributes. So when we say that God is infinite, we do not mean that he can sin, be powerless, or be unfaithful, for he is holy, all-powerful, and faithful.[7]

Voices from Church History: Herman Bavinck

Bavinck (1854–1921), a Dutch theologian and a leading thinker in the Reformed tradition, is best known for his *Reformed Dogmatics*, an authoritative four-volume systematic theology. Here he shows that God is both far above (transcendent) and near to (immanent) his creation:

> The same God who in his revelation limits himself, as it were, to certain specific places, times, and persons is at the same time infinitely exalted above the whole realm of nature and every creature. Even in the parts of Scripture that stress this temporal and local manifestation, the sense of his sublimity [exaltedness] and omnipotence is not lacking. The Lord who walks in his garden is the Creator of heaven and earth. The God who appears to Jacob is in control of the future. Although the God of Israel dwells in the midst of his people in the house that Solomon built for him, he cannot even be contained by the heavens (1 Kings 8:27). . . . In a word, throughout the Old Testament these two elements occur hand in hand: God is with those who are of a contrite and humble spirit, and nevertheless is the high and lofty One who inhabits eternity (Isa. 57:15).[8]

God's infinity also characterizes other attributes. He is infinitely holy, infinitely powerful, and so on. Multiple depictions of God in Ephesians

---

[7] That God cannot make a square circle or a married bachelor has nothing to do with his infinity or power, for these are examples of nonsense; by definition, they do not exist.

[8] Herman Bavinck, *Reformed Dogmatics*, John Bolt and John Vriend, vol. 2: *God and Creation* (Grand Rapids: Baker Academic, 2004), 33–34.

relate the infinity or greatness of God's perfections. Paul speaks of the "riches of his grace" (1:7), "the immeasurable greatness of his power" to us, and "the mighty working of his strength" (v. 19), and says that he is "far above" every other authority (v. 21). God is "rich in mercy," characterized by "great love" (2:4), and will display "the immeasurable riches of his grace" to us (v. 7). Paul proclaims "the incalculable riches of Christ" (3:8); the church displays "God's multi-faceted wisdom" (v. 10); our strength is according to "the riches of his glory" (v. 16). Paul's prayer is that we would comprehend what is "the length and width, height and depth of God's love," a love that "surpasses knowledge" (vv. 18–19). Indeed, this infinite and glorious God "is able to do above and beyond all that we ask or think" (v. 20).

Our God Is Present (Omnipresent)

By *omnipresent* we mean that God is fully and simultaneously present everywhere. God's omnipresence interrelates to all his attributes, but two are noteworthy here: God as spirit and God as infinite. He is spirit, not physical, so his presence is as spirit, but genuine nonetheless. God is infinite, and his omnipresence is essentially his infinity related to the category of space. Where is God? He is here right now. And he is there right now. God is everywhere. There is nowhere God is not. God cannot be contained by a set of coordinates on a GPS; God exists as fully and simultaneously present in all sets of coordinates.

The Bible speaks of how God is both near and far: "'Am I a God who is only near'—this is the LORD's declaration—'and not a God who is far away? Can a person hide in secret places where I cannot see him?'—the LORD's declaration. 'Do I not fill the heavens and the earth?'—the LORD's declaration" (Jer 23:23–24).

God is transcendent ("far away," v. 23), beyond his creation and not trapped in it. "God is enthroned above the circle of the earth" (Isa 40:22) so that "even heaven, the highest heaven, cannot contain" him (1 Kgs 8:27; 2 Chr 6:18). God is also immanent ("near"), present in his creation, though not a part of it, for "in him we live and move and have our being" (Acts 17:28). Indeed, Isaiah comforts God's people with his caring presence: "he

gathers the lambs in his arms and carries them in the fold of his garment"
(Isa 40:11).

Contemplating God's omnipresence raises several questions. God is
present in and with Christ in a unique way, for Jesus is God incarnate. As
the *God*-man, Christ is God himself. As the God-*man*, he is endued with
the Spirit beyond measure (Isa 61:1–3; John 3:34).[9] The Holy Spirit is with
Christ as he is with no one else. As we will see, the Spirit is upon Jesus
from his conception through his resurrection, enabling him to accomplish
the work of salvation.[10]

Although the Spirit is with Jesus as Lord and Savior in an absolutely
unique way, he is also present in a special way with those Jesus saves. God
is everywhere present in the sense of existing fully and simultaneously
everywhere. But he is not equally present everywhere or with everyone in
terms of his covenantal or special presence. Importantly, he is with believers in a special way, including as we carry out his Great Commission to
make disciples of all nations. Jesus reassures us: "I am with you always,
to the end of the age" (Matt 28:20). And the Spirit is in and with us as the
Spirit of life and truth (John 6:63; 14:17). The Spirit joins us to Christ in
salvation and indwells us, keeping us saved (Eph 4:30).

Though God is omnipresent, he manifests his presence in a special
way at certain times and places. In the Old Testament he dwells in tabernacle and temple, where he chose for his name (presence) to dwell (1 Kgs
8:13, 16, 20). Now believers corporately and individually are God's temple,
where he especially dwells (1 Cor 3:16; 6:19).

Distinguishing between God's general omnipresence and his special
presence helps us answer the common question of whether God is in hell.
The answer is yes, because he is everywhere present. But he is present in
heaven (and will be in the new heavens and earth) in a different way than
he is present in hell. He is present in heaven in grace, comfort, and blessing. He is not in hell in those ways (2 Thess 1:9), but instead is present in

---

[9] See D. A. Carson, *The Gospel According to John* (Grand Rapids: Eerdmans,
1991), 213.

[10] See chapter 9, "The Holy Spirit."

holiness, justice, and wrath (Rev 14:10 ESV). Indeed, hell is a place of banishment, a place of exile, a place outside of God's kingdom and special, covenantal presence (Matt 7:21–23; 25:31–46; Rev 22:15).

God's omnipresence and special presence with us are great encouragements. We cannot get away from God, even on days we might want to (Ps 139:7–9). Everywhere his hand leads and holds us (v. 10). Some days we may ask, "Where is God?" Scripture is clear: he is right here, fully present with us.

Our God Is All-Powerful (Omnipotent)

By *all-powerful* or *omnipotent* we mean that God has unlimited power to do anything he wants to do, as Scripture teaches when it calls him "the Almighty" (Gen 49:25, for example). God's omnipotence interrelates with all his attributes, but two require mention here: God's sovereignty and God's infinity. We will interact with God's sovereignty later in this section, but note here that sovereignty emphasizes authority or domain; omnipotence stresses power or ability. They overlap but are not identical.

God is also infinite, and his omnipotence is essentially his infinity related to the category of power. What is God able to do? Anything he pleases. There is no power in the universe that compares to his. No one is his equal. Indeed, there is no use trying to quantify infinite power in terms of wattage, ergs, horsepower, or the like, because God's power is unlimited and beyond any measure.

Some interpret omnipotence in peculiar ways that we should avoid, however. God's omnipotence does not mean that he can make a rock too large for him to lift. That is a logical impossibility. God's being all-powerful means he can do anything that power can do. Power cannot make a square circle. As C. S. Lewis famously said, "Nonsense remains nonsense, even when we talk it about God."[11]

Further, God's power is not disconnected from who he is. His power is not only related to his sovereignty and infinity but also to his holiness,

---

[11] C. S. Lewis, *The Problem of Pain* (New York: Macmillan, 1962), 28.

love, and so forth. God can do whatever he wants, but what he wants is not free-floating or capricious. It is linked to his love, holiness, goodness, and all that he is. God is holy, and he does not use his power to do evil. God is loving, and he does not use his power to betray his people. God is true, and he does not use his power to deceive (Titus 1:2). God's power is harnessed for good and is united with his other perfections.

The Bible describes God's power in many ways and with consider-able frequency. Images of God that pertain to omnipotence include potter (Isa 29:15–16) and warrior (Exod 15:3).

Every section of both Testaments declares that God is all-powerful.

Law
Because he loved your fathers, he chose their descendants after them and brought you out of Egypt by his presence and great power. (Deut 4:37)

Writings
You have a mighty arm; your hand is powerful; your right hand is lifted high. (Ps 89:13)

Prophets
He brings out the stars by number; he calls all of them by name. Because of his great power and strength, not one of them is missing. (Isa 40:26)

Gospels
Jesus looked at them and said, "With man this is impossible, but with God all things are possible." (Matt 19:26)

Acts
"By what power or in what name have you done this?" Then Peter was filled with the Holy Spirit and said to them, ". . . Let it be known to all of you . . . that by the name of Jesus Christ of Nazareth—whom you crucified and whom God raised from the dead—by him this man is standing here before you healthy." (Acts 4:7–8, 10)

Epistles

. . . the immeasurable greatness of his power to us who believe, according to the mighty working of his strength. (Eph 1:19)

Revelation

The twenty-four elders . . . fell facedown and worshiped God, saying: "We give you thanks, Lord God, the Almighty, who is and who was, because you have taken your great power and have begun to reign." (Rev 11:16–17)

God manifests his awe-inspiring might in many spheres. In fact, the Lord, who "is great, vast in power" (Ps 147:5), displays it in creation (65:6), providence (107:23–43), and redemption (77:15). In addition, Scripture ascribes to Christ divine power exercised in creation (John 1:3), providence (Heb 1:3), healing and exorcism (Acts 10:38), raising himself from the dead (John 10:17–18), and transforming our bodies in resurrection (Phil 3:21).

The ramifications of God's being all-powerful are magnificent. The Almighty loves us as sons and daughters (2 Cor 6:18), protects us (Ps 91:1), and keeps us saved (1 Pet 1:5). He empowers us to live for him (Isa 40:29; 2 Pet 1:3), especially in our weakness (2 Cor 12:9), and specifically to spread the gospel (Acts 1:8). For all of this and more, our omnipotent Lord deserves our praise now and forever (1 Chr 29:11; Rev 4:8).

Our God Is All-Knowing (Omniscient)

By *all-knowing* or *omniscient* we mean that God is limitless in knowledge and understanding; he knows all things. Omniscience is essentially God's infinity interrelated with his knowledge.[12]

---

[12] In a way that is similar to the language of presence, the Bible uses the language of knowledge in multiple ways. God knows in the sense of cognition, perception, or understanding (the focus of this section). And God knows in the sense of loving or being in covenant relationship (e.g., John 17:3: "This is eternal life: that they may know you, the only true God, and the one you have sent—Jesus Christ").

The psalmist praises God because "his understanding is infinite" (Ps 147:5), and Isaiah says "there is no limit to his understanding" (Isa 40:28). God's knowledge of his creation is comprehensive, "for he looks to the ends of the earth and sees everything under the heavens" (Job 28:24). His "perfect knowledge" (37:16) includes observing from heaven all human beings and their works (Ps 33:13–15). Images of God that pertain to his being all-knowing include the first and the last (Isa 44:6–7), bookkeeper (Ps 139:16), and potter (Isa 29:15–16).

According to the Bible, God knows the past, present, and future.[13] In Isaiah, God asserts his deity over against idols when he affirms his ability to predict future events: "Remember what happened long ago, for I am God, and there is no other; I am God, and no one is like me. I declare the end from the beginning, and from long ago what is not yet done, saying: my plan will take place, and I will do all my will" (46:9–10; see also 42:8–9; 44:6–7).

God is the omniscient Lawgiver and Judge, and "no creature is hidden from him, but all things are naked and exposed to the eyes of him to whom we must give an account" (Heb 4:13). His eyes "are everywhere, observing the wicked and the good" (Prov 15:3). He does not merely observe external actions, "for the LORD searches every heart and understands the intention of every thought" (1 Chr 28:9). This is bad news for sinners, for "the heart is more deceitful than anything else, and incurable," the heart that the Lord examines and tests (Jer 17:9–10). But it can also be transformative for us, as God's complete knowledge of our hearts, thoughts, and actions may lead us to repentance (Ps 51:4). Remembering God's infinite knowledge can also reassure us since he sees, hears, knows, cares about, and acts for his people (Exod 3:7–10).

Scripture teaches that there are "hidden things" (Dan 2:22) that belong to the all-knowing Lord alone, some of which he reveals that we may know him and do his will (Deut 29:29). Most important, this includes "God's hidden wisdom in a mystery," made known through his apostles

---

[13] For more on God's knowledge of the future, see Frame, *The Doctrine of God*, 469–512.

in the gospel. This wisdom, unknown apart from the Spirit's revelation, concerns the crucified Christ (1 Corinthians 2). As Paul contemplates the marvel of God's gracious dealings with Jews and Gentiles, he exclaims, "Oh, the depth of the riches both of the wisdom and of the knowledge of God! How unsearchable his judgments and untraceable his ways! For who has known the mind of the Lord? Or who has been his counselor?" (Rom 11:33–34).

Jesus is also depicted with this infinite knowledge, for "in him are hidden all the treasures of wisdom and knowledge" (Col 2:3). Like us, his first disciples are sometimes slow to learn, but both Peter (John 21:17) and his fellows (16:29–30) confess Christ's omniscience.

God's omniscience comforts us, for he knows the details of our lives (Luke 12:7), and he knows what we need before we even ask him (Matt 6:8).

Our God Is Eternal

By *eternal* we mean that the living and true God is the Lord of time. He is infinite in relationship to time. Indeed, God exists before time. Time itself has a beginning, but God does not. Time was created by God, along with the rest of the cosmos. God is both beyond time and voluntarily enters into it to relate to us who live in it.

Both Testaments ascribe this attribute to God. Moses, the author of one psalm, says, "Before the mountains were born, before you gave birth to the earth and the world, from eternity to eternity, you are God" (Ps 90:2). Paul bursts forth in praise: "Now to the King eternal, immortal, invisible, the only God, be honor and glory forever and ever. Amen" (1 Tim 1:17). Revelation recounts, "'I am the Alpha and the Omega,' says the Lord God, 'the one who is, who was, and who is to come, the Almighty'" (1:8). Images of God that pertain to his being eternal include the first and the last (Isa 44:6–7).

Scripture teaches that God is Lord over time and stands outside of it. He is not trapped in time but controls it (Ps 90:4; 2 Pet 3:8). Yet desiring to relate to us as his time-bound creatures, God also enters into time so that he experiences before-and-after relationships with respect to creation (Gen 1:1), for the creation is not eternal. God also plans our salvation in eternity past but accomplishes it and applies it in space and time: salvation is historical, for God saves in history, and thus in time. The Son of God was not always incarnate but became a man at a point in time (John 1:14). Jesus lives in time, dies on the cross in time, rises from the dead in time, ascends in time, reigns in time, and will return in time. The Spirit is also with us in time, convicting us, drawing us, and uniting us to Christ at our conversions, which occur in time. So God relates to time.

A comparison to God's relationship to space may help. God is both transcendent and immanent with respect to space. That is, he is both beyond space and present at each point in it. We can say that he is also both transcendent and immanent with respect to time. As its Creator, he stands outside of time and is not trapped within it. But he also is immanent with respect to time. He truly relates to it in loving and saving us.[14]

Before Moses affirms God's eternity, he says, "Lord, you have been our refuge in every generation" (Ps 90:1). Though our lives are transient and beset by sin (vv. 3–11), God is our Keeper and Protector. Therefore, Moses later prays, "Teach us to number our days carefully so that we may develop wisdom in our hearts" (v. 12). Although even "youths" grow weary, "the everlasting God" does not, but "gives strength to the faint" (Isa 40:28–30). As a result, "those who trust in the LORD will renew their strength; they will soar on wings like eagles; they will run and not become weary, they will walk and not faint" (v. 31). We face the future

---

[14] Evangelicals debate whether this means that God is timeless or that he is everlasting. The timeless view holds that God lives endlessly outside of time in the eternal present. The everlasting view holds that God exists endlessly backward and forward through all time. The former says that he is timelessly infinite, and the latter that he is temporally infinite. For brief discussion, see Ronald H. Nash, *The Concept of God: An Exploration of Contemporary Difficulties with the Attributes of God* (Grand Rapids: Zondervan,1983), 73–83. For a defense of divine timelessness, see Paul Helm, *Eternal God: A Study of God without Time*, 2nd ed. (Oxford: Oxford University Press, 2011). For a defense of the everlasting view, see Feinberg, *No One Like Him*, 375–436.

with confidence in "the eternal God" (Rom 16:26), who simultaneously inhabits eternity and dwells with us.

Our God Is Unchanging (Immutable)

By *unchanging* or *immutable* we mean that God does not change in his character or nature, unlike God's changing creation: "You are the same, and your years will never end" (Ps 102:27). As a result, we "will dwell securely" amid a changing world (v. 28). Though we rebel against him, God remains our steadfast Rock. In the midst of words denouncing Israel for disobedience, God states, "Because I, the LORD, have not changed, you descendants of Jacob have not been destroyed" (Mal 3:6). The Lord's unchanging character is a basis for his faithful commitment to his people. God is stable. Images of God that pertain to his being unchanging include a rock (Ps 62:1–2) and Father of lights (Jas 1:17).

While God's character remains constant, he is also a personal being who enters into a formal relationship with us via covenant: "I will confirm my covenant that is between me and you and your future offspring throughout their generations. It is a permanent covenant to be your God and the God of your offspring after you" (Gen 17:7). God does not change in who he is, *and* he genuinely relates to us. He answers our prayers, desires our praise, and is pleased when we love and obey him.

This is the proper context in which to address the so-called problem of God repenting. The King James Version (KJV) correctly translates two passages denying that God repents (Num 23:19; 1 Sam 15:29), but it translates others as saying that he does (Gen 6:6–7; Exod 32:12, 14; Judg 2:18; 1 Sam 15:11, 35; Jonah 3:10; 4:2). These and similar passages are to be understood in light of Scripture's clear affirmation of God's stable character as expressions of his genuinely relating to people.[15] Modern translations handle these passages better, as the Christian Standard Bible (CSB) shows, translating "the LORD regretted" (Gen 6:6–7; 1 Sam 15:11, 35) as "the

---

[15] For more on God as unchanging but responsive to humans in time, see Frame, *The Doctrine of God*, 543–75.

LORD relented" or "God relented" (Exod 32:12, 14; Jonah 3:10; see also 4:2) or "the LORD was moved to pity" (Judg 2:18). In each of these passages, it is not God's character or nature that changes. In each case, who God is remains the same. The passages stress that God is genuinely responsive to human beings. When we sin, he is deeply disturbed. When we are hurting, he is truly compassionate. Similarly, when we draw near to God, he draws near to us (Jas 4:8). When we pray, he acts on our behalf (Jas 4:2; 5:13–18). When we confess our sin, he forgives us (Jas 5:15–16; 1 John 1:9). Who God is remains fixed, but God's actions toward us are historical and related to our responses to him.

As with other attributes of God, Scripture ascribes this one to Christ: "Jesus Christ is the same yesterday, today, and forever" (Heb 13:8). Such words are true only of God, and they thus remind us that Christ is divine.

James insists that God is neither tempted nor tempts others; instead, our evil desires lead us into sin. He warns, "Don't be deceived, my dear brothers and sisters. Every good and perfect gift is from above, coming down from the Father of lights, who does not change like shifting shadows" (Jas 1:16–17). God is the Creator of the heavenly lights, and unlike them, he does not vary or change. He is stable in his nature. He is always good and has no dark side.

God's stability of character gives us great security (Ps 102:27). Unlike us, God is not fickle, and we can always rely on him. His unchangeableness undergirds the gospel. We will enjoy final salvation because our immutable Lord has promised and will not go back on his Word: "Through two unchangeable things," God's promise and oath, "we have this hope as an anchor for the soul, firm and secure" (Heb 6:18–19).

Our God Is Great

Our God is also *great*, which means that God is of utmost significance and beyond comparison. His majesty is infinite. He alone is the High and Exalted One, and there is no one like him. As the Song of Moses proclaims after the exodus, "LORD, who is like you among the gods? Who is like you, glorious in holiness, revered with praises, performing wonders?" (Exod 15:11). Images of God that pertain to his being great include King (Isa 40:21–24).

This attribute emphasizes the Lord's uniqueness, especially over against the so-called gods of the nations, which are only idols: "Lord, there is no one like you among the gods, and there are no works like yours. All the nations you have made will come and bow down before you, Lord, and will honor your name. For you are great and perform wonders; you alone are God" (Ps 86:8–10; see also 96:3–5).

At times Scripture combines expressions of God's greatness with other attributes. The following passages do this for his sovereignty, faithfulness, and power, respectively:

> For I know that the LORD is great; our Lord is greater than all gods. The LORD does whatever he pleases in heaven and on earth, in the seas and all the depths. (Ps 135:5–6)

> The LORD, the God of the heavens, the great and awe-inspiring God who keeps his gracious covenant with those who love him and keep his commands . . . (Neh 1:5)

> LORD, there is no one like you. You are great; your name is great in power. Who should not fear you, King of the nations? It is what you deserve. For among all the wise people of the nations and among all their kingdoms, there is no one like you. (Jer 10:6–7)

The Psalms praise God for the greatness of his name, his person (8:1, 9; 148:13). They also praise him for the greatness of his works:

> The LORD is great and is highly praised; his greatness is unsearchable. One generation will declare your works to the next and will proclaim your mighty acts. I will speak of your splendor and glorious majesty and your wondrous works. They will proclaim the power of your awe-inspiring acts, and I will declare your greatness. (Ps 145:3–6)

God's greatness leads us to worship him and him only (Ps 86:8–10; 96:3–5; Luke 1:46–48). It leads us to fear him (Ps 96:3–5; Jer 10:6–7), submit to his sovereign hand (Ps 135:5–6), and trust in his covenant faithfulness (Neh 1:5). God's greatness also inspires us to bear witness of him to others (Ps 145:3–6).

Our God's Shared Attributes (Communicable)

As we previously discussed, God's communicable attributes refer to his qualities or characteristics that he shares with his people. By creating us in his image, saving us by his grace, uniting us with Christ, and transforming us into the image of Christ, God increasingly forms believers in his character. Of course, he is perfect in degree in each of these, and we are dependent creatures, always works in progress. Further, God is naturally all of these attributes, and we are only becoming these by his grace and through being in Christ.

Our God Is Personal

The self-existent, infinite, unchanging, and great God is not an impersonal force but a divine person. As human beings, we are persons because he made us in his image. God has the attributes of personality: intellect, self-awareness, and the ability to relate to others.

God has intellect, for he "has perfect knowledge" (Job 37:16). In fact, God "knows all things" (1 John 3:20; see also Heb 4:13). God has self-awareness, for he says, "Turn to me and be saved, all the ends of the earth. For I am God, and there is no other" (Isa. 45:22). God relates to others. He knows his people, as Paul says: "The Lord knows those who are his" (2 Tim 2:19). And God's people know him: "Love is from God, and everyone who loves has been born of God and knows God" (1 John 4:7). Jesus tells of mutual knowledge between him and believers: "I am the good shepherd. I know my own, and my own know me" (John 10:14).

That God is personal has ramifications, including great blessings. Because God is a divine person with all his attributes, he loves us everlastingly (Jer 31:3), saves us by grace (Eph 2:8), keeps us (Rom 8:1), answers our prayers (Matt 7:7–8), and comforts us in affliction (2 Cor 1:3–4).

The personal God made us personal as well. We think, feel, and choose, and we are built for relationships: with God, one another, and creation.

Our God Is Sovereign

Our personal God is also sovereign. By *sovereign* we mean that God has supreme authority and reigns over all things. God is the King, and he plans and guides all things to his goals, for "the LORD has established his throne in heaven, and his kingdom rules over all" (Ps 103:19). Images of God that pertain to his being sovereign include Lord of Armies (Isa 2:12–18) and King of kings (1 Tim 6:15).

He has unlimited authority over nature, human life, and history. The psalmist proclaims, "The LORD does whatever he pleases in heaven and on earth, in the seas and all the depths" (Ps 135:6). Indeed, God's attributes of "faithful love," "truth," and sovereignty distinguish him from lifeless idols and bring glory to his name (Ps 115:1–8).

God ordains our lives, as David testifies of God's knowledge of him in the womb: "Your eyes saw me when I was formless; all my days were written in your book and planned before a single one of them began" (Ps 139:16). God also governs the history of nations, as Paul attests: "From one man he has made every nationality to live over the whole earth and has determined their appointed times and the boundaries of where they live" (Acts 17:26).

Although God holds us all accountable for our actions, his sovereign plan is never ultimately foiled (Job 42:2). The Creator-creature distinction underlines his sovereignty, as God naturally has authority over his creation. Though mighty nations plan, none can succeed apart from God's will: "The LORD frustrates the counsel of the nations; he thwarts the plans of the peoples. The counsel of the LORD stands forever, the plans of his heart from generation to generation" (Ps 33:10–11; see also Dan 4:34–35).

Scripture teaches that we make real and meaningful decisions, just as it also teaches that God is sovereign, "the one who works out everything in agreement with the decision of his will" (Eph 1:11). Human responsibility and divine sovereignty are twin truths that are both affirmed in the

Scripture.[16] As will become clearer in the chapter on humanity and sin, we humans have genuine freedom, which is a gift of God, flows from being created in the image of God, is related to our creaturely identity, is temporarily expressed through our fallen condition, and will be ultimately completely good in the new creation.

Biblical examples of these twin truths abound. One remarkable example is when Joseph's brothers sin heinously against him, selling him into slavery (Gen 37:26–28). Yet Joseph says that God is in control (45:4–8) and tells them, "You planned evil against me; God planned it for good" (50:20). Though we cannot fully comprehend it, the same actions that the brothers intend for evil, God overrules for good. Joseph's brothers sin and oppose God in doing so. Yet God sovereignly uses their freely chosen sin to orchestrate his deliverance of Joseph, which leads to the sparing of his covenant people. The brothers' sin does not hinder God's plan, but in some mysterious way it is one of the means by which God brings about his plan.

The most striking example is Christ's crucifixion. This event is the worst crime in human history (i.e., the illegal execution of the only sinless person, the murder of the Son of God). But in this event God accomplishes the greatest good in human history—redemption. Peter says to the Jewish leaders, "Though [Jesus] was delivered up according to God's determined plan and foreknowledge, you used lawless people to nail him to a cross and kill him" (Acts 2:23). Later, the apostles pray, "For, in fact, in this city both Herod and Pontius Pilate, with the Gentiles and the people of Israel, assembled together against your holy Servant Jesus, whom you anointed, to do whatever your hand and your will had predestined to take place" (4:27–28).

"Lawless people" (Acts 2:23) kill Christ when Jews and Gentiles approve of his death. God's sovereignty does not nullify human responsibility, and those who murder Jesus are culpable. At the same time,

---

[16] For a brief discussion of these twin truths, see D. A. Carson, *How Long, O Lord?* 2nd ed. (Grand Rapids: Baker Academic, 2006), 177–220. For a more detailed treatment, see D. A. Carson, *Divine Sovereignty and Human Responsibility* (Grand Rapids: Zondervan, 1994).

inexplicably, God uses their own freely chosen and hateful evil for good, without himself approving of or committing the evil. Jesus's crucifixion happens "according to God's determined plan and foreknowledge" (2:23). The evildoers do what God "had predestined to take place" (4:28).

As is true of all of God's attributes, we will make mistakes in our view of God's sovereignty if we fail to see how it relates to and is united to his other attributes. After all, we are not studying the concept of "sovereignty," but our God, who is sovereign. His sovereignty is personal, infinite, powerful, good, wise, loving, just, and so forth. His sovereignty is not dark or capricious, but it is a good sovereignty because he is good, has no dark side, is never evil, and never commits evil (Jas 1:13–18; 1 John 1:5). His rule is not that of an aloof autocrat but that of our personal and tender Father to whom we can pray (Matt 6:9–13). His kingship is not vying for influence but is the universal and effective sovereignty of an infinite and powerful God. His lordship is comprehensive, guiding all things, even our freely chosen sin, for his intended purposes, which are for our good (Rom 8:28).

Christ, too, possesses "all authority in heaven and earth" (Matt 28:18). In fact, the Father sits his Son "at his right hand in the heavens—far above every ruler and authority, power and dominion, and every title given, not only in this age but also in the one to come. And he subjected everything under his feet" (Eph 1:20–22).

The fact that our God is sovereign gives us joy: "The LORD reigns! Let the earth rejoice; let the many coasts and islands be glad" (Ps 97:1). God's rule brings us comfort. Recalling Noah, David sings, "The LORD sits enthroned over the flood; the LORD sits enthroned, King forever. The LORD gives his people strength; the LORD blesses his people with peace" (Ps 29:10–11). God's kingly reign drives our hope, as we know that ultimately God wins, evil loses, and justice prevails. In his unique sovereign rule, God creates humans and gives them a measure of rule under his almighty hand (Gen 1:26–31).[17] And God's loving sovereignty guides our service, as we serve his creation responsibly, expressing our dominion as stewards, not tyrants.

---

[17] Arguably, God's sovereignty belongs among his incommunicable attributes; we placed it here because he shares his rule with us, even in small measure.

Our God Is Wise

By *wise* we mean that our all-knowing God puts his knowledge to work to accomplish his ends. J. I. Packer observes, "Wisdom is the power to see, and the inclination to choose, the best and highest goal, together with the surest means of attaining it. Wisdom is, in fact, the practical side of moral goodness. As such, it is found in its fullness only in God. He alone is naturally and entirely and invariably wise."[18]

The practicality of wisdom shines when God gives it to people. He gives Bezalel wisdom, skill in craftsmanship, to make furnishings for the tabernacle (Exod 31:1–5), Joshua wisdom to lead Israel (Deut 34:9), and Solomon wisdom to rule Israel (1 Kgs 3:12).

Both Testaments extol God's great wisdom. Job declares, "Wisdom and strength belong to God; counsel and understanding are his" (Job 12:13). God's wisdom is unsearchable and unquestionable, as Paul exclaims: "Oh, the depth of the riches both of the wisdom and the knowledge of God! How unsearchable his judgments and untraceable his ways!" (Rom 11:33).

God displays his wisdom in all his works, especially creation and redemption. Proverbs proclaims his wisdom in creation: "The LORD founded the earth by wisdom and established the heavens by understanding" (Prov 3:19; see also Ps 104:24; Jer 10:12).

Redemption shows God's wisdom too. By grace God saved us in Christ "with all wisdom and understanding" (Eph 1:8). Although contradicting the world's wisdom, the apostles tell of "Jesus Christ and him crucified" (1 Cor 2:2) and "speak God's hidden wisdom in a mystery" (v. 7). God makes known his wisdom in the gospel, and Paul tells Timothy, "From infancy you have known the sacred Scriptures, which are able to give you wisdom for salvation through faith in Christ Jesus" (2 Tim 3:15).

Christ, too, possesses the divine attribute of wisdom. The Old Testament predicts of the Messiah, "The Spirit of the LORD will rest on him—a Spirit of wisdom and understanding, a Spirit of counsel and

---

[18] J. I. Packer, *Knowing God* (Downers Grove, IL: InterVarsity Press, 1973), 80.

strength, a Spirit of knowledge" (Isa 11:2). Paul tells believers, "You are in Christ Jesus, who became wisdom from God for us—our righteousness, sanctification, and redemption" (1 Cor 1:30). Indeed, the apostle says of Christ, "In him are hidden all the treasures of wisdom and knowledge" (Col 2:3).

God's wisdom fortifies his Word. As a result, we grow in wisdom as we read and meditate on Scripture (Ps 119:98–99). Furthermore, as we "let the word of Christ dwell richly among" us, we teach and admonish "one another . . . in all wisdom . . . through psalms, hymns, and spiritual songs, with gratitude . . . to God" (Col 3:16).

God's wisdom deserves praise, as Paul acknowledges: "To the only wise God, through Jesus Christ—to him be the glory forever! Amen" (Rom 16:27). John tells of virtues ascribed to Christ in praise, including wisdom (Rev 5:12). He also includes wisdom in the praise that angels, elders, and the four living creatures offer to God (Rev 7:11–12).

Generously "the Lord gives wisdom; from his mouth come knowledge and understanding" (Prov 2:6). In response, we are called to seek wisdom from him in faith: "Now if any of you lacks wisdom, he should ask God, who gives to all generously and ungrudgingly, and it will be given to him" (Jas 1:5). God's wisdom begins with "the fear of the Lord" (Prov 9:10), is the skill of godly living (4:11), and results in all that is "first pure, then peace-loving, gentle, compliant, full of mercy and good fruits, unwavering, without pretense" (Jas 3:17).

Our God Is Truthful

By *truthful* we mean two things: God is the only true God, and he always speaks the truth.[19] There is only one living and true God, as Scripture affirms:

> But the Lord is the true God; he is the living God and eternal King. (Jer 10:10; see also 2 Chr 15:3)

---

[19] We thank Feinberg, *No One Like Him*, 372, for these insights.

. . . for they themselves report what kind of reception we had from you: how you turned to God from idols to serve the living and true God. (1 Thess 1:9; see also 1 John 5:20)

An image of God that pertains to his being truthful is light (Ps 27:1).

The one genuine God is truthful, as he affirms: "I the LORD speak the truth; I declare what is right" (Isa 45:19 ESV); or as John puts it, "God is true" (John 3:33). David finds solace in him alone: "You have redeemed me, LORD, God of truth" (Ps 31:5; see also Isa 65:16). Paul is offended by the thought of unbelief canceling God's faithfulness: "Absolutely not! Let God be true, even though everyone is a liar" (Rom 3:4). Because God is truthful, he does not lie, as Samuel insists: "Furthermore, the Eternal One of Israel does not lie or change his mind, for he is not man who changes his mind" (1 Sam 15:29; see also Num 23:19). Paul is succinct: "God . . . cannot lie" (Titus 1:2).

The true God always speaks the truth and never lies. Therefore, his Word is true, as it abundantly affirms:

Lord GOD, you are God; your words are true. (2 Sam 7:28)

Guide me in your truth and teach me, for you are the God of my salvation. (Ps 25:5)

Sanctify them by the truth; your word is truth. (John 17:17)

You have already heard about this hope in the word of truth, the gospel. (Col 1:5)

By his [God's] own choice, he gave us birth by the word of truth. (Jas 1:18)

In fact, all of God's Word is true: "The entirety of your word is truth, each of your righteous judgments endures forever" (Ps 119:160). Paul tells why this is so: "All Scripture is inspired by God" (2 Tim 3:16). Consequently, his Word is the standard of truth.[20]

---

[20] For discussion of views of truth, and argument that Scripture assumes the correspondence theory of truth, see Feinberg, *No One Like Him*, 38–148, 370–74.

God's promises are also true, as Joshua emphasizes: "You know with all your heart and all your soul that none of the good promises the Lord your God made to you has failed. Everything was fulfilled for you; not one promise has failed" (Josh 23:14; see also 21:45).

The Bible ascribes the divine attribute of truthfulness to the Son and the Holy Spirit, thereby underlining their deity. The Son is the truth (John 14:6), is full of grace and truth (1:14), and speaks the truth (8:40; 18:37) that sets people free (8:32). The Holy Spirit is "the Spirit of truth" (14:17; 15:26; 16:13), who "is true and is not a lie" (1 John 2:27).

The true God does not lie; we can take him at his Word, and he will fulfill his promises. Scripture regularly and variously applies God's truthfulness in character and word. His truth convicts and leads us to confession (1 John 1:8–9). The one whose fellowship God seeks "lives blamelessly, practices righteousness, and acknowledges the truth in his heart" (Ps 15:1–2). God's truth guards (40:11) and guides us (25:5). God enjoins us to "speak truth to one another" (Zech 8:16; Eph 4:25) and not to "love in word or speech, but in action and in truth" (1 John 3:18). Diligence in Scripture equips us to correctly teach "the word of truth" (2 Tim 2:15).

Our God Is Faithful

By *faithful* we mean that God is reliable in his character, actions, and words. God redeems Israel because the Lord sets his love on them and chooses them (Deut 7:7–8). He wants Israel to "know that the Lord your God is God, the faithful God who keeps his gracious covenant loyalty for a thousand generations with those who love him and keep his commands" (v. 9). Images of God that pertain to faithfulness include husband (Hos 3:1), strength, rock, fortress, mountain (HCSB), shield, horn, and stronghold (all found in Ps 18:1–2).

When God sends Israel to occupy the Promised Land, he gives them "all the land he had sworn to give to their fathers" (Josh 21:43). Israel bears responsibility for failure to remove all the Canaanites and their idols from the land, for "none of the good promises the Lord had made to the house of Israel failed. Everything was fulfilled" (v. 45).

All God's people can join the psalmist in celebrating God's great faithfulness:

> I will proclaim your faithfulness to all generations with my mouth. . . . The LORD said, "I have made a covenant with my chosen one; I have sworn an oath to David my servant: 'I will . . . build up your throne for all generations.'" LORD, the heavens praise your wonders—your faithfulness also—in the assembly of the holy ones. . . . LORD God of Armies, who is strong like you, LORD? Your faithfulness surrounds you. (Ps 89:1, 3–5, 8)

Israel in Babylonian exile feels forgotten by the Lord. But he comforts: "Can a woman forget her nursing child, or lack compassion for the child of her womb? Even if these forget, yet I will not forget you. Look, I have inscribed you on the palms of my hands; your walls are continually before me" (Isa 49:15–16). In covenant faithfulness God remembers the destroyed walls of Jerusalem and will act on behalf of his people.

Even when things look hopeless, each believer can say with true Old Testament saints, "Yet I call this to mind, and therefore I have hope: Because of the LORD's faithful love we do not perish, for his mercies never end. They are new every morning; great is your faithfulness! I say, 'the LORD is my portion, therefore I will put my hope in him'" (Lam 3:21–24).

Paul assures New Testament believers that God will sustain us to the end, "blameless in the day of our Lord Jesus Christ" (1 Cor 1:8). What is the basis for our confidence? "God is faithful; you were called by him into fellowship with his Son, Jesus Christ our Lord" (v. 9).

We are not to repeat the sins of the Israelites in the wilderness: idolatry, sexual immorality, testing God, and grumbling. We must guard against overconfidence with this assurance: "No temptation has come upon you except what is common to humanity. But God is faithful; he will not allow you to be tempted beyond what you are able, but with the temptation he will also provide a way out so that you may be able to bear it" (1 Cor 10:13).

Proper responses to God's faithfulness include our gratefulness, obedience, and faithfulness. When we sin and repent, God's faithfulness still undergirds us: "If we confess our sins, he is faithful and righteous to forgive us our sins and to cleanse us from all unrighteousness" (1 John 1:9).

This attribute of God means that we can fully trust him and his Word in all circumstances. Even our assurance of final salvation resides not in us but in his faithfulness: "Now may the God of peace himself sanctify you completely. And may your whole spirit, soul, and body be kept sound and blameless at the coming of our Lord Jesus Christ. He who calls you is faithful; he will do it" (1 Thess 5:23–24). The Holy Spirit links us to Christ and produces the fruit of the Spirit in us, and that includes faithfulness (Gal 5:22–23).

Our God Is Holy

By God's *holiness* we mean two things: that God is unique and that God is morally pure, separate from all sin. Images of God that pertain to his being holy include lawgiver (Exodus 20), consuming fire (Exod 24:17), judge (Amos 9:7–10), and light (1 John 1:5).

God's holiness speaks of God's otherness, uniqueness, and incomparability. Moses celebrates God's victory over the Egyptians: "Who is like you, O Lord, among the gods? Who is like you, majestic in holiness, awesome in glorious deeds, doing wonders?" (Exod 15:11). And Hannah exults, "There is no one holy like the Lord. There is no one besides you! And there is no rock like our God" (1 Sam 2:2).

The "Holy One of Israel" is not only profoundly distinct from us in being; he is also morally perfect (Isa 1:4). He is totally pure and sinless, and separate from all that is not holy. Because God is separate from sin, he "is not tempted by evil, and he himself doesn't tempt anyone" (Jas 1:13). Furthermore, when God's holiness comes in contact with human sinfulness, the result is predictable. This is why Joshua warns the Israelites who do not seem to be repentant: "You will not be able to worship the Lord, because he is a holy God. He is a jealous God; he will not forgive your transgressions and sins" (Josh 24:19). This is also seen when the Philistines, Israel's enemies, take the ark of the Lord, and he visits their cities with judgment and death. Even when the ark is returned to Israel, God strikes dead seventy of the men of Beth-shemesh who disrespect the ark, and the people ask, "Who is able to stand in the presence of the Lord this holy God?" (1 Sam 6:20).

God's holiness is also transformative for the prophet Isaiah. He has a vision of the Lord as an exalted King, sitting in the temple. Angels cry, "Holy, holy, holy is the Lord of Armies; his glory fills the whole earth" (Isa 6:3). By this threefold repetition, God's transcendent holiness is displayed gloriously throughout the whole earth. God's moral holiness instantly exposes Isaiah's impurity as dreadful, leading to Isaiah's distress: "Woe is me for I am ruined because I am a man of unclean lips and live among a people of unclean lips, and because my eyes have seen the King, the Lord of Armies" (v. 5). God's holiness exposes human sin, but the holy God is also characterized by mercy and faithfulness. As such, he forgives Isaiah and calls him into service as his prophet (vv. 6–8).

The holy Lord is worthy of adoration:

> The Lord is great in Zion; he is exalted above all the peoples. Let them praise your great and awe-inspiring name. He is holy. The mighty King loves justice. You have established fairness; you have administered justice and righteousness in Jacob. Exalt the Lord our God; bow in worship at his footstool. He is holy. . . . Exalt the Lord our God; bow in worship at his holy mountain, for the Lord our God is holy. (Ps 99:2–5, 9)

Scripture ascribes the divine attribute of holiness to Christ too, even calling him the "Holy One" (Mark 1:24; John 6:69; Acts 3:14; Rev 3:7). Jesus is also described as "holy, innocent, undefiled, separated from sinners, and exalted above the heavens," which makes him fit to save us as our high priest (Heb 7:26). Obviously the Holy Spirit is also characterized by holiness, even identified by it in his name.

Praise of God's holiness will occupy us through all eternity: "Each of the four living creatures had six wings; they were covered with eyes around and inside. Day and night they never stop, saying, 'Holy, holy, holy, Lord God Almighty, who was, who is, and who is to come'" (Rev 4:8).

In the meantime, both Testaments declare God's will to build holiness into our lives. God tells Israel, "I am the Lord your God, so you must consecrate yourselves and be holy because I am holy" (Lev 11:44). Peter quotes this passage when he urges believers to live new lives for God: "As obedient children, do not be conformed to the desires of your former ignorance. But as the one who called you is holy, you also are to be holy in all your conduct; for it is written, Be holy, because I am holy'" (1 Pet 1:14–16; see also 1 Thess 4:2–8).

Our God Is Righteous (Just)

By *righteous* or *just*, we mean that God has established a moral order, governs the world morally, and treats all creatures justly. Scripture often states that "the Lord is righteous" (Ps 11:7; see also 116:5; 129:4; 145:17). While pleading with God to spare any godly people in Sodom and Gomorrah, Abraham exclaims, "Far be it from you . . . to put the righteous to death with the wicked . . . ! Shall not the Judge of all the earth do what is just?" (Gen 18:25 ESV). Scripture so associates righteousness with God that it says, "Righteousness and justice are the foundation of his throne" (Ps 97:2) and "the Lord is righteous in all his ways" (145:17). Moreover, as the psalmist sings, "[God's] righteousness is an everlasting righteousness, and [his] instruction is true" (119:142). Images of God that pertain to his being righteous (or just) include warrior (Exod 15:3), farmer (Isa 5:1–7), a bear and a lion (Lam 3:10–11), and a consuming fire (Heb 12:25–29).

Because God is righteous, he is a just Judge, as the Psalms proclaim: "The heavens proclaim his righteousness, for God is the Judge" (50:6). As King over all, "he has established his throne for justice, and he judges the world with righteousness; he judges the peoples with uprightness" (9:7–8 ESV). Moreover, he will judge at the end: "He is coming to judge the earth. He will judge the world with righteousness, and the peoples with his faithfulness" (96:13).

In justice God is concerned for the poor and downtrodden. He tells the Israelites about to enter the Promised Land, "[T]here will never cease to be poor people in the land; that is why I am commanding you, 'Open your hand willingly to your poor and needy brother in your land'" (Deut 15:11). Through the prophet Amos, God condemns those "who oppress the poor and crush the needy" (Amos 4:1). God's concern for the poor continues in the New Testament, as James demonstrates: "Pure and undefiled religion before God the Father is this: to look after orphans and widows in their distress and to keep oneself unstained from the world" (Jas 1:27). And

John warns, "If anyone has this world's goods and sees a fellow believer in need but withholds compassion from him—how does God's love reside in him?" (1 John 3:17).

God's righteousness brings conviction and prompts repentance (Dan 9:7–14). God's righteousness brings salvation (Isa 46:13; 51:5–6, 8; 56:1; Rom 3:21–26). And God's righteousness pervades the last judgment, when his "righteous judgment is revealed" (Rom 2:5). God "has set a day when he is going to judge the world in righteousness by the man he has appointed. He has provided proof of this to everyone by raising him from the dead" (Acts 17:31).

That man is the Lord Jesus, who is likewise righteous. Isaiah foretells that the coming Servant of the Lord will produce justice and righteousness (Isa 9:7; 42:1–4), and Jesus fulfills such predictions in word and deed (John 5:30; Heb 1:9). Jesus serves as the righteous Judge, assigning eternal destinies for the righteous and the wicked on the last day (Matt 25:34, 41, 46).

As God's people, we too are to be characterized by righteousness. In the Sermon on the Mount, Jesus teaches that his community hungers and thirsts for righteousness (Matt 5:6), is persecuted for righteousness (v. 10), will have righteousness greater than the Pharisees' (vv. 17–20), and will practice real, internal righteousness (6:1–18).

A treatment of God's holiness and justice is incomplete without discussing his wrath.[21] God is inherently holy and just but not inherently wrathful. Rather, his wrath is his response to sin and rebellion. As his personal, active, and settled anger toward and opposition to sin, God's wrath is an extension of his holiness and justice. Specifically, God's wrath is occasioned by the fall of Adam and Eve into sin. *Wrath* is his holy revulsion against all that is unholy, his righteous judgment against unrighteousness, his firm response to covenant unfaithfulness, his good opposition to the cosmic treason of sin. God first displays his wrath in the garden of Eden, and as his people continue to sin, his wrath follows. Cain murders Abel and receives God's curse (Gen 4:8–16). God brings the flood in response

---

[21] This section largely depends on the more extensive material in Christopher W. Morgan, "Wrath" in the *NIV Zondervan Study Bible*, 2681–83 (see chap. 1, n. 25).

to widespread human rebellion (Genesis 6–9). He destroys wicked Sodom and Gomorrah with sulfur and fire from heaven (19:23–29). God punishes Pharaoh and his people with the plagues and in the sea (Exodus 7–15), and so the story goes: people rebel and God visits them with his wrath.

However, even in the midst of these many demonstrations of God's wrath, his grace relentlessly shines through. No sooner does he confront Adam and Eve for their sin than he gives the first promise of redemption (Gen 3:15). It is true that when he proclaims his name, his identity, he says that "he will not leave the guilty unpunished . . . to the third and the fourth generation" (Exod 34:7). But in contrast, because God's "mercy triumphs over judgment" (Jas 2:13), he first announces he is "the LORD . . . a compassionate and gracious God, slow to anger and abounding in faithful love and truth, maintaining faithful love *to a thousand generations*, forgiving iniquity, rebellion, and sin" (Exod 34:6–7).

Astoundingly, God in grace deals with his own wrath toward sin and sinners in order to rescue them. Jesus voluntarily saves us from God's wrath by bearing that wrath for us on the cross. Paul says that "in his restraint God passed over the sins previously committed" in Old Testament times (Rom 3:25). He forgave sins based on animal sacrifice, knowing that ultimately "it is impossible for the blood of bulls and goats to take away sins" (Heb 10:4). Thus, God really forgave Old Testament saints in light of the future sacrifice of his Son. All need Christ's sacrifice, for "all have sinned and fall short of the glory of God" (Rom 3:23). When Christ died on the cross, "God presented him as an atoning sacrifice in his blood . . . to demonstrate his righteousness" (v. 25). Christ thus dies as our propitiation, to meet God's holy demands for justice and to make atonement for sins.

Christ's death as a propitiation maintains trinitarian harmony. "Propitiation—Christ's loving, atoning self-sacrifice that satisfies God's wrath on our sin and reconciles us to God (see Rom 3:25; Heb 2:17; 1 John 2:2; 4:10 [all ESV])—does not pit the wrathful Father against the loving Son (as some allege); rather it underscores that the cross both supremely showcases God's love and perfectly satisfies God's wrath."[22] God's love

---

[22] Morgan, "Wrath," 2682.

sends Christ to the cross (Rom 5:8), and Christ's sacrifice demonstrates God's "righteousness at the present time, so that he would be righteous and declare righteous the one who has faith in Jesus" (Rom 3:26).

Salvation is already enjoyed by believers, but greater blessing awaits in the resurrection and eternal bliss. It is similar for unbelievers and God's wrath. At present, God's wrath is revealed against ungodliness (Rom 1:18) and already is on those outside of Christ (John 3:18, 36). But the full demonstration of God's wrath is still future (Rom 2:5–8; 2 Thess 1:5–9; Rev 14:9–11). Scripture presents the coming wrath as both tragic and good. Jesus weeps over Jerusalem's unbelief and coming judgment (Matt 23:37; Luke 19:41). Paul laments that most Jews reject their Messiah, longs for their salvation, and is willing to give himself for them (Rom 9:2–3; 10:1). But at the same time wrath, judgment, and hell also represent God's victory over evil, Satan, and all his foes. God will avenge his people (2 Thess 1:5–9). God and his people will win in the end, and he will ensure that justice prevails. Through his righteous judgment and ultimate victory, God will glorify himself, displaying his greatness and receiving the worship he is due.

Our God Is Loving

By *loving* we mean that God genuinely desires the good of others and gives of himself to bring about that good. The loving God cares deeply for us. His love is great in its commitment to us. When Moses asks to see God's glory, God reveals himself as "the LORD, the LORD, a God merciful and gracious, slow to anger, and abounding in *steadfast love* and faithfulness, keeping *steadfast love* for thousands, forgiving iniquity and transgression and sin" (Exod 34:6–7 ESV). Images of God that pertain to his being loving include a bird (Ps 36:7), a shepherd (Psalm 23), a husband (Hos 3:1), and a parent (Hosea 11).

God's love is also great in its extent, so David sings, "LORD, your faithful love reaches to heaven" (Ps 36:5). Though Israel's rebellion deserves God's anger, he proclaims to her, "I have loved you with an everlasting love; therefore, I have continued to extend faithful love to you" (Jer 31:3). In response, the godly long for God: "My lips will glorify you because your faithful love is better than life. So I will bless you as long as I live"

(Ps 63:3–4). The greatness of God's love is multiplied by his loving a world that hates him (John 3:16, 19–20).

Both Testaments declare that his love is also undeserved. David says, "He has not dealt with us as our sins deserve or repaid us according to our iniquities. For as high as the heavens are above the earth, so great is his faithful love toward those who fear him" (Ps 103:10–11). Hosea's life with his adulterous wife, Gomer, is a living allegory of the Lord's relationship with idolatrous Israel. As God tells the prophet to take her back amid her adulteries, so the Lord faithfully loves his unfaithful people (Hos 2:19–20).

The New Testament also publishes the undeserved nature of God's love. Paul remarks how unusual it is in human affairs for people to die for someone they value (Rom 5:7). We are astonished, then, to hear that "God proves his own love for us in that while we were still sinners, Christ died for us" (v. 8). God's love for those who are spiritually dead is the epitome of grace: "God, who is rich in mercy, because of his great love that he had for us, made us alive with Christ even though we were dead in trespasses. You are saved by grace!" (Eph 2:4–5).

Moreover, God's love is trinitarian. Jesus likens the Father's love for believers to that of the Father's love for him: "You have sent me and have loved them as you have loved me" (John 17:23). He expands: "You loved me before the world's foundation" (v. 24). The Father's love for the Son includes the Son's redemptive mission (10:17). Moreover, the relationship is reciprocal (14:31). The Father, Son, and Spirit love each other eternally.

Trinitarian love spills over to us, as these passages show, concerning the Father, Son, and Holy Spirit, respectively:

He loved us and sent his Son to be the atoning sacrifice for our sins. (1 John 4:10)

"As the Father has loved me, I have also loved you." (John 15:9)

This hope will not disappoint us, because God's love has been poured out in our hearts through the Holy Spirit who was given to us. (Rom 5:5)

God's love received brings great responsibility. John is clear on two counts: love comes from God, not us, and it claims us. "Love consists in this: not that we loved God, but that he loved us and sent his Son to be the atoning sacrifice for our sins. Dear friends, if God loved us in this way, we also must love one another" (1 John 4:10–11). Jesus explains: "I give you a new command: Love one another. Just as I have loved you, you are also to love one another" (John 13:34).

The Spirit produces fruit in us as we walk in the Spirit (Gal 5:16, 25), and the first fruit is "love" (v. 22). Such love is an indication of true faith: "Everyone who loves has been born of God and knows God. The one who does not love does not know God, because God is love" (1 John 4:7–8).

God's love brings incredible privileges. He welcomes us into his family: "See what great love the Father has given us that we should be called God's children" (1 John 3:1). God's love moves him to correct us as his children: "Those whom I love, I reprove and discipline" (Rev 3:19 ESV). God's love removes our fear of final judgment (1 John 4:17) and assures us that nothing "will be able to separate us from the love of God that is in Christ Jesus our Lord" (Rom 8:39). No wonder, then, that we contemplate, sing about, and tell of God's faithful love:

> God, within your temple, we contemplate your faithful love. (Ps 48:9)

> I will sing about the LORD's faithful love forever; I will proclaim your faithfulness to all generations with my mouth. (Ps 89:1)

Our God Is Gracious

By *gracious* we mean that God has deep compassion for all, especially his own people, and gives them undeserved favor and thus the opposite of what they deserve—he gives them the knowledge of him and eternal life. God's identity includes grace: "The LORD is a compassionate and gracious God" (Exod 34:6). God's love, grace, and mercy are often linked and treated almost synonymously (vv. 6–7; Eph 2:4–10; Titus 3:3–8). Images of God that pertain to his being gracious include father of orphans and widows, champion (Ps 68:5), husband (Hos 3:1), and parent (Hosea 11).

God's grace shines as Ezra rejoices that God's grace preserves "a remnant for [the Jews]" (Ezra 9:8). Ezra is thankful that God "has extended grace to [them] in the presence of the Persian kings, giving [them] new life, so that [they] can rebuild the house of our God and repair its ruins" (v. 9). The psalmist, too, delights in the God of grace: "Better a day in your courts than a thousand anywhere else" for "the LORD grants favor and honor" (Ps 84:10–11).

Grace characterizes the Trinity. The Father is the "God of all grace" (1 Pet 5:10), the Son is "full of grace and truth" (John 1:14), and the Spirit is "the Spirit of grace" (Heb 10:29). The Bible links Jesus and grace. "God's grace was on him" as a boy (Luke 2:40), his humility in becoming a man shows grace (2 Cor 8:9), and he makes atonement "by God's grace" (Heb 2:9). Peter teaches that Jews and Gentiles "are saved through the grace of the Lord Jesus" (Acts 15:11). Indeed, the apostles confess that they "all received grace upon grace from his fullness" (John 1:16). Also, at the start and end (Rom 1:7; 16:20; 1 Cor 1:3; 16:23) of his letters, Paul often prays that the Father and the Son will grant readers grace.

God is gracious to unbelievers. The display of his grace in the New Testament even eclipses that in the Old Testament, as the prophets foretell (1 Pet 1:10–11). Salvation is not just for Israel but also for the world (Titus 2:11). The message of salvation in Jesus is so concerned with grace that it is called "the gospel of God's grace" (Acts 20:24) and "the message of his grace" (14:3; "word" of his grace, 20:32). Grace reaches the unlikely, including Paul, a chief foe of the early church (1 Tim 1:13–14). God saves us by giving us his grace "in Christ Jesus before time began" (2 Tim 1:9). Peter, a Jewish believer, learns that Gentiles are saved in the same way as Jews (Acts 15:11), "by grace through faith" (Eph 2:8). God's grace produces salvation, viewed from many angles, including our new birth (vv. 4–5), calling (Gal 1:15–16), justification (Rom 3:24), and forgiveness (Eph 1:7).

God's grace drives the Christian life. We must "approach the throne of grace with boldness" to receive mercy and "grace to help us" (Heb 4:16). But we come humbly, for "God resists the proud, but gives grace to the humble" (Jas 4:6; 1 Pet 5:5). Grace is God's unmerited love *and* his power (2 Tim 2:1), called enabling grace. Paul says that God's grace makes him what he is and is effective through him. By it he works harder than the other apostles (1 Cor 15:10), and learns a hard lesson: "[God's] grace is sufficient for [us], for [his] power is perfected in weakness" (2 Cor 12:9).

God's grace is active and fruitful. As Adam's sin results in humankind dying, so grace "overflowed to the many . . . by . . . the grace of . . .
Christ" (Rom 5:15). "Where sin multiplied, grace multiplied even more"
(v. 20). God's grace triumphs over sin, and as a result, so do we (v. 21).
Grace produces holiness, for our union with Christ's death breaks sin's
sway over us, and our union with his resurrection produces a new way
of life (6:1–4).

The Holy Spirit dispenses spiritual gifts to us in grace (Rom 12:6), and
we must use them "to serve others, as good stewards of the varied grace
of God" (1 Pet 4:10). God's grace is reflected in our lives (Titus 2:11–15),
which includes using gracious words that build up others (Eph 4:29–32).

God's grace pertains to the past (Eph 2:8), present (Heb 4:16), and
future (1 Pet 5:10). His goal for the church is "so that in the coming ages
he might display the immeasurable riches of his grace through his kindness to us in Christ Jesus" (Eph 2:7). He urges us to set our "hope completely on the grace to be brought . . . at the revelation of Jesus Christ"
(1 Pet 1:13).

Our God Is Merciful

By *merciful* we mean that God sees our affliction and moves to relieve
it. God's qualities of love, grace, mercy, goodness, and patience overlap.
Mercy is an expression of God's love and goodness. God shows mercy
when he sees "the misery" (Exod 3:7) of his people in Egyptian bondage. He rescues them through his servant Moses and brings them to the
Promised Land. An image of God pertaining to his mercy is husband (Hos
2:14–23; 11:9–11).

At times God displays mercy by withholding deserved punishment:
God "has not dealt with us as our sins deserve or repaid us according
to our iniquities" (Ps 103:10). Sometimes mercy is only received upon
repentance (Deut 13:17), and at other times God's mercy is the motive for
repentance (Joel 2:13).

After Mary learns she will give birth to the Messiah, she sings of
God: "His mercy is from generation to generation on those who fear him"
(Luke 1:50). God's mercy, evident in the Old Testament, overflows in the

New Testament. This is especially true of Jesus, who has compassion for the crowds "because they were distressed and dejected, like sheep without a shepherd" (Matt 9:36). Jesus shows abundant mercy to the afflicted. In duress, they cry out to him as "Son of David" (Messiah), and repeatedly in mercy he heals the blind (Matt 9:27–29; Luke 18:35–43) and casts out demons (Matt 15:22–28; 17:15–18; Mark 5:1–20).

Supremely, God's mercy brings salvation. God freely gives it, as Moses states: "I will be gracious to whom I will be gracious, and I will have compassion on whom I will have compassion" (Exod 33:19). Paul later cites Moses to show that salvation "does not depend on human will or effort but on God who shows mercy" (Rom 9:16). God plans "to make known the riches of his glory on objects of mercy that he prepared beforehand for glory," Jewish and Gentile believers (vv. 23–24).

Paul joins mercy, love, and grace: "But God, who is rich in mercy, because of his great love that he had for us, made us alive with Christ even though we were dead in trespasses. You are saved by grace!" (Eph 2:4–5). God's mercy excludes human effort to save: God "saved us— not by works of righteousness that we had done, but according to his mercy—through the washing of regeneration . . . by the Holy Spirit" (Titus 3:5). God's mercy elicits praise: "Blessed be the God and Father of our Lord Jesus Christ. Because of his great mercy he has given us new birth into a living hope through the resurrection of Jesus Christ" (1 Pet 1:3–4). Because we have received God's mercy and because we always stand in need of mercy, we freely and generously give it to others (Matt 6:9–13; 18:21–35; Eph 4:32). Indeed, Jesus asserts that his people are marked by mercy: "Blessed are the merciful" (Matt 5:7).

Our God Is Good (Generous)

By *good* or *generous*, we mean that God cares about and cultivates the well-being of all his creatures. "Goodness" is used of God's name, his whole character (Exod 33:19), but usually it speaks of his attribute of dealing benevolently and liberally with his creatures. Indeed, "every good and perfect gift is from above, coming down from the Father of lights" (Jas 1:17). He is good to both believers and unbelievers, "for he causes his sun to rise on the evil and the good, and sends rain on the righteous and the unrighteous" (Matt 5:45). Images of God that pertain to his being generous include parent (Ps 145:19; Matt 6:26, 30) and shepherd (Psalm 23).

Simply put, "the LORD is good to everyone; his compassion rests on all he has made" (Ps 145:9). Besides, God's goodness is not confined to people. He also cares for and provides for the animals. David even sings of God's goodness in feeding them: "All eyes look to you, and you give them their food at the proper time. You open your hand and satisfy the desire of every living thing" (vv. 15–16).

God's goodness leads his people to the Promised Land, where he shows special care for the poor: "You provided for the poor by your goodness" (Ps 68:10). God's goodness, which lasts forever, contrasts with that of humankind, for "all humanity is grass, and all its goodness is like the flower of the field" in its brevity (Isa 40:6–7).

Creation and redemption reveal God's goodness. After creating, "God saw all that he had made, and it was very good" (Gen 1:31). Nehemiah attests to God's goodness when the Lord leads Israel to possess the Promised Land: "They ate, were filled, became prosperous, and delighted in [God's] great goodness" (Neh 9:25). Paul, offended when the people of Lystra mistake Barnabas and him for gods, points them to the good Creator: "He did what is good by giving you rain from heaven and fruitful seasons and filling you with food and your hearts with joy" (Acts 14:17).

God's great goodness gleams in redemption. It pleases his Old Testament people, as he declares: "My people will be satisfied with my goodness" (Jer 31:14). He invites them to "taste and see that the LORD is good" (Ps 34:8). Therefore, believers cry out to him, "Do not remember the sins of my youth or my acts of rebellion; in keeping with your faithful love, remember me because of your goodness, LORD" (Ps 25:7). Walking with God, each one trusts that "only goodness and faithful love will pursue [him] all the days of [his] life" (23:6). Though not as pronounced as its New Testament counterpart, God's future goodness is something the Old Testament saints trust in: "How great is your goodness that you have stored up for those who fear you" (31:19).

The flower of God's goodness comes to full bloom in the New Testament. Paul chastens hypocrites: "Do you despise the riches of his kindness, restraint, and patience, not recognizing that God's kindness is intended to lead you to repentance?" (Rom 2:4). Believers are ecstatic that "when the kindness of God our Savior and his love for mankind appeared, he saved us" (Titus 3:4–5). As we anticipate future and final redemption, we have confidence because God "has given us everything required for life and godliness through the knowledge of him who called us by his own glory and goodness" (2 Pet 1:3).

How shall we respond to God's goodness? We praise, "for he is good; for his faithful love endures forever" (2 Chr 7:3). We suffer in hope, for "we know that all things work together for the good of those who love God" (Rom 8:28). As we remember God's care for the birds and the wildflowers, we trust his goodness to provide the necessities of life (Matt 6:25–34). We reflect God's goodness by loving and praying for enemies (5:44–45). And we walk in the Spirit and yield "the fruit of the Spirit," which includes "goodness" (Gal 5:22).

Our God Is Patient (Long-Suffering)

By *patient* or *long-suffering*, we mean that God is slow to get angry and does not always immediately punish sin. This neglected quality of God is also called "forbearance." When God reveals his identity (his "name") to Moses, he includes patience, proclaiming of himself: "The LORD—the LORD is a compassionate and gracious God, *slow to anger* and abounding in faithful love and truth" (Exod 34:6; see also Ps 103:8; 145:8). Under attack from ruthless men who hate him, David prays, "But you, Lord, are a compassionate and gracious God, *slow to anger* and abounding in faithful love and truth. Turn to me and be gracious to me" (Ps 86:15–16). An image of God that reflects his patience is that of a shepherd, who patiently searches for one lost sheep (Matt 18:10–14).

God's patience is evident in Old Testament history. Genesis recounts that when God sees the widespread corruption of humanity, he prepares to judge it in the form of a flood to drown humankind and the world over which it is to rule (6:5–13). Peter recalls the Noahic flood but notes God's patience: "God patiently waited in the days of Noah while the ark was being prepared" (1 Pet 3:20). In another event, when God is so angry with his rebellious people that he wants to destroy them, Moses pleads with God not to do so for the sake of his reputation: "The LORD is slow to anger and abounding in faithful love, forgiving iniquity and rebellion" (Num 14:18). Isaiah warns the people against trying the patience of God (Isa 7:13). Levites survey Israel's history leading to captivity and pray to God: "You were patient with them for many years, and your Spirit warned them through your prophets, but they would not listen. Therefore, you handed them over to the surrounding peoples" (Neh 9:30).

Though not cited as often as God's love and grace, his patience also relates to salvation. Paul slams abusers of it: "Do you despise the riches of his kindness, restraint, and patience, not recognizing that God's kindness is intended to lead you to repentance?" (Rom 2:4). Christ's cross is a propitiation that satisfies God's righteousness, because Jesus needed to make full atonement for human sin: "in his restraint God passed over the sins previously committed" (3:25). Paul tells why God withholds judgment for those who rebel against him: he "endured with much patience objects of wrath prepared for destruction[.] And what if he did this to make known the riches of his glory on objects of mercy that he prepared beforehand for glory?" (9:22–23).

As with many of God's attributes, Scripture ascribes divine patience to Christ too. Paul thanks Christ for putting him, "formerly a blasphemer, a persecutor, and an arrogant man" (1 Tim 1:13), in the ministry. Paul rejoices in Christ's patience: "I received mercy for this reason, so that in me, the worst of them, Christ Jesus might demonstrate his extraordinary patience as an example to those who would believe in him for eternal life" (v. 16).

Patience comes readily to the apostles' minds as they await Christ's return. Peter teaches Christians to "regard the patience of our Lord as salvation, just as our dear brother Paul has written to you according to the wisdom given to him" (2 Pet 3:15; see also 3:9). James urges, "Therefore, brothers and sisters, be patient until the Lord's coming" (Jas 5:7).

God wants his patience to be seen in the lives of his people. Patience is, therefore, a fruit of the Spirit (Gal 5:22), and Paul first describes both Christian love and hope as "patient" (1 Cor 13:4; see also Rom 8:25). Like God, we too are to be "slow to anger" (Jas 1:19).

Our God Is Glorious

Our loving, gracious, merciful, generous, and patient God is also glorious. God's glory is notoriously hard to define, although it is as grand as any truth in Scripture. Every major section of Scripture treats the glory of God, and it impacts every major doctrine.

Sometimes the glory of God designates God himself, as when Peter calls God the Father "the Majestic Glory" (2 Pet 1:17). This rare phrase is apparently a Hebrew way of referring to God without stating his name.

At other times the glory of God refers to "an attribute, or a summary attribute of God."[23] Examples include David's speaking of God as the "King of glory" (Ps 24:8–10) and "the God of glory" (29:3). Stephen calls him "the God of glory" (Acts 7:2), and Paul calls him "the glorious Father" (Eph 1:17). Jesus is "the Lord of glory" (1 Cor 2:8) and "our glorious Lord Jesus Christ" (Jas 2:1). The Holy Spirit is called "the Spirit of glory and of God" (1 Pet 4:14).

Glory often expresses God's special presence.[24] This understanding of glory is emphatic in the events surrounding the exodus, for example. The glory cloud (Exodus 13–14; 16:7; 20; 24; see also Rev 15:8), the manifestations to Moses (Exodus 3–4; 32–34), and God's presence in the tabernacle (Exod 29:43; 40:34–38) all highlight God's covenant presence. This connotation of God's glory also emerges in passages related to the ark of the covenant (1 Samuel 4–5), the temple (1 Kgs 8:10–11; 2 Chronicles 5–7), the eschatological temple in Ezekiel (43:1–5), the person of Christ (John 1:1–18; Colossians 1–2; Hebrews 1), the Holy Spirit (John 14–16), and even heaven itself (Revelation 21–22).

Scripture joins God's glory and its display to a number of his attributes: holiness (Lev 11:44; Isa 6:1–8), uniqueness (42:8), power

---

[23] Christopher W. Morgan, "Toward a Theology of the Glory of God," in *The Glory of God*, vol. 2 of Theology in Community, ed. Christopher W. Morgan and Robert A. Peterson (Wheaton, IL: Crossway, 2010), 157. For a more detailed treatment of this attribute, see Morgan, 153–87, which we follow here.

[24] C. John Collins, "*kabod*," in *New International Dictionary of Old Testament Theology and Exegesis*, Willem A. VanGemeren, ed. (Grand Rapids: Zondervan, 1997), 2:577–87.

(Exod 13:21–22; 16:10–15; Rom 6:4), beauty, majesty, and goodness. God's glory is also tied to his works: creation (Genesis 1–2; Psalm 19), salvation (Exod 13:21–22; Ephesians 1), providence (Exod 16:10–12; 40:36–38), judgment (Num 14:10–23; 16:41–45; 2 Thess 1:8–9), and achieving victory (Exod 16:7–12; Ps 57:5–11; Isa 2:10–21). Even more astounding is that Scripture links our triune God's glory with more holistic ideas that emphasize his very nature: God's presence (Exod 33:13–18; 40:34), name, holiness (Lev 11:44; Isa 6:1–8), face, Spirit, fullness, and honor (1 Tim 1:17).

Since God's glory is the extrinsic (external) display of so many attributes, of a panorama of God's works, and of holistic terms related to God's nature, it is clear that God's intrinsic (internal) glory must be viewed holistically. Put differently, if the display of God's power is a display of his glory, if a display of God's holiness is a display of his glory, and if his presence is a central meaning of his glory, then glory must be something broad enough to cover such wide-ranging depictions.

This also makes sense of other biblical data, that which relates to the ultimate end of all things. The Bible repeatedly affirms that God's activities of creation, providence, salvation, and judgment are all for his glory. Yet the Bible offers various attributes that will be set forth in display to be marveled at, and displays of those attributes are not subsumed under a primary attribute but are depicted as ultimate. For example, in Exodus, God acts so that others will recognize his utter uniqueness and power. In Romans, God's saving action displays his righteousness, justice, wrath, power, mercy, and the riches of his glory (3:21–26; 9:20–23). In Ephesians, God acts for the ultimate display of at least three attributes: grace (1:6, 12, 14), kindness (2:4–10), and wisdom (3:10–11). Such biblical data suggests that God's glory is broader than a single attribute. His glory corresponds to his very being and sometimes functions as a sort of summation of his attributes.

Even more, the glory of God frames the biblical story and worldview. *"The triune God who is glorious displays his glory largely through his creation, image bearers, providence, and redemptive acts. God's people respond by glorifying him. God receives glory and, through uniting his people to Christ, shares his glory with them—all to his glory."*[25] Let's look at each aspect of this definition in the following paragraphs.

First, "the triune God who is glorious." God's glory is intrinsic (internal) and extrinsic (external) glory. God's intrinsic glory is his majesty, worth, beauty, and splendor. His extrinsic glory is his glory revealed.

Second, God "displays his glory, largely through his creation, image bearers, providence, and redemptive acts." God reveals his glory in creation: "The heavens declare the glory of God, and the expanse proclaims the work of his hands" (Ps 19:1). He shows his glory in human beings, his image bearers: "What is a human being that you remember him, a son of man that you look after him? You made him little less than God and crowned him with glory and honor" (Ps 8:4–5). The Lord discloses his glory in providence, for after speaking of God's providential care for the world and its creatures, the psalmist exclaims, "May the glory of the Lord endure forever; may the Lord rejoice in his works" (104:31). God makes known his glory in his redemptive acts, including the exodus (Exod 14:13–18) and Christ's resurrection (Acts 3:13–15).

Third, "God's people respond by glorifying him," as Scripture often reminds us: "Not to us, Lord, not to us, but to your name give glory" (Ps 115:1; see also Eph 1:5–6; Rev 19:1).

Fourth, "God receives glory," as we see in both Testaments (Ps 29:1–2, 9; 57:5, 11; Rev 4:8–11; 5:12–14). He delights in the sincere worship of his people (Ps 51:19).

Fifth, "and through uniting his people to Christ, [God] shares his glory with them." Paul explains: "He called you to this through our gospel, so that you might obtain the glory of our Lord Jesus Christ" (2 Thess 2:14; see also Col 3:4).[26]

---

[25] See Morgan, "Toward a Theology of the Glory of God," *The Glory of God*, 159, italics in original.

[26] See the section "We Are Glorious in Christ" in chapter 8, "Salvation," pp. 384–87. See also the section, "We Will Partake of God's Glory" in chapter 11, "The Future," pp. 548–49.

Sixth, "all to his glory." God's extrinsic glory is the communication of God's intrinsic fullness and sufficiency. In Rom 11:36, Paul concludes, "For from him and through him and to him are all things. To him be glory forever" (see Col 1:16 [of Christ]; Heb 2:10). God is the Creator ("from him"), sustainer ("through him"), and goal ("to him") of all things. The self-sufficient and independent God creates out of fullness, guides out of fullness, and receives back according to his communicated fullness. Jonathan Edwards captures it well: "The whole is *of* God, and *in* God, and *to* God; and he is the beginning, middle, and end."[27]

Our God's Works

The glorious God is known by his works, which both accomplish his purposes and display his glory. His works are many, but four stand out as primary: creation, providence, redemption, and consummation. Since we address redemption and consummation in subsequent chapters, we will focus on creation and providence here.

Our God Creates Everything (Creation)

The Bible begins with God creating the heavens and the earth, and the Bible ends with God bringing about a new heaven and a new earth (Gen 1:1; Revelation 21–22). As such, the doctrine of God as Creator frames the biblical story and plays a key role in Christian theology.

At its core, the doctrine of creation is that God, without the use of any preexisting material (ex nihilo), brings into being all that is. Creation is a completely free act of God to communicate his excellence. He alone has no beginning (Ps 90:2). God creates all that is, including light, the earth, sky, water, vegetation, marine life, animals, angels, and everything else (Gen 1:1–25; Ps 148:1–5; Col 1:16; Rev 4:11). God is also directly creating men and women, whom he specially creates in his image (Gen 1:27; 2:7;

---

[27] See Jonathan Edwards, "The End for Which God Created the World," in *God's Passion for His Glory*, ed. John Piper (Wheaton, IL: Crossway, 1998), 247, italics in original.

Mark 10:6; Rom 5:12–21; Jas 3:9–12). All of creation reflects the design and order of God's eternal plan and comes into being by the wisdom of God (Jer 10:12), the will of God (Rev 4:11), and the word of God (Ps 33:6–9).

Creation reveals God as it bears witness of his power and handiwork to all people, at all times, and in all places (Ps 19:1–6; Rom 1:18–32). Creation also brings glory to God as it displays his kingship, power, goodness, wisdom, love, and beauty (Gen 1:1–28; Isa 43:7; Rom 11:33–36). Revelation 4:11 links God's role as Creator to his reception of worship and glory: "Worthy are you, our Lord and God, to receive glory and honor and power, for you created all things, and by your will they existed and were created" (ESV).[28]

Indeed, the eternal God exists before creation (Ps 90:2), and he alone brings all things into being. He creates without the use of previously existing materials, for "the universe was created by the word of God, so that what is seen was made from things that are not visible" (Heb 11:3).

God creates by speaking his word: "Then God said, 'Let there be light,' and there was light" (Gen 1:3 and seven more times in Genesis 1; see also 2 Pet 3:5). He makes human beings capable of understanding his words and responding to him.[29] Moreover, God makes the whole of reality, which is what "the heavens and the earth" mean in Gen 1:1. He creates "all things" (Eph 3:9; Rev 4:11), including everything "visible and . . . invisible" (Col 1:16). John stresses this point by affirming the positive and denying the negative: "All things were created through him, and apart from him not one thing was created that has been created" (John 1:3).

The Trinity inseparably performs the work of creation, namely the Father (1 Cor 8:6; Rev 4:11), the Son (John 1:3; 1 Cor 8:6; Col 1:16; Heb 1:2, 10), and the Holy Spirit (Gen 1:2; Job 33:4). God does not create out of a sense of loneliness or a need for fellowship because the three trinitarian persons love one another from all eternity (John 17:24). God the Father is the source of creation, and the Son is the agent of creation: "There is

---

[28] David S. Dockery, "Creation," in *Systematic Theology Study Bible*, ed. Christopher W. Morgan, Robert A. Peterson, and Stephen J. Wellum (Wheaton, IL: Crossway, 2017), 1674.

[29] For more on God's creation of humans, see chapter 5, "Humanity and Sin."

one God, the Father. All things are from him, and we exist for him. And there is one Lord, Jesus Christ. All things are through him, and we exist through him" (1 Cor 8:6). The Spirit of God is also active in creation (Gen 1:2; Psalm 104).[30]

In creation, as in everything since, God is both transcendent and immanent. He alone exists before creation and thus stands outside of and above it. He is also immanent in his creation because he cares for it, draws near, and enters into a covenant relationship with his people.

The Christian doctrine of creation rejects the errors of dualism, emanationism, pantheism, and deism. Dualism holds that there are two eternal principles of good and evil. To the contrary, God, the all-powerful Creator, is the ultimate reality. Evil is not a competing eternal principle with God, but is a distortion, an aberration, of God's good creation. Emanationism holds that the world is an emanation or extension of God himself, his substance. Contrary to this, the Creator is distinct from his creation. Creation is not an overflow of his being. Rather, he, who alone exists from eternity, brings his world into being by his word. It remains as distinct from him as the creature is distinct from its Creator. Pantheism confuses God and his world. It says God is everything, and everything is God. While pantheism erroneously equates God with his world, deism removes God from the world. It teaches that the Creator builds into the world the ability to run on its own according to human insight, without his involvement. The doctrines of creation and providence refute both pantheism and deism: God not only makes the world but continues to uphold it and direct it.

The chief purpose of God's work of creation is his own glory. Paul affirms this when he contemplates God's works of creation, providence, and consummation: "For from him and through him and to him are all things. To him be the glory forever. Amen" (Rom 11:36). Paul also writes of Christ: "All things have been created through him and for him" (Col 1:16). When Paul says "for him," he means for his purposes and glory.

The fact that Scripture declares God's work of creation "very good" (Gen 1:31) has great ramifications. Everything he makes is intrinsically good, not evil, including physical things. Indeed, the human body and sexuality are not sinful but are gifts from God, to be used according to his

---

[30] Dockery, "Creation," *Systematic Theology Study Bible*, 1675.

will. Asceticism, the idea that holiness is achieved by rough treatment of the human body, is misguided, as Paul teaches (Col 2:20–23).

Because human beings are creatures of the eternal Creator, we have both great gifts and many limitations. He "crowned" us "with glory and honor" and gives us dominion "over the works of" his "hands" (Ps 8:5–6). Our creatureliness brings great responsibility to fulfill the purposes for which he made us. These include as stewards taking an ecological interest in the world God gives us as our home. He gives us wonderful minds and bodies, enabling us to enjoy him and his beautiful world. But only God is self-sufficient and eternal, and we are his creatures who depend on him, for "in him we live and move and have our being" (Acts 17:28). We also praise the Creator for his majestic and lovely world (Ps 19:1; 33:1–9), which has meaning, unity, and intelligibility and points to God's wisdom, power, goodness, glory, and beauty.[31]

Our God Guides History (Providence)

Creation is God's original act of bringing all things into existence, while providence is his ongoing work of maintaining and directing his creation. The Westminster Shorter Catechism defines providence well: "Providence is God's most holy, wise and powerful preserving and governing all his creatures and all their actions."[32]

Providence includes both preservation and government. Preservation is God's work of maintaining his creation, to which both Old and New Testaments bear witness (Ps 104:10–30; 148:7–14; Col 1:17; Heb 1:3 [both of Christ]). God's preservation especially pertains to his people, whom he loves, saves, and keeps according to his plan (Psalm 23; Isa 40:11, 27–31; Rom 8:28–39; 1 John 5:18). Government is God's work of directing his creation toward his goals, which Scripture abundantly affirms (Ps 33:10–22; Isa 40:22–26; Dan 4:34–35; Acts 4:23–31; 14:12–17).

Besides preservation and government, providence also involves concurrence, in which God acts and his creatures act, both unto his intended

---

[31] Gerald Bray, *God Is Love: A Biblical and Systematic Theology* (Wheaton, IL: Crossway, 2012), 226–27.

[32] Westminster Shorter Catechism, answer to question 11.

purposes. God does not always guide history by his direct action, but often uses the free actions of people and other secondary causes. Scripture reflects this idea, asserting that God uses human agents (Gen 1:26–30; 2 Sam 12:1–15; John 6:1–13; Acts 1:8), nations (Isa 10:5–11; Ezra 1), creation (Psalm 104), angels (Gen 16:6–14; Luke 1:26–38), and more.

God's providence extends to every area of his creation:

the universe (Ps 103:19; Dan 4:35; Eph 1:11)
nature (Job 37:5, 10; Ps 104:14; 135:6; Matt 5:45; 6:25–30)
people's lives (1 Sam 16:1; Ps 139:16; Isa 45:5; Gal 1:15–16)
Satan and angels (Job 1:12; Ps 103:20–21; Luke 22:31)
nations (Job 12:23; Ps 22:28; 66:7; Acts 17:26)
animals (1 Kgs 17:4–6; Ps 104:21, 28; Matt 6:26; 10:29)
accidents (Prov 16:33; Jonah 1:7; Matt 10:29)
free actions (Gen 45:5; Exod 10:1, 20; Isa 10:5–7; Acts 4:27–28)
sinful actions (Gen 50:20; Exod 14:17; Acts 2:22–24; 2 Thess 2:11)[33]

God's providence reflects his greatness, wisdom, power, truth, justice, and grace. And his providence inspires our praise, delight, confidence, trust, awe, fear, and wisdom (Psalm 111).

Our God Creates Angels, and Some Rebel

God creates all things, and that includes angels. Does God, then, create Satan and demons? God creates them as good angels, but they rebel against him and become evil angels. Although we do not fully understand, God in his providence allows their rebellion. Sovereignly and mysteriously, he uses even evil for ultimate good. Scripture does not present a complete angelology, satanology, or demonology, but teaches some truths on these topics.

---

[33] Louis Berkhof, *Systematic Theology* (Grand Rapids: Eerdmans, 1939), 168. In his providence God rules over sin, although he is not its cause. Of their own will, evil people oppose Jesus and crucify him. Yet Peter and John stress that this is according to God's eternal plan (Acts 2:22–24; 4:23–30).

ANGELS

God creates angels to worship and serve him. Apparently, many angels rebel before the creation of human beings, and this is the origin of Satan and his demons. Scripture does not give us a complete doctrine of angels, Satan, or demons, but speaks of them all in relation to God. Unlike the Trinity, angels play no part in creation or redemption, but the good angels have important roles as God's messengers, judges, and preservers. They appear before God (Job 1:6; 2:1) and praise (Ps 148:1–2; Isa 6:3) and worship him (Heb 1:6; Rev 4:8).

God creates angels as spiritual beings (Ps 148:1–5; Col 1:16; Heb 1:14) in large numbers (Deut 33:2; Matt 26:53; Heb 12:22; Rev 5:11). They have some organization, because there are archangels (1 Thess 4:16; Jude v. 9). Scripture names two angels: Michael (Dan 12:1) and Gabriel (Dan 8:16; Luke 1:19, 26). Although angels sometimes appear in human form (Gen 18:1–2), they do not have physical bodies, do not marry or procreate (Matt 22:30), and do not die (Luke 20:36). Contrary to common misrepresentations, angels in Scripture do not appear as women or infants, but sometimes appear as mighty human warriors. Angels have great intellectual prowess, but unlike God, their knowledge is limited (Mark 13:32). They are stronger than human beings (Ps 103:20; 2 Pet 2:11), but unlike God, their power is limited, for they are his creatures. As creatures of God, angels are not divine and are not to be worshipped (Rev 19:10; 22:8–9).

Good angels are God's servants who do his will (Ps 103:20–21) and perform four main functions: (1) They adore and praise God (Ps 148:2; Luke 2:13–14; Rev 5:11–12). (2) They serve as God's messengers (Dan 9:21–22; Luke 1:19; Acts 10:22; Rev 1:1). (3) They bring God's judgment on rebellious human beings (2 Kgs 19:35; Acts 12:23; Rev 9:15). (4) They serve God's people (Heb 1:14; Acts 5:19), especially by preserving them (Matt 2:13; Acts 5:17–21).

The eternal Son creates the angels (Col 1:16) along with everything else (John 1:3). The devil tempts Christ (Matt 4:1–11), attempting to thwart his work (Matt 16:23; Luke 22:31; John 8:44), and incites (John 13:2) and empowers (v. 27) Judas to betray Jesus. Good angels play roles in the life of Christ: predicting his birth (Matt 1:20; Luke 1:26–38), announcing it (2:13–15), serving him after his temptation (Mark 1:13) and in Gethsemane (Luke 22:43), announcing his resurrection (Matt 28:2, 5; John 20:12), witnessing his ascension (Acts 1:10–11), and they will accompany his return (Matt 16:27; 25:31; 2 Thess 1:7).

SATAN AND DEMONS

God creates the angels holy, but many of them join Satan and rebel against God. Many think that the prophets describe this rebellion symbolized in the kings of Babylon and Tyre (Isa 14:12–14; Ezek 28:12–17). Satan, "the great dragon . . . the ancient serpent" or "the devil" (Rev 12:9), the leader of the unholy angels or demons (Matt 12:26), is a liar, murderer (John 8:44), accuser (Rev 12:10), and deceiver (12:9). The unfallen or elect angels (1 Tim 5:21) are still holy (Mark 8:38), but the rebellious ones are apparently to be identified with unclean spirits (Matt 10:1; Mark 3:11). Demons, "the spiritual forces of evil in the heavens" (Eph 6:12), carry out Satan's evil plans (2 Cor 11:15) by promoting idolatry (Deut 32:16–17; Ps 106:36–38; 1 Cor 10:19–20) and false teaching (1 Tim 4:1) and possessing and afflicting people (Matt 8:28; 17:15, 18).

Satan and his demons hate God and his people and seek to destroy them (1 Pet 5:8). The devil sometimes disguises himself as an angel of light (2 Cor 11:14–15). Satan blinds unbelievers' minds to prevent them from believing the gospel (2 Cor 4:4). The devil tempts believers to materialism (1 Tim 6:10), pride (3:6), immorality (1 Cor 7:5), lying (Acts 5:3), sinful anger (Eph 4:26–27), lack of forgiveness (2 Cor 2:6–8), and divisiveness (Titus 3:10–11). He promotes false teaching (1 John 4:1–4). Thankfully, believers, by God's strength, can resist the devil, who is subject to the rule of God (Job 1:9–12; Luke 22:31; Jas 4:7). Satan and demons' rebellion against God seals their fate: eternal punishment in hell (Matt 25:41; Rev 20:10).

"I am God, and there is no other; I am God, and no one is like me" (Isa 46:9). God the Trinity alone is God: Father, Son, and Holy Spirit. He alone possesses all the attributes of deity, both his unique ones and those he shares in part with human beings. He alone performs his wonderful works of creation and providence. He alone creates all things, including the angels, some of whom rebel. He alone is the Lord, who in the end will save his people and triumph over all his enemies.

▨ KEY TERMS

angels

aseity

atheism

communicable attributes

creation

deism

demons

dualism

emanationism

eternity of God

ex nihilo

faithfulness of God

generosity of God

glory of God

goodness of God

grace of God

greatness of God

holiness of God

immutability of God

incommunicable attributes

infinity of God

justice of God

love of God

mercy of God

mutual indwelling

omnipotence of God

omnipresence of God

omniscience of God

pantheism

patience of God

personality of God

providence

righteousness of God

Satan

sovereignty of God

spirituality of God

Trinity

truthfulness of God

union with Christ

unity of God

wisdom of God

▨ RESOURCES FOR FURTHER STUDY

Allison, Gregg R. *Historical Theology: An Introduction to Christian Doctrine*. Grand Rapids: Zondervan, 2011, 187–318.

Bray, Gerald. *The Doctrine of God*, Contours of Christian Theology. Downers Grove, IL: InterVarsity, 1993.

Carson, D. A. *The Difficult Doctrine of the Love of God*. Wheaton, IL: Crossway, 2000.

Feinberg, John. *No One Like Him: The Doctrine of God*, Foundations of Evangelical Theology. Wheaton, IL: Crossway, 2001.

Frame, John. *The Doctrine of God*. Phillipsburg, NJ: P&R, 2002.

Helm, Paul. *The Providence of God*, Contours of Christian Theology. Downers Grove, IL: InterVarsity, 1993.

Kaiser, Christopher B. *The Doctrine of God: A Historical Survey*. Revised ed. Eugene, OR: Wipf and Stock, 2001.

Letham, Robert. *The Holy Trinity: In Scripture, History, Theology, and Worship*. Phillipsburg, NJ: P&R, 2004.

Morgan, Christopher W., ed. *The Love of God*. Vol. 7 of Theology in Community. Wheaton, IL: Crossway, 2016.

Morgan, Christopher W., and Robert A. Peterson, eds. *The Glory of God*. Vol. 2 of Theology in Community. Wheaton, IL: Crossway, 2010.

Nash, Ronald H. *The Concept of God: An Exploration of Contemporary Difficulties with the Attributes of God*. Grand Rapids: Zondervan, 1983.

Packer, J. I. *Knowing God*. Downers Grove, IL: InterVarsity, 1993.

Sanders, Fred. *The Deep Things of God: How the Trinity Changes Everything*. 2nd ed. Wheaton, IL: Crossway, 2017.

5

HUMANITY
AND SIN

The Bible is filled with teaching about our identity as humans. God creates us directly and personally, and we experience the Creator-creature distinction. He is our Maker, who creates us in his image. As such, he distinguishes us from himself, animals, and the rest of creation. And though the details are not always clear, being made in God's image concerns who we are: specially created people who can know God. It speaks of what we do: serve God's purposes, one another, and his creation. And it concerns our relationships: with God, ourselves, others, and creation. Our identity is further clarified as we learn that God makes us as holistic, unified persons with immaterial (souls) and material parts (bodies). And most important, God creates us for his glory: to worship, love, delight in, serve, and reflect him.

Sadly, since Adam's fall, sin has entered human experience. Though never our essential nature, sin is our quasi-nature. We are fallen. We are sinners and guilty before God. We all suffer and we all die. We are morally polluted and experience estrangement in all our relationships. We find ourselves unable to escape sin's dominion, and we stand desperately in need of God's help. Wonderfully, God sends his Son to save us from our sinful condition, initially, then gradually; he will finally restore us completely to what God originally created us to be: spiritually alive to him and conformed to the image of Christ, reflecting and serving God through serving others and his creation.

OBJECTIVES

- To lay a biblical foundation for understanding humanity and sin
- To establish our identity as persons made in God's image with great significance and responsibility
- To motivate us to value our status and roles as God's creatures unified in body and soul
- To understand the fall and its terrible consequences
- To encourage us to recognize our actual sins, repent of them, and seek God

OUTLINE

Humanity and Sin in the Biblical Story
Humanity and Sin in Selected Passages
    Psalm 8
    Psalm 51
    Mark 7:20–23
    1 Corinthians 15:45–49
The Doctrine of Humanity
    God Creates Us
        Our Triune God Creates Us
        God Richly Blesses Us
        Views on Humanity's Origin
    God Creates Us in His Image
        Genesis 1:26–28
        Genesis 5:1–2; 9:6
        James 3:9
        Colossians 3:9–10
        Ephesians 4:22–24

Humanity and Sin in the Biblical Story

The Bible's story is first and foremost God's story. He is by far the most important character in the biblical drama. By God's goodness, human beings are his costars in the story. So it is not surprising that humanity plays an early role in the story, but unfortunately, so does sin. The apex of the creation story is God's creation of Adam and Eve, our first parents. God saves their creation for last (Gen 1:26–31; 2:4–25). Of all his creatures, God makes only them in his image. They are like him in unique ways. He makes them with minds to know him and do his will. He makes them morally upright and puts them over the other creatures, to steward and care for them.

God makes Adam and Eve holy and in fellowship with him. However, when they listen to Satan instead of God, they plunge themselves and the rest of us into guilt and corruption. Subsequently, all are born condemned in God's sight and polluted by sin. Death, not a part of God's original creation, now has dominion over us.

God delivers us from sin's guilt and corruption through Christ's saving work, although our total deliverance awaits the resurrection. God declares us righteous when we trust his Son as our sin bearer. In addition, God renews us in his image in knowledge and holiness so that we come to know, love, and serve him out of grateful hearts. We still fight with sin, but God gives us victory through Christ.

At the resurrection of the dead, God will fulfill in us the purposes for which he has created us. He will perfect us in Christ's image and confirm us in perfect holiness. We will love and serve God as his representatives for eternity over the new earth, from which he will banish sin and death. "The kings of the earth will bring their glory into" the city, the new Jerusalem (Rev 21:24, 26), and all redeemed humanity will enjoy redeemed culture forever.

Humanity and Sin in Selected Passages[1]

In the passages below, God displays the glory of his name worldwide in his exaltation of humans made in his image. The Lord of all gives us

---

[1] We treat significant portions of Genesis 1–3, Romans 1–5, Ephesians 2, and more later in this chapter.

responsibility to steward and care for his creation, and for this he is to be praised. God creates humans as holy, but we fall in Adam. David, therefore, confesses his sin and asks God to forgive him and cleanse him within. David is born a sinner and commits sins of adultery and murder against humans and God. David's sin is terrible, but God's love is greater.

Jesus teaches that sins defile us and come from the center of our being. He penetrates to the evil desires behind outward sins and lists sins that come from within. God's inbreathing animates Adam, but Christ, the second Adam, animates believers with eternal life. He gives us eternal life now and will raise our bodies from the grave at his return. Now we have mortal human bodies, like Adam's after the fall. Only in the resurrection will we have immortal resurrection bodies, like Jesus's after his resurrection.

Psalm 8

This psalm applauds humans, over whom their Creator exults. Indeed, God creates, remembers, loves, crowns with honor, and blesses humans with responsibilities over creation. The psalm concerns human beings, but its matching bookends adore God, who has highly elevated humanity: "Lord, our Lord, how magnificent is your name throughout the earth!" (vv. 1, 9). The splendor and grace of God's name are displayed worldwide in his exaltation of human beings, made in his image. God exhibits his glory over all the *earth* and dresses the *heavens* with his majesty (v. 1). And yet he condescends to enter into covenant with us so that we may call him "our Lord"!

Twice the psalmist contrasts God's world on macro and micro levels to put the spotlight on humanity. God adorns the skies with his majesty and brings strength from babies' mouths to silence his foes (vv. 1–2). God has created marvelous heavenly bodies and cares for puny human beings (vv. 3–4). God highly favors us.

The psalmist exults, "You made [mankind] little less than God and crowned him with glory and honor" (v. 5). The psalm establishes God's magnificence compared to his human creatures. Here he compares us, under our Maker, to the lower creation. God, the Lord of the heavens and earth, delegates to us responsibility for domesticated and wild land animals, birds, and fish (vv. 6–8). Indeed, God "put everything under [man's] feet" (v. 6). God gives us leadership over his creation to rule and care for it in his name. For all this God is to be praised (v. 9).

Psalm 51

In this famous psalm David confesses his sin (see also Psalm 32). He does not hide his sin from God, but he openly acknowledges it, labeling it "rebellion" (v. 1), "guilt" (v. 2), "sin" (v. 2), and "evil" (v. 4). He asks God to remove his sin by blotting it out (v. 1) and washing it away (v. 2). David wants God to make him clean within by cleansing (v. 2), purifying (v. 7), and washing him (v. 7).

David realizes that his sin is not superficial; it runs deep and concerns the heart. He is born a sinner: "Indeed, I was guilty when I was born; I was sinful when my mother conceived me" (v. 5). Therefore, he needs a cleansed heart and renewed spirit (v. 10). David perceptively knows that his sins of adultery and murder are ultimately sins against God himself: "Against you—you alone—I have sinned and done this evil in your sight" (v. 4).

David knows that his sin before God requires forgiveness. David's appeal for forgiveness is based on God's "faithful love" and "abundant compassion" (v. 1). David's principal motive for confessing his sins is for God's righteousness to be vindicated in judgment (v. 4). David also longs for his integrity to be restored and the joy of his salvation to be renewed (v. 8), as well as for inward cleansing (v. 10), a willing spirit (v. 12), and the ability to help others (v. 13).

The backdrop for David's prayer includes God's rejection of King Saul after his willful and persistent rebellion against the Lord. David sees God remove the Spirit of kingship from Saul and fears that God might deservedly do the same to him (v. 11). As is often the case, heartfelt confession brings increased wisdom (v. 6), steadfastness (v. 10), praise (v. 15), humility (v. 17), and purity of worship (v. 19). David's sin is terrible, but God's love is greater.

Mark 7:20–23

When Pharisees and scribes complain to Jesus about his disciples' neglecting the traditions of the elders and eating with unclean (unwashed) hands, Jesus offers an insight to the crowd: "Nothing that goes into a person from outside can defile him but the things that come out of a person are what defile him" (Mark 7:15). Foods do not defile people, but sins do, as they come from our "hearts," the center of our being. As he does in the Sermon on the Mount (Matt 5:21–22, 27–28), here Jesus penetrates to the evil desires behind outward sins. Jesus lists sins that come from within. He includes "evil thoughts" ("deceit," "envy," "pride," "foolishness"), evil words ("slander"), and "evil actions" that pertain to sex ("immoralities," "adulteries"), excess ("self-indulgence," "greed"), and crimes against others ("thefts," "murders").

Jesus's sober indictment of the heart points to our need for redemption, which he himself later accomplishes in his death and resurrection.

1 Corinthians 15:45–49

Paul here contrasts the two Adams and their respective people. Adam, the first man, is the father of humanity. God fashions his body from the earth and breathes into his nostrils "the breath of life," and as a result Adam "became a living being" (Gen 2:7; 1 Cor 15:45). Paul calls Christ "the second man" and "the last Adam."

God makes Adam "a living being," but "the last Adam becomes a life-giving spirit" (v. 45). God's inbreathing animates Adam. Christ animates with eternal life all who believe in him. After his crucifixion, Jesus rises from the tomb to live forever. As the Living One, he gives eternal life to us now and will raise our bodies from the grave at his return.

Paul explains that God's order is first the natural and then the spiritual (v. 46). Adam comes first and then comes Christ, the second and last Adam.

Paul contrasts the origins of the two Adams. God creates Adam "out of the dust from the ground" (Gen 2:7); therefore, Adam is "from the earth," that is, natural or ordinary (1 Cor 15:47). Adam comes from dust, and because of his rebellion, his body returns to dust in death. By contrast, Christ is "from heaven." He is the eternal Son of God, who becomes a man in the incarnation. Adam is earthly in origin; Christ, heavenly.

In v. 48, Paul applies these truths to humanity: all of Adam's descendants like him are "of dust," and all of Christ's descendants like him are "of heaven." The bodies of the two groups follow the pattern of the respective Adams. Now we live with natural or ordinary human bodies, like Adam's after the fall. Only in the resurrection will we live in resurrection bodies, like Jesus's after his resurrection.

"Just as we have borne the image of the man of dust, we will also bear the image of the man of heaven" (v. 49). We will bear the image of Christ, the second Adam, in immortality, even as we have borne the image of Adam in mortality. God makes Adam in his image (Gen 1:26–27), and this image, though marred, has persisted in Adam's descendants since the fall (9:6). Since then, Adam and his posterity have bodies that are susceptible to corruption, dishonored (in death), weak, and natural (ordinary) (1 Cor 15:42–44). After resurrection, Christ and his people will have incorruptible, glorious, powerful bodies ruled by the Holy Spirit ("spiritual," v. 44).

The Doctrine of Humanity

God Creates Us

Every part of the Bible testifies to God as Creator:

> Law: "On the day that God created man, he made him in the likeness of God; he created them male and female." (Gen 5:1–2)

> Writings: "Your hands made me and formed me." (Ps 119:73)

> Prophets: "I made the earth, and created humans on it." (Isa 45:12)

> Gospels: "'Haven't you read,' [Jesus] replied, 'that he who created them in the beginning made them male and female?'" (Matt 19:4)

> Acts: "From one man he has made every nationality to live over the whole earth." (Acts 17:26)

Paul's Epistles: "They exchanged the truth of God for a lie, and worshiped and served what has been created instead of the Creator, who is praised forever. Amen." (Rom 1:25)

General Epistles: "So then, let those who suffer according to God's will entrust themselves to a faithful Creator while doing what is good." (1 Pet 4:19)

Revelation: "He swore by the one who lives forever and ever, who created heaven and what is in it, the earth and what is in it, and the sea and what is in it." (Rev 10:6)

OUR TRIUNE GOD CREATES US

If we listen to the whole of Scripture, we learn that our triune God makes all things. Praise is due God the Father for his work of creation: "Our Lord and God, you are worthy to receive glory and honor and power, because you have created all things, and by your will they exist and were created" (Rev 4:11).

The Son creates "everything . . . in heaven and on earth" (Col 1:16). Indeed, "all things were created through him, and apart from him not one thing was created that has been created" (John 1:3). Moreover, the Son is not only Creator of all but also its heir: "God has appointed him heir of all things and made the universe through him" (Heb 1:2).

The Holy Spirit also takes part in creation, as Elihu rightly declares to Job and his friends: "The Spirit of God has made me, and the breath of the Almighty gives me life" (Job 33:4).[2]

GOD RICHLY BLESSES US

God makes humans, male and female, uniquely like him: "God created man in his own image; he created him in the image of God; he created them male and female" (Gen 1:27). God richly blesses us in our physical and spiritual makeup, as David acknowledges: "I will praise you because

---

[2] For more on the Spirit of God in the Old Testament, see Bruce K. Waltke, with Charles Yu, *An Old Testament Theology* (Grand Rapids: Zondervan, 2007), 619–23.

I have been remarkably and wondrously made. Your works are wondrous, and I know this very well" (Ps 139:14). This passage should inspire us to view the body as God's good creation. Scripture teaches that God makes all things "very good indeed" (Gen 1:31), including Adam and Eve's bodies and marital intimacy. Our bodies, not just our souls, are the temple of the Holy Spirit (1 Cor 6:12–20). God the Son takes on humanity and therefore has a genuine physical body (John 1:1–18). Jesus's resurrection is bodily, and ours will be too (1 Cor 15:12–58).

God also richly blesses us in the place he gives us in his world. David is stunned as he contemplates this in light of God's vast heavens: "When I observe your heavens, the work of your fingers . . . what is a human being that you remember him . . . ? You made him little less than God and crowned him with glory and honor" (Ps 8:3–5).

God creates us to serve him and his creation. He is our Maker and Lord; we are his creatures and servants. Moreover, he is our Father, and we are his children by faith in Christ (Gal 3:26). Our motivation for service is love for who he is and what he has done (Ps 150:2). And after resurrection on the new earth, we will serve God forever: "For this reason they are before the throne of God, and they serve him day and night in his temple" (Rev 7:15).

The Creator blesses us with work: "The LORD God took the man and placed him in the garden of Eden to work it and watch over it" (Gen 2:15). Work is a part of God's design for humanity. The dignity of our God-given work is striking, as Tim Keller observes:

> We share in doing the things that God has done in creation—bringing order out of chaos, creatively building a civilization out of the material of physical and human nature, caring for all that God has made. This is a major part of what we were created to be. . . .
>
> While Greek thinkers saw ordinary work, especially manual labor, as relegating human beings to the animal level, the Bible sees all work as distinguishing human beings from animals and elevating them to a place of dignity.[3]

---

[3] Keller, *Every Good Endeavor*, 36 (see chap. 1, n. 21).

Further, we do not live, serve, or work alone, for God creates us for community. He knows it is not good for Adam to be alone, so he makes Eve to be his wife (Gen 2:18). God makes a covenant with Abraham and his family (Gen 17:7; see also 1 Cor 7:14). We are thus blessed with the communal blessings of marriage, family, and church. Indeed, God relates to his people as Israel in the Old Testament and as the church in the New.

We are never to forget the greatest blessing: the Creator claims us for himself. "Acknowledge that the Lord is God. He made us, and we are his—his people, the sheep of his pasture" (Ps 100:3).

Views on Humanity's Origin

There are at least five views of humanity's origin, which are subsets of two main views: evolution and creationism. Evolution holds that human beings evolved from primates, while creationism holds that humans are special creations of God.

Naturalistic evolution holds that all that exists, including humans, has come into being through natural processes. "Naturalistic" means anti-supernaturalistic, omitting any place for God.

Deistic evolution holds that God plans the evolutionary process to accomplish his goals. After God creates the first form, he removes himself from the process.

Theistic evolution is similar to deistic evolution but with significant differences. It holds that God plays a role both in the beginning of the process and also at key points within it. It posits that God directly and supernaturally creates human beings by infusing a human soul into a higher primate.

Fiat creationism holds that God by a direct act creates everything immediately. It stresses both God's direct action and a short time span for creation.

Progressive creationism views "the creative work of God as a combination of a series of de novo creative acts and an immanent or processive operation."[4] At points in time God creates new creatures without using previously existing life. Between these special acts of creation, development occurs. Progressive creationists hold that God creates man directly;

---

[4] Erickson, *Christian Theology*, 505–7 (see chap. 1, n. 18).

he does not use a previously existing primate. This view rejects macro-evolution but accepts some development.

EVALUATION

The first two views plainly contradict biblical teaching. Evangelicals have held each of the last three views, though we believe that theistic evolution also falls short on biblical grounds, as we will see.

Adam and Eve Are Historical Persons. While some modern theologians take Adam and Eve as symbolic, the accounts in Genesis treat them as historical figures (2:4). The witness of the New Testament also points to their historicity. Jesus's genealogy in Luke 3 begins with the fact that he is "thought to be the son of Joseph" (v. 23) and ends with his being "son of Enos, son of Seth, son of Adam, son of God" (v. 38). Luke regards the people in this genealogy, including Adam, as historical persons.

In 1 Tim 2:11–15 the apostle Paul addresses pastoral roles. He gives as a basis for his position the facts that (1) Adam, not Eve, is created first by God; and (2) Eve, not Adam, is deceived. What force would this argument have if Paul were referring to myths, the very thing he speaks against (1:4; 4:7)?

Paul's uses of the Adam/Christ parallel in Romans 5 and 1 Corinthians 15 are also convincing. He contends for the redemptive historical significance of the death and resurrection of Christ: "just as through one man's disobedience the many were made sinners, so also through the one man's obedience the many will be made righteous" (Rom 5:19). Would this be true if Adam were merely a symbol for humankind and not a historical person? Because of the way the Old and New Testaments speak of Adam and Eve, we regard them as historical figures.[5]

Adam and Eve Are Directly Created by God. Genesis 1 gives an overview of creation, while Genesis 2 focuses on the creation of humans:

---

[5] For more on the historicity of Adam and its theological importance, see John W. Mahony, "Why an Historical Adam Matters for a Biblical Doctrine of Sin," *Southern Baptist Journal of Theology* 15 (Spring 2011): 60–79; C. John Collins, *Did Adam and Eve Really Exist? Who They Were and Why You Should Care* (Wheaton, IL: Crossway, 2012).

"Then the LORD God formed the man" (v. 7). God the divine potter fashions a man from the dust "from the ground" (v. 7). Some theistic evolutionists interpret "dust" here as symbolic, allowing for their view that God uses a previously existing animal to create Adam. This misses the plain sense of 2:7 and the use of "dust" in 3:19. There God curses Adam for his sin: "You are dust, and you will return to dust." "Dust" here does not mean a previously existing creature. Humans are made from the dust of the earth, and at death their bodies decay and return to dust. Eve, too, was a special creation: "The LORD God caused a deep sleep to come over the man, and he slept. God took one of his ribs and closed the flesh at that place. Then the LORD God made the rib he had taken from the man into a woman and brought her to the man" (2:21–22).

Genesis 2:7 adds that God "breathed the breath of life into his nostrils, and the man became a living being." The word "became" is important. Man *became* a living creature as a result of God's breathing life into him. This is not the impartation of a soul into a living primate. Man is not alive before God breathes into him. He becomes a living being because of God's action.

God Creates Us in His Image[6]

GENESIS 1:26–28

God's crowning act of creation is to make human beings. This is true for five reasons.

First, God makes us after the other creatures. The narrative builds up to this. The first things God makes are "sea-creatures," "every winged creature," and "livestock, creatures that crawl, and the wildlife of the earth" (Gen 1:21, 24). Then God makes Adam and Eve (v. 27). Therefore, "with the creation of man the creation account reaches its climax."[7]

Second, on four of the previous five days, God sees that his work is "good" (vv. 4, 10, 12, 18, 25). But on the sixth day—when God creates

---

[6] We were helped by Anthony A. Hoekema, *Created in God's Image* (Grand Rapids: Eerdmans, 1995), 11–101.

[7] Wenham, *Genesis 1–15*, 27 (see chap. 1, n. 14).

human beings—"God saw all that he had made, and it was *very good indeed*" (v. 31).

Third, God gives human beings alone dominion over the rest of creation. Gordon Wenham explains:

> God's purpose in creating man was that he should rule over the animal world (v. 26). . . . Because man is created in God's image, he is king over nature. He rules the world on God's behalf. This is of course no license for the unbridled exploitation and subjugation of nature. . . . Mankind is here commissioned to rule nature as a benevolent king, acting as God's representative over them [the animals] and therefore treating them in the same way as God who created them.[8]

Fourth, humanity's creation is more personal than are God's previous acts of creation. Previously, he says, "Let there be" or "Let the earth produce" (v. 24), but when he creates the first humans, he uses the words "Let us make man" (v. 26).

Fifth, God makes man and woman alone in his image and likeness (vv. 26–27). We devote a section to the image of God below, but for now we quote Derek Kidner, who says of human beings, "This living creature, then, and not some distillation from him, is an expression or transcription of the eternal, incorporeal creator in terms of temporal, bodily, creaturely existence—as one might attempt a transcription of, say, an epic into a sculpture, or a symphony into a sonnet."[9]

God reveals his intention to create humans in verse 26 but does not actually create until verse 27. God creates and makes humans in his image. "Image" and "likeness" are parallel words in Hebrew that are synonymous—God intends to make his highest creature, man, like himself in some special sense(s). God then executes his plan: "So God created man in his own image; he created him in the image of God" (v. 27). Moses adds, "He created them male and female." God makes humans male and female

---

[8] Wenham, *Genesis 1–15*, 33.

[9] Derek Kidner, *Genesis*, Tyndale Old Testament Commentaries (Downers Grove, IL: InterVarsity, 1967), 51.

from the beginning. This teaches the equality of man and woman before God, for he makes both in his image. "God blessed them, and God said to them, 'Be fruitful, multiply, fill the earth'" (v. 28). Adam and Eve are to have children to populate the earth; sexuality and procreation are thus part of God's blessing.

In verse 28, we also see the idea of dominion. Dominion is a result of being made in God's image. God makes humans like himself in giving them leadership over the rest of the created order. As a result, humanity should be committed to human justice for fellow humans and resolved to serve our ecological responsibilities.

GENESIS 5:1–2; 9:6

Moses rehearses previous statements: "On the day that God created man, he made him in the likeness of God; he created them male and female. When they were created, he blessed them and called them mankind" (Gen. 5:1–2). God tells Noah and his sons after the flood, "Whoever sheds human blood, by humans his blood will be shed, for God made humans in his image" (9:6). Fallen humanity is still (in some senses) in the image of God.

JAMES 3:9

Like Gen 9:6, James teaches that fallen humans are still in some senses in the image of God. In Jas 3:9, James speaks of the inconsistency often found in our speech: "With the tongue we bless our Lord and Father, and with it we curse people who are made in God's likeness." James calls for consistency in our faith, with our words matching our walk, and our faith in Christ resulting in visible and tangible acts of love for others. James's ethical arguments on how to use words are rooted in his view that humans are created in God's image. Because we are created in God's image, James asserts, we ought not to curse one another. Notice also that the contrast with blessing God is not cursing God but cursing humans. Why? Because humans are created in the image of God. Humans still bear God's image, even after the fall. This makes humans valuable and worthy of loving and just treatment. People matter to God; they should also matter to God's people. Why? Not because of status or abilities but simply because individuals are humans, created in the image of God.

COLOSSIANS 3:9–10

The larger context of this passage emphasizes believers' union with Christ in his death (Col 2:20; 3:3), resurrection (3:1), ascension (v. 3), and second coming (v. 4). We are spiritually joined to the Son of God so that the benefits of his saving work becomes ours.

Since we are united to Christ, we are to consider our bodily members as dead to sins (v. 5). God's wrath will come upon unbelievers on account of such sins (v. 6). Before their salvation, the Colossian Christians committed these sins (v. 7). Besides putting away the sins of v. 5, the believers in Colossae are exhorted also to put aside sins of anger and evil speaking (v. 8). Specifically, they are not to lie to one another because they have "put off [as clothing] the old [sinful] self with its [sinful] practices" (v. 9). A further reason for not returning to their former ungodly lives of lying is given in v. 10: you "have put on [as clothing] the new self" and "are being renewed in knowledge according to the image of your Creator" (v. 10).

The Colossian Christians have had a change of spiritual clothing. They have taken off the old man and put on the new. They have put away their sinful lifestyle and begun to live a holy life. The new man is "being renewed"; there is a divine and ongoing remaking of believers in Christ.[10] This is Paul's theme of re-creation. He uses the language of Genesis 1–2 to speak of Christ as the Re-Creator, who initiates the new creation of God. Christ is the second Adam, who gives life to his people through his resurrection from the dead.[11]

The renewal affects the way a person thinks—he is "being renewed in knowledge" (Col 3:10). Christians are being renewed according to the image of God, their Creator, in knowledge. Since this renewal accords

---

[10] This is a divine passive. See J. P. Louw, *Semantics of New Testament Greek* (Atlanta: Society of Biblical Literature, 1982), 67–68. This is a progressive present tense. So F. F. Bruce, *The Epistles to the Colossians, to Philemon, and to the Ephesians*, 2nd ed., New International Commentary on the New Testament (Grand Rapids: Eerdmans, 1984), 146n80.

[11] For a good summary, see Herman Ridderbos, *Paul: An Outline of His Theology*, trans. John Richard de Witt (Grand Rapids: Eerdmans, 1997), 78–86.

with God's image in man, and since the renewal is a renovation "in knowledge," knowledge must have been an aspect of the original image of God. The "knowledge" spoken of here is "the ability to recognize God's will and command."[12] It is knowledge of his will (1:9). This "knowledge" includes cognition but is more: the ability to think used to serve God.

Adam and Eve come from the hand of their Creator able to think; they can love God with their minds by obeying him. They are able to understand and obey God's word that prohibits them from eating the forbidden fruit (Gen 2:16–17). Adam is able to name the animals (vv. 19–20). The first pair is able to use language and respond intelligently (v. 23). There is thus a cognitive aspect to the image of God in humanity.

Since the fall, our reason is darkened, and we use our minds to engage in the sins of Col 3:5, 8–9 (see also Cain's slaying of Abel and humankind's sinful condition before the flood). When we are saved in Christ, we undergo a lifelong process of sanctification, of gradual growth in practical holiness. Part of this is having our thinking conformed to the will of God (putting away falsehood and the other sins mentioned earlier; see Rom 12:2). In this way we are "being renewed in knowledge according to the image of [our] Creator."

EPHESIANS 4:22–24

Paul exhorts his readers not to live in sin, as the unsaved do (Eph 4:17–19). His readers have not been taught to live in an ungodly manner when they learned of Christ in the gospel (vv. 20–21). Rather, they are taught to live a holy life. Paul uses three infinitives (in vv. 22–24) to teach this new godly living that replaces the old sinful life.

Paul tells readers "to take off [as clothing] your former way of life, the old self that is corrupted by deceitful desires" (v. 22). He then instructs them to "be renewed in the spirit of your minds" (v. 23). Paul also urges them "to put on the new self, the one created according to God's likeness in righteousness and purity of the truth" (v. 24). Here is the new spiritual

---

[12] Peter T. O'Brien, *Colossians-Philemon*, Word Biblical Commentary (Nashville: Thomas Nelson, 1982), 192.

creation in Christ, a corporate concept with individual application (see 2:10, 15; Col 3:10; 2 Cor 5:17).

The "new self, the one created according to God's likeness," is very similar to "the new self . . . according to the image of your Creator" (Col 3:10). Although the image of God is not specifically mentioned in Eph 4:24, the verse likely speaks of that concept for the following reasons: (1) the close parallelism to Col 3:10; (2) the use of "to create" in both passages to refer to the new creation; (3) the phrase "likeness of God," which approximates "image of God."[13]

Ephesians 4:24 and Col 3:10, then, speak of the same topic: the re-creation of people in Christ according to the original image of God in humans. In Eph 4:24 we learn that the new humanity is created according to God "in true righteousness and holiness" (ESV). Since the restoration of the image involves true righteousness and holiness, the original image must have included the same. This is a moral aspect of the original image of God; God made humans like himself in original purity. This fits with Genesis, where Adam and Eve live in fellowship with God before the fall. Only holy beings can live in fellowship with a holy God.

CHRIST AND THE IMAGE OF GOD

Paul also teaches that Christ is the image of God. He speaks of "the light of the gospel of the glory of Christ, who is the image of God" shining upon sinners in the proclamation of the Word (2 Cor 4:4). It is the glorious Christ who is the subject of the gospel. God the Creator re-creates sinners by illumining them through the saving message. Christ is the image of God in that he reflects the glory of God when the gospel is preached (vv. 4, 6).

---

[13] Mitton agrees: "The wording here in Ephesians differs from that of Col 3:10, but clearly the meaning is intended to be the same." C. Leslie Mitton, *Ephesians*, New Century Bible Commentary (Grand Rapids: Eerdmans, 1981), 166. Bruce, *The Epistles to the Colossians, to Philemon, and to the Ephesians*, 359, adds, "The phrase 'according to God' means 'in the image of God.'"

Paul calls Christ "the image of the invisible God" (Col 1:15). Jesus is the visible representation of God, who is invisible. Jesus is God incarnate, who makes God visible.

In two other texts Paul does not call Christ "the image of God" but regards him as the image to which believers will conform. In Rom 8:29 Paul presents the goal of salvation as our conformity to Christ's image. Jesus is the preeminent Son of God, and as the children of God, we will increasingly and eschatologically conform to his image. He is our older Brother, and by virtue of family resemblance, we will be like him in glory. Speaking of re-creation, Paul teaches that we will bear the image of Christ, the second Adam, in immortality, even as we have borne the image of Adam in mortality (1 Cor 15:49). Here conformity to Christ's glorified body is the goal of salvation.

What do these passages add to our understanding of the image of God? Two passages teach that Jesus *is* the image of God. Through gospel preaching he reveals God's image (2 Cor 4:4). In his incarnation he reveals the invisible God (Col 1:15). God creates Adam and Eve in his image; as the God-*man*, Jesus Christ is the image of God. The incarnate Christ is a perfect example of what human beings are to be.

Paul also teaches that Christ is the eschatological goal to which the redeemed will conform. God's children will share the glory of the firstborn Son (Rom 8:29). The image bearers of Adam will be the image bearers of the second Adam when they are clothed with immortality (1 Cor 15:49).

Christ is thus the model (2 Cor 4:4; Col 1:15) and the final goal (Rom 8:29; 1 Cor 15:49) of the image of God in humanity.

HISTORICAL INSIGHTS

Three views of the image of God have predominated in church history. *Substantive* or *structural* views were predominant until the Enlightenment. Such views hold that the image of God is what we *are* as humans, rather than the image being expressed in our roles or relationships. The image is in our makeup, often in our power of cognition. A substantive view of the image points to our ability to think as distinguishing us from animals. Thomas Aquinas is a representative of this view.

The *functional* view of the image is more recent. It holds that the image of God centers on our roles, not our being. Advocates, including Leonard Verduin,[14] point to God's granting Adam and Eve dominion over the other creatures as prime evidence for the functional view. As we exercise dominion, we image God.

The *relational* view of the image is also recent. It maintains that the image of God is found in our relationships, not in our being or roles. We image God in our relationships with him, fellow humans, and creation. Love is regarded as the chief expression of the image in this view, which Emil Brunner advocates.[15]

SYNTHESIS[16]

First, *the image has substantive, functional, and relational aspects* that we must hold together. God creates Adam and Eve like him in their makeup. He endows them with cognition to do his will. He makes them in his image, in righteousness. As humans, we are partially able to think God's thoughts after him and to do his will. We are holy beings created for fellowship with our Maker. This is the substantive aspect of the image. The Bible also speaks (more often) of functional and relational aspects of the image. God gives Adam and Eve dominion over creation. They are to represent their Lord as his representatives over the earth. They are also to relate to God, their fellow humans, and creation in ways that please God. It seems best to view the functional and relational aspects of the image as rooted in the substantive. Because of who we are, we have certain roles. Because of who we are as humans, we have certain relationships.

Second, *Jesus Christ is the perfect image of God*. He is both our ultimate model and our eschatological goal. Jesus substantively is the image of God, and in his incarnation he perfectly models God's image. Erickson explains: "Jesus had perfect fellowship with the Father. . . . Jesus obeyed the Father's will perfectly . . . and Jesus always displayed a strong love for

---

[14] Leonard Verduin, *Somewhat Less Than God: The Biblical View of Man* (Grand Rapids: Eerdmans, 1970).

[15] Emil Brunner, *The Christian Doctrine of Creation and Redemption*, Dogmatics, vol. 2 (Philadelphia: Westminster, 1952), 58–59.

[16] We were helped considerably by Hoekema, *Created in God's Image*, 66–101.

humans."[17] In addition, Jesus is the final goal for his people. God will one day conform us to Christ's image when we put on immortality and glory.

Third, *the image should also be viewed along the biblical story line*, as Hoekema stresses.[18] We view the image of God in human beings in these redemptive-historical stages:

Stage	Description of the Image of God in Humanity
At creation	The original image
After the fall	The marred image
After redemption	The image being restored in Christ
In the eternal state	The perfected image

Viewing the image of God along Scripture's story line, we note that at creation God makes Adam and Eve in his original image. Our first parents are creatures of God, their Maker; and of all his creatures, they alone are like him in important ways. After the fall, the image is marred but not erased. Fallen human beings retain the image; they do not become less than human. But the image is tainted, and humans no longer reflect God as they were made to do. When people come to Christ, God begins a lifelong process of restoring them in the image. In Christ, God works a gradual renewal of the image in believers. The image is not perfect as at creation, but it is truly and progressively restored. Only in the eternal state will the image be perfected. In fact, our last state will be better than the first, for we will not be able to sin or again suffer a marred image.

Voices from the Global Church: Lausanne Covenant

"Something needs to be said at this point about the collectivist view of humanity in the Bible that is so alien to our individualistic western culture. The Bible teaches that the meaning and purpose of human life is worked out in the relational context of collectivities—of family, tribe, people, nation, and humanity."[19]

---

[17] Erickson, *Christian Theology*, 533–34.

[18] Hoekema, *Created in God's Image*, 82–96.

[19] The Lausanne Covenant, https://www.lausanne.org/content/lop/following-jesus-as-his-community-in-the-broken-world-of-ethnic-identity-lop-62-d (no longer accessible).

Fourth, *the image includes relationships to God, fellow human beings, and creation,* as Hoekema teaches.[20] By God's enabling grace we can grow in our reflection of the image of God in these areas. God's creating us male and female is an expression of this relational aspect of the image, as are human friendships and marriage. A larger expression of this relational aspect is the local church, and the largest expression is the sum total of redeemed humanity. Therefore, the image of God in humanity will be completely revealed only when all of God's people are resurrected and glorified to live on the new earth. Revelation 7:9 anticipates "every nation, tribe, people, and language" being united into one redeemed humanity in the new heavens and the new earth.

Fifth, *the image of God relates to humans holistically,* as Hoekema says.[21] It is inadequate to locate the image exclusively in the soul. As we will see below, God creates Adam and Eve in his image as holistic beings, made of bodies and souls. He creates us to image him in our roles and relationships, which requires bodies. When we do, others see the image of the invisible God embodied in human beings with faces, hands, and feet. The perfected image will involve resurrected human beings, united in body and soul, glorifying the Trinity in loving service on the new earth.

God Creates Us as Holistic Beings

Passages

God creates Adam and Eve as whole beings with bodies and souls united. Genesis relates, "The Lord God formed the man out of the dust from the ground and breathed the breath of life into his nostrils, and the man became a living being" (2:7). This speaks not of God's imparting a soul to Adam but of his causing him to come alive. It is not from Genesis but from the whole of Scripture that we learn that God makes humans with material and immaterial parts. Genesis emphasizes our wholeness without speaking of the parts.

---

[20] Hoekema, *Created in God's Image,* 75–82.

[21] Hoekema, 68.

Scripture does distinguish body and soul. Jesus warns, "Don't fear those who kill the body but are not able to kill the soul; rather, fear him who is able to destroy both soul and body in hell" (Matt 10:28).

Scripture reveals that we have material and immaterial parts when it tells of their separation at death. Jesus assures the dying thief, "Today you will be with me in paradise" (Luke 23:43). The thief will join Jesus later that day in God's presence. Since their bodies stay on the cross, are taken down, and are buried, there must be an immaterial part of humanity that survives death. I. Howard Marshall is right: "Jesus' reply assures him of immediate entry into paradise."[22] The thief's journey matches Christ's, who prays, "Father, into your hands I entrust my spirit" (v. 46).

Paul expresses his desire "to depart and be with Christ" (Phil 1:23). In context he is speaking of departing the body at death, as he contrasts living and dying (v. 21), speaks of continued living "in the flesh" (v. 22), and speaks of remaining "in the flesh" (v. 24). Paul expects to go into the presence of Christ when he dies. His body will be buried and will decay; his immaterial part will go to be with the Lord.

In 2 Cor 5:6–8 Paul contrasts being "at home in the body" and "away from the Lord" with being "away from the body and at home with the Lord." Assumed here is that human nature is composed of material and immaterial parts. When one is at home in the body (living in the body on earth), one is not in the presence of Christ in heaven. When a believer departs the body, he goes to be with the Lord. Plainly, the body he departs does not yet go into Christ's presence. There is an immaterial part that survives the death of the body and enters into the Lord's presence.

TERMINOLOGY

Scripture frequently refers to our material part as "body" or "flesh." It speaks of our immaterial part as "soul" or "spirit," but more often does so by using personal pronouns:

---

[22] I. Howard Marshall, *The Gospel of Luke*, New International Greek Testament Commentary (Grand Rapids: Eerdmans, 1978), 873.

"Truly I tell you, today *you* will be with me in paradise." (Luke 23:43)

I long to depart and be with Christ. (Phil 1:23)

While *we* are at home in the body *we* are away from the Lord . . . and *we* would prefer to be away from the body and at home with the Lord. (2 Cor 5:6, 8)

VIEWS

Monism holds that human beings are indivisible. Accordingly, one must have a body to be human. Monism denies that there is a disembodied existence in an intermediate state.

Dichotomy holds that human beings are composed of two parts: a material one (the body) and an immaterial one (the soul or spirit).

Trichotomy holds that humans consist of three parts: a body, a soul ("the seat of the affections, desires, emotions, and the will"), and a spirit (which "knows and is capable of God-consciousness and communication with God"[23]).

Conditional unity is also called *psychosomatic unity* or *holistic dualism*. It holds that our normal state is as beings composed of bodies and souls united. This unity is altered at death, where the immaterial part lives on while the material part decomposes. This disembodied intermediate state is abnormal, temporary, and incomplete. In the resurrection, people will again be unified.

SYNTHESIS

The passages surveyed (Luke 23:43, 46; Phil 1:23; 2 Cor 5:6, 8) refute the monistic view. Human nature is not such a unity that a disembodied existence is impossible. Such an existence becomes actual in the intermediate state.[24] Yet if we view death in light of the Bible's story, then the intermedi-

---

[23] *New Scofield Reference Bible* (New York: Oxford University Press, 1967), 1293n2 on 1 Thess 5:23.

[24] The parable of the rich man and Lazarus in Luke 16:22–26 teaches the reality of the disembodied existence of the lost after death, as does 2 Pet 2:9.

ate existence is an anomaly, for God creates Adam and Eve as embodied beings, we are embodied now, and after the resurrection we will live as embodied beings for all eternity. Indeed, our final state is not a disembodied existence. Our final state will be in glorified bodies on the new earth.

Scripture describes our material and immaterial parts in various ways, sometimes adding further nuance. In 1 Thess 5:23 Paul states, "Now may the God of peace himself sanctify you completely. And may your whole spirit, soul, and body be kept sound and blameless at the coming of our Lord Jesus Christ." There is some difference between spirit and soul here. But two distinct immaterial constituents of human nature are not implied any more here than they are in similar expressions of our total being in Deut 6:5 and Luke 10:27 (i.e., heart, soul, mind, and strength). Hebrews 4:12 states, "The word of God is living and effective and sharper than any double-edged sword, penetrating as far as the separation of soul and spirit, joints and marrow." This speaks of God's Word penetrating deep within to expose our disobedience. His Word is so penetrating that it pierces to the division of soul and spirit and the separation of joints and marrow. Again, there is some sort of distinction between soul and spirit here, but such a distinction is so subtle that the passage uses it as an example of the amazing probing features of God's Word.

In sum, humanity has material and immaterial parts. However, the union of body and soul is normal. That is how God makes us, how we live now, and how we will live for eternity. Scripture teaches an intermediate state in which our immaterial part lives an incorporeal existence. But this state is abnormal, temporary, and incomplete. God will raise us from the dead and unite body and soul. Our final state will be eternal life as unified persons with glorified bodies on a new earth.

God Creates Us for His Glory

The living and true God created us in his image as holistic beings. And he did this for his glory. Although we were made to glorify God as his image bearers, through Adam's original sin and our actual sins, we rebelled against him. We all rejected God's glory and sought our own in its place. God finds us "without excuse" because his creation broadcast knowledge that reached to us, but we failed to "glorify him as God or show gratitude" (Rom 1:20–21). We thought we were wise without God, but in fact we became "fools and exchanged the glory of the immortal God" for worthless idols (vv. 22–23).

Mercifully, God does not leave us in our lost estate, but by his grace and for his glory he restores his image in us by spiritually joining us to Christ, the true image. God delivers believers not only *from* the penalty and power of sin but also *unto* his glory. God progressively restores in Christians the original divine image tarnished by sin. Paul recalls the Israelites, who insisted that Moses veil his face because they cannot bear to see God's glory. Astonishingly, Paul, by contrast, says of all new covenant believers, "We all, with unveiled faces, are looking as in a mirror at the glory of the Lord and are being transformed into the same image from glory to glory; this is from the Lord who is the Spirit" (2 Cor 3:18).

God gives glory to us, who despise his glory and defile his image in us. He not only works his glory into the lives of us who know and love his Son but also promises to give us future glory, including conformity to the image of that Son. "Thus, we are recipients of glory, are undergoing transformation through glory, and will be sharers of glory."[25] All of this can be fully appreciated only against the ugliness of our sin, the topic to which we turn next.

The Doctrine of Sin

Biblical Descriptions

We begin with biblical descriptions of sin as set forth by John Mahony.[26]

---

[25] Morgan, "Toward a Theology of the Glory of God," 186 (see chap. 4, n. 23).

[26] This section relies on John W. Mahony, "A Theology of Sin for Today," in *Fallen: A Theology of Sin*, vol. 5 of Theology in Community, ed. Christopher W. Morgan, and Robert A. Peterson (Wheaton, IL: Crossway, 2013).

Sin Is a Failure to Glorify God and Rebellion against Him

The Bible uses many words for sin. Many are expressions that view sin as a failure or a "falling short." In this sense, sin is a failure to keep God's law ("lawlessness," 1 John 3:4), a lack of God's righteousness (Rom 1:18), an absence of reverence for God (Rom 1:18; Jude v. 15), a refusal to know (Eph 4:18), and, most notably, a coming "short of the glory of God" (Rom 3:23). Thus, sin is the quality of any human action that causes it to fail to glorify the Lord fully.

Sin Is Offense against God and Violation of His Law

The title of Psalm 51 indicates that its occasion was David's adultery with Bathsheba, which implies his murder of Uriah, her husband, to cover up his sin. But David confesses, "Against you—[God] alone—I have sinned and done this evil in your sight" (Ps 51:4). Why does he say this? Because ultimately all sin is against God. When Potiphar's wife tries to seduce Joseph, his rebuff reveals the same principle: "How could I do this immense evil, and . . . sin against God?" (Gen 39:9). God's law reveals his character and will as the Lawgiver. Violation of his law, then, is an attack on his character. Paul equates hostility toward God with disobeying his law (Rom 8:7), and John says tersely, "Sin is the breaking of law" (1 John 3:4 HCSB).

Sin Is a Willful Act and the Present State of Human Existence

Sin encompasses our whole rebellious existence: what we do and who we are. Sin is a personal act. It arises from individual choice and is, therefore, a matter of personal responsibility (Ezek 18:4). Every willful act of sin, however, flows from a sinful condition, which is also sin. Personal sins are not simply isolated events. All of our actions and words reflect who we are: "a bad tree produces bad fruit" (Matt 7:17).

Sin Is Personal and Social

Sin in Scripture is primarily personal but also societal. Social sin has two dimensions. First, every sin disturbs the entire human network by setting in motion social consequences (Joshua 7). Today we can trace the repercussions of domestic violence, hate crimes, and divorce in families and the larger cultural context. Second, social sin also appears in societal structures that proliferate the evils of prejudice, hate, greed, and thirst for power.

A major task of Israel's prophets is to confront societal sins. Isaiah exposes the apostasy of the nation from God (Isa 1:2–4), as well as the corruption in Israel's legal system (10:1–4). Jeremiah indicts the nation for its treatment of the fatherless (Jer 5:28–29). Amos preaches against injustice: "I know your crimes are many and your sins innumerable. They oppress the righteous, take a bribe, and deprive the poor of justice at the city gates" (Amos 5:12).

Sin Involves Commission, Omission, and Imperfection

Sin can be categorized as commission (a deed done), omission (a deed left undone), or imperfection (a deed done with wrong motives). Sin as commission does or says or thinks the wrong thing. Sin as omission, on the other hand, fails to do or say or think the right thing. Imperfection refrains from doing the wrong thing but does the right thing with the wrong motive.

God judges all moral acts by the standard of his holiness expressed in his good law. As John Mahony explains, the Ten Commandments are published expressions of God's moral law. Lying, stealing, killing, committing adultery, and disrespecting the Lord are overt acts. Breaking them constitutes the commission of a crime against him. God states eight of the commandments negatively to mark moral boundaries. But he also intends the commandments to be moral guides. For example, the prohibition against murder also includes the principle of the sanctity of human life. Each sin in varying degree includes commission, omission, and imperfection simultaneously.[27] Jesus also comments on what constitutes obedience to the commandments: we must love God with all our hearts, souls, and minds (Matt 22:37).

---

[27] See Mahony, "A Theology of Sin for Today," 198–99.

Sin Is a Rogue Element in Creation

Good characterizes God's creation (Gen 1:31), and as Augustine under-stood, sin is the negation of that good. Mahony clarifies:

> [S]in is not a substance created by God but is an absence within the good which he did create.[28] Further, sin arose through will-ful choices made by creatures whom God had created. The only avenue through which sin appears in creation is the open door of free choice. Consequently, sin is parasitic, a negative quality which has no actual existence in the created world but usurps the moral structures which God has instituted. In the similar case of viruses, the parasite requires a host to live. In the same way, sin is a moral virus and exists only in the context of the good purposes of God.[29]

Sin Is a Failure to Image the Creator to the World

We are created in the image of God to glorify God. When we sin, we exchange the glory of the incorruptible God for idols (Jer 2:11–12; Rom 1:23). Richard Gaffin explains: Although human beings are God's image bearers, with "foolish, darkened hearts (see 1 Cor 1:18–25), they have idolatrously exchanged God's glory for creaturely images, human and otherwise (Rom 1:21–23). Having so drastically defaced the divine image, they have, without exception, forfeited the privilege of reflecting his glory (Rom 3:23). This *doxa*-less condition, resulting in unrelieved futility, cor-ruption and death, permeates the entire created order (Rom 8:20–22)."[30]

---

[28] Mahony cites Albert M. Wolters, *Creation Regained: Biblical Basics for a Reformational Worldview* (Grand Rapids: Eerdmans, 1985), 44–56.

[29] Mahony, "A Theology of Sin for Today," 202–3.

[30] Richard B. Gaffin Jr., "Glory, Glorification," in *Dictionary of Paul and His Letters*, ed. Gerald F. Hawthorne and Ralph P. Martin (Downers Grove, IL: InterVarsity, 1993), 348. See also Gaffin, "The Glory of God in Paul's Epistles," in *The Glory of God*, vol. 2 of Theology in Community, ed. Christopher W. Morgan and Robert A. Peterson (Wheaton, IL: Crossway, 2010).

Sin Includes Guilt and Pollution

Sin involves guilt. All sin is against God, earns his wrath, and makes us guilty in his sight. This guilt is not to be reduced to guilty feelings, though they may be involved. Rather, this is objective guilt before a holy and just God, whether or not accompanied by guilty feelings. Paul explains: "God's wrath is revealed from heaven against all godlessness and unrighteousness of people" (Rom 1:18; see also 3:19–20). Since the fall, human beings are born guilty in God's sight: "we were by nature children under wrath as the others were also" (Eph 2:3, where "by nature" means "by birth"; see also Gal 2:15).[31]

Sin involves not only guilt but also pollution or corruption. Guilt is a legal category and pollution a moral one. Sin pollutes or corrupts us so that we are sinners. And because we are sinners, we sin (Mark 7:21–23). Sin condemns us before God (guilt) and stains us and our lives (pollution or corruption).

Sin Includes Thoughts, Words, and Actions

Sin expresses itself in thoughts. When the tenth commandment condemns coveting, it extends to the thought life (Exod 20:17). Jesus teaches that hatred is directly related to murder (Matt 5:22, in violation of the sixth commandment) and that lust is directly related to adultery (5:28, in violation of the seventh commandment).

Sin expresses itself in words. When Isaiah sees a vision of God's exalted holiness in the temple, he is convicted of his and his people's sins of speech (Isa 6:5). James addresses how sin expresses itself in words in Jas 3:1–18. His treatment of the instrument of speech, the tongue, warns of its great influence compared to its size, and of its being evil, untamable, and fickle (vv. 1–12). Indeed, the tongue "stains the whole body, sets the course of life on fire, and is itself set on fire by

---

[31] Bruce, *The Epistles to the Colossians, to Philemon, and to the Ephesians*, 284. "Children of wrath" means "worthy to receive divine judgment." It is a Hebrew idiom; see 2 Sam 12:5, where being "a son of death" means one "deserves to die" (284–85).

hell" (v. 6). The one good thing James has to say about the tongue is that we use it to praise God. But this is not unmitigated good news: "With the tongue we bless our Lord and Father, and with it we curse people who are made in God's likeness. Blessing and cursing come out of the same mouth. My brothers and sisters, these things should not be this way" (vv. 9–10). James 3:13–18 then directly ties the sin of words to the source: the heart.

Sin is expressed in actions. Paul summarizes:

> The works of the flesh are obvious: sexual immorality, moral impurity, promiscuity, idolatry, sorcery, hatreds, strife, jealousy, outbursts of anger, selfish ambitions, dissensions, factions, envy, drunkenness, carousing, and anything similar. I am warning you about these things—as I warned you before—that those who practice such things will not inherit the kingdom of God. (Gal 5:19–21)

SIN IS DECEITFUL

Of many passages depicting sin's deceitfulness, here are three:

> The heart is more deceitful than anything else, and incurable— who can understand it? (Jer 17:9)

> "Why do you look at the splinter in your brother's eye but don't notice the beam of wood in your own eye? Or how can you say to your brother, 'Let me take the splinter out of your eye,' and look, there's a beam of wood in your own eye? Hypocrite! First take the beam of wood out of your eye, and then you will see clearly to take the splinter out of your brother's eye." (Matt 7:3–5)

> Watch out, brothers and sisters, so that there won't be in any of you an evil, unbelieving heart that turns away from the living God. But encourage each other daily, while it is still called today, so that none of you is hardened by sin's deception. (Heb 3:12–13)

Sin's deceitfulness can often be seen in how what is right in the world is often entangled with what is wrong. What is wrong can flow in people and systems apparently committed to the good. Henri Blocher astutely asks,

If humans are capable of so much evil, how is it that they also reach heights of heroism, performing admirable deeds of selfless service and devotion to the truth? . . . We have to acknowledge the complexity of the human phenomenon. . . . Actually the complexity is worse than many imagine; one may discover worthy motives in outrageous actions, and ugly roots under the flowering of virtue. How can we make sense of the entanglement of these things?[32]

Sin Has a Beginning in History and Will Have an End

The biblical story sheds much light on sin: sin did not exist before creation, enters human history in the fall, is defeated by Christ, and will one day be utterly eliminated. Sin emerges in God's good creation as a temporary intruder, causes much havoc, and holds many in its clutches. But it is no match for the work of God in Christ. Through Jesus's sinless life, sin-bearing death, sin-defeating resurrection, and sin-crushing second coming, sin and its offspring of suffering and death are given the deathblow. In the end, *sin will be judged, and sin will be defeated.* Sin abounded, but grace superabounds! In the biblical story, God has the first word. And thankfully, God also has the last word, as the apostle Paul so marvelously proclaims:

"Where, death, is your victory?
    Where, death, is your sting?"
    The sting of death is sin, and the power of sin is the law. But thanks be to God, who gives us the victory through our Lord Jesus Christ! (1 Cor 15:55–57)

The Fall and Sin

God does not create sin but creates a good universe and good human beings. Sadly, Adam and Eve do not obey God's command not to eat from the tree of the knowledge of good and evil, but "they fall." The tempter

---

[32] Henri Blocher, *Original Sin: Illuminating the Riddle*, New Studies in Biblical Theology, ed. D. A. Carson (Grand Rapids: Eerdmans, 1997), 11–12.

calls into question God's truthfulness, sovereignty, and goodness. The "cunning" tempter deflects the woman's attention from the covenantal relationship God has established. In the central scene, the fall reaches its climax. The fatal sequence unfolds rapidly: Eve "saw," "took," "ate," and "gave" (Gen 3:6), and the sequence culminates in "he ate." In striking contrast, the forbidden fruit does not deliver what the tempter promises but brings new dark realities, as the good, truthful, covenant Lord had warned.

This initial rebellious act brings divine justice. The consequences of man's sin are fitting and devastating. The couple immediately feels shame, realizing they are naked (3:7). They sense their estrangement from God, foolishly trying to hide from him (vv. 8–10). They fear God and his response (vv. 9–10). Their alienation from each other emerges as Eve blames the serpent, while Adam blames Eve and, by intimation, even God (vv. 10–13). Pain and sorrow ensue. The woman will experience pain in childbirth; the man will toil trying to grow food in a land with pests and weeds; and both discover dissonance in their relationship (vv. 15–19). Worse, God banishes them from Eden, away from his glorious presence (vv. 22–24).

How they wish they would have heeded God's warning: if you eat of the tree of the knowledge of good and evil, "you will certainly die"! (2:17). Upon eating the forbidden fruit, they do not immediately die from something like cardiac arrest. But they do die. They die spiritually, and their bodies also begin to experience the gradual decay that leads ultimately to their physical death as God's judgment states: "You will return to dust" (3:19).

Most devastating is that these consequences not only befall Adam and Eve but extend to their descendants. The scene is dismal: none of their children "enjoyed marriage relationships without some degree of rivalry or resentment, and they inevitably ate bread produced by the sweat of their brow. . . . Adam and Eve sinned alone, but they were not the only ones locked out of the Garden. Cut off from the tree of life, they and their descendants were all destined to die."[33]

So, in the beginning, God creates a good cosmos with good humans who have good relationships with him, themselves, one another, and

---

[33] Robert A. Pyne, *Humanity and Sin* (Dallas: Word, 1999), 162.

creation. But sin enters the picture and disrupts each human relationship—with God, self, one another, and creation.

As we will see, Paul's well-known remarks in Rom 5:12–21 also shed light on the fall. This passage is not primarily about sin but is instructive, setting Christ's work against the backdrop of Adam's sin. In Adam, sin enters, death spreads and reigns, and condemnation is sentenced. In contrast, in Christ there is righteousness, new life, and justification.

Reflecting on the fall leads us to several truths about humanity and sin.

Adam's Sin Brings Sin into the World

That sin is an intruder, entering the human experience in Adam's sin, is clear historically from Genesis. That sin enters human history in Adam's sin is also clear theologically in Rom 5:12: "sin entered the world through one man." But much about the intrusion of sin is not clear, as Hoekema suggests: "One of the most important things we must remember about sin . . . is that it is inexplicable. The origin of evil is . . . one of the greatest riddles of life."[34]

The riddle centers on the question of why Adam and Eve would sin. Augustine teaches that Adam was able not to sin and able to sin, so that there was an inherent possibility to sin in him. This is helpful, but, as Hoekema advises, "how this possibility became actuality is a mystery that we shall never be able to fathom. We shall never know how doubt first arose in Eve's mind. We shall never understand how a person who had been created in a state of rectitude, in a state of sinlessness, could begin to sin."[35]

Adam and Eve are created good and do not initially have corrupt hearts to lead them astray. They have a close relationship with the Lord, enjoy intimacy with each other, and retain authority over creation. It would seem that they have everything in Eden; they live, after all, in paradise! Collins notes,

---

[34] Hoekema, *Created in God's Image*, 130–31.
[35] Hoekema, 131.

In 3:6, as [Eve] regards the tree and sees that it is "good for food, a delight to the eyes, and desirable for giving insight," the irony of the parallel with 2:9 (there was already "every tree desirable to the sight and good for food" in the garden) should not escape us. She already had everything she could possibly want, and she even had the resources to get everything she thought the tree had to offer.[36]

The first couple has everything they could ever want, and yet history records that, in unfaithfulness to God and disobedience to his one prohibition, they absurdly throw it all away. As Augustine notes, trying to determine reasons for such foolishness is like trying to see darkness or hear silence. Or, as Plantinga describes, sin is like sawing off a branch that supports us—it cuts us off from our only help.[37] We cannot make sense of such folly or find clear-cut explanations for the irrationality of this primal sin.

ADAM'S SIN RESULTS IN THE FALL

Although clarity on the reason(s) for Adam's sin remains out of reach, Scripture does indicate that Adam's sin not only results in his own punishment but also has dire consequences for all of humanity. Adam sins not merely as the first bad example but as the representative of all humanity.[38] Recall Rom 5:12–21 and the contrast between Adam's representation of us and Christ's representation of us. In Adam there is sin, death, and condemnation. In Christ there is righteousness, life, and justification. In Adam there is the old era, the dominion of sin and death. In Christ there is a new reign, marked by grace and life (see 1 Cor 15:20–57). Note the outcomes of Adam's representative trespass:[39]

---

[36] Collins, *Genesis 1–4*, 172 (see chap. 1, n. 8).

[37] Cornelius Plantinga, *Not the Way It's Supposed to Be: A Breviary of Sin* (Grand Rapids: Eerdmans, 1995), 123.

[38] For a historical overview of Pelagius and Augustine's responses, see Allison, *Historical Theology*, 342–52 (see chap. 1, n. 26).

[39] Thomas R. Schreiner, *Romans*, Baker Exegetical Commentary on the New Testament (Grand Rapids: Baker, 1998), 268.

- "many died" because of his sin (Rom 5:15)
- his sin brought "condemnation" to all (v. 16)
- "death reigned" over all human beings (v. 17)
- all people were condemned because of his one trespass (v. 18)
- by virtue of his sin "many were made sinners" (v. 19)

Note also the greater outcomes of Christ's representative work:

- his grace and gift abounded for many (v. 15)
- his grace brought "justification" where Adam introduced "condemnation" (v. 16)
- instead of death reigning, believers now "reign in life" by virtue of the grace of Jesus Christ (v. 17)
- the righteous act of Jesus Christ brought "justification leading to life" for all (v. 18)
- through Christ's obedience, the many are now "made righteous" (v. 19)

And note four particular effects that result from Adam's sin and representation:

1. Many/all were constituted sinners (v. 19).
2. Many/all died (v. 15).
3. Condemnation is upon all (v. 16, 18).
4. Death reigned over all humans (v. 17).

Thus, and as we will see, in Adam all are sinners; all die; all are under the domain of death; and all are condemned.

Paul begins a contrast between Adam and Christ in v. 12. He speaks of the effects of Adam's sin but does not finish the contrast by speaking of Christ. Later he completes the unfinished contrast: "So then, as through one trespass there is condemnation for everyone, so also through one righteous act there is justification leading to life for everyone" (v. 18). Paul draws his argument to a conclusion. Adam's transgression results in condemnation for all. The one sin of Adam is the basis for the condemnation of all humanity. "So also" establishes the similarity between the two Adams and their respective effects. Christ's "one righteous act" parallels Adam's "one trespass." As Adam's sin brings punishment to all, so Christ's righteous deed, his saving death, brings justification that results in life to all.

Paul repeats his message: "For just as through one man's disobedience the many were made sinners, so also through the one man's obedience the many will be made righteous" (v. 19). This verse parallels the previous one. Adam's sin is the means whereby we became sinners. Paul deliberately sets the second Adam over against the first. Christ's obedience offsets Adam's disobedience. Christ's obedience (in going to the cross) is the means whereby his people will become righteous.

"Everyone" (v. 18) and "many" (v. 19) tell the effects of the two Adams on humanity. "Everyone" and "all" do not stand in contradiction. Rather, Paul contrasts Adam's "one" act with its widespread effects upon "many" (humanity). Likewise, Paul contrasts Christ's "one" act with its incalculable effects on "many." Paul uses "everyone" similarly here. To determine the extent of the effects of the two Adams' deeds, we must view the whole passage (and all Scripture). Adam's sin affects the whole human race; this is shown by the fact that all die. Christ's righteousness avails for "those who receive . . . the gift" (v. 17).

A chart depicts the comparison of Adam and Christ in Rom 5:12–21:

	ADAM	**CHRIST**
THE ACT	Sin	Righteousness
GOD'S VERDICT	Condemnation	Justification
THE RESULT	Death	Life

WE ARE ALL SINNERS

That the fall of Adam results in universal human sinfulness is suggested by Genesis 3–11 and emphasized by Rom 5:12–21. In particular, v. 19 clarifies, "For just as by the one man's disobedience the many were made sinners, so also through the one man's obedience the many will be made righteous."

That all are sinners is no surprise to Christians. The universality of sin is well known and famously expressed in Rom 3:23: "All have sinned and fall short of the glory of God," which crystallizes Paul's more developed case in 1:18–3:20. Note also the universal scope of sin reiterated by Paul as he concludes his argument in 3:9–20:

> What then? Are we any better off? Not at all! For we have already charged that *both Jews and Gentiles are all under sin*, as it is written:
>> There is *no one* righteous, *not even one*.
>>> There is *no one* who understands;
>>> there is *no one* who seeks God.
>> *All* have turned away; *all alike* have become worthless.
>>> There is *no one* who does what is good,
>>> *not even one*.
>> Their throat is an open grave;
>>> they deceive with their tongues.
>> Vipers' venom is under their lips.
>>> Their mouth is full of cursing and bitterness.
>> Their feet are swift to shed blood;
>>> ruin and wretchedness are in their paths,
>> and the path of peace they have not known.
>>> There is no fear of God before their eyes.
>
> Now we know that whatever the law says, it speaks to those who are subject to the law, so that *every mouth* may be shut and the *whole world* may become subject to God's judgment. For *no one* will be justified in his sight by the works of the law, because the knowledge of sin comes through the law.

The way all are constituted sinners in Adam is harder to understand and is the subject of many discussions.[40] A view holding to the forensic

---

[40] There have been several views, including Pelagianism, mediate imputation, realism, and immediate imputation. In broad strokes, *Pelagianism* envisions Adam as merely setting a bad example for his descendants; it denies that humans are sinful, corrupt, or guilty in Adam. *Mediate imputation* holds that humans derive sinful corruption from Adam through their parents and that Adam's guilt is mediated through the condition in which people are born. *Realism* (or *natural headship*) holds that all humans are guilty of Adam's sin because everyone is a

(legal) nature of Adam's representation is most plausible, due to the comparison with Christ as the other unique representative, whose work for us is not merely moral but also judicial, substitutionary, representative. In an essay on Rom 5:12–21, Lewis Johnson puts forward several arguments for this perspective (also called federal headship). Three stand out. First, he maintains, "Just as the act of the Last Adam is a representative act, becoming the judicial ground of the justification of believers, it follows that the act of the first Adam is a representative act, becoming the judicial ground of the condemnation of those united in him."[41] Second, Johnson argues,

> In v. 12, the apostle makes the point that all die because all sinned. In the following verses, vv. 13–19 (including both the parenthesis of vv. 13–17 and the apodosis of vv. 18–19), he makes the point that all die because one sinned. Can the apostle be dealing with two different things? Hardly. The one fact may be expressed in terms of both plurality and singularity. The sin of all is the sin of one. There must be some kind of solidarity. It is that of federal representation.[42]

Third, Johnson suggests that immediate imputation "enables us to see why only the first sin of Adam and not his subsequent sins, nor the sin of Eve, is imputed to men."[43]

The salvation historical nature of Adam's representation of humanity is also significant. Herman Ridderbos comments on Paul's argument in Rom 5:12–21 and "the reckoning of many as sinners on the grounds of Adam's sin and their share in it":

---

part of his generic human nature. *Immediate imputation* (or *federal headship*) holds that Adam is both the physical progenitor and representative of all humans; when Adam sins, he does so as the representative of all, and therefore his condemnation is applied to all. See Hoekema, *Created in His Image*, 154–67.

[41] S. Lewis Johnson Jr., "Romans 5:12—An Exercise in Exegesis and Theology," in *New Dimensions in New Testament Study*, ed. Richard N. Longenecker and Merrill C. Tenney (Grand Rapids: Zondervan, 1974), 312.

[42] Johnson, 313.

[43] Johnson.

This is apparent not only from the parallel expression in verse 19b: "will be constituted righteous," which likewise has a forensic and not a moral significance, but also from the preceding pronouncements, which describe the share of all in Adam's sin again and again as a sentence extending to all. . . .

By the entrance of sin into the world the situation has been profoundly changed. Sin has begun its calamitous regime. To be constituted sinners also means to have been placed under the power of sin and death (cf. v. 21).[44]

WE ARE ALL GUILTY

Romans 5:12–21 displays our guilt in Adam, particularly in verses 16 and 18: "the judgment following one trespass brought condemnation" (v. 16 ESV); "as one trespass led to condemnation for all men" (v. 18 ESV). Paul's teaching in Eph 2:1–3 speaks similarly: we are all "by nature children under wrath" (v. 3). Blocher puts it well: "Sinfulness has become our quasi-nature while remaining truly our anti-nature."[45] Humans are universally guilty, in that state by nature (by birth; see Gal 2:15), and thereby condemned under the wrath of God.

The biblical material addressing the relationship of sin and guilt is complex. Take, for example, sin and guilt in Romans. In Rom 1:18–32, Paul highlights that everyone is guilty because everyone suppresses and rejects God, who communicates himself universally and persistently through creation. In Romans 2, Paul reiterates the universality of guilt, pointing to human guilt's emergence from failure to follow the law written in the hearts of people. In Romans 3, Paul underlines the guilt of the Jews for failure to follow God and his ways, even though they are blessed with God's clear revelation—his very oracles. Paul further concludes that all actively sin and are judged guilty, and the law plays a significant role in this (vv. 19–20). And here in Romans 5, he points to the entrance of sin, death, and condemnation—all three of which are interrelated and enter through Adam, as we have seen. So, humans are universally

---

[44] Ridderbos, *Paul*, 98–99.
[45] Blocher, *Original Sin*, 30.

guilty—through rejection of God's general revelation in creation, failure to embrace God's general revelation in the internal law of conscience, and failure to live according to God's Word in the law; and they are guilty in Adam.

Passages such as John 3 also illustrate the complexities of the biblical portrait of human guilt. Take John 3:18, for example: "Whoever believes in him is not condemned, but whoever does not believe is condemned already, because he has not believed in the name of the only Son of God" (ESV). John 3:19–20 underlines that condemnation comes because people love darkness. John 3:36 points to the present wrath of God upon the current state of unbelievers. So, according to John's Gospel, everyone who does not believe in Jesus is already spiritually dead (3:3–5) and presently condemned; they are now under God's wrath. Further, they do not believe because they love darkness, and they are judged because they love darkness.

The complexity of sin and guilt can also be seen in passages that relate guilt to factors of knowledge (Matt 10:15; Luke 9:13–14; 12:47–48; John 19:11; 1 Tim 1:13)[46] or intention (Lev 4:22; Num 15:27–30) and in those passages that focus God's judgment upon an individual's sin (Deut 24:16; Jer 31:30; Ezek 18:20). But while guilt may be spoken of in various ways and in varied degrees (see Rom 2:5), all humans are guilty in Adam.

We All Die

The death of all is evident from Genesis, beginning with God's warning in 2:17: "You must not eat from the tree of the knowledge of good and evil, for on the day you eat from it, you will certainly die." The death of all is also evident from God's judgment upon Adam: "You will eat bread by the sweat of your brow until you return to the ground, since you were taken from it. For you are dust, and you will return to dust" (3:19). The

---

[46] See Hoekema, *Created in God's Image*, 177–86. For the state of infants and the mentally challenged, see Ronald H. Nash, *When a Baby Dies: Answers to Comfort Grieving Parents* (Grand Rapids: Zondervan, 1999); Robert A. Peterson, *Hell on Trial: The Case for Eternal Punishment* (Phillipsburg, NJ: P&R, 1995), 235–36. For the status of those who have not heard the gospel, see Morgan and Peterson, eds., *Faith Comes by Hearing* (see chap. 2, n. 10).

entrance of death is also clear from the banishment of Adam and Eve from Eden and from access to the tree of life (vv. 22–24). For humans, death first becomes a physical reality in Cain's murder of Abel, then soon after in Lamech, "an arrogant bully who openly boasted of his murderous exploits" (4:23–24).[47] Death, originally abnormal to humanity, becomes so commonplace that it seems ordinary.[48] Genesis 5 testifies to the regularity of death through the refrain "then he died" (vv. 5, 8, 11, 14, 17, 20, 27, 31).

Romans 5:12–21 also presents Adam's sin as causing universal human death. It enters human history through Adam's sin and spreads to all (v. 12). Paul is stark: "By the one man's trespass the many died" (v. 15); "sin reigned in death" (v. 21); and later, "the wages of sin is death, but the gift of God is eternal life in Christ Jesus our Lord" (6:23). These texts view death as a penalty or judgment for Adam's sin.

Physical death is included in these texts, but too often we forget *the domain of sin and death* that results from the fall. Ridderbos is right: "the sin of Adam" has brought all men "under the dominion and power of sin and death. . . . Death is thereby not only a punishment that puts an end to life, but a condition in which the destiny of life outside of Christ is turned into its opposite."[49] The domain of sin and death is central in Eph 2:1–3:

> You were dead in your trespasses and sins in which you previously lived according to the ways of this world, according to the ruler of the power of the air, the spirit now working in the disobedient. We too all previously lived among them in our fleshly desires, carrying out the inclinations of our flesh and thoughts, and we were by nature children under wrath as the others were also.

This passage is replete with teachings related to sin. But notice especially how the domain of sin and death is central: the text mentions the

---

[47] T. V. Farris, *Mighty to Save: A Study in Old Testament Soteriology* (Nashville: B&H, 1993), 40.

[48] Farris, 52–53.

[49] Ridderbos, *Paul*, 96, 99, 112–13. See also J. Julius Scott Jr., "Life and Death," in *Dictionary of Paul and His Letters*, ed. Gerald F. Hawthorne and Ralph P. Martin (Downers Grove, IL: InterVarsity, 1993), 553–55.

state of spiritual death; the lifestyle that flows from it; the environmental influence of the world, Satan, and the flesh on human behavior; the designation of sinners as those characterized by sin ("the disobedient" and "children under wrath"); and the universal guilt of all by nature.

We Are All Corrupt

The corruption of all is directly related to the domain of sin and death just mentioned. Indeed, Rom 5:12–21 conjoins Adam's sin, humans constituted as sinners, universal guilt, universal death, and the domain of death. The domain of sin and death is the macro-environmental condition in which life occurs; particular human corruption is one of the personal and individual aspects of the domain of sin and death.

As we noted earlier, Eph 2:1–3 relates these factors. Spiritual death is a condition "in which you once walked" (v. 1 ESV). It includes a following after the way of the world, the present evil age, and Satan (vv. 1–2). There is a spirit that is at work in sinners (v. 2), leading to a living after the passions of the flesh, a carrying out of improper mental and physical desires (v. 3).

Scripture speaks of this corruption in various ways. It uses numerous metaphors to indicate our corruption: spiritual death, darkness, hardness, bondage, blindness, flesh, and more.

- *Death*: "You were dead in the trespasses and sins in which you once walked" (Eph 2:1 ESV).
- *Darkness*: "Now this I say and testify in the Lord, that you must no longer walk as the Gentiles do, in the futility of their minds" (Eph 4:17 ESV).
- *Hardness*: "They [unbelievers] are darkened in their understanding, alienated from the life of God because of the ignorance that is in them, due to their hardness of heart. They have become callous and have given themselves up to sensuality, greedy to practice every kind of impurity" (Eph 4:18–19 ESV).
- *Bondage*: "We know that our old self was crucified with [Christ] in order that the body of sin might be brought to nothing, so that we would no longer be enslaved to sin" (Rom 6:6 ESV).

- *Blindness*: "Even if our gospel is veiled, it is veiled to those who are perishing. In their case the god of this world has blinded the minds of the unbelievers, to keep them from seeing the light of the gospel of the glory of Christ, who is the image of God" (2 Cor 4:3–4 ESV).
- *Flesh*: "If you live according to the flesh you will die, but if by the Spirit you put to death the deeds of the body, you will live" (Rom 8:13 ESV).

Scripture also links corruption to a wide range of human faculties and behaviors: mind, will, actions, words, ways, attitudes, and inaction. In Rom 3:9–20, for example, the overall condition of sinners is bleak: all are "under sin" (v. 9); "none is righteous, no, not one" (v. 10 ESV); the whole world will be judged guilty before God (v. 19); no human being will be justified by the works of the law (v. 20). But notice also the wide range in how this fallenness is depicted:

- *Mind*: "No one understands" (v. 11 ESV).
- *Will*: "No one seeks for God" (v. 11 ESV).
- *Actions*: "All have turned aside. . . . No one does good, not even one" (v. 12 ESV).[50]
- *Words*: "Their throat is an open grave; they use their tongues to deceive. The venom of asps is under their lips. Their mouth is full of curses and bitterness" (vv. 13–14 ESV).
- *Ways*: "Their feet are swift to shed blood; in their paths are ruin and misery, and the way of peace they have not known" (vv. 15–17 ESV).
- *Attitude*: "There is no fear of God before their eyes" (vv. 18 ESV).

Paul stresses that the corruption is pervasive—from head to toe, as it were—and includes the mind, will, throat, tongue, mouth, and feet. Jonathan Edwards perceptively observes, "Their heads and their hearts are totally depraved; all the members of their bodies are only instruments of sin, and all their senses (seeing, hearing, tasting) are only inlets and

---

[50] See Gal 5:16–25.

outlets of sin, channels of corruption. . . . There are breaches of every command in thought, word, and deed."[51]

Scripture locates this universal corruption not merely environmentally in the domain of sin and death but as directly as is conceivable, even within the person. In Mark 7:20–23 Jesus teaches that evil thoughts, actions, desires, attitudes, and ways of life are all rooted in the corrupt human heart. And as Jesus teaches his disciples about prayer in Luke 11:13, one of his examples compares the generosity of the good God with that of humans, who are designated quite starkly as "evil."

James's teaching about temptation also demonstrates that this corruption is rooted in the very core of all people (Jas 1:13–15). When tempted, we need not look to God or others for the source; we need look no further than our own polluted hearts, as our "own desire" is the root and the core problem. Such evil desire gives birth to sin, and when sin grows into adulthood, the outcome is death.[52]

That this corruption is not only pervasive but internally driven suggests its radical power. We sin according to our sinful hearts, and our minds, wills, desires, actions, and attitudes are shaped by such sin. We cannot disentangle them from sin's grip but need something or someone from the outside to rescue us and change our hearts. All humans are sinful, guilty, under the domain of death, fundamentally corrupt, and therefore in desperate need of grace, as Philip Hughes observes:

> Original sin, however mysterious its nature may be, tells us that the reality of sin is something far deeper than the mere outward commission of sinful deeds. . . . It tells us there is an inner root of sinfulness which corrupts man's true nature and from which his

---

[51] Jonathan Edwards, "The Eternity of Hell Torments," in *The Wrath of Almighty God: Jonathan Edwards on God's Judgment against Sinners*, ed. Don Kistler (Morgan, PA: Soli Deo Gloria, 1996), 91–92.

[52] For an introduction to the related doctrines of total depravity and inability, see Hoekema, *Created in God's Image*, 147–54. For the Arminian and Reformed views of human inability, and for exposition of related passages, see Robert A. Peterson and Michael D. Williams, *Why I Am Not an Arminian* (Downers Grove, IL: InterVarsity, 2004), 162–72.

sinful deeds spring. Like a deadly poison, sin has penetrated to and infected the very center of man's being: hence his need for the total experience of rebirth by which, through the grace of God in Christ Jesus, the restoration of his true manhood is effected.[53]

WE ALL SUFFER

As sin enters through Adam, so do its effects, suffering included. And just as God is not the author of sin, so is he not the author of suffering. Suffering is not a part of God's good creation but is sin's by-product, as Carson writes: "Between the beginning and the end of the Bible, there is evil and there is suffering. But the point to be observed is that from the perspective of the Bible's large-scale story line, the two are profoundly related: evil is the primal cause of suffering, rebellion is the root of pain, sin is the source of death."[54] Since we live in a fallen world, we suffer and "reap sin's consequences in the home, the workplace, and the cemetery."[55]

Thus, sin is not the only intruder, but its evil children—suffering and death—intrude as well. We intuitively know this but often do not weigh its significance. When we encounter suffering, something within cries out: "This is wrong. The world should not be like this. Children should not be abused! Missionaries should not be tortured!" Or, on a more personal level, we might protest, "Why me? What did I do to deserve this?" Such instincts are valid, for they recognize that the world is not the way it is supposed to be. We know this when we consider sin; we know to hate rape, murder, bigotry, and child abuse. We oppose sin and refuse to be at ease with it. Similarly, we are not to be comfortable with the reality of suffering (though we are to be at peace with God in the midst of it) and should do our best to alleviate it. Like sin, suffering is an intruder and

---

[53] Philip E. Hughes, "Another Dogma Falls," *Christianity Today*, May 23, 1969, 13. Cited in Hoekema, *Created in God's Image*, 154.

[54] Carson, *How Long, O Lord?*, 42 (see chap. 4, n. 16).

[55] Pyne, *Humanity and Sin*, 160.

cannot be treated as natural. The horror of suffering's intrusion points to the horror of sin, its fundamental source.[56]

WE ARE ALL ESTRANGED

Voices from the Global Church: Benyamin F. Intan

Intan from Indonesia wrote, "One result of our fallenness is the way we are naturally welcoming to those like us and hostile toward those unlike us. The answer to such ethnic bias is not to flatten out ethnic differences as if they did not exist (note Rev. 7:9; 21:24–26). Rather, the gospel ignites an impulse of love for those who are different from us. For in the gospel, God came to earth in his Son, Jesus, and loved those who were different from him—indeed, those who were hostile toward him (John 3:16; Rom. 5:8). This is a model for us. In Christ, 'there is neither Jew nor Greek' (Gal. 3:28). No ethnic group has any inherent advantage over another in receiving the blessings of the gospel (Eph. 2:13–19; 3:6–10). Yet this is not to obliterate all racial distinction—indeed, in the new earth, racial distinction will be celebrated and will bring glory to God (Rev. 5:9–10; 7:9–10)."[57]

As noted, God creates a good cosmos with good human beings who have good relationships with God, themselves, one another, and creation. But sin enters the picture and brings disruption and estrangement in each human relationship: with God, self, one another, and creation.

Genesis shows the first couple's ruined relationship with God. Previously they had enjoyed God's presence, but after eating the forbidden fruit, they hide from him (3:8). They realize they are naked (vv. 7–11), lie to God (vv. 12–13), are judged by him (vv. 16–19), face death (v. 19), and are banished from his temple-garden (vv. 22–24).

Genesis also depicts how sin hurts its perpetrators. Adam and Eve find themselves naked and ashamed. Being fruitful and multiplying will

---

[56] For more on suffering, see Christopher W. Morgan and Robert A. Peterson, eds., *Suffering and the Goodness of God*, vol. 1 of Theology in Community (Wheaton, IL: Crossway, 2008).

[57] Benyamin F. Intan, "Personal Ethics," in *ESV Global Study Bible*, 1907 (see chap. 2, n. 35).

now require pain in childbirth, and exercising dominion will now require toil. Further, they fail to live out the image of God—to be what God has intended them to be, to do what he has created them to do, and even to want and will rightly. Marguerite Shuster observes:

> These paradoxes reveal something corrupt at the root of our acts and impulses: our "natural" desires for pleasure and for a goodness of our own are deeply self-centered and so twisted that they cannot reach their own proper ends but tend to destroy self and others. Even the effort to rid oneself of excessive self-concern may intensify it. Thus, at the superficial level, the paradox is simply the observation that we cannot reach certain goals by aiming at them; at a deeper level, the paradox points to our profound moral inability to do that which we ought to do, to love what we ought to love, or to will as we ought to will.[58]

Sin also disorders interpersonal relationships. Adam blames Eve for the sin and, in telling stupidity and self-justification, even insinuates that God is somehow at fault. Adam and Eve's previous intimate relationship is replaced by enmity, evasion of responsibility, and blame of each other. Cain kills Abel (Genesis 4), societal evil becomes rampant (Genesis 6), and social sin marches on as mistreatment leads to further mistreatment and as victims become perpetrators. That sin results in estrangement is evidenced today in evils such as persecution, abortion, exploitation, oppression, racism, sexism, gang violence, corruption, and abuse.

The fallout is also seen in human relations with the creation and cosmos. As previously mentioned, there is new pain in being fruitful and multiplying, new toil in working the ground. As Farris explains: "History's first family now faced a fallen and perverted order that featured hostile death-dealing conditions, a violent world of chaos and destruction."[59]

---

[58] Marguerite Shuster, *The Fall and Sin: What We Have Become as Sinners* (Grand Rapids: Eerdmans, 2004), 166. See also her perceptive comments on pp. 163–65; 190–207.

[59] Farris, *Mighty to Save*, 40.

Indeed, God judges: "The ground is cursed because of you" (Gen 3:17). Paul clarifies and gives hope:

> The creation eagerly waits with anticipation for God's sons to be revealed. For the creation was subjected to futility—not willingly, but because of him who subjected it—in the hope that the creation itself will also be set free from the bondage to decay into the glorious freedom of God's children. For we know that the whole creation has been groaning together with labor pains until now. Not only that, but we ourselves who have the Spirit as the firstfruits—we also groan within ourselves, eagerly waiting for adoption, the redemption of our bodies. (Rom 8:19–23)

Even creation is affected by the fall, being "subjected to futility" and "the bondage to decay," longing for full freedom, and groaning for final redemption (see Rev 22:3).

WE ALL NEED GOD'S GRACE

These truths about sin underline our desperate condition: we all need help; we cannot save ourselves, so we need God's grace to rescue us. Paul often teaches this reality, but three particular passages stand out in showing that, apart from Christ, we all are spiritually dead, lack the Holy Spirit, and are blinded by the devil.

Ephesians 2:1–3, 8–9. Paul paints a dismal picture of our situation before God saved us:

- We are spiritually dead (v. 1).
- We live sinful lives (v. 2).
- We follow the ways of the sinful world system (v. 2).
- We follow the ways of Satan (v. 2).
- We follow our sinful desires (v. 3).
- We are by nature condemned, children of God's wrath (v. 4).

Our plight is desperate. Being spiritually dead, we are devoid of the life of God (v. 1). Fulfilling our sinful desires (v. 3), we live sinful lives and follow the ways of the world system that opposes God (v. 2). Though we do not realize it, Satan works in our lives (v. 2). By nature, which means by birth, we are under God's wrath (v. 4). The result: ruled by Satan and sin, opposed to God and deserving his judgment, we are unable to deliver ourselves from this condition.

As former rebels, unable to rescue ourselves, we as believers can thank God that he,

> who is rich in mercy, because of his great love that he had for us, made us alive with Christ even though we were dead in trespasses. You are saved by grace! He also raised us up with him and seated us with him in the heavens in Christ Jesus, so that in the coming ages he might display the immeasurable riches of his grace through his kindness to us in Christ Jesus. For you are saved by grace through faith, and this is not from yourselves; it is God's gift—not from works, so that no one can boast. (vv. 4–9)

1 Corinthians 2:14–16. Paul draws a key distinction between the "unspiritual" person (v. 14 RSV) and the "spiritual" one (v. 15). What makes the difference? The former lacks the Holy Spirit, while the latter has the Spirit. As we will see, this difference is huge, for those without the Spirit do not accept "what comes from God's Spirit" (v. 14). This refers to the gospel, expressed in many ways in this passage, including as "Jesus Christ and him crucified" (v. 2), "what has been freely given to us by God" (v. 12), and "spiritual things" (v. 13).

The "unspiritual man" (RSV) as a matter of course rejects the gospel "because it is foolishness to him" (v. 14). Lacking the Spirit, lost people do not welcome the message of salvation, for they regard it as foolish. Paul explains further: the person without the Spirit "is not able to understand it since it is evaluated spiritually" (v. 14b). In contrast to those who have the Holy Spirit and therefore can evaluate spiritual things (vv. 15–16), those who lack the Spirit reject the gospel and are unable to save themselves.

2 Corinthians 4:1–6. Unsaved people are spiritually dead and lack the Holy Spirit. And Paul teaches that their plight is even worse, for Satan blinds their minds so they will not believe the gospel. Paul's enemies claim that unbelief shows that the gospel is false. By contrast, he explains that people reject the gospel because they are lost and perishing: "In their case, the god of this age has blinded the minds of the unbelievers to keep them from seeing the light of the gospel of the glory of Christ" (v. 4). Satan blinds unsaved people's thoughts or minds so that they will not believe the gospel.

Paul uses a metaphor of light and darkness to show that a being more powerful than sinners blinds their unbelieving thoughts. They are unable to "see" the gospel until a greater One comes to illumine them: "God who said, 'Let light shine out of darkness,' has shone in our hearts to give the light of the knowledge of God's glory in the face of Jesus Christ" (v. 6). Sinners are blinded by the devil and in need of divine light, but they cannot illumine themselves. Thankfully, God our Creator shines in hearts with the light of the gospel, and thus we see Christ and come to know him.

Conclusion. The Bible sets forth some bad news about its bad news. Humans not only are sinners and guilty before God, but even more, we are unable to deliver ourselves out of our sinful condition. We are spiritually dead, devoid of God's life and unable to give ourselves eternal life (Eph 2:1). We lack the Holy Spirit and do not accept the gospel, for it seems foolish to us (1 Cor 2:14). We are blinded by the devil and cannot illumine ourselves in order to believe (2 Cor 4:4). We are in deep trouble and in desperate need of help.

Thankfully, help is exactly what our gracious heavenly Father provides. Scripture gives us good news about the bad news: while we are still sinners, guilty, and enemies of God, God offers grace (Rom 5:6–11). This grace centers on Jesus's person and work, the subject of our next two chapters. Even before God becomes a man in Jesus's birth, the angel tells Joseph to name him Jesus ("the Lord saves") because he will rescue his people from their sins (Matt 1:21). Jesus himself says that he has come to serve us and to give his life to ransom ours (Mark 10:45). Jesus demonstrates the depth of his love for us when he redeems us "from the curse of the law by becoming a curse for us," dying on the cross (Gal 3:13).

▓ KEY TERMS

accountability

body

Christ as image of God

corruption

creationism

curse

death

deistic evolution

devil

dichotomy

federal headship

fiat creationism

flesh

free will

functional view of image

guilt

immediate imputation

inability

intermediate state

likeness

monism

natural headship

naturalistic evolution

original sin

progressive creationism

relational view of image

responsibility

soul

spirit

substantive view of image

suffering

temptation

theistic evolution

total depravity

trichotomy

world

▓ RESOURCES FOR FURTHER STUDY

Allison, Gregg R. *Historical Theology: An Introduction to Christian Doctrine*. Grand Rapids: Zondervan, 2011, 321–62.

Blocher, Henri. *Original Sin: Illuminating the Riddle*. New Studies in Biblical Theology. Grand Rapids: Eerdmans, 1997.

Carson, D. A. *How Long, O Lord? Reflections on Suffering and Evil*. Grand Rapids: Baker, 1990.

Collins, C. John. *Did Adam and Eve Really Exist?* Wheaton, IL: Crossway, 2011.

Edwards, Jonathan. Paul Ramsey, ed. *Freedom of the Will*. New Haven, CT: Yale University Press, 1957.

Hoekema, Anthony A. *Created in God's Image*. Grand Rapids: Eerdmans, 1986.

Hughes, Philip Edgcumbe. *The True Image: The Origin and Destiny of Man in Christ*. Grand Rapids: Eerdmans, 1989.

Luther, Martin. *The Bondage of the Will*. Trans. J. I. Packer and O. R. Johnston. Old Tappan, NJ: Revell, 1957.

Machen, J. Gresham. *The Christian View of Man*. Edinburgh, UK: Banner of Truth, 1984.

McConville, J. Gordon. *Being Human in God's World: An Old Testament Theology of Humanity*. Grand Rapids: Baker, 2016.

Morgan, Christopher W., and Robert A. Peterson, eds. *Fallen: A Theology of Sin*. Vol. 5 of Theology in Community. Wheaton, IL: Crossway, 2013.

———. *Suffering and the Goodness of God*. Wheaton, IL: Crossway, 2008.

Morris, Leon. *The Wages of Sin*. London: Tyndale, 1954.

Plantinga, Cornelius. *Not the Way It's Supposed to Be: A Breviary of Sin*. Grand Rapids: Eerdmans, 1995.

Sherlock, Charles. *The Doctrine of Humanity*. Contours of Christian Theology. Downers Grove, IL: InterVarsity, 1997.

6

JESUS

The Bible is the greatest story ever told, and God is its teller. He uses human beings to write the story, but he guides them as they write. God tells the story in four parts: (1) creation, (2) the disastrous fall, (3) redemption, featuring Israel and the church, and (4) restoration and consummation. From the beginning, human beings are the costars of God's story.

The hero of the story is the Lord Jesus Christ. He is the Father's agent in the creation of the heavens and the earth. Nothing is made apart from him. When Adam and Eve rebel, God announces his plans to rescue humanity through Eve's offspring, the second Adam, Jesus Christ (Gen 3:15).

Jesus is the Redeemer, who heads up God's reclamation project. He is the hope of Old Testament Israel and the head of the church. God the Son becomes a human being to deliver his people and his creation. He is the Lamb of God, who makes purification for sins. He is the firstborn from the dead, and because he lives, believers will live too. His death and resurrection are the most important events in history. People gain salvation from sin and hell only by trusting him.

Jesus is also the Restorer and Consummator. Because of his incarnation and saving work, there will be a new heavens and a new earth, the place of the eternal consummation of God's story. Jesus will return in glory, raise the dead, officiate at the last judgment, and join his Father on his eternal throne, with the Holy Spirit before the throne.

Jesus is the Alpha and the Omega, the beginning and the end, Creator, God of providence, Lord and Savior, and heir of all things. He is the Father's beloved Son, who loves us and gives himself for us; he is the One deserving eternal praise, and he will rightly come to have first place in everything.

OBJECTIVES

- To build a biblical foundation for understanding the person of Christ
- To overwhelm us with the miracle of the Son of God's incarnation
- To ground our faith in the mystery of Christ as God and man in one person
- To help us appreciate the connection between Christ's person and work
- To motivate us to trust, worship, and serve Jesus as Lord and Savior
- To establish our identity in Christ as individuals and as the church

OUTLINE

Our Lord in the Biblical Story
Our Lord in Selected Passages
    Isaiah 9:6–7
    John 1:1–18
    Philippians 2:5–11
    Colossians 1:15–20
    Hebrews 1
Our Lord Is Eternal and Preexistent
Our Lord Becomes a Man
Our Lord Is Born of a Virgin
Our Lord Remains Sinless
Our Lord Is Divine

Our Lord in the Biblical Story

God's grace shines even in the story of Adam's fall. No sooner do our first parents sin against the Lord than he gives the first promise of a Redeemer. God curses the devil's instrument, the serpent. He says he will put hostility between the serpent and Eve and between their offspring. Then God says to the serpent concerning the woman's offspring, "He will strike your head, and you will strike his heel" (Gen 3:15). The woman's Seed will defeat the devil. The devil will deal the woman's Seed a serious blow, but the Seed will deal the devil a fatal blow, which Jesus certainly does (Heb 2:14–15).

The Old Testament priests, sacrificial animals, and sacrifices point toward Jesus. The high priests are types of Christ, the "merciful and faithful high priest," who will "make atonement for the sins of the people" and "help those who are tempted" (Heb 2:17–18). The unblemished animals that the priests offer as sacrifices (Lev 1:3; 3:1; 4:3) prefigure Christ, "an unblemished and spotless lamb" (1 Pet 1:19), the "righteous" One who suffers "for the unrighteous" to bring them to God (3:18). The sacrifices of Leviticus point toward a great and final sacrifice of "the Lamb of God, who takes away the sin of the world" (John 1:29).

God rejects David's request to build a house, a temple, for him. Instead, David's son (Solomon) will build the temple. David will not build a house for God, but God will build a house, a dynasty, for David. God says concerning David's descendant, "I will establish the throne of his kingdom forever" (2 Sam 7:13). God promises that his faithful love will never leave David's descendants as it had Saul, who disobeyed the Lord. Rather, God tells David, "Your house and kingdom will endure before me forever, and your throne will be established forever" (v. 16). These promises are fulfilled ultimately in Jesus Christ, "who was a descendant of David according to the flesh and was appointed to be the powerful Son of God according to the Spirit of holiness by the resurrection of the dead" (Rom 1:3–4). Indeed, as God's unique divine Son, Jesus alone is the Davidic King, and he will reign forever on the new earth (Heb 1:5, 8, 13).

Isaiah foretells the Servant of the Lord, who will die vicariously to deliver his people (Isa 52:13–53:12). The Servant will grow up inconspicuously (53:2) and will not sin in word or deed (v. 9). He will be despised and rejected (v. 3), be disfigured beyond recognition (52:14), suffer for others (53:5–6), quietly endure oppression and affliction (v. 7), die as a "guilt offering," live after death (v. 10), and as a result win a great victory (52:13; 53:12). Isaiah predicts this Servant's death between two thieves and his burial in a rich man's tomb: "He was assigned a grave with the wicked [plural], but he was with a rich man [singular] at his death" (v. 9).

When Daniel, in a courtroom scene, prophesies of "one like a son of man" (Dan 7:13), he refers to mortal man (as in Ps 8:4). Indeed, this human being, apparently representing humanity, fulfills the goal of Gen 1:28, for he exercises dominion (Dan 7:14). However, matters are complicated for four reasons. First, this "son of man" is given universal and everlasting dominion, which is not fitting for a mere human being.

Second, he comes "with the clouds of heaven" (v. 13), a portrayal fitting God. Third, his deity is implied when he goes into the very presence of the "Ancient of Days," God himself. Fourth, the son of man receives divine worship, for God gives him "dominion, and glory, and a kingdom," with the result that "those of every people, nation, and language" serve him (v. 14). Daniel's son of man is thus a human and divine figure who will rule over all people forever in his eternal kingdom. Daniel's figure is elusive, and it will take the coming of the Christ to clarify that Jesus is that divine-human Son of Man.

This is exactly what happens, for, at the appointed time, "God sent his Son, born of a woman, . . . to redeem those under the law" (Gal 4:4–5). Through the Holy Spirit, the eternal Son becomes incarnate in Mary's womb. God announces his Son's birth not to kings but to humble shepherds: "Today in the city of David a Savior was born for you, who is the Messiah, the Lord" (Luke 2:11). Jesus's baptism at the age of thirty launches his public ministry: "God anointed Jesus of Nazareth with the Holy Spirit and with power, and . . . he went about doing good and healing all who were under the tyranny of the devil" (Acts 10:38). Jesus lives a sinless life, preaches the good news of the kingdom, casts out demons, and heals many. The high point of his ministry is his dying for our sins and rising from the dead, promising eternal life to all who trust him as Savior. He ascends to heaven, sits down at the right hand of the Father, and pours out the Holy Spirit on the church. He prays for us now in heaven and one day will come again to bless his people and judge his enemies. Jesus is the central character in the biblical story. Because of his resurrection he lives forever and "is able to save completely those who come to God through him" (Heb 7:25).

Our Lord in Selected Passages

We will see that Isaiah foretells the birth of David's heir, who will be both God and man and will reign over the world forever. The eternal Son of God, himself God, is the Father's agent in creation. The Son becomes a man of flesh and blood and lives on earth. The apostles see the divine glory of the Father's unique Son. Israel rejects Jesus, but some people believe in him, and he gives them the right to become God's children. The Son is the revealer of God, who makes the invisible God visible.

The eternal Son shows great humility, for while existing as God, he becomes a servant. He relinquishes his divine rights and chooses to become a genuine human being and to suffer the horrible death of the cross. But God raises Jesus, exalts him, and at his return all will bow before him and acknowledge his lordship. God wills for Christ to be supreme over creation and the church. The eternal Son is supreme over creation because he is the Creator, sustainer, Redeemer, and heir. He is also supreme over the new creation, including the church, for he is its head, giving it spiritual life and direction. As the risen One, he begins the new creation.

Christ fulfills three Old Testament offices. He is the great prophet through whom God speaks as never before. He is the great high priest who provides cleansing for sins. He is the great King, whose coronation means sitting at God's right hand. Christ, the Mediator of the new covenant, is superior to prophets and angels—Old Testament mediators of revelation—because he is God who does the works of creation, providence, redemption, and consummation. He is of the essence of God, is worshipped by angels, and has divine names, including "God" and "Lord."

Isaiah 9:6–7

The prophet Isaiah foretells deliverance for the northern areas of the Promised Land (including "Galilee of the nations"), where enemies traditionally attacked first. When he liberates his people, God will replace "gloom" and distress with "honor." God will send to the people "a great light" (Isa 9:1–3). That light will shine brilliantly on a people previously engulfed by darkness. As a result, boundless rejoicing will replace sadness, and peace will replace war (vv. 3–5). What is the light of which the prophet speaks? How will God bring all this joy and peace?

Surprisingly, the light will be a child. God will accomplish Isaiah's predictions through a male infant. This baby boy will be different from all others. David's heir, both divine and human, will reign over the world forever (vv. 6–7). Isaiah ascribes to the male child startling titles: "Wonderful Counselor, Mighty God, Eternal Father, Prince of Peace" (v. 6). We will ponder these in turn.

The baby will grow up to be a "Wonderful Counselor." Isaiah here describes a very wise king. Rejecting human folly, which is so prevalent (1:3; 27:11), this king will display God's wisdom, ruling in "justice and righteousness" (v. 7).

Shocking us, Isaiah calls the infant "Mighty God" (v. 6). Biblical writers in various parts of the Old Testament use the adjective "mighty" to describe God (Gen 49:24; Josh 22:22; Neh 9:32; Ps 24:8). Isaiah does the same (Isa 1:24; 49:26; 60:16). Moreover, Isaiah and Jeremiah use the expression found in Isa 9:6 as a title for God:

The remnant will return, the remnant of Jacob, to the *Mighty God*. (Isa 10:21)

You show faithful love to thousands but lay the fathers' iniquity on their sons' laps after them, great and *mighty God* whose name is the LORD of Armies. (Jer 32:18)

Although Isaiah does not explain how this will come about, the baby will be both divine and human. As an adult, he will have divine strength to accomplish God's will.

The promised child will be "Eternal Father." It is important that we do not misunderstand Isaiah. He does not here speak of God the Father. Rather, he speaks of the child, who will grow up to be King, one who will protect his people as a good father protects his children. The promised one will kindly protect his people forever.

The fourth title recalls the absence of war in Isa 9:4–5, but in positive terms: "Prince of Peace" (v. 6). It is fitting for this title to be last, "for it is the climactic one," as the next verse shows. He is a ruler who brings peace, and although Isaiah does not now explain, "somehow through him will come the reconciliation between God and man that will then make possible reconciliation between man and man (53:5; 57:19; 66:12; Luke

2:14; John 16:33; Rom. 5:1; Heb. 12:14)."[1] This prince's rule will know neither limits nor end, for its "dominion will be vast, and its prosperity will never end. He will reign on the throne of David and over his kingdom, to establish and sustain it with justice and righteousness from now on and forever" (Isa 9:7).

Taken together, Isaiah's titles point to One who will be God and man in one person, filled with divine wisdom, having "almighty" power to protect his own, and reigning universally without end. The emphasis is on the child's growing up to be a ruler, for, after announcing his birth and before listing his titles, Isaiah writes, "the government will be on his shoulders" (v. 6).

To prevent misunderstanding, the prophet asserts that God's "zeal" (v. 7), his "passionate involvement with his people," will bring this about— not human strength.[2]

In this passage Isaiah predicts the birth of Jesus and his coming to Galilee, as Matthew makes plain (Matt 4:12–16). Jesus alone is the "light of the world" (John 8:12; 9:5). Isaiah prophesies of the One of whom Paul also writes, in whom "are hidden all the treasures of wisdom and knowledge" (Col 2:3), who is God and man in one person (Rom 1:3–5), who gives his people eternal life and promises that "they will never perish" (John 10:28), and who will occupy David's throne forever in peace and righteousness on the new earth (Rev 1:5; 17:14).

John 1:1–18

The theme of this incredible passage is the incarnation of the Son of God and its results. First, in words reminiscent of the Bible's first verse (Gen 1:1), John teaches that the Word is in the beginning, before creation, with God, and even that the Word is God (John 1:1). John thus distinguishes God and the Word, yet he also equates them. Here are the rudiments of the doctrine of the Trinity.

---

[1] John N. Oswalt, *The Book of Isaiah, Chapters 1–39*, New International Commentary on the Old Testament (Grand Rapids: Eerdmans, 1986), 248.

[2] Oswalt, 248.

John affirms the Word's deity by ascribing to him the creation of all things (v. 3). Eternal life resides in the Word, and this life reveals God to human beings when he creates all things (v. 4). God's revelation in creation continues after the fall. Ever since the fall, light (truth and holiness) and darkness (falsehood and evil) have battled, but the darkness has not been able to overcome the light.

God sends John the Baptist to be a witness to the Light, who is Jesus, so people might trust him as Savior (vv. 6–8). The Light comes into the world when the Son of God becomes incarnate in Jesus Christ (v. 9). After the incarnation, the Son is in the world he had created, but it rejects him (v. 10). Moreover, he comes to his covenant people Israel, but they reject him too (v. 11).

However, some believe in Jesus, and he gives the right to become God's children to all who do. They experience a spiritual birth, not as the result of human endeavor but as the work of God (vv. 12–13). The eternal Creator, who is equal with God, becomes a human being of flesh and blood and lives on earth for more than thirty years. The apostles see the divine glory of God the Father's unique Son, glory "full of grace and truth" (v. 14; see also Ps 100:5; 117:2).

John the Baptist witnesses to the fact that although Jesus is born six months after him and begins his ministry six months later, "he existed before" John because he is God (v. 15). The apostles testify that Jesus from his fullness gave them "grace upon grace" (v. 16). Although no one has seen God's invisible essence, "the one and only Son, who is himself God and is at the Father's side—he has revealed him" (v. 18). The Son, who reveals God by virtue of his work in creation before his incarnation, is abundantly qualified to reveal God after becoming a man, for he is God and man in one person. He, the revealer of God, makes the invisible God visible.

Philippians 2:5–11

Paul wants the Philippian believers to adopt Jesus's attitude of humility (Phil 2:5). Paul demonstrates this attitude when he says that although Christ exists "in the form of God" (v. 6), he does not hesitate to assume "the form of a servant" (v. 7).

To be "existing in the form of God" is true only of God himself. Thus Paul teaches the deity of Christ at the beginning of this passage. As we will see, he does the same thing at its end also. The eternal Son of God "did not consider equality with God as something to be exploited" (v. 6). He does not demand his divine rights but chooses to become a human being and to suffer.

"He emptied himself" (v. 7) does not mean that the Son divests himself of divine qualities. Rather, as Paul explains in the very next words, "he emptied himself by assuming the form of a servant, taking on the likeness of humanity" (v. 7). Christ does not insist on his rights as God but instead humbles himself by becoming a man, like Adam before the fall. Although as God he is King, the Son also becomes a servant. As such, "he humbled himself by becoming obedient to the point of death—even to death on a cross" (v. 8).

Thus far Paul teaches what theologians call Christ's state of humiliation, which stretches from his incarnation to his burial. Next Paul describes Christ's state of exaltation, which encompasses everything from his resurrection to his return. Because the Son humbles himself to the point of crucifixion, God the Father "highly exalted him and gave him the name that is above every name" (v. 9). This is not the name "Jesus," which he receives at birth (Matt 1:21), but the title "Lord," given to him in a new sense when he dies and arises.

It is God's will that at Christ's return, all human beings will bow before Jesus and confess that he is Lord (Phil 2:10–11). This means not that all will worship Jesus and be saved but that all will acknowledge Jesus's universal lordship. Jesus is Lord, not Caesar nor anyone else. Paul here references Isaiah 45, which teaches that all will bow, those "who are enraged against" God "will come to him and be put to shame" in condemnation (v. 24), and only spiritual "descendants of Israel will be justified and find glory through the LORD" (v. 25).

Colossians 1:15–20

In Colossians, Paul opposes the poison of false teaching and ungodly living. His antidote to both is Christ, who because of his identity and accomplishments deserves "to have first place in everything" (1:18). By "everything" the apostle has in mind two spheres: creation (vv. 15–17) and the church (vv. 18–20). The Son "is the image of the invisible God" (v. 15). Paul means that in the incarnation Jesus reveals God's invisible nature as never before.

This is not surprising because, as Paul shows, the Son is the eternal Creator, sustainer, and Redeemer. The divine Christ is supreme over creation; he is "the firstborn over all creation" (v. 15). Paul means not that the Son is God's first creature but that he is foremost over creation. The Old Testament background to this idea includes the story of Jacob, who is not the firstborn of twins but nevertheless usurps his brother, Esau, to gain the rights of the firstborn. Psalm 89:27 also provides insight into "firstborn" here. There God says of the messianic King, "I will also make him my firstborn, greatest of the kings of the earth."

The Son creates everything in heaven and earth (an allusion to Gen 1:1), "the visible and the invisible," including angels (Col 1:16). In addition, "by him all things hold together" (v. 17), which means that he performs the divine work of providence, maintaining the creation he brings into being. Furthermore, "all things have been created . . . for him" (v. 16), which means that he is not only Creator but also heir of all. Paul adds that "he is before all things" (v. 17) to indicate the Son's eternity, an attribute of God alone.

Christ is also supreme over the new creation, including the church, for "he is also the head of the body, the church" (v. 18). As the church's head, he gives both spiritual life and direction to its members. Again Paul alludes to Scripture's first verse when he says of Christ, "He is the beginning" (v. 18). As God, the Son creates all things in the beginning. As the risen One, he is "the beginning" (the origin) of the new creation. Even as he has priority over creation, so does he have priority over the new creation as "the firstborn from the dead" (v. 18). Paul thus exalts the Son as preeminent over both creation and the new creation, which includes the church.

Hebrews 1

This chapter is replete with teaching concerning the person of Christ. The writer is preparing his readers for the truth that they must heed the gospel, brought by Christ and his apostles, because it is weightier than the law given by God through angels to Moses (Heb 2:1–4). Chapter 1 presents Christ's three offices. He is the great prophet through whom God has spoken to us in the last days (v. 2). He is the great high priest, who has made "purification for sins" and has "sat down at the right hand of the Majesty on high" (v. 3). Above all, Hebrews 1 treats Christ's coronation as the great King who sits at God's right hand (vv. 5–13).

In showing that Christ is superior to Old Testament mediators of revelation (prophets and angels), Hebrews 1 presents five strong witnesses to Christ's deity. First, Christ performs works unique to God: creation (vv. 2, 10), providence ("sustaining all things," v. 3), redemption (v. 3), and consummation (he is "heir of all things," v. 2). Second, the Son is essentially God, for he "is the radiance of God's glory and the exact expression of his nature" (v. 3). Third, he is the proper object of worship, for at his coronation he sits at the right hand of him who declares, "Let all God's angels worship him" (v. 6). Fourth, he has names fitting for God alone, for the Father calls him "God," whose "throne . . . is forever and ever" (v. 8), and addresses him as the "Lord" who created the heavens and the earth (v. 10). Fifth, the Son has attributes that only God possesses. Unlike the creation, which perishes, the Son remains and is "the same"; his "years will never end" (vv. 10–12).

Our Lord Is Eternal and Preexistent

By *preexistent* we mean that the Son of God lived before his incarnation. By *eternal* we mean that the Son of God has always existed and will always exist. Jesus's life as a man began in Bethlehem, but his life as God did not. Rather, he had a preexistence before his earthly life. In fact, as a person of the Trinity, the Son's eternal life had no beginning. Instead, he, the Father, and Holy Spirit are eternal. The eternal Son preexisted his incarnation.

Is it correct to speak of the preexistence of the Father or Holy Spirit? No, although it is correct to speak of their eternity, because they are God. But only the Son had a change in his manner of existence. Preexistence views the Son from the perspective of the incarnation and looks back.

The Son who had an eternal preexistence became a human being permanently at Bethlehem. Such is the depth of his love for us.

Jesus teaches his own preexistence. Jewish leaders are offended at Jesus's claim to give eternal life to anyone who keeps his word (John 8:51) and his claim to have seen Abraham: "You aren't fifty years old yet, and you've seen Abraham?" (v. 57), they ask. At this Jesus replies, "Truly I tell you: Before Abraham was, I am" (v. 58). Then the leaders pick up stones to stone him (v. 59). Although the leaders' response to Jesus is very wrong, they understand his claim. He claims to have existed before becoming a man—to be preexistent. He likely refers to God's statements in Isaiah that begin with "I am" (45:5, 6, 7, 18, 22). When Jesus applies such language to himself, he is claiming to be equal to God.[3]

John also teaches that Jesus was preexistent. John writes of how the Son (whom he calls "the Word") before his incarnation was with God, was himself God, and created all things (John 1:1–3). John later identifies the "Lord," whom Isaiah saw in his temple vision (Isa 6:1), as Jesus (John 12:40–41).

Paul teaches the same truth when he says that before his incarnation Christ existed "in the form of God" (Phil 2:6). The Son, who created everything "in heaven and on earth, . . . is before all things" (Col 1:16–17) and thus had preexistence before his life as a man. Hebrews affirms the Son's preexistence when it says that God "made the universe through him" (1:2).

Our Lord Becomes a Man

The preincarnate "Word became flesh" in the incarnation (John 1:1–3, 14). The eternal Son becomes a man of flesh and blood. The preexistent One who exists "in the form of God" humbles himself to assume "the form of a servant" (Phil 2:6–7). This means that he takes "on the likeness of humanity" in order to submit himself "to death on a cross" for sinners

---

[3] Vern S. Poythress, *Theophany: A Biblical Theology of God's Appearing* (Wheaton, IL: Crossway, 2018), 419, provides other Old Testament examples of the Son's preexistence as recognized in Rev 1:12–16 (Ezek 1:27; Dan 7:9–10, 13; 10:5–6) and Luke 9:28–36 (Exod 24:15–18).

(Phil 2:7–8). When Paul calls Christ "the image of the invisible God" (Col 1:15), he indicates that the incarnate Son reveals God, who is invisible. As God incarnate, Jesus makes God known as never before. Moreover, Paul assures the Colossians that, contrary to the false teachers' claims, believers are complete in Christ (2:10). Because they have Jesus as Savior, Christians do not need secret teachings or practices, "for the entire fullness of God's nature dwells bodily in Christ" (v. 9). That is, Christ is God incarnate, and he is all we need for eternal "life and godliness" (2 Pet 1:3).

Voices from Church History: Athanasius and Anselm

Athanasius (c. 296/298–373) was a Christian theologian, church father, and the chief defender of trinitarianism against Arianism. He endured five exiles because of his unwavering commitment to Christ's deity. His chief argument was that Christ must be God to be able to save sinners. Opposing Arius and several Roman emperors, he was embattled during his lifetime. Christians later esteemed his writings for their deep devotion to the Word-become-flesh and pastoral concern. He wrote, "For this purpose, then, the incorporeal and incorruptible and immaterial Word of God comes to our realm, howbeit he was not far from us before. For no part of Creation is left void of Him: He has filled all things everywhere, remaining present with His own Father. But He comes in condescension to shew loving-kindness upon us, and to visit us."[4]

Anselm of Canterbury (1033/4–1109) was a Benedictine monk, abbot, and theologian who originated the ontological argument for God's existence. His approach was "faith seeking understanding," using the mind to understand theology already believed. His most famous work, *Cur Deus Homo* (*Why God Became a Man*), was a response for requests to discuss the incarnation. God had to become a man to make atonement for humanity, because the Savior had to be both fully divine and fully human. He wrote, "So, if, as I showed earlier, the heavenly kingdom must be filled with men, and if this cannot happen unless the satisfaction is

---

[4] Athansius of Alexandria (1892), "On the Incarnation of the Word," in P. Schaff and H. Wace, eds., A. T. Robertson, trans., *St. Athanasius: Select Works and Letters* (Grand Rapids: Eerdmans, 1987), 4:40.

made for sin—satisfaction which no one can make but God, and no one ought to make but man—then it is necessary for the God-man to make it."[5]

Hebrews includes a statement of the incarnation before each of three pictures of Christ's atonement. First, Jesus is the second Adam, who through his death and resurrection restores the creational glory and dominion that Adam forfeited in the fall (Ps 8:5–8). Christ's incarnation makes this possible: "We do see Jesus—made lower than the angels for a short time so that by God's grace he might taste death for everyone— crowned with glory and honor because he suffered death" (Heb 2:9).

Second, Christ our champion defeats our enemies: Satan, demons, sin, death, and hell. He wins a mighty victory through his victorious life, death, resurrection, exaltation to heaven, and return. The essential prerequisite for this is his incarnation: "Since the children have flesh and blood in com- mon, Jesus also shared in these, so that through his death he might destroy the one holding the power of death—that is, the devil—and free those who were held in slavery all their lives by the fear of death" (Heb 2:14–15).

Third, the dominant picture of the Savior in Hebrews is Christ as our divine-human great high priest. Again the writer introduces this by speak- ing of the incarnation: "It is clear that he does not reach out to help angels, but to help Abraham's offspring. Therefore, he had to be like his brothers and sisters in every way, so that he could become a merciful and faithful high priest in matters pertaining to God, to make atonement for the sins of the people" (Heb 2:16–17).

The incarnation of the Son of God is an essential precondition for redemption. Without it there is no crucifixion and resurrection, Christ's central saving events. Two errors highlight the importance of our Lord's incarnation, *adoptionism* and *kenoticism*. Adoptionism was a second- century attack on the incarnation and Christ's deity. It held that Jesus was merely a man until his baptism, at which point God adopted him as his son. Kenoticism was a nineteenth-century error that taught a reduction

---

[5] Anselm, *Cur Deus Homo*, quoted in "#205: Anselm on the Incarnation," Christian History Institute website, accessed June 21, 2019, https://christian historyinstitute.org/study/module/anselm.

of Christ's deity in the incarnation by wrongly using Paul's words that
describe how "Christ Jesus, who, existing in the form of God, did not
consider equality with God as something to be exploited. Instead *he emptied himself* by assuming the form of a servant, taking on the likeness of
humanity" (Phil 2:5–7).

Kenoticism taught that there was a reduction of Christ's deity in the
incarnation and that the second person of the Trinity laid aside some of
his divine attributes when he became a man. The historic Christian faith,
however, rightly insists that the Son retained all of his divine attributes in
the incarnation. He did not give up any of them but gave up the independent exercise of them, using them only in accordance with the Father's
will. The "emptying" (of Phil 2:7, *kenosis* in Greek) is clarified by the next
two clauses, which describe his taking the form of a servant and being
born in the likeness of men.

Our Lord Is Born of a Virgin

Jesus's birth is normal, but his conception is miraculous. Luke tells the
story from Mary's perspective, while Matthew does from Joseph's. Mary
and Joseph are engaged when the angel Gabriel appears to her with startling news of God's blessing:

> You will conceive and give birth to a son, and you will name him
> Jesus. He will be great and will be called the Son of the Most High,
> and the Lord God will give him the throne of his father David. He
> will reign over the house of Jacob forever, and his kingdom will
> have no end. (Luke 1:31–33)

Mary is to be the mother of the promised One, the messianic King!

Mary does not disbelieve, as Sarah, Isaac's mother, and Zechariah, John
the Baptist's father, had done, but she does ask an honest question: How can
this be, since she is a virgin? Gabriel explains: "The Holy Spirit will come
upon you, and the power of the Most High will overshadow you. Therefore,
the holy One to be born will be called the Son of God" (v. 35). Gabriel tells
how Mary's elderly aunt Elizabeth has conceived, asserting, "Nothing will
be impossible with God" (v. 37). Humbly, Mary submits to the Lord (v. 38).

Matthew tells how godly Joseph, learning of Mary's pregnancy, decides to divorce her quietly rather than subjecting her to public disgrace. As he thinks about this, no doubt very sadly, an angel appears to him in a dream and says, "Joseph, son of David, don't be afraid to take Mary as your wife, because what has been conceived in her is from the Holy Spirit. She will give birth to a son, and you are to name him Jesus, because he will save his people from their sins" (Matt 1:20–21). Joseph is greatly encouraged by these unexpected words. Matthew, more concise than Luke, merely says that Jesus is conceived "from the Holy Spirit" (vv. 18, 20). Jesus's conception is supernatural, as befits his name and task—Jesus, Savior of his people.

The Son of God assumes genuine humanity, and as the second Adam, he is sinless and never sins. The incarnation of God the Son is the Holy Spirit's work. He works in Mary's womb, and she conceives Jesus's humanity.

Our Lord Remains Sinless

Our Lord is born of a virgin, assumes genuine humanity, and as the second Adam, is holy and never sins. The Scripture testifies:

> They made his grave with the wicked and with a rich man in his death, although he had done no violence and had not spoken deceitfully. (Isa 53:9 ESV; see also v. 11)

> [An evil spirit cried out,] "I know who you are—the Holy One of God!" (Mark 1:24)

> [Gabriel told Mary,] "The holy one to be born will be called the Son of God." (Luke 1:35)

> We have come to believe and know that you are the Holy One of God. (John 6:69)

> Lord, consider their threats, and grant that your servants may speak your word with all boldness, while you stretch out your hand for healing, and signs and wonders are performed through the name of your holy servant Jesus. (Acts 4:29–30)

> He made the one who did not know sin to be sin for us, so that in him we might become the righteousness of God. (2 Cor 5:21)

> We do not have a high priest who is unable to sympathize with our weaknesses, but one who has been tempted in every way as we are, yet without sin. (Heb 4:15)

> Christ also suffered for sins once for all, the righteous for the unrighteous, that he might bring you to God. (1 Pet 3:18)

> You know that he was revealed so that he might take away sins, and there is no sin in him. (1 John 3:5)

> Write to the angel of the church in Philadelphia: Thus says the Holy One, the true one . . . (Rev 3:7)

Jesus's holiness and sinlessness are evident through an Old Testament prophet and every major section in the New Testament: Gospels, Acts, Pauline Epistles, General Epistles, and Revelation. Such an array of those bearing witness to this truth include Isaiah the prophet, the angel Gabriel, an evil spirit through a demon-possessed man, several apostles, and Jesus himself.

As we will see in the chapter "Jesus's Saving Work," Jesus's sinlessness is important not only to his identity but also for the effectiveness of his work. He is the new Adam, succeeding where Adam failed (Rom 5:12–21). Jesus passes the tests in the wilderness, where Israel failed (Matt 4:1–11). He can successfully die in our place for our sins and grant us his righteousness because he is righteous and without sin (2 Cor 5:21; 1 Pet 3:18). Jesus can be our high priest, who sympathizes yet is holy and able to represent us (Heb 4:15).

Our Lord Is Divine

Jesus Is Identified with God

The New Testament continues to affirm Old Testament monotheism (the reality that there is only one God) and at the same time identifies Jesus with the one true God in at least three ways: the fact that Old Testament passages that refer to "Yahweh" are applied to Jesus, the interchangeability of Jesus and God in the New Testament, and the fact that Jesus is called "God."

The New Testament Applies Yahweh Passages to Jesus

New Testament writers apply to Jesus Old Testament texts that use God's name, Yahweh. Mark's Gospel quotes Mal 3:1, which says, "'See, I am going to send my messenger, and he will clear the way before me. . . .' says the Lord of Armies." Mark writes, "See, I am sending my messenger ahead of you; he will prepare your way" (Mark 1:2). Mark applies this passage to Christ, portraying him as the Lord and John the Baptist as his messenger.

At Pentecost, Peter cites Joel to explain that the ascended Lord Jesus pours out the Holy Spirit on the church: "Then everyone who calls on the name of the Lord will be saved" (Joel 2:32). In the same sermon, Peter identifies this "Lord" as Jesus: "Therefore let all the house of Israel know with certainty that God has made this Jesus, whom you crucified, both Lord and Messiah" (Acts 2:36). He offers salvation "in the name of Jesus" (v. 38) as a direct echo of salvation in the "name of the Lord" in Joel 2.

Paul quotes Jer 9:24: "The one who boasts should boast in this, that he understands and knows me—that I am the Lord," and says, "in order that, as it is written: Let the one who boasts boast in the Lord" (1 Cor 1:31). Shortly, Paul identifies the "Lord" in whom believers are to boast: he is "the Lord of glory," whom the foolish rulers of this age "crucified" (2:8)—that is, Jesus.

Peter cites Isa 8:12–13, "Do not fear what they fear; do not be terrified. You are to regard only the Lord of Armies as holy. Only he should be feared," when he writes, "Do not fear what they fear or be intimidated, but in your hearts regard Christ the Lord as holy" (1 Pet 3:14–15). Peter puts "Christ the Lord" in place of Isaiah's "Lord of Armies."

Jesus's words in Revelation 1 are reminiscent of Yahweh's words in Isaiah: "I am the Lord, the first, and with the last—I am he" (41:4); "I am the first and I am the last. There is no God but me" (44:6); "I am he; I am the first, I am also the last" (48:12). Echoing the prophet's words, in which Yahweh alone speaks, Jesus says, "Don't be afraid! I am the First and the

Last, and the Living One. I was dead, but look—I am alive forever and ever, and I hold the keys of death and Hades" (Rev 1:17–18). Isaiah's eternal Yahweh is Revelation's eternal Christ.

All portions of the New Testament apply Old Testament texts that speak of Yahweh to the Lord Jesus, thereby identifying Jesus with Yahweh. We have cited five such texts, but there are more.[6]

THE NEW TESTAMENT INTERCHANGES JESUS WITH GOD

New Testament writers, especially Paul, also identify Jesus with God. Here is a sample from David Wells, who shows that Paul linguistically identifies Christ with Yahweh:

- God's kingdom (1 Thess. 2:12) is Christ's (Eph. 5:5).
- God's love (Eph. 1:4–5) is Christ's (Rom. 8:35).
- God's Word (Col. 1:25; 1 Thess. 2:13) is Christ's (1 Thess. 1:8; 4:15).
- God's Spirit (1 Thess. 4:8) is Christ's (Phil. 1:19).
- God's peace (Gal. 5:22; Phil. 4:9) is Christ's (Col. 3:15; Phil. 1:2; 4:7).
- God's "day" of judgment (Isa. 13:6) is Christ's "day" of judgment (Phil. 1:6, 10; 2:16).
- God's grace (Eph. 2:8, 9; Col. 1:6; Gal. 1:15) is Christ's grace (1 Thess. 5:28; Gal. 1:6; 6:18).[7]

THE NEW TESTAMENT CALLS JESUS GOD

Six New Testament passages plainly call Jesus God:

In the beginning was the Word, and the Word was with God, and the Word was God. (John 1:1)

Thomas responded to [Jesus], "My Lord and my God!" (John 20:28)

---

[6] For more, see Christopher W. Morgan and Robert A. Peterson, eds., *The Deity of Christ*, vol. 3 of Theology in Community (Wheaton, IL: Crossway, 2011). See also Robert M. Bowman Jr. and J. Ed Komoszewski, *Putting Jesus in His Place: The Case for the Deity of Christ* (Grand Rapids: Kregel), 157–70.

[7] David F. Wells, *The Person of Christ: A Biblical and Historical Analysis of the Incarnation* (Westchester, IL: Crossway, 1984), 65.

The ancestors are theirs, and from them, by physical descent, came the Christ, who is God over all, praised forever. Amen. (Rom 9:5)

We wait for the blessed hope and appearing of the glory of our great God and Savior, Jesus Christ. (Titus 2:13)

... but to the Son: "Your throne, O God, is forever and ever, and the scepter of your kingdom is a scepter of justice." (Heb 1:8)

Simeon Peter, a servant and an apostle of Jesus Christ: To those who have received a faith equal to ours through the righteousness of our God and Savior Jesus Christ. (2 Pet 1:1)

When the New Testament writers apply the title "God" (*theos*) to Christ, they explicitly assert his deity.[8]

Jesus Performs the Works of God

Christ demonstrates his deity by performing many works that only God can perform. These include the works of creation, providence, judgment, and salvation.

JESUS AND CREATION

Both Old (Gen 1:1) and New Testaments (Acts 4:24) proclaim that God alone does the work of creation. Yet the New Testament ascribes the work of creation to Jesus Christ, thereby showing that he is divine (John 1:3; Col 1:16; Heb 1:2).

JESUS AND PROVIDENCE

Both Old (Ps 104:24–30) and New Testaments (Acts 17:24–28) teach that providence is the work of God alone. God not only creates all things, he alone sustains and directs them to his appointed ends. The New

---

[8] Murray J. Harris, *Jesus as God: The New Testament Use of* Theos *in Reference to Jesus* (Grand Rapids: Baker, 1992).

Testament ascribes the work of providence to Jesus Christ (Col 1:16; Heb 1:3), thereby affirming that he is God.

Jesus and Judgment

Both Old (Ps 96:13) and New Testaments (Rom 14:10) teach that only God does the work of judgment. Yet the New Testament ascribes judgment to the Son of God (Matt 16:27; Acts 10:42). Jesus declares, "The Father, in fact, judges no one but has given all judgment to the Son, so that all people may honor the Son just as they honor the Father" (John 5:22–23). Paul speaks of "the revelation of the Lord Jesus from heaven with his powerful angels, when he takes vengeance with flaming fire on those who don't know God and on those who don't obey the gospel of our Lord Jesus" (2 Thess 1:7–8).

Jesus and Salvation

One of the strongest arguments for Christ's deity is that he saves. God alone is the Savior who does the work of salvation (Exod 15:2; 1 Tim 1:1). Yet the New Testament ascribes the work of salvation to Jesus Christ in at least six ways.

Jesus Is Savior. The New Testament often calls Jesus "Savior" (Luke 2:11; John 4:42; Acts 5:31; 13:23; Eph 5:23; Phil 3:20; Titus 1:4; 2:10, 13; 3:6; 2 Pet 3:2; 1 John 4:14). Additionally, in many places it presents him as the only Savior without using the word (Matt 1:21; 11:27; John 14:6; Acts 16:31; Heb 5:9; 1 Cor 15:3–4).

Jesus Forgives Sins. Forgiving sins is a divine prerogative (Exod 34:6–7; Ps 103:10, 12; Isa 43:25). In every section of the New Testament, forgiving sins is also Jesus's divine prerogative (Luke 7:47–49; Acts 5:31; Col 1:13–14; Rev 1:5–6). Jesus is divine.

Jesus Does the Work That Saves Us Forever. Scripture extols the Son of God's magnificent work. Hebrews testifies that "the Messiah . . . entered the most holy place once for all . . . by his own blood, having obtained eternal redemption" (9:11–12). It also says that "by one offering he has perfected forever those who are sanctified" (10:14).

Jesus Is the Object of Saving Faith. In the Old Testament, God alone is the proper object of his people's faith (Gen 15:6; Exod 14:31). And one of the basics of the Christian religion is "faith in God" (Heb 6:1).

The New Testament, however, proclaims an additional message: repeatedly it presents Jesus as the proper object of saving faith. John teaches that whoever believes in Christ will have eternal life (John 3:16–18, 36). Paul teaches that "a person is not justified by the works of the law but by faith in Jesus Christ" (Gal 2:16). Scripture is unequivocal. Concerning Jesus, it declares, "There is salvation in no one else, for there is no other name under heaven given to people by which we must be saved" (Acts 4:12).

Jesus Gives the Holy Spirit to His Church. Pentecost is Jesus's saving work, and it is a *divine* saving work. Joel foresees that in the last days God himself will pour out his Spirit on all flesh (Joel 2:28–31). John the Baptist announces that the Messiah will baptize the church with the Spirit (Matt 3:11; Luke 3:16; John 1:32–34). In Acts 2, Jesus fulfills these prophecies.

At Pentecost the Jewish pilgrims are shocked to hear the apostles reciting God's mighty works in their languages (vv. 7–8), and Peter says, "This is what was spoken through the prophet Joel" (v. 16). He quotes Joel's prophecy and says that Jesus fulfills it: "This Jesus God raised up, and of that we are all witnesses. Being therefore exalted at the right hand of God, and having received from the Father the promise of the Holy Spirit, he has poured out this that you yourselves are seeing and hearing" (v. 33 ESV). Jesus, the Messiah, the Christ, the anointed One, pours out the Spirit on the church at Pentecost. This is God's work, according to Joel; indeed, it is a work of the Lord Jesus. As Peter explains, this event proves that Jesus is both Christ and Lord (Acts 2:36).

Jesus Consummates Salvation. God alone puts people to death and brings them to life (1 Sam 2:6; Deut 32:39).[9] The New Testament speaks similarly, but of eternal destinies. Jesus warns us to "fear him who is able to destroy both soul and body in hell" (Matt 10:28; see also Jas 4:12).

The New Testament ascribes these same divine prerogatives to the returning Christ. It is he who will "make alive" the dead, assign eternal destinies, and bring final salvation, including the new heavens and the

---

[9] Bowman and Komoszewski, *Putting Jesus in His Place*, 228, pointed us to these texts.

new earth. Jesus will raise the dead (John 5:28–29; 6:40, 44, 54), something only God can do.

Jesus also assigns saints and sinners their final destinies (Matt 7:21–
23; 25:31–46). He will welcome true believers into everlasting life and banish unbelievers to everlasting punishment.

Jesus brings final salvation (Phil 3:20–21; Heb 9:27–28), including cosmic restoration. Through Jesus "God was pleased . . . to reconcile everything to himself, whether things on earth or things in heaven, by making
peace through his blood, shed on the cross" (Col 1:20). Jesus's death and
resurrection save all God's people *and* bring about new heavens and a
new earth (Isa 65:17; 66:22–23; Revelation 21–22). This cosmic restoration, a work of God himself, is accomplished by the returning Son of God.

Jesus Saves Us in Union with Him

Salvation is God's work from beginning to end. The Father plans it before
creation (Eph 1:4–5; 2 Tim 1:9). The Son accomplishes salvation when he
dies and arises (Rom 4:25; 1 Cor 15:3–4). The Holy Spirit applies it when
he opens hearts to the gospel (Acts 16:14; 1 Cor 12:3). The triune God will
consummate salvation when he raises the dead for final salvation (Rom
8:11; Heb 9:28).

As we will see later in the chapter "Salvation," Paul speaks of the
application of salvation as union with Christ. Union with Christ is the
Holy Spirit's joining believers spiritually to Christ and his salvation. Paul
tells of union in two main ways. First, he speaks of being "in Christ." This
phrase most often pertains to union with Christ. Second, Paul speaks of
being united to Christ in his saving deeds, namely, his death (Rom 6:2–6, 8;
Col 2:20), resurrection (Rom 6:4–5, 8; Eph 2:5–6; Col 3:1), ascension (Col
3:3), session (sitting at God's right hand, Eph 2:6), and second coming
(Rom 8:19; Col 3:2).

Union with Christ is a comprehensive way of speaking of God's
applying salvation to us.[10] Being joined to Christ, we receive regeneration

---

[10] John Murray, *Redemption Accomplished and Applied* (Grand Rapids:
Eerdmans, 1955), 161, 170.

(Eph 2:4–5), justification (2 Cor 5:21; Phil 3:9), adoption (Gal 3:26–29), perseverance (Rom 8:1, 38–39), resurrection (1 Cor 15:22), and glorification (Col 3:4). We are given new life, righteousness, adoption, perseverance, resurrection, and glory in Christ.

We have seen that union with Christ, as an aspect of salvation, is the work of God alone. In it the Holy Spirit joins believers to all of Christ's spiritual accomplishments. And this union is comprehensive, including all of the various elements that constitute the application of salvation. But how does this union constitute an argument for Christ's deity? David Wells answers definitively: "To speak of being 'in' a teacher, and of participating at an ontological and ethical level in that teacher's capacities, would be preposterous if that teacher were not divine."[11] It makes no sense to say we are "in the angel Gabriel" or that "we died, were buried, and raised with the apostle Paul." It is senseless to say that we are spiritually joined to mere creatures, whether angelic or human. Christ's place in saving union is the place occupied by God alone. Union with Christ, then, is a sweeping and powerful demonstration of our Lord's deity.

Jesus Brings the Age to Come

The New Testament contrasts the "present age" (1 Tim 6:17; Titus 2:12) with the "age to come" (Mark 10:30; Luke 18:30). The "present age," the one between Christ's advents, looks back on the Old Testament and ahead to the "age to come," the eschaton. The "present age" is characterized by evil (Gal 1:4), spiritual blindness (2 Cor 4:4), and spiritual death (Eph 2:1–2). The "age to come" is characterized by the resurrection (Luke 20:3–36), eternal life (Luke 18:30), and the riches of God's grace (Eph 2:7). From an Old Testament vantage point, the fulfillment of the ages has come already (1 Cor 10:11; Heb 1:2; 9:26). Amazingly, believers living in the "present age" experience the "powers of the age to come" (6:5 ESV), a present foretaste of future, greater blessings.

Another key distinction is that between the "already" and the "not yet." From an Old Testament outlook, the New Testament presents the

---

[11] Wells, *The Person of Christ*, 61.

"already," the fulfillment of prophetic predictions in the coming of Christ. Nevertheless, along with the "already" in the New Testament is the "not yet," the reality that many prophecies are yet to be fulfilled. The common tension between the "already" and the "not yet" contributes to the New Testament's special character.

The transitions from the Old Testament era to the "present age" and from the "present age" to the "age to come" are the works of God Almighty alone. And yet it is evident that in the New Testament, Jesus Christ brings both the "already" and the "not yet." In doing this, the Scripture powerfully identifies Jesus with God.

Jesus Christ brings both ages. The Gospels primarily present the "already" and the "not yet" as the coming of the kingdom of God, present and future. Jesus inaugurates the kingdom in his preaching, for he tells his disciples, "To you it has been given to know the secrets of the kingdom of heaven" (Matt 13:11 ESV). Jesus brings the kingdom in his exorcisms: "If it is by the Spirit of God that I cast out demons, then the kingdom of God has come upon you" (12:28 ESV). Jesus, the Son of Man, will also bring the consummated kingdom. He will return in great glory, sit on his glorious throne, judge the nations, and assign eternal destinies (25:41, 46).

It is the same in Acts. There Jesus, exalted to heaven, gives gifts of repentance and forgiveness now, as Peter says: "God exalted him at his right hand as Leader and Savior, to give repentance to Israel and forgiveness of sins" (5:31 ESV). But the "times of refreshing . . . from the presence of the Lord" are future, and they will come when the Father sends "the Christ appointed for you, Jesus, whom heaven must receive until the time for restoring all the things about which God spoke by the mouth of his holy prophets long ago" (3:20–21 ESV).

In the Epistles, too, Jesus brings the "already" and the "not yet." God the Father already "has delivered us from the domain of darkness and transferred us to the kingdom of his beloved Son, in whom we have redemption, the forgiveness of sins" (Col 1:13–14 ESV). But our resurrection will occur only when Christ returns and transfers the kingdom to the Father (1 Cor 15:22–25).

Finally, Revelation testifies to the same truths. Already Christ is the One "who loves us and has freed us from our sins by his blood" (1:5–6

ESV). But that day is still to come when his kingdom will be established outwardly and eternally in the new heavens and the new earth.
Believers long for the day when "the kingdom of the world has become
the kingdom of our Lord and of his Christ, and he will reign forever and
ever" (11:15).

The fact that Jesus brings the "present age" and the "age to come" as
well as the "already" and the "not yet" is a vivid demonstration of his deity.

Jesus Receives Devotion Due to God

Against the backdrop of the Old Testament, which commands worship
of the one living and true God while condemning all other worship, the
New Testament's practice is amazing. It continues to affirm monotheism
but also affirms that it is proper and necessary to offer religious devotion
to Jesus. He is worshipped, praised in doxologies, adored in hymns, and
addressed in prayer.

WORSHIP

Religious devotion to Jesus includes worship. After healing a lame man,
Jesus puts his deeds, including judgment, on par with the Father's: "The
Father judges no one, but has given all judgment to the Son, that all
may honor the Son, just as they honor the Father" (John 5:22–23 ESV).
Jesus deserves divine honor for himself. Such honor is given in John 9
by a man born blind. Jesus gives him sight and asks if he believes in the
Son of Man. When Jesus identifies himself as that Son of Man, the man
replies, "'Lord, I believe,' and he worship[s] him" (v. 38 ESV). Perhaps
the most famous example of worship in the Gospels is that of Thomas,
who, when the resurrected Christ appears to him, exclaims, "My Lord
and my God!" (20:28).

Paul teaches that one day all will bow before Jesus and confess his
lordship (Phil 2:9–11). The background in Isaiah 45 makes it clear that all
will bow, but those who hate God will be condemned, while only spiritual
Israelites will be saved (Isa 45:23–25; Phil 2:10–11).

Hebrews 1 teaches that the Father directs the angels to worship the
Son: "When he brings the firstborn into the world, he says, '. . . Let all

God's angels worship him'" (v. 6). The writer speaks of Christ's session (sitting down) in the heavenly world, as the surrounding context demonstrates. When the victorious Son returns to God's presence, there is much worship in heaven. The good angels relate to Christ not as to a peer but as creatures to their Maker—they worship him.

Revelation also speaks of worship of Christ. John introduces his favorite designation for Christ—the Lamb—in chapter 5 and describes worship: Jesus as "a Lamb standing, as though it had been slain," before whom angels and leading men "fell down" in worship (v. 6 ESV, 8; see also 4:10). They sing a song of worship to him, after which, accompanied by innumerable angels, they cry "with a loud voice" a doxology to the Lamb. Indeed, they repeat the worship and ascribe to the Father and Son "blessing and honor and glory and might forever and ever!" (5:11–13 ESV).

Redeemed human beings and good angels refuse to be worshipped (Acts 14:11–16; Rev 19:10; 22:8–9). But Jesus is Lord, and he rightly accepts worship from human beings and angels.

DOXOLOGIES

Religious devotion to Jesus includes doxologies (liturgical statements of praise and worship). Peter writes, "Grow in the grace and knowledge of our Lord and Savior Jesus Christ. To him be the glory both now and to the day of eternity. Amen" (2 Pet 3:18; see also Heb 13:20–21). Revelation does the same when John presents angels and human beings as praising Christ, shouting, "Worthy is the Lamb who was slain to receive power and wealth and wisdom and might and honor and glory and blessing!" (Rev 5:12 ESV). Only God is the subject of doxologies, and in Heb 13:20–21 and 2 Pet 3:18, Jesus alone is praised!

HYMNS

Religious devotion to Jesus includes hymn singing. Paul commands, "Be filled with the Spirit, addressing one another in psalms and hymns and spiritual songs, singing and making melody to the Lord with your heart" (Eph 5:18–19 ESV). Christian singing is done "to the Lord," here in reference to Christ. Hymns are addressed to Christ, further underlining his deity.

PRAYERS

Religious devotion to Jesus includes prayers. Jesus states, "Whatever you ask in my name, this I will do, that the Father may be glorified in the Son" (John 14:13 ESV). To ask in Jesus's name is to approach the Father confidently based on the work of Jesus (see 16:23–24). Disciples are also to ask the Son himself: "If you ask me anything in my name, I will do it" (14:14). Father and Son alike are the objects of Christian prayer.

We find the same thing in other New Testament books: people pray to Jesus as they would pray to God. Stephen, as he is being stoned to death, cries out, "Lord Jesus, receive my spirit!" (Acts 7:59). The Bible ends with a prayer to Jesus. After John records Jesus's words, "Surely I am coming soon" (Rev 22:20 ESV), he adds a prayer to Christ: "Amen! Come, Lord Jesus!"

Conclusion

Two significant historical denials of Christ's deity deserve mention, *Ebionism* and *Arianism*. The former is blatant and the latter subtle. Ebionism was a Jewish monotheistic denial that Christ is God. It held that at Jesus's baptism, the Christ descended upon Jesus in the form of a dove. Near the end of Jesus's life, the Christ withdrew from him. Unlike Ebionism, Arianism arose within the church. Arius (died 336), for whom the heresy is named, was an elder in the church in Alexandria. Emphasizing the absolute uniqueness and transcendence of God, he denied the full deity of Christ. Instead, he held that Christ (the Word, the Son) was God's first and highest creature. The Father worked and works through the Word, but unlike God, the Word had a beginning. The Son is different in essence from the Father. The Council of Nicaea in 325 rightly condemned Arianism as a heresy by affirming Christ's deity.

The creed from the Council of Nicaea is commonly called the Nicene Creed:

> We believe in one God the Father Almighty, maker of heaven and earth and of all things visible and invisible;
>
> And in one Lord Jesus Christ, the Son of God, the Only-begotten, begotten by his Father before all ages, Light from Light,

true God from true God, begotten not made, consubstantial with the Father, through whom all things came into existence, who for us men and for our salvation came down from the heavens and became incarnate by the Holy Spirit and the Virgin Mary and became a man, and was crucified for us under Pontius Pilate and suffered and was buried and rose again on the third day in accordance with the Scriptures and ascended into the heavens and is seated at the right hand of the Father and will come again with glory to judge the living and the dead, and there will be no end to his kingdom;

And in the Holy Spirit, the Lord and life-giver, who proceeds from the Father, who is worshipped and glorified together with the Father and the Son, who spoke by the prophets;

And in one holy, catholic and apostolic church;

We confess one baptism for the forgiveness of sins;

We wait for the resurrection of the dead and the life of the coming age. Amen.[12]

The church rightly teaches the deity of Christ because Scripture so plainly does:

- The New Testament identifies Jesus with God.
- Jesus performs the works of God.
- Jesus saves us in union with him.
- Jesus brings the age to come.
- Jesus receives devotion due to God alone.

In fact, Jesus bears witness to his own deity. We do not make this a separate category because it runs through all five categories. Jesus identifies himself with God when he applies Old Testament Yahweh passages to himself (Rev 1:17–18). He says that he performs the works of God: judgment (John 5:22–23), raising the dead (John 5:28–29), and

---

[12] This translation appears in Letham, *The Holy Trinity*, 171–72 (see chap. 3, n. 1), and credits Hanson, *The Search for the Christian Doctrine of God*, 815–16 (see chap. 3, nn.1, 3).

assigning final destinies (Matt 25:31–46). He saves believers who are in union with him (John 14:20; 17:23). He says that he brings the age to come (Matt 12:28; 25:34, 41). And he receives devotion due only to God (John 14:13–14; 20:28).

Voices from Church History: John Newton

Newton (1725–1807), after serving as a captain on slave ships, was converted and later became an evangelical Anglican clergyman. He supported abolitionism, and lived to see slavery abolished in England just before his death. He is most remembered for writing "Amazing Grace."

> He with whom we have to do, our great High Priest, who once put away our sins by the sacrifice of himself, and now for ever appears in the presence of God for us, is not only possessed of sovereign authority and infinite power, but wears our very nature, . . . He is still the same in his exalted state; compassions dwell within his heart. In a way inconceivable to us, but consistent with his supreme dignity and perfection of happiness and glory, he still feels for his people. . . . Still more, besides his benevolent, he has an experimental, sympathy. He knows our sorrows, not merely as he knows all things, but as one who has been in our situation, and who, though without sin himself, endured when upon earth inexpressibly more for us than he will ever lay upon us. . . . What then shall we fear, or of what shall we complain; when all our concerns are written upon his heart, and their management, to the very hairs of our head, are under his care and providence?[13]

Our Lord Is Human

Christ's deity is necessary for salvation because only *God* can rescue us. Christ's humanity is also essential for salvation because only a human can represent *us* (as we will see). Only the God-*man* can be our Mediator, rescuing us by dying in our place and making atonement for our sins.

---

[13] John Newton and Richard Cecil, *The Works of John Newton*, vol. 2 (London: Hamilton, Adams & Co., 1824), 20–21.

Scripture teaches Christ's humanity in many ways, including through the recognition that

- Jesus Becomes a Human Being
- Jesus Has Human Needs
- Jesus Displays Human Emotions
- Jesus Has Human Experiences
- Jesus Has a Human Relationship with His Father
- Jesus Is "Made Perfect"
- Jesus's Humanity Is Genuine

Jesus Becomes a Human Being

The incarnation stresses Jesus's genuine humanity (see previous section titled "Our Lord Became a Man" on p. 236 for more detail). "The Word became flesh" (John 1:14); the eternal Son of God became a man of flesh and blood. Why? "Since the children have flesh and blood in common, Jesus also shared in these" (Heb 2:14) in order to die, defeat Satan, and deliver his people (v. 15). He who existed "in the form of God" assumed the "form of a servant" and took "on the likeness of humanity" (Phil 2:6–7) so that he could die on the cross for us sinners (v. 8).

Jesus Has Human Needs

Jesus's genuine humanity is shown in his human weaknesses and needs. He became "worn out" from walking and therefore rested by Jacob's well (John 4:6). When the devil tempted him, "he ate nothing" and after forty days "was hungry" (Luke 4:2). On the cross, he said he was thirsty. The soldiers held up to his mouth a sponge full of sour wine (John 19:29). Although he faced danger when it was the Father's will (7:30), when it was not his will, Jesus avoided danger: "he did not want to travel in Judea because the Jews were trying to kill him" (v. 1).

Although "God is not tempted by evil" (Jas 1:13), the God-man was tempted and never succumbed. This enabled Jesus to be our empathetic high priest: "We do not have a high priest who is unable to sympathize with our weaknesses, but one who has been tempted in every way as we are, yet without sin" (Heb 4:15). As a man, Jesus successfully endured every type of temptation; as God, he is able to give us grace and mercy when we struggle (v. 16).

At the beginning of his ministry, Jesus faced major temptations. After the Spirit led him into the wilderness, the devil tempted him (Luke 1:1). Jesus withstood the evil one not by using his divine powers but by opposing Satan's three temptations with the inspired words of Deuteronomy.

Jesus Displays Human Emotions

Jesus shows human emotions. Near Passover he is angry at seeing commerce in the temple complex. He makes a whip and drives out those selling animals for sacrifice. He pours out the money changers' coins and overturns their tables. He shouts at those selling doves: "Get these things out of here! Stop turning my Father's house into a marketplace!" (John 2:16).

Another event elicits anger and sadness. As is customary, he attends synagogue, and while there, sees a man with a paralyzed hand. When his accusers watch to see if he would heal on the Sabbath, "he was grieved at the hardness of their hearts" and heals the man's hand (Mark 3:5).

Jesus experiences intense grief as he contemplates crucifixion and separation from the Father's fellowship. In Gethsemane, unsupported in prayer by his closest disciples, he cries out in pain: "I am deeply grieved to the point of death" (Matt 26:38).

The emotions of anger, love, and sorrow intermingle in Jesus's heart when he comes face-to-face with the death of his friend Lazarus. When he sees Mary and other Jews weeping, "he was deeply moved in his spirit and troubled" (John 11:33). As he approached the tomb, "Jesus wept" (v. 35), at which the Jews remark, "See how he loved him!" (v. 36).

Jesus Has Human Experiences

Our Lord's humanity is also shown by the fact that he has normal experiences. Though his conception is miraculous, his birth is normal. Joseph and Mary travel to Bethlehem, and "while they were there, the time came for her to give birth. Then she gave birth to her firstborn Son, and she wrapped him tightly in cloth and laid him in a manger, because there was no guest room available for them" (Luke 2:6–7).

Furthermore, the incarnate Son of God experiences normal human growth: "Jesus increased in wisdom and stature, and in favor with God and with people" (Luke 2:52). Let us consider how Jesus grew. He grows in wisdom: Jesus understands more at age seven than at age two, more at twenty-one than at seven, and so on. He experiences normal human intellectual growth.

Jesus grows in stature: if Mary makes marks on the doorframe, measuring her son's height, the marks will go higher with age. It is not irreverent to note that Jesus experiences puberty, and if young Jewish men normally get pimples in first-century Palestine, he does too.

Jesus grows in favor with God: although as God he enjoys eternal fellowship with the Father, in the incarnation Jesus grows spiritually. His prayers are more fervent at twenty than at five. He better understands God's will at thirty, when his ministry begins, than at twenty-one.

Jesus grows in favor with people, that is, socially: Jesus's social skills are more advanced at seventeen than at seven, and so on.

Jesus's humanity is especially clear in that he dies. Crucifixion is not the normal way for people to die. This terrible method of execution is reserved for criminals, yet the sinless Son of God endures the cross and dies, as John records:

> There they crucified him and two others with him, one on either side, with Jesus in the middle. (John 19:18)

> He said, "It is finished!" Then bowing his head, he gave up his spirit. (v. 30)

> When they came to Jesus, they did not break his legs since they saw that he was already dead. (v. 33)

Jesus Has a Human Relationship with His Father

As the God-*man*, Jesus has a human relationship with God, his Father. This is evident in many ways; we will mention three. First, Jesus affirms that he is subordinate to God: "The Father is greater than I" (John 14:28). The Father gives his Son work to do on earth, work that the Son completes (17:4). This is a subordination of role, not of essence. A subordination of essence would mean that the Son is not fully divine; a subordination of role or work means the divine-human Son submits to the Father to accomplish salvation.

Second, Jesus honors his Father as a man honors God. When he receives a mixed response from his hearers, he replies, "The one who speaks on his own seeks his own glory; but he who seeks the glory of the one who sent him is true" (John 7:18). He opposes Jewish leaders, who accuse him of having a demon: "'I do not have a demon,' Jesus answered. 'On the contrary, I honor my Father and you dishonor me'" (8:49).

Third, Jesus obeys God's commands. He does not speak in disobedience to the Father, "but the Father himself who sent [him had] given [him] a command to say everything [he has] said" (John 12:49). Furthermore, Jesus explains from where he receives the right to die and rise: "I have received this command from my Father" (10:18).

In these three ways and more, Jesus's relationship with the Father underscores his humanity.

Jesus Is "Made Perfect"

Uniquely, Hebrews says that Jesus is "made perfect." Two references state this fact:

> In bringing many sons to glory, it was entirely appropriate that God . . . should make the source of their salvation perfect through sufferings. (Heb 2:10)

> The law appoints as high priests men who are weak, but the promise of the oath, which came after the law, appoints a Son, who has been perfected forever. (7:28)

A third reference helps us understand the expression: "Although he was the Son, he learned obedience from what he suffered. After he was perfected, he became the source of eternal salvation for all who obey him" (5:8–9). The Son is already perfect in his deity and sinless humanity. His being perfected concerns his obedience in suffering according to the Father's will. Our divine Redeemer not only has to become man; he also has to obey "to the point of death—even to death on a cross" (Phil 2:8).

Jesus's Humanity Is Genuine

Jesus's humanity is so raw in three places that some Christians try to explain them away. First, believers sometimes cringe at on-screen depictions of Jesus's temptation by the devil (Matt 4:1–11). We do not endorse every such depiction of Jesus, but his temptations were real, and his overcoming them contributes to our salvation (Heb 4:15).

Second, beginning with the church fathers, Christians have been nervous at Jesus's not knowing the time of his return (Matt 24:36). For reasons not revealed, it was not the Father's will for Jesus to exercise his divine knowledge in this area while on earth. Of course, now in heaven he knows when he will return.

Third, Jesus's asking in Gethsemane to be spared the cross makes some Christians uneasy (Matt 26:36–46). But it should not, for once more his humanity comes to the fore, and with it our salvation. We cannot imagine the Son's horror at contemplating the Father's punishing him with the punishment we deserve. Jesus shrinks at this but does not sin; he submits to the Father's will (vv. 39, 42, 44). Rather than being something of which we should be ashamed, this epitomizes Jesus's love for us sinners. That he would suffer the pains of hell for us on the cross is incredible!

Conclusion

Two historical denials of Christ's humanity warrant mention: *Docetism* and *Apollinarianism*. Greek philosophy held to gradations of reality, with spirit being the highest and matter less real. Ethical gradations corresponded to these ontological ones, so spirit was good and matter bad. It was thus considered impossible for God to become a human being. Docetism (from the Greek *dokeō*, "I think, seem, appear") therefore claimed that Christ only appeared to be human.

Apollinarianism, named after Apollinarius (fourth century AD), denied the completeness of Christ's humanity. It held that Jesus had a human body but not a human soul, with the Word taking the place of a soul. This heresy was condemned at the Council of Constantinople in 381. The council's creed affirms both Christ's deity and his humanity:

> We believe . . . in one Lord, Jesus Christ, the only-begotten Son of God, eternally begotten of the Father, Light from Light, true God from true God, begotten, not made, of one being with the Father. Through him all things were made. For us, humans, and for our salvation, he came down from heaven, was incarnate of the Holy Spirit and the virgin Mary, and became fully human.[14]

While Christians reject Docetism and Apollinarianism, it is sometimes hard for us, who rightly affirm Christ's deity, to affirm his humanity wholeheartedly as well. But two things stand out. First, our salvation depends on his humanity, his being one with us, just as it does on his deity, his being God for us. Jesus's humanness enables him to identify with and to die for his fellow human beings in order to rescue them from their sins. Second, we confess mystery in the person of Christ. We cannot fully understand how he is God and man in one person. But he is, and the unity of his person matters, as we will see.

Our Lord Is One

Errors about His Unity

This is best understood against the background of two historical errors, *Nestorianism* and *monophysitism* (*Eutychianism*). Nestorianism is associated with tearing the person of Christ into two, destroying his unity. This is ironic because Nestorius, installed as patriarch of Constantinople in 428, was not a Nestorian. He did teach ambiguously

---

[14] Creed of the Council of Constantinople, 381, on the website Fourth Century Christianity, accessed June 24, 2019, http://www.fourthcentury.com /constantinople-381-creed-english.

concerning Christ, however, and opened himself up to attack by his opponent, Cyril of Alexandria.

Monophysitism ("one nature"-ism) denies the distinction between Christ's two natures. It is also called Eutychianism, after Eutyches (c. 378–454), who erroneously taught that the Son had two natures before the incarnation and one after, as Christ's humanity was gradually absorbed into his deity and virtually eliminated.

One Person with Two Natures

In contrast to Nestorianism's dividing Christ in two and monophysitism's eliminating the distinction between his natures, orthodox Christianity teaches that Christ is one person with two natures joined in a personal (hypostatic) union. Before the incarnation the Word, the Son, the second person of the Trinity, existed for all eternity with the Father and the Holy Spirit. In the incarnation the Word took to himself genuine humanity so that Christ was one person with two natures, one divine and one human. The basis of Christ's personhood is the divine Son's becoming a man.

Jesus's humanity did not exist before the incarnation. Further, Jesus's humanity never existed alone but from conception was joined to the Son in Mary's womb. The creed of the most famous Christological council, Chalcedon (451), states that the incarnate Son is one person "in two natures without confusion, without change, without division, without separation":

> Therefore, following the holy fathers, we all with one accord teach men to acknowledge one and the same Son, our Lord Jesus Christ, at once complete in Godhead and complete in manhood, truly God and truly man, consisting also of a reasonable soul and body; of one substance with the Father as regards his Godhead, and at the same time of one substance with us as regards his manhood; like us in all respects, apart from sin; as regards his Godhead, begotten of the Father before the ages, but yet as regards his manhood begotten, for us men and for our salvation, of Mary the Virgin, the Godbearer; one and the same Christ, Son,

Lord, Only-begotten, recognized in two natures, without confusion, without change, without division, without separation; the distinction of natures being in no way annulled by the union, but rather the characteristics of each nature being preserved and coming together to form one person and subsistence, not as parted or separated into two persons, but one and the same Son and Only-begotten God the Word, Lord Jesus Christ; even as the prophets from earliest times spoke of him, and our Lord Jesus Christ himself taught us, and the creed of the fathers has handed down to us.[15]

Communication of Attributes

The communication of attributes highlights the unity of Christ's person. The church fathers note that sometimes Scripture refers to the person of Christ with a title that corresponds to his divine nature while attributing to him a quality that pertains to his human nature. Peter tells the Jews, "You killed the Author of life" (Acts 3:15 ESV; see also 20:28), referring to Christ by the divine title "Author of life" while ascribing human mortality to him.

Paul says that none of this age's rulers understood God's wisdom in Christ, "for if they had, they would not have crucified the Lord of glory" (1 Cor 2:8 ESV). Paul refers to Christ with the divine title "Lord of glory" while attributing to him the human quality of mortality.

John calls Christ the "Word of life" (a divine title) while testifying that the apostles heard, saw, and touched him—things that could not be said of God (1 John 1:1). But they were said of God incarnate. In each case there is a communication, a sharing, of attributes. Christ is called God, but what is said of him pertains to his being a man. In this way Scripture underlines the unity of his person, putting both natures together in a single sentence.

---

[15] "The Chalcedon Formula," Anglicans Online, accessed July 19, 2018, http://anglicansonline.org/basics/chalcedon.html.

Exercise of Attributes

Christ exercises his divine and human attributes as one person. How can
we conceive of his use of both his divine and his human attributes while
not harming the unity of his person? First, all biblical statements speaking of the Son of God incarnate are to be attributed to the whole person,
although some make special reference to one nature. So, the person of
Christ was crucified, not merely his humanity, because his two natures
are inseparable from his person. God in heaven cannot die, but God the
Son becomes a man precisely so that he could (Heb 2:14). So, the person
of Christ is crucified with special reference to his human nature. Similarly,
Jesus's ability to forgive sins (Luke 5:20; 7:48) pertains to his whole person, with special reference to his divine nature.

Second, our Lord incarnate voluntarily subordinates the exercise of
his divine attributes (which he retains in full) in obedience to the Father's
will. This is no reduction of, but a veiled manifestation of, his divine powers. In the incarnation he is fully God, retaining all of his divine powers.
He does not give them up but gives up his independent use of them, using
them only in obedience to the Father. So, when it is the Father's will, Jesus
exercises divine knowledge while on earth (John 1:48–49; 2:24–25; 4:17–
19). But for reasons not revealed, it is not the Father's will for the Son to
know the time of his return while he is on earth (Matt 24:36). Of course,
he knows it now.

Third, we respect the miracle of the incarnation and the resulting
mystery of Christ's person. We do not fully understand how he can be
God and man in one person. Nevertheless, we can know truly without
knowing fully (Eph 3:14–21).

Our Lord Is Exalted

Although we are unable to understand fully the person of the God-man,
Jesus Christ, we can know many truths concerning him. One such truth
answers this question: How can we explain the difference between Christ
on earth in the first century and Christ in heaven now? A common but
incorrect answer is that he gives up his human nature when he is raised

from the dead. This is a mistake, for the incarnation is permanent. When God became a man, he did so forever. Christ in heaven today is still God and man in one person:

> Since we have a great high priest who has passed through the heavens—Jesus the Son of God—let us hold fast to our confession. For we do not have a high priest who is unable to sympathize with our weaknesses, but one who has been tempted in every way as we are, yet without sin. (Heb 4:14–16)

"Jesus, the Son of God" is a divine title; it points to his deity. The divine Christ "has passed through the heavens" and returned to his Father in heaven. And this divine Christ remains a human being, for the writer says Jesus can sympathize with our infirmities because he was tempted and never sinned. These words describe a genuine human being. If someone protests that Jesus is sinless and therefore not human, we reply, "He is indeed sinless, but sin is not a necessary part of human nature but an aberration. Adam was created without sin, and believers will be sinless when God raises them for eternal life on the new earth."

The correct way to distinguish between Christ on earth and Christ in heaven is with the two-states doctrine. The states are two chronological phases and corresponding conditions through which the Son of God passes in accomplishing salvation. The state of humiliation includes Jesus's birth, earthly life, temptation(s), sufferings, trials, crucifixion, death, and burial. The state of exaltation includes Jesus's resurrection, ascension, session (sitting at God's right hand), present heavenly ministry, and second coming. Never again will the exalted Son of God suffer, be tempted, or die. Rather, he will return in power and glory to redeem his people and punish his enemies.

The classic passage on Jesus's two states is Phil 2:6–11. The first paragraph (vv. 6–8) describes Jesus's state of humiliation. While existing as God, Jesus humbles himself and becomes a man. Again he humbles himself, even to the point of giving himself to die on a cross. Paul elsewhere sums it up well: "You know the grace of our Lord Jesus Christ: Though he was rich, for your sake he became poor, so that by his poverty you might become rich" (2 Cor 8:9).

The second paragraph (Phil 2:9–11) describes Jesus's state of exaltation. The Father raises his Son and exalts him to heaven so that at his return, all people will bow before him and acknowledge his lordship. Some will bow in worship and some in defeat, but all will bow before Jesus Christ the Lord. Paul also sums up this state in Ephesians: God "exercised this power in Christ by raising him from the dead and seating him at his right hand in the heavens—far above every ruler and authority, power and dominion, and every title given, not only in this age but also in the one to come" (1:20–21).

Incredibly, because of his great love for us and in obedience to the Father, the preexistent, eternal, and glorious Son of God humbles himself and voluntarily becomes a man. As one person with two natures (fully divine and fully human), Jesus is uniquely able to save us and represent us. Only God can save, and only a human can represent us as the new Adam. In response to Jesus's work on our behalf, the Father exalts him to the highest place, which in turn also glorifies the Father.

KEY TERMS

Alpha and Omega

Apollinarianism

Arianism

Christophany

Christ's deity

Christ's exercise of attributes

Christ's humanity

Christ's incarnation

Christ's states of humiliation and exaltation

Christ's unity

communication of attributes

cornerstone

Docetism

Ebionism

Eutychianism

firstborn from the dead

Good Shepherd

head of the church

heresy

hypostatic union

kenosis doctrine

Lamb of God

Lord Jesus

Mediator

monophysitism

Nestorianism

person of Christ

preexistence of Christ

Savior

second Adam

sinlessness

Son of God

Son of Man

true vine, the

virgin birth

work of Christ

▨ RESOURCES FOR FURTHER STUDY

Allison, Gregg R. *Historical Theology: An Introduction to Christian Doctrine*. Grand Rapids: Zondervan, 2011, 365–88.

Bauckham, Richard. *Jesus and the God of Israel: God Crucified and Other Studies on the New Testament's Christology of Divine Identity*. Grand Rapids: Eerdmans, 2008.

Blomberg, Craig L. *Jesus and the Gospels: An Introduction and Survey*, 2nd ed. Nashville: B&H, 2009.

Bock, Darrell L. *Jesus according to Scripture: Restoring the Portrait from the Gospels*. Grand Rapids: Baker Academic, 2002.

Bowman, Robert M. Jr., and J. Ed Komoszewski. *Putting Jesus in His Place: The Case for the Deity of Christ*. Grand Rapids: Kregel, 2007.

Erickson, Millard J. *The Word Became Flesh: A Contemporary Incarnational Christology*. Grand Rapids: Baker, 1981.

Fee, Gordon D. *Pauline Christology: An Exegetical-Theological Study*. Peabody, MA: Hendrickson, 2007.

Gathercole, Simon J. *The Preexistent Son: Recovering the Christologies of Matthew, Mark, and Luke*. Grand Rapids: Eerdmans, 2006.

Harris, Murray J. *Jesus as God: The New Testament Use of* Theos *in Reference to Jesus*. Grand Rapids: Baker, 1992.

Hurtado, Larry W. *Lord Jesus Christ: Devotion to Jesus in Earliest Christianity*. Grand Rapids: Eerdmans, 2003.

Machen, J. Gresham. *The Virgin Birth of Christ*. New York: Harper, 1930.

Macleod, Donald. *The Person of Christ*. Contours of Christian Theology. Downers Grove, IL: InterVarsity, 1998.

Morgan, Christopher W., and Robert A. Peterson, eds. *The Deity of Christ*. Vol. 3 of Theology in Community. Wheaton, IL: Crossway, 2011.

Wells, David F. *The Person of Christ: A Biblical and Historical Analysis of the Incarnation*. Westchester, IL: Crossway, 1984.

Wellum, Stephen J. *God the Son Incarnate: The Doctrine of Christ*. Foundations of Evangelical Theology. Wheaton, IL: Crossway, 2016.

7

JESUS'S
SAVING
WORK

The Word of God is clear that salvation is not based on human merit; no one will ever be saved by good works offered to God (Eph 2:8–9; 2 Tim 1:8–9). But Scripture also teaches that all Christians *are* saved by good works—Christ's own good works, especially his death and resurrection.

After seeing the role of Jesus's saving work in the biblical story, we here examine selected passages that present his work. Next, we expand our idea of what Jesus does to save us, including his incarnation, life, death, resurrection, ascension, sitting at God's right hand, sending the Spirit at Pentecost, intercession, and return. Then we look at biblical pictures of Jesus's salvation: he is our substitute, victor, sacrifice, Redeemer, reconciler, and new Adam. After considering Jesus's offices of prophet, priest, and King, we note how his work is directed toward God, our enemies, human beings, and heaven and earth. And throughout the journey, we show how understanding what Jesus does for us shapes our understanding of who we are.

▦ OUTLINE

Jesus's Saving Work in the Biblical Story
Jesus's Saving Work in Selected Passages

▓ OBJECTIVES

- To expand our understanding of the breadth and depth of Christ's saving work
- To ground our faith in Christ's death and resurrection
- To move us to trust, love, and worship Jesus as Lord and Savior
- To motivate us to give God all the glory for such a great salvation
- To establish our identity in Christ as individuals and as the church

Jesus's Saving Work in the Biblical Story

Jesus's saving work is the center of the biblical story. God creates all things and pronounces them "very good indeed" (Gen 1:31). He makes Adam and Eve in his own likeness, holy, and in fellowship with him. Tragically, our first parents rebel against their Maker and friend by disobeying his word. No sooner does this happen than God makes the first promise of redemption (3:15).

The rest of the Old Testament builds on God's promise in Eden. The sacrifices of Leviticus point toward a great sacrifice that will end all sacrifices. Psalm 22 speaks of the innocent sufferer par excellence, whose hands and feet will be pierced (v. 16) and who will cry, "My God, my God, why have you abandoned me?" (v. 1; see also Matt 27:46). Isaiah foretells the servant of the Lord, who will die vicariously to deliver his people (Isaiah 53). Jonah's experience with the great fish foreshadows "the Son of Man," who will "be in the heart of the earth three days and three nights" (Matt 12:40).

The four Gospels report the coming of this promised One, whose saving work climaxes his story. The eternal Son of God becomes a human being, as he is conceived by the Holy Spirit in Mary's womb (Gal 4:4). He grows to be a man, John the Baptist baptizes him in the Jordan River, and immediately the Spirit thrusts him into the desert, where he successfully endures the devil's temptations (Matt 4:1). After gathering twelve disciples, he preaches, teaches, casts out demons, heals many diseases, and trains the Twelve for three years. The heart and soul of his ministry is his death and resurrection.

Jesus is crucified between two thieves, and after promising the penitent thief, "Today you will be with me in paradise" (Luke 23:43), Jesus shouts, "It is finished" (John 19:30), and commits his spirit to God the Father in death (Luke 23:46). Three days later, by Jewish reckoning, he is raised from the dead and appears to many believers, including his disciples and five hundred Christians at once (1 Cor 15:6). For forty days he teaches his followers the meaning of his ministry from the Old Testament and, after promising to pour out the Spirit, ascends before them to the Father's presence in heaven (Luke 24:51), from which he promises to return in his second coming (John 14:3).

Jesus's Saving Work in Selected Passages

The following passages show that holy God dwells in the midst of his people Israel, and their sin defiles both them and the tabernacle, his dwelling place. In grace God provides the Day of Atonement to cleanse and remove their sins. The high priest offers sacrifices for the altar, the tent of meeting, and the people, so the people can continue in fellowship with their covenant Lord. In the Gospel of Mark, Jesus as a prophet predicts his death and resurrection three times. In John's Gospel, he also predicts the same two events. Jesus willingly dies, showing his love for and obedience to the Father. In Acts, the apostles preach that the crucified Jesus is alive. His redemptive events include everything from his incarnation to his return, and the center is his death and resurrection. Though Jesus is a formidable Judge, he is also a wonderful Savior who saves his people from beginning to end. God saves all who turn from their own righteousness and trust Christ for salvation.

We distinguish between Christ's states of humiliation and exaltation. His humiliation shows his humanity, which is essential for our salvation, for only a fellow human could die in our place. Christ's exaltation shows his deity, which is also essential for our salvation, for only God could rescue us. When Paul summarizes the gospel, he stresses Jesus's death and resurrection. But if we take the big picture, we see nine events: Jesus's becoming a man, his sinless life, his death, his resurrection, the ascension, sitting at God's right hand, sending the Spirit at Pentecost, interceding for us, and coming again. Peter teaches that Jesus dies as our substitute, is raised victoriously, ascends to heaven, and sits down at God's right hand, the place of greatest honor and power.

Leviticus 16

The first verse in this chapter recalls Leviticus 10, which treats the death of two of Aaron's sons, who, when serving as priests, dare to approach God carelessly and suffer the consequences—the divine judgment of death. Leviticus 16 teaches the high priests how they are to carry out their activities so as to avoid the same fate (v. 2). R. K. Harrison underscores the great importance of the Day of Atonement, the subject of Leviticus 16: "This chapter comprises the ceremonial and theological pivot upon which the entire book of Leviticus turns."[1]

---

[1] R. K. Harrison, *Leviticus*, Tyndale Old Testament Commentaries (Downers Grove, IL: InterVarsity, 1980), 166.

The chapter regulates the ceremonies on the Day of Atonement, including sacrificial animals, priestly garments, and the rites themselves in outline (vv. 1–10). Next, it describes the three sacrificial rites (vv. 11–28). Finally, it describes the duty of God's people (vv. 29–34). Our focus is on the three rites discussed in verses 11–28. Three sacrifices are to be offered on this holy day: a sin offering for Aaron and his family; two male goats as a sin offering for the people; and two rams for burnt offerings, one for Aaron and one for the people.

First, Aaron is to approach the mercy seat in the most holy place only after having made atonement with a sin offering of a bull (vv. 6, 11). He is to slaughter the bull (v. 11). Next, he is to make an incense cloud to cover the mercy seat. He must take a censer full of coals from the altar of the burnt offering in the outer court, add two handfuls of finely ground fragrant incense, and take it inside the veil. "He is to put the incense on the fire before the LORD, so that the cloud of incense covers the mercy seat that is over the testimony, or else he will die" (v. 13). Why must Aaron do this? The purpose of the incense cloud is to shield Aaron from seeing God's glory, for no one can see his face and live (Exod 33:20).[2] Following this, with his finger Aaron is to sprinkle some of the bull's blood on the top of the mercy seat and some blood seven times before the mercy seat (Lev 16:14). The blood of the bull applied to the mercy seat will make atonement for Aaron and his family (v. 6).

Second, Aaron is to present goats as a sin offering. God tells him to take two live male goats, cast lots over them, and handle them in different ways. Aaron is to sacrifice one as a sin offering; he is to send away the other into the wilderness. Aaron is to slaughter the first goat as an offering for the people's sins and to sprinkle its blood on the mercy seat, as with the bull's blood. "He will make atonement for the most holy place in this way for all their sins because of the Israelites' impurities and rebellious acts" (v. 16). He will also make atonement for the tent of meeting (vv. 16–17). In addition, "he will go out to the altar that is before the LORD and make atonement for it" (v. 18). Israel's sin pollutes the place where God

---

[2] Gordon J. Wenham, *The Book of Leviticus*, The New International Commentary on the Old Testament (Grand Rapids: Eerdmans, 1979), 231.

dwells, with its altar and holy place. In grace God makes atonement for these as well as for the people's sins.

God instructs Aaron concerning the second goat:

> Aaron will lay both his hands on the head of the live goat and confess over it all the Israelites' iniquities and rebellious acts—all their sins. He is to put them on the goat's head and send it away into the wilderness by the man appointed for the task. The goat will carry all their iniquities into a desolate land, and the man will release it there. (vv. 21–22)

The high priest's actions symbolize substitutionary sacrifice, as Allen Ross explains: "Aaron laid both hands on the goat to ensure the transference of sin to the goat. He then confessed all of the wickedness and rebellion of Israel—all their sins. And these sins were placed on the goat to bear them away into the wilderness."[3] Moreover, the goat sent away into the wilderness symbolizes expiation, the taking away of the people's sins, for "the goat will carry all their iniquities into a desolate land" (v. 22). The two goats sacrificed on the Day of Atonement, then, are substitutionary sacrifices for the people.

Third, Aaron is to select from the herd "a ram for a burnt offering" for himself (v. 3) and also to take "from the Israelite community . . . one ram for a burnt offering" for the people (v. 5). After handling the two goats, and leaving his linen garments in the holy place and bathing, he is to "go out and sacrifice his burnt offering and the people's burnt offering; he will make atonement for himself and for the people" (v. 24).

The Israelites have a seemingly insurmountable obstacle: their sin and impurity defile both them and God's dwelling place. Jay Sklar summarizes the Day of Atonement as God's solution:

> The Israelites were faced with a serious problem: the holy Lord now dwelt in their midst, but their sins and impurities defiled his holy dwelling. True, they would have atoned for many of these

---

[3] Allen P. Ross, *Holiness to the LORD: A Guide to the Exposition of the Book of Leviticus* (Grand Rapids: Baker Academic, 2002), 320–21.

properly (Leviticus 4–5, 11–15), but they would have missed many others, which then, defiled the tabernacle more and more. . . . How could the holy Lord continue in their midst without bringing his justice to bear against them? By means of a regular atonement ceremony—the Day of Atonement—that would cleanse and remove the Israelites' sins and impurities so they could continue in covenant fellowship with him.

Three rites formed the heart of the ceremony, each making atonement in its own way. . . . Taken together, these rites fully atoned for the Israelites; their sins and impurities were no longer there; the slate was completely clean (cf. Ps. 103:12). The holy God who is offended by sin and impurity is also the compassionate and gracious God who delights to cleanse and forgive it.[4]

Mark 8:31–33

Jesus is a prophet who makes many predictions while on earth. Chief among them are his death and resurrection: "Then he began to teach them that it was necessary for the Son of Man to suffer many things and be rejected by the elders, chief priests, and scribes, be killed, and rise after three days" (Mark 8:31; see also 9:31; 10:33–34).

Three times in Mark's Gospel, Jesus predicts his rejection by the Jewish leaders, his death, and his resurrection. Peter's rebuke is born of love for Jesus but reveals ignorance of the reason he comes into the world. Jesus corrects Peter, seeking to orient him to God's plan, which focuses on the cross and the empty tomb.

John 10:17–18

John's Gospel links Jesus's death and his love for God: "This is why the Father loves me, because I lay down my life so that I may take it up again. No one takes it from me, but I lay it down on my own. I have the right to

---

[4] Jay Sklar, *Leviticus*, Tyndale Old Testament Commentaries (Downers Grove, IL: InterVarsity Press, 2014), 215–16.

lay it down, and I have the right to take it up again. I have received this command from my Father" (10:17–18). Jesus here predicts his death and resurrection, both of which are motivated by his love for and obedience to the Father. Jesus is not coerced into death but willingly dies. This is one of two places in Scripture that teaches that Jesus raises himself from the dead (the other is 2:19–22).

Acts 2:32–33

The apostles in Acts lay heavy emphasis on the fact that the crucified Jesus is alive: "God has raised this Jesus; we are all witnesses of this. Therefore, since he has been exalted to the right hand of God and has received from the Father the promised Holy Spirit, he has poured out what you both see and hear" (Acts 2:32–33). Peter here counts among Christ's saving deeds his death (implied), resurrection, ascension, sitting at God's right hand, and pouring out the Spirit at Pentecost. We will see that the Savior's redemptive acts include everything from his incarnation to his return and that the core of his saving accomplishment is his death and resurrection.

Romans 10:9–10

What constitutes a saving response to the gospel? Paul answers: "If you confess with your mouth, 'Jesus is Lord,' and believe in your heart that God raised him from the dead, you will be saved. One believes with the heart, resulting in righteousness, and one confesses with the mouth, resulting in salvation" (Rom 10:9–10). The gospel includes Jesus's death and resurrection (1 Cor 15:3–4). God saves all who turn away from their own righteousness and trust Christ, crucified and risen, for salvation.

Philippians 2:5–11

As we saw in the previous chapter, it is important to distinguish between Christ's states of humiliation and exaltation, as Paul does in Phil 2:5–11. The eternal Son of God humbles himself by leaving heaven to become a man, even a servant, and to die the horrible death of crucifixion (vv. 6–8). Why did he do this? Because he loves us, considers us more important than himself (though we are not), and looks out for our interests instead of his own (see vv. 3–4). As a result of his obeying the Father "to the point of . . . death on a cross . . . God highly exalted him" (vv. 8–9).

The apostle takes words that God speaks about people's bowing before him and swearing allegiance to him (Isa 45:23) and applies them to Jesus. Christ's exaltation thus shows his deity, which is essential for our salvation, for only God could rescue us. Christ's humiliation shows his humanity, which is also essential for our salvation, for only a fellow human could die in our place. Thus this great passage proclaims the humanity and deity of the crucified, risen, and exalted One. In this way, Paul highlights the bond between the person and the work of the Mediator.

Romans 8:34

The role of divine Judge in the New Testament judgment passages is evenly split between the Father and the Son. So, when Paul asks, "Who is the one who condemns?" and answers, "Christ Jesus," we would expect him to tell of the Son's sending sinners to hell. But instead he speaks of the Son as Savior of his people: "Christ Jesus is the one who died, but even more, has been raised; he also is at the right hand of God and intercedes for us" (Rom 8:34). Paul here lists four of Christ's saving works: his death, resurrection, sitting at God's right hand, and intercession for his own. Although Jesus is a formidable Judge, he is also the wonderful Savior who does all that is necessary to save us, from beginning to end.

1 Peter 3:18, 21–22

When Paul summarizes the gospel, he includes Jesus's death and resurrection (1 Cor 15:3–4). In fact, if we take the big-picture approach to what Jesus did to rescue us, we see nine events—everything from his incarnation to his second coming. These events are his becoming a man, his sinless life, his death, the resurrection, the ascension, sitting at God's right hand, sending the Spirit at Pentecost, interceding for us, and coming again.

Peter brings together four of Christ's saving deeds: "Christ also suffered for sins once for all, the righteous for the unrighteous, that he might bring you to God. . . . through the resurrection of Jesus Christ, who has gone into heaven and is at the right hand of God with angels, authorities, and powers subject to him" (1 Pet 3:18, 21–22).

Peter thus includes Jesus's death, resurrection, ascension, and sitting at God's right hand among the deeds Christ performs to deliver us. Jesus dies as our substitute: "the righteous" One suffers "for the unrighteous" ones (v. 18). He is raised victoriously, ascends to heaven, and sits down at God's right hand, the place of greatest honor and power.

Jesus's Saving Events

The persons of the Trinity work together to save us. Before creation the Father plans salvation. In the first century AD, the Son does the work necessary to save us. The Holy Spirit applies Christ's saving work through uniting us to Christ.

Voices from Church History: John Calvin

Calvin (1509–1564), a French theologian and pastor in Geneva, was a leader in the Protestant Reformation. In addition to his famous systematic theology, *Institutes of the Christian Religion*, Calvin wrote commentaries on most books of the Bible. He founded a school that trained many students, including missionaries to France, who planted hundreds of churches. His influence continues through his example of expository preaching and the theology that bears his name (Calvinism), which stresses God's glory and sovereignty. Calvin made this classic statement of the breadth of Christ's saving work:

> If we seek salvation, we are taught by the very name of Jesus that it is "of him" [1 Cor. 1:30]. If we seek any other gifts of the Spirit, they will be found in his anointing. If we seek strength, it lies in his dominion; if purity, in his conception; if gentleness, it appears in his birth. For by his birth he was made like us in all respects [Heb. 2:17] that he might learn to feel our pain [cf. Heb. 5:2]. If we seek redemption, it lies in his

passion; if acquittal, in his condemnation; if remission of the curse, in his cross [Gal. 3:13]; if satisfaction, in his sacrifice; if purification, in his blood, if reconciliation, in his descent into hell; if mortification of the flesh, in his tomb; if newness of life, in his resurrection; if immortality, in the same; if inheritance of the Heavenly Kingdom, in his entrance into heaven; if protection, if security, if abundant supply of all blessings, in his Kingdom; if untroubled expectation of judgment, in the power given him to judge. In short, since rich store of every kind of goods abounds in him, let us drink our fill from this fountain, and from no other.[5]

At the center of Jesus's accomplishments are his atoning death and victorious resurrection. But they are not alone. Two essential events (prerequisites) precede them, and five essential results follow. The two prerequisites are his incarnation and his sinless earthly life. The five results are his ascension, his session (sitting at God's right hand), his pouring out of the Spirit at Pentecost, his present intercession (prayer) for the church, and his second coming.[6]

- Our Lord Becomes a Human
- Our Lord Lives a Sinless Life
- Our Lord Dies for Us
- Our Lord Rises from the Dead
- Our Lord Ascends to Heaven
- Our Lord Sits at God's Right Hand
- Our Lord Sends the Holy Spirit
- Our Lord Intercedes for Us
- Our Lord Returns in Victory
- Viewing the Events Together

---

[5] John Calvin, *Institutes of the Christian Religion*, ed. John T. McNeill, trans. Ford Lewis Battles, 2 vols. (Philadelphia: Westminster, 1960), 1:527–28; 2:16, 19.

[6] We follow the structure of and condense the more thorough treatment in Robert A. Peterson, *Salvation Accomplished by the Son: The Work of Christ* (Wheaton, IL: Crossway, 2012), 21–269.

Our Lord Becomes a Human

In the middle of the night, angels gloriously appear to shepherds in their fields and announce Jesus's birth: "Today in the city of David a Savior was born for you, who is the Messiah, the Lord" (Luke 2:11). Luke thus indicates that this unique baby is the Savior from sin, Israel's promised Messiah or Christ, and God himself (Lord).

Luke tells Jesus's story from the perspective of the earth, but John begins in heaven. There the One he calls "the Word" is with God and is God (John 1:1). The "Word became flesh and dwelt among us. We observed his glory, the glory as the one and only Son from the Father, full of grace and truth" in the incarnation (v. 14). The eternal Son of God becomes a man of flesh and blood and reveals God as never before. He also comes to give believers "the right to be children of God" (v. 12).

The apostle Paul also includes Jesus's incarnation among his saving events: "When the time came to completion, God sent his Son, born of a woman, born under the law, to redeem those under the law, so that we might receive adoption as sons" (Gal 4:4–5). At the right time in redemptive history, the Father sends his eternal Son into the world to be born a baby. Moreover, Jesus is "born under the law," that is, as a Jewish man obligated to keep the law, which he does perfectly his whole life. Not only so, but by suffering the law's penalty, Jesus also redeems lawbreakers who believe in him, for "Christ redeemed us from the curse of the law by becoming a curse for us" in death (3:13). As a result of the Redeemer's death (and resurrection), all who believe "receive adoption as sons" (4:5), which means God himself welcomes us into his family.

Paul says that the One who exists "in the form of God" humbles himself and assumes "the form of a servant" (Phil 2:6–7). This means that Jesus takes on "the likeness of humanity" in order to submit himself "to the point of death, even to death on a cross" for sinners (vv. 7–8). But God "highly exalted him" by raising him from the dead and giving him glory (v. 9). When he returns, all will bow before him and confess his lordship (vv. 10–11).

The book of Hebrews likewise presents the incarnation as an essential part of Jesus's saving work: "since the children have flesh and blood in common, Jesus also shared in these" (2:14). The Son of God partakes of the same humanity shared by God's children when he becomes a man. Why does he do this? So he could die. What does he accomplish by dying? Two things: he becomes a man "so that through his death he might destroy the one holding the power of death—that is, the devil—and free those who were held in slavery all their lives by the fear of death" (vv. 14–15). Jesus's death is a mighty victory over our enemy Satan, who uses death to terrorize us. Jesus's death is also a mighty deliverance for all who trust him, who previously were slaves to the fear of God's judgment after death.

The incarnation by itself does not save. Rather, it is a necessary precondition for Jesus's saving death and resurrection. And there is another necessary precondition: Jesus's sinless earthly life.

Our Lord Lives a Sinless Life

Isaiah foresees that the Servant of the Lord will neither do "violence" nor speak "deceitfully"; consequently, the "righteous servant will justify many, and he will carry their iniquities" (Isa 53:9, 11). Even before Jesus's birth the angel Gabriel announces to Mary, "The holy one to be born will be called the Son of God" (Luke 1:35).

Unlike any of us, the Son of God lives a sinless life during his thirty-three years on earth. Indeed, he is "tempted in every way as we are, yet without sin" (Heb 4:15). In fact, he undergoes more severe temptations than we will ever know when the evil one tempts him in the wilderness after he'd gone forty days without food (Matt 4:1–11; Luke 4:1–13). Still, he does not yield and sin. For these reasons, Luke repeatedly testifies in Acts to Jesus's moral purity. Various speakers call him "the Holy and Righteous One" (Peter in Acts 3:14), "your holy servant Jesus" (believers in Acts 4:27, 30), and "the Righteous One" (Stephen in Acts 7:52; Ananias in Acts 22:14).

Paul attests to Christ's moral perfection when he speaks of the great transaction: "He made the one who did not know sin to be sin for us, so that in him we might become the righteousness of God" (2 Cor 5:21). God the Father reckons our sin to the sinless Christ's spiritual bank account so that the Father might reckon Christ's perfect righteousness to our accounts. The result, of course, is that by trusting Christ as Savior, we are accepted forever by God.

The apostles Peter and John add their voices to the chorus proclaiming Christ's purity: "Christ also suffered for sins once for all, the righteous for the unrighteous, that he might bring you to God" (1 Pet 3:18). Peter here depicts Christ's substitutionary suffering and death for sinners—the righteous One died for the unrighteous ones to close the gap separating us from God. John adds, "There is no sin in him" (1 John 3:5), and "If anyone does sin, we have an advocate with the Father—Jesus Christ the righteous one" (1 John 2:1).

Jesus's sinlessness was a necessary prerequisite for his atoning death and resurrection. If he had sinned, he would not have been able to rescue us. But thanks be to God, he never sinned, but instead made full atonement so that we can know God now and forever.

Our Lord Dies for Us

Without the Son's incarnation and spotless life, we would not be saved, for the Son had to be a sinless man to die as our perfect substitute. But Jesus's incarnation and sinless life do not accomplish salvation; only Jesus's death and resurrection do that. Although Scripture joins his death and resurrection, and so should we, we will examine them separately to understand better what he did for us.

The prophet Isaiah foretells that the Servant of the Lord, whom we know to be Jesus, will rescue sinners by dying in their place. Four times Isa 53:5 says that his sufferings save us: he "was pierced because of our rebellion, crushed because of our iniquities; punishment for our peace was on him, and we are healed by his wounds." And v. 6 presents him as the sacrifice for sin on whom God places our iniquity.

The New Testament broadcasts the same message: "Even the Son of Man did not come to be served, but to serve, and to give his life as a ransom for many" (Mark 10:45). When the Son of God came from heaven, he deserved to be served by his creatures, but that is not why he came. Rather, he came to serve humankind, and the epitome of that service is his giving his life as the ransom price to free us from slavery to sin.

Jesus saves as the Lamb of God who takes away the sins of the world. The sacrificial system plays a vital role in the Old Testament. The various Levitical offerings prescribe the sacrifice of innumerable animals. Against this background, John the Baptist, when he sees Jesus approaching, proclaims, "Here is the Lamb of God, who takes away the sin of the world!" (John 1:29; see also v. 36). That is, Jesus's death is the culmination of all the Old Testament sacrifices and is universal in scope.

Paul commands, "[W]alk in love, as Christ also loved us and gave himself for us, a sacrificial and fragrant offering to God" (Eph 5:2). Christ's love is seen in his willingness to die for us. Paul describes Jesus's self-giving in terms of Old Testament sacrifice. As food offerings are sometimes described as "a pleasing aroma to the LORD" (Lev 1:9), so Paul describes Christ's priestly sacrifice of himself as "a sacrificial and fragrant offering to God," which God accepts.

With the imagery of Old Testament sacrifice, the writer to the Hebrews ascribes astounding results to Jesus's crucifixion: "By one offering he has perfected forever those who are sanctified" (Heb 10:14). Those whom Jesus saves are identifiable: they are the ones "who are sanctified," that is, who believe in Christ and are growing in practical holiness. So then, is their progress in the Christian life the basis for God's acceptance of them? Never, for "by one offering" Jesus "has perfected" them "forever." Jesus's single sacrifice replaces a million Old Testament animal sacrifices, and it makes perfect in God's sight all who trust Christ as Lord and Savior. And it does this "forever." Christ's blood, his atoning death, secures "eternal redemption" (9:12).

Peter also teaches that Jesus's death saves: "You were redeemed from your empty way of life inherited from your fathers, not with perishable things like silver or gold, but with the precious blood of Christ, like that of an unblemished and spotless lamb" (1 Pet 1:18–19). Redemption from sin requires payment of a steep price: "the precious blood of Christ." Christ is God's sacrificial Lamb, whose death ransoms believers once lost in sin and purchases us for God.

We have separated Christ's death and resurrection for the sake of our study, but we also must keep them together, as Scripture does (Mark 8:31; 9:31; 10:33–34; John 2:19; 10:17–18; Acts 2:22–24; Rom 4:25; 10:9–10; 1 Cor

15:3–4; 2 Cor 5:15; Phil 3:10; Heb 1:3; 1 Pet 1:11). Jesus's death and resurrection are the core of his saving work. They are distinct events and yet are inseparably joined.

Our Lord Rises from the Dead

Unlike other religious leaders who died, Jesus arose. Christians believe this, but few can tell how Jesus's resurrection saves them. Scripture comes to our aid. John teaches that believers already have eternal life and will experience it more fully in the age to come (John 3:36; 12:25). Why? Jesus explains: "Because I live, you will live too" (14:19). Jesus's resurrection saves because it brings us eternal life now and guarantees our everlasting life after we are raised from the dead.

Our divine-human Mediator saves us by his death *and* resurrection, as Paul explains: "If Christ has not been raised, your faith is worthless; you are still in your sins" (1 Cor 15:17). If Jesus was not raised, his death would lack atoning power, for he would not have overcome sin and the grave. But because he not only died for us but also lives as Conqueror over all our enemies, he saves us forever.

Jesus's resurrection is the cause of our being raised to eternal life: "since death came through a man, the resurrection of the dead also comes through a man. For just as in Adam all die, so also in Christ all will be made alive" (vv. 21–22). Paul contrasts the first and second Adams. Adam's sin in Eden brought death to the human race (Rom 5:12). Christ, "the last Adam," "the second man" (1 Cor 15:45, 47), brings resurrection to all who are joined to him by grace through faith. His resurrection saves in that it results in resurrection and everlasting life for all believers.

Paul declares, "[Christ] is also the head of the body, the church" (Col 1:18). As a human head controls its body, so Christ rules his church. Paul's next words are difficult at first: "He is the beginning" (v. 18). The beginning of what? His previous statement provides a clue: "everything was created by him, in heaven and on earth" (v. 16). This points us to Gen 1:1: "In *the beginning*, God created the heavens and the earth." Christ is Lord over creation because in the beginning he was God's agent in creating everything. He is Lord over his church because it is a part of God's re-creation. Jesus is the new beginning, the source of the church's eternal life. In what capacity does he play this role? As "the firstborn from the dead" (Col 1:18). It is Jesus's powerful resurrection from the dead that enables him to be Lord over the church, to rule it as head, and to give life to each of its members. Paul follows immediately with these words: "that in everything he might be preeminent" (v. 18 ESV). "Everything" corresponds to the two spheres just discussed: the creation (vv. 15–17) and the re-creation (v. 18), of which the church is part. Christ is Lord of all and Savior of his church by virtue of his death and resurrection.

Unlike Old Testament priests, who died and were replaced, Jesus is alive, and therefore "he holds his priesthood permanently" (Heb 7:24). This is "because he remains forever" as the risen One. "Therefore, he is able to save completely those who come to God through him, since he always lives to intercede for them" (v. 25). Jesus saves us forever because he continually presents his atoning sacrifice to the Father in heaven.

Jesus's resurrection is also the ground of the Holy Spirit's giving new life to us who are spiritually dead. According to the Father's "great mercy he has given us new birth into a living hope" (1 Pet 1:3). What is Jesus's role? We are born again "through the resurrection of Jesus Christ from the dead" (v. 3b). His resurrected life is the source of the eternal life that the Spirit applies to us.

Our Lord Ascends to Heaven

Jesus came from heaven to earth in the incarnation, and after he dies and arises, he ascends from earth to heaven (Acts 1:11). After saying that Jesus has ascended, Peter affirms that we must "know with certainty that God has made this Jesus, [who was] crucified, both Lord and Messiah" (2:36). Christ's ascension, then, confirms his identity. He truly is the Son of God, who comes into the world to save us and restore creation, and an indication of this is that after he rises from the dead, he ascends into heaven into God's presence to reign.

The ascension is also the prerequisite for the subsequent saving works of Christ: his session, Pentecost, intercession, and second coming. Christ has to ascend in order to sit down at the right hand of the Father, thereby beginning his heavenly session (Ps 110:1; Acts 2:33–36). By his ascension, then, Christ is able to take his place as King over all creation until the time when all things will be subjected to him. The ascension is also necessary for Christ to send the Spirit at Pentecost, as Jesus explains in John 16:7: "It is for your benefit that I go away, because if I don't go away the Counselor will not come to you. If I go, I will send him to you."

The ascension is essential for the completion of Christ's priestly work. It qualifies him for a greater priesthood and enables him to present in heaven the sacrifice he made on earth. By his ascension beyond the earthly realm, he is able to take his sacrifice into the heavenly sanctuary, of which the earthly temple is a shadow (Heb 8:15; 9:11–12, 23–24). Old Testament sacrifice is not completed by the slaying of the sacrificial offering but also involves the presentation of this offering before God (see Leviticus 1–7, 16). This is also true of the perfect sacrifice that Christ offers on the cross. Christ accomplishes this through his ascension, when he passes into heaven into the presence of God the Father and presents in the heavenly sanctuary what he has accomplished (Heb 6:19). After doing so, Christ sits down, indicating that his priestly work of earthly sacrifice and heavenly presentation is complete and perfect (10:12). As a result, because Christ presents his one perfect sacrifice before God, we are assured that his sacrificial blood purifies us and that our sins will never again separate us from God.

Christ ascends into heaven with the full human nature that he has during his incarnation (Acts 1:11). In heaven, Christ becomes our forerunner (Heb 6:19–20). Through Christ's ascension he does everything necessary to reestablish a close relationship between human beings and God. This is a source of great hope for us, because one of our own kind ascends to the right hand of God, guaranteeing that we will one day follow him there. In addition, the ascension enables Christ to present in heaven the sacrifice that he accomplishes on earth (Heb 9:11–12). For Christ enters "into heaven itself, so that he might now appear in the presence of God for us" (v. 24).

Our Lord Sits at God's Right Hand

Jesus's session is his sitting at God's right hand, the place of highest honor and authority. His session saves because from there he fulfills his threefold office of prophet, priest, and King, which is bestowed on him when he receives the Spirit at baptism. Jesus sits down as the great prophet. The risen, ascended, seated Christ pours out the Holy Spirit on the day of Pentecost in fulfillment of Joel's prophecy (Joel 2:28–32; Acts 2:33). He acts as a heavenly prophet who sends the Spirit to his disciples, enabling them to spread the word of his saving death and resurrection, fulfilling his prediction of Acts 1:8. Hebrews affirms the superiority of the Son-prophet to Old Testament mediators of special revelation (prophets and angels, Hebrews 1). Indeed, "in these last days, [God] has spoken to us by his Son" (Heb 1:2).

Jesus sits down as our great high priest: "After making purification for sins, he sat down at the right hand of the Majesty on high" (Heb 1:3). These words speak of the finality, perfection, and efficacy of the Son's sacrifice, as Hebrews later makes explicit. The Old Testament priests never sit in their service, "but this man, after offering one sacrifice for sins forever, sat down at the right hand of God" (10:12). As a result, amazingly, "by one offering he has perfected forever those who are sanctified" (v. 14). In fact, Christ, unlike any other priest, takes the fruits of his earthly priestly ministry permanently into God's heavenly presence (8:1–8).

Jesus sits down as the great King. In his Pentecost sermon, Peter interprets Christ's session as God's coronation of him as Lord and Christ (Acts 2:32–36). God displays his power in raising Christ from the dead and seating him at God's right hand. From here Christ makes immense power available to the church (Eph 1:19–23). Though Christ's session pertains to all three of his messianic offices, it pertains especially to his royal office. Jesus overcomes our foes and sits down at God's right hand (Heb 12:1–2). He triumphs over the evil powers and rules over them all at God's right hand. And his triumph gives us confidence that we too will triumph (1 Pet 3:21–22; Rev 3:21).

Our Lord Sends the Holy Spirit

Jesus's sending of the Spirit on the day of Pentecost is a part of his saving work. With word and actions he anticipates Pentecost for his disciples when "he breathed on them and said, 'Receive the Holy Spirit. If you forgive the sins of any, they are forgiven them; if you retain the sins of any, they are retained'" (John 20:22–23). Jesus thus joins his sending of the Spirit in newness and power with the forgiveness of sins, an important feature of the promised new covenant (Jer 31:34).

The work needed to ratify the new covenant is performed by Christ in his death and resurrection. But this good news is not broadcast until fifty days after his resurrection. Jesus, the Mediator of the new covenant, publicly heralds that covenant at Pentecost. He does this through the Holy Spirit, whom he pours out on his apostles.

Christ forms a new community, the New Testament church, when he gives the Spirit at Pentecost; this marks a great transition in redemptive history (Acts 2). And this affects believers' relationship with the Son and the Spirit. Faith in Christ is never so explicit. Only "now Jesus can be believed on as the risen, vindicated Lord."[7] And the Spirit comes with newness and power. This is because, "beginning with the Pentecost converts themselves, the receiving of the Spirit in full new-covenant blessing has been one aspect of their conversion and new birth."[8]

How are we to account for the fact that more people are saved during the week following Pentecost than in Jesus's entire three-and-a-half-year public ministry? By pointing to the Spirit of Christ filling and empowering the apostles and drawing their converts to Christ.

---

[7] Graham A. Cole, *He Who Gives Life: The Doctrine of the Holy Spirit*, Foundations of Evangelical Theology (Wheaton, IL: Crossway, 2007), 195.

[8] Cole, 196.

Our Lord Intercedes for Us

Another aspect of Jesus's saving work is his intercession, which includes his praying for us and presenting his sacrifice to God on our behalf. First, Christ's intercession involves prayer. Explaining the eternal security of our salvation, Paul asks who will bring a charge against God's chosen people. He answers that no one will, since God already declares us righteous and Christ will not condemn us either: "Christ Jesus is the one who died, but even more, has been raised; he also is at the right hand of God and intercedes for us" (Rom 8:34). Far from condemning us, Christ our Savior dies for us, is raised for us, and now prays for us at God's hand. And in doing so, he preserves our salvation.

Second, Christ's intercession includes presenting his completed sacrifice in heaven. Hebrews portrays Christ the priest as superior to Old Testament priests. In fact, unlike them, whose ministries were discontinued by death, he is a permanent priest because he arises from the dead and "remains forever" (Heb 7:24). For this reason, as Mediator he saves forever all who come to God through him because "he always lives to intercede for them" (v. 25). His atoning work, forever in God's presence, saves forever all who trust him for salvation.

Christ's intercession is the aspect of his priestly work that continues. Theologians discuss the finished work of Christ and thereby emphasize Christ's sacrifice on the cross. However, it would be a mistake to conclude that all of Christ's saving work is completed, for he actively intercedes for us now and will return to save those who are eagerly waiting for him (Heb 9:28). Christ performs ongoing work in heaven. He prays and advocates in the Father's presence.

Christ's priestly intercession is also effective. God the Father listens to his Son, and the Father always answers his requests (John 11:42). This means that Christ's intercessory prayers are successful. As Jesus prays for Peter (Luke 22:31–32), he prays for all his people, including us. He prays that his people will persevere until final salvation, and God answers his prayers. He always lives to make intercession for us (Heb 7:25). Jesus Christ is a perfect Savior.

Our Lord Returns in Victory

Christ's return is the grand finale of his saving work. When teaching about the sheep and the goats, Jesus promises great blessings to the saints at his return. Before he condemns the goats, he comforts the sheep: "Come, you who are blessed by my Father; inherit the kingdom prepared for you from the foundation of the world" (Matt 25:34). God is our Father, and all who trust his Son for salvation become God's children and receive an inheritance. God is also King, as is his Son, and believers' inheritance is "the kingdom prepared for" them from creation.

Jesus's return saves in that it results in our being with him and the Father: "In my Father's house are many rooms; if not, I would have told you. I am going away to prepare a place for you. If I go away and prepare a place for you, I will come again and take you to myself, so that where I am you may be also" (John 14:2–3). Here heaven is likened to a large house with many rooms. Jesus has returned to the Father's house to prepare a place for each of us, for the Father loves us, and we will be "home" in his heavenly presence.

Paul teaches the same truth when he clears up the Thessalonians' confusion concerning Jesus's return. They have the mistaken idea that their fellow believers who have died might miss out on final salvation. But Paul tells the Thessalonians that they are not to grieve, as the unsaved do, when their loved ones die. Those who believe in Christ will not miss out on final salvation, for Jesus will raise them from the grave. "Then we who are still alive, who are left, will be caught up together with them in the clouds to meet the Lord in the air, and so we will always be with the Lord" (1 Thess 4:17). Jesus's second coming brings salvation for living and deceased believers.

Paul declares that the Second Coming will mean glory for Christians. Though we live on earth, "our citizenship is in heaven, and we eagerly wait for a Savior from there, the Lord Jesus Christ. He will transform the body of our humble condition into the likeness of his glorious body, by the power that enables him to subject everything to himself" (Phil 3:20–21). Our bodies are lowly because they are subject to sickness and death. At his return Christ will exercise his great power and cause our lowly bodies to share his resurrection glory. It is no wonder, then, that Paul describes Christ's "appearing" as our "blessed hope" (Titus 2:13), for its anticipation fills us with joy.

Peter teaches us not to have mixed emotions about the Second Coming but urges us, "Set your hope completely on the grace to be brought to you at the revelation of Jesus Christ" (1 Pet 1:13). Christ's return will involve an outpouring of God's grace on us such as we have never seen.

The Bible ends on a joyful note, for Jesus says, "Look, I am coming soon, and my reward is with me to repay each person according to his work" (Rev 22:12). Jesus will come again and reward his people (and punish the wicked). John follows with a beatitude: "Blessed are those who wash their robes, so that they may have the right to the tree of life" (v. 14). Here again Scripture pronounces Christians as "blessed," filled with joy, at the end. Why? Because they are cleansed by the blood of the Lamb, and as a result have "the right to the tree of life." The tree representing eternal life with God is found in the garden of Eden and reappears at the end of the biblical story. God banishes Adam and Eve from Eden so they would not eat from the tree and live forever in a sinful state. But at the end all sin will be removed from us, and we will have free access to the tree, which symbolizes abundant life (v. 2).

Viewing the Events Together

A wide-angle lens helps us view all Christ's saving events together. The gospel focuses on the central two events: his death and resurrection. The rest are either preparations for or results of these two events. The eternal Son's incarnation is necessary for all that follows because God has to become a human being to live and die to rescue the lost. The arithmetic is simple: no incarnation, no redemption. Christ's sinless life is another essential precondition for his death and resurrection. Sin would disqualify Jesus from being our Savior.

Scripture is clear that our good works will never rescue us. But Jesus's works do. And his death in the place of sinners and triumphant resurrection are the nucleus of his saving accomplishments.

Five essential results of Jesus's death and resurrection follow. His ascension moves him, a genuine human being (who is also God), from the limited earthly sphere to the transcendent heavenly one. He sits down at the Father's right hand, signifying that he has made a full and finished atonement. As John the Baptist announces in all four Gospels, Christ, the anointed One, pours out the Holy Spirit on his church. In addition, Jesus continues to pray for us and to present his sacrifice in heaven to preserve us and our salvation. Christ's final saving event is his return, when he will subdue all our foes and raise us from the dead to eternal life with him on the new earth forever.

Christ's Saving Events

ESSENTIAL PREREQUISITES

1. The Incarnation of the Son of God: Luke 2:11; Gal 4:4–5; Heb 2:14–15
2. Jesus's Sinless Life: 2 Cor 5:21; Heb 4:15; 1 Pet 3:18

CORE EVENTS

1. Jesus's Death: Isa 53:5–6; Mark 10:45; Heb 9:12; 10:14; 1 Pet 1:18–19
2. Jesus's Resurrection: John 14:19; 1 Cor 15:17; Heb 7:24–25; 1 Pet 1:3

ESSENTIAL RESULTS

1. Jesus's Ascension: John 14:2–3; Acts 2:36; 5:31; Heb 6:19–20; 9:11–12, 24
2. Jesus's Session: Col 3:1–3; Heb 1:3; 10:11–14
3. Jesus's Sending of the Holy Spirit at Pentecost: John 20:22–23; Acts 1:8
4. Jesus's Intercession: Rom 8:34; Heb 7:25
5. Jesus's Second Coming: Matt 25:34; John 14:2–3; Phil 3:20–21; Titus 2:13; 1 Pet 1:13

Jesus's Saving Work in Church History

Events must be interpreted for us to understand them—even God's events. Graciously, God both accomplishes our salvation through Jesus's saving deeds and explains the meaning of those deeds with six major biblical pictures. Before we turn our attention to those, we will ponder theological pictures that the church has painted over the ages. These theological pictures, also called theories of the atonement, sometimes reflect the biblical pictures better than at other times. Regardless, we can learn as we consider and evaluate them.

In the early church in the West, the ransom-to-Satan view held sway. Gregory of Nyssa taught that Satan took possession of humanity in the fall; as a result, we became his slaves. Satan demanded Christ, weakened on the cross, as a ransom price for humans. But God deceived the devil, for hidden under Christ's humanity was his deity, which made him too powerful for Satan to hold. Christ not only freed the slaves but overcame the enemy. This flawed view contains some truth: Christ in death gave himself as "a ransom for many" (Mark 10:45). And Christ's death and victorious resurrection were directed at Satan and the rest of our enemies. But God did not deceive Satan, and Christ did not pay a ransom to him. Rather, Christ died to "destroy . . . the devil" (Heb 2:14) and "triumphed over" the demons (Col 2:15).

In the early church in the East, deification predominated. Eastern fathers viewed sin not primarily as bringing condemnation and guilt, as the West did, following Augustine. Rather, they viewed sin as bringing corruption and death. Unlike Western theologians, who concentrated on the death of Christ, Athanasius affirmed the cross but highlighted Christ's saving deeds of incarnation and resurrection. In becoming a man, dying as our representative, and especially rising from the grave, Christ gained eternal life for humans. Christ in his resurrection destroyed death. Those teaching deification often appealed to 2 Pet 1:4: God "has given us very great and precious promises, so that through them you may share in the divine nature." The church East and West was careful to maintain the distinction between the Creator and his creatures. Although the East did not teach that we become a part of God, deification sounds strange to our

ears. We come closest to it when teaching the final result of union with
Christ in his death and resurrection: we will partake of Christ's glory and
be transformed into his image.

In the Middle Ages, Anselm advanced understanding of the atonement by rejecting the ransom-to-Satan view. In its place he put the satisfaction view. Whereas the ransom-to-Satan view was directed toward the
devil, Anselm insisted that Christ's work was primarily directed to God.
He stated that the fall offended God's honor and that the Son of God had
to become a man to rectify the situation. Anselm thus underscored the
necessity of the incarnation for salvation. To save humanity, God faced
a dilemma: there must either be satisfaction or punishment. God chose
satisfaction, and the death of Jesus Christ, the *God*-man, had infinite
value and thus could render satisfaction to restore God's offended honor.
Anselm's advances included teaching the necessity of both the incarnation and the crucifixion and teaching that the cross was directed toward
God. The Reformers improved his view by teaching that God in Christ satisfied his justice, not primarily his honor. They rejected Anselm's dilemma
of satisfaction *or* justice and taught that God in the cross accomplished
satisfaction *through* punishment of Christ on the cross.

With Anselm, Abelard rejected the ransom-to-Satan theory. Against
Anselm, he taught the moral influence theory. He held that the cross was
not directed toward God but toward human beings. God could forgive
sinners apart from Christ's cross. There was no need for divine satisfaction, but of a change in humans. The main effects of sin were making us
ignorant and fearful of God. God sent his Son to live and to die to show
God's love for us and to remove our fear and ignorance of him. Although
Abelard taught other atonement themes, he interprets Rom 3:25–26 in
terms of the moral influence theory in his Romans commentary, a mature
work. Scripture certainly teaches that the cross is God's great revelation
of his love for us (Rom 5:8; 1 John 4:10). But God's main purpose in sending Christ was not to change us within. Instead, the cross satisfies God's
justice, defeats our enemies, and makes atonement for our sins.

In the sixteenth century, the Reformers Luther and Calvin taught
many atonement motifs. They held that as high priest, Christ in crucifixion offered the perfect sacrifice to God (John 1:29). They taught that his

death also accomplished reconciliation (Rom 5:10) and redemption (Eph 1:7). But their favorite atonement pictures were Christus Victor and penal substitution. As Christus Victor, Christ our champion in his death and resurrection overcame our enemies of sin, death, and Satan. In penal substitution, Christ our substitute gave himself in death to rescue us by paying the penalty we lawbreakers could not pay (Col 2:14). These Reformers' work on the atonement was characteristic of the Reformation, which turned to Scripture and produced biblical preaching, biblical commentaries, biblical worship, and theology based on the Bible.

Late in the sixteenth century, Faustus Socinus rejected Luther and Calvin's view of the atonement as penal substitution. His theology had a weak foundation, for he rejected the Trinity, the deity of Christ, and the idea that Adam's sin made us guilty and corrupt. When discussing Christ's work, Socinus denied that God's justice had to be satisfied. He set God's justice against his love, rejecting the former for the latter. He said that if God punishes sin, he does not forgive it. Socinus thus denied that God's justice is satisfied in the cross and instead affirmed that the cross is the revelation of God's love. Christ did not die for our sins, he felt, because in love God freely forgives without atonement. Christ is the great example, whose death showed perfect love for God. The man Jesus's devotion to God on the cross moves us to repentance and to imitate Jesus's love in order for us to be saved from annihilation (Socinus rejected eternal punishment). His views greatly influenced later Unitarianism. He erred in rejecting the Trinity, Christ's deity, our condemnation in Adam, and the New Testament's main message—Christ died for our sins to save us.

In the first half of the seventeenth century, Hugo Grotius promoted the governmental (or Grotian) view of the atonement. He outwardly agreed with the Reformers by asserting that Christ had to die for God in justice to save sinners. Although Grotius's language seems to follow the Reformation, his teaching did not. He held that God is governor, not judge. As ruler, God can cancel or change the law. Socinus held that God canceled it, and Grotius held that he changed it. God punishes sin in Christ, not because his justice demands it, but because it is in the best interests of his moral government. Christ died to meet the requirements of God's relaxed law. Christ did not die as our penal substitute, but as a substitute for a penalty. His death does not make atonement, but shows God's hatred toward sin. It does not pay the penalty that sin deserves, but shows what sin deserves. Grotius's theory thus reduces to a sophisticated presentation of Christ dying as an example, a penal example, but an example nonetheless. Though it is true that Christ's death is an example and that it upholds God's moral government, it does much more. It propitiates God, defeats our powerful enemies, and delivers us from hell.

In the nineteenth and twentieth centuries, liberalism sought to make Christianity acceptable to modern people. Thus, it often adopted the moral influence theory of the atonement and presented Christ as our example. R. S. Franks followed in the train of Abelard and set forth the moral influence theory as the heart of the New Testament's teaching concerning Christ's saving work. Franks held that Paul had other ideas but his primary one was that Christ's death revealed God's love for sinners. Franks also followed Abelard in the doctrine of sin, for he defined sin as distrust of God's love. The main accomplishment of Christ's cross, in his view, is to move us to trust God. Christ's powerful love, revealed on the cross as nowhere else, draws us into God's love too. Christ is God's prime example of love, which we must imitate. Our evaluation of Franks is similar to our evaluation of Abelard, his medieval hero. Christ's death reveals God's love, but it does so as God's means of making atonement for those unable to rescue themselves. Christ is first of all Lord and Savior, and then, an example for Christians.

Evangelicalism has worked hard to understand Scripture's teaching concerning Christ's saving accomplishment. We will summarize some of its ideas in light of previous historical theology. Evangelicals reject the ransom-to-Satan theory of the early church. They accept Christ as Redeemer, "who gave himself as a ransom for all" (1 Tim 2:6). They also teach that Christ is our mighty victor, who in his death and resurrection routed our enemies (sin, death, hell, and the devil). Evangelicalism has not accepted deification, but with it, longs for final union with Christ, when all believers will be conformed to Christ's glory. With Anselm, evangelicals hold that Christ's incarnation and death are necessary for salvation. Anselm's pointing of the cross toward God to make satisfaction influenced the Reformers' understanding of penal substitution, which has been the dominant teaching on Christ's atonement among evangelicals. They follow Luther and Calvin in teaching that God's justice was satisfied by Christ's enduring the cross. Evangelicals reject liberalism's view that the cross was mainly a revelation of God's love. It was a great revelation of God's love because through it God satisfied his justice, overthrew our enemies, and delivered us from the punishment that our sins deserved.

We do not have to understand these theories of the atonement in competition with one another. Rather, we prefer to view most of them as supplemental to the results of studying Christ's saving work from six major biblical vantage points.

Jesus's Saving Work in Pictures

Scripture paints six main pictures to show what Jesus has done to rescue us:[9]

- Jesus Is Our Substitute
- Jesus Is Our Victor
- Jesus Is Our Sacrifice
- Jesus Is Our New Adam
- Jesus Is Our Redeemer
- Jesus Is Our Reconciler

Jesus Is Our Substitute

The most foundational of these pictures involves penal substitution. By *penal substitution*, we mean that the Lord Jesus willingly suffers the penalty that we sinners deserve when he dies to satisfy divine justice. Jesus loves us and gives himself for us by dying in our place and taking our punishment to save us from hell.

---

[9] We follow the structure and condense the more thorough treatment in Peterson, *Salvation Accomplished by the Son*, 273–549.

Isaiah 53

The prophet Isaiah powerfully predicts the substitutionary atoning sacrifice of the Christ. Isaiah foretells the coming of the righteous Servant of the Lord, who willingly suffers and dies in the place of others, enduring the suffering they deserve:

> He was pierced because of our rebellion,
> crushed because of our iniquities;
> punishment for our peace was on him,
> and we are healed by his wounds. . . .
> The Lord has punished him for the iniquity of us all. . . .
> For he was cut off from the land of the living;
> he was struck because of my people's rebellion. . . .
> and he will carry their iniquities. (vv. 5–6, 8, 11)

Christopher Wright is correct:

> [The Servant's] vicarious suffering and death will "bear" the iniquities of those who, having thought he was suffering under the judgment of God for his own sin, now realize that it was actually *our* sorrows, transgressions, iniquities and sins that were laid upon him. The language of sacrificial substitution and of vicarious sin-bearing runs through Isaiah 53 unmistakeably.[10]

Romans 3:25–26

God saves believing sinners "freely by his grace" (Rom 3:24) through Christ's death as a redemption and propitiation. Paul mentions the former and develops the latter. Propitiation and expiation are both ways of depicting Jesus's cross, but they are pointed in different directions and have different aims. Propitiation is directed toward God, while expiation is directed toward sin. Propitiation is the turning away of God's wrath; expiation is the putting away of sin.

---

[10] Christopher J. H. Wright, "Atonement in the Old Testament," in *The Atonement Debate*, ed. Derek Tidball, David Hilborn, and Justin Thacker (Grand Rapids: Zondervan, 2008), 80, italics in original.

God presents Christ publicly as a propitiation in his violent death. He did so "to demonstrate his righteousness, because in his restraint God passed over the sins previously committed" (v. 25). God forgives Old Testament believers who present sacrifices (through priests). In so doing, he "passed over" those sins without actually making atonement because animal blood was insufficient. Rather, the blood shed portrays the gospel for believing worshippers. God forgives them, writing spiritual IOUs to himself, so to speak.

But if we are to be saved, God actually has to make atonement. He does this by presenting his Son as a propitiation, as Paul explains: "God presented [Jesus] to demonstrate his righteousness at the present time, so that he would be righteous and declare righteous the one who has faith in Jesus" (v. 26). God punishes Christ with the punishment that we deserve, thereby satisfying his justice. The sinless Son of God endures God's wrath on the cross to save us. God thus justly declares righteous all who trust Jesus, for he pays our penalty. In this way, God maintains his moral integrity and rescues those who cannot rescue themselves.

Some argue that the word in Rom 3:25 should be rendered "means of expiation," not "propitiation."[11] The latter is considered unworthy of God and pagan in origin, involving ideas of vengeful deities demanding blood. Scripture does teach that Christ's death accomplishes the expiation of sin (in, e.g., Heb 9:26). Though that is not debated, the meaning of *hilasterion* in Rom 3:25 is. We must distinguish the biblical portrayal of propitiation from pagan notions. In paganism, humans take the initiative to make fickle gods willing to forgive by appeasing (propitiating) them through various means. In Scripture, a loving and holy God takes the initiative and

---

[11] C. H. Dodd, *The Bible and the Greeks* (London: Hodder & Stoughton, 1935). This is a reprint of an earlier article, "*Hilasterion*, Its Cognates, Derivatives and Synonyms in the Septuagint," *Journal of Theological Studies* 32 (1931): 352–60. The words are *hilasterion* (Rom 3:25), *hilaskesthai* (Heb 2:17), and *hilasmos* (1 John 2:2; 4:10). For cases for propitiation, see Leon Morris, *The Apostolic Preaching of the Cross*, 3rd ed. (Grand Rapids: Eerdmans, 1965), 155–78; and Roger Nicole, "C. H. Dodd and the Doctrine of Propitiation," *Westminster Theological Journal* 17 (1955): 117–57.

propitiates his own justice by bearing the brunt of his wrath against sin to forgive his rebellious creatures freely.

For two reasons we take *hilasterion* in Rom 3:25 to mean propitiation, not expiation. First is Paul's argument in Romans. The gospel is the revelation of God's saving righteousness (1:16–17). God reveals his wrath against sinners (1:18–3:20). In 3:21 Paul revisits his theme of God's saving righteousness. But if verses 25–26 do not teach that God's wrath is satisfied in Christ's cross, then where does the wrath of 1:18–3:20 go? How do believers "have peace with God through our Lord Jesus Christ" (5:1) if God does not deal with his holy hatred of sin? Douglas Moo answers: "When to the linguistic evidence we add the evidence of the context of Rom. 1–3, where the wrath of God is an overarching theme (1:18; cf. 2:5), the conclusion that *hilasterion* includes reference to the turning away of God's wrath is inescapable."[12]

Second, Rom 3:25–26 teaches propitiation and not expiation due to the meaning of these very verses. Consider the redemptive historical difference between "the sins previously committed" and "the present time" (vv. 25–26). God exhibits Jesus as a *hilasterion* in his blood because in mercy he "passed over" former sins (v. 25). Until Jesus's death, God forgives sins without actually making atonement for them. The animal sacrifices depict the gospel, and God forgives Old Testament saints (e.g., Ps 103:12). But "it is impossible for the blood of bulls and goats to take away sins" (Heb 10:4). In his patience God forgives Old Testament believers on the basis of Christ's work to come. Before that, the sacrifices anticipate the atonement through Christ's blood. This is what Christ does "at the present time." It is necessary for Christ to die in order for God to maintain his moral integrity, to settle accounts he had made with himself before Christ's death.

Therefore, verses 25–26 say, "God put forward [Christ Jesus] as a propitiation by his blood . . . to show God's righteousness," and "It was to show his righteousness at the present time, so that he might be just and the justifier of the one who has faith in Jesus" (ESV). Though the meaning

---

[12] Douglas J. Moo, *The Epistle to the Romans*, New International Commentary on the New Testament (Grand Rapids: Eerdmans, 1996), 235.

of "righteousness" is debated, Moo argues convincingly that here "it means God's 'consistency' in always acting in accordance with his character."[13]

The problem is not what is so easily assumed today: how could a loving God condemn anyone? Genesis 1–3 and Romans 1–3 easily answer that question. A loving and holy God could condemn the world for its rebellion. The biblical problem is more difficult: how could a loving and holy God maintain his moral integrity and pardon sinners? The answer is by displaying Christ "as a propitiation in his blood." God settles accounts accumulated in the Old Testament. He satisfies his holy anger against sin by pouring out that wrath on Christ, who willingly gives himself for his people.[14]

D. A. Carson also concludes that Rom 3:25–26 speaks of penal substitution:

> In short, Romans 3:25–26 makes a glorious contribution to Christian understanding of the "internal" mechanism of the atonement. It explains the need for Christ's propitiating sacrifice in terms of the just requirements of God's holy character. This reading not only follows the exegesis carefully, but it brings the whole of the argument from Romans 1:18 on into gentle cohesion.[15]

GALATIANS 3:10–14

Paul is quick to describe the poison of sin and even quicker to offer its antidote, as he does in Galatians 3. The passage begins and ends with blessing (vv. 7, 14); in between are five occurrences of cursing. Paul specifies what he means by "curse": it is the threat of the punishment that all lawbreakers deserve. "Everyone who does not do everything written in the book of the law is cursed" (v. 10).

Within this context of blessing and curse, Paul speaks of Christ's atoning death: "Christ redeemed us from the curse of the law by becoming a

---

[13] Moo, *The Epistle to the Romans*, 240. See his discussion beginning on page 237.

[14] See the excellent treatment of this passage by D. A. Carson, "Atonement in Romans 3:21–26," in *The Glory of the Atonement: Biblical, Theological, and Practical Perspectives*, ed. Charles E. Hill and Frank A. James III (Downers Grove, IL: InterVarsity Press, 2004), 119–39.

[15] Carson, 138.

curse for us" (v. 13). This is a strong statement of Christ's being our legal penal substitute, as Christ delivers sinners from the law's threat of punishment *by becoming* a curse for them!

Paul demonstrates that Christ dies the death of an accursed man by citing Deut 21:23, which curses the executed person whose body is left hanging on a tree "because it is written, 'Cursed is everyone who is hung on a tree'" (Gal 3:13). Christ takes the penalty that we lawbreakers deserved— he becomes a curse—that we might gain the blessing of eternal life. He dies an accursed death on the tree to rescue us from the punishment of the law.

Paul's words need to be interpreted in light of his own experience. Before his conversion, Deut 21:23 convinced him that Jesus could not be the Messiah, for his death shows he is cursed by God and this precludes him from being the Messiah. Paul, however, comes to a radical new understanding of Deut 21:23 and Jesus in light of the resurrection. Gordon Fee explains: "What he came to realize, as the argument in Gal. 3:10–14 indicates, is that Christ's having been hanged on a cross did indeed involve God's curse but not on Christ himself. Rather, the whole human race, in its sin and rebellion against the eternal God, came under God's curse and in effect was hung on the cross through the one perfect sacrifice."[16]

Paul defines the blessing as the fulfillment of the covenant promise that God made to Abraham: "All the nations will be blessed through you" (Gal 3:8; citing Gen 12:3). Paul views this promise as fulfilled in the gospel coming to the Gentiles: he writes that Christ died for us so "that the blessing of Abraham would come to the Gentiles by Christ Jesus" (Gal 3:14). Then he describes an aspect of that blessing: "so that we could receive the promised Spirit through faith" (v. 14b). The blessings of the Abrahamic covenant culminate in the blessings of the gospel, including a relationship with God through Christ, eternal life, receiving the Holy Spirit, and so on.

COLOSSIANS 2:14

We were morally unclean, "dead in . . . the uncircumcision of" our "flesh" (Col 2:13). God's cure? Forgiveness (v. 13b). But how does God forgive us

---

[16] Gordon D. Fee, *Pauline Christology: An Exegetical-Theological Study* (Peabody, MA: Hendrickson, 2007), 535.

all our trespasses? Paul answers: "he erased the certificate of debt, with its obligations" (v. 14). "Certificate of debt" translates *cheirographon*, which "refers literally to something that is written by hand and more specifically to the certificate of indebtedness issued by the debtor in his or her own hand as an acknowledgment of debt," as Margaret MacDonald explains.[17] Paul says that the record of debt opposes us "with its obligations." The same expression appears in Eph 2:15, where it is rendered "the law consisting of commands and expressed in regulations." This shows that the expression refers to the Ten Commandments.

We all sign, so to speak, a handwritten note confessing our breaking of the commandments. This record of debt, with its legal demands, "was against us" because it exposes us as guilty lawbreakers; it condemns us. But Paul says that God forgives us: "he erased the certificate of debt, with its obligations" (Col 2:14). The word "erased" here means to blot out or remove. Paul does not say that God merely overlooks our disobedience to the commandments and forgives us, as his next words reveal: God "has taken it away by nailing it to the cross" (v. 14c).

Paul draws imagery from the Roman practice of nailing to crosses the charges against those being executed, as occurred on Jesus's cross (John 19:19). Moo explains: "In causing him to be nailed to the cross, God . . . has provided the full cancellation of the debt of obedience that we had incurred. Christ took upon himself the penalty that we were under because of our disobedience, and his death fully satisfied God's necessary demand for due punishment of that disobedience."[18] Paul thus paints a vivid picture of penal substitution.

1 PETER 3:18

After exhorting believers to be willing to suffer for doing good, Peter speaks of Christ's suffering in a forthright manner: "For Christ also suffered for sins once for all, the righteous for the unrighteous, that he might bring you

---

[17] Margaret Y. MacDonald, *Colossians and Ephesians*, Sacra Pagina Series (Collegeville, MN: Liturgical Press, 2000), 17:102.

[18] Douglas J. Moo, *The Letters to the Colossians and to Philemon*, Pillar New Testament Commentary (Grand Rapids: Eerdmans, 2008), 211–12.

to God" (1 Pet 3:18). Jesus's call for Christians to suffer is a call to follow in his steps, for he suffers first. As Peter says earlier, "Christ also suffered for you, leaving you an example, that you should follow in his steps" (2:21).

So, there is a sense in which Christ's suffering is similar to ours. But more important, it is unlike ours in at least two ways. First, he suffers "once," and his suffering is unique. The writer to the Hebrews shows the superiority of Christ's sacrifice to those of the Old Testament: "Every priest stands day after day ministering and offering the same sacrifices time after time, which can never take away sins. But this man, after offering one sacrifice for sins forever, sat down at the right hand of God" (10:11–12).

Second, and more important, unlike our suffering, Christ's is redemptive. "Christ also suffered for sins once for all." Peter explains: "the righteous for the unrighteous" (1 Pet 3:18). Literally, the words read this way: "the righteous one for the unrighteous ones." Jesus dies in the place of sinners, as Peter Davids observes: "Christ's substitutionary death for those who deserved death comes across clearly."[19]

The apostle tells the purpose of Christ's death: "that he might bring you to God" (v. 18). Christ dies to bring to God those who are far away from him. He, our substitute, dies as Mediator of the new covenant to bridge the gulf between God and us and to lead us into the presence of the Father.[20]

1 John 4:10

John teaches the idea of propitiation in a great biblical passage on God's love. He encourages his readers to love one another because God is love and new life shows itself in love for fellow believers (1 John 4:7). The converse is also true: a lack of love is a bad sign, because God is love (v. 8). If we ask how God shows his love supremely, John answers: "God's love was revealed among us in this way: God sent his one and only Son into the world so that we might live through him" (v. 9).

---

[19] Peter H. Davids, *The First Epistle of Peter*, New International Commentary on the New Testament (Grand Rapids: Eerdmans, 1990), 136.

[20] Davids, 136, helped us.

But in what way does Christ show God's love? John replies: "In this is love, not that we have loved God but that he loved us and sent his Son to be the propitiation for our sins" (v. 10 ESV). This is the fourth occurrence of "propitiation" in the New Testament (following Rom 3:25; Heb 2:17; and 1 John 2:2). Here John uses the term to define God's love. James Denney's words are helpful:

> So far from finding any kind of contrast between love and propitiation, the apostle can convey no idea of love to anyone except by pointing to the propitiation—love is what is manifested there; and he can give no account of propitiation but by saying, "Behold what manner of love." For him, to say "God is love" is exactly the same as to say, "God has in His Son made atonement for the sin of the world."[21]

John Stott underlines the distinguishing features of a biblical understanding of propitiation: "It is God himself who in holy wrath needs to be propitiated, God himself who in holy love undertook to do the propitiating, and God himself who in the person of his Son died for the propitiation of our sins."[22]

Jesus Is Our Victor

Voices from the Global Church: John Mbiti

Mbiti from Kenya said, "The greatest need among African peoples is to see, to know, and to experience Jesus Christ as the victor over the powers and forces from which Africa knows no means of deliverance."[23]

---

[21] James Denney, *The Death of Christ* (London: Hodder and Stoughton, 1911), 152, cited in I. Howard Marshall, *The Epistles of John* (Grand Rapids: Eerdmans, 1978), 215.

[22] John R. W. Stott, *The Cross of Christ* (Downers Grove, IL: InterVarsity, 1986), 173–75.

[23] Timothy C. Tennent, *Theology in the Context of World Christianity* (Grand Rapids: Zondervan, 2007), 116, citing "Some African Concepts of Christology," *Christ and the Younger Churches*, ed. Georg F. Vicedom (London: SPCK, 1972), 53.

Jesus is our mighty champion, who overpowers enemies much too powerful for us. Sin, death, hell, the devil, and demons are all dedicated to our demise. Even all God's people together could not defeat these powerful foes. But the Son of God becomes a human being and accomplishes that very feat. This is known as the Christus Victor theme of Christ's work.[24]

COLOSSIANS 2:15

Paul writes, "[Christ] disarmed the rulers and authorities and disgraced them publicly; he triumphed over them in him" (Col 2:15) The apostle here speaks of Christus Victor. The apostle portrays God as the mighty Conqueror, who through Christ's cross routes and disgraces the demons. The imagery comes from the triumphal Roman military procession in which, during a lavish parade, the victorious Roman army would march ahead of its defeated foes—including the defeated king and some surviving enemy warriors—through the streets of Rome, to cheers for the victors and jeers for the defeated (see 2 Cor 2:13–14).[25]

Paul writes that Christ's triumph is related to how he "disarmed" the rulers and authorities (Col 2:15). This word means "stripped," and when used of human warriors, refers to the conquered being stripped of either clothes or weapons. In the former case, the emphasis is on embarrassment; in the latter, on subjection. It comes down to a matter of emphasis, because each idea implies the other: for the conquered are humiliated and weaponless. And this is the same for the conquered demons: they are embarrassed and powerless.

God in Christ "disgraced" the defeated spiritual powers "publicly" (v. 15). God shames the demons when "he triumphed over them in him"

---

[24] The name comes from Gustaf Aulén's *Christus Victor: An Historical Study of the Three Main Types of the Idea of the Atonement*, trans. A. G. Hebert (New York: Macmillan, 1931, 1969). For an excellent survey of views/theories of the atonement, see Erickson, *Christian Theology*, 800–17 (see chap. 1, n. 18). For major views on the extent of the atonement, see Andrew David Naselli and Mark A. Snoeberger, ed., *Perspectives on the Extent of the Atonement: Three Views* (Nashville: B&H, 2015).

[25] We received help from Scott Hafemann's note in the *ESV Study Bible* (Wheaton, IL: Crossway, 2008), on 2 Cor 2:14 (p. 2226).

(v. 15b). God leads a triumphal procession over the evil powers; he routes them in Christ and his saving work.

Thus, Christ our champion defeats the spiritual forces of evil in the heavenly places by his cross. What is the implied connection between Col 2:14 and 2:15? By nailing our bond of indebtedness to Christ's cross (v. 14), God defeats the demons (v. 15), as F. F. Bruce notes:

> Not only has he blotted out the record of . . . indebtedness but he has subjugated those powers whose possession of the damning indictment was a means of controlling [us]. The very instrument of disgrace and death by which the hostile forces thought they had him in their grasp and had conquered him forever was turned on them into the instrument of their defeat and disablement.[26]

That is, the Christus Victor motif in v. 15 is grounded on penal substitution in v. 14. Christ our substitute is also our victor.

HEBREWS 2:14–15

Hebrews combines the incarnation and Christ's work as a colossal victory: "Since the children have flesh and blood in common, Jesus also shared in these, so that through his death he might destroy the one holding the power of death—that is, the devil—and free those who were held in slavery all their lives by the fear of death" (Heb 2:14–15). Christ's crucifixion routs the devil and liberates believers from his power.

This theme of the atonement and resurrection appears in many other Scriptures.[27] This is Hebrews' principal Christus Victor passage. It begins with the incarnation (v. 14): the One who defeated the devil and delivers us is God and man in one person. Christ the mighty victor attains two goals: first, by dying he breaks the power of the devil, who held sway over death; and second, through this same death he rescues us who lived in bondage to the fear of judgment.

---

[26] Bruce, *The Epistles to the Colossians, to Philemon, and to the Ephesians*, 110–11 (see chap. 5, n. 10).

[27] These include Matt 12:22–29; John 12:31–33; 1 Cor 15:4, 54–57; Eph 1:19–22; 1 Pet 3:21–22; 1 John 4:4; Rev 3:21; 5:5; 12:11; 19:11–16.

First, Christ becomes incarnate so that "through his death he might destroy the one holding the power of death—that is, the devil" (v. 14). The devil and death are powerful foes. We are so familiar with the cross that we miss the irony of Christ's death: his seemingly shameful defeat constitutes a mighty victory! Nevertheless, appearances notwithstanding, Christ our victor's death vanquishes the evil one by already depriving him of his power and by one day resulting in his being cast into an eternal hell (Rev 20:10). Hughes comments:

> We should carefully consider *whose* death it was that achieved this triumph and *what kind of* death it was that he died. . . . The spectacle of the cross is not that of any man enduring the pains of death, but of the incarnate Son of God in his pure innocence suffering a death which is not his due. . . . In Christ, the Son of man and only law-keeper, dying in the place of man the guilty law-breaker, the justice and love of God prevail together.
>
> Thus the death of Christ for us was the defeat of the devil; but it is not the end of the story, for it was followed by his resurrection. . . . [T]he victory is Christ's and, as the next verse declares, he is indeed our all-powerful deliverer.[28]

Second, because Christ is our all-powerful deliverer, our victor, his death delivers us from death and hell: "Jesus also shared in these, so that through his death he might . . . free those who were held in slavery all their lives by the fear of death" (Heb 2:14–15). The devil "has the power of death" as the usurper who deceived Adam and Eve and occasioned the fall (v. 14 ESV). The "death" spoken of here is not only physical death but includes spiritual death, including the "fear" that "involves punishment" (1 John 4:18). Such fear of death enslaves those who do not know the Lord. Christ the Redeemer, through his death and resurrection, delivers from this bondage all who trust him for deliverance. He is our mighty champion.

---

[28] Philip Edgcumbe Hughes, *A Commentary on the Epistle to the Hebrews* (Grand Rapids: Eerdmans, 1977; repr., 1990), 112–13, italics in original.

Jesus Is Our Sacrifice

Hebrews 1:3

Hebrews 1 treats Christ's coronation as divine Davidic King, who sits at God's right hand. It begins by speaking of Christ as prophet (vv. 1–2). And although this section has only one sentence on Christ as priest, it is powerful: "After making purification for sins, he sat down at the right hand of the Majesty on high" (v. 3). Anticipating chapters 9 and 10, the author implies that Christ, our great high priest, renders Old Testament rites of purification obsolete.

The need for salvation is here viewed as defilement requiring cleansing or purification, which is central to Old Testament worship. And yet, according to Hebrews, the very repetition of the sacrifices bears witness to their lack of efficacy (10:1). Jeremiah foresees that the forgiveness of sins will be an essential mark of the new covenant (31:34). How will final purification be accomplished, and when will a day of complete forgiveness come? The answer to both questions lies in the work of Christ, our high priest.

As Hebrews later clarifies, "he did this once for all time when he offered himself" in death (7:27). In a characteristic contrast between old and new covenants, the author praises the purifying power of Christ's blood (9:13–14). But the writer does not wait to tell of the cleansing power of the Son of God's blood. He extols it at the beginning: "After making purification for sins, he sat down at the right hand of the Majesty on high" (1:3). The author will wait to draw out the implications of his opening statement of Christ's work, speaking of its finality and perfection. These are implied in the place Christ sits—at God's right hand. As Hughes states, "The description of the Son as being now seated signifies the completion of the work of purification. . . . His session, moreover, is 'on high'. . . . This is the seal of divine acceptance of his work of purification."[29]

Another astounding result of Christ's unique accomplishment is that, unlike Old Testament sacrifices considered in themselves, his is effective, as F. F. Bruce eloquently reminds us. Christ's death exhibits "the grace

---

[29] Hughes, *A Commentary on the Epistle to the Hebrews*, 47.

which has provided a remedy for the defilement of sin by a life freely offered up to God on our behalf. The underlying emphasis here . . . is that by making purification for sins the Son of God has accomplished something incapable of achievement by anyone else."[30]

HEBREWS 9:11–15

Unlike high priests of the old covenant, who went into a tent on earth yearly on the Day of Atonement, "Christ has appeared as a high priest of the good things that have come. In the greater and more perfect tabernacle not made with hands (that is, not of this creation), he entered the most holy place once for all time" (Heb 9:11–12). Christ, our high priest, enters heaven itself, the very presence of God. Christ goes into the true holy places in heaven, which the most holy place on earth typified (v. 12).

Furthermore, unlike the Levitical high priests, Christ approaches God not with animal blood "but by his own blood" (v. 12). His blood, his sacrificial death, is the antitype to which the Old Testament sacrifices point. Astoundingly, his self-offering, accomplished on earth and presented in heaven, secures "eternal redemption" (v. 12). Unlike the numerous and repeated sacrifices performed in the Old Testament, Christ's single sacrifice does all the work necessary to save his people forever.

Only here in Hebrews does Scripture teach that Christ sacrifices himself "through the eternal Spirit." Despite some disagreement, we believe this refers to the Holy Spirit and, as Lane says, "indicates what makes Christ's sacrifice absolute and final."[31] The results of Christ's Spirit-anointed self-offering are spelled out: to "cleanse our consciences from dead works so that we can serve the living God" (v. 14). Here "conscience" speaks of human beings' God-given faculty for distinguishing good and evil. The definitive sacrifice of Christ, the Mediator of the new covenant, fulfills Jeremiah's promise that the new covenant will involve a work on believers' "hearts" (Jer 31:33). Christ's atoning death cleanses

---

[30] F. F. Bruce, *The Epistle to the Hebrews*, New International Commentary on the New Testament (Grand Rapids: Eerdmans, 1964), 7.

[31] William L. Lane, *Hebrews 9–13*, Word Biblical Commentary (Dallas: Word, 1991), 240.

dirty consciences and renews hearts so that we are liberated to "serve the living God."

The author declares, "He is the mediator of a new covenant, so that those who are called might receive the promise of the eternal inheritance" (Heb 9:15). Because Christ mediates the new covenant and enters heaven itself to secure "eternal redemption" (v. 12), we who trust Christ "receive the promise of the eternal inheritance" (v. 15b). The next words astonish: "because a death has taken place for redemption from the transgressions committed under the first covenant" (v. 15c).

As we have seen, God ordains the Old Testament sacrificial system to provide forgiveness and purification for his people Israel. And yet "it is impossible for the blood of bulls and goats to take away sins" (10:4). So, God forgives and cleanses believing Israelites who trust him to do as he promises that the animal sacrifices would. But those sacrifices are not the basis for the people's forgiveness and cleansing. They instead look forward to "the Lamb of God, who takes away the sin of the world" (John 1:29).

It is Christ, the Mediator of the new covenant, whose sacrifice redeems Old Testament saints "from the transgressions committed under the first covenant" (Heb 9:15). Christ's "redemptive sacrifice is retrospective in its effects and is valid for all who trusted God for the forgiveness of sins in ancient Israel."[32] And Christ's redemptive sacrifice is prospective, saving all who have believed since his crucifixion, all who believe now, and all who will believe in him.

Hebrews 10:10–14

Hebrews 10:5–10 argues that Christ's one sacrifice supersedes the many repeated Old Testament sacrifices; verses 11–14 argue that the one high priest of the new covenant supersedes the many priests of the old covenant. "Every priest stands day after day ministering and offering the same sacrifices time after time, which can never take away sins. But this man, after offering one sacrifice for sins forever, sat down at the right hand of God" (vv. 11–12).

---

[32] Lane, *Hebrews 9–13*, 328.

Note the dissimilarities. First, the posture of the unique priest of the new covenant contrasts dramatically with that of the old covenant priests. They stand, showing that their work is not done; Jesus sits, showing that his work is finished (vv. 11–12). Second, they "day after day" perform their priestly service (v. 11); he offers "one sacrifice for sins forever" (v. 12). Third, they offer "the same sacrifices time after time" (v. 11); Jesus offers "one sacrifice" (v. 12). Fourth, their sacrifices are not efficacious—they "can never take away sins" (v. 11); his sacrifice "has perfected forever" his people (v. 14).

The writer says that Christ, having made his unique and unrepeatable sacrifice and having sat at God's right hand, waits "until his enemies are made his footstool" (v. 13). His session does not render him inactive. Rather, it enables him to pursue actively his heavenly new covenant ministry of intercession and help. He will do so until, according to Ps 110:1, God overthrows his enemies forever. Christ sits as God's enthroned priest; there is no doubt as to the outcome, for Christ only waits for the certain, final overthrow of his foes.[33]

Hebrews 10:14 adds, "By one offering he has perfected forever those who are sanctified." This is a tremendous statement of the efficacy of Christ's sacrifice (along with 9:12, 15, 23; 10:10), combining two theological ideas. On the one hand, believers contribute nothing to their salvation—it is all of grace and all of Christ, for by his self-offering "he has perfected" them "forever." On the other hand, they are identifiable—those for whom this sacrifice has availed "are being sanctified." This verse, then, further emphasizes the decisive character of the completed work of the Mediator of the new covenant, as Hughes relates: "The sacrifice of himself in our place on the cross was *the sacrifice to end all sacrifices* (cf. v. 26 below)."[34] As a result, this verse ties Christ's work to his people so as to make their final salvation certain.

The author situates his discussion of the superiority of Christ's sacrifice and priesthood by reminding his readers of his citation (in 8:7–12) of Jeremiah's new covenant prophecy. The quotations and applications of

---

[33] Lane, *Hebrews 9–13*, 267.

[34] Hughes, *A Commentary on the Epistle to the Hebrews*, 400, italics added.

Jer 31:33–34 in the following four verses of Hebrews (10:15–18) accentu-ate two results of Christ's priestly sacrifice. By God's declaration, these are obedience from the heart—"I will put my laws on their hearts and write them on their minds"—and forgiveness of sins—"I will never again remember their sins and their lawless acts" (vv. 16–17). Verse 18 is an aphorism emphasizing forgiveness: "Now where there is forgiveness of these, there is no longer any offering for sin."

Christ is priest and sacrifice; his work on our behalf is incomparable. Present worship is preparation for eternal songs of praise sung to the Lamb, who was "slaughtered, and . . . purchased people for God . . . from every tribe and language and people and nation" (Rev 5:9).

Jesus Is Our New Adam

Jesus is our substitute, victor, and sacrifice, and he is our new Adam, who by his death and resurrection brings about the new creation. We must view this picture in light of Adam, the original creation, and the fall. Adam and Christ (the second and last Adam) greatly affect their respective peo-ple, as Paul explains:

> As through one trespass there is condemnation for everyone, so also through one righteous act there is justification leading to life for everyone. For just as through one man's disobedience the many were made sinners, so also through the one man's obedi-ence the many will be made righteous. (Rom 5:18–19)

Paul here contrasts the two Adams and their influence on their respective people. Adam's one trespass brings condemnation to all of his people. Christ is the second Adam, who through "one righteous act," his death on the cross, brings justification and eternal life to everyone who believes in him (v. 18). Adam's disobedience causes his descendants to be made sinners in God's sight. Christ's "becoming obedient to the point of death—even to death on a cross" (Phil 2:8) causes all who trust him to be made righteous in God's sight.

The two Adams bring death and life, respectively: "Since death came through a man, the resurrection of the dead also comes through a man. For just as in Adam all die, so also in Christ all will be made alive" (1 Cor 15:21–22). Adam's sin brings death, both physical and spiritual, into the world (Rom 5:12). Christ's obedience, however, brings eternal life to believers now and forever. To have eternal life now is to know the Father and the Son (John 17:3). To have eternal life forever is to be raised from the dead to enjoy life on the new earth with all the saints of all the ages.

In Colossians 1, while presenting Christ as head of his body, the church, Paul calls him "the beginning" (v. 18), an allusion to Scripture's first verse and the theme of creation. Paul has just set forth Christ as "the firstborn over all creation," that is, first in rank over the realm of creation because he was the Father's agent in the creation of everything (vv. 15–16).

Now, when speaking of the church, Paul calls Christ "the beginning" of the new creation as "the firstborn from the dead" (v. 18). As the Living One, the risen Christ inaugurates the new creation now ("already") because his resurrection life is the source of our new birth (1 Pet 1:3). Christ is also "the beginning" of the new creation, which will come in its fullness (which is "not yet") only at his return to establish the new heavens and new earth.

In sum, Christ, the second and last Adam, undoes what Adam did. Christ, in his death and resurrection, effects a new creation, which means new life for the spiritually dead who place faith in him now and their resurrection to eternal life at the end of the age. God's goal is that his beloved Son "might come to have first place in everything," creation and new creation (Col 1:18).

Jesus Is Our Redeemer

Redemption begins in the Old Testament with God's deliverance of the Israelites from Egyptian bondage and Isaiah's message of a new exodus for Jewish captives in Babylon (Exod 3:8; Isa 43:1–2). People in New Testament times also knew of redemption because of the custom of manumission, the freeing of slaves. In both Testaments, God takes the initiative in redeeming his people (Exod 6:6; Mark 10:45) out of love for them (Deut 4:37; Rev 1:5–6). Redemption depicts Christ as crucified

Redeemer freeing people from spiritual bondage to "the domain of darkness" (Col 1:13).

We all are in need of redemption, as Ps 49:7 declares: "Truly no man can ransom another, or give to God the price of his life" (ESV). We can therefore be grateful that "the Son of Man came . . . to give his life as a ransom for many" (Mark 10:45 ESV). Indeed, Christ is the Mediator of redemption: "there is one God and one mediator between God and humanity, the man Christ Jesus, who gave himself as a ransom for all" (1 Tim 2:5–6). At least nine passages portray Christ's death as the redemption price.[35]

John presents one such powerful passage, in which Christ, the Lamb, is worshipped (Rev 5:9–10):

> You are worthy to take the scroll and to open its seals, because you were slaughtered and you purchased people for God by your blood from every tribe and language and people and nation. You made them a kingdom and priests to our God, and they will reign on the earth.

Christ's violent death on the cross is the ransom price by which he purchases slaves to sin from every culture. He liberates all who trust him as Redeemer and makes them citizens of the kingdom of God and his representatives on earth.

Redemption highlights Christ's willingness to give himself to deliver us from bondage (1 Tim 2:5–6; Titus 2:13–14). Because Christ, the Mediator of redemption, voluntarily gives himself as a ransom for all, his death secures forgiveness for all who believe, and for this reason Scripture joins redemption and forgiveness (Eph 1:7; Col 1:13–14).

Redemption concerns the past, present, and future. It has to do with the past: "You are not your own, for you were bought at a price. So glorify God with your body" (1 Cor 6:19–20). It pertains to the present, for the Father "has rescued us from the domain of darkness and transferred us into the kingdom of the Son he loves. In him we have redemption, the

---

[35] Mark 10:45; Acts 20:28; 1 Cor 6:19–20; 7:23; 1 Tim 2:5–6; Heb 9:12; 1 Pet 1:18–19; Rev 1:5–6; 5:9–10.

forgiveness of sins" (Col 1:13–14). Redemption has to do with the future as well: "we ourselves who have the Spirit as the firstfruits—we also groan within ourselves, eagerly waiting for adoption, the redemption of our bodies" (Rom 8:23).

The results of redemption are far-reaching, for Christ redeems individuals (1 Cor 6:18–20), the church (Acts 20:28; Rev 5:9), and the cosmos (Rom 8:19–22). Christ's death frees us from bondage: "you are no longer a slave but a son, and if a son, then God has made you an heir" (Gal 4:7). At the same time, he purchases us for God so that now we belong to him (1 Cor 6:19–20; see also 7:23; Rev 14:4).

Jesus Is Our Reconciler

The sixth image of Christ's saving accomplishment is reconciliation, or peacemaking. Reconciliation is a picture of salvation drawn from the field of personal relations. The need for reconciliation is due to broken personal relationships. We need reconciliation because we are alienated from God, as Paul explains: "once you were alienated and hostile in your minds expressed in your evil actions" (Col 1:21). Our sins put us at odds with our Maker, and we could not make peace with him. As with every atonement motif (theme), here too God takes the saving initiative. Also, as with every motif, Christ is the Mediator of reconciliation: "he is our peace" (Eph 2:14).

How does he reconcile us to God? He dies for us and rises again. Paul is explicit: "If, while we were enemies, we were reconciled to God through the death of his Son, then how much more, having been reconciled, will we be saved by his life" (Rom 5:10). The apostle points to Jesus's death and resurrection ("life") as the basis for our peace with God. Paul communicates with an "if/then" clause: if, when we were God's enemies, he made us his friends by his Son's death, then, now that we are his friends, we can be certain that he will keep us saved by his Son's resurrection. In verse 9, Paul tells us what we shall be saved from: God's wrath.

Christ's work of reconciliation not only reconciles us to God but, even more basically, reconciles God to us. Although we alone are the blameworthy parties, our rebellion offends God. Graciously, he reconciles himself to us and us to him in the work of his Son, Jesus the peacemaker. In addition, when Christ reconciles us to him, he also reconciles us to one another. In this way he unites believing Jews and Gentiles to each other (Eph 2:12–17).

As a result of God's peacemaking work, he gives us "the ministry of reconciliation" (2 Cor 5:18). God "committed the message of reconciliation to us. Therefore, we are ambassadors for Christ, since God is making his appeal through us. We plead on Christ's behalf: 'Be reconciled to God'" (vv. 19–20).

Christ's work of reconciliation is greater yet. "God was pleased to have all his fullness" of deity "dwell in" Christ (Col 1:19; see also 2:9). God is also pleased through Christ "to reconcile everything to himself, whether things on earth or things in heaven, by making peace through his blood, shed on the cross" (1:20). Christ's work has cosmic implications. His reconciliation is God's means to remove the curse of the fall on creation and to bring in the new heavens and new earth.

Viewing the Pictures Together

We have explored six biblical pictures that express the meaning of Jesus's death and resurrection. These images do not describe six different things; instead, in six ways they describe the same thing: how Jesus's saving events rescue sinners. Each picture portrays our need for salvation, magnifies the person and work of Christ, and communicates interrelated results.

Three remarks are in order. First, each picture is important if we are to do justice to the scriptural breadth of Christ's work. Therefore, our familiarity with them will lead to new ways for us to present the gospel and make disciples. The pictures are tools in our ministerial toolboxes, various ones of which are well suited to particular occasions. Second, we put penal substitution first for a reason. It occupies pride of place among the pictures and helps explain the others. Third, the pictures are incomplete, for Scripture's presentation of Christ's work is inexhaustible.

Picture	Need	Christ's Person and Work	Results	Texts
Substitution	Guilt	<u>Substitute</u> pays penalty	Justification	Gal 3:13; Col 2:14
Victory	Foes	<u>Champion</u> defeats enemies	Victory	Col 2:15; Heb 2:14–15
Sacrifice	Filth	<u>High priest</u> offers himself	Purification	John 1:29; Heb 9:12, 15
Restoration	Death	<u>Second Adam</u> obeys	Life	Rom 5:18–19; 1 Cor 15:22
Redemption	Bondage	<u>Redeemer</u> frees slaves	Freedom	Mark 10:45; 1 Cor 6:19
Reconciliation	Alienation	<u>Mediator</u> makes peace	Peace	2 Cor 5:18–20; Col 1:20

Jesus's Three Offices

God gives his Old Testament people the three offices of prophet, priest, and king. He sends prophets as his mouthpieces to declare his word to his people. People do not volunteer to be prophets, but God chooses them. He sometimes enables his prophets to perform miraculous signs so that the people would believe their words. The way to tell a true prophet from a false one was (and still is) that the words of God's prophets always came to pass (Deut 18:22). When prophets make false prophecies, God instructs the people to stone them to death (v. 20). God's prophets include Moses, Elijah, Elisha, David, Isaiah, Jeremiah, Ezekiel, Daniel, and many others.

God chooses the tribe of Levi to serve him as priests, which involves taking care of all matters related to sacrifice, the tabernacle, and later the temple. God chooses Moses's brother, Aaron, to be Israel's first high priest

and for his descendants to follow him in that office. God carefully regulates the priesthood and sacrifices. He gives detailed instructions concerning priests' ordination, clothing, and how they are to perform each
type of sacrifice.

Jacob's dying prophecy foretells that kings will come from the tribe
of Judah (Gen 49:10). Israel sins not in wanting a human king but in their
motivation for wanting one (1 Samuel 8). God's plan was to rule over his
people through godly kings like David. Sadly, the kingdom divides after
David's son Solomon's death, and the northern kingdom of Israel largely
deserts God, devising its own idolatrous religion (1 Kings 12). Even the
southern kingdom of Judah, to which God gave the temple and many
prophets, has more unfaithful kings than faithful ones.

From the beginning God plans to unite the three offices in one person—the promised Messiah, who will be an unparalleled prophet, priest,
and King. How is this possible, however, because although prophets have
no tribal requirement, priests come from Levi and kings from Judah? How
could the promised One be from two tribes at once?

The Lord solves this problem by instituting a second priesthood. He
sends the mysterious figure Melchizedek, king of Salem and priest of God
Most High, to receive tithes from and to bless Abraham (Gen 14:18–20).
Melchizedek disappears from the biblical story as silently as he enters,
reappearing in Ps 110:4, where God says concerning the promised One,
"You are a priest forever according to the pattern of Melchizedek." This
is the first that we learn of such a priestly order, which is exclusive, for it
only has two members: Melchizedek and Jesus.

Hebrews identifies Jesus as the priest that Psalm 110 predicts. He,
like Melchizedek, is both a king and a priest, and is made a priest by
God's oath (Heb 5:5–6; 7:20–21). Uniquely, he makes final atonement for
sins in his death, and because of his resurrection remains a priest forever
(10:12–14; 7:24–25). This means he saves forever all who trust him as
Lord and Savior.

Jesus is the great prophet of God, who brings God's final word (Heb
1:1–2). He does this in his earthly ministry by calling his hearers to repentance and by preaching the good news of the kingdom of heaven (Matt
4:17, 23). At the Father's right hand, as heavenly prophet, he sends the

Spirit to empower the apostles to preach and write the New Testament (Acts 2:16–17, 33).

Jesus is the great King of kings, foretold by David, Isaiah, and others (2 Sam 7:14–17; Ps 89:29; Isa 9:6–7), and announced by the angel Gabriel to Mary (Luke 1:32–33). He reigns now in heaven and in the hearts and lives of his people (Eph 1:20–23), and he will reign over his people on the new earth forever (Rev 22:3; see also 19:16).

Jesus's Work and Its Directions

We have explored the events Jesus performed to rescue us, Scripture's pictures that interpret those events, and Christ's offices of prophet, priest, and King. Another way to view Christ's saving work is to consider the directions to which it points. His work accomplishes things pertaining to God, our foes, human beings in general, and the entire creation.[36]

Toward God

Most important, in three ways Christ's saving work is directed toward God and affects him. First, the Son propitiates God, as we explained when treating Rom 3:25–26 regarding penal substitution on pages 297–300.

Second, Christ reconciles God to us. Although Scripture always says that God reconciles us to himself and never that he reconciles himself to us, Scripture's theology implies this truth. We offend God; he does not offend us. But our rebellion offends him, so he also needs to be reconciled. Christ's death, then, reconciles God to us and also reconciles us to him. He makes peace between us. It is very gracious of God to work on our behalf in such a way.

Third, astonishingly, Christ atones for heaven itself, God's dwelling place. It sounds absurd for heaven to need cleansing. But not when we consider Old Testament background. The sacrifices on the Day of Atonement purifies both the people and the most holy place, which needs

---

[36] We received help from Peterson, *Salvation Accomplished by the Son*, 560–64.

atonement because Israel's sin defiles it, as God's words to the high priest tell:

> When he slaughters the male goat for the people's sin offering and brings its blood inside the curtain, he must do the same with its blood as he did with the bull's blood: He is to sprinkle it against the mercy seat and in front of it. He will make atonement for the most holy place in this way for all their sins because of the Israelites' impurities and rebellious acts. He will do the same for the tent of meeting that remains among them, because it is surrounded by their impurities. (Lev 16:15–16)

Hebrews draws a parallel between the high priest's making atonement for the most holy place and Christ's death purifying the heavenly sanctuary:

> According to the law almost everything is purified with blood, and without the shedding of blood there is no forgiveness. Therefore it was necessary for the copies of the things in the heavens to be purified with these sacrifices, but the heavenly things themselves to be purified with better sacrifices than these. For Christ did not enter a sanctuary made with hands (only a model of the true one) but into heaven itself, so that he might now appear in the presence of God for us. (Heb 9:22–24)

After his death and resurrection, Christ ascends and presents his finished work to purify the presence of God in heaven.

Toward Our Enemies

God meets all our needs and so "rescued us from the domain of darkness and transferred us into the kingdom of the Son he loves" (Col 1:13). The Divine Warrior of the Old Testament becomes incarnate in Jesus our champion, who dies and rises again to deliver us from our enemies. Because we treated this under the picture of Jesus's saving work as a mighty victory (see pages 304–7), here we summarize. Jesus, our divine-human champion, defeats our adversaries: Satan, demons, and the world system opposed to God, sin, death, and hell.

Toward Human Beings

Scripture richly testifies that Jesus has come to deliver us:

> He was pierced because of our rebellion, crushed because of our iniquities; punishment for our peace was on him, and we are healed by his wounds. (Isa 53:5)

> She will give birth to a son, and you are to name him Jesus, because he will save his people from their sins. (Matt 1:21)

> Believe in the Lord Jesus, and you will be saved—you and your household. (Acts 16:31)

> In him we have redemption through his blood, the forgiveness of our trespasses. (Eph 1:7)

> Christ Jesus came into the world to save sinners. (1 Tim 1:15)

> Jesus Christ the righteous one. . . . is the atoning sacrifice for our sins, and not only for ours, but also for those of the whole world. (1 John 2:1–2)

> To him who loves us and has set us free from our sins by his blood . . . (Rev 1:5)

Toward Heaven and Earth

Remarkably, Christ's work also rescues the heavens and the earth. God does not give up on his people or his planet, and he forecasts a new heaven and a new earth (Isa 65:17–25; 66:22–23; Matt 19:28; Rom 8:20–22; 2 Pet 3:10–13; Revelation 21–22). Adam's fall brings the curse on the earth, which Jesus's cross and empty tomb reverses. His saving work thus has universal and cosmic effects. Paul highlights this using the pictures of reconciliation and redemption: "God was pleased . . . to reconcile everything to himself, whether things on earth or things in heaven, by making peace through his blood, shed on the cross" (Col 1:19–20). In addition, Jesus's work redeems God's world: "the creation itself will also be set free from the bondage to decay into the glorious freedom of God's children" (Rom 8:21).

Conclusion

God is on a mission to bring salvation to the world. At the center of that mission is the gospel, and at the center of the gospel is Jesus's work of salvation. It is impossible to capture the greatness of that work. We have only hit some highlights, including Jesus's saving events; biblical pictures explaining the meaning of those events; Jesus's three offices of prophet, priest, and King; and the directions of Jesus's work. Jesus's death and resurrection are the most important events in history. They please God himself, rescue us from our sin, crush our enemies, and will usher in the new heavens and the new earth.

KEY TERMS

ascension

atonement

Christ as peacemaker

Christ's offices

Christus Victor

Day of Atonement

death of Christ

expiation

governmental view of the atonement

intercession

Jesus as King

Jesus as priest

Jesus as prophet

Mediator

new heavens and new earth

penal substitution

Pentecost

propitiation

ransom

reconciliation

redemption

restoration

resurrection of Christ

sacrifice

second Adam

Second Coming

session

sinlessness of Christ

substitution

RESOURCES FOR FURTHER STUDY

Allison, Gregg R. *Historical Theology: An Introduction to Christian Doctrine*. Grand Rapids: Zondervan, 2011, 389–429.

Cole, Graham A. *God the Peacemaker: How Atonement Brings Shalom*. New Studies in Biblical Theology. Downers Grove, IL: InterVarsity, 2009.

Demarest, Bruce A. *The Cross and Salvation: The Doctrine of Salvation.* Foundations of Evangelical Theology. Wheaton, IL: Crossway, 1997.

Gaffin, Richard. *Resurrection and Redemption,* 2nd ed. Phillipsburg, NJ: P&R, 1987.

Hill, Charles E., and Frank A. James III, eds. *The Glory of the Atonement: Biblical, Theological, and Practical Perspectives.* Downers Grove, IL: InterVarsity, 2004.

Jeffrey, Steve, Michael Ovey, and Andrew Sach. *Pierced for Our Transgressions: Recovering the Glory of Penal Substitution.* Wheaton, IL: Crossway, 2007.

Letham, Robert. *The Work of Christ.* Contours of Christian Theology. Downers Grove, IL: InterVarsity, 1993.

Marshall, I. Howard. *Aspects of the Atonement: Cross and Resurrection in the Reconciling of God and Humanity.* London: Paternoster, 2007.

Morris, Leon. *The Cross in the New Testament.* Grand Rapids: Eerdmans, 1965.

Murray, John. *Redemption Accomplished and Applied.* Grand Rapids: Eerdmans, 1955.

Peterson, David, ed. *Where Wrath and Mercy Meet: Proclaiming the Atonement Today.* Carlisle, Cumbria, UK: Paternoster, 2001.

Peterson, Robert A. *Salvation Accomplished by the Son: The Work of Christ.* Wheaton, IL: Crossway, 2012.

Stott, John R. W. *The Cross of Christ.* Downers Grove, IL: InterVarsity, 1986.

8

SALVATION

"For God so loved the world, that he gave his only Son, that whoever believes in him should not perish but have eternal life" (John 3:16 ESV). This monumental passage helps millions around the globe understand salvation. Clearly and wonderfully, in one verse we learn of God's love as the motivation for our salvation: "God so loved the world." We discover the ground of salvation: the coming of the Son of God, who dies and rises for us. We uncover a major aspect of our salvation: eternal life. We find our responsibility concerning salvation: to believe in Christ, which means to trust in him alone to save us. We also are amazed and overjoyed at the universal offer of salvation: because God loves the world, he invites all to come and receive the blessing of salvation—"whoever believes." That surely includes us! We then learn from verses that proceed and follow John 3:16 that we all need this salvation. No one will see or enter the kingdom of God without being born again, which is to receive new spiritual life from God (vv. 3–5). Indeed, all of us are already condemned (v. 18), live presently under the wrath of God (v. 36), and need the salvation found only in Jesus (vv. 12–18).

We find later in other passages that by God's grace and through our faith in Christ we have a new identity: we are joined spiritually to Christ and are recipients of new life. We are accepted as righteous because of Christ; we are God's sons and daughters; and we are being transformed into holy people. Our salvation changes everything: how we relate to and view God, ourselves, other believers, and those without Christ.

OBJECTIVES

- To help us appreciate union with Christ and its fruit of fellowship with him
- To bring us to realize that God takes the initiative in applying salvation
- To help us enjoy the results of salvation applied, expressed in various pictures
- To motivate us to look forward to final salvation as the culmination of God's gracious work

OUTLINE

Salvation in the Biblical Story
Salvation in Selected Passages
    Genesis 15
    Psalm 103
    Romans 8
    Ephesians 1:3–14
    1 Peter 1:3–9
We Are in Christ
We Are Chosen in Christ
We Are Called to Christ
We Are Alive in Christ
We Believe in Christ
We Are Righteous in Christ
We Are Adopted in Christ
We Are Holy in Christ
We Are Kept in Christ
We Are Glorious in Christ
We Are Saved for God's Glory
Key Terms
Resources for Further Study

Salvation in the Biblical Story

God creates Adam and Eve in his image as holy beings who know him and enjoy a peaceful relationship with him. But they rebel against his leadership. Yet God graciously takes the initiative to intervene, confronts them about their sin, and even promises a restoration. God calls Abraham from a family of idolaters (Josh 24:2–3) to belong to him (Gen 17:7). Abraham believes in the Lord, and God saves him (Gen 15:6). God also makes a covenant with Abraham, promising to give him the Promised Land, to make him into a great nation, and to bless all peoples though him (Gen 12:1–3). God changes the name of Abraham's grandson Jacob to Israel and from him brings twelve tribes. God makes these tribes his people and blesses them greatly. However, they continually rebel against the Lord and break his covenant, even though he sends them prophets to call them to repentance and to promise a future Redeemer (Psalm 110; Isa 52:13–53:12).

God sends the promised Redeemer, his Son, Jesus Christ (Gal 4:4–5). Christ lives a sinless life, dies in the place of sinners, and is raised to life. After he ascends to the Father, he sends the Holy Spirit to empower the church to spread the gospel. The Holy Spirit applies salvation to all believers by spiritually uniting them to Christ. The roots of our salvation go even deeper than these events. Indeed, God saves us "not according to our works, but according to his own purpose and grace, which was given to us in Christ Jesus before time began" (2 Tim 1:9). God the Father plans salvation; Jesus does the work necessary to save all who believe; and the Holy Spirit brings God's grace to bear on our lives as we trust Christ.

The apostles describe our salvation not only in black and white but in Technicolor. They paint many pictures to teach that our triune God rescues us, and we could not rescue ourselves. The overarching picture is union with Christ, God's joining believers to his Son by grace through faith so that all of his saving benefits become ours. When the Holy Spirit unites us spiritually to the Son, we receive many other benefits as well. The Father effectively summons us to the Son through the gospel (calling). The Spirit makes us alive spiritually (regeneration). He turns us from sin (repentance) and to the Son (faith) as he is offered in the gospel (conversion). The Father declares us righteous in his sight because of the Son's righteousness (justification). The Father places us into his family as his children (adoption). The Spirit purifies us, setting us apart from sin unto holiness once and for all and progressively working holiness into us (sanctification). The Father keeps us (preservation) so that we continue to walk with him (perseverance) and do not turn away from the Son (apostasy). Because the Father chooses us in the Son (election) and he dies and rises to save us, he will share his glory with us on the last day (glorification).

Salvation in Selected Passages

In the following passages we see that Abraham believes, and God regards him as righteous, showing that justification is by grace through faith. God commits himself to Abraham in a gracious covenant, promising him a land and a son through whom God will bless the world. Later, David calls God's people to remember the Lord's benefits, especially his immense love and total forgiveness.

Our Maker treats us frail humans as a caring father does his children. We in this fallen world are short-lived, but God's covenant love spans eternity toward those who reverence and obey him. Paul declares that God the Judge will not condemn those of us who are united to Christ by faith, for he dies in our place, the perfect sacrifice for sins. In gratitude, we are to live godly lives. The Holy Spirit gives us eternal life now and will raise our bodies in the future. By grace God the Father welcomes us into his family, as the Spirit of adoption enables us to call him "Father." The Spirit assures our hearts that we are God's children now, and our future adoption will be even greater! Adam and Eve's rebellion brings God's judgment on human beings and creation, but he will save the church and liberate his creation from its curse. Because believers have the Holy Spirit, we live in hope, longing for resurrection. God, who saves us freely by his grace, promises to keep us saved until the end. Indeed, nothing will ever separate us from Christ's love.

The three persons of the Trinity work in harmony to save us. The Father chooses us in Christ, the Son redeems us through his cross, and the Father seals us in union with Christ by giving us the Spirit as a guarantee of final salvation. The Father in mercy plans our regeneration, Jesus's resurrection provides its power, and the Holy Spirit makes us alive. God gives us a living hope of a magnificent inheritance that is enduring, holy, brilliant, and reserved for us. God's power keeps us saved, and his power works through faith. We rejoice in such a salvation, even though we may have to suffer, for God uses our suffering to prove the genuineness of our faith and to bring glory to himself at Jesus's return.

Genesis 15

In Genesis 15, God appears to Abram (who is known later as Abraham) in a vision and promises to be his shield and to reward him greatly (v. 1). Abram naturally asks God how this is possible, since he is elderly and childless. God promises that Abram's own son will be his heir. God takes him outside and promises that his offspring will be as numerous as the stars (vv. 3–5). The next sentence is striking: "Abram believed the LORD, and he credited it to him as righteousness" (v. 6; see also 14:22). Abram's only reason for believing this seemingly far-fetched claim is God's promise, but that is reason enough. Abram trusts God—who he is and, therefore, what he says. God promises, Abram believes, and God regards him as righteous. The New Testament often quotes this verse to show that justification has always been by faith, an active trust in God (Rom 1:16–17; 4:3, 22; Gal 3:6; Jas 2:23).

God declares to Abram, "I am the LORD," the covenant Lord who brings him out of Ur to give him a new land (Gen 15:7). God assures Abram of the Promised Land via a formal covenant (vv. 7–21) made in blood (vv. 9–10). God tells Abram how his descendants will come to possess the land (vv. 13–16), sealing the covenant by moving between the pieces of the sacrificed animals as "a smoking fire pot and a flaming torch" (v. 17). This covenant is a solemn promise that Abram will come to possess what God has shown him (12:6–9), and it crystallizes the relationship. The promised son, the Promised Land, and God's gracious covenant underline God's commitment to Abram. As the biblical story unfolds, it becomes increasingly clear that through the promised son/Son (Matt 1:1), the Promised Land, and the covenant with Abram, God will bless all nations (Gen 12:1–3; Matt 28:18–20).

Psalm 103

David begins and ends Psalm 103 with lavish praise (vv. 1, 22) extolling God's abundant benefits to his people. Human praise is insufficient, so David invites the angels (vv. 20–21) and "all [the LORD's] works" (v. 22) to join the chorus. God's people are to remember and celebrate his benefits (v. 2), especially his love and forgiveness.

God rules over everything in heaven and earth (v. 19). His dealings with rebellious Old Testament Israel and us today are righteous and loving, for he acts justly yet "is compassionate and gracious, slow to anger and abounding in faithful love" (vv. 6, 8). As a result, he does not deal with us as our sins deserve but shows us grace (v. 10). The result is forgiveness, which is total—"He forgives all your iniquity" (v. 3)—and permanent: "As far as the east is from the west, so far has he removed our transgressions from us" (v. 12).

God's great love is as amazing as his forgiveness: "As high as the heavens are above the earth, so great is his faithful love toward those who fear him" (v. 11). He deals with us compassionately, giving us good things for our enjoyment and rejuvenation (vv. 4–5). Because the Lord our Maker knows that we are frail, he treats us as a caring father does his children (vv. 13–14). Fallen human beings are short-lived—here today and gone tomorrow—and this makes the comparison with God's covenant love so remarkable, for it is "from eternity to eternity" toward those who reverence and obey him (vv. 15–18).

Romans 8

This chapter overflows with teaching about salvation, including the work of Christ (Rom 8:34), justification (vv. 1–3, 33–34), adoption (vv. 14–17), sanctification (vv. 4–10), perseverance (vv. 28–39), resurrection (vv. 11, 23–25), and the new heavens and the new earth (vv. 18–22). Paul begins by declaring that God the Judge will not condemn those of us who are united to Christ by faith (v. 1), for Christ liberates us from the condemnation that we lawbreakers deserve. Because we cannot keep the law perfectly, it is unable to rescue us. But God does what the law could not "by sending his own Son in the likeness of sinful flesh as a sin offering" (v. 3). Christ dies in our place, the perfect sacrifice for sins, to bring us to God. It follows that in gratitude we live godly lives, obeying the Holy Spirit (v. 4).

The Holy Spirit is essential both to salvation and to the Christian life: "If anyone does not have the Spirit of Christ, he does not belong to him" (v. 9). The Spirit gives us eternal life now and will raise our bodies in the future (vv. 10–11). Because the Spirit has given us life, we live for God and not for sin. Indeed, obedience to the Spirit characterizes us as God's adopted children (vv. 12–14).

Before God the Father welcomes us into his family, we are slaves of sin. But God replaces fear with faith. He shows us mercy and gives us the Spirit of adoption, who enables us to call God "Father" in truth (v. 15). The Spirit plays another important role, for he also assures our hearts that we are God's children (v. 16). Adoption pertains to the present—we are already God's children. It also points to the future—his children are "heirs of God and coheirs with Christ" (v. 17). Jesus is the eternal Son of God. By God's grace we become God's sons and daughters. God's plan is to conform us "to the image of his Son, so that he [is] the firstborn among many brothers and sisters" (v. 29). Adoption brings responsibilities, including suffering; it also brings blessings, including the Spirit's guidance and eternal glory (vv. 14, 17–18).

When Adam and Eve rebel against God, they bring God's judgment not only on human beings but also on creation. God's salvation, likewise, includes not only individuals and the church but also creation. He will deliver his creation from its curse, liberating it "from the bondage to decay into the glorious freedom of God's children" (v. 21). Paul portrays creation as awaiting its deliverance like a woman groaning in childbirth. Because believers have the Holy Spirit, we also groan, longing for resurrection, "the redemption of our bodies" (v. 23). And because God gives us his Word and Spirit, we live in hope, waiting patiently for God to fulfill his promises. And although we are weak and do not even always know what to pray for, we are not alone, for "the Spirit himself intercedes for us with unspoken groanings" (v. 26).

Romans 8 ends with Scripture's strongest affirmation that God keeps his people saved and will not allow them to perish (vv. 28–39). Paul gives four reasons why God preserves us. First, we are safe because God plans our salvation from beginning (foreknowing us) to end (glorifying us) (vv. 28–30). Second, we are safe because almighty God, who gives his own Son for us, is on our side, and nothing will defeat him or us (v. 32). Third, we are safe because in God's justice our case reaches heaven's Supreme Court, where God declares us righteous! The Son will not condemn us but save us (vv. 33–34). Fourth, we are safe because nothing will ever separate us from Christ's love: nothing in our life or death, no demon, no persecution, nothing present or future, "nor any other created thing" (v. 39).

Ephesians 1:3–14

Paul praises God the Father for heaping the blessings of salvation upon us (Eph 1:3). The apostle celebrates the work of the three persons of the Trinity as they cooperate in harmony to bring about our salvation. The Father chooses us in Christ, resulting in our holiness and adoption (vv. 4–5). The Son redeems us through his work on the cross and brings us forgiveness (v. 7). The Father seals us in union with Christ by giving us the Holy Spirit as a guarantee of our final salvation (vv. 13–14). All of this is for our good (blessings) and his glory (vv. 6, 12, 14).

Ephesians 1 portrays salvation in terms stretching from eternity past to eternity future. "Before the foundation of the world" the Father plans our salvation (v. 4). In the first century AD, Christ loves us and redeems us "through his blood," his violent death on the cross (v. 7). We are saved when we hear the message of salvation and trust Christ as Lord and Savior (v. 13). All this is according to "the mystery" of God's will, which centers on his bringing "everything together in Christ, both things in heaven and things on earth." This will occur after Jesus's second coming (vv. 9–10), the resurrection of the dead, and the last judgment. Then we who know Christ will enter into our final "inheritance," eternal life on the new earth, which will contribute to the praise of God's glory (v. 14).

1 Peter 1:3–9

One scriptural picture that describes how God touches our lives with his saving grace is the new birth, in which God makes alive those who were spiritually dead. The Father, who shows us "great mercy," is the source of our new life (1 Pet 1:3). Jesus's resurrection provides the power for our new life (v. 3). And the Holy Spirit actually makes us alive (John 3:8).

Peter rejoices in the results of God's gift of new life. First, we believers have a "living hope" (1 Pet 1:3). Our hope of resurrection and eternal life with God on the new earth will not disappoint because Jesus, who loves us and gives himself for us, is raised from the dead and is alive. Another benefit is the magnificent inheritance our Father plans for us, which Peter describes in four ways that distinguish it from all earthly inheritances (v. 4). Our inheritance is "imperishable," for it will never be destroyed. It is "undefiled," not tarnished by sin but holy. Our inheritance is "unfading," never lacking in brilliance. It is also "kept in heaven for [us]": God reserves it for us, and by his grace we will not fail to receive it.

Not only is our inheritance "kept," but so are we: "You are being guarded by God's power through faith for a salvation that is ready to be revealed in the last time" (v. 5). God's power keeps us saved, and his power works through faith. We rejoice in such a salvation, even though we may have to suffer, as Peter's readers did (v. 6; 4:12). God uses our suffering to prove the genuineness of our faith and to bring glory to himself at Jesus's return (1:7). We cannot see Jesus now, but we trust him, love him, and greatly rejoice because we experience his salvation even now (vv. 8–9).

As we have seen, even if briefly, the biblical doctrine of salvation is grounded in the love of God. And this loving God is on a mission, sending his Son to accomplish this mission: God thus loves the world by giving his Son, who freely gives himself for us and our salvation. God bids us to believe in the Son and then blesses us with eternal life in the Son when we do. In and through it all, God brings about our good and glorifies himself.

This salvation is multifaceted, as it addresses our multifaceted sin problem and flows from Jesus's multifaceted saving work. Indeed, we learn that our salvation means that God unites us to Christ. It means that God chooses and calls us in Christ. It means that we receive new life and a new direction, turning from our sin and trusting in Christ. It means that God justifies us, adopts us, makes us holy, keeps us, and will glorify us in Christ. These truths about our salvation, more than anything else, define who we really are. We are in Christ! We are chosen and called by God. We are believers in Christ, new in Christ. We are right with God. We are children of God. We are holy, preserved, and glorious in Christ.

We will look at each of these amazing truths in turn.

We Are in Christ

We Are United to Christ

Voices from the Global Church: Ajith Fernando

Fernando from Sri Lanka wrote, "The doctrine of fellowship in Christ's sufferings is a natural extension of the doctrine of our union with Christ. Christ is a suffering Savior, and if we are to be truly one with him, we too must suffer. There is a depth of union with Christ that comes to us only through suffering. But not only do we share in his sufferings; he also shares in our sufferings. The exalted Christ, sharing in the glory of God, is not deaf to our cries of pain as we suffer; he himself suffers with us when we suffer. Paul came to understand this on the road to Damascus when he heard Jesus ask, 'Saul, Saul, why are you persecuting me?' (Acts 9:4). He had been hitting the church, but Christ had been feeling the pain."[1]

As is clear from Eph 1:3–14, our union with Christ is the comprehensive category for the application of salvation.[2] The Father plans salvation; the Son accomplishes it; and the Spirit applies it to believers. What Christ does for us is connected to us through union with him. Union with Christ is the Holy Spirit's work of joining to Christ all of us who believe so that all his saving benefits become ours.

All the riches of God's grace and blessings are located in Christ (Eph 1:3). Therefore, as long as we are apart from him, we are far away

---

[1] Christopher W. Morgan and Robert A. Peterson, eds., *Heaven*, vol. 6 of Theology in Community (Wheaton, IL: Crossway, 2014), 6:232.

[2] We follow the structure and condense the more thorough treatment of union with Christ in Robert A. Peterson, *Salvation Applied by the Spirit: Union with Christ* (Wheaton, IL: Crossway, 2014).

from those blessings. Before salvation we were "separated from Christ . . . having no hope and without God in the world" (2:12 ESV). But now the Spirit graciously joins us to Christ, so that we who were previously separated from him are now united with him. This happens in history, in space and time. Union with Christ is not some mystical fusing of ourselves with the universe but is historical and transformative, applying salvation to us.

We Are United to the Father, Son, and Spirit

This startling truth must be understood against the background of the Trinity. There is one God (Deut 6:4; 1 Tim 2:5), who exists eternally in three persons as Father, Son, and Holy Spirit. The three are inseparable but distinguishable (Matt 3:16–17). At the same time, we do not confuse the persons. The Father never dies on the cross, for example. Only the Son becomes incarnate, dies, arises, returns to the Father, and will come again. We distinguish the three persons, then, without separating or confusing them.

In addition, the three trinitarian persons mutually indwell one another. This is called *perichoresis, circumincession,* or *co-inherence.* The three persons are one God and live in one another. The Father is in the Son (John 17:23); the Father indwells the Son (14:10). The Son is in the Father (14:20); the Father and Son are in one another (10:38; 14:10–11, 20; 17:21).

Furthermore, God indwells us as believers. Paul usually says that the Holy Spirit indwells us (in at least eight texts), but six times he says that the Son indwells us (Rom 8:10; 2 Cor 13:5; Gal 2:20; Eph 3:17; Col 1:27; 3:11), and even twice that the Father does so (2 Cor 6:16; Eph 2:22). Christians, then, are indwelt by the Father, Son, and Holy Spirit. Jesus promises that the Spirit will come to indwell God's people (John 14:16–17). He adds that the Father (John 17:21) and the Son are in believers (14:20; 17:23, 26) and will come to make their home with them (14:23). Even more, Jesus and believers are in one another (John 14:20). He and his true disciples mutually abide in one another (6:56; 15:4–5). They are in the Father and the Son (John 17:20–21). Paul teaches the same thing (1 Thess 1:1; 2 Thess 1:1).

How are we to understand such a teaching? We respect the Holy Trinity by observing the Creator/creature distinction. We do not become gods or part of God. God is always the Savior; we are always the saved. Jesus is always the head of the church, and we are never the head but always the body. Further, the trinitarian mutual indwelling is eternal, whereas ours begins at conversion. The Trinity's mutual indwelling is by nature, whereas ours is by grace through faith in Christ. And what grace this is, that Jesus speaks of us as being "in" the Father and the Son (John 17:21)!

We Are United to Christ Definitively, Intimately, and Permanently

Our union with Christ is definitive, intimate, and permanent. It is definitive in that it defines our very existence as God's people, for we are chosen in him, adopted in him, justified in him, made holy in him, kept in him, glorious in him, and so on. Indeed, we are "saints in Christ Jesus" (Phil 1:1). Our identity includes the fact that, because of union, we belong to Jesus and he belongs to us.

Our union is intimate: Paul uses a most intimate picture to describe union—sexual relations between husband and wife. "Don't you know that your bodies are a part of Christ's body? So should I take a part of Christ's body and make it part of a prostitute? Absolutely not!" (1 Cor 6:15). Paul goes on to explain that, because of union, Christians enjoy a spiritual marital relationship with Christ: "But anyone joined to the Lord is one spirit with him" (v. 17).

Union with Christ is also permanent. As we have previously seen, the Father seals believers in Christ "with the promised Holy Spirit" (Eph 1:13). We can be certain that this union is unbreakable and will last forever, for believers are sealed with the Spirit "for the day of redemption" (4:30).

Our union with Christ is definitive, intimate, and permanent, and as such we do *everything* in union with Christ. It is definitive: because union defines who we are, we always act joined to Jesus. It is intimate: because we are spiritually married to Christ, we bring our "husband" with us whenever we act. And it is permanent: because union is unbreakable, everything we do is in union with Christ. We live in union with Christ: "I have been crucified with Christ, and I no longer live, but Christ lives in me. The life I now live in the body, I live by faith in the Son of God, who loved me and gave himself for me" (Gal 2:20). Even death does not separate us from Christ, for we die in union with him: "I heard a voice from heaven saying, 'Write: Blessed are the dead who die in the Lord from now on'" (Rev 14:13). Indeed, we live godly lives (2 Tim 3:12), speak (2 Cor 2:17), and are strong in grace (2 Tim 2:1) in him.

We Are United to Christ and His Story

By God's grace we participate in many aspects of Jesus's story. We do not participate in his incarnation or sinless life, although in justification his righteousness is credited to our spiritual bank accounts. We do participate, however, in his death, resurrection, session, and return.

Scripture abundantly testifies to the fact that we die with Christ (Rom 6:3–8; 7:4; 2 Cor 4:10; Gal 2:20; Phil 3:10; Col 2:20; 3:3). As God the Son incarnate, only he dies to make atonement for sins. But when the Spirit unites us to Christ, we are joined to his death. In a similar manner, the Spirit unites believers to Jesus's resurrection (Rom 6:4–8; 7:4; 2 Cor 4:10–14; Eph 2:6; Col 2:12; 3:1).

Jesus's death and resurrection are the very substance of his saving work. They are God's antidote to the poison of sin past, present, and future. In regard to the past, sin wants to condemn us. In regard to the present, it wants to dominate us. In regard to the future, it wants to ruin us forever.

Concerning the past, Jesus's death and resurrection solve via justification the problem of sin's *penalty*: "There is now no condemnation for those in Christ. . . . [God] condemned sin in the flesh by sending his own Son in the likeness of sinful flesh as a sin offering" (Rom 8:1, 3).

Concerning the present, Jesus's death and resurrection solve via progressive sanctification the problem of sin's *power*: "We were buried with him by baptism into death, in order that, just as Christ was raised from the dead by the glory of the Father, so we too may walk in newness of life" (Rom 6:4).

Concerning the future, Jesus's death and resurrection solve via glorification the problem of sin's *presence*: "We rejoice in the hope of the glory of God. . . . For if, while we were enemies, we were reconciled to God through the death of his Son, then how much more, having been reconciled, will we be saved by his life" (Rom 5:2, 10).

Scripture goes one step further and teaches that the Father enables us to participate in Jesus's resurrection and session: "he also raised us up with him and seated us with him in the heavens in Christ Jesus" (Eph 2:6). Spiritually, we have sat down with Christ in heaven. This is one way that God assures us of salvation and promises us a place in his final kingdom.

In two passages the Bible even says we will participate in Jesus's second coming:

> The eager expectation of the creation awaits eagerly the revelation of the sons of God. (Rom 8:19, authors' translation)

> When Christ, who is your life, appears, then you also will appear with him in glory. (Col 3:4)

In the first text Paul uses the word "revelation," the same word used often to speak of Jesus's return (1 Cor 1:7; 2 Thess 1:7; 1 Pet 1:7, 13; 4:13 [HCSB]; Rev 1:1). There is a sense in which believers have a revelation, a return. The second passage uses the same word, "appear," to speak of Jesus's and believers' second coming. We are so tied to Jesus that our true identity will be perfectly revealed only when he comes again.

We Receive the Blessings of Salvation in Christ

The aspects of the application of salvation are aspects of union with Christ. The blessings God provides for believers are "with Christ" or "in Christ," that is, by virtue of union with him.

> *Regeneration*: "God, who is rich in mercy, because of his great love that he had for us, made us alive with Christ even though we were dead in trespasses." (Eph 2:4–5)

> *Justification*: "He made the one who did not know sin to be sin for us, so that in him we might become the righteousness of God." (2 Cor 5:21)

Adoption: "Through faith you are all sons of God in Christ Jesus. For those of you who were baptized into Christ have been clothed with Christ." (Gal 3:26–27)

Sanctification: "We are his workmanship, created in Christ Jesus for good works, which God prepared ahead of time for us to do." (Eph 2:10)

Perseverance: "There is now no condemnation for those in Christ Jesus." (Rom 8:1)

Resurrection: "Since death came through a man, the resurrection of the dead also comes through a man. For just as in Adam all die, so also in Christ all will be made alive." (1 Cor 15:21–22)

Glorification: "When Christ, who is your life, appears, then you also will appear with him in glory." (Col 3:4)

Regeneration, justification, adoption, sanctification, perseverance, resurrection, and glorification are ours, not apart from Christ but in union with him. When the Spirit joins us to Christ, all of his spiritual benefits become ours. God applies salvation to us precisely by joining us spiritually to his Son.

We Are Chosen in Christ

Instead of focusing on the frequent debates and perennial questions surrounding the overwhelming doctrine of election, we will focus on what we can know. Our structure here primarily flows from Eph 1:3–14, though other passages are addressed too.

The Author of Election: God Chooses Us

There is a significant place for our freedom and responsibility in salvation, but when speaking of election, Paul states simply as he speaks concerning God:

He chose us (Eph 1:4).

He predestined us (v. 5).

God has chosen you for salvation (2 Thess 2:13).

In love God chooses Old Testament Israel out of all the nations to be his people (Deut 7:6–8; 10:14–15; 14:2). God also chooses the Messiah: "This is my Son, the Chosen One" (Luke 9:35; see also Isa 42:1; Matt 12:18; Luke 23:35; 1 Pet 1:20; 2:4). Jesus, the Chosen One, chooses his disciples to belong to him instead of the world: "You did not choose me, but I chose you. . . . You are not of the world, but I have chosen you out of it" (John 15:16, 19).

Against the darkness of human depravity, God's initiative shines. If we receive what we deserve for our sins, we will be condemned. But God in grace chooses us, who did not seek him (Rom 3:9–20), and gives us what we do not deserve: eternal life (Acts 13:48; Eph 2:4–5). Thus our salvation is based "on God who shows mercy" (Rom 9:16). The initiative in salvation belongs to God (v. 15, quoting Exod 33:19). As a result, God is glorified for his marvelous grace (Eph 1:6, 12).

The Recipients of Election: God Chooses Us

God chooses us (Eph 1:4); God predestines us (v. 5). In Ephesians 1, this clearly refers to believers, saints, the ones receiving every spiritual blessing in the heavenlies; the ones adopted, becoming holy, being forgiven, receiving an inheritance, and being sealed.

The language concerning the recipients of election in Scripture is commonly plural, making it hard to detect whether the focus is individual or corporate. New Testament letters like Ephesians are written to churches to be read to churches and should be interpreted as such. Indeed, here and elsewhere these depictions of salvation are also identified with the church. The church is the chosen people of God, the holy people of God, the children of God (adoption), the redeemed people of God, the ones with an inheritance. Yet so are we as individual believers: I am adopted; I am being made holy; I am forgiven; I am sealed; I receive an inheritance. It seems natural to interpret election similarly. The fact that God chooses us, then, apparently refers to the church as well as to us as individual believers. It seems to be both collective and individual.

Other passages are similar. Believers, the people of God, are the recipients of God's election. Jesus calls them his "sheep" (John 10:26–27) and, praying to the Father, "those you have given me" (17:9, 24). Luke calls them "all who had been appointed to eternal life" (Acts 13:48), and God calls them his "people" (18:10). Paul refers to election's recipients as "God's chosen ones" (Col 3:12), "brothers and sisters loved by the Lord" (2 Thess 2:13), and "the elect" (2 Tim 2:10). Often, he uses personal pronouns, calling them "you" (2 Thess 2:13) and, adding himself, "us" (Eph 1:4–5; 2 Tim 1:9).

The Sphere of Election: God Chooses Us in Christ

In Ephesians 1, Paul combines election and union with Christ: "He chose us *in him*, before the foundation of the world" (v. 4). Paul speaks similarly in 2 Timothy: "He has saved us and called us with a holy calling . . . according to his own purpose and grace, which was given to us *in Christ Jesus* before time began" (1:9). God chooses us for salvation before creation and also plans the means to save us: he plans to send his Son to die, rise, and send the Spirit to unite believers to Christ in salvation. This plan is for our salvation, for the creation of his church, and for the restoration of the cosmos (Eph 1:3–11).

The Time of Election: God Chooses Us before Creation

Paul teaches that God chooses us for salvation before he creates the world. Paul tells the Ephesian church that the Father "chose us in him, before the foundation of the world" for sanctification (Eph 1:4). He also tells Timothy that God saves us not because of "our works, but according to his own purpose and grace, which was given to us in Christ Jesus before time began" (2 Tim 1:9). God chooses us before we exist—even before space and time exist. When Paul says that God chooses us before creation, he locates election in God, not us.

The Motivation of Election: In Love God Chooses Us

Paul traces our election to God's love and grace. He chooses us "in love" and "according to the good pleasure of his will," which is directly related to the display of his grace (Eph 1:4–6). This is similar to Deut 7:6–8, where God declares that he chooses Israel not based on her strength or abilities but because of his love for her.

Paul similarly traces election to God's purpose or will. He speaks of "the good pleasure of his will" (Eph 1:5) and "the plan of the one who works out everything in agreement with the purpose of his will" (v. 11). The apostle sets forth the reason for election both negatively and positively. Negatively, election is not based on human desire or endeavor, for, Paul explains, salvation "does not depend on human will or effort" (Rom 9:16). Positively, Paul completes the sentence to state that salvation does depend "on God who shows mercy" (v. 16).

The reason for election is also depicted as God's "purpose and grace" (2 Tim 1:9) and "God's purpose according to election" (Rom 9:11). God chooses us based on his "mercy" (Rom 9:15–16, 18, 23), "compassion" (v. 15), and "grace" (11:5–6). In love he chooses us (Eph 1:4).

Voices from Church History: Charles Haddon Spurgeon

Spurgeon (1834–1892), English Baptist preacher, still influential among many Christians, was pastor of the Metropolitan Tabernacle in London for thirty-eight years. He defended the 1689 London Baptist Confession of Faith and opposed the liberal theologies of his day. Spurgeon is the author of many works but is most remembered for powerful sermons of biblical exposition and penetrating application. He wrote,

> I cannot expect to understand the mysteries of God, neither do I wish to do so. If I understood God, He could not be the true God. A doctrine which I cannot fully grasp is a Truth of God which is intended to grasp me. When I cannot climb, I kneel. Where I cannot build an observatory, I set up an altar. . . . How idle it is to dream of our ever running parallel in understanding with the infinite God! His knowledge is too wonderful for us. It is so high—we cannot attain to it.[3]

---

[3] Charles H. Spurgeon, "The Hairs on Your Head Numbered," in *Metropolitan Tabernacle Pulpit*, vol. 34, 1888 (Pasadena, TX: Pilgrim Publications, 1974), 54.

Goals of Election: God Chooses Us to Holiness and Adoption

Paul teaches that God chooses us in Christ "to be holy and blameless in love before him" (Eph 1:4). So election is for our sanctification. Paul also adds that God "predestined us to be adopted as sons through Jesus Christ for himself" (v. 5). So election is for our adoption, which includes not only our initial salvation but also our future inheritance (v. 11; see also Rom 8:18–27). We learn elsewhere that God predestines us for conformity to Christ's image and glorification (Rom 8:29–30). Indeed, God chooses believers for "glory" (Rom 9:23), even "eternal glory" (2 Tim 2:10).

So, God chooses us in Christ not only to receive initial salvation but to bring about the whole of our salvation: past, present, and future (in addition to the passages above, see also 2 Thess 2:13). How should we respond to these things? With praise (Eph 1:3, 6, 12, 14)! We must respond also with thanksgiving (2 Thess 2:13), humility (Rom 9:15–16), renewed service (Acts 18:9–10; 2 Tim 2:8–10), bolstered assurance (John 10:27–29), and passionate evangelism (Rom 9:1–6; 10:1–17).

The Ultimate End of Election: God Chooses Us for His Glory

In Eph 1:3–14 Paul clarifies the ultimate end of our election: the glory of God. Paul explicitly incorporates a refrain: "to the praise of his glorious grace" (1:6), "praise to his glory" (v. 12), and "to the praise of his glory" (v. 14). Paul's point is unmistakable: the ultimate end of our election is not our salvation, as important as that is. God chose us to glorify himself. And as we will see later in this chapter, our salvation as a whole is also for the glory of God.

The Missionary Mandate of Election: God Chooses Us, and We Hear the Gospel

It is important to remember that Ephesians does not end at 1:6. Paul continues to speak of how we are saved: through the redeeming work of Jesus. His blood is the ground of our salvation and forgiveness (vv. 7–11). And Paul teaches that salvation comes through hearing "the word of truth, the gospel of your salvation" (v. 13). Anyone speaking of election without speaking of missions fails to do justice to the Bible.

In Gen 12:1–3 God chooses Abraham, saying, "I will make you into a great nation, I will bless you, I will make your name great." And God commissions him: "you will be a blessing . . . and all the peoples on earth will be blessed through you."

Abraham is chosen for the sake of mission. In Exod 19:5–6 God expresses his choice of Israel. They are his covenant people—his treasured possession, his kingdom of priests, his holy nation. The particularity is striking: out of all the nations, you are mine, God says. Even more striking is that God's particularity is for the sake of universality: out of all the nations, you are mine; *and* the whole earth is mine, so you will be for me a kingdom of priests and a holy nation. God is on a mission, and he plans to reach the nations through his covenant people. They will witness to him and his ways through their distinctiveness as his holy nation. And they will witness to him through their proclamation as a kingdom of priests, "bringing the knowledge of God to the nations, and bringing the nations to the means of atonement with God."[4]

Paul writes similarly in Romans 9–10. Note how he begins and ends this incredibly complex treatment on salvation history, Israel, the church, divine election, and human responsibility. He begins this theological discourse by stating his intense and unceasing burden for the salvation of his people, the Jews. He so longs for their salvation that he would almost be willing to go to hell in order for them to be saved, if that were actually possible (9:1–5). After a heavy and detailed treatise, Paul stresses his deep desire and prayer for the conversion of the Jews. He then reminds his readers that "everyone who calls on the name of the Lord will be saved" (10:13). But how will others call on Jesus without believing in Jesus? How will they believe without hearing the gospel? And how will they hear without someone telling them? Paul then reiterates the necessity of the gospel: faith comes through hearing, and hearing through the word of God, the gospel (vv. 14–17).

---

[4] Christopher J. H. Wright, *The Mission of God: Unlocking the Bible's Grand Narrative* (Downers Grove, IL: IVP Academic, 2006), 331. Wright also helped us overall on Genesis 12 and Exodus 19.

Human Responsibility and Election: God Chooses Us, and We Believe

After speaking of how God chooses us in Christ, redeems us through the blood of Christ, and sends us the gospel of Christ, Paul notes, "You believed" (Eph 1:13). Our salvation is always tied to God's love, Christ's death, the Spirit's work, *and* our faith in Christ. Our faith does not save us; God saves us through Christ. But our faith receives what God has done for us in Christ. We are never the source, ground, or cause of our salvation; God is. He is the Savior; we are the saved. He is the Redeemer; we are the redeemed. But salvation is by grace through *faith*, so we trust, we believe, we have faith, we repent (Eph 2:8–9). We are active as we receive salvation through faith.

We Are Called to Christ

As we maintained above, God uses the proclamation of the gospel to bring us to faith. We see this again in Acts when Paul and Barnabas preach the gospel: "When the Gentiles heard this, they rejoiced and honored the word of the Lord, and all who had been appointed to eternal life believed. The word of the Lord spread through the whole region" (Acts 13:48–49). We see here the inseparable interweaving of God's mission, God's purpose, our response of faith, and our commitment to evangelism.

Note how again and again, calling is God's means of bringing people to salvation:

> Those he predestined, he also called; and those he called, he also justified; and those he justified, he also glorified. (Rom 8:30)

> What if he did this to make known the riches of his glory on objects of mercy that he prepared beforehand for glory—on us, the ones he also called, not only from the Jews but also from the Gentiles? (9:23–24)

> But we ought to thank God always for you, brothers and sisters loved by the Lord, because from the beginning God has chosen you for salvation through sanctification by the Spirit and through

belief in the truth. He called you to this through our gospel, so that you might obtain the glory of our Lord Jesus Christ. (2 Thess 2:13–14; see also 2 Tim 1:9)

Sometimes *calling* refers to the sharing and hearing of the gospel and its invitation and promises. Such calling includes the gospel: we are lost and cannot rescue ourselves, Christ dies and arises to rescue sinners, and we must trust him to be rescued. It includes an invitation, summoning people to trust Christ for salvation. God calls the lost to believe in Jesus's death and resurrection for deliverance. It includes promises: the forgiveness of sins and eternal life to believers. Many biblical texts issue the gospel call, such as these:

Believe in the Lord Jesus, and you will be saved—you and your household. (Acts 16:31)

If you confess with your mouth, "Jesus is Lord," and believe in your heart that God raised him from the dead, you will be saved. (Rom 10:9)

Sometimes *calling* also refers to God's summoning people to him so that they trust in Christ. Examples include Rom 8:29–30, which links five verbs of salvation in such a way that those whom God foreknows he also predestines, calls, justifies, and glorifies. The "called" here are believers who trust Christ, love God, and will be glorified (see also v. 28). Another example of calling in this sense is 2 Tim 1:9: "He has saved us and called us with a holy calling, not according to our works, but according to his own purpose and grace, which was given to us in Christ Jesus before time began" (see also John 6:44).

We Are Alive in Christ

The Nature of Our New Birth: New Life in Christ

We not only are united to Christ, chosen in Christ, and called to Christ but also have new life in Christ. We are born again, or regenerated.

Regeneration is an aspect of the initial application of salvation: God's giving us new life. Before our new births, we are spiritually dead, devoid of the life of God, and unable to make ourselves alive (Eph 2:1). Graciously and instantaneously, "God, who is rich in mercy, because of his great love that he had for us, made us alive with Christ even though we were dead in trespasses. You are saved by grace!" (vv. 4–5). God's making the spiritually dead alive is the epitome of grace.

Regeneration is likened to circumcision of the heart (Rom 2:29). Israel, stubborn and unwilling to love God, suffers from an uncircumcised heart and needs heart surgery that only God could perform (Deut 10:16; 30:6). This is exactly what God promises when he restores them to their land and cleanses them from idolatry: "I will give you a new heart and put a new spirit within you; I will remove your heart of stone and give you a heart of flesh. I will place my Spirit within you" (Ezek 36:26–27). God revives his people inwardly by replacing hard hearts with responsive ones. He gives believers his Spirit to indwell them and to motivate their obedience.

The Source of Our New Birth: The Triune God

The whole Trinity is involved in our new birth. God the Father is to be praised for his "great mercy" that is the source of our new life. God the Son is the ground of our new birth, as we are regenerated "through the resurrection of Jesus Christ from the dead" (1 Pet 1:3). God the Spirit is the agent of the new birth, as we are born again when the Spirit unites us to Jesus's death and resurrection (Rom 6:1–10; Eph 2:4–7).

The Basis of Our New Birth: Jesus's Saving Work

As we just noted, we have new life "through the resurrection of Jesus Christ from the dead" (1 Pet 1:3). The Holy Spirit connects us to Jesus's death and resurrection (Rom 6:1–10; Eph 2:4–7). His resurrection moves us from spiritual death to life. Our living Lord shares his new life with us now and promises that we will enjoy its fullness in the future. Our regeneration brings with it "living hope" because the risen Christ conquers death, and through him we too will be raised (1 Cor 15:26) and look forward to a matchless inheritance (1 Pet 1:4).

The Agent of Our New Birth: The Holy Spirit

The Holy Spirit is the agent of regeneration. Jesus expands on the fact that the new birth is not because of human willingness but is God's work (John 1:12–13) when he tells Nicodemus that new birth is necessary to enter God's kingdom. Religion, status, heritage, or interest is insufficient, for "you must be born again" (3:7). Jesus makes a play on words (the same Greek word means "breath," "wind," or "spirit"): "The wind blows where it pleases, and you hear its sound, but you don't know where it comes from or where it is going. So it is with everyone born of the Spirit" (v. 8). As we cannot control or predict the blowing of the wind, so it is with the work of the Spirit of God. He cannot be seen, but he effects change.

The Instrument of Our New Birth: The Word of God

The Spirit uses the instrument of the Word of God to give us new life. The gospel not only is information; it is God's effective word, a tool to accomplish his purposes. God creates by his word (Genesis 1), sustains by his word (Heb 1:3), calls us to salvation by his word (2 Tim 1:9), and sanctifies us by his word (John 17:17). We should not be surprised, then, when God uses the gospel to give life: "You have been born again—not of perishable seed but of imperishable—through the living and enduring word of God" (1 Pet 1:23; see also Jas 1:18).

Corollary to Our New Birth: Entering the Kingdom

Regeneration enables us to see the kingdom in Jesus and even to taste (experience) it now (John 3:3–5). Through regeneration we enter the kingdom, the reign of God begun in the Messiah's arrival. Through our new birth, we experience the kingdom and become citizens of the kingdom, part of the community of Christ's reign. Like the kingdom, regeneration reflects the New Testament emphasis on the "already" and the "not yet." We receive new life in Christ now, but regeneration in its fullness is still future in the resurrection of the body and the new heavens and the new earth (Matt 19:28).

Fruit of Our New Birth: New Lifestyle

First John emphasizes regeneration's results, the fruit it bears in the lives of true believers. Those who have been born of God believe that Jesus is the promised Messiah (5:1), follow God as a way of life (2:29; 3:9; 5:18), and love God's people (4:7–12). Our new life from God results in a new, Godward lifestyle.

We Believe in Christ

Our Conversion

Conversion involves turning *from* something *to* something else. Biblical conversion is God's turning people from sin to Christ (Acts 20:21). Turning from sin is repentance, and turning to Christ is faith. So conversion is shorthand for repentance and faith.

Scripture tells of both Paul's dramatic conversion and Timothy's quiet one. Paul, whose name is Saul, is on the road leading to Damascus with authorization from the high priest to persecute Christians there. On the way, the living Christ meets him in power, knocking him to the ground. Paul knows he had encountered God and asks his identity. The reply from heaven is as shocking as any in Scripture: "I am Jesus, the one you are persecuting" (Acts 9:5).

By contrast, Timothy, whose father is an unsaved Greek (Acts 16:1), grows up with a Christian mother, Eunice, and grandmother, Lois (2 Tim 1:5). Timothy has the great advantage of knowing from childhood "the sacred Scriptures, which are able to give . . . wisdom for salvation through faith in Christ Jesus" (2 Tim 3:15).

Scripture tells of the conversion of both individuals and families. Paul and Timothy's conversions are examples of the former. We see the latter when whole families turn to Christ in Acts (16:14–15, 31–34).

Voices from the Global Church: Orlando Costas

Costas from Costa Rica wrote, "The concept of multi-individual decisions gives a sociological orientation to the experience of conversion because it affirms that conversion, which depends on a personal act of faith in Christ, can take place in a group setting, where all the members of a given group (family, clan, tribe or mutual interest group) participate in a similar experience with Christ after considering it together and deciding to turn to Christ at the same time."[5]

Our Repentance and Faith

Repentance and faith are not identical and must be distinguished. They differ in their direction. Repentance is directed toward sin and involves a rejection of and movement away from it. Faith is belief directed toward God or, more specifically, toward Christ as he is offered in the gospel. Sometimes Scripture names both repentance and faith as conditions of salvation. This is not customary, but it occurs several times:

> John baptized with a baptism of repentance, telling the people that they should believe in the one who would come after him, that is, in Jesus. (Acts 19:4)

> I testified to both Jews and Greeks about repentance toward God and faith in our Lord Jesus. (Acts 20:21)

> Therefore, let us leave the elementary teaching about Christ and go on to maturity, not laying again a foundation of repentance from dead works, faith in God . . . (Heb 6:1)

---

[5] Orlando Costas, *The Church and Its Mission: A Shattering Critique from the Third World* (Wheaton, IL: Tyndale, 1974), 128.

Although sometimes Scripture names both repentance and faith as conditions of salvation, frequently it mentions repentance alone:

> From then on Jesus began to preach, "Repent, because the kingdom of heaven has come near." (Matt 4:17)

> [Jesus said,] "This is what is written: The Messiah would suffer and rise from the dead the third day, and repentance for forgiveness of sins would be proclaimed in his name to all the nations, beginning at Jerusalem." (Luke 24:46–47)

> For godly grief produces a repentance that leads to salvation without regret, but worldly grief produces death. (2 Cor 7:10)

Even more frequently, Scripture describes faith as the sole condition of salvation:

> I am not ashamed of the gospel, because it is the power of God for salvation to everyone who believes, first to the Jew, and also to the Greek. (Rom 1:16)

> For we conclude that a person is justified by faith apart from the works of the law. (Rom 3:28)

> You are saved by grace through faith, and this is not from yourselves; it is God's gift. (Eph 2:8)

Therefore, Scripture sometimes names both repentance and faith as conditions of salvation, but much more frequently it mentions either repentance or faith as the sole condition. Repentance and faith are distinguishable but inseparable in God's plan. They are not two separate conditions but two sides of one coin. Repentance is turning from and to. When we turn from something, we automatically turn toward something else. When we turn from sin, we turn toward Christ. So, when Scripture names only repentance or faith as the correct response to the gospel, the other one is implied. As John Murray famously writes,

> The question has been discussed: which is prior, faith or repentance? It is an unnecessary question and the insistence that one

is prior to the other is futile. There is no priority. The faith that is unto salvation is a penitent faith and the repentance that is unto life is a believing repentance.[6]

Our Repentance

Repentance often refers to our initial turning from sin toward Christ, leading to our salvation. By his grace, God enables us to repent:

> When they heard this they became silent. And they glorified God, saying, "So then, God has given repentance resulting in life even to the Gentiles." (Acts 11:18)

> . . . instructing his opponents with gentleness. Perhaps God will grant them repentance leading them to the knowledge of the truth. (2 Tim 2:25)

These two verses show that repentance is a gift from God. Earlier verses cited also show that it is the responsibility of humans (Matt 4:17; 2 Cor 7:10).

Repentance is also a regular part of the Christian life and is a fruit of our initial repentance. Christian repentance is turning from sins out of love for Jesus and a desire to promote God's glory. Repentance is a way of life, as we repeatedly battle sin, succumb to temptation, and repent to walk rightly. This process lasts until death. It involves spurning sinful thoughts, speech, and actions again and again.

> I now rejoice, not because you were grieved, but because your grief led to repentance. For you were grieved as God willed. (2 Cor 7:9)

> [Jesus said,] "As many as I love, I rebuke and discipline. So be zealous and repent." (Rev 3:19)

---

[6] Murray, *Redemption Accomplished and Applied*, 113 (see chap. 6, n. 10).

The concept of Christian repentance occurs often in Scripture without the word "repent" or "repentance" (see Rom 6:15–23; Eph 4:25–32; Col 3:5–10; Heb 3:12–15; 1 Pet 2:1–3; 1 John 1:8–10).

Our Faith

Voices from Church History: John Wesley

Wesley (1703–1791), was a minister and theologian who, with his brother Charles and friend George Whitefield, founded Methodism. After an evangelical conversion, though facing opposition, Wesley traveled and preached the gospel outdoors. His ministry spanned many years and covered thousands of miles on horseback. He organized small Christian discipleship groups that stressed accountability, and he appointed itinerant evangelists to do the same. Under his leadership, Methodists became leaders in many social issues, including prison reform and the abolition of slavery. He wrote,

> Christian faith is then not only an assent to the whole gospel of Christ, but also a full reliance on the blood of Christ, a trust in the merits of his life, death, and resurrection; a recumbency on him as our atonement and our life, as given for us and living in us. Saving faith is a "sure confidence which a man hath in God, that through the merits of Christ his sins are forgiven, and he is reconciled to the favour of God; and, in consequence hereof, a closing with him and cleaving to him as our 'wisdom, righteousness, sanctification, and redemption,' or, in one word, our salvation."[7]

Faith is positively trusting in Christ, depending on him as Savior, and recognizing him as Lord. Scripture regards faith as vital, asserting that it is impossible to please God without it (Heb 11:6) and that we are saved by

---

[7] John Wesley, "Salvation by Faith," in *The Works of John Wesley*, 3rd ed. (Grand Rapids: Baker, 2007), 5:9–10; reprinted from the 1872 edition issued by the Wesleyan Methodist Book Room, London.

faith in Christ. Indeed, faith in Christ is necessary for salvation, as John 14:6; Acts 4:12; and Rom 10:9–10 stress.[8]

There are many Old Testament descriptions of faith, including believing the Lord (Gen 15:6), taking refuge in him (Ps 5:11), trusting him (9:10), relying on him (21:7), waiting for him (27:14), putting hope in him (42:5, 11), and more. It is the same for the New Testament, as the Gospel of John alone speaks of faith predominantly as believing (1:7), believing in Jesus's name (v. 12), believing in him (3:16), and believing his word (4:50), but also as receiving Christ (1:12), accepting his testimony (3:33), coming to him (6:35), and remaining in him (15:4–7).

Faith involves knowledge, assent, and trust. We must hear and *know* the facts of the gospel. But it is not enough to know the facts, for many know the truth but do not believe it. We must *assent* to (say yes to) the gospel as God's truth. And yet it is possible to accept the facts of the gospel without commitment to Christ. We must *trust* Jesus and rest in his finished work to be saved.

Faith is only as good as its object. Our faith can be misplaced, as we can trust in people or things we should not. However, faith in Jesus Christ crucified and risen saves, as Paul explains: "Faith comes from what is heard, and what is heard comes through the message about Christ" (Rom 10:17).

As we distinguish initial repentance from lifelong Christian repentance, so we distinguish saving faith from Christian faith. The passages cited above depicting faith as a condition of salvation show the reality of saving faith. There is also lifelong Christian faith, for the Christian life is not only begun by faith but lived by faith as well:

We walk by faith, not by sight. (2 Cor 5:7)

---

[8] See Morgan and Peterson, eds., *Faith Comes by Hearing*, 185–89, 194–97 (see chap. 2, n. 10).

The life I now live in the body, I live by faith in the Son of God, who loved me and gave himself for me. (Gal 2:20)

As repentance is both the gift of God and the responsibility of human beings, the same is true regarding faith. It is God's gift:

When the Gentiles heard this, they rejoiced and honored the word of the Lord, and all who had been appointed to eternal life believed. (Acts 13:48)

[Jesus said,] "No one can come to me unless the Father who sent me draws him, and I will raise him up on the last day." (John 6:44)

Faith is God's gift, but it is also the responsibility of human beings, a truth to which many texts bear witness, including:

Hearing this, Jesus was amazed and said to those following him, "Truly I tell you, I have not found anyone in Israel with so great a faith." (Matt 8:10)

Believe on the Lord Jesus, and you will be saved—you and your household. (Acts 16:31)

Therefore, we thank God for his gifts of initial repentance and saving faith. And we lean on his grace to empower us for lifelong repentance and faith.

We Are Righteous in Christ

As we have seen, we are chosen in Christ and called to Christ. We have new life in Christ and are believers in Christ. We are also righteous, justified in Christ by grace through faith, to the glory of God. Justification is a legal image of salvation that presents God as the Judge who justifies (declares righteous) everyone who trusts Christ for salvation.

The doctrine of justification is of primary importance. This doctrine was a major reason for the sixteenth-century Reformation, as the

Reformers correctly regarded it as central to the New Testament books of Romans and Galatians. Martin Luther considered justification to be the article on which the church stands or falls.[9] John Calvin called it the "main hinge" or "principal axis" on which Christianity turns.[10]

Our Need for Justification: Sin and Guilt

Romans broadcasts our need for justification: "both Jews and Gentiles are all under sin" (3:9), and "all have sinned and fall short of the glory of God" (v. 23). Paul announces his theme, the gospel, the revelation of God's saving righteousness (1:16–17), and then treats the revelation of something very different: God's wrath (1:18–3:20). Why? Because we appreciate the gospel—God's good news of salvation—only against the backdrop of the bad news of our sin and what it deserves: God's judgment.

In Romans, Paul begins by showing our guilt through the actual sins we all commit (1:18–3:20). None of us escapes Paul's indictment: "There is no one righteous, not even one. There is no one who understands; there is no one who seeks God. All have turned away; all alike have become worthless. There is no one who does what is good, not even one" (3:10–12).

After rejoicing in God's justification of all who trust Christ as substitute (3:21–5:11), Paul again underlines our need for justification: Adam's original sin. Paul contrasts Adam and Christ, as well as their effects: Adam's one original sin condemns all his descendants; Christ's "one righteous act" of dying brings justification and eternal life to all who trust him (5:18). We are guilty; we cannot rescue ourselves but need a Redeemer.

---

[9] Martin Luther, *What Luther Says: An Anthology*, ed. Ewald M. Plass, 3 vols. (St. Louis: Concordia: 1959), 2:704n5. More precisely, Luther said, "If this article stands, the church stands; if this article collapses, the church collapses." See also Justin Taylor, "6 Quotes That Luther Didn't Actually Say," Gospel Coalition, February 20, 2014. https://www.thegospelcoalition.org/blogs/justin-taylor/5-quotes-that-luther-didnt-actually-say.

[10] Calvin, *Institutes of the Christian Religion*, 3.11.1, vol. 2:726 (see chap. 7, n. 5).

The Source of Our Justification: God's Grace

God is the source of our justification, as he justifies us "freely by his grace" (Rom 3:24). God's grace, his goodwill when we deserve his ill will, shines in justification. But the matter is more complicated. Most wonder, *How can a loving God judge anyone?* Reading the first three chapters of the Bible or of Romans answers that question: a holy God punishes sin, and we all are guilty. In Romans, Paul asks a different question: How could a holy and loving God declare guilty sinners to be righteous?

The answer lies in God's grace and justice, displayed in the crucifixion of his beloved Son. We will examine this in more detail below, but now we note that God sends his Son to die on the cross "to demonstrate his righteousness at the present time, so that he would be righteous and declare righteous the one who has faith in Jesus" (Rom 3:26). Through Christ's substitutionary work, God's moral integrity shines, and he forgives all who believe in Christ.

The Basis of Our Justification: Christ

Paul stresses that the basis for God declaring sinners righteous is Jesus's death and resurrection (Rom 4:25). Paul presents the cross as both negatively turning away God's judgment (3:25–26) and positively obtaining his righteousness (5:18–19). In both cases, Jesus is our substitute, the one who takes our place to save us.

In Rom 3:21 Paul returns to his announced theme: the revelation of God's saving righteousness. All lack this righteousness, because "all have sinned" and fail to earn God's favor (v. 23). God credits saving righteousness to everyone who believes in Jesus. God does so because Christ's death satisfies his justice. "In his restraint God passed over the sins previously committed" (v. 25). God shows restraint, not bringing the judgment that his Old Testament people deserve but instead forgiving those who believe. Although animal sacrifices could never remove sins (Heb 10:4), they picture the gospel, and God forgives Old Testament saints based on Christ's work to come (9:15). That time comes when

"God put forward" Christ "as a propitiation by his blood to be received by faith. This was to show God's righteousness" (v. 25 ESV). God punishes his holy Son with the penalty our sins deserve. In this way God demonstrates "his righteousness at the present time, so that he would be righteous and declare righteous the one who has faith in Jesus" (v. 26). Christ also redeems us (v. 24), purchasing us by his blood and freeing us from our bondage to sin.[11]

The Means of Our Justification: Faith

Paul highlights faith as justification's means. In his purpose statement in Romans, he affirms three times that faith in Christ is how we are justified (1:16–17). Both Jews and Gentiles are justified the same way: by faith (3:27–31). Both Old and New Testament believers are saved by grace through faith (Romans 4). Justification is not by works (4:1–8), circumcision (4:9–12), or law keeping (4:13–15) but only by faith in Christ (3:22, 25–26; 4:23–25).

As we saw in the preceding section, faith is trusting in Christ, depending on him as Savior and yielding to him as Lord. It includes belief in the gospel, genuine sorrow for sin, and a commitment to Christ. In exercising faith, we illustrate the Creator-creature distinction: God gives; we depend. In exercising faith, we illustrate God's holiness and our sin: God alone can save; we can only offer God our sin. In exercising faith, we illustrate how God acts for his glory and our good: God is the Supreme One, who displays his greatness as the Giver; we are blessed as we receive from him. Since justification is by grace through faith, God meets our needs and gets the glory.

---

[11] For more on propitiation and redemption, see the previous chapter, "Jesus's Saving Work," pages 297–304 and 313–315.

The Nature of Our Justification: Imputed Righteousness

Voices from Church History: Martin Luther

Luther (1483–1546), professor of theology and preacher, questioned the Roman Catholic view on indulgences in his Ninety-five Theses of 1517 and unwittingly sparked the Reformation. Luther came to oppose Catholic teaching by regarding Scripture more highly than the church and by holding that justification is received as a gift of God's grace alone through faith alone in Christ alone. His translation of the Bible into German impacted both the church and German culture. His hymns influenced the development of singing in Protestant churches. He wrote,

> The first is alien righteousness, that is the righteousness of another, instilled from without. This is the righteousness of Christ by which he justifies through faith, as it is written in 1 Cor. 1:30. . . . Therefore a man can with confidence boast in Christ and say: "Mine are Christ's living, doing, and speaking, his suffering and dying, mine as much as if I had lived, done, spoken, suffered, and died as he did.". . . Through faith in Christ, therefore, Christ's righteousness becomes our righteousness and all that he has becomes ours; rather, he himself becomes ours. . . . This is an infinite righteousness, and one that swallows up all sins in a moment, for it is impossible that sin should exist in Christ.[12]

Justification is a legal picture of the application of salvation, portraying God as the Judge who declares righteous all who believe in Jesus. God's declaration of us as righteous is based on imputation, the act of crediting something to someone.

There are three related imputations. First, God imputes Adam's original sin to all of us (Rom 5:18–19). Second, God imputes our sin to Christ: "He made the one who did not know sin to be sin for us" (2 Cor 5:21). God reckons our sin to the sinless One, who dies as a condemned person for

---

[12] Martin Luther in Timothy F. Lull, ed. *Martin Luther's Basic Theological Writings* (Minneapolis: Fortress, 1989), 155–56.

us. He pays our penalty. Third, God also imputes Christ's righteousness to us, as the combination of three passages reveals:

> Abraham believed God, and it was credited to him for righteousness. (Rom 4:3)

> Just as through one man's disobedience the many were made sinners, so also through the one man's obedience the many will be made righteous. (5:19)

> He made the one who did not know sin to be sin for us, so that in him we might become the righteousness of God. (2 Cor 5:21)

The first passage depicts God as imputing righteousness to Abraham, who believes him. The second passage shows that just as Adam's original sin is imputed to his people, so Christ's saving righteousness is imputed to all believers. As Luther emphasizes, the righteousness of God that saves us (Phil 3:8–9) is Christ's righteousness credited to us. For people to be "made" sinners or righteous (Rom 5:19) means God judges or declares them to be sinners or righteous. The third passage says God imputed our sins to Christ, that God might impute Christ's righteousness to us in union with Christ.[13]

Together these passages teach that God declares us righteous based not on our righteousness but on Christ's righteousness, attributed to us when the Spirit joins us to Christ. The righteousness that saves us is not ours. It is outside of us, the righteousness of another, even Christ's "alien righteousness," as Luther taught.[14] This is how God justifies the ungodly (Rom 4:5). This is why Paul says believers "are justified freely by his grace" as a gift from God (3:24).

---

[13] See Brian Vickers, *Jesus' Blood and Righteousness: Paul's Theology of Imputation* (Wheaton, IL: Crossway, 2006); and Vickers, *Justification by Grace through Faith*, Explorations in Biblical Theology (Phillipsburg, NJ; P&R, 2013).

[14] See Martin Luther, "Third Disputation Concerning Justification, 1536," *Luther's Works* (St. Louis: Concordia, 1955–2019), 34:151–53.

The Roman Catholic View of Justification

Although Roman Catholicism and evangelicalism agree on many things, such as the doctrine of the Trinity, they differ significantly over several things, including justification. The Roman Catholic Church's position was set forth through the Council of Trent, 1545–63. The Roman Catholic Church rejected many of the Reformation's teachings and taught that justification is both forgiveness and an infusion of grace that grants a new nature. Faith is viewed as the first of seven preparations for justification, including baptism, "the instrumental cause," which is considered necessary and regenerating.[15] Justification can be lost if one commits serious sin. Furthermore, the righteousness received in justification can be increased, and grace enables believers to "merit" an increase in grace and eternal life. Merit is construed as something we do to which God responds favorably, and the Catholic Church's position is thus a synergism, in which God and human beings work together for justification.[16] Canon 32 of the Council of Trent states,

> If any one saith, that the good works of one that is justified are in such manner the gifts of God, as that they are not also the good merits of him that is justified; or, that the said justified, by the good works which he performs through the grace of God and the merit of Jesus Christ, whose living member he is, does not truly merit increase of grace, eternal life, and the attainment of that eternal life . . . let him be anathema.[17]

---

[15] Council of Trent, session 6, "On Justification," First Decree, chap. 7, http://www.thecounciloftrent.com/ch6.htm.

[16] We found much help on this from Anthony A. Hoekema, *Saved by Grace* (Grand Rapids: Eerdmans, 1989), 152–91; see also Gregg R. Allison, *Roman Catholic Theology and Practice: An Evangelical Assessment* (Wheaton, IL: Crossway, 2014), 413–51.

[17] Council of Trent, session 6, Canon 32, http://www.thecounciloftrent.com/ch6.htm.

More recently, a Roman Catholic publication, Rahner and Vorgrimler's *Dictionary of Theology*, has included a definition of justification that closely resembles the conclusions of the Council of Trent:

> Justification is the event in which God, by a free act of love, brings man . . . into that relationship with him which a holy God demands of man. . . . He does so by giving man a share of his divine nature . . . through the word of faith and the signs of the sacraments. This justice, which is not merely imputed in juridical fashion but makes a man truly just, is at the same time the forgiveness of sins. . . . There can be no reflexive certainty of salvation for any individual. . . . This justice, God-given and received, can also be lost if man rejects divine love by serious sin. . . . Man can both preserve and continually increase [justification].[18]

A more significant recent document is *The Catechism of the Catholic Church*, 1992, promulgated by Pope John Paul II and commended by Cardinal Joseph Ratzinger (later, Pope Benedict XVI). There is much to agree with, but its view of justification essentially reflects the Council of Trent. For example, article 2, "Grace and Justification," states,

> 1987 The grace of the Holy Spirit has the power to justify us, that is, to cleanse us from our sins and to communicate to us "the righteousness of God through faith in Jesus Christ" and through Baptism.

> 1988 . . . By the participation of the Spirit, we become communicants in the divine nature.

> 1989 . . . Justification is not only the remission of sins, but also the sanctification and renewal of the interior man.

> 1990 Justification detaches man from sin. . . . It frees from the enslavement to sin, and it heals.

---

[18] Karl Rahner and Herbert Vorgrimler, *Dictionary of Theology*, 2nd ed. (New York: Crossroad, 1981), 260–61. Cited in Hoekema, *Saved by Grace*, 168–69.

1991 Justification is at the same time the acceptance of God's righteousness through faith in Jesus Christ. Righteousness (or "justice") here means the rectitude of divine love. With justification, faith, hope, and charity are poured into our hearts, and obedience to the divine will is granted us.

1992 . . . Justification is conferred in Baptism, the sacrament of faith. It conforms us to the righteousness of God, who makes us inwardly just.

1993 Justification establishes cooperation between God's grace and man's freedom.

1995 The Holy Spirit is the master of the interior life. By giving birth to the "inner man," justification entails the sanctification of his whole being.[19]

The Roman Catholic Church views the evangelical Protestant view of justification as a legal fiction, a robe thrown over a corpse that leaves sinners unchanged and does not save them from sin. This criticism is incorrect for two reasons. First, the evangelical view is not a legal fiction but a legal reality. It is an aspect of the application of salvation that is legal or forensic in character. God the righteous Judge declares righteous all who trust Jesus as their substitute. Much like adoption, this is not merely a mental shift but a real declaration, a verdict, a change in status. Justification addresses actual guilt and brings actual forgiveness.

Second, it is wrong to claim that the Protestant view of salvation leaves sinners unchanged and does not save them from sin. Instead, it saves us from both sin's penalty (justification) and its power (regeneration and progressive sanctification). While justification is an aspect of the application of salvation that is relational and does not in itself morally change sinners, it is linked with other aspects of the application of salvation that are transformational. Union with Christ is both forensic and

---

[19] *Catechism of the Catholic Church*, pt. 3, sec. 1, chap. 3, art. 2, "Grace and Justification" (1992). http://www.vatican.va/archive/ccc_css/archive/catechism/p3s1c3a2.htm. Paragraph numbers begin each paragraph.

transformative. Regeneration and progressive sanctification affirm that God changes sinners, making us spiritually alive (regeneration) and causing us to grow in personal holiness (progressive sanctification).

The Reformation and Justification

The Protestant Reformation of the sixteenth century was a political, social, economic, and cultural event with widespread and enduring results.[20] Above all, however, the Reformation was a theological event that focused on the rediscovery of the gospel. The Reformation was not monolithic (uniform), but produced various views of doctrine and church life, including Lutheran, Calvinist, Anglican, Anabaptist, and, in response to Protestant ideas, the Catholic Counter-Reformation. But at its core the Reformation in its various Protestant expressions united around the gospel.

Undergirding the gospel was the Reformation's emphasis on Scripture alone as the supreme authority in the church (*sola Scriptura*).[21] Rejecting Roman Catholicism's view that placed Scripture and tradition on equal footing, Martin Luther, Ulrich Zwingli, John Calvin, and others insisted that the Word of God is the ultimate norm for both teaching and the Christian life. Of course, the Reformers appealed to reason, tradition, and experience, but their goal was to deliberately and consistently subordinate these lesser authorities to the Bible.

When the Reformers gave Scripture the last word concerning faith and practice, they understood that its central message was one

---

[20] We gladly acknowledge help from Timothy George, "What the Reformers Thought They Were Doing," in *Celebrating the Legacy of the Reformation*, ed. Kevin L. King, Edward E. Hindson, and Benjamin K. Forrest (Nashville, TN: B&H, 2019), 9–25.

[21] *Sola Scriptura* is the first of five Reformation *solas*. The others are (2) *sola fide* ("faith alone"): we are saved through faith in Christ alone, not good works; (3) *sola gratia* ("grace alone"): we are saved by God's grace alone; (4) *solus Christus* ("Christ alone"): Christ alone is our Lord and Savior and the only Mediator between God and men; and (5) *soli Deo gloria* ("to the glory of God alone"): all glory belongs to God alone.

of forgiveness conveyed by justification by grace alone through faith alone in Christ alone. Luther's teaching on justification, accepted by the major Reformers, was radical, and it struck at the heart of the medieval Roman Catholic Church's merit theology. The Catholic Church taught that grace was only given through its sacraments of baptism, penance, and Eucharist. Luther protested against this view and devoted his life and energies to promoting the gospel of God's free grace.

Evangelicals and others are in debt to the Reformation when they teach that justification is a legal picture of the way God applies salvation to his people. It is not transformational, and it is not a process. Justification is God's judicial act in which he once for all declares righteous and forgives those who believe in Jesus. Justification, viewed alone, means that a Christian is at the same time righteous (in God's sight) and a sinner (*simul justus et peccator*, as Luther said). But justification is never alone, because everyone God justifies he also regenerates and sanctifies. Justification always results in progressive sanctification but must be distinguished from it.

Because justification is all of grace, it is received by faith alone: "This is why the promise is by faith, so that it may be according to grace" (Rom 4:16). We cannot earn God's favor by any means. Instead, we look entirely away from ourselves and to Christ alone for salvation (4:25).

Justification is based on Christ's substitutionary atonement. He is our propitiation, saving us from God's wrath. Luther put it plainly:

> There was no remedy [for guilt and wrath] except for God's only Son to step into our distress and himself become man, to take upon himself the load of awful and eternal wrath and make his own body and blood a sacrifice for sin. And so he did, out of the immeasurably great mercy and love towards us, giving himself up and bearing the sentence of unending wrath and death.[22]

---

[22] Martin Luther, "Epistle Sermon: Twenty-Fourth Sunday after Trinity," cited in John Nicholas Lenker, ed., *The Precious and Sacred Writings of Martin Luther* (Minneapolis: Luther Press, 1909), 9:43–45. We owe this quote to Stephen

Justification also involves imputation. As noted above, because of Christ's "one righteous act" on the cross, our sin is imputed to him, and his righteousness is imputed to us. In fact, theologians describe Christ's obedience that saves us (Rom 5:19) as "active" and "passive." Christ's active obedience is his lifelong obedience to the Father and the law. His passive obedience refers not to passivity but to his Passion, his sufferings on the cross. This is his obedience to death (Phil 2:8). Jesus's sinless life and death deliver us from our sins.

If we confuse justification with our lifelong Christian growth in love and holiness, we confuse the order of salvation and thereby undercut our assurance of salvation. We are declared righteous *before* we perform good works of love and holiness (Eph 2:8–10). God expects us to love him and live for him, but we do not gain or keep his favor by loving him or living for him. He accepts freely by his grace all who trust Christ as their substitute. Having been justified by grace through faith, we eagerly love him, serve him, and know that we know him (1 John 5:11–20).

Further, if we confuse justification with our lifelong Christian growth in love and holiness, we confuse more than the order. We miss the heart of the matter. We are justified on account of Christ alone, by his grace alone, through faith alone, to the glory of God alone. The repetition of the word *alone* is important. Justification is on account of Christ alone, not Christ and the church. Justification is by grace alone, not grace and baptism. And justification is through faith alone, not faith and works. And because justification is in Christ alone, by grace alone, through faith alone, it highlights God's glory alone.

We Are Adopted in Christ

As Christians, we are in Christ, chosen in Christ, and called to Christ. We are alive in Christ, believe in Christ, and are righteous in Christ. We are also adopted in Christ. Adoption is the act of God the Father in which he places former slaves of sin into his family by grace though faith in Christ

---

J. Wellum, *Christ Alone: The Uniqueness of Christ as Savior* (Grand Rapids: Zondervan, 2017), 174.

the Redeemer. We are accepted by God and adopted by God as the children of God.

Our Need for Adoption: Slaves to Sin

Some say that before adoption we were spiritual orphans, but the Bible paints a more dismal picture. Before the Father adopted us, we were in bondage to Satan, sin, and self. John divides the world into two groups, marked by godly and sinful lifestyles, respectively: "This is how God's children and the devil's children become obvious" (1 John 3:10). Before adoption we were Satan's children, often doing his will unwittingly.

Our plight was even worse: before Christ we "were in slavery under the elemental forces of the world" (Gal 4:3). Paul likely portrays "the elemental forces of the world" as the demonic realm standing behind world ideologies. Before adoption we were orphans in that we did not know God as our Father. But sadly, we also were in subjection to the devil, the demonic realm, and our own sinful selfishness. Thanks be to God, however, for his great grace; by it we are no longer slaves but children (v. 7).

The Source of Our Adoption: God's Love

Scripture describes adoption's source as God's love. In love the Father plans for us to be his children before he creates the world, as Paul stresses (Eph 1:3–6).

John also teaches about our adoption: "To all who did receive him, he gave them the right to be children of God" (John 1:12); "See what great love the Father has given us that we should be called God's children" (1 John 3:1). Indeed, 1 John 3:1 calls us to marvel at God's boundless love for us, expressed in calling us his "children."

The Basis of Our Adoption: Christ

The basis of our salvation, viewed from any perspective, is always Christ's death and resurrection. The Son of God's incarnation, death, and resurrection are necessary for salvation. Paul's time of "completion" (Gal 4:4) refers to the new covenant, which fulfills the covenants God made with Abraham and Moses: "When the time came to completion, God sent his Son, born of a woman, born under the law, to redeem those under the law, so that we might receive adoption as sons" (4:4–5; see also 3:14–18). The Father sends his Son to be born as a Jew. As such he is obligated to keep the law, which he does perfectly. Moreover, Christ comes to redeem those condemned by the law, that we might enjoy adoption into God's family.

After highlighting the curse (threat of punishment) of the law that hangs over the heads of lawbreakers, Paul exclaims, "Christ redeemed us from the curse of the law by becoming a curse for us" (Gal 3:13). Christ's saving work, seen through the lens of adoption, is a redemption that frees us from the slavery of sin.

The Means of Our Adoption: Faith

Christ's saving work is the basis of adoption, and faith in Christ is our means of receiving it. John tells of the Son of God's incarnation as "the true light . . . coming into the world" (John 1:9). Christ, the true Light, causes a separation among humankind. Sadly, although he is the Creator who comes as Savior, most reject him (vv. 10–11). Still, many believe in him, with startling results: "to all who did receive him, he gave them the right to be children of God, to those who believe in his name" (v. 12).

Paul agrees: "for through faith you are all sons of God in Christ Jesus" (Gal 3:26). The Spirit enables us to believe and be adopted: "you received the Spirit of adoption, by whom we cry out, 'Abba, Father!'" (Rom 8:15). "Abba" is an Aramaic word used by children to address a loved father, much like "Daddy" or "Papa."

Justification and adoption are two pictures of salvation taken from the courtroom. Justification is in the criminal division; adoption is in the family court. Both are by God's grace and received through faith.

Justification involves God's declaring us righteous through imputing Christ's righteousness to us, while adoption deals with the Father's welcoming us into his family as his beloved children.

The Results of Our Adoption: Children of God

Adoption brings delightful results, all related to being the children of God. The same Holy Spirit who enables us to call God "Father" bears witness within our hearts to our adoption: "The Spirit himself testifies together with our spirit that we are God's children" (Rom 8:16).

We also bear a family resemblance to our heavenly Father. Paul teaches this at the beginning and end of his passage on adoption in Romans 8: "All those led by God's Spirit are God's sons" (v. 14). To be "led" here refers not to receiving guidance from God's Spirit but to obeying him. In other words, as God's children we are identifiable, for we obey the Spirit of sonship. Paul again teaches that God's children show a family resemblance, for those whom God will glorify with Christ are those who "suffer with him" (v. 17).

Another result of adoption is the fatherly discipline that God gives us as his children: "the Lord disciplines the one he loves and punishes every son he receives" (Heb 12:6). Why does our Father do this? "He does it for our benefit, so that we can share his holiness" (v. 10).

Like other aspects of our salvation, adoption is both "already" and "not yet": "Dear friends, we are God's children now, and what we will be has not yet been revealed. We know that when he appears, we will be like him because we will see him as he is" (1 John 3:2).

Paul also teaches that adoption is both a present and a future reality: "you are no longer a slave but a son, and if a son, then God has made you an heir" (Gal 4:7). We are now sons and daughters, and we are also heirs of a future inheritance. In fact, we long for our final adoption: "we ourselves who have the Spirit as the firstfruits—we also groan within ourselves, eagerly waiting for adoption, the redemption of our bodies" (Rom 8:23).

We Are Holy in Christ

Voices from the Global Church: Lausanne Covenant

"Following Jesus is a change process. Following Jesus means enrolling ourselves in the school of change. . . . Following Jesus means answering the Master's beckoning hand that lovingly declares, 'Come and follow me and I will make you. . . .' Following him is an appointment with change, one that makes us what he always wants us to be or become."[23]

Sanctification is a picture of the application of salvation focusing on our holiness in Christ. God alone is absolutely holy, separate from his creatures and morally perfect. All other holiness derives from God, including the holiness of angels, human beings, the temple, and even heaven. The giving of the Ten Commandments shows that God's holy people display holiness by loving him and others (Exod 19:4–6; 20:2–6; Lev 19:1–18; Matt 22:37–40). Scripture therefore intertwines holiness and love. Holiness is not merely separation from sin but is also consecration to God, which at its core is love for God and others.

Our sanctification occurs in union with Christ; is the work of the Trinity; involves our responsible participation; is past, present, and future; occurs individually and in life together; and is marked by tensions.

Our Sanctification Occurs in Union with Christ

As is true of every aspect of the application of salvation, sanctification occurs in union with Christ. God sanctifies us not apart from him but in spiritual union with him. Paul teaches this when he says that we participate in Christ's story. We have died with him so that the sin that dominated us "was crucified with him . . . so that we may no longer be enslaved to sin" (Rom 6:6). When the Holy Spirit unites us to Christ, he

---

[23] Isaiah M. Dau, "Following Jesus in a World of Suffering and Violence (LOP 62 F)," Lausanne Movement, accessed June 24, 2019, https://www.lausanne.org /content/lop/following-jesus-in-a-world-of-suffering-and-violence-lop-62-f.

sets us free from the stranglehold of sin. And because we are raised with Christ (vv. 5, 8), God empowers us to "walk in newness of life" (v. 4). Union with Christ in his death and resurrection drives our sanctification and enables us to consider ourselves "dead to sin and alive to God in Christ Jesus" (v. 11).

Our Sanctification Is the Work of the Trinity

All three persons of the Godhead are active in our sanctification. The Father providentially guides us through difficult circumstances "so that we can share his holiness" (Heb 12:10). The Son of God dies on the cross to sanctify us: "Christ loved the church and gave himself for her to make her holy" (Eph 5:25–26). And the Holy Spirit brings about our sanctification: "God has chosen you for salvation through sanctification by the Spirit and through belief in the truth" (2 Thess 2:13). In love the Father, Son, and Spirit each promote our holiness.

Our Sanctification Involves Our Active Participation

God alone makes the first move in our salvation, and he is likewise the Author of our sanctification. But this does not mean that we passively sit back. No, we are actively involved in our growth in holiness. Jesus says, "Remain in me, and I in you. Just as a branch is unable to produce fruit by itself unless it remains on the vine, neither can you unless you remain in me" (John 15:4). Paul urges Christians "in view of the mercies of God . . . to present [their] bodies as a living sacrifice, holy and pleasing to God" (Rom 12:1). Peter admonishes, "Above all, maintain constant love for each other, since love covers a multitude of sins" (1 Pet 4:8).

In fact, it is because God is the Author of our sanctification that we are enabled to be active participants. In Philippians, Paul commands us, "Work out your own salvation with fear and trembling" (2:12). But the Christian life is not a self-help project, as Paul's next words show: "for it is God who is working in you both to will and to work according to his good purpose" (v. 13). God is the Lord who saves, keeps, and works in us, and he enables us to pursue holiness.

In Colossians, Paul similarly teaches that we *labor* for him who saves us by his grace. And we do so by his mighty power. Paul strives to attain his goal of presenting "everyone mature in Christ . . . striving with his strength that works powerfully in [him]" (Col 1:28–29).

Our Sanctification Is Past, Present, and Future

More precisely, our sanctification is definitive, progressive, and final. *Definitive* (or *initial*) *sanctification* is the Holy Spirit's work of setting us apart as holy unto Christ, constituting us as saints. This is a past event that occurred when we trusted Christ. Paul surprises us by addressing the troubled Corinthian church as "those sanctified in Christ Jesus, called as saints" (1 Cor 1:2). Although there were false believers among them (5:9–13), most of the Corinthians were "washed," "sanctified," and "justified" (6:11). Paul uses the same past tense to speak of their justification and their sanctification.[24] Our sanctification has a past element: in Christ we have been constituted as saints.

Our sanctification is also present. *Progressive sanctification* is the Spirit's work of enabling us to grow in practical holiness. This is what is most commonly connoted by the term *sanctification* in theology. Paul tells the Thessalonians, "This is God's will, your sanctification: that you keep away from sexual immorality" (1 Thess 4:3). Those who are already saints are urged to pursue God's will for their lives, which is to pursue holiness. This is a daily activity in the Christian life. We fight temptation, oppose sin, and strive toward holiness. The idea of progressive sanctification is a major theme in the Bible (see Romans 12–14; Galatians 5–6; Ephesians 4–6 for just a few examples), communicated in many ways: as walking with God, following God, being a disciple, growing, obeying, abiding, and so on.

Our sanctification is also future. *Final sanctification* is the Spirit's work of conforming us to Christ's image at his return, at which point Christ

---

[24] Paul also speaks of definitive sanctification in 2 Thess 2:13. Peter does the same in 1 Pet 1:1–2, as is seen if we recognize that there Peter uses "obedient" to speak of obeying Christ as he is offered in the gospel (see 4:17).

will "present the church to himself in splendor, without spot or wrinkle or anything like that, but holy and blameless" (Eph 5:27). Paul promises that our entire sanctification will occur when Christ returns (1 Thess 5:23), assuring us, "He who calls you is faithful; he will do it" (v. 24). First John likewise celebrates our final sanctification: "We know that when he appears, we will be like him because we will see him as he is" (3:2).

We are holy now. We are growing in holiness. And we will be completely holy. Seeing all three aspects of our sanctification benefits us. First, it highlights the fact that salvation is God's work from beginning (in definitive sanctification) to end (in final sanctification). Highlighting that God alone saves does not diminish our activity in progressive sanctification but puts it in proper theological context. We work under God and by his strength when we "strain forward" and "press on" toward the "prize" (Phil 3:13–14 ESV).

Second, seeing sanctification's three aspects offers us hope in the midst of our struggles. We can look back: our past struggles remind us that we are not now what we once were. We can also look forward: we all struggle, and the hope of final sanctification assures us that God will complete the good work that he began in us (Phil 1:6).

Our Sanctification Occurs Individually and in Life Together

God sanctifies us individually and corporately as his people. Jesus promises to preserve each one of God's people: "This is the will of him who sent me: that I should lose none of those he has given me but should raise them up on the last day" (John 6:39). He also prays to the Father for his disciples as representatives of the church: "Sanctify them by the truth; your word is truth" (17:17).

Additionally, God addresses his people as individuals when he exhorts them to godliness: "Now we desire each of you to demonstrate the same diligence for the full assurance of your hope until the end, so that you won't become lazy but will be imitators of those who inherit the promises through faith and perseverance" (Heb 6:11–12). God also speaks to us as church members: "Encourage each other daily . . . so that none of you is hardened by sin's deception" (3:13).

God treats us as individuals: "Pursue . . . holiness—without it no one will see the Lord" (Heb 12:14). At the same time, we belong to other believers, who care for us and give us opportunity to care for them. "And let us watch out for one another to provoke love and good works, not neglecting to gather together, as some are in the habit of doing, but encouraging each other, and all the more as you see the day approaching" (10:24–25).

Our Sanctification Involves Tensions

Intellectual and Experiential Knowledge. An awareness of tensions in sanctification benefits us. As with other aspects of the Christian life, a tension exists between knowing and doing. We need to learn theologically how to pursue holiness. Simultaneously, we need to learn experientially about sanctification through life—in marriage, parenting, work, suffering, and much more.

"Already" and "Not Yet." Sanctification is both "already" (realized) and "not yet" (not fully realized). In definitive sanctification, the Spirit has already set us apart from sin to holiness as saints. But as we all painfully know, perfect holiness in thought, speech, and actions is still future; final sanctification is not yet realized.[25] So we live between definitive and final sanctification, experiencing progressive sanctification's joys and frustrations. We *have been* made holy and also *will be* completely holy. And while we wait for that day, we persistently and patiently grow in love and holiness.

Divine Sovereignty and Human Responsibility. God sovereignly sanctifies us, and we are active, responsible agents. God alone is holy, and he is the sanctifier of all who are sanctified. Because of his action on our behalf, we now act. We bear the fruit of the Spirit, his fruit in and through us (Gal 5:22–23). We yield, submit, depend, and trust God for our holiness while also daily confessing, repenting, believing, walking, and fighting.

---

[25] Wesleyan "Christian perfection" or "entire sanctification" holds that believers may love God so totally in this life as to be freed from sin, defined as deliberate transgression of a known law of God.

Indicative and Imperative. Colossians 3:9–10 and Eph 4:22–24 illustrate Paul's teachings on the indicative and the imperative.[26] In the former
passage, Paul tells the Colossians what has already happened: they have
taken off the old man and put on the new. In Eph 4:22–24 he exhorts his
readers to take off the old ways and put on the new. This is a pattern in
Paul. He often speaks of what God in Christ has done for his people (the
indicative). In another context, he exhorts God's people to do the very
things that he says God has done for them (the imperative). This tension is
Paul's way of teaching that (1) the Christian life is based on God's saving
work; (2) the Christian life is reflective of what God has done for us; and (3)
we are actively involved in the Christian life. God's free salvation becomes
ours, and we experience it by living in the light of what he has done for us.

Victory and War, Freedom and Slavery. The collision of grace and
sin produces tensions. God's grace brings victory and freedom; our sin
brings war and slavery. Many cry with Paul, "What a wretched man I am!
Who will rescue me from this body of death?" (Rom 7:24). While a final
answer escapes us, two points deserve mention. First, God humbles us
in progressive sanctification. In Christ we have attained "every spiritual
blessing in the heavens" (Eph 1:3), but in practice we also stumble and
fall. Our struggles, then, undercut our pride and self-reliance. Second, the
battles of progressive sanctification drive us back to Christ's grace. We
need grace at the beginning of the Christian life and at every step along its
path. Martin Luther explains:

> Sin remains in the spiritual man, in order that he might exercise
> himself in grace, put off his pride, and check his arrogance. He
> who confesses his sins should not believe that he can thereby
> shake off the burden of sin and quietly live on in sin. But he
> should know that when he puts off the burden of sin, he enters
> the warfare for God and takes up a new burden for God against
> the Devil and his own remaining faults.[27]

---

[26] Ridderbos, *Paul*, 253–58, 270–71 (see chap. 5, n. 11).

[27] Martin Luther, *Commentary on Romans*, trans. J. Theodore Mueller (Grand
Rapids: Zondervan, 1954), 116.

Positive and Negative. Sanctification involves positively pursuing holiness out of love for Christ. It also involves negatives: daily turning away from sin out of that same love for Christ. Another way of capturing this tension is to say that the Christian life involves passion for God and holiness (positives) and also discipline in rejecting what opposes God's glory (negatives).

Living with the Tensions.[28] As followers of Christ, our lives are marked by both a sincere longing for holiness and a struggle with sin. We live with the tensions related to realizing genuine growth and experiencing frequent failure. We are all works in progress; we are under construction. "He's Still Working on Me" is not just the name of a song children sing at church; it is a reality that clarifies our spiritual journey on this side of heaven. Our salvation has begun and will be completed; in the meantime, we are in the process of growing in holiness, love, and Christlikeness. As strange as it feels, we are now saints and are also not yet fully holy in our day-to-day lives, though we are increasingly so. We are, as Martin Luther stressed 500 years ago, simultaneously justified and sinners. Hence the tensions.

One day, though, by God's grace, we will be thoroughly transformed. God's grace has begun our journey; God's grace sustains our journey; and God's grace will lead us home, completing our journey. On that day, we will be completely characterized by holiness and love, and all our current battles with sin will be a distant memory. In the meantime, we persevere in faith, knowing that we are kept by God.

We Are Kept in Christ

Unlike other aspects of the application of salvation, perseverance deals only with ongoing salvation. The phrase "the perseverance of the saints" refers both to God's preservation of the saints—his keeping them—and the saints' perseverance—their continuing to live for God. We will call the first "preservation" and restrict "perseverance" to the saints' continuing to believe and serve God. Related concepts include "assurance," confidence

---

[28] For more practical teaching on the Christian life, see chapter 12, "The Christian Life."

of final salvation, and "apostasy," defection from a professed faith. We will explore preservation, perseverance, assurance, and apostasy in turn.[29]

Preservation: God Keeps Us

God graciously saves us, and he graciously keeps us saved. Jesus affirms concerning his sheep:

> I give them eternal life, and they will never perish. No one will snatch them out of my hand. My Father, who has given them to me, is greater than all. No one is able to snatch them out of the Father's hand. I and the Father are one. (John 10:28–30)

Jesus gives his people eternal life, unending life with God. Emphatically Jesus declares that we will *never* perish (v. 28). He reinforces this teaching by stating that he and the Father hold us, and no one can snatch us away from them (vv. 28–29). "Snatch" indicates violent attempts to tear us from the arms of the Father or the Son, robbing us of salvation. Jesus categorically promises that no such attempts will succeed. The Father and Son are one, and here their unity is focused on preserving us, keeping us saved (v. 30). Jesus gives us eternal life, and we are safe in the strong arms of him and the Father.[30]

Paul likewise affirms God's preservation of us as his saints: "There is now no condemnation for those in Christ Jesus" (Rom 8:1). God the Judge will not condemn us to hell; rather, he will save us to the end. In Romans 8, Paul marshals four arguments for preservation. First, God promises us final salvation because of his sovereign plan. He has planned and will execute our salvation from beginning to end. Those whom God foreknew (loved before time) he also predestined (chose to be saved). These same people he also called to Christ, justified in Christ, and glorified, or made sharers of his glory in Christ (8:29–30). Paul includes glorification, which

---

[29] We follow and condense the more thorough treatment in Robert A. Peterson, *Our Secure Salvation: Preservation and Apostasy*, Explorations in Biblical Theology (Phillipsburg, NJ: P&R, 2009).

[30] See also Luke 22:31–34; John 6:35–44; and 17:9–24.

is still future, among the past events God has performed for his people. In God's sovereign plan, we are as good as glorified. God began our salvation, and he will complete it.

Paul's second argument for our preservation is based on God's lordship: "If God is for us, who is against us?" (v. 31). God is the supreme Being, the Lord of all, and he is on our side. God shows that he is for us by giving his beloved Son to die for us. Having gone to such lengths to make us his own, he will surely now keep us saved (v. 32).

The third argument is from the courtroom. Paul asks who will bring an accusation against God's people and make it stick. The answer is no one, for "God . . . justifies" (v. 33). The Judge, knowing our sins perfectly, has already declared us righteous in his Son. No accusations of guilt, then, will stand. Paul asks who will condemn us and mentions Christ, who shares with the Father the role of Judge. Will the Son condemn us? No, he will save us. The Judge of all is our Savior, who died, rose, and intercedes for us (v. 34).

Paul's last argument concerns God's amazing love. The apostle asks rhetorically what can divorce God's people from Christ's love (v. 35). He cites seven threats, from "affliction" to "sword" (death), and concludes, "No, in all these things we are more than conquerors through him who loved us" (v. 37). Eloquently, he affirms that nothing at all will ever "be able to separate us from the love of God that is in Christ Jesus our Lord" (vv. 38–39). In these four ways, Paul assures us that God will keep us saved. He does the same in other passages.[31]

Hebrews also teaches preservation. It contrasts Christ with Old Testament priests, whose ongoing priesthood depended on continuing generations: "But because he remains forever, he holds his priesthood permanently" (7:24). Jesus gave himself as the final sacrifice for sins and then arose. His priesthood, therefore, never ends but is as eternal as his life. The writer concludes, "Therefore, he is able to save completely those who come to God through him, since he always lives to intercede for them" (v. 25). Because Christ arose, he saves forever all who trust him as

---

[31] These include Rom 5:9–10; 1 Cor 1:4, 8–9; 11:27–33; Eph 1:13–14; 4:30; Phil 1:6; and 1 Thess 5:23–24.

Savior. He always presents his finished sacrifice in the Father's presence to keep us saved.

Peter, too, affirms preservation. He praises the Father for mercifully giving us new birth, which provides a living hope. The basis for the new birth is Christ's resurrection, which unleashes eternal life (1 Pet 1:3). Peter says our grand inheritance "is imperishable, undefiled, and unfading, kept in heaven for" us (v. 4). Unlike earthly inheritances, it will last forever, and it is "kept" (reserved) for us. And we too are kept: "You are being guarded by God's power through faith for a salvation that is ready to be revealed in the last time" (v. 5). God's power, mediated by faith, protects us for final salvation. Our salvation is reserved in heaven, and by God's power we will not fail to enjoy it. Other authors of the General Epistles teach this same truth.[32]

Perseverance: We Continue in the Faith

Scripture teaches that true believers must continue in the faith. In fact, our perseverance (continuance) in three areas underlines the reality of our profession: in faith, love, and holiness.

True believers persevere in faith. We not only make a profession of faith; we continue to believe the gospel. Paul says that though the Colossians were once alienated from God, "now he has reconciled [them] by his physical body through his death, to present [them] holy, faultless, and blameless before him" (Col 1:22). He adds a condition: "if indeed you remain grounded and steadfast in the faith and are not shifted away from the hope of the gospel that you heard" (v. 23). We may waver in faith but will never completely and totally reject the gospel.[33]

True believers persevere in love. When God gives us new life in Christ, he gives us a new heart that loves him and others. Of course, our

---

[32] See Heb 6:17–20; 1 John 2:18–19; and 5:18. For more detail on how the Trinity, attributes of God, and Christ's saving work secure our preservation, see Peterson, *Our Secure Salvation*, 196–99.

[33] Other texts indicating that believers must persevere in faith include Matt 24:13; John 6:66–69; Heb 10:36; and 12:1.

love for God and others is never perfect in this life, but it is real, as 1 John attests (3:10, 13–15). A lack of love reveals a lack of salvation (v. 10, 14–15). Steadfast love boosts our assurance (v. 14).

First John also traces our love to its source:

> Dear friends, let us love one another, because love is from God, and everyone who loves has been born of God and knows God. The one who does not love does not know God, because God is love. God's love was revealed among us in this way: God sent his one and only Son into the world so that we might live through him. (4:7–9)

Indeed, God is the source of love (v. 7). Again we see that love is evidence of the new birth and that a heart without love is a bad sign (v. 7–8). God is characterized by love, and he shows it preeminently in sending his Son to die and give us eternal life (vv. 8–9). As his children, we too will be characterized by love.

True believers persevere in holiness. God accepts us in justification, not because of our righteousness but because of Christ's. God saves us not *according to* our holiness but *unto* holiness: "You are saved by grace through faith, and this is not from yourselves; it is God's gift—not from works, so that no one can boast. For we are his workmanship, created in Christ Jesus for good works, which God prepared ahead of time for us to do" (Eph 2:8–10). People saved by God's grace, not their works, are eager nevertheless to do good works (Titus 3:4–8). Those professing Christ must pursue peace with one another and holiness, without which "no one will see the Lord" (Heb 12:14). Consistently failing to live for God is a bad sign. We are not saved by our holiness, but everyone God saves seeks holiness.

Assurance: God Gives Us Confidence of Our Salvation

God wants his children to have assurance, confidence of final salvation, as is clear from the conclusion to 1 John. John calls us to have assurance through knowing several things. We can know that we have the Son and eternal life in the Son (5:11–13). We can know that we are heard by God, our loving Father who enjoys and answers our prayers (vv. 14–15). We can know that we are born of God, changed by God, and kept by God (v. 18). We can know that we are children of God (v. 19). We can know the truth of God and the true God, and that we are in the Son, who is the true God and eternal life (v. 20). Indeed, we can know we have eternal life in the Son (vv. 11–13), for knowing the Son is having eternal life (v. 20). Such assurance is not presumption but humility, for as we submit to God's Word, he gives us confidence of salvation.

We also learn from 1 John and other passages that God assures us in three ways: by his Word, by his Spirit's witness within us, and by changing our lives.

God Assures Us by His Word. The most important way God assures his people is by promising salvation to all of us who believe. This is assurance based on his Word, his promise, the gospel. The texts we examined above that teach preservation belong here, as do gospel promises: "This is the testimony: God has given us eternal life, and this life is in his Son. The one who has the Son has life" (1 John 5:11–12).

God pledges that all who trust Christ as Savior will not go to hell but will gain eternal life (John 3:16). We need not wait until the end to hear the Judge's verdict. Instead, we can and should know now the last day's verdict: not condemned (v. 18). God's Word gives us this confidence.[34]

God Assures Us by His Spirit. God assures the hearts of everyone who believes the gospel. He gives his Holy Spirit to all who trust Christ for salvation. One of the Spirit's ministries is to give us confidence that we belong to God. Paul warmly instructs, "The Spirit himself testifies together with our spirit that we are God's children" (Rom 8:16). John speaks similarly: "This is how we know that we remain in him and he in us: he has given us of his Spirit" (1 John 4:13; see also 3:24; 5:6–9). The Holy Spirit is God's internal witness of salvation. He testifies in our hearts that God is our Father and we are his cherished children.

---

[34] Other passages belonging in this category include John 6:37–40; 17:15–24; Rom 5:9–10; 1 Cor 11:31–32; Phil 1:6; 1 Thess 5:23–24; and Heb 6:17–20. See Robert A. Peterson, *The Assurance of Salvation* (Grand Rapids: Zondervan, 2019).

God Assures Us by Changing Our Lives. God also assures us by working in our lives. First John stresses that we can know that we are born again, in part, because we love God and his people (2:7–11; 4:7–12). We are still a work in progress, so we struggle with sin (1:8–10; Jas 3:2). But we do obey God (2:3–6; 5:1–5) and live on a Godward trajectory (2:15–17; 3:4–6; 5:16–21).

The three persons of the Trinity change our lives and reinforce our assurance. We must "work out [our] own salvation with fear and trembling." How will this occur? "It is God who is working in [us] both to will and to work according to his good purpose" (Phil 2:12–13). The Father works, giving us godly desires and the power to carry them out. The Son is the vine, and we are the branches, of which Jesus says, "The one who remains in me and I in him produces much fruit, because you can do nothing without me" (John 15:5). The Spirit works in all of us "who belong to Christ Jesus" and "have crucified the flesh with its passions" to produce his fruit in our lives: "love, joy, peace, patience, kindness, goodness, faithfulness, gentleness, and self-control" (Gal 5:24, 22–23).

God saves us by Jesus's work, not our own. But God saves us to do good works. And as he works in us to produce the "good works, which God prepared ahead of time" for us to do (Eph 2:10), he strengthens our assurance. "But," we may protest, "we still sin; that is not a good work, and it does not help our assurance but hinders it." It is true that no one should claim assurance who does not follow Christ as a way of life (as the previous section on perseverance stressed). But it is also true that being consistently bothered by sin and longing to be rid of it may indicate that God is at work in our lives to produce godliness. Those who are insensitive to sin and not burdened by it are the most likely to be deceived. Those who are sensitive to sin are the most likely to be honest followers of Christ. God convicts his children of sin; he reminds us that we still have sin; and he invites us to confess it. When we do (and as his children we will), he graciously promises to forgive and cleanse us (1 John 1:8–10). This is encouraging in light of the rest of 1 John's stress on our perseverance in faith, love, and holiness as evidence of eternal life.

Synthesis. Paul combines the three means of assurance in Rom 5:1–11. God assures us by working in our lives. He uses affliction, rightly handled, to produce endurance and the character quality of steadfastness. Seeing God change us now breeds hope for future heavenly glory (vv. 3–4). God also assures us by his Spirit: our hope of heaven does not disappoint, for his "love has been poured out in our hearts through the Holy Spirit who was given to us" (v. 5). The Spirit assures us deep within of the Father's love.

Most of all, God assures us by his Word. When we were "helpless," "ungodly," "sinners" (vv. 6, 8), God loved us and "Christ died for us" (v. 8). Since God reconciled us to himself when we were foes, "how much more, having been reconciled, will we be saved by his life" (v. 10)? Repeatedly God promises to save and keep us. We can rest in his Word.

Apostasy: Some Deny the Faith

Scripture teaches that some who profess Christ will deny the faith and perish. The major function of the Bible's many warning passages is to distinguish true believers from false ones.[35] Christ the Judge will reject some who profess his lordship and do miracles in his name because he has never known them with the knowledge of salvation (Matt 7:21–23).[36]

Many texts unmask inadequate faith (John 2:23–25; 1 Tim 1:3–7, 18–20; 2 Tim 2:11–13). Scripture says God will reject those who reject the gospel (Matt 10:33; 1 Tim 4:1–5; 2 Tim 2:17–19). It warns that some who appear to be saved will in fact not be (2 Pet 2:20–22; Rev 22:18–19).

Scripture links lack of perseverance and apostasy: "They went out from us, but they did not belong to us; for if they had belonged to us, they would have remained with us. However, they went out so that it might be made clear that none of them belongs to us" (1 John 2:19). After false teachers fail to persuade John's readers of errors concerning Christ (4:1–6) and

---

[35] See Peterson, *Our Secure Salvation*, 101–94, for exposition of many warning passages.

[36] See also Matt 7:16, 20; Luke 8:4–15; John 15:1–8; and Acts 8:13, 20–24.

the Christian life (1:5–10), the false teachers reject the believers. Although the teachers outwardly associate with the church, their departure shows they are not really saved. If they belong to God's people, John teaches, they would remain (v. 19). True believers persevere.

We Are Glorious in Christ

We Are Restored to Glory

We are created in the image of God to worship and display God, but we all refuse to acknowledge God's glory and instead seek our own glory. Through this we forfeit the glory God intends for us as his image bearers. However, by his grace and through union with Christ, the perfect image, God saves us, restoring us as full image bearers to participate in and reflect the glory we longed for the whole time. Thus we are recipients of glory, are undergoing transformation through glory, and will be sharers of glory. Our salvation is not merely from sin but is also unto glory. We who exchange the glory of God for idols, we who rebel against God's glory, have been, are being, and will be completely transformed by the very glory we despise and reject (Rom 1:18–31; 3:23; 8:28–30; 9:23; 2 Cor 3:18).

We Are Characterized by Glory, Past, Present, and Future

Our glory in Christ is past, present, and future. We have already been given glory, as Jesus states: "I have given them the glory you have given me, so that they may be one as we are one" (John 17:22). We are being transformed from glory to glory, as Paul expresses: "We all, with unveiled faces, are looking as in a mirror at the glory of the Lord and are being transformed into the same image from glory to glory; this is from the Lord who is the Spirit" (2 Cor 3:18). And we await glory, as Paul describes: "We rejoice in the hope of the glory of God" (Rom 5:2). Our future glorification follows Christ's glorious return (Titus 2:13; 1 Pet 4:13) and is coupled to the renewal of the cosmos (Rom 8:19–22; 2 Pet 3:13). All of us as God's people, both the living and the resurrected dead, will be glorified together (1 Cor 15:51–52; 1 Thess 4:15–18).

We Are Conformed to Christ's Image

The image of God, in which we are created (Gen 1:26–27), still exists in our being. Its function is tarnished in the fall but is gradually restored in Christ (Eph 4:22–24; Col 3:9–10). It will be perfected only when Christ, the true image (2 Cor 4:4; Col 1:15), powerfully conforms us to his image in resurrection: "He will transform the body of our humble condition into the likeness of his glorious body, by the power that enables him to subject everything to himself" (Phil 3:21). Ferguson points out, "The image and image-bearers are one in Spirit to the end, so that when Christ appears in glory image-bearers are one with him in that glory (Col 3:4). We are raised in Christ, with Christ, by Christ, to be like Christ."[37] In the meantime, we know "Christ in [us], the hope of glory" (Col 1:27).

We Will Share Christ's Glory

Paul writes, "I consider that the sufferings of this present time are not worth comparing with the glory that is going to be revealed to us" (Rom 8:18). Astoundingly, *glorification* means resurrected saints' seeing Christ's glory and being transformed by it, so as to partake of it. God will produce "for us an absolutely incomparable eternal weight of glory" (2 Cor 4:17). In answer to Jesus's prayer, we will see his glory (John 17:24), and that vision will transform us (Phil 3:21; 1 John 3:2) so that we will actually partake of his glory (1 Pet 5:2). God has "prepared [us] beforehand for glory" (Rom 9:23) from the beginning, and by his grace he will bring his "many sons and daughters to glory" (Heb 2:10) in the end.

---

[37] Sinclair Ferguson, *The Holy Spirit*, Contours of Christian Theology (Downers Grove, IL: InterVarsity, 1996), 251.

We Will Receive Glorified Bodies

Though at death our spirits are "made perfect" (Heb 12:23), glorification
involves our *bodies* being redeemed (Rom 8:23). There will be continuity
between our present bodies and our resurrection bodies (v. 11). But there
will also be discontinuity, for our new bodies will be imperishable, glorious, powerful, and immortal (1 Cor 15:42–54). They will be both physical
and "spiritual" (v. 44), ruled by the Spirit.

We Will Inhabit a Renewed Creation

As believers, we are a microcosm of the final redemption of the cosmos.
The macrocosm is this: "the creation itself will also be set free from the
bondage to decay into the glorious freedom of God's children" (Rom
8:21). God will fulfill his purposes for his creation by delivering it from
the curse (Rev 22:3) and perfecting us (1 Thess 5:23) and it (2 Pet 3:13).
Ferguson puts it well: "The consummation of this glorification awaits the
eschaton and the Spirit's ministry in the resurrection. Here, too, the pattern of his working is: as in Christ, so in believers and, by implication, in
the universe."[38]

We Are Saved for God's Glory

As we have previously seen, in Eph 1:3–14 Paul praises the triune God for
our salvation: the Father chooses us, the Son redeems us, and the Spirit
is our seal. These blessings of salvation are comprehensive: we have
"every spiritual blessing" (v. 3), which includes being chosen, adopted,
redeemed, forgiven, reconciled, given an inheritance, sealed, and more.
(From other passages, we could add: called, made alive, justified, sanctified, kept, and glorified.) God accomplishes all of this through the saving work of Christ, and he applies it through our union with Christ. And
at key intervals, Paul explicitly incorporates a refrain:

---

[38] Ferguson, *The Holy Spirit*, 249.

to the praise of his glorious grace (v. 6)

praise to his glory (v. 12)

to the praise of his glory (v. 14)

Paul's point is unmistakable: *the ultimate end of our salvation is not our salvation,* as important as that is. God chooses us, adopts us, redeems us, unites us, gives us an inheritance, and seals us *to the praise of his glory* (1:6, 12, 14).

The Application of Salvation

Aspect	Problem	Description	Scripture
Union with Christ	Separation	God joins us to Christ	Eph 1:3–14
Calling	Deafness	God enables us to hear	2 Tim 1:9
Regeneration	Death	God makes us alive	Eph 2:1–5
Conversion	Lostness	God turns us from sin (repentance) to Christ (faith)	Acts 20:21
Justification	Condemnation	God declares us righteous	Eph 2:15–16
Adoption	Slavery	God brings us into his family	Gal 3:26
Sanctification	Uncleanness	God makes us holy	Eph 5:25–27
Preservation	Unfaithfulness	God keeps us saved	Rom 8:28–39
Glorification	Shame	God gives us his glory	2 Cor 3:18

Paul is emphatic: God's glory is his ultimate end.[39] But what does this mean? Ephesians discloses two aspects of this. First, God acts unto the praise of his glory, or to the praise of the glory of his grace (1:6, 12, 14). Thus, God's glory as his ultimate end means that God acts to receive the worship and praise of his creation, especially his people. Second, God acts to display himself throughout creation. He displays his love, mercy, grace, kindness, creative work, and wisdom (2:4–10; 3:8–10). Thus, God's glory as his ultimate end also means that God acts to display himself, and as he displays himself he communicates his greatness and fullness. That, in and of itself, glorifies him. So, according to Ephesians, God's glory as his ultimate end means that he acts to display himself and communicate his greatness and that he acts to receive worship.

Ephesians also reminds us of a related pitfall in understanding the glory of God: that God acts with his glory as his ultimate end does not imply that other ends are excluded. Those ends remain important and should not be marginalized. The Bible teaches that the ultimate end of our salvation is God's glory, and it puts forward additional reasons. For example, Eph 1:4–6 is instructive:

> In *love* he predestined us for adoption to himself as sons through Jesus Christ, according to the purpose of his will, to the praise of his glorious *grace*, with which he has blessed us in the Beloved. (ESV)

Notice also Eph 2:4–7:

> But God, who is rich in *mercy*, because of his great *love* that he had for us, made us alive with Christ even though we were dead in trespasses. You are saved by *grace*! He also raised us up with him and seated us with him in the heavens in Christ Jesus, so that

---

[39] God's glory is the goal of creation; the exodus; Israel; Jesus's ministry, life, death, resurrection, and reign; our salvation; the church; the consummation; and all of salvation history. See Edwards, "The End for Which God Created the World," 125–36 (see chap. 4, n. 27).

in the coming ages he might display the immeasurable riches of his *grace* through his *kindness* to us in Christ Jesus.

In the same Ephesians passages that underline that God acts unto his glory, we also see that God acts out of a genuine love for us. So, our conviction that God acts with glory as his ultimate end must be linked to our recognition that God acts out of love for our good.

Other passages highlight this as well. John 3:16 states, "God loved the world in this way: he gave . . ." (see also 1 John 4:9–10). Titus 3:4–7 ties our salvation to God's mercy. Romans 8:28 also makes it clear that redemptive history is, in large part, for the good of God's people.

Exodus is also noteworthy. Why does God redeem his people from slavery in Egypt? One might quickly reply, "For his glory." Certainly God redeems his people from slavery to glorify himself. But other concerns also play a part. The book of Exodus presents God's reasons for deliverance in a multifaceted way: love for his oppressed people (3–4); faithfulness to the covenant promises made to Abraham, Isaac, and Jacob (3:15; 4:5; 6:8; 32:13; 34:6); so that Israel would serve Yahweh (4:23; 6:5); so that the people would know that he is Yahweh (6:7; 10:2; 13:1); to give the Promised Land (6:8); so that the Egyptians would know that he is Yahweh (5:2; 7:5; 14:3–4, 15–18); so that Pharaoh would know Yahweh as incomparable (7:17; 8:10–18); to display his power (9:16); so that his name might be proclaimed in all the earth (9:16); to pass down a heritage to the children (10:1–2); so that his wonders might be multiplied (11:9); to receive glory over Pharaoh and his army (14:3–18); and for Israel's sake (18:8). So God delivers his people out of love, covenant faithfulness, and jealousy. He does so for his glory, for Israel's good, for judgment on Egypt, and for the continuance of his covenant people.

Realizing these multiple ends does not detract from an emphasis on God's glory but actually highlights it. Indeed, in the exodus God displays his love, covenant faithfulness, jealousy, providence, and power through his wonders, salvation, and judgment. In doing so, God communicates himself and thus glorifies himself.

Understanding this truth is significant, as it helps us address a common question concerning God's glory: if God seeks his own glory above all things, does this mean that he is selfish? After all, if we as humans seek our own glory, we are deemed selfish. The standard answer to this line of questioning is that God is the ultimate Being and the highest end, and we are not. Good behavior seeks the highest end, so God's making himself his own ultimate end is fitting. If we make ourselves the highest end, we act wrongly because we treat ourselves as the highest end when we are not.

That argument is valid and significant. But it omits God's genuine desire for the good of his creatures and fails to show how God's love and his glory are united. It is important to stress that God saves us out of love, displays his kindness toward us for all eternity, and is glorified by putting his greatness, goodness, and fullness on display. As God displays himself, he glorifies himself. In this way, God is self-giving and self-exalting. He gives himself to us and acts on our behalf, which simultaneously meets our needs and demonstrates his sufficiency.[40] Through it all, he saves us for our good and, ultimately, for his glory.

---

[40] For more on how God's self-giving and self-exalting cohere, especially in the mutual glorification of the persons of the Trinity, see Morgan, "Toward a Theology of the Glory of God," 175–87 (see chap. 4, n. 23).

▦ KEY TERMS

active obedience

adoption

alien righteousness

apostasy

application of salvation

assurance

calling

children of God

conversion

election

eternal life

faith

forgiveness of sins

glorification

glory of God

gospel

heirs of God

Holy Spirit

imputation

in Christ

inheritance

justice of God

justification

kingdom of God

love of God

passive obedience

perfectionism

perseverance

predestination

preservation

regeneration

repentance

resurrection

sanctification

simul justus et peccator

union with Christ

witness of the Spirit

▦ RESOURCES FOR FURTHER STUDY

Allison, Gregg R. *Historical Theology: An Introduction to Christian Doctrine*. Grand Rapids: Zondervan, 2011, 453–561.

Burke, Trevor. *Adopted into God's Family*. Downers Grove, IL: InterVarsity, 2006.

Campbell, Constantine R. *Paul and Union with Christ*. Grand Rapids: Zondervan, 2012.

Carson, D. A., Peter T. O'Brien, and Mark A. Seifrid, eds., 2 vols. *Justification and Variegated Nomism*. Grand Rapids: Baker Academic, 2001, 2004.

Demarest, Bruce A. *The Cross and Salvation: The Doctrine of Salvation*. Foundations of Evangelical Theology. Wheaton, IL: Crossway, 1997.

Ferguson, Sinclair B. *Children of the Living God*. Carlisle, PA: The Banner of Truth Trust, 1989.

Hoekema, Anthony E. *Saved by Grace*. Grand Rapids: Eerdmans, 1989.

Marshall, I. Howard. *Jesus the Saviour: Studies in New Testament Theology*. Downers Grove, IL: InterVarsity, 1990.

Murray, John. *Redemption Accomplished and Applied*. Grand Rapids: Eerdmans, 1955.

Packer, J. I. *Evangelism and the Sovereignty of God*. Chicago: InterVarsity, 1961.

Peterson, Robert A. *Adopted by God*. Phillipsburg, NJ: P&R, 1987.

———. *The Assurance of Salvation*. Grand Rapids: Zondervan, 2019.

———. *Election and Free Will*. Phillipsburg, NJ: P&R, 2001.

———. *Our Secure Salvation: Perseverance and Apostasy*. Phillipsburg, NJ: P&R, 2005.

———. *Salvation Applied by the Spirit: Union with Christ*. Wheaton, IL: Crossway, 2014.

Schreiner, Thomas R. *Faith Alone: The Doctrine of Justification*. Grand Rapids: Zondervan, 2015.

9

THE HOLY SPIRIT

Living between Jesus's first and second comings is quite a blessing. We as believers have the completed Bible of Old and New Testaments; a personal knowledge of Christ; the instruction, discipline, and fellowship of the church; and, in focus here, the greatest revelation of the person and work of the Holy Spirit in the history of redemption. Since Jesus pours out the Spirit at Pentecost, God provides in the New Testament unprecedented teaching on the Spirit and makes available unprecedented power to his people. Our identity as believers is shaped in many ways by the Holy Spirit, and this chapter aims to make us more aware of these ways.

After tracing the Holy Spirit through the biblical story, we will examine selected passages on the Spirit. Then we will see that the Holy Spirit is a divine person, the Third Person in the Trinity. Next we will ponder the Spirit's works in creation, in inspiring Scripture, in the Old Testament, in the apostles, in the world, and in Jesus. Investigating the Spirit's ministries to believers, we begin with his most important one—union with Christ. We conclude by studying the ministries of the Holy Spirit in the church. The Spirit indwells, empowers, produces fruit, enables worship, and gifts us to build up the church.

▒ OBJECTIVES

- To lay a biblical foundation for understanding the person and work of the Holy Spirit
- To demonstrate that the Holy Spirit is a person, not an impersonal force
- To show that the Holy Spirit is God
- To increase understanding that the Holy Spirit is a member of the Trinity
- To enlarge our appreciation of the Holy Spirit's works and ministries
- To motivate us to grow in worship of, reliance on, and obedience to the Holy Spirit
- To establish our identity as individuals and a church indwelled, gifted, and empowered by the Spirit

▒ OUTLINE

The Holy Spirit in the Biblical Story
The Holy Spirit in Selected Passages
     John 14:15–17
     Acts 1:8
     1 Corinthians 2:10–16
     1 Corinthians 12:1–13
     1 Thessalonians 1:5–6
The Person of the Holy Spirit
     The Holy Spirit Is a Person
     The Holy Spirit Is God
     The Holy Spirit Is a Person of the Trinity
The Work of the Holy Spirit
     The Spirit Works in Creation
     The Spirit Inspires the Scriptures
     The Spirit Works in the Old Testament
     The Spirit Works in the Apostles
     The Spirit Works in the World
     The Spirit Works in Jesus

The Holy Spirit in the Biblical Story

The Spirit of God is active in the Old Testament.[1] He is "hovering over" the waters of creation as a bird does her nest (Gen 1:2). The Spirit empowers individuals for service, including the artist Bezalel (Exod 31:3), Joshua (Num 27:18), judges such as Gideon and Samson (Judges 6:34; 15:14), King David (1 Sam 16:13), and prophets such as Ezekiel (Ezek 11:5). The Spirit speaks through the prophets. Joel prophesies that God will pour out his "Spirit on all humanity" (Joel 2:28). God speaks through Zechariah to remind Israel that God's work is accomplished not by human "strength or by might, but by [his] Spirit" (Zech 4:6).

The prophets foretell the Spirit's work in and through the Messiah. The Spirit will give him wisdom and strength to execute justice for the oppressed and to slay the wicked (Isa 11:1–4). The Messiah will be the Lord's chosen servant, strengthened by the Spirit, to act inconspicuously, while bringing justice to the nations and teaching them (42:1–4). The Lord

---

[1] Certain New Testament passages equate the Holy Spirit of the New Testament with the Spirit of God in the Old Testament (Luke 4:18/Isa 61:1–2; Acts 2:17–18, 33/Joel 2:28–29). In addition, Peter says that "the Spirit of Christ" in the Old Testament prophets predicted Christ's sufferings and glory (1 Pet 1:10–11).

will anoint the Messiah with the Spirit, and as a result the Messiah will "bring good news to the poor . . . [and] proclaim the year of the Lord's favor, and the day of our God's vengeance" (61:1–2).

The prophets Jeremiah and Ezekiel foretell that God will make a new covenant with his people. This covenant will not be broken as the Israelites broke the one God made with Moses (Jer 31:32). Instead, in the new covenant God promises to write his word on their hearts, to be their God and to make them his people, to bring them all to know him, and to forgive their sins forever (vv. 33–34). How will this be accomplished? Jesus comes to ratify the new covenant by his death and resurrection. Ezekiel sees that God will put his Spirit within his people to cleanse them and give them a new heart that is responsive and obedient to God (Ezek 36:25–27).

As the Old Testament prophets foretell, the Holy Spirit plays a major role in Jesus's life and ministry. In fact, the Spirit is active in Jesus from his conception to his resurrection. The Spirit is at work in his conception (Luke 1:35), baptism (Matt 3:16), temptation (4:1), teaching (Luke 4:18, 21, quoting Isa 61:1), healings and exorcisms (Matt 12:22, 28; Acts 10:38), crucifixion (Heb 9:14), and resurrection (Rom 1:3–4).

Jesus is the Messiah or Christ, which means "anointed one." The Father anoints Jesus with the Spirit at his baptism (Matt 3:16), and Jesus bestows the Spirit on the church, fulfilling prophecies of Joel (Joel 2:28) and John the Baptist (Matt 3:11). After his death and resurrection, Jesus pours out the Holy Spirit on the church in newness and power with two great results (Acts 2). First is the missionary activity of the early church, with the gospel spreading across the Roman world. Second, especially in Paul's letters, God provides in-depth teaching concerning the person and activities of the Spirit. We will study that teaching in this chapter.

The Holy Spirit also takes part in the culmination of the biblical story. In exile John is "in the Spirit" on a Sunday when he receives the message of the book of Revelation from Jesus (1:10). The phrase "in the Spirit," taken from Ezekiel, shows John has the same authority as the Old Testament prophets. Along with the Father and Jesus Christ, the Spirit grants divine gifts of grace and peace to the churches to which John writes (1:4–5). "The seven spirits" is "a figurative designation of the effective working of the Holy Spirit."[2] Elsewhere John uses "seven spirits of God" with the same meaning (3:1; 4:5; 5:6). The Spirit serves the Father (he is "before his throne," 1:4; 4:5) and the Son (5:6).

Christ refers to himself as "the one who has the seven spirits of God" (3:1), showing the close connection between him and the Holy Spirit. Christ addresses the seven churches in 2:7–3:22. At the same time, the Spirit does as well, for near the end of each letter we read, "He who has an ear, let him hear what the Spirit says to the churches" (2:7, etc.).

In contrast to the lost, who will never experience rest from the torments of hell, the Spirit pronounces a blessing on all who die in union with Christ: "They will rest from their labors, since their works follow them" (14:13). The Spirit transports John to a mountain, where he sees the vision of the new Jerusalem clothed with God's glory, a picture of God's dwelling in the midst of his people forever (21:10). John ends his book as he began it, praying that the Father, the Spirit, and Jesus would bless his readers (22:16–17, 21).

The Holy Spirit in Selected Passages

In the following passages we see that Jesus promises to send the Spirit, another Counselor like Jesus, who does many things that he does, including teaching, bringing conviction, and giving eternal life. The Spirit will abide with the disciples as their companion and will indwell them. In fulfillment of prophecies of Joel and John the Baptist, Jesus pours out the Holy Spirit on the disciples in newness and power at Pentecost. In Acts, as the Holy Spirit leads the apostles, they preach the gospel, do miracles, suffer persecution, and win converts. Acts presents the Spirit as having personal attributes and as a divine person, for his name is used interchangeably with "God," and he does things only God can do.

Paul says the Holy Spirit empowers the apostles' preaching, revealing God's thoughts to them, and making the difference between believers and unbelievers. The Spirit enables people to recognize Christ's

---

[2] G. K. Beale, *The Book of Revelation*, New International Greek Testament Commentary (Grand Rapids: Eerdmans, 1999), 189.

lordship and reject idolatry. God's working in the church reflects the
unity and diversity of the Trinity. As there is diversity in the Trinity, so in
the church there are diverse gifts, ministries, and workings. These gifts,
ministries, and workings are unified, however, because as the Trinity
is one God, so the one Spirit gives different gifts; the one Lord Jesus is
served by different ministries; and the one God and Father works in the
gifts and ministries. God gifts each of us, and we must use our gifts to
serve others. Although a human body has many members, together they
constitute one body. Similarly, Christ's church has many members but
is one. Paul underscores the church's oneness by speaking of the Holy
Spirit's most important ministry: uniting believers to Christ in salvation.
When Paul preaches the gospel in Thessalonica, the Holy Spirit works
through his human words, and the hearers believe and gain assurance
of salvation.

John 14:15–17

After encouraging his disciples in prayer and obedience (John 14:13–15),
Jesus promises to send the Spirit. In response to Jesus's request, the
Father will give the disciples "another Counselor to be with [them] forever" (v. 16). The Spirit is another Counselor like Jesus, and he does many
things that Jesus does. Actually, John presents the Spirit as taking Jesus's
place and assuming his ministries. Jesus gives eternal life (10:28), and
so does the Spirit (6:63). Jesus is the truth (14:6), and the Counselor is
the Spirit of truth (14:17). Jesus convicts the world of sin (7:7), and he
promises that the Spirit will do the same (16:8–11). Jesus teaches the disciples (13:34–35), and the Spirit will continue his teaching ministry (14:26;
16:13–14). Jesus spends time with the disciples (1:39), and the Spirit will
be with them forever (14:16). Jesus bears witness to himself (8:14), and
the Spirit will also bear witness to Jesus (15:26).

Jesus says that, unlike the disciples, the world does not know
the Holy Spirit (14:17). The world will not accept the Spirit because it
only believes what it can see. The Spirit is invisible and thus outside
the world's frame of knowledge. By contrast, Jesus tells the disciples,
"You do know him, because he remains with you and will be in you" (v.

17). The Spirit will abide with the disciples as their companion and will indwell them.

Acts 1:8

After his death and resurrection, Jesus appears to his disciples at different times over forty days, and he teaches them. He instructs them to stay in Jerusalem and to wait for the promise made by the Father and John the Baptist (Acts 1:4–5). Jesus here refers to words at the beginning and end of his earthly ministry. At the beginning John the Baptist denies that he himself was the Messiah and points to one far greater than himself who would "baptize . . . with the Holy Spirit and fire" (Luke 3:16). Toward the end of his time on earth, Jesus says, "I am sending you what my Father promised. As for you, stay in the city until you are empowered from on high" (24:49).

Now Jesus says that this promise will be fulfilled "in a few days" (Acts 1:5). He asserts, "You will receive power when the Holy Spirit has come on you, and you will be my witnesses in Jerusalem, in all Judea and Samaria, and to the end of the earth" (v. 8). During his three-and-a-half-year public ministry, Jesus trains his disciples in preparation for this day. Now, as he prepares to return to the Father in heaven, he commissions and equips them to spread the gospel. He tells them that they will witness in increasing concentric circles, beginning in Jerusalem and gradually expanding their outreach until they reach "the end of the earth." Most important, he promises to send the Holy Spirit to enable them to witness effectively in his name.

On the day of the Jewish Feast of Pentecost, Jesus pours out the Holy Spirit on the disciples in newness and power (Acts 2:1–13). Jesus's words in 1:8 provide a general outline to the book of Acts. As the Holy Spirit leads and empowers the apostles, they preach the gospel, perform miracles, endure persecution, and gain converts in Jerusalem (2:14–7:60), Samaria (8:1–40), and beyond (9:1–26:32), leading to Rome (27:1–28:31).

Acts presents the Spirit as a divine person. He has attributes that only personal beings possess: he speaks (10:19), forbids (16:6), compels (20:22), and can be lied to (5:3), tested (v. 9), and resisted (7:51). He is a divine person, for his name is used interchangeably with "God" (5:3–4). Furthermore, he does things only God can do. He speaks through the Old Testament prophets (1:16; 28:25), gives repentance (11:15–18), and appoints overseers in the church (20:28). The Spirit is a major player in Acts. He speaks (11:12; 13:2), guides (13:4; 16:6–7), encourages (9:31), empowers (1:8; 10:38), transports (8:39), grants wisdom (6:10), fills believers (4:8; 13:9), and energizes speaking for God (4:31; 19:6).

1 Corinthians 2:10–16

The Holy Spirit performs valuable ministries, and Paul presents four of them in 1 Cor 2:10–16. First, the Spirit empowers the apostles' preaching. Certain topics are considered unfit for polite Greek society, and crucifixion is certainly among them. It is a dreadful form of public execution, and Greeks speak of it little. Nevertheless, in Corinth the focus of Paul's preaching is "Jesus Christ and him crucified" (v. 2). Although Greeks prize rhetoric and grand oratory, Paul displays neither in Corinth. Instead, there his words are not full of human wisdom and persuasion but are "a demonstration of the Spirit's power" (v. 4).

Second, the Spirit reveals the gospel to the apostles. Paul preaches not human wisdom but divine. The world's rulers do not know God's wisdom, for if they did, they would not crucify Jesus, the Son of God and Savior of the world (v. 8). God's wisdom is not found by human efforts to know his mind. Rather, God makes known his wisdom to Old Testament prophets and New Testament apostles. As a result, they preach and write the very words of God. How does God reveal to Paul and the other apostles his wisdom found in the gospel? "God has revealed these things . . . by the Spirit" (v. 10).

Third, just as no one knows another person's thoughts unless he or she chooses to reveal them, so God must reveal his thoughts if we are to know him (vv. 10–11). And that is just what he has done. The Holy Spirit, who alone knows God's deep thoughts (v. 10), reveals God's thoughts to the apostles, with the result that they convey their messages not in words of human wisdom "but in those taught by the Spirit" (v. 13). When the apostles preach the gospel or write Scripture, they preach or write the very words of God. Consequently, the Bible is God's words in human language.

Fourth, Paul teaches that the Holy Spirit makes the difference between a believer and an unbeliever. Paul describes unsaved people frankly: they lack the Holy Spirit, and as a result do not accept what comes from him, which in context means the message of Christ. They reject the gospel and regard it as "foolishness" because it is only understood spiritually, that is, with the Spirit's help (v. 14). By contrast, believers are "spiritual" people because they have the Holy Spirit. As a result, they have spiritual discernment (v. 15). Paul repeats the ideas that we can know God only as he reveals himself to us (as Isa 40:13 says), that he has done so, and that therefore by the Spirit we know God's wisdom found in Jesus Christ and him crucified (1 Cor 2:16).

1 Corinthians 12:1–13

Paul instructs his readers concerning spiritual things, including gifts in 1 Corinthians 12. He emphasizes that it is the Spirit who enables his readers to recognize Christ's lordship and reject idolatry.[3] Their prior spiritual experiences as unbelievers did little to prepare them to understand Christian worship. Before salvation they were deceived and "led astray by mute idols" (v. 2). Paul thinks of Old Testament denunciations of idols, who can neither hear and answer prayer nor speak God's word as his prophets do (see Ps 115:4–5; Isa 41:21–24).

Paul then speaks about elementary spiritual discernment. He insists, "No one speaking by the Spirit of God says, 'Jesus is cursed,' and no one can say, 'Jesus is Lord,' except by the Holy Spirit" (1 Cor 12:3). The Spirit prompts people to acknowledge Jesus's lordship. In fact, confession of Jesus Christ as Lord is only possible by the Spirit.

Next, Paul teaches that God's working in the church reflects the unity and diversity of the Trinity (vv. 4–6). There is diversity in the Godhead:

---

[3] We received help from Roy E. Ciampa and Brian S. Rosner, *The First Letter to the Corinthians*, Pillar New Testament Commentary (Grand Rapids: Eerdmans, 2010), 560–66.

Father, Son, and Holy Spirit are distinct and not to be confused. Similarly, in the church there are diverse gifts, ministries, and activities. They are unified, however, because they reflect the unity of the Trinity. The Father, Son, and Spirit are one God. Similarly, the one Spirit gives different gifts. The one Lord Jesus is served by different ministries. And the same God and Father "empowers them all in everyone" (v. 6 ESV).

Paul applies his message by reminding believers that God gifts each of us. He urges us to use our gifts "for the common good" (v. 7; see also 1 Pet 4:10). Paul then gives a representative list of spiritual gifts: "a message of wisdom . . . , a message of knowledge . . . , faith . . . , gifts of healing . . . , the performing of miracles, . . . prophecy, . . . distinguishing between spirits, . . . different kinds of tongues, . . . interpretation of tongues" (vv. 8–10). Paul stresses that the same Holy Spirit who gives these various gifts is active in each one. Furthermore, the Spirit gives the gifts "as he wills" (v. 11).

Paul likens the church to a human body with its many parts. Although a body has many members, together they constitute one body (v. 12). Similarly, Christ's church is one but has many members. Paul underscores the church's oneness by speaking of the Holy Spirit's most important ministry: uniting believers to Christ in salvation (v. 13). Paul uses the images of baptism and the drinking of liquid to teach that the Spirit joins *all* believers to Christ. In the midst of our cultural distinctions, we are one in Christ because we share the Spirit.

1 Thessalonians 1:5–6

Paul also speaks of the Holy Spirit as he gives thanks to God for his dear Thessalonians (1 Thess 1:2). He fondly remembers their faith, love, and hope, which has inspired their work, labor, and perseverance, respectively (v. 3). Paul says that he knows that God has chosen his readers for salvation, because they believe the gospel.

Paul describes his readers' reception of the gospel: "Our gospel did not come to you in word only, but also in power, in the Holy Spirit, and with full assurance" (v. 5). Paul, Silvanus, and Timothy preach the gospel in Thessalonica. The people hear the gospel in human words. But God is working in and through those words. Consequently, the hearers believe. Paul tells how the gospel comes to them: the Holy Spirit uses the preached Word and works powerfully in the hearers. As a result, they "welcomed the message with joy from the Holy Spirit" (v. 6) and gained "full assurance" (v. 5). "Full assurance" is "the Thessalonians' deep inward persuasion of the truth of the gospel, a token of the Holy Spirit's work in their hearts."[4]

The Person of the Holy Spirit[5]

The Spirit is a person and is God, a person of the Trinity.

The Holy Spirit Is a Person

Scripture presents the Holy Spirit as a person, not an impersonal force. That the Spirit is personal is seen in how he has personal traits, performs personal ministries, and is affected as a person.

The Holy Spirit Has Personal Traits

The elements of personality are intelligence, volition, and emotion, and Scripture ascribes all three to the Spirit. The Spirit has intelligence, for Jesus promises that the Spirit will speak through his disciples when they are persecuted because of Jesus (Matt 10:19–20). He promises that after he returns to the Father, the Spirit will teach the disciples, remind them of Jesus's words (John 14:26), and guide them "into all the truth" (16:13). Paul teaches that the Spirit alone "knows the thoughts of God" (1 Cor 2:11).

The Spirit has volition, for although believers are told to seek spiritual gifts, "one and the same Spirit is active in all these, distributing to each person as he wills" (1 Cor 12:11). The Spirit allocates spiritual gifts as he sees fit.

---

[4] F. F. Bruce, *1 & 2 Thessalonians*, Word Biblical Commentary (Waco, TX: Word, 1982), 14.

[5] We acknowledge help in this section from Erickson, *Christian Theology*, 873–79 (see chap. 1, n. 18).

The Spirit has emotion, because only persons can be grieved, and Paul says the Spirit can be grieved. He warns, "And don't grieve God's Holy Spirit. You were sealed by him for the day of redemption" (Eph 4:30).

THE HOLY SPIRIT PERFORMS PERSONAL MINISTRIES

The Spirit performs ministries that only persons perform. John's Gospel portrays the Spirit as taking Jesus's place when he returns to the Father. Jesus promises, "I will ask the Father, and he will give you another Counselor to be with you forever" (14:16). The Spirit perpetuates Jesus's teaching, testifies to him, and glorifies him:

> He will take from what is mine and declare it to you. (John 16:14; see also 14:26)

> When the Counselor comes, the one I will send to you from the Father—the Spirit of truth who proceeds from the Father—he will testify about me. (15:26)

> He will glorify me. (16:14)

Impersonal forces also do not convict people of sin, but the Spirit does, as Jesus says: "When he comes, he will convict the world about sin, righteousness, and judgment" (John 16:8).

Paul also teaches that the Spirit engages in personal ministries, such as prayer: "the Spirit himself intercedes for us with unspoken groanings" (Rom 8:26). The Spirit assures: "The Spirit himself bears witness with our spirit that we are children of God" (v. 16 ESV). And he gives life: "the letter kills, but the Spirit gives life" (2 Cor 3:6).

THE HOLY SPIRIT IS AFFECTED AS A PERSON

The Spirit can be blasphemed (Mark 3:29), lied to (Acts 5:3), tested (v. 9), resisted, (7:51), grieved (Eph 4:30), quenched (1 Thess 5:19), and insulted (Heb 10:29).

In sum, the Holy Spirit is not an impersonal force but a person whom believers know, as Jesus foretells: "You do know him, because he remains with you and will be in you" (John 14:17). And he is a person with whom we fellowship: "The grace of the Lord Jesus Christ, and the love of God, and the fellowship of the Holy Spirit be with you all" (2 Cor 13:13).

The Holy Spirit Is God

The Holy Spirit is a person, even a divine person. He is God. The deity of the Spirit is seen in that he has divine qualities, does divine works, and has a name interchangeable with God's.

THE HOLY SPIRIT HAS DIVINE QUALITIES

Scripture ascribes to the Spirit qualities that only God has, including truth, holiness, power, knowledge, and eternity. Two of the Spirit's divine qualities are tied to his names. He is "the Spirit of truth" (John 14:17; 15:26; 16:13) because he does God's work of revealing Jesus to his disciples (15:26; 16:13–15). He is the "Holy Spirit" because his name connects him to God's holiness in a way only fitting for God himself. Truth and holiness, then, are bound to the Spirit's names so as to show him to be a divine person.

When the Holy Spirit works mightily through Paul to perform apostolic miracles (Rom 15:19), he reveals his divine power. Furthermore, the Spirit possesses divine knowledge, for only "the Spirit searches everything, even the depths of God" (1 Cor 2:10).

The Holy Spirit also possesses God's attribute of eternity, as Hebrews demonstrates when it links the Spirit and Christ's sacrifice: he "through the eternal Spirit offered himself without blemish to God" (Heb 9:14).

THE HOLY SPIRIT DOES DIVINE WORKS

The Spirit performs certain works that only God does. The Spirit plays a part in the work of creation (Gen 1:1–2) and the production of Holy Scripture (2 Pet 1:20–21), but his most famous work deals with salvation. The Spirit raises Jesus from the dead. Although Scripture usually credits the Father for this work, the Holy Spirit has a part to play too. In fact, Jesus "was appointed to be the powerful Son of God according to the Spirit of holiness by the resurrection of the dead" (Rom 1:4).

God the Spirit also applies our salvation. He unites us to Christ (1 Cor 12:13). He applies to us adoption (Rom 8:15), regeneration (John 3:8; Titus 3:5), sanctification (2 Thess 2:13), and justification (1 Cor 6:11). He also plays a part in raising us from the dead (Rom 8:11). In fact, having the Spirit is synonymous with having salvation: "If anyone does not have the Spirit of Christ, he does not belong to him" (v. 9).

Only God indwells his people. Jesus predicts that the Spirit will indwell us (John 14:16–17). And in at least six places, Paul says the Holy Spirit indwells us (Rom 8:9, 11; 1 Cor 3:16; 6:19; 2 Cor 1:21–22; 2 Tim 1:14).

THE HOLY SPIRIT'S NAME IS INTERCHANGEABLE WITH GOD'S

Luke implies this in Acts 5 when Peter confronts Ananias and Sapphira about their lies. Peter rebukes Ananias and says that when he lies "to the Holy Spirit," he lies not "to people but to God" (vv. 3–4). Paul teaches that Christians are "God's temple" (1 Cor 3:16) and a "temple of the Holy Spirit" (6:19). The Spirit is thus interchangeable with God. His name is equated with God's.

The Holy Spirit Is a Person of the Trinity

The Spirit is distinct from the Father and the Son but is equal to them. He is associated with the Father and the Son as only God can be.[6]

THE SPIRIT IS DISTINCT FROM THE FATHER AND THE SON

The Gospels, the Epistles, and Revelation show this: the Spirit is a distinct person of the Godhead. After Jesus's baptism, "the heavens suddenly opened for him, and he saw the Spirit of God descending like a dove and coming down on him. And a voice from heaven said: 'This is my beloved Son, with whom I am well-pleased'" (Matt 3:16–17). The Father, Son, and Spirit are simultaneously present at Jesus's baptism. Jesus comes out of the water, the Spirit descends on him, and the Father speaks words of love and delight.

---

[6] For more on the Trinity, see chapter 3, "God the Trinity."

At the end of John's Gospel, the risen Jesus blesses his disciples: "'Peace be with you. As the Father has sent me, I also send you.' After saying this, he breathed on them and said, 'Receive the Holy Spirit'" (20:21–22). As he sends the disciples, Jesus distinguishes himself from the Father who sent him. And, in a prophetic action, he breathes the Holy Spirit on them to empower them to preach the gospel.

After declaring that all of God's promises find their fulfillment in Christ, Paul writes, "Now it is God who strengthens us together with you in Christ, and who has anointed us. He has also put his seal on us and given us the Spirit in our hearts as a down payment" (2 Cor 1:21–22). As he defends himself against adversaries' attacks with words of assurance, the apostle distinguishes God the Father, Christ, and the Spirit.

In Revelation, which bears features of a prophecy and an epistle, John opens with a salutation: "To the seven churches in Asia. Grace and peace to you from the one who is, who was, and who is to come, and from the seven spirits before his throne, and from Jesus Christ, the faithful witness, the firstborn from the dead and the ruler of the kings of the earth" (Rev 1:4–5). Along with "Jesus Christ" we find the eternal One on the throne, God the Father, and "the seven spirits," the Holy Spirit. "The seven spirits" and "the seven spirits of God" (4:5; 5:6) are "figurative designations for the effective working of the Holy Spirit, since this is the characteristic identification of Spirit in the New Testament when found in conjunction with or as part of an apparent formula with God and Christ."[7]

All parts of the New Testament, then, distinguish Father, Son, and Holy Spirit. They teach us not to confuse the persons. We do not put the Father or the Spirit on the cross, for example. The three trinitarian persons are distinct, but mysteriously, they are also equal. This is proven when Scripture associates the Spirit with the other two persons so as to imply his deity.

---

[7] Beale, *The Book of Revelation*, 189.

Before his ascension, the risen Christ gives the Great Commission to his church, telling the disciples to make other disciples, baptize, and teach all nations. They are to baptize believers "in the name of the Father and of the Son and of the Holy Spirit" (Matt 28:19). The Spirit is here combined with the other two persons of the Trinity in a way fitting for God alone. It makes no sense to speak of baptism in the name of an apostle (1 Cor 1:13) or of an angel. Rather, baptism is performed in the name of the triune God.

Paul writes, "There are varieties of gifts, but the same Spirit; and there are varieties of service, but the same Lord; and there are varieties of activities, but it is the same God who empowers them all in everyone" (1 Cor 12:4–6 ESV). Paul teaches that there are varieties of gifts, service, and activities but the same Holy Spirit, the same Lord Jesus, and the same God the Father. That is, the unity of the persons of the Trinity undergirds the church's ministries. The Spirit gives different spiritual gifts, which are used in different types of service done for the Lord Jesus, and which result in different activities performed by the Father. The Holy Spirit is tied to the other two trinitarian persons in various aspects of the church's life. Only God gives spiritual gifts, and he is here called "the same Spirit" (v. 4).

Paul's most famous benediction—"The grace of the Lord Jesus Christ, and the love of God, and the fellowship of the Holy Spirit be with you all" (2 Cor 13:13)—shows the Spirit's deity. Here Christ is the source of grace for God's people, the Father is the source of love, and the Holy Spirit is the source of fellowship. Divine blessings are given by the Son, the Father, and the Spirit.

The Work of the Holy Spirit

The Spirit's works powerfully demonstrate his deity, for only God creates, gives Scripture, and moves supernaturally in the lives of Old Testament figures, Jesus, his apostles, and people in the world. And the Spirit does all these things.

The Spirit Works in Creation

The Bible begins, "In the beginning God created the heavens and the earth. Now the earth was formless and empty, darkness covered the surface of the watery depths, and the Spirit of God was hovering over the surface of the waters" (Gen 1:1–2). The word translated "Spirit" (*ruakh*) means "breath," "wind," "spirit," or "Spirit." Though some have understood v. 2 to refer to wind, this is incorrect, as Collins shows, pointing to "contextual factors" in support of the translation "Spirit."[8]

Similar to the Holy Spirit's "descending like a dove" on Jesus after his baptism (Matt 3:16), Genesis 1 here speaks of the Spirit using bird imagery. The fact that "the Spirit of God was hovering over the surface of the waters" (v. 2) refers to the Holy Spirit's role in the divine activity of creation. Bruce Waltke explains: "Hovering eaglelike over the primordial abyss, the almighty Spirit prepares the earth for human habitation."[9] Elihu's words in Job also presuppose the Spirit's part in creation: "The Spirit of God has made me, and the breath of the Almighty gives me life" (Job 33:4).

Scripture frequently assigns the work of creation to God the Father. A number of times the New Testament assigns it also to the Son as the Father's agent (John 1:3; 1 Cor 8:6; Col 1:16; Heb 1:2). When Genesis and Job indicate that the Spirit played a part in creation, they imply his deity, because only God is Creator.

The Spirit Inspires the Scriptures

In his farewell discourses, Jesus foretells the writing of the New Testament. Before his crucifixion he promises to send "the Spirit of truth" (John 14:17; 15:26; 16:13), who will minister in keeping with his name:

---

[8] See Collins, *Genesis 1–4*, 45 n. 17 (see chap. 1, n. 8).

[9] Waltke, *Genesis*, 60 (see chap. 1, n. 7).

The Counselor, the Holy Spirit, whom the Father will send in my name, will teach you all things and remind you of everything I have told you. (John 14:26)

When the Counselor comes, the one I will send to you from the Father—the Spirit of truth who proceeds from the Father—he will testify about me. (15:26)

When the Spirit of truth comes, he will guide you into all the truth. For he will not speak on his own, but he will speak whatever he hears. He will also declare to you what is to come. He will glorify me, because he will take from what is mine and declare it to you. (16:13–14)

Jesus promises that the Spirit will teach the disciples, remind them of Jesus's words, testify of Jesus, and guide them into the truth. He will take what comes from the Father through the Son and make it known to the disciples. The Savior thus pre-authenticates the apostles' writing of the New Testament by the Spirit.

Twice Peter teaches that the Holy Spirit is the ultimate Author of Scripture. First, when discussing Old Testament prophecy, he says, "No prophecy of Scripture comes from the prophet's own interpretation, because no prophecy ever came by the will of man; instead, men spoke from God as they were carried along by the Holy Spirit" (2 Pet 1:20–21). Peter asserts that prophecies are not the product of mere human impulse but that the Holy Spirit works in the prophets so that they speak from God himself. When the prophets write, God speaks forth his word.

Second, Peter indicates the source of the prophets' predictions of Christ's humiliation and exaltation: "The prophets . . . inquired into what time or what circumstances the Spirit of Christ within them was indicating when he testified in advance to the sufferings of Christ and the glories that would follow" (1 Pet 1:10–11). The prophets do not fully comprehend their predictions of the Christ. But "the Spirit of Christ" within them does. When Scripture calls the Holy Spirit the "Spirit of Christ," it either anticipates or recalls Christ's pouring out of the Spirit on the church at

Pentecost. The prophets are spokesmen for God because the Spirit works through them.

The Spirit Works in the Old Testament[10]

THE HOLY SPIRIT EQUIPS AND EMPOWERS

The Spirit engages in many activities after creation (Gen 1:2). He gives the master craftsman Bezalel "ability in every craft to design artistic works" to adorn the tabernacle (Exod 31:3; 35:31). He equips people for leadership, including Joshua and David (Num 27:18; 1 Sam 16:13). He empowers judges, such as Othniel (Judg 3:10), Gideon (6:34), Jephthah (11:29; 13:25), and Samson (14:6, 19; 15:14). He anoints and empowers kings, enabling them to undertake successful military exploits (1 Sam 11:6).

God's Spirit is ever-present with his people (Ps 139:7), and David asks God's "good Spirit" to lead him in righteousness (143:10 ESV). After Samuel anoints youthful David for kingship, the Spirit takes control of him (1 Sam 16:13); elderly David's last words praise God that the Spirit has spoken through him (2 Sam 23:2).

THE HOLY SPIRIT ENABLES PEOPLE TO PROPHESY

The Spirit enables people to speak for God, including elders in Israel (Num 11:17, 25–26, 29); kings, including Saul (1 Sam 10:6, 10; 19:23) and David (2 Sam 23:2); and of course, the prophets, even Balaam (Num 24:2).

THE HOLY SPIRIT STRENGTHENS AND ENCOURAGES

Through the prophet Azariah, the Spirit encourages King Asa to bring spiritual renewal to Judah (2 Chr 15:1), and through the priest Jahaziel, he motivates King Jehoshaphat to stand against Judah's enemies and watch the Lord's victory (20:14). The Spirit moves the priest Zechariah to rebuke the idolatrous people of Judah under King Joash (24:20). In spite of Israel's rejection of the words of earlier prophets (Zech 7:12), God

---

[10] See Christopher J. H. Wright, *Knowing the Holy Spirit through the Old Testament* (Downers Grove, IL: InterVarsity Academic, 2006); Leon J. Wood, *The Holy Spirit in the Old Testament* (Grand Rapids: Zondervan, 1976).

strengthens the people to rebuild the temple: "My Spirit is present among you; don't be afraid" (Hag 2:5), for such things are accomplished "not by strength or by might, but by my Spirit, says the LORD of Armies" (Zech 4:6).

THE HOLY SPIRIT MAKES FUTURE PROMISES

Isaiah, whom the incomprehensible Spirit of the Lord sends to Israel (Isa 40:13; 48:16) prophesies that the Spirit will rest on the Messiah and give him wisdom and strength (11:2) to bring justice to the nations (42:1), to preach "good news to the poor . . . to heal the brokenhearted," and "to proclaim liberty to the captives" (61:1).

Isaiah prophesies that although Israel rebels and grieves his Holy Spirit after the exodus (63:10), the Spirit will bring prosperity, transformation, and deliverance to Israel (32:15; 44:3; 59:21) and complete destruction to Edom (34:16).

Through Ezekiel God promises to replace Israel's heart of stone with one of flesh and to place his Spirit within them so that they might obey him (Ezek 36:26–27). By putting his Spirit within them, he will cause them to "live," to be reborn nationally (37:14). He will pour out his Spirit and bring restoration to Israel (39:29). Joel foresees God's pouring out of his Spirit at Pentecost with amazing spiritual results (Joel 2:28–32).

The Spirit Works in the Apostles

The Spirit is also active in the apostles' ministries. He speaks through them (Matt 10:20; Luke 12:12), grants them "wisdom" (Luke 21:15), and empowers them to witness to Jesus's death and resurrection (24:49). He indwells them and will be their Helper forever (John 14:16–17 ESV).

The Spirit directs the apostles in God's work (Acts 13:2, 4) and leads them to make wise decisions for the church (15:28). He shuts and opens doors of ministry for them, steering them to preach the Word where God calls (16:6–10).

Using the apostles' ministry, the Spirit erects the church (that is, the body of believers) as the Lord's temple. Surprisingly, God takes Gentiles—foreigners to God and his covenants—and integrates them into his people (Eph 2:19–22). The Holy Spirit builds the church on the foundation of Christ and the apostles. He does this by adding believing Jews and Gentiles to God's people, joining them to Christ as individuals to form "a holy temple in the Lord . . . for God's dwelling in the Spirit" (vv. 21–22).

The Spirit Works in the World

Voices from the Global Church: Lausanne Covenant

"We love the Holy Spirit within the unity of the Trinity, along with God the Father and God the Son. He is the missionary Spirit sent by the missionary Father and the missionary Son, breathing life and power into God's missionary Church. We love and pray for the presence of the Holy Spirit because without the witness of the Spirit to Christ, our own witness is futile. Without the convicting work of the Spirit, our preaching is in vain. Without the gifts, guidance and power of the Spirit, our mission is mere human effort. And without the fruit of the Spirit, our unattractive lives cannot reflect the beauty of the gospel."[11]

In addition, the Spirit works in the world. Jesus tells the disciples that it is good for him to leave because after he does, he will send the Helper. Moreover, "when he comes, he will convict the world about sin, righteousness, and judgment: About sin, because they do not believe in me" (John 16:8–9). Because Jesus is full of mercy, he will send the Spirit to convict sinners "because they do not believe in" him (v. 9). Left to their own devices, sinners would not believe, but one of the Spirit's ministries is to show the world its need for Christ.

Furthermore, John's Gospel includes the Spirit among the witnesses to Jesus: "When the Counselor comes, the one I will send to you from the Father—the Spirit of truth who proceeds from the Father—he will testify about me" (15:26). The Spirit joins the Father, Jesus's miracles, the Old Testament, John the Baptist, the disciples, and Jesus himself in testifying of Jesus.

---

[11] The Cape Town Confession of Faith, pt. 1, no. 5, Lausanne Movement, accessed June 24, 2019, https://www.lausanne.org/content/ctc/ctcommitment.

The Spirit also invites people to come to Christ. In the last chapter of the New Testament, John writes, "Both the Spirit and the bride say, 'Come!' Let anyone who hears, say, 'Come!' Let the one who is thirsty come. Let the one who desires take the water of life freely" (Rev 22:17). God graciously ends the biblical story with both the Spirit and the church summoning readers to come to Jesus to satisfy their spiritual thirst.

Moreover, when people trust Jesus as Redeemer, the Spirit has worked within to enable faith, as Paul says: "No one can say, 'Jesus is Lord,' except by the Holy Spirit" (1 Cor 12:3). This is the early Christian confession (see also Rom 10:9–10). The Spirit empowers people to say "Jesus is Lord" in truth.

The Spirit Works in Jesus

The Spirit is at work in Old Testament predictions of Christ and in his conception, baptism, temptation, teaching, healing, exorcisms, crucifixion, and resurrection.

Old Testament Prophesies

The Old Testament predicts that the Spirit will be at work in the promised One. He will come from the line of King David, the son of Jesse. God's Spirit will rest on him and give him great wisdom and strength. As a result, his life will be marked by "the fear of the Lord" (Isa 11:1–3). The Lord will choose him to be his servant and will delight in him. The Lord's gift of the Spirit will enable him to show justice, to be gentle, and to persist in pursuing justice among the nations (42:1–4). The Lord will anoint the Messiah with his Spirit. This divine enablement will lead to the Messiah's preaching good news to the poor, the despondent, and prisoners. His message will comfort some hearers and warn of a day of vengeance for others (61:1–2).

Jesus's Conception

The Holy Spirit works from the very beginning of Jesus's life. The Spirit brings about his conception in Mary's womb. As the Spirit came upon people in the Old Testament, the angel Gabriel tells Mary that the Spirit will come upon her (Luke 1:35). The angel's message continues: "The power of the Most High will overshadow you. Therefore, the holy one to be born will be called the Son of God" (v. 35). The Spirit overshadows Israel in the pillars of cloud and fire in the wilderness, and he dwells in the tabernacle and the temple. However, the glorious cloud of the Spirit's presence is absent from the second temple.

Ezekiel foretells that as he sees the glory depart from the temple, so it will reappear in the new temple (Ezek 43:1–5).[12] Jesus is that promised glory. And from his conception the Spirit of glory "overshadowed" Mary so that her baby boy is born the "holy . . . Son of God" (Luke 1:35). Even before Jesus's birth, therefore, the Spirit prepares for him a human body and soul so that through death and resurrection he can save his people.

Jesus's Baptism and Temptation

The Holy Spirit is involved in Jesus's baptism and temptation. At his baptism by John the Baptist in the Jordan, Jesus sees "the Spirit of God descending like a dove and coming down on him" (Matt 3:16). The Spirit is anointing him to fulfill his threefold messianic office of prophet, priest, and King. The Spirit also leads him "into the wilderness to be tempted by the devil" (4:1). Jesus successfully resists the tempter's three enticements by rebuking him three times from Holy Scripture.

Jesus's Teaching, Healing, and Exorcisms

The incarnate Son of God is God and man in one person. When it is the Father's will, Christ exercises divine prerogatives and powers. And he also receives the Holy Spirit at his baptism to equip him for ministry. The Father gives his Son the Holy Spirit without measure so that Jesus can teach as no one has before.

After going to synagogue in Nazareth, as is customary, Jesus stands, takes the Isaiah scroll, and reads: "The Spirit of the Lord is on me, because he has anointed me to preach good news to the poor. He has sent me to proclaim release to the captives and recovery of sight to the blind, to set

---

[12] We were helped by Ferguson, *The Holy Spirit*, 39 (see chap. 8, n. 37).

free the oppressed" (Luke 4:18, quoting Isa 61:1). When he finishes reading and sits down, Jesus astonishes his listeners by saying, "Today as you
listen, this Scripture has been fulfilled" (Luke 4:21).

When Jesus heals a demon-possessed man, enabling him to speak
and see (Matt 12:22), Jesus elicits two responses. Some wonder aloud if
Jesus could be the promised Son of David (v. 23). The Pharisees, however,
claim that Jesus casts out demons by Satan (v. 24). Against this response
Jesus argues logically, insisting that Satan does not fight against himself. Jesus has no part with Satan; rather, he says, "If I drive out demons
by the Spirit of God, then the kingdom of God has come upon you" (v.
28). The Spirit works through Jesus's exorcisms to defeat the devil, free
the demonized, and usher in the kingdom of God. With holy anger Jesus
pronounces as an unforgivable sin the Pharisees' knowingly ascribing the
Spirit's work to the evil one (vv. 31–32).

The Spirit, then, is active in all aspects of Jesus's earthly ministry, as
Peter recaps: "God anointed Jesus of Nazareth with the Holy Spirit and
with power, and . . . he went about doing good and healing all who were
under the tyranny of the devil, because God was with him" (Acts 10:38).

Jesus's Crucifixion

Jesus is conceived by the Spirit and empowered by the Spirit for ministry.
And the Spirit plays a role in his atoning death as well. We distinguish the
persons of the Trinity but never separate them. The Father takes part in
Christ's atonement: "in Christ, God was reconciling the world to himself"
(2 Cor 5:19). And the Spirit also takes part, for "through the eternal Spirit"
Christ "offered himself . . . to God" (Heb 9:14). This means that Christ's
sacrifice is the great and final sacrifice, making all other sacrifices obsolete. Jesus is divinely empowered when he offers himself as a sacrifice
for sin.[13]

Jesus's Resurrection

Paul teaches that the Spirit is active also in Jesus's resurrection. Romans
begins by declaring the gospel concerning God's "Son, Jesus Christ our

---

[13] Lane, *Hebrews 9–13*, 240 (see chap. 7, n. 31).

Lord, who was a descendant of David according to the flesh, and was appointed to be the powerful Son of God according to the Spirit of holiness by the resurrection of the dead" (1:3–4). Paul contrasts Jesus's humanity (as David's descendant, v. 3) and deity (which God declared by raising him, v. 4). His resurrection was done "according to the Spirit of holiness," that is, the Holy Spirit. The Father proclaims that his Son is God by powerfully raising him from the dead through the Spirit's agency.

Paul also teaches that the Spirit is active in Jesus's resurrection in his confession of "the mystery of godliness": "He was manifested in the flesh, vindicated in the Spirit, seen by angels, preached among the nations, believed on in the world, taken up in glory" (1 Tim 3:16). Paul here includes Christ's incarnation, resurrection, being proclaimed, being the object of faith, and ascension. Our focus is Jesus's "vindication" from the dead "in the Spirit." Because Jesus dies the death of a condemned man, his resurrection is his justification (vindication). The Father justifies his Son by raising him from the dead. And he does so "by the Spirit" (ESV).

The Ministries of the Holy Spirit: Union with Christ

The Holy Spirit joins us to Christ in salvation and enables us to live for God as the church. The two key ministries of the Spirit to us are thus uniting us to Christ and enabling us to live for Christ in the community of faith. We will examine these in turn.

The Spirit is the bond of our union with Christ. The Spirit is so indispensable for salvation that people who lack the Spirit do not belong to Christ. Furthermore, the Spirit brings about aspects of salvation that occur in union with Christ, including regeneration, justification, adoption, sanctification, preservation, and glorification.

The Spirit Unites Us to Christ

As we previously noted, the Holy Spirit is essential to spiritual union between us and Christ: "For we were all baptized by one Spirit into one body—whether Jews or Greeks, whether slaves or free—and we were all given one Spirit to drink" (1 Cor 12:13). The Spirit is the necessary link between believers and Christ (v. 13). Though the church has many members, it is one body because all its members participate in one Holy Spirit when we are incorporated into Christ's body.

The Spirit Causes Us to Belong to Christ

Paul reinforces that the Holy Spirit is indispensable for our union with Christ by teaching that to lack the Spirit means not to belong to Christ. Paul contrasts two antithetical realms: the realm of the flesh and that of the Spirit (Rom 8:5–11). To be "in the flesh" is to be unsaved, to hate God, to be unable to please God, and to be headed for condemnation. To be "in the Spirit" is to be saved, to love God, to be able to please God, and to be headed for salvation.

Paul assures his readers that they do not belong to the group of those "in the flesh": "You, however, are not in the flesh, but in the Spirit, if indeed the Spirit of God lives in you" (v. 9). He teaches that they are not in the flesh but in the Spirit because the Spirit indwells them.

Moreover, "if anyone does not have the Spirit of Christ, he does not belong to him" (v. 9). Though it is negative in form, the purpose of this statement is mainly positive, seeking to underline "that every Christian is indwelt by the Spirit."[14] However, its secondary purpose is to insist that no one lacking the Spirit could be a Christian, regardless of a profession of faith. The point again is that possession of the Holy Spirit is necessary to salvation.

Because the Holy Spirit is the bond of our union with Christ, both negative and positive implications follow. Negatively, those who lack the Spirit do not belong to Christ. Positively, the Spirit brings about aspects of our salvation that occur in union with Christ.

---

[14] C. E. B. Cranfield, *The Epistle to the Romans*, ICC (Edinburgh: T&T Clark, 1975), 388.

The Spirit Applies Our Salvation in Christ

The Holy Spirit is the person of the Godhead who joins believers to Christ. Therefore, we are not surprised to find the Spirit active in these aspects of the application of our salvation. Union is the all-embracing category to which these elements belong: regeneration, justification, adoption, sanctification, preservation, and glorification. They all occur in union with Christ and are all brought about by the Spirit.

The Spirit brings about our *new birth* (*regeneration*), which occurs in union with Christ, as Paul teaches: "God, being rich in mercy, because of the great love with which he loved us . . . made us alive together with Christ" (Eph 2:4–5 ESV). The Holy Spirit applies Jesus's work to us so that we are "born of the Spirit" (John 3:8; see also Titus 3:4–5).

The Spirit brings about our *justification*, which occurs in union with Christ, as Paul teaches. Our sin is imputed, or reckoned, to Christ, and his righteousness is imputed to us. When Paul writes, "so that *in him* we might become the righteousness of God" (2 Cor 5:21), he indicates that we are justified in union with Christ.[15] Justification is also the Holy Spirit's work. After listing ungodly lifestyles, Paul tells the Corinthians that they are "justified . . . by the Spirit of our God" (1 Cor 6:11).

The Spirit brings about our *adoption*, which occurs in union with Christ. Paul speaks of our adoption by faith: "through faith you are all sons of God in Christ Jesus" (Gal 3:26). Verse 27 makes adoption a subset of a larger category, union with Christ: "For those of you who were baptized into Christ have been clothed with Christ." Adoption is also the Holy Spirit's work, as Paul teaches: "You did not receive a spirit of slavery to fall back into fear. Instead, you received the Spirit of adoption, by whom we cry out, 'Abba, Father!'" (Rom 8:15). The Spirit acts in adoption to unite us to Christ and bring us all the rights, privileges, and responsibilities that accompany it.

The Spirit brings about our *sanctification*, which occurs in union with Christ, as Paul teaches: "Therefore we were buried with him by

---

[15] So Constantine R. Campbell, *Paul and Union with Christ: An Exegetical and Theological Study* (Grand Rapids: Zondervan, 2012), 186–87. So also Phil 3:8–9.

baptism into death, in order that, just as Christ was raised from the dead by the glory of the Father, so we too may walk in newness of life. For if we have been united with him in the likeness of his death, we will certainly also be in the likeness of his resurrection" (Rom 6:3–5). Sanctification is also the Holy Spirit's work, as Paul teaches: "We ought to thank God always for you, brothers and sisters loved by the Lord, because from the beginning God has chosen you for salvation through sanctification by the Spirit and through belief in the truth" (2 Thess 2:13).

The Spirit brings about our *preservation* (God's keeping his people), which occurs in union with Christ, as Paul teaches: "I am persuaded that neither death nor life, nor angels nor rulers, nor things present nor things to come, nor powers, nor height nor depth, nor any other created thing will be able to separate us from the love of God that is in Christ Jesus our Lord" (Rom 8:38–39). Because of God's love in Christ, nothing will ever separate us from our Lord. Paul uses comprehensive language, for everything is included in "death nor life," "things present nor things to come," and "any other created thing." Preservation is also the Holy Spirit's work, as Paul teaches: "Do not grieve the Holy Spirit of God, with whom you were sealed for the day of redemption" (Eph 4:30 NIV). The Spirit himself is God's seal protecting us for final salvation.

The Spirit brings about our *glorification*, which occurs in union with Christ. Rejoicing in the Father's adoption of believers, Paul focuses on the Spirit. The Spirit enables us to cry out to the Father in saving faith (Rom 8:15), and he also testifies within our hearts that God is our Father (v. 16). Paul next speaks of our inheritance as God's children, affirming that we are "heirs of God and coheirs with Christ" (v. 17; see also Gal 4:7). Paul then makes a qualification: we are children and heirs "if indeed we suffer with him so that we may also be glorified with him" (Rom 8:17). Because we are joined to Christ in his resurrection, we will "also be glorified with him." Glorification is also the Holy Spirit's work, as the Spirit of glory acts to unite believers to Christ "when his glory is revealed" (1 Pet 4:13).

In conclusion, three facts relate the Spirit's work in our salvation as union with Christ. First, Paul ascribes union to the Spirit via two pictures (1 Cor 12:12–13). Christ baptizes all believers into his body with the same

Spirit, and all believers drink of the one Spirit. It makes sense, then, that the Spirit is indispensable to our union with Christ, as the next point clearly says. Second, Paul writes candidly, "If anyone does not have the Spirit of Christ, he does not belong to him" (Rom 8:9). That is, the Spirit is the bond of union with Christ, and this has negative and positive implications. Negatively, it is as straightforward as this: no Spirit, no union. Positively, and third, Paul attributes to the Spirit aspects of our salvation that transpire in union with Christ. Various ways of talking about our salvation include regeneration, justification, adoption, sanctification, preservation, and glorification. Each of these takes place in union with Christ, and each is the work of the Holy Spirit.

The Ministries of the Holy Spirit: The Church

Having explored the Holy Spirit's ministry of uniting us to Christ, we turn our attention to the Spirit's enabling us to live for God as the church. This involves many gracious ministries of the Spirit: indwelling, empowering, producing fruit, providing leaders, enabling worship, and giving spiritual gifts.

The Spirit Indwells Us

In fourteen passages Paul reveals that God dwells within believers as individuals and as the church. We customarily think of indwelling as the Holy Spirit's work, and that is correct. But five times Paul says the Son indwells us (Rom 8:10; 2 Cor 13:5; Gal 2:20; Eph 3:17; Col 1:27), and twice that the Father does so (2 Cor 6:16; Eph 2:22). Thus the Father, Son, and Holy Spirit indwell Christians. This should not surprise us, because although we distinguish the persons of the Trinity, we never separate them.

The Trinity indwells us as individuals and together as the church:

Indwelling individuals: "Don't you know that your body is a temple of the Holy Spirit who is in you, whom you have from God? You are not your own, for you were bought at a price. So glorify God with your body." (1 Cor 6:19–20)

Indwelling the church: "Don't you yourselves know that you are
God's temple and that the Spirit of God lives in you? If anyone
destroys God's temple, God will destroy him; for God's temple is
holy, and that is what you are." (3:16–17)

The first text addresses God's people as individuals and treats sexual
ethics. Our bodies are temples of the Holy Spirit. The Spirit joins us to
Christ, the temple. God expects us to live according to our exalted status
(1 Cor 6:20).

The second passage depicts believers corporately as God's temple.
Once more it is the indwelling Spirit who makes the temple a temple. And
because the Spirit is holy, so are God's people, the church (3:17). Because
the church belongs to God and is thus valuable to him, to damage others'
spiritual welfare brings God's judgment.

Scripture applies these truths to Christian living in at least three
ways. First, we know that God loves us: "because [we] are sons, God
sent the Spirit of his Son into our hearts, crying, 'Abba, Father!'" (Gal
4:6). Second, our hope for salvation is solid, for "if the Spirit of him
who raised Jesus from the dead lives in [us], then he who raised Christ
Jesus from the dead will also bring [our] mortal bodies to life through
his Spirit who lives in [us]" (Rom 8:11; see also 5:5). Third, we must
strive vigorously for godliness, for, as Paul tells the Romans, "your body
is a temple of the Holy Spirit who is in you, whom you have from God[.]
You are not your own, for you were bought at a price. So glorify God
with your body" (6:19–20).

The Spirit Empowers Us

The Spirit not only indwells us; he also empowers us. The New Testament
portrays the power for Christian living in three ways, and each is related
to the Spirit's work. First, it simply calls it "power." Paul prays for the
Ephesians to know "the immeasurable greatness of his [the Father's]
power toward us who believe" (Eph 1:19). Paul extols this power as that
which raised Christ from the dead and which he now exercises at God's

right hand above all things, with everything under his feet. This is the power at work within us (vv. 19–23).

Voices from Church History: John Owen

Owen (1616–1683), an English Nonconformist church leader, theologian, and academic administrator, earned great respect for his character and keen intellect. He was a great preacher, and his abundant writings include *Doctrine of the Saints' Perseverance* (1654); *On the Mortification of Sin in Believers* (1656); *Of Temptation* (1658); a massive commentary on the Epistle to the Hebrews; a probing book on *Indwelling Sin*; *On the Holy Spirit* (1677–1678); and *The Doctrine of Justification* (1677). He wrote,

> [T]his whole work [of mortification] which I have described as our duty, is effected, carried on, and accomplished by the power of the Spirit, in all the parts and degrees of it; as—He alone clearly and fully convinces the heart of the evil and guilt and danger of the corruption, lust, or sin to be mortified. . . . The Spirit alone reveals unto us the fullness of Christ for our relief. . . . The Spirit alone establishes the heart in expectation of relief from Christ. . . . The Spirit alone brings the cross of Christ into our hearts with its sin-killing power. . . . The Spirit is the author and finisher of our sanctification; gives new supplies and influences of grace for holiness and sanctification. . . . In all the soul's addresses to God in this condition, it has support from the Spirit.[16]

Scripture also speaks of power for Christian living as enabling grace. When Paul receives "a thorn in the flesh" (2 Cor 12:7), he prays for its removal. But God denies his requests and adds, "My grace is sufficient for you, for my power is perfected in weakness" (v. 9). "Grace" is parallel with God's "power" here, and it is God's grace that enables Paul to

---

[16] John Owen, "Of the Mortification of Sin in Believers," in *Overcoming Sin and Temptation: Three Classic Works by John Owen*, ed. Kelly M. Kapic and Justin Taylor (Wheaton, IL: Crossway, 2006), 138–39.

overcome despite weaknesses. Because of enabling grace the apostle can say, "When I am weak, then I am strong" (v. 10).

A third way of viewing the power we need to live for Christ is to speak of the Holy Spirit. The New Testament often associates the Holy Spirit and God's power. The same Spirit who empowers Jesus in his earthly ministry (Acts 10:38), works as he makes atonement (Heb 9:14), and raises him from the dead (Rom 1:4) strengthens us to live for him. The same Spirit who applies salvation to us, enabling us to embrace the gospel (1 Thess 1:5), and regenerating (Titus 3:5) and justifying us (1 Cor 6:11), gives us power to serve Christ.

The empowering Holy Spirit works both inside and outside of God's people. He empowers the church through giving each of us spiritual gifts (1 Cor 12:11). He empowers us to grow in holiness (Rom 8:13), "overflow with hope" (15:13), and gain strength and encouragement (Eph 3:16). The Spirit also works outside of us to deliver us from difficult circumstances (Phil 1:19), to empower us for witness (Acts 1:8), and to produce fruit from our evangelistic efforts (Rom 15:18–19).

The Spirit Produces Fruit in Us

The Spirit also graciously produces fruit in and through our lives. The classic passage on the fruit of the Spirit, Gal 5:22–24, is at the center of a chiasm that runs from 5:13 through 6:2. Regular parallelism follows the pattern ABAB, ABCABC, and so on, where the letters represent words or ideas. Inverted parallelism, or chiasm, reverses the pattern: ABBA, ABCCBA, and so forth. Galatians 5:13–6:2 follows this form:

> **A** Command to love, 5:13–14
> > **B** Interpersonal abuses, 5:15
> > > **C** Walk in the Spirit, 5:16–18
> > > > **D** Works of the flesh, 5:19–21
> > > > **D** Fruit, 5:22–24
> > > **C** Walk in the Spirit, 5:25
> > **B** Interpersonal abuses, 5:26
> **A** Command to love, 6:1–2

Paul is livid because his opponents in Galatia "are troubling" the churches by seeking to turn them to "a different gospel" (Gal 1:6–7) that adds elements of the law to faith in Christ. Paul argues from his own experience and the Old Testament that salvation is by grace through faith in Christ, apart from law keeping (1:11–5:12). At 5:13 Paul begins a practical section that teaches that the Christian life is likewise lived by grace through faith. Although the law is part of the content of the Christian life, the power for Christian living comes from the Spirit, not the law.

We return to the chiasm above. Paul borders it with commands to love.

> Serve one another through love. For the whole law is fulfilled in one statement: Love your neighbor as yourself. (5:13–14)

> Carry one another's burdens; in this way you will fulfill the law of Christ. (6:2)

As he begins this section, Paul commands the Galatians to "serve one another through love" (5:13). He reminds them that love of neighbor is the essence of the law's ethic (v. 14). He ends this section by urging godly brothers to restore erring ones gently. By bearing each other's burdens they fulfill the law of Christ, especially Jesus's love command (Matt 22:37–40).[17] Paul's opponents' stress on law keeping produces not love but strife. This is why the apostle borders the chiasm as he does and why the first fruit of the Spirit is love. Love is paramount.

Moving in one position on the chiasm yields these two texts:

> But if you bite and devour one another, watch out, or you will be consumed by one another. (Gal 5:15)

> Let us not become conceited, provoking one another, envying one another. (v. 26)

Paul describes love's antithesis, the fruit of his opponents' defective teaching: dissension, fighting (v. 15), pride, provocation, and jealousy (v.

---

[17] "He said to him [a lawyer], 'Love the Lord your God with all your heart, with all your soul, and with all your mind. This is the greatest and most important command. The second is like it: Love your neighbor as yourself.'"

26). It is not by accident that most of the "works of the flesh" (v. 19) are interpersonal sins, such as those mentioned here.

At the next stage of the chiasm Paul treats the way to produce love and to avoid interpersonal abuses—by walking in the Spirit:

> I say then, walk by the Spirit and you will certainly not carry out the desire of the flesh. (5:16)

> If we live by the Spirit, let us also keep in step with the Spirit. (v. 25)

To walk by the Spirit and to follow the Spirit overlap. They refer to going step-by-step with the Spirit and to following in his footsteps, respectively. Both images point to trusting the Spirit for energy to produce love and the other fruits. Of course, this trust in the Spirit is inseparable from obeying him. The Spirit empowers us by applying Christ's death to us (v. 24).

At the center of the chiasm are the works of the flesh and the fruit of the Spirit. The former can be categorized this way:

Sexual sins: sexual immorality, moral impurity, promiscuity (v. 19)

Religious sins: idolatry, sorcery (v. 20)

Interpersonal sins: hatreds, strife, jealousy, outbursts of anger, selfish ambitions, dissensions, factions, envy (vv. 20–21)

Sins of excess: drunkenness, carousing, and anything similar (v. 21)

We may not be surprised to see sexual sins first in the list, but we may find "religious sins" striking. The same two topics appear (in reverse) in Rom 1:22–27. Both concern human identity. We are religious beings, made to worship God. And we are sexual beings. Next, in light of Paul's opponents' views, the largest category of works of the flesh is interpersonal sins. He ends with sins of indulgence.

The fruit of the Spirit are to be understood within their historical and literary contexts. Historically, love and the other fruits contradict the lifestyles created by the adversaries' teaching. Literarily, we must interpret the fruit against the works of the flesh. It is instructive to read the works of the flesh with any one fruit in mind. The fruit of the Spirit and the works of the flesh clash as much as the flesh and the Spirit do: "these are opposed to each other" (Gal 5:17).

Capturing the theme of 5:14 and 6:2, love is listed first because it is foremost. It holds pride of place in interpersonal relations throughout the New Testament.[18] Where there is love, there is joy, which is absent when legalism dominates. Although Scripture promises inner peace to God's people (Isa 26:3; Phil 4:6–7), the peace mentioned here is harmony among members of the congregation. The rest of the Spirit's fruit also contributes to interpersonal love and harmony: "kindness, goodness, faithfulness, gentleness, and self-control" (Gal 5:22–23).

Several conclusions follow. First, the fruit of the Spirit concern interpersonal relations, love in the church. Second, the fruit are character qualities the Spirit produces. We cannot produce this fruit on our own. Third, believers are commanded (5:16) and exhorted (v. 25) to rely on the Spirit, and this involves human responsibility. Fourth, the Spirit produces fruit in all those who are united to Christ (v. 24). Fifth, we must view the fruit against the works of the flesh, about which Paul warns: "Those who practice such things will not inherit the kingdom of God" (v. 21).

The Spirit Guides Our Leaders

The Holy Spirit plays important roles concerning leaders for Christ's church. He appoints and enables us and our leaders to engage effectively in new covenant ministry. He gives us wisdom, faith, power, and joy for ministry, enables us to speak for God, gives us wisdom for decision-making, and enables us to guard the gospel.

THE HOLY SPIRIT APPOINTS AND ENABLES OUR LEADERS FOR NEW COVENANT MINISTRY

Paul warns the Ephesian elders to keep watch over themselves and the congregations over which "the Holy Spirit has appointed" them "as overseers, to shepherd the church of God" (Acts 20:28). Though Paul likely

---

[18] See Matt 22:39; John 13:34–35; 1 Cor 13:13; Eph 3:17–19; 1 Pet 1:22; 4:8; 1 John 3:11–18; and 4:7–12.

chooses these leaders based on their character, reputation, and service, ultimately the Spirit chooses them. Christ the Redeemer buys the church with his sacrificial death, and as a result it belongs to him. When he entrusts its pastoral care to redeemed leaders, he gives them the Spirit to enable them to fulfill their responsibilities.

The Spirit enables leaders for new covenant ministry. Compared to the surpassing glory of the new covenant, the glory of the Mosaic covenant "is not glorious now" (2 Cor 3:10). What makes the new covenant so great? The answer is Christ, the Mediator of the new covenant (Heb 8:6; 9:15), and the Holy Spirit. Paul characterizes the new covenant as "the ministry of the Spirit" (2 Cor 3:8), to which God calls leaders since Jesus arose. New covenant leaders depend on the Spirit to give new life to unbelievers and to empower believers and help them grow.

The Holy Spirit Gives Us Wisdom, Faith, Power, and Joy

The Spirit gives these wonderful gifts to the young church. When a complaint arises concerning neglect of Hellenistic Jewish widows in the daily distribution of food, the apostles tell the believers to choose godly men to handle these matters (Acts 6:1–6). The men have good reputations and are "full of the Spirit and wisdom" (v. 3). Dealing with dissension requires the wisdom that the Spirit provides. Stephen is named first as "a man full of faith and the Holy Spirit" (v. 5). God gives him "grace and power" and performs miracles through him (v. 8). When Jews challenge Stephen's message, "they [are] unable to stand up against his wisdom and the Spirit by whom he [is] speaking" (v. 10).

The persecution that scatters the believers does not halt the church's witness but spreads it. When the leaders in the Jerusalem church hear reports of many people turning to Christ among Hellenists in Antioch, they send Barnabas to investigate (11:19–22). Luke describes him as "a good man, full of the Holy Spirit and of faith" (v. 24), for again the Spirit has brought gifts; this time, faith to Hellenists. Barnabas sees results of God's grace at work, and being a great encourager, "he [is] glad and encourage[s] all of them to remain true to the Lord with devoted hearts" (v. 23).

Persecution brings physical and mental anguish but does not stop the gospel. Each time the gospel bears fruit, enemies oppose the apostles and their message. So it is at Antioch in Pisidia, from which Paul and Barnabas are forced to flee (13:48–51). Although we might expect the believers to be downhearted, the Spirit has other ideas: "And the disciples were filled with joy and the Holy Spirit" (v. 52).

THE HOLY SPIRIT ENABLES OUR LEADERS TO SPEAK FOR GOD

Jesus promises that when his disciples face persecution, he will provide words for them: "But when they hand you over, don't worry about how or what you ought to speak. For you will be given what to say at that hour, because it isn't you speaking, but the Spirit of your Father is speaking through you" (Matt 10:19–20).

Similarly, the apostles put their confidence not in their speaking ability or wisdom but in the Holy Spirit's using the gospel. When Paul goes to Corinth, he relies not on persuasive oratory, which the people love, but on God's gospel, power, and Holy Spirit:

> When I came to you . . . , I did not come with brilliance of speech or wisdom. I decided to know nothing among you except Jesus Christ and him crucified. I came to you in weakness, in fear, and in much trembling. My speech and my preaching were not with persuasive words of wisdom but with a demonstration of the Spirit's power, so that your faith might not be based on human wisdom but on God's power. (1 Cor 2:1–5)

Before his ascension, Jesus instructs his disciples to wait in Jerusalem for the promised Holy Spirit. Christ promises that the Spirit's coming will mean power for evangelism: "You will receive power when the Holy Spirit has come on you, and you will be my witnesses in Jerusalem, in all Judea and Samaria, and to the ends of the earth" (Acts 1:8). Acts shows the fulfillment of this promise, especially through the ministries of Peter and Paul. The Spirit enables God's people to speak for him and spread the good news to the nations.

THE HOLY SPIRIT GIVES US WISDOM FOR DECISION-MAKING

The Spirit also is at work guiding the church to make wise decisions. At times the apostles make decisions "in the Spirit," as Paul does on his third missionary journey: "After these events, Paul resolves by the Spirit to pass through Macedonia and Achaia and go to Jerusalem. 'After I've been there,' he said, 'It is necessary for me to see Rome as well'" (Acts 19:21).

Similarly, the Jerusalem Council deliberates before reaching a decision concerning how to direct Gentile believers. They hear reports from Peter and Paul and Barnabas telling how the Spirit has worked to convince them to accept Gentile believers without requiring obedience to the law. They hear James's confirming words from the Old Testament prophets. The preface to their decision indicates that their actions are implications drawn from the Spirit's working in the apostles to fulfill Scripture and lead the church in the love and truth of the gospel:

> For it was the Holy Spirit's decision—and ours—not to place further burdens on you beyond these requirements: that you abstain from food offered to idols, from blood, from eating anything that has been strangled, and from sexual immorality. You will do well if you keep yourselves from these things. Farewell. (Acts 15:28–29)

The Spirit also initiates the first missionary journey: "The Holy Spirit said, 'Set apart for me Barnabas and Saul for the work to which I have called them.' Then after they [the church in Antioch] had fasted, prayed, and laid hands on them, they sent them off" (Acts 13:2–3). The Spirit leads the church to set apart Saul and Barnabas to the mission to which the Spirit has called them. The church heeds the direction of the Spirit, and the result is history.

THE HOLY SPIRIT ENABLES OUR LEADERS TO GUARD THE GOSPEL

Heretics attack Paul's message, and he urges his understudy to guard what God entrusts to him (1 Tim 6:20). Now he reinforces this theme: "Hold on to the pattern of sound teaching that you have heard from me, in the faith and love that are in Christ Jesus. Guard the good deposit through the Holy Spirit who lives in us" (2 Tim 1:13–14). Timothy, Paul's handpicked successor for ministry to the Gentiles, is to stick faithfully to Paul's message. The apostle entrusts the gospel to Timothy, and he must retain Paul's healthy teaching and protect the message.

Paul addresses Timothy in personal responsibility as a minister of the Word. He must actively teach, live, and guard the gospel through the indwelling Holy Spirit (v. 14). The Spirit enables us to preserve the gospel in the face of false teaching. Ultimately, he is the one who safeguards the accomplishment of God's mission.

The Spirit Enables Our Worship

The same Spirit who enables us to confess Jesus as Lord (1 Cor 12:3), assures us within that God is our Father (Rom 8:16), and gives us joy and hope (14:17; 15:13) also enables us to worship. The Spirit grants us access to the Father, prompts our thanksgiving and songs of worship, and helps us to pray.

THE SPIRIT GRANTS US ACCESS TO THE FATHER THROUGH THE SON

Christian worship is thoroughly trinitarian. Christ is the reconciler, who by his death and resurrection makes peace between believing Jews and Gentiles. As a result, "through him we both have access in one Spirit to the Father" (Eph 2:18). Christ is the Mediator between God and human beings (1 Tim 2:5), and the Spirit unites both Jewish and Gentile believers to God and to one another. Reconciled and united to God and each other, together we approach the Father in worship and prayer.

THE SPIRIT PROMPTS OUR THANKSGIVING AND SONGS OF WORSHIP

Paul commands the Ephesians to avoid drunkenness and to "be filled by the Spirit" instead (Eph 5:18). Although we unavoidably live in the world, we are not to live as if we belong to it but are to live in the Spirit's domain, as those he makes alive to God and directs. Spiritual, heartfelt worship will result, characterized by "psalms, hymns, and spiritual songs" (v. 19) that teach and admonish as they convey wisdom about Christ (Col 3:16). Being filled by the Spirit will also result in great thanksgiving "to God the Father in the name of our Lord Jesus Christ" (Eph 5:20), again stressing that Christian worship is trinitarian.

THE SPIRIT HELPS US TO PRAY

The Spirit ministers to us by praying for us when we do not know what to pray and by empowering our own prayers. We struggle now while anticipating future glory (Rom 8:18). We groan as we await our final adoption, the redemption of our bodies, and God encourages us by giving us the Spirit as the firstfruits of the final harvest of salvation (v. 23). The Spirit helps us in another way too: "In the same way the Spirit also helps us in our weakness, because we do not know what to pray for as we should, but the Spirit himself intercedes for us with unspoken groanings" (v. 26). What a blessing to know that even when we pray by ourselves, we are not alone. And what a blessing to know that when we do not know how to pray, the Spirit does, and prays for us.

The Spirit also empowers our prayers. As he concludes his exhortation for believers to "put on the full armor of God" (Eph 6:11) to fight the devil and demons, Paul introduces another weapon—prayer: "Pray at all times in the Spirit with every prayer and request, and stay alert with all perseverance and intercession for all the saints" (v. 18). Here the apostle urges that we pray repeatedly, attentively, and persistently. He also insists that we pray "in the Spirit." Frank Thielman explains: "This is not merely prayer 'in the sphere of the Spirit' . . . or 'spirited' or heartfelt prayer . . . but prayer that the Spirit has given the believer the strength to utter."[19] Paul thus ends his treatment of the armor of God the way he began it: by pointing us to God's "vast strength" (v. 10).

Jude also teaches that the Spirit empowers our prayers. After announcing his theme—defending the Christian faith (v. 3)—Jude goes after false teachers who twist and deny the faith (vv. 4–19). Not until the climax of the letter does he return to his theme of contending for the faith (vv. 20–23). He tells us how to wage spiritual war: "But you, dear friends, as you build yourselves up in your most holy faith, praying in the Holy Spirit, keep yourselves in the love of God, waiting expectantly for the mercy of our Lord Jesus Christ for eternal life" (vv. 20–21). Jude wants us to strengthen ourselves, to pray, and to remain in God's love as we trust Christ's mercy. Specifically, he wants us to "pray in the Holy Spirit." These instructions contrast sharply with the identity of the false teachers, who

---

[19] Frank Thielman, *Ephesians*, Baker Exegetical Commentary on the New Testament (Grand Rapids: Baker, 2010), 433.

do not have the Holy Spirit (v. 19). Prayer in the Spirit is "prayer stimulated by, guided by, and infused by the Holy Spirit."[20]

The Spirit Grants Us Gifts

Although the Corinthian church has an abundance of spiritual gifts (1 Cor 1:7), Paul has to address difficulties with them in 1 Corinthians 12–14. Note the Spirit's role in seven areas here. First, the divine sovereignty/human responsibility tension, so evident in Paul's thought, appears. The Spirit sovereignly assigns our gifts "as he wills" (12:11), and Paul commands us to "desire spiritual gifts" (14:1; see also 12:31). Should we covet gifts that we do not have, we must bow to the Spirit's sovereignty. And when we are inactive, we must obey God's call to serve him by using whatever gifts we have.

Second, Paul warns, "No one speaking by the Spirit of God says, 'Jesus is cursed,' and no one can say, 'Jesus is Lord,' except by the Holy Spirit" (12:3).

Third, our spiritual gifts reflect the Trinity's unity and diversity: "Now there are different gifts, but the same Spirit. There are different ministries, but the same Lord. And there are different activities, but the same God activates each gift in each person" (vv. 4–6). There is one Holy Spirit, one Lord Jesus, and one God the Father. Church unity is thus based on the unity of the Trinity. The different gifts, ministries, and activities reflect the differences between the three persons. And there is a process: the same Spirit's different gifts are used in different ministries to serve the same Lord Jesus, as the same Father activates the gifts. When we serve the church, the triune God uses us as his means of blessing others.

Fourth, Paul gives the purpose of our spiritual gifts: "A manifestation of the Spirit is given to each person for the common good" (v. 7). Peter says much the same thing: "Just as each one has received a gift, use it to serve others, as good stewards of the varied grace of God" (1 Pet 4:10). God in his grace gives us gifts (Rom 12:6–8) that we might serve others and benefit them.

---

[20] Douglas J. Moo, *2 Peter, Jude*, NIV Application Commentary (Grand Rapids: Zondervan, 1996), 285.

Fifth, Paul uses body imagery, comparing the unity in diversity of our bodies with the unity in diversity that the Spirit brings to the church (1 Cor 12:12–13; Rom 12:4–5). Inconspicuous church members are not unnecessary or unimportant (1 Cor 12:14–20). And conspicuous church members are not more necessary or more important than others (vv. 21–24). It is God's will "that there would be no division in the body, but that the members would have the same concern for each other" (v. 25).

Sixth, our love for one another is vital for the proper functioning of the gifts in the body of Christ. Amazing gifts without love are "nothing" (1 Cor 13:1–3). Paul's description of love is both wonderful and too high for anyone to attain without the Spirit's working through the Word (vv. 4–7). In contrast to the spiritual gifts, love endures forever (vv. 8–12). Love is not to be underestimated, for "now these three remain: faith, hope, and love—but the greatest of these is love" (v. 13).

Seventh, prophecy and tongues call for care. Paul urges first-century believers to pursue love and spiritual gifts, especially prophecy (1 Cor 14:1, 39) to edify the church (v. 12). Prophecy is more profitable in the first-century church than tongues-speaking (vv. 2–25). Prophecy is spoken to people, with the mind not the spirit, to edify, encourage, and teach them (vv. 3–4, 31). Prophecy is a sign for unbelievers that God uses to demonstrate his reality to them (vv. 22–25).

Tongues are spoken to God (v. 28), with the spirit not the mind (v. 14) in mysteries by the Spirit (v. 2) to edify the speaker (vv. 4, 28). When tongues are interpreted, they edify the church (v. 5), but uninterpreted tongues do not (vv. 5–12). Paul speaks in tongues, but not in church unless there is interpretation (vv. 15–19). Paul teaches that the church is not to forbid speaking in tongues (v. 39).

Paul insists that there must be order in worship services (vv. 26–39). A key principle is that all must be done for edification (v. 26). There must be no more than three people speaking in tongues, they must speak one at a time, and there must be interpretation (vv. 27–28). There must be no more than three prophets who speak, and the others must weigh what the prophets say (vv. 29–33). They too must speak one at a time (v. 31). Speakers must keep under control, for this is God's will (vv. 32–33, 40).

Evangelicals largely agree on primary matters concerning the gifts but disagree on secondary ones. We agree that certain gifts have ceased; there are no more apostles and prophets as those who speak authoritative new revelation from God. We also agree that certain gifts continue, including service, teaching, exhorting, giving, leading, and showing mercy (Rom 12:6–8). We disagree concerning the cessation or continuation of the so-called sign gifts, including healing, miracles, prophecy, and tongues (1 Cor 12:9–10). We should agree that no one spiritual gift is essential for either salvation or service (all the Corinthians are baptized with the Spirit, though not all of them speak in tongues; 1 Cor 12:13, 30).

The same Holy Spirit gives each of us various spiritual gifts. We use them in various ministries in service of our same Lord Jesus and his church. We serve others, and they serve us. We need them, and they need us. Though we have different gifts, we are united in Christ and can serve alongside each other to strengthen his church. Though "there are varieties of activities . . . it is the same God and Father who empowers them all in everyone" (1 Cor 12:6 ESV).

▓ KEY TERMS

adoption

application of salvation

baptism of the Holy Spirit

Counselor

empowering of the Spirit

exorcism

fruit of the Spirit

gifts of the Spirit

glorification

healing

Holy Spirit's deity

Holy Spirit's filling

Holy Spirit's indwelling

Holy Spirit's ministries

Holy Spirit's personality

Holy Spirit's works

inspiration

Messiah's ministry and the Spirit

new covenant

Pentecost

persecution

prayer

preaching

prophecy

regeneration

sanctification

temptation

tongues

Trinity

union with Christ

virgin birth

walking in the Spirit

▓ RESOURCES FOR FURTHER STUDY

Allison, Gregg R. *Historical Theology: An Introduction to Christian Doctrine.* Grand Rapids, Zondervan, 2011, 430–49.

Allison, Gregg R., and Andreas J. Köstenberger. *The Holy Spirit.* Theology for the People of God. David S. Dockery, Nathan A. Finn, and Christopher W. Morgan, eds. Nashville: B&H Academic, 2020.

Carson, D. A. *Showing the Spirit: A Theological Exposition of 1 Corinthians 12–14.* Grand Rapids: Baker, 1987.

Cole, Graham A. *Engaging with the Holy Spirit: Real Questions, Practical Answers.* Wheaton, IL: Crossway, 2008.

———. *He Who Gives Life: The Doctrine of the Holy Spirit.* Foundations of Evangelical Theology. John S. Feinberg, ed. Wheaton, IL: Crossway, 2007.

Fee, Gordon. *God's Empowering Presence. The Holy Spirit in the Letters of Paul.* Peabody, MA: Hendrickson, 1994.

Ferguson, Sinclair. *The Holy Spirit.* Contours of Christian Theology. Downers Grove, IL: InterVarsity, 1996.

Hamilton, James M., Jr., *God's Indwelling Presence: The Holy Spirit in the Old and New Testaments.* New American Commentary Studies in Bible and Theology. Nashville: B&H, 2006.

Morris, Leon. *Spirit of the Living God.* Downers Grove, IL: InterVarsity, 1960.

Packer, J. I. *Keep in Step with the Spirit.* 2nd ed. Grand Rapids: Baker, 2005.

Sanders, Fred. *The Deep Things of God. How the Trinity Changes Everything.* 2nd ed. Wheaton, IL: Crossway, 2017.

Schreiner, Thomas R. *Spiritual Gifts: What They Are and Why They Matter.* Nashville: B&H, 2018.

Stott, John R. W. *Baptism and Fullness: The Work of the Holy Spirit Today.* Downers Grove, IL: InterVarsity, 2006.

Thiselton, Anthony C. *The Holy Spirit: In Biblical Teaching, Through the Centuries, and Today.* Grand Rapids: Eerdmans, 2013.

10

THE CHURCH

As the church, we are the new covenant community of Jesus, rooted in Israel, built by Jesus, and inaugurated by the Holy Spirit. We are the people of God, chosen by the Father and graciously brought into a relationship with the triune God and one another. We are the redeemed communion of saints bought by the blood of Christ, universal and invisible, including all believers throughout all ages—those now on earth and those already in heaven. We are the adopted family of God, once slaves to sin but now brought into a loving relationship with God as Father and each other as brothers and sisters in Christ. We are the body of Christ, having him as head, dependent on him, gifted by the Holy Spirit, created as a unity with diversity, and dependent on one another, functioning as Christ's agents in the world.

As the church, we are the bride of Christ, expressly loved by him, saved by his sacrificial work on the cross, exclusively devoted to him, and increasingly adorned in beauty for him, the Bridegroom. We are the temple of the Spirit, filled with the fullness of Christ, marked by God's presence. We are the new humanity, composed of Jewish and Gentile Christians united in Christ and displaying the way life was always supposed to be. We are the gathered covenant community, regularly coming together for worship, discipleship, fellowship, ministry, and mission. We are the kingdom community, existing in the "already" and the "not yet," living out God's eternal purpose of cosmic unity.[1]

OBJECTIVES

- To ground our understanding of the church in Scripture
- To help us understand and appreciate what the church is
- To move us to join a Bible-believing local church
- To encourage us to worship in a local church
- To encourage us to serve the Lord in a local church
- To help us benefit from our baptism and participation in the Lord's Supper
- To motivate us to participate in the church's mission

OUTLINE

The Church in the Biblical Story
The Church in Selected Passages
      Genesis 12:1–3
      Exodus 19:4–6
      Matthew 5–7
      Matthew 16:16–19
      Acts 2:37–47
      1 Corinthians 12:14–31
      Ephesians 2:11–22
Biblical Pictures of the Church
    We Are the Body of Christ
    We Are the Bride of Christ
    We Are the Temple of the Spirit
    We Are the New Humanity
    We Are the Family of God
    We Are the People of God

---

[1] See Bruce Riley Ashford and Christopher W. Morgan, "The Church," in *ESV Systematic Theology Study Bible*, 1713 (see chap. 1, n. 25).

The Church in the Biblical Story

The people of God begin with Adam and Eve in the garden of Eden. He makes them in his image, which means in part that they are created in fellowship with their Maker (Gen 1:27). They know the sound of him walking in the garden (3:8). Even after they rebel against him, he does not abandon them but promises to send a Redeemer (3:16).

Later, God calls Abraham from a family of idol worshippers and enters into a covenant with him, promising to be God to him and his descendants (Gen 17:7). God promises to give Abraham a land, to make him into a great nation, and through him to bless all peoples (12:3). From Abraham come Isaac and Jacob, whose name God changes to Israel and from whom God brings twelve tribes of his people. The rest of the Old Testament concerns God's dealings with these twelve tribes of Israel.

Through great plagues and a dramatic exodus, God calls Israel out of Egyptian bondage to be his people. He gives them the Ten Commandments, claims them as his people, and gives them the Promised Land, which they occupy after defeating the Canaanites. Later, God gives them David as king in Jerusalem. God promises to make David's descendants into a dynasty and to establish the throne of one of them forever (2 Sam 7:14–16).

In mercy God sends many prophets to warn his Old Testament people of the judgment that will come if they do not repent of their sins and turn to the Lord. Nevertheless, they repeatedly rebel against him and his prophets. In response, he sends the northern kingdom of ten tribes into captivity in Assyria in 722 BC and the southern kingdom of two tribes, Judah and Benjamin, into captivity in Babylon in 586 BC. Through the prophets, God also promises to send a Deliverer (Isa 9:6–7; 52:13–53:12).

God promises to restore his people to their land from Babylonian captivity after seventy years (Jer 25:11–12), and he brings this about under Ezra and Nehemiah. The people rebuild the walls of Jerusalem and build a second temple. Yet the Old Testament ends with God's people continuing to turn away from him (see Malachi).

After 400 years God sends his Son as the promised Messiah, Suffering Servant, King of Israel, and Savior of the world. Jesus tells the purpose of his coming: "the Son of Man did not come to be served, but to serve, and to give his life as a ransom for many" (Mark 10:45). He chooses disciples, spends time with them, teaches them about the kingdom of God, casts out demons, performs miracles, and predicts his death and resurrection. After he is raised, he directs his disciples to take the gospel to all nations to fulfill God's promise to Abraham to bless all peoples. On the day of Pentecost, Jesus sends his Spirit, who forms the church as the New

Testament people of God. The Spirit empowers the disciples to spread the gospel to the world.

Paul and Peter often describe churches in Old Testament terms (Gal 6:16; Phil 3:3; 1 Pet 2:9–10). There is continuity and discontinuity between Old Testament Israel and the church. On one hand, the church as the people of God is spiritual Israel, consisting of believing Jews and Gentiles. On the other hand, Paul teaches that "since God's gracious gifts and calling are irrevocable" (Rom 11:29), there is still a future for ethnic Israel, blood descendants of Abraham and Sarah (vv. 26–29). God is bringing and will yet bring many Jews to salvation.[2]

When God joins us to Christ in salvation, he also joins us to everyone else joined to Christ. The New Testament depicts the church in union with Christ in many ways. He is the vine, and the church is the branches (John 15). He is the groom, and the church is his bride (1 Cor 6:15–17; Eph 5:22–32). He is the head, and the church is his body (Eph 5:23, 29–30; Col 1:18). The church abides in the Father and the Son (John 17:20–21; 1 John 4:16). The church is a living temple (1 Cor 3:16–17; Eph 2:19–22; 1 Pet 2:6–8). The church is "in Christ" (1 Cor 1:30; 2 Cor 5:21). The church participates in Jesus's story (Rom 6:3–8; Col 2:20; 3:1–4). Jude rejoices that the church comprises "those who are the called, loved by God the Father and kept for Jesus Christ" (Jude v. 1). As God's people, we belong to him, and, amazingly, he belongs to us. This will be fully realized only in the new heavens and earth, after God raises us from the dead, glorifies us, and dwells among us (Rev 21:1–4).

The Church in Selected Passages

In the following passages, by God's grace Abraham knows him, and God promises him a land, which ultimately means the new earth, on which all God's resurrected people will spend eternity. As he promises, God gives childless Abraham and Sarah a son, Isaac, who is father to Jacob,

---

[2] To pursue this issue, see John Feinberg, ed., *Continuity and Discontinuity (Essays in Honor of S. Lewis Johnson, Jr.): Perspectives on the Relationship Between the Old and New Testaments* (Wheaton, IL: Crossway, 1988).

whose name God changes to Israel and from whom springs the promised nation. God promises to bless all peoples through Abraham. This promise is fulfilled ultimately in Christ, for Abraham is the father of all believers, regardless of ethnicity, and all believers are his sons.

After freeing Jacob/Israel's descendants from Egypt, God meets Moses on Mount Sinai and tells him to remind Israel of God's deliverance of them and of his covenant with them. God promises to make them his own people, who worship him and serve him among the nations, and to make them a godly nation. God is on a mission, and he plans to reach the nations through his covenant people.

In the Sermon on the Mount, Jesus sets forth his vision for his new kingdom community. In the Beatitudes, Jesus associates God's kingdom with spiritual poverty, mourning, meekness, hunger for godliness, mercy, peace, and persecution. Jesus says that for those who embrace such things, the kingdom of heaven is now, and greater blessings will come in the future consummation. His disciples are not to withdraw from the world or be contaminated by it, but are to pursue a mission of holy living and gospel witness. After Peter confesses that Jesus is the Messiah and God's Son, Jesus declares that Peter will be a key leader in building Jesus's church. Jesus is Lord and Messiah, who builds his messianic community, which he will cause to triumph over its enemies, including death. By preaching the gospel, the disciples will invite believers into God's kingdom.

When Peter preaches Christ crucified and risen on Pentecost, 3,000 people believe and are baptized. Luke explains that the early church was dedicated to the apostles' instruction, fellowship, the Lord's Supper, and prayer. The church is characterized by joy, praise, a good reputation, and growth. In salvation the Spirit unites all believers to Christ, making us a part of his body so that we belong to him and one another. God designed the church to be unified and wants members to share each other's suffering and joys. Paul orders gifts according to importance and shows something better than gifts—love. God sent his Son, whose death and resurrection made peace between God and us. His reconciling work unifies believing Jews and Gentiles into one new humanity, and together they enter into relationship with the Trinity.

Genesis 12:1–3

"The history of redemption, like that of creation, begins with God speaking."[3] Genesis 1 says that God speaks creation into being, and here he calls Abram ("exalted father"), whose name God later changes to Abraham ("father of a multitude," Gen 17:5 ESV). God commands him to leave his home in Ur of the Chaldees and go to a land God will show him (12:1). Unlike his father, Terah, who worshipped idols (Josh 24:2), Abraham knows the true God because of his gracious initiative. In God's plan, Abraham will become the father of God's people.

Along with God's one command to Abraham, God makes amazing promises to him. The idea of blessing pervades the promises, occurring five times. These promises are foundational to all of God's dealings with his people. God promises (1) to give Abram a land, (2) to bring a great nation from him, (3) to bless him and make his name great, (4) to protect him, and (5) to bless "all the peoples on earth" through him (Gen 12:1–3).

These five foundational promises warrant our attention. First, God promises Abraham a land. This is the Promised Land, which Israel finally enters after forty years of wilderness wandering. Under Joshua, Israel displaces the Canaanites and possesses the land. And we will live in the new earth (Rom 4:13), on which all the resurrected people of God will spend eternity (Heb 11:10).

Second, God promises to bring a great nation from Abraham. This was humanly impossible because Sarah was barren (11:30). Bruce Waltke comments: "Through this childless couple, God will bring into being a new humanity that is born not of the will of a husband but by the will of God."[4] God gives Abraham and Sarah Isaac, who is father to Jacob, whose name God changes to Israel and from whom God brings the promised nation. Ultimately Christ comes from Israel, and he is the head of the new humanity comprising believing Jews and Gentiles and rooted in God's promise to Abraham (Gal 3:7–9).

---

[3] Kidner, *Genesis*, 113 (see chap. 5, n. 9).

[4] Waltke, *Genesis*, 201 (see chap. 1, n. 7).

Third, in contrast to those building the Tower of Babel, who seek to "make a name for [them]selves" (11:4), God promises Abraham a great name. This is remarkable, for Scripture ascribes greatness only to the name of God, with two exceptions. One is David: "I will make a great name for you" (2 Sam 7:9); the other is Abraham, here.

Fourth, God promises to protect Abraham. God will bless people who bless Abraham and curse anyone who treats him with contempt.

Fifth, God promises to bless "all the peoples on earth" through Abraham (Gen 12:3). Gordon Wenham shows that there is a buildup in God's blessing. First, only Abraham is blessed. Then, he will be a blessing. Next, those who bless him are blessed. Finally, all families are blessed through him. Though God's original promise to Abraham is "In you all the *families* of the earth shall be blessed" (v. 3 ESV), later we read that "all the *nations* of the earth will be blessed" (18:18; 22:18; 26:4).[5] This promise is fulfilled ultimately in Christ, for Abraham is "the father of all who believe," Jew and Gentile (Rom 4:11–12); he is "our father in God's sight" (v. 17). Therefore, believers in Christ are "Abraham's sons" (Gal 3:7) and "Abraham's seed, heirs according to the promise" (v. 29).

In sum, God promises Abraham: "I will make you a great nation, I will bless you, and I will make your name great" (Gen 12:2). And God commissions him: Be a blessing to the nations. I will bless you, so that you will be a blessing to the nations. Abraham is chosen for the sake of mission.

Exodus 19:4–6

Three months after leaving Egypt, the Israelites come to Mount Sinai in fulfillment of God's promise to Moses (Exod 3:12). He goes up to meet with God, who speaks to him and tells him what to say to the people (19:1–3).

God tells Moses to remind the people what God has done to the Egyptians. He has defeated the gods of Egypt and Pharaoh in the ten plagues and destroyed Pharaoh's army in the sea. God remarks, "I carried you on eagles' wings" (v. 4). The metaphor of an eagle's flight highlights

---

[5] Wenham, *Genesis 1–15*, 275 (see chap. 1, n. 14).

God's deliverance of his people in the exodus. The care of eagles for their young underscores God's abundant protection and care. In love he has powerfully redeemed them from 430 years of slavery in Egypt.

When the Lord says, "I . . . brought you to myself" (v. 4), he speaks of entering into covenant with the Israelites. A covenant is a formal relationship between the living God and his people.[6] Here it is expressed in the words, "I will . . . be your God, and you will be my people" (Lev 26:12; Jer 7:23). Previously he told them who he is; now he tells them who they are.[7] He sets forth the terms of their relationship. He charges the people to obey him and to be faithful to their covenant with him (Exod 19:5).

In return God makes three great promises to them. First, although he is Creator of "the whole earth," he will make them alone his "own possession" (v. 5). Although all the nations belong to God, only the Israelites will be his own people. Ryken notes that the word used for "treasured possession" (ESV) designates property belonging to a king. He explains that because of God's grace (Deut 7:6–8), "Israel was God's royal property, his most prized possession."[8]

Second, the Israelites will be his "kingdom of priests." This focuses both within and without Israel. Within the nation, each Israelite is to worship and serve God. Outside Israel, the Israelites are to be dedicated to God's service among the nations as priests. God's people are not to be a people who cut themselves off from the rest of the world. Rather, as priests stand between God and people, so the Israelites are to represent him to the nations. How is Israel to do this? Paul House answers: "This priestly ministry included teaching God's word accurately (Hos 4:1–14; Mal 2:7–9), praying for others (Jer 15:1–2), and helping people worship God through offering sacrifices appropriately (see Mal 1:6–14)."[9]

---

[6] We acknowledge considerable help from Douglas K. Stuart, *Exodus*, New American Commentary (Nashville: B&H, 2006), 422–23.

[7] We learned from Philip Graham Ryken, *Exodus: Saved for God's Glory*, Preaching the Word (Wheaton, IL: Crossway, 2015), 458.

[8] Ryken, 459.

[9] Paul R. House, "God Walks with His People: Old Testament Foundations," in *The Community of Jesus*, 6 (see chap. 4, n. 4).

Third, they will be his "holy nation" (Exod 19:6), as befits a people in fellowship with the holy God of the covenant. The Israelites' covenant responsibility, as laid out in the Ten Commandments (Exod 20:1–17), embraces all of life, including dealings with God, neighbors, and the nations. If the Israelites live in light of these three promises, they will help bring to pass God's blessing to Abraham: "All the peoples on earth will be blessed through you" (Gen 12:3).

Peter shows continuity between the people of God in the Old and New Testaments when he applies Moses's words from Exod 19:4 to the church: "You are a chosen race, a royal priesthood, a holy nation, a people for his possession" (1 Pet 2:9). Peter adds, "so that you may proclaim the praises of the one who called you out of darkness into his marvelous light." Living out our identity as the people of God matters; it brings glory to God and is central to the mission of God.

In sum, God expresses his choice of Israel. They are his covenant people—his treasured possession, his kingdom of priests, his holy nation. The particularity is striking: out of all the nations, you are mine, God says. Even more striking is that God's particularity is for the sake of universality: out of all the nations, you are mine; *and* the whole earth is mine, so you will be for me a kingdom of priests and a holy nation. God is on a mission, and he plans to reach the nations through his covenant people. They will witness to him and his ways through their distinctiveness as his holy nation. And they will witness to him through their proclamation as a kingdom of priests, "bringing the knowledge of God to the nations, and bringing the nations to the means of atonement with God."[10]

Matthew 5–7

In the Sermon on the Mount, Jesus sets forth his vision for his new kingdom community.[11] In the Sermon's Beatitudes, Jesus reorients his

---

[10] Wright, *The Mission of God*, 331 (see chap. 8, n. 4). Wright helped us on Genesis 12 and Exodus 19.

[11] For more on this passage, see Christopher W. Morgan and Justin L. McLendon, "A Trajectory of Spirituality," in *Biblical Spirituality*, Theology in

community's values. His people are to be driven not by wealth, power, honor, or comfort but by faith, hope, and love. Jesus begins by pronouncing God's blessings on his kingdom community (Matt 5:3–12). Jesus expresses these blessings in a pattern, first by pronouncing "blessed" those who are marked by particular characteristics: the poor in spirit, those who mourn, the meek, those who hunger and thirst for righteousness, the merciful, the pure in heart, the peacemakers, and the persecuted for righteousness' sake. Jesus here links God's blessing, his kingdom community, and true spirituality. Jesus's people live out a spirituality marked by dependence on God, longing for repentance, humility, desire for true righteousness, integrity, reconciliation with others, and persecution for faithfully following Christ.

Jesus then relates the blessings themselves: theirs is the kingdom of heaven, they shall be comforted, they shall inherit the earth, they shall be satisfied, they shall receive mercy, they shall see God, they shall be called the sons of God, and theirs is the kingdom of heaven. The first and last beatitude end with the same overarching blessing: "theirs is the kingdom of heaven" (vv. 3, 10 ESV). The six beatitudes in the middle relate future blessings (note the recurring "shall be" in vv. 4–9 ESV). God blesses Jesus's people, who are a community of the kingdom now ("theirs is the kingdom") that awaits a fuller, final display of the kingdom ("shall be"). John Stott puts it well: "The blessing promised . . . is the gloriously comprehensive blessing of God's rule, tasted now and consummated later, including the inheritance of both earth and heaven, comfort, satisfaction and mercy, the vision and sonship of God."[12]

The rest of the Sermon on the Mount expands Jesus's vision of his kingdom community. In Matt 5:17–48 he calls his people to holistic holiness as he highlights that true righteousness is Word-saturated, internal,

---

Community, ed. Christopher W. Morgan (Wheaton, IL: Crossway, 2019), 19–54. For more on how spirituality, the church, and mission relate, see Anthony L. Chute and Christopher W. Morgan, "Missional Spirituality as Congregational," in *Spirituality for the Sent: Casting a New Vision for the Missional Church*, ed. Nathan A. Finn and Keith S. Whitfield (Downers Grove, IL: InterVarsity, 2017), 75–95.

[12] John R. W. Stott, *The Message of the Sermon on the Mount*, The Bible Speaks Today (Downers Grove, IL: InterVarsity, 1985), 38.

and external (see also Lev 19:1–18). In Matt 6:1–18 Jesus calls for genuine worship as he stresses that God (not others or ourselves) is to be the sole audience of worship (using the examples of three spiritual disciplines: giving, praying, and fasting) and that living all of life in light of God's kingdom is the central focus of kingdom prayer. In Matt 6:19–34 Jesus sets forth kingdom values as he contrasts earthly treasures with kingdom significance. In Matthew 7 Jesus focuses on the centrality of generous love as he overturns judgmentalism and advances the golden rule. Along the way, Jesus clarifies what it means to be his disciple. Jesus's community possesses true righteousness and lives out true spirituality, which is marked by kingdom character, holistic holiness, genuine worship, kingdom values, and generous love.

A community so enthusiastic about the Messiah's arrival and committed to live out such a spirituality might be expected to be self-focused and separated from the rest of society. Jesus, however, interweaves the spirituality and the mission of his people. Indeed, spirituality fuels mission. From the beginning of Jesus's ministry, "discipleship and mission are inseparably linked."[13] Jesus's disciples are called and sent, called to follow the way of the kingdom and sent to call others to do the same. The inherently missional nature of his kingdom community is striking as he bids it to be the "salt of the earth" (Matt 5:13) and the "light of the world" (v. 14). These images build on the Beatitudes, in which Jesus associates God's kingdom not with human strength and honor but with spiritual poverty, mourning, meekness, hunger, mercy, peace, and persecution. Fundamental to these images is distinctiveness as the holy kingdom community (vv. 3–12). The world is in decay, and Jesus's people are the salt. The world is in darkness, and Jesus's people are the light. Both images not only assume the community's distinctiveness but also clarify the community's mission of holy living and gospel witness.

---

[13] Eckhard J. Schnabel, *Early Christian Mission: Jesus and the Twelve* (Downers Grove, IL: InterVarsity, 2004), 1:272–79.

Matthew 16:16–19

Voices from the Global Church: Lausanne Covenant

"We affirm that God is calling the whole church to take the whole gospel to the whole world. So we determine to proclaim it faithfully, urgently, and sacrificially until he comes."[14]

This passage is famous for its teaching about Jesus and the church.[15] Jesus asks the disciples to tell him who people think he is. Their answers include John the Baptist, risen from the dead; Elijah, predicted in the Old Testament (Mal 4:5); and Jeremiah or another prophet (Matt 16:14). Then Jesus asks them as a group who they think he is. Simon Peter, who often serves as leader, answers for them: "You are the Messiah, the Son of the living God" (v. 16). Jesus says that Peter speaks not with human wisdom, but with divine. Jesus's Father in heaven has revealed Jesus's identity to Peter (v. 17). Only after Jesus's resurrection and appearances to the disciples will they fully understand these words.

Jesus makes a play on words between "Peter" and "rock" and declares that Peter will be a key leader in building Jesus's church. D. A. Carson is insightful: "If it were not for Protestant reactions against extremes of Roman Catholic interpretation, it is doubtful whether many would have taken 'rock' to be anything or anyone other than Peter."[16] The heart of Jesus's claim is often missed: "I will build my church" (v. 18). This is an astounding declaration in light of Israel's being the people of Yahweh. Here Jesus asserts himself as Lord and Messiah, the one building a messianic community and the Lord of his people. These covenant people of God will be the people of Jesus. Like Peter, they will acknowledge that Jesus is the Christ, the Son of God. "The gates of Hades" is an Old Testament

---

[14] The Manila Manifesto, Lausanne Movement website, accessed June 24, 2019, https://www.lausanne.org/content/manifesto/the-manila-manifesto.

[15] We received help from D. A. Carson, "Matthew," in *The Expositor's Bible Commentary* (Grand Rapids: Zondervan, 1984), 8:61–62, 365–75.

[16] Carson, "Matthew," 368. Carson cautions, "The text says nothing about Peter's successors, infallibility, or exclusive authority."

expression referring to death (Job 17:16; Ps 9:13; Isa 38:10).[17] Despite the fact that it is at war, Jesus's church will not die. Because of who he is and what he will accomplish, his church will be victorious over its enemies, including the archenemy: death.

Jesus gives Peter (and the other disciples) "the keys of the kingdom of heaven," the ability to admit or refuse admittance into it (Matt 16:19). By preaching the gospel, the disciples will invite believers into God's kingdom and exclude unbelievers from it. Their actions on earth will mirror God's prior action in heaven. God will use them and their increasing understanding of Jesus's identity to extend his kingdom by gospel proclamation. Note how Jesus speaks of the church in both universal and local terms here. The church's ultimate victory points to some sort of universal church that will stand the test of time, while the proclamation of the gospel and the keys point to a concrete, visible group of people.

Acts 2:37–47

On the day of Pentecost, the apostle Peter preaches that his hearers have rejected and crucified Jesus but God has raised the crucified Jesus from the dead and exalted him to his right hand, publicly proclaiming him to be Lord and Christ (Acts 2:36). These words convict those who hear of their sins, and they ask the apostles how they should respond. Peter urges them to turn from their sins and be baptized (v. 38). He explains that the gospel is for his hearers, their children, and "all who are far off, as many as the Lord our God will call" (v. 39).

Three thousand people believe the gospel and are baptized (v. 41). Luke summarizes activities they engage in together as the church: "They devoted themselves to the apostles' teaching, to the fellowship, to the breaking of bread, and to prayer" (v. 42). The believers dedicate themselves to the apostles' instruction, the heart of church life. The Christians get involved in each other's lives, as their fellowship with the Father and the Son (1 John 1:3) results in fellowship with one another, including sharing material possessions (Acts 2:44–45). The early church is committed to "the breaking of bread" (v. 42), which refers either to taking meals together or to the Lord's

---

[17] Carson, "Matthew," 370.

Supper. They certainly share meals (v. 46), and Acts 20:7 refers to the observance of the Lord's Supper at Sunday worship. In addition, the believers dedicate themselves to prayer, a valuable part of their shared life.

The early church is characterized by meeting and eating together, joy, praise, a good reputation with unbelievers, and growth in numbers (vv. 46–47).

1 Corinthians 12:14–31

In salvation the Holy Spirit unites all believers to Christ and one another. The Spirit makes us a part of Christ's body (1 Cor 12:12–13). That means that we, along with all other Christians, belong to Christ and one another. We are all members of Christ's body (v. 14). Therefore, less conspicuous church members are just as much a part of Christ's body as are conspicuous ones (vv. 15–16). Even if the inconspicuous do not think they belong to Christ, they still do, for the body needs the contributions of each member (v. 17). Paul sets forth a key principle of divine design: "God has arranged each one of the parts in the body just as he wanted" (v. 18).

Having addressed those who think they are unimportant, Paul turns to address those who overestimate their importance. Regardless of what they think, every member of the body needs the other members (vv. 21–24). Indeed, God has ordered the body "so that there would be no division in the body, but that the members would have the same concern for each other" (v. 25). God wants church members to enter into the suffering of one another and to rejoice when other members are honored (v. 26).

Paul repeats that the church is the body of Christ and individually his members (v. 27). He orders gifts according to importance and urges the Corinthians to seek them in light of this ordering. Plainly, apostles, prophets, and teachers are most important and tongues least important (v. 28). Then in verses 29–30 Paul reinforces "the point that no gift is common to all believers."[18] It is thus an error to teach that possession of any particular spiritual gift is essential for salvation, empowerment, or service.

---

[18] Ciampa and Rosner, *The First Letter to the Corinthians*, 609 (see chap. 9, n. 3).

Paul leaves the best for last when he promises to show his readers "an even better way" (v. 31), the way of love. He devotes the next chapter to this theme, which strengthens his argument by setting forth the way believers are to relate to each other in the body of Christ: with the love the Old Testament commands and that Christ displays in word and deed (see also Lev 19:18; John 13:34).

Ephesians 2:11–22

Paul addresses Gentiles and reminds them of their situation before they came to know Christ: they were "without Christ . . . without hope and without God in the world" (Eph 2:12). But now God joins them to Christ, and they are no longer far from God but close to him through Christ's blood, his atoning death on the cross (v. 13). Before salvation, our sins alienate us from God and his love, but he takes the initiative and sends his Son as the peacemaker. Jesus's death and resurrection make peace between God and us, and us and God. His reconciling work also unifies believing Jews and Gentiles, making us "one new man from the two, resulting in peace" (vv. 14–15).

Because of the work of Jesus the Mediator, Jews and Gentiles who trust him as Lord and Savior have peace with God (v. 17). Both become part of Christ's church and obtain a relationship with the Trinity. Through Christ both groups come into God the Father's presence "in one Spirit" (v. 18 ESV). As a result of Christ's reconciling death and resurrection, Gentile believers are not on the outside looking in. Rather, they are fellow citizens of God's kingdom and belong to the church, the people of God. Indeed, they are "members of God's household" (v. 19).

Paul then expands on the church using house and temple imagery. God incorporates believing Gentiles into his family and also makes them a part of his house. This house, which turns out to be a temple where God dwells, is built on a foundation with a cornerstone. That foundation is the apostles and New Testament prophets, who preach the gospel to the Gentiles. The cornerstone, the most important part of the building, is Christ Jesus himself (v. 20). The church is thus built upon Jesus, crucified and risen, and his apostles and prophets, who bear his message.

Paul reveals that the building is a temple dedicated to Christ. The building is under construction, being built so that it "grows into a holy temple in the Lord" (v. 21). Therefore, all who believe in Jesus are members of God's family and a part of his temple, the place where he dwells in the Holy Spirit (v. 22).

Biblical Pictures of the Church

The Bible portrays the church in multiple pictures or images. We will consider some of the most significant ones.

We Are the Body of Christ

Paul teaches that the church is the body of Christ. This picture extols Christ as preeminent: "He is also the head of the body, the church" (Col 1:18). As head of his body, Christ is the source of our spiritual life. "He is the beginning, the firstborn from the dead" (v. 18b). Risen, he inaugurates the new creation and gives us eternal life. The new heavens and earth await their fullness, but Christ's death and resurrection have initiated the new creation so that we have eternal life now in mortal bodies as we await our immortal bodies (Rom 8:10–11). His headship also means that he is the church's ultimate authority (Col 2:19), whom we must obey in the world.

The Holy Spirit joins us to Christ and to one another in one body (1 Cor 12:13). Christ is the head of his body, and we are its members (1 Cor 12:27). Christ is united with the church, yet distinct: he is always the head, and we are always the body. The image of the body conveys the relationship of believers, the members, not only to Christ, their head (Rom 12:6–8), but also to one another (1 Cor 12:14–27). Just as our bodily members belong to us, so we belong to Christ. And by virtue of our union with him, we belong to each other and are interdependent on one another. Christ desires that "there would be no division in the body, but that the members would have the same concern for each other" (v. 25).

God entrusts the work of Christ's church to him and his people. Church leaders are to train members to engage in ministry to edify

Christ's body (Eph 4:12). Christ provides the stimulus for growth, but both the head of the body and its members are active in bodily growth (vv. 15–16). The body image is dynamic, for the body grows and matures (v. 19; Col 2:19) as it operates as Christ's instrument in the world.

We Are the Bride of Christ

Paul portrays the church as Christ's bride. He uses this most intimate picture of union with Christ to teach that we are spiritually wedded to Christ. This image is replete with God's grace, for Christ initiates the marriage, offering himself up in death for his bride, the church, who is the object of his love and care (Eph 5:25).

This picture stresses God's grace and sovereignty but does not omit our responsibility. Paul speaks as he who "promised" the Corinthians "in marriage to one husband," Christ (2 Cor 11:2). Paul aims to present the Corinthians in purity to Jesus when he comes again. With godly jealousy Paul fears, lest his readers "be seduced from a sincere and pure devotion to Christ" into spiritual adultery (v. 3). Instead, as a bride submits to her loving husband exclusively in marriage, so the church must submit to Christ, its loving husband (Eph 5:23–24).

John, too, builds on the Old Testament picture of God's people adorning themselves as a bride for her husband (Isa 61:10) to depict the fulfillment of God's covenantal promises of affection for his saints. John proclaims delight in heaven at the magnificent expectation of the wedding of Christ and his church, preceded by the joyful marriage supper: "Let us be glad, rejoice, and give him glory, because the marriage of the Lamb has come, and his bride has prepared herself. . . . 'Blessed are those invited to the marriage feast of the Lamb!'" (Rev 19:7, 9). John interprets the wedding imagery of 19:6–8 in terms of the ultimate union between Christ and the church: "I also saw the holy city, the new Jerusalem, coming down out of heaven from God, prepared like a bride adorned for her husband. Then I heard a loud voice from the throne: Look, God's dwelling is with humanity, and he will live with them. They will be his peoples, and God himself will be with them and will be their God" (Rev 21:2–3).

We Are the Temple of the Spirit

Paul depicts the church, God's people, as a temple. Against the background of Solomon's magnificent temple, he boldly calls Christians "God's temple" (1 Cor 3:16–17). Paul teaches that the Spirit occupies the place of the god or goddess in a Greco-Roman temple. In fact, in passages treating the church as a temple (including 1 Cor 6:19–20; 2 Cor 6:16; and Eph 2:19–22), Paul says it is God's presence that makes a church a church. This temple of God's people is dynamic and organic, a building growing into a temple before our eyes (vv. 21–22). Paul affirms that God dwells in his people individually, but his emphasis falls on his dwelling in them communally as God's temple. In Christ we are the temple of the living God, worshipping the triune God (v. 18).

Peter also presents the church as a temple, a living temple with Christ as "a living stone" (1 Pet 2:4). Recalling Jesus's reference to himself as the "cornerstone" (of Ps 118:22 in Matt 21:42), Peter presents Christ as the "cornerstone" who saves those who believe and judges those who reject him (1 Pet 2:6–8). Peter presents the risen Christ as the "living stone" (v. 4). He is alive from death and the source of spiritual life for his people (see 1:3, 23). Peter extends his "stone" imagery to encompass God's people: as believers in Christ, the "living stone," we are "living stones" ourselves, deriving spiritual life from him (2:4–5).

God uses these stones to build a building, a "spiritual house," where we serve as believer-priests to "offer spiritual sacrifices acceptable to God through Jesus Christ" (v. 5). Peter thus portrays the church as an organism. We are alive with the resurrection life of Jesus. Through union with Christ, God "has given us new birth into a living hope" (1:3) and forms us as the church, a living temple where God is worshipped.

We Are the New Humanity

The church is also the new humanity. Christ is the new Adam, and God's reconciliation of Jews and Gentiles in him is the creation of a new humanity. Christ our peace removes the hostility between Jews and Gentiles, and God creates one new humanity out of the two divided peoples. Paul uses new creation language to describe the church as a living display of what humanity is supposed to be (Eph 2:13–16).

Voices from the Global Church: James H. O. Kombo

Kombo from Kenya wrote, "While the Bible recognizes and ultimately rejoices in racial distinction (Rev. 5:9–10; 7:9–10), it also teaches the equality of all peoples regardless of race or ethnicity (Eph. 2:14–18). In Christ, there is only one people, one nation, one 'tribe' . . . (Gal. 3:28–29). . . . [I]dentity in Christ supersedes all other identities. Moreover, all people are created in the image of God (Gen. 1:26–27; 9:6). And so, as we learn to resist the exaltation of ourselves or our ethnicity that our sin nature promotes, we can joyfully exult in the wonder of being included in the one nation that the Christian gospel produces—the 'tribe' of Christ (Eph. 4:3–7)."[19]

Although he is created in God's image, Adam fails to display God to the cosmos, and Israel, also the image of God, does the same. But Christ comes as the new Adam and the perfect image of God, succeeding where they fail. Through his death and resurrection, he re-creates a people into that same image. Through union with Christ, the church is now the image of God. We are the one new people, the new humanity, called to display God to the world (Eph 2:15; 4:13, 24).

The church is already the new humanity (2:14–18) but is to attain unto a mature humanity (4:13). This is because God's eternal purpose of cosmic reconciliation is not yet fully realized—sin and injustice still occur. However, God will bring about a new creation. And, strikingly, God's new creation is already underway—in the church! The church is the firstfruits of the ultimate new creation still to come. We are both the genuine reality of the new creation and the foretaste of more to come. Thus, the church is the new humanity, a glimpse of the way things are supposed to be, and a glimpse of the way the cosmos ultimately will be.

---

[19] James H. O. Kombo, "Social Ethics," in *ESV Global Study Bible*, 1903–4 (see chap. 2, n. 35).

We Are the Family of God

By virtue of our adoption in Christ, we are also the family of God. Before adoption we were children of the devil and slaves of sin (Gal 4:3; 1 John 3:10). But our gracious God saves us and gives us a new identity as his children, as John exults: "See what great love the Father has given us that we should be called God's children" (1 John 3:1). This happens because "God sent his Son, born of a woman, born under the law, to redeem those under the law, so that we might receive adoption as sons" (Gal 4:4–5). Christ dies as our substitute, becoming a curse for us in his accursed death on the cross to redeem us from the curse of the law (3:13). We are now "heirs of God and fellow heirs with Christ" (Rom 8:15, 17; see also Gal 4:6–7). We will inherit God himself and the new heavens and new earth (1 Cor 3:21–23; Rev 21:3).

Our adoption in Christ permanently relates us to God and connects us to each other as the family of God. James teaches that the church is a spiritual family. It is a community of family-like relationships, where love, truth, and service are to mark its members (Jas 1:18–27). James's use of "brothers and sisters" (1:2 to 5:19) depicts the church as a family, where people love one another and are bound to one another. And this family gathers to encourage one another in following Christ, which involves teaching truth, living in holiness, and ministering to the poor.[20]

We Are the People of God

God enters into covenant with Abraham and his descendants to be their God (Gen 17:7). Because God redeems the Israelites from Egyptian slavery, they belong to him. He pledges himself to them and claims them as his own (Lev 26:12). God promises that in the new covenant, "[He would] be their God, and they [would] be [his] people" (Jer 31:33).

The New Testament applies God's new covenant promises to the church, the people of God (Heb 8:10). Israel was the Lord's vineyard (Isa 5:1–7); the church remains in Jesus, the true vine (John 15:1–8). Israel

---

[20] Morgan, *A Theology of James*, 161 (see chap. 2, n. 3).

had the temple; the church is God's temple (1 Cor 3:16). Peter applies Old Testament descriptions of Israel to the church: "You are a chosen race, a royal priesthood, a holy nation, a people for his possession. . . . Once you were not a people, but now you are God's people; you had not received mercy, but now you have received mercy" (1 Pet 2:9–10). There is thus continuity between believing Israelites and the church. But this is not an absolute identity, for Paul teaches that there is still a future for ethnic Jews, blood descendants of Abraham (Rom 11:25–32). They will be brought to Christ and become part of his church.

God takes the gracious initiative in choosing, saving, keeping, and perfecting his people. He chooses us for salvation apart from our works (2 Tim 1:9–10). He saves us by giving Christ to die and rise for us (John 10:14–18). He keeps us in his love (Rom 8:35–39). In the end he will present the church to himself in perfect holiness (Eph 5:27).

The church is the united people of God, not a collection of individuals. The Spirit indwells God's people individually (1 Cor 6:19–20) and corporately (3:16–17). The Spirit gives us spiritual gifts "as he wills" (12:11). He empowers us to live for God and spread the gospel (Acts 1:8; 2 Cor 12:9; Eph 6:10). God leads us to worship and serve him in mission.

At the end, we "will be his peoples, and God himself will be with [us] and will be [our] God" (Rev 21:3). Only here does God use the plural "peoples," highlighting that ethnic diversity will characterize us as his final people.

The Nature of the Church

The Church and the Churches

The word "church" (*ekklesia*) in the New Testament refers to the church in its many manifestations. It refers to churches meeting in homes (house churches):

> Aquila and Priscilla send you greetings warmly in the Lord, along with the church that meets in their home. (1 Cor 16:19)

To Philemon our dear friend and coworker, to Apphia our sister,
to Archippus our fellow soldier, and to the church that meets in
your home. (Phlm vv. 1–2)

New Testament writers sometimes use the word "church" to point to
citywide or metropolitan churches:

On that day a severe persecution broke out against the church in
Jerusalem, and all except the apostles were scattered throughout
the land of Judea and Samaria. (Acts 8:1)

Now from Miletus, he sent to Ephesus and summoned the elders
of the church. (Acts 20:17)

The churches in a Roman province (provincial churches) are corporately referred to as the church:

So the church throughout all Judea, Galilee, and Samaria had
peace and was strengthened. (Acts 9:31)

The churches of Asia send you greetings. (1 Cor 16:19)

On a few occasions the word "church" refers to the whole ecumenical
church:

Then the apostles and the elders, with the whole church, decided
to select men who were among them and to send them to Antioch
with Paul and Barnabas: Judas, called Barsabbas, and Silas, both
leading men among the brothers. (Acts 15:22)

Sometimes "church" is used to depict what some may call the invisible or universal church, which speaks of the unity of all believers everywhere, both living and dead:

And he subjected everything under his feet and appointed him as
head over everything for the church. (Eph 1:22)

Now to him who is able to do above and beyond all that we ask or
think according to the power that works in us—to him be glory

in the church and in Christ Jesus to all generations, forever and ever. Amen. (3:20–21)

He did this to present the church to himself in splendor, without spot or wrinkle or anything like that, but holy and blameless. (5:27)

Voices from the Global Church: Chuang Chua

Chua from Singapore wrote, "The church is the worldwide people of God, the community of those who have been redeemed by the work of Jesus Christ. The church transcends ethnic, cultural, and racial lines, being comprised of all those who have repented of their sin and trusted in Christ alone for their salvation. The church is the single most important institution on earth, the organism through which God advances his kingdom. . . . Indeed, the essential identity of the church as communal and relational is rooted in the eternal and blessed community of the Godhead. . . . While the church is created through the redemptive work of the triune God, it finds diverse expressions in different contexts in the form of local congregations. . . . [T]he ultimate goal of the church is nothing less than the glory of God, expressed from every corner of the globe."[21]

The church in this sense is not identical with any one local church, denomination, or association. It is not entirely visible to human beings and refers to the sum total of all believers from all places and all times.

Most of the time in the New Testament, "church" refers to the local, visible church—the gathered community of God's people who are covenanted together to worship the triune God, love one another, and witness to the world.

When they had appointed elders for them in every church . . . (Acts 14:23)

So the churches were strengthened in the faith and grew daily in numbers. (Acts 16:5)

---

[21] Chuang Chua, "The Importance of the Global Church," in *ESV Global Study Bible*, 1863–64.

This is the predominant usage of *church*, and the biblical emphasis: the church is a local group of identifiable believers committed to Christ and one another, working together to glorify God and to serve his mission. The local church is the primary locus of fellowship and worship; it's the primary means God uses for evangelism, disciple making, and ministry. This is why Paul plants local churches, appoints leaders for them, sends delegates to them, and writes letters to them. Local churches are key in his theology, and they are key in his mission strategy. In the local church, we share life together, grow in maturity together, minister together, worship together, and witness together.

The Church as Believers

Under the old covenant, Israel is a mixed community composed of believers and unbelievers. By contrast, under the new covenant the church is composed of believers. Of course, unbelievers sometimes identify with the church, but true members of the church have been born again, believe in Jesus, and are indwelt by the Spirit.

Jeremiah predicts the superiority of the new covenant to the old. Because of their sins and unbelief, the Israelites whom God delivers from Egypt break the old Mosaic covenant and die in the wilderness. The new covenant will be much greater because it will center on God's work. The Lord promises that he will be his people's God, and they will belong to him. He will write his law on their hearts, and they will obey him. Even more, the Lord promises, "They will all know me" (Jer 31:34). *All* under the new covenant will know God and enjoy the forgiveness of sins he graciously provides (vv. 31–34). The new covenant community is thus not identical to the old covenant community. The new covenant community, the church, will not be a mixture of believers and unbelievers but filled with people who all know the Lord, his new life, and his forgiveness.

Jesus teaches that his death ratifies the new covenant (Luke 22:20), and Paul does the same (1 Cor 11:25). Although Scripture teaches that there is one people of God through the ages, Jesus's death and resurrection bring great changes to those who know him. He is "the mediator of a new covenant" and ushers in the promises that Jeremiah made. This has great ramifications for the New Testament church, as Stephen Wellum explains: "True members of the new covenant community are only those who have professed that they have entered into union with Christ by repentance and faith and are thus partakers of all the benefits and blessings of the new covenant age."[22]

The images of the church also point to the church as being composed of believers. Only Christians can be the body of Christ, since it refers to people united to Christ. Only Christians can be the bride of Christ, since it refers to people who are increasingly holy in Christ. Only Christians are the temple of the Spirit, since it refers to people who are saints and indwelt by the Spirit. Only Christians are the new humanity, since it refers to people who are reconciled to God. Only Christians are the family of God, since it refers to people who know God as Father and each other as brothers and sisters. Only Christians are the people of God, since it refers to people who know God.

The attributes of the church discussed next also point to the church as believers. Only Christians are one with Christ and one another. Only Christians are holy in Christ. Only Christians are characterized by truth.

Attributes of the Church

In the Niceno-Constantinopolitan Creed of 381, early Christians confess belief in "one, holy, catholic, and apostolic church." This important statement skillfully summarizes the biblical teaching about the attributes of Christ's church: unity, holiness, universality (catholicity), and apostolicity (truth).

- We Are One: United in Christ
- We Are Holy: Set Apart by the Spirit
- We Are Universal: Spread over the World
- We Are Apostolic: Founded on the Truth

---

[22] Stephen J. Wellum, "Beyond Mere Ecclesiology: The Church as God's New Covenant Community," in *The Community of Jesus*, 194.

We Are One: United in Christ

Voices from Church History: Dietrich Bonhoeffer

Bonhoeffer (1906–1945), a German pastor and theologian, was a founding member of the Confessing Church, which opposed Hitler and Nazism. He left a safe teaching position in America to return to Germany to teach in an underground seminary. His most famous book, *The Cost of Discipleship* (1937), shows how the Sermon on the Mount speaks to life today. *Life Together* (1939), written while living in shared community amid danger, continues to speak to the church. His opposition to Hitler cost him his life. He wrote,

> Because God already has laid the only foundation of our community, because God has united us in one body with other Christians in Jesus Christ long before we entered into common life with them, we enter into that life together with other Christians, not as those who make demands, but as those who thankfully receive. . . . We thank God for giving us other Christians who live by God's call, forgiveness, and promise. . . . And is not what has been given us enough: other believers who will go on living with us through sin and need under the blessing of God's grace?[23]

The church is one because believers have been united in the same Lord Jesus Christ and are to promote visibly this eternal, spiritual union (John 17:20–23; Rom 12:3–8). The church's unity transcends all earthly distinctions of ethnicity, social status, or gender (Gal 3:27–28).

Adam's sin brings disorder and disunity, but God's plan is to glorify himself through a full-scale restoration of cosmic unity in Christ. Ephesians tells us that God will do this by bringing all things together in Christ. God's new creation—including the church—is related to all three spheres of his plan for cosmic unity.[24] First, the church is composed of

---

[23] Dietrich Bonhoeffer, *Life Together and Prayerbook of the Bible*, English ed. (Minneapolis: Fortress, 2005), 39–40.

[24] See Christopher W. Morgan, "Toward a Theology of the Unity of the Church," in *Why We Belong: Evangelical Unity and Denominational Diversity*,

believers who were alienated from God but through Christ's saving work are united to him by the Holy Spirit (2:1–10). Second, the church is also the people of God reconciled to one another (vv. 11–22). Third, the church is a demonstration of God's plan of cosmic reconciliation (3:8–11). God creates the church to display and glorify himself (2:7, 10; 3:10). Church unity declares that "there is one body and one Spirit . . . one hope . . . one Lord, one faith, one baptism, one God and Father of all, who is above all and through all and in all" (4:4–6).

The unity of the church is a reality, for God has created one new people, one with Christ and one another (Eph 2:11–22). Unity marks the whole or universal church. The reconciliation of Jews and Gentiles into one new people is global and thus requires belief in a universal church. Unity also marks the local church, for the reconciliation of Jews and Gentiles showcases God's purposes of cosmic unity and requires the church's visibility, and thus the local church.

The church's unity is both a current reality and a perennial pursuit. This means that the unity of the church bears witness to "the already and the not yet" of the kingdom. Thus, Paul urges the church toward specific behaviors and grounds those exhortations on the theological realities of the church's identity. Ephesians regularly points to the already/not yet aspect of the church.

Unity is hard to come by, so Paul exhorts readers to live out unity "with all humility and gentleness, with patience, bearing with one another in love, making every effort to keep the unity of the Spirit through the bond of peace" (Eph 4:2–3). Church unity is built on the theological foundations of one God, one Lord, one Spirit, and so on (vv. 4–6). Paul stresses that being united to one another means that we must speak truth, not nurse anger, give generously, avoid hurtful words, edify others, and not grieve the Spirit (vv. 25–30). He urges unity, emphasizing removal of "all bitterness, anger and wrath, shouting and slander . . . along with all malice." Christians are to "be kind and compassionate to one another,

---

ed. Anthony L. Chute, Christopher W. Morgan, and Robert A. Peterson (Wheaton, IL: Crossway, 2013), 19–36.

forgiving one another" (vv. 31–32). The church's unity is summed up by love (5:1–2).

The unity of the church is an important doctrine and a practical challenge. We often forget that unity is a doctrine. The Christian church is created in and through the gospel. Unity is broken by those who deny the gospel, the deity of Christ, or other core truths (see Gal 1:6–10). The doctrine of church unity shapes the church's praxis (Eph 4:1–6, 17–32). Church unity can exist in the midst of differences of opinion on culture and tradition. It is striking that Paul never urges the church at Rome to agree on food laws and customs; rather, he urges them to worship God with one voice despite such differences (Rom 15:5–7). The day-to-day practice of church unity is shown in our relationships to the church as a whole and to individual believers. Paul later shows how the holiness (5:3–18) and the worship of the church (vv. 18–21) are to display God and church unity. Unity is also displayed in our Christian family/household relationships, including those of husband and wife, parents and children, and even master and bondservant (6:5–9).

We Are Holy: Set Apart by the Spirit

Holiness is another attribute of the church. Salvation as sanctification or holiness is initial, progressive, and final. Initial sanctification is the work of the Holy Spirit in setting apart sinners to God and holiness once and for all (1 Cor 6:11). It is also called definitive sanctification because God defines as his saints those initially sanctified (1:2). Progressive or Christian sanctification is God's working actual holiness into the lives of members of his body the church by turning them more and more away from sin and toward him (1 Thess 4:3–5). The Spirit works progressive holiness into believers, using the Word, the church, and prayer (John 17:17; 2 Thess 2:13). Final sanctification is the Holy Spirit's work of confirming the saints in perfect holiness when Jesus comes again (Eph 5:27; 1 Thess 5:23–24).

The church is holy because God comes to dwell in believers corporately and individually. Viewing the church as a whole, Paul declares, "God's temple is holy, and that is what you are" (1 Cor 3:17). Viewing believers' bodies as temples, Paul says, "Don't you know that your body is a temple of the Holy Spirit who is in you, whom you have from God?" (6:19). Sanctification of the church is the work of all three trinitarian persons. It is the work of God the Father, for "the Father of spirits" disciplines us "for our benefit, so that we can share his holiness" (Heb 12:9–10). It is the work of the Son, for "Christ loved the church and gave himself for her to make her holy, cleansing her with the washing of water by the word" (Eph 5:25–26). And sanctification is the work of the Holy Spirit, as Paul teaches when he speaks of "salvation through sanctification by the Spirit and through belief in the truth" (2 Thess 2:13).

Although Scripture usually says that the Spirit indwells believers, because God is three in one, we are not surprised to learn that the Son and Father indwell believers too. Paul ascribes indwelling six times to the Son (Rom 8:10; 2 Cor 13:5; Gal 2:20; Eph 3:17; Col 1:27; 3:11) and twice to the Father (2 Cor 6:16; Eph 2:22). Christians, then, are indwelt by the Father, Son, and Holy Spirit and are thus holy in God's sight; in response, they are to live holy lives.

In his high priestly prayer, Jesus asks his Father to sanctify the church: "Sanctify them by the truth; your word is truth" (John 17:17). We can be confident that God will sanctify us because of Jesus's consecration of himself to be our priestly sacrifice (v. 19). Because the Father welcomes Jesus to his right hand after his sacrifice, we know that his sacrifice is final, perfect, and effective (Heb 1:3). As a result, Paul describes the church's final sanctification in staggering terms: Christ gives himself in death for the church, "to present the church to himself in splendor, without spot or wrinkle or anything like that, but holy and blameless" (Eph 5:27).

In sum, the church is holy because we have been set apart to God and constituted as his saints, are indwelt by the Holy Spirit, are consecrated to the service of God, and walk in his ways. At Christ's return the church will be perfected in holiness.

We Are Universal: Spread over the World

The church is universal, or catholic, in that it is not confined to any one place or people. Instead, it is composed of all God's people spread over the whole earth. The roots of the church's universality sink deep into Old Testament soil in God's promises to make Abraham a blessing to all peoples (Gen 12:3) and nations (22:18). The Old Testament hints at the universality of God's people when some Egyptians leave their land with the Israelites (Exod 12:38), in Rahab and her family (Josh 6:22–25), in Ruth's becoming an Israelite by marriage (Ruth 4:13), in Elisha's healing Naaman the leper (2 Kgs 5:13–14), in reluctant Jonah's successful ministry to Nineveh (Jonah 3), and in Daniel's ministry in Babylon (Dan 6:25–28). The prophets foretell that the Messiah will minister to the nations (Isa 42:1–9; 49:1–7; 52:15).

These promises and hints are fulfilled in the New Testament, when Jesus comes as the Redeemer of Jews and Gentiles. God directs Gentile "wise men from the east" to worship him after his birth (Matt 2:2). Although Jesus comes first to the "lost sheep of the house of Israel" (Matt 15:24), he also ministers to a Canaanite woman (vv. 21–28), Samaritans (John 4:1–42), and Greeks (12:20–26). Ironically, not Jews but Samaritans confess that he is "the Savior of the world" (John 4:42). Once again these are biblical hints of what would transpire.

Jesus's Great Commission leaves no doubt as to his worldwide intentions: "Go, therefore, and make disciples of all nations, baptizing them in the name of the Father and of the Son and of the Holy Spirit, teaching them to observe everything I have commanded you. And remember, I am with you always, to the end of the age" (Matt 28:19–20).

The apostles obey their Lord and evangelize and disciple "all nations." Though the gospel is preached "first to the Jew," it is taken "then to the Gentile" (Rom 1:16 NIV). God enlarges Peter's thinking and uses him to bring salvation to Gentiles (Acts 10). Paul, the apostle to the Gentiles, is also God's instrument in fulfilling his promises to Abraham to bless the world. He writes,

> You know, then, that those who have faith, these are Abraham's sons. Now the Scripture saw in advance that God would justify the Gentiles by faith and proclaimed the gospel ahead of time to Abraham, saying, All the nations will be blessed through you. (Gal 3:7–8)

> You have already heard about this hope in the word of truth, the gospel that has come to you. It is bearing fruit and growing all over the world, just as it has among you since the day you heard it and came to truly appreciate God's grace. (Col 1:5–6)

In time it became a settled principle of church teaching: "The Father has sent his Son as the world's Savior" (1 John 4:14). As a result of the worldwide preaching of the gospel and church planting in numerous nations, the church is spread around the globe.

Local churches exist in communities in most countries, and the sum totals show that the church is global and multinational. A corollary of the church's catholicity is the fact that ethnic, racial, or gender discrimination is sinful. Not only are all human beings made in God's image, but God brings into his family people "from every tribe and language and people and nation" (Rev 5:9; see also 7:9–10; 21:24; 22:1–4).

We Are Apostolic: Founded on the Truth

Roman Catholics believe that the description "one, holy, catholic and apostolic Church" applies only to their church. The Roman Catholic Church claims that it alone is apostolic because of apostolic succession of a continuous line of bishops stretching back to the apostles. This concerns especially the church of Rome, whose first bishop Rome regards to have been Peter. Rome holds that Christ makes Peter head of the apostles and also chooses him as the first pope, Christ's representative on earth. Apostolicity guarantees the Roman church's valid authority, teaching, and sacraments.

Contrary to this, evangelicals maintain that the church is apostolic because it is founded on the preaching and teaching of the apostles, including Peter. Apostolicity, then, is based on fidelity to the gospel as found in the New Testament. Indeed, the church is "built on the foundation of the apostles and prophets, with Christ Jesus himself as the cornerstone" (Eph 2:20). The early church devotes itself to the apostles' teaching, which is in accord with the Word of God (Acts 2:42). Apostolicity is reflected in the apostles' commitment to God's truth (2 Tim 3:14–4:4). Paul writes, "I am not ashamed, because I know whom I have believed and am persuaded that he is able to guard what has been entrusted to me until that day. Hold on to the pattern of sound teaching that you have heard from me, in the faith and love that are in Christ Jesus" (2 Tim 1:12–13). The gospel is true and God's Word is true, so our beliefs, teaching, and lives are grounded on it.[25]

Furthermore, Jesus promises that he and the Father will send to his disciples the Spirit of truth, who will "testify about" Jesus and guide them "into all the truth" (John 15:26; 16:13). The Spirit does this, and, as a result, the apostles believe and preach the gospel, placing it at the center of their apostolic ministries:

> Christ died for our sins according to the Scriptures . . . he was buried . . . he was raised on the third day according to the Scriptures. (1 Cor 15:3–4)

> Christ also suffered for sins once for all, the righteous for the unrighteous, that he might bring you to God. (1 Pet 3:18)

Apostolicity is so serious a matter that, according to the New Testament, preaching a different gospel, even if preached by angels or apostles, brings down curses from God on the preachers' heads: "Even if we or an angel from heaven should preach to you a gospel contrary to what we have preached to you, a curse be on him! As we have said before, I now say again: If anyone is preaching to you a gospel contrary to what you received, a curse be on him!" (Gal 1:8–9). As far as the apostle Paul is concerned, he subordinates himself to the gospel. He is only the messenger and is to be trusted only as he is faithful to the message—the gospel of God revealed. God's Word has supreme authority, even over apostles like Paul. Indeed, the New Testament binds all teachers and preachers to receive, believe, guard, and pass on the truth of God. They are to "preach the word; be ready in season and out of season; rebuke, correct, and encourage with great patience and teaching" (2 Tim 4:1–3).

---

[25] For more on the truthfulness of Scripture, see chapter 2, "God's Revelation."

Synthesis

As an agent of the kingdom, the church reflects the already-and-not-yet nature of the kingdom. As such, the church is already one, holy, catholic, and apostolic. However, the church is also not yet complete in these attributes but is growing in each of them (Eph 2:11–22; 4:11–16; 5:22–33). When Christ returns, he will confirm his church in perfect unity, holiness, catholicity, and truth.

Marks of the Church

The attributes were formulated in the early centuries of the church, the patristic period. They were a part of the biblical faith that the church confessed. The marks arose in the sixteenth-century Protestant Reformation, and the Reformers used them to separate truth from error. Churches of the Reformation derived three marks from Scripture to distinguish true churches. They needed these marks to differentiate between their churches and those of Rome and various sects. They identified the marks of the church as the pure preaching of the Word/gospel, the proper administration of the ordinances (sacraments), and the faithful exercise of church discipline. Jesus's Great Commission contains two of the marks. Discipleship includes baptism (Matt 28:19) and observance of his commands (the Word) (v. 20). In the same Gospel, Jesus taught the importance of church discipline (18:15–17) and instituted the Lord's Supper (26:26–30).

We Preach the Word

Preaching the Word means proclaiming the gospel according to biblical teaching in the power of the Holy Spirit. This involves teaching that salvation is by God's grace alone through faith alone in Christ alone (Eph 2:8–9). It sets forth Jesus as the only Savior of the world (John 14:6; Acts 4:12) and his death and resurrection as the only means of salvation from sin and hell (1 Cor 15:3–4). Although all believers are to share their faith (1 Thess 1:8), God gives to his church pastors and teachers (Eph 4:11), whose responsibilities include to "preach the word" (2 Tim 4:2). This mark of the church allows Christians to unite around core biblical teachings.

We Observe the Ordinances

Jesus is the origin of the two New Testament ordinances, baptism and the Lord's Supper (Matt 26:26–28; 28:19–20). Both ordinances are ceremonies that visibly portray the gospel: baptism once (Eph 4:5) and the Lord's Supper until Jesus returns (1 Cor 11:26). Baptism and the Lord's Supper show union with Christ (Gal 3:27; Matt 28:19) and forgiveness (Acts 22:16; Matt 26:28). The church must faithfully observe the two ordinances that Jesus gives to it. We will offer a more thorough treatment on these ordinances later in this chapter.

We Exercise Discipline

Jesus and his apostles insist that the church must discipline professing Christians who depart from core teachings or whose lives dishonor Christ (Matt 18:15–17; 1 Cor 5:11–13; Gal 6:1–2; Titus 3:10–11). The goals of church discipline are to glorify God, reclaim the sinner (2 Cor 2:5–8), and warn the church (1 Tim 5:19–20). Erring church members who refuse to repent risk ultimate excommunication from the Lord's Table and church membership. Church discipline must be exercised in love and gentleness (Gal 6:1–3) and is a God-given means to help those who stray and to keep others from straying.

Ordinances of the Church

Jesus our Lord has given two ordinances to us as the church: baptism and the Lord's Supper. God ministers to our five senses. The Word addresses our ears and eyes, and God reinforces the spoken and written Word with touch, taste, and smell. Israel had its annual feasts and sacrificial system. The New Testament has the gospel dramatized in the ordinances of baptism and the Lord's Supper. The term *ordinance* underlines that the Lord

Jesus commands the church to observe both practices. God preaches the gospel to us in baptism (Acts 2:38) and the Lord's Supper (1 Cor 11:26).

Baptism

John the Baptist preaches a baptism of repentance in preparation for the Messiah (Mark 1:4). Both Jesus and John speak of a baptism with the Spirit that is to come and that indeed comes at Pentecost (Luke 3:16; Acts 1:4–5). Jesus teaches that baptism is a part of being a disciple and of making disciples (Matt 28:18–20). Paul teaches that baptism identifies someone with the dying and rising of Christ (Rom 6:3–4). It symbolizes dying to an old life and turning to a new one in a new sphere of divine influence. Some churches incorrectly believe that people must be baptized to be saved. But in Paul's mind, preaching the gospel takes priority over the practice of baptism: "Christ did not send me to baptize, but to preach the gospel" (1 Cor 1:17).

VIEWS OF BAPTISM

Churches have different views of Christian baptism. We will survey Roman Catholic, Lutheran, Reformed, and Baptist views.

Roman Catholicism baptizes infants and adults who have not been baptized. According to the Catechism of the Roman Catholic Church (section 1213):

> Through Baptism we are freed from sin and reborn as sons of God; we become members of Christ, are incorporated into the Church and made sharers in her mission: "Baptism is the sacrament of regeneration through water in the word."

According to the website of the Lutheran Church, Missouri Synod (LCMS):

> Lutheranism holds that baptism is a miraculous means of grace (another is God's Word as it is written or spoken), through which God creates and/or strengthens the gift of faith in a person's heart. . . . Although we do not claim to understand fully how this

happens, we believe that when an infant is baptized God creates faith in the heart of that infant. We believe this because the Bible says that infants can believe (Matt. 18:6) and that new birth (regeneration) happens in Baptism (John 3:5–7; Titus 3:5–6). . . .

Lutherans do not believe that only those baptized as infants receive faith. Faith can also be created in a person's heart by the power of the Holy Spirit working through God's (written or spoken) Word. . . .

The LCMS does not believe that Baptism is ABSOLUTELY necessary for salvation.

According to the Westminster Confession of Faith (chapter 28), the Reformed view of baptism is this:

Baptism is a sacrament of the New Testament, ordained by Jesus Christ, not only for the solemn admission of the party baptized into the visible Church; but also to be unto him a sign and seal of the covenant of grace, of his ingrafting into Christ, of regeneration, of remission of sins, and of his giving up unto God, through Jesus Christ, to walk in the newness of life. Which sacrament is, by Christ's own appointment, to be continued in His Church until the end of the world. . . .

Not only those that do actually profess faith in and obedience unto Christ, but also the infants of one, or both, believing parents, are to be baptized.

Although it is a great sin to contemn or neglect this ordinance, yet grace and salvation are not so inseparably annexed unto it, as that no person can be regenerated, or saved, without it: or, that all that are baptized are undoubtedly regenerated.

According to the Baptist Faith and Message 2000 (article 7):

Christian baptism is the immersion of a believer in water in the name of the Father, the Son, and the Holy Spirit. It is an act of obedience symbolizing the believer's faith in a crucified, buried, and risen Savior, the believer's death to sin, the burial of the old life, and the resurrection to walk in newness of life in Christ

Jesus. It is a testimony to his faith in the final resurrection of the dead. Being a church ordinance, it is prerequisite to the privileges of church membership and to the Lord's Supper.

A comparison is in order. Roman Catholicism and Lutheranism hold that baptism regenerates those being baptized, while the Reformed and Baptist churches do not. Roman Catholic, Lutheran, and Reformed churches baptize infants and adults, while Baptists baptize believers only. Roman Catholic, Lutheran, and Reformed churches allow baptism by sprinkling, pouring, or immersion (rarely done), while Baptists baptize only by immersion.

BAPTISM OF BELIEVERS

Mark Dever encapsulates believer's baptism, the position taken here:

> Baptism itself is a summary of our faith. Baptism is a confession of sin and a picture of repentance. Baptism is a profession of faith in Christ. It reminds us of Christ's humiliation and death as he identified with sinners and of his resurrection from the dead. Baptism presents a preview of the bodily resurrection, and it portrays the radical nature of conversion. When rightly practiced, it distinguishes believers from unbelievers, the church from the world.[26]

Baptism is for believers for at least six reasons.

First, the New Testament teaches that people must believe in Christ before being baptized. Robert Stein explains:

> The individual's responsibility, which is always portrayed as preceding baptism, involves repentance, faith in Jesus Christ, and the confession of Jesus as Christ and Lord. The interrelatedness of this single, three-fold response to the gospel message is

---

[26] Mark E. Dever, "Baptism in the Context of the Local Church," in *Believer's Baptism: Sign of the New Covenant in Christ*, ed. Thomas R. Schreiner and Shawn D. Wright, NAC Studies in Bible & Theology (Nashville: B&H Academic, 2006), 33.

such that often only one of these components of the individual's responsibility may be described in a particular account. Yet repentance always assumes the presence of faith and confession; faith always assumes repentance and confession; and confession always assumes repentance and faith.[27]

People must hear the gospel and respond properly to be saved, and baptism follows this response.

Second, Jesus's Great Commission points to believer's baptism (Matt 28:18–20). Note the order: "Go . . . and make disciples, . . . baptizing, . . . teaching . . ." We are to go and make disciples, whom we then baptize and teach. Those baptized are the new disciples, the new believers in Jesus.

Third, believer's baptism best fits the pattern of the book of Acts. Consistently, Acts presents repentance/faith/confession as a prerequisite for baptism and consistently records the baptism of believers:

> Those who accepted his message were baptized, and that day about three thousand people were added to them. (Acts 2:41)

> When they believed Philip, as he proclaimed the good news about the kingdom of God and the name of Jesus Christ, both men and women were baptized. (8:12)

> A God-fearing woman named Lydia, a dealer in purple cloth from the city of Thyatira, was listening. The Lord opened her heart to respond to what Paul was saying. After she and her household were baptized, she urged us, "If you consider me a believer in the Lord, come and stay at my house." And she persuaded us. (16:14–15)

> Crispus, the leader of the synagogue, believed in the Lord, along with his whole household. Many of the Corinthians, when they heard, believed and were baptized. (18:8)

Note the order for each: the gospel is heard, the person or persons believe(s) in Jesus, and then they are baptized. Acts 2:47: the message is

---

[27] Robert H. Stein, "Baptism in Luke-Acts," in *Believer's Baptism*, 64.

given; the message is accepted; people are baptized. Acts 8:12: the gospel is preached; the men and women believe; they are baptized. Acts 16:14–15: Lydia hears the gospel, she responds to the gospel, and she is baptized. Acts 18:8: Crispus, his household, and many Corinthians believe and are baptized.

Fourth, the interrelationship of believer's baptism and the believer's church points to believer's baptism, as seen in the texts above. In Acts 2, 16, and 18 the new believers are baptized and become a part of the local church.

Fifth, there is no clear example of infant baptism in Acts. Rather, those baptized are believers. It is true that sometimes believers' families are baptized, but this presupposes faith. Consider the Philippian jailer and his family:

> [Paul and Silas] said, "Believe in the Lord Jesus, and you will be saved—you and your household." And *they spoke the word of the Lord to him along with everyone in his house.* [The jailer] took them the same hour of the night and washed their wounds. Right away he and all his family were baptized. He brought them into his house, set a meal before them, and rejoiced because *he had come to believe in God with his entire household.* (Acts 16:31–34)

Again, the gospel first comes to the jailer and his household; then the jailer and his entire household believe, and then they are baptized. The story of Crispus in Acts 18:8 follows the same pattern.

Sixth, believer's baptism best fits the meaning of baptism. David Dockery explains: "For Paul, baptism was primarily an act of identification with the death, burial, and resurrection of Christ (Rom 6:1–4). Baptism also served as a sign of covenant relationship with Christ and his people (Col 2:9–13)."[28] Only believers can identify with Jesus crucified and risen and enter into a covenant relationship with him.

---

[28] David S. Dockery, "The Church in the Pauline Epistles," in *The Community of Jesus*, 113.

Baptism by Immersion

Although many churches baptize by pouring or sprinkling water on those being baptized, immersion more closely reflects the biblical teaching. Baptism by immersion means that the pastor or church leader submerges the one baptized under the water. Three reasons stand out.

First is the meaning of the word "to baptize" in the NT. Most, including Martin Luther and John Calvin, consider the ordinary meaning of this word to be "to immerse." The Orthodox churches, including Greek Orthodox churches, have always practiced baptism by immersion. The standard dictionary of the Greek NT lists immersion as the primary meaning of "baptize."[29] While we do not claim that "to baptize" could only mean "to immerse" in NT times, "immersion does seem to be the most straightforward meaning of the word itself (thus the unbroken practice of immersion among Greek-speaking churches) and to best fit the uses of the word in the New Testament."[30]

Second, examples of baptism in Scripture are often linked to the presence of a body of water, which would seem to fit with baptism by immersion. John the Baptist baptizes Jesus in the Jordan River and, after being baptized, Jesus "came up out of the water" (Mark 1:10). Philip baptizes the Ethiopian high official and both "went down into the water" and "came up out of the water" after baptism (Acts 8:38–39).[31]

Third, immersion portrays the essential meaning of baptism. Baptism has several meanings in the NT, but its most important and comprehensive meaning is union with Christ. Immersion best portrays union with Christ in his death, burial, and resurrection, as the following two passages in Paul show.

---

[29] Arndt, Gingrich, and Danker, *A Lexicon of the New Testament and Other Early Christian Literature*, 2nd ed. (Chicago: Chicago University Press, 1979), 131–32.

[30] Mark E. Dever, "The Church," in *A Theology for the Church*, Daniel L. Akin, ed. (Nashville: B&H Academic, 2007), 786.

[31] Wayne Grudem offers this argument in his *Systematic Theology* (Grand Rapids: Zondervan, 1994), 967–68.

> Are you unaware that all of us who were baptized into Christ Jesus were baptized into his death? Therefore we were buried with him by baptism into death, in order that, just as Christ was raised from the dead by the glory of the Father, so we too may walk in newness of life. For if we have been united with him in the likeness of his death, we will certainly also be in the likeness of his resurrection. (Rom 6:3–5)

> You were buried with him in baptism, in which you were also raised with him through faith in the working of God, who raised him from the dead. (Col 2:12)

The most natural reading of these passages involves immersion. Paul teaches that believers are buried with Christ into death when they are put under the waters of baptism. They are raised with Christ when they come up out of the water.

The Lord's Supper

Jesus gives his church another ordinance: the Lord's Supper (Luke 22:19–20). The Lord's Supper draws attention to Jesus's sacrifice on our behalf. The practice is retrospective: it looks back to the cross. And it is prospective: it looks forward to Christ's return and proclaims his death until he returns. In the world to come, there will be no need for either baptism or the Lord's Supper (though we will participate in the wedding supper of the Lamb; see Rev 19:9).

Augustine taught that in the Lord's Supper the risen Christ preaches to our senses. It is the Word made visible, as it were. The Reformers insisted that scriptural explanation of the Supper is needed. Paul stresses that the Lord's Supper indicates our union with Christ and one another (1 Cor 10:16–17). It therefore calls for our faith and love (11:17–34).

The meal has come to be known by a number of names. It is a *Eucharist*, or thanksgiving (v. 24). It is a *Communion*, an invigoration of union with Christ (10:16). It is the *Lord's Table* (v. 21), and he is the host at this fellowship meal. It is the *Lord's Supper*, which he ordained, turning the Passover into a symbol of his sacrifice (11:17–34).

VIEWS OF THE LORD'S SUPPER

Four views of the Lord's Supper predominate: Roman Catholic, Lutheran, Reformed, and Zwinglian. The Roman Catholic view of the Supper is called *transubstantiation*. In Roman Catholic theology, when priests are ordained, they receive the authority to offer Christ in the sacrifice of the mass. The Roman Catholic Church teaches that when the priest consecrates the elements, they miraculously become the body and blood of Christ. Their outward appearance does not change, but miraculously the invisible essence of the elements changes into Christ's body and blood. The priest offers a non-bloody sacrifice of Christ to God in the mass.

The Lutheran view of the Lord's Supper rejects the Roman Catholic ideas of sacrifice and transubstantiation and instead embraces *consubstantiation*. The Supper is not a priestly sacrifice made to God, but a benefit that he bestows on the worshippers. In Communion, the elements do not change. Instead, Christ is bodily present in, with, and under the elements of bread and the fruit of the vine. Lutherans hold that in his resurrection, the divine attribute of omnipresence is supernaturally transferred from Christ's deity to his humanity. This enables his body to be everywhere present, including in the elements of Communion.

The Reformed view of the Lord's Supper differs from both the Roman Catholic and Lutheran views. It is sometimes called the doctrine of the *real presence* of Christ. It rejects both transubstantiation and consubstantiation. The elements do not change, and Christ's body is in heaven. Instead, the Reformed hold that Christ is present in the Supper when the Holy Spirit brings the benefits of the risen Christ from his place at the Father's right hand to believing participants in Communion.

The Zwinglian view of the Supper differs from the other three views. Although it is debatable whether it was actually the view of Ulrich Zwingli, it remains attached to his name. It is called the *memorial* view because it emphasizes the church's remembering Jesus in his death. The Supper is a commemoration that brings to mind Christ's death and its effectiveness in taking away our sins. In distinction from the other views, it holds that Christ is not present in the Supper in a distinctive or supernatural way.

THEOLOGY OF THE LORD'S SUPPER

First, the Lord's Supper follows Jesus's commands. It is an ordinance. The church observes the Lord's Supper for the same reason it practices Christian baptism: Jesus commands his disciples to do so. Matthew is representative of the Synoptic Gospels:

> As they were eating, Jesus took bread, blessed and broke it, gave it to the disciples, and said, "Take and eat it; this is my body." Then he took a cup, and after giving thanks, he gave it to them and said, "Drink from it, all of you. For this is my blood of the covenant, which is poured out for many for the forgiveness of sins." (Matt 26:26–28)

Second, the Lord's Supper remembers Jesus's death. It is a memorial. In it, we remember Jesus's historical, unique, and unrepeatable death, as Paul relates:

> On the night when he was betrayed, the Lord Jesus took bread, and when he had given thanks, broke it, and said, "This is my body, which is for you. Do this in remembrance of me." In the same way also he took the cup, after supper, and said, "This cup is the new covenant in my blood. Do this, as often as you drink it, in remembrance of me." (1 Cor 11:23–25)

Remembrance is more meaningful than many realize, as David Dockery explains:

> When the church celebrated the Supper, it did so to remember Jesus' broken body and shed blood and the love that motivated his bearing the cross. The Supper visibly represented the body and blood of Christ in the partaking of the bread and the cup. . . . As the bread and cup were taken, the Lord's presence was to be recalled in the words "in remembrance of Me" (1 Cor 11:24). To recall means to transport an action buried in the past in such a

way that its original potency and vitality are not lost but are carried over into the present. Paul emphasized the remembrance of the life and death of the Lord.[32]

Third, the Lord's Supper clarifies Jesus's sacrifice. It is covenantal. Jesus's death is the sacrifice of the new covenant, as Jesus and Paul both state. It is for the church, observed by the church, and taken by believers. Jesus loves his church and gives himself for it. And in the Lord's Supper, he reminds us that "as often as" we partake of the Supper we proclaim the message that saves, keeps, and motivates us as his people.

Fourth, the Lord's Supper unites Jesus's church. It is communal. It celebrates Christ's saving work and underlines our union with Christ and unity with one another as the community of Jesus (1 Cor 10:16–17). It bids us to love one another, show deference to one another, and include one another (11:17–34).

Fifth, the Lord's Supper broadcasts Jesus's gospel. It is missional: "as often as you eat this bread and drink the cup, you proclaim the Lord's death" (1 Cor 11:26). Again, David Dockery is helpful: "The Lord's Supper served as an announcement of the gospel (1 Cor 11:26), a sermon in silence by the entire church."[33] The Lord's Supper does not have inherent power, but it does share the gospel, which is the power of God for salvation and a seed that brings forth life (Rom 1:16; 10:14–17; Jas 1:18).

Sixth, the Lord's Supper celebrates Jesus's provision. It is a participation (see also 1 Cor 10:14–22). We bring nothing to the Table but our sin. We come and receive—receive from the saving work of Jesus, receive from the generous grace of God who accepts sinners who believe in Jesus.[34] There is enough grace at the cross for our past. There is enough grace for our present. And there is enough grace for our future too. The Lord's Supper does not accomplish this grace. Jesus has. The Lord's Supper is

---

[32] Dockery, "The Church in the Pauline Epistles," in *The Community of Jesus*, 114.

[33] Dockery, 115.

[34] See Andreas J. Köstenberger, "The Church According to the Gospels," in *The Community of Jesus*, 49.

not a sacrifice. Jesus has already completed the sacrifice. But the Lord's Supper testifies to God's provision for his people—grace upon grace. And in the Supper we participate; we receive.[35]

Seventh, the Lord's Supper forecasts Jesus's return. It is eschatological. It looks to the future, for at its institution Jesus promised, "I will not drink from this fruit of the vine from now on until that day when I drink it new with you in my Father's kingdom" (Matt 26:29). Paul connects the Supper with Jesus's second advent: eating the bread and drinking the cup proclaims "the Lord's death *until he comes*" (1 Cor 11:26).

Government of the Church

Christians vary significantly concerning church government, but they share belief in several common features. Before exploring these features, we will summarize the various kinds of church government.

Various Types

The Roman Catholic Church is a worldwide hierarchy under the pope, the bishop of Rome based in Vatican City. Catholicism locates the church's ultimate authority in Peter, whom they regard as the first pope, or representative of Christ on the earth. Authority is transmitted through apostolic succession from the church in Rome. Roman Catholic teaching

---

[35] The Second London Confession, 1689, a Baptist confession that follows closely both the Westminster Confession and the Savoy Declaration, states that the "Supper of the Lord Jesus, was instituted by him, the same night wherein he was betrayed, to be observed in his Churches unto the end of the world, for the perpetual remembrance, and shewing forth the sacrifice in his death, confirmation of the faith of believers in all the benefits thereof, their spiritual nourishment, and growth in him; and to be a bond and pledge of their communion with him, and with each other." Second London Confession 30.1, in W. J. McGlothlin, *Baptist Confessions of Faith* (Philadelphia: American Baptist Publication Society, 1911), 270. See also Michael A. G. Haykin, "Baptists, the Lord's Supper, and the Christian Tradition," in *Baptists and the Christian Tradition: Towards an Evangelical Baptist Catholicity*, ed. Matthew Y. Emerson, Christopher W. Morgan, and R. Lucas Stamps (Nashville: B&H Academic, 2020).

includes sacerdotalism, which maintains that the power to forgive sins is passed from the pope to bishops by the laying on of hands. Bishops also possess much derived authority and rule over priests and deacons, who assist them. The Roman church's strength is rooted in its priests, serving in local parishes.

Churches with episcopal church government are governed by bishops, in whom the church locates its authority. Bishops may be subject to higher-ranking bishops (called archbishops, metropolitans, or patriarchs). They also meet in synods. Episcopal church government is not a simple chain of command, and some authority resides in lay church councils.

Presbyterian church government is representative, locating authority in a hierarchy of councils. The lowest level, called the session or consistory, is composed of elders, who govern a local church. The minister of the church (or teaching elder) is a member of and presides over the session. The congregation elects lay representatives (ruling elders). The session sends elders to the next level of council, called the presbytery or classis. The highest council is the general assembly or synod, to which each presbytery sends representatives.

Congregational church government locates authority in the congregation. The local congregation rules itself and elects its own leaders. These churches may be pastor led, staff led, elder led, or otherwise, but in each case the congregation retains the final authority. Local churches may be completely independent or belong to a denomination. If the latter, neither the congregations nor the associations exercise any control over each other, other than having the ability to end membership in the association. The associations or conventions are relational and financial networks of like-minded churches that usually exist to promote church health, missions, and theological education. Churches that traditionally practice congregational church government include Baptists, Congregationalists, and many forms of nondenominational Christianity.

Core Features

Despite the variety in forms of church government, we note several common core features.

First and foremost, Christ is the head of the church (Matt 16:18–19; Eph 5:25–28). As such, he possesses ultimate authority over the church as a whole and over local congregations.

Second, the Bible retains authority over the church (see Gal 1:8–9 above).

Third, Christ expresses his authority through the leadership of the church (Matt 18:15–20; Acts 6:3).

Fourth, the church has two offices. The first is *pastor/elder/bishop*. The term "pastor" denotes care and nurture with the Word (1 Pet 5:1–4), "elder" denotes maturity and wisdom (Titus 1:5–9), and "bishop" or "overseer" denotes leadership and administrative abilities (1 Tim 3:1–7). A qualified pastor is a Christian of sound character who leads his family well, has a good reputation in the community, is able to teach the church (1 Tim 3:1–7; Titus 1:5–9), and is marked by wisdom, love for others, humility, and self-control (Jas 3:1–18). Pastors/elders shepherd the church (1 Pet 5:2), lead the church (1 Tim 3:5), teach the Word (1 Tim 3:2), oppose error (Titus 1:9), pray for the church's members (Jas 5:13–15), and set an example for the others to follow (1 Pet 5:3). The second office is that of *deacon* (Phil 1:1). Deacons' main responsibilities concern service to the church. The qualifications for deacons (1 Tim 3:8–13) are similar to those for pastors, without the requirement to be able to teach.

Fifth, the spiritually gifted congregations themselves are central in fulfilling the ministries of the church. Pastors and other leaders teach and lead, but all members of the congregation bear responsibilities and are ministers too (Eph 4:12–16). They actively use their diverse gifts (teaching, leadership, mercy, giving, etc.) to serve the Lord, the church, and others.[36] All of us are given spiritual gifts. All of us are to use them to strengthen the body of Christ. We need to use our gifts to serve the church so that others will be helped. And we need others to use their spiritual gifts to serve the church so that we will be helped. We give and receive; others give and receive. In and through it all, God is glorified, as he is the giver of the gifts, the one empowering the gifts, and the one being praised through the church's increased health.

---

[36] For more on spiritual gifts, see chapter 9, "The Holy Spirit."

Finally, decisions in church life should reflect the church's nature (i.e., its unity, holiness, truth, and love) and mission.[37]

Mission of the Church

Voices from Church History: William Carey

Carey (1761–1834) was a British Baptist missionary, translator, social reformer, and the "father of modern missions." After rejection by non-Baptist missionaries in West Bengal, India, he joined Baptist missionaries in Serampore, India. He founded schools and translated the Bible into many languages. He opposed sati, the practice of Indian widows throwing themselves onto their husbands' funeral pyres. His essay, *An Enquiry into the Obligations of Christians to Use Means for the Conversion of the Heathens*, sparked the founding of the Baptist Missionary Society. He wrote,

> As our blessed Lord has required us to pray that his kingdom may come, and his will be done on earth as it is in heaven, it becomes us not only to express our desires of that event by words, but to use every lawful method to spread the knowledge of his name. . . . Expect great things; attempt great things. . . . Do not the goodness of the cause, the duties incumbent on us as the creatures of God, and Christians, and the perishing state of our fellow men, loudly call upon us to venture all and use every warrantable exertion for their benefit?[38]

In Matt 28:18–20, Jesus gives the Great Commission to his disciples. He begins by asserting that he is the exalted Son, who is Lord over all, both in heaven and on earth, and over all nations (see also Dan 7:14). The universality of the commission is striking: Jesus has all authority, directs the

---

[37] See Ashford and Morgan, "The Church," in *ESV Systematic Theology Study Bible*, 1713–15.

[38] William Carey, "An Enquiry into the Obligations of Christians to Use Means for the Conversion of the Heathens," in Timothy George, *Faithful Witness: The Life and Mission of William Carey* (Worcester, PA: Christian History Institute, 1998), E.3, E.49.

disciples to make disciples of all nations, instructs them to teach all that he commands them, and promises to be with them "always, to the end of the age" (Matt 28:20). The particularity of the commission is also striking: Jesus uniquely is Lord, he alone is worthy of worship by all nations, his teachings have binding authority, and his presence is with his people as they participate in his mission.[39]

The essence of Jesus's Great Commission is found in its command to make disciples of all nations. Jesus calls his disciples to make other disciples, who are also expected to follow Jesus, listen to his teaching, and reflect his ways. Such disciples live in community, in fellowship with the teacher and with each other as fellow followers of Jesus, the Teacher. Eckhard Schnabel comments: "The directive to 'make disciples' demonstrates the ecclesiological dimension of the mission of the Twelve: missionary work and church must not be separated, since the very goal and purpose of missionary work is the creation of a community of disciples."[40] Making disciples of all nations expands the mission beyond that of Israel to all Gentile peoples. "Nations" does not refer to geopolitical nation-states but connotes Gentiles and something akin to peoples, families, clans, and tribes (see also Gen 12:3; Dan 7:13–14; Matt 24:14; Rev 5:9–10).

The central command of making disciples is clarified by three participles: going, baptizing, and teaching. Matthew apparently uses "go" as an introductory circumstantial participle that is rightly translated as coordinate to the main verb—here "Go and make" (see also 2:8; 9:13; 11:4; 17:27; 28:7).[41] The participle establishes the motion that is necessary for the accomplishment of the command. So "go" here is the necessary action to accomplish the command of making disciples. This makes good sense of the context, since the disciples can make other disciples of all nations only if they go to people who do not yet know Jesus.

---

[39] Schnabel, *Early Christian Mission*, 1:353–55.

[40] Schnabel, 356.

[41] David W. Chapman, "The Great Commission as the Conclusion of Matthew's Gospel," in *All for Jesus: A Celebration of the Fiftieth Anniversary of Covenant Theological Seminary*, ed. Robert A. Peterson and Sean Michael Lucas (Fearn, Ross-shire, UK: Mentor, 2001), 91.

Jesus calls the disciples to make disciples of all nations also by "baptizing them in the name of the Father and of the Son and of the Holy Spirit" (28:19). Those who follow Christ depict their new allegiance to Jesus through baptism. Through baptism, the new disciple publicly identifies with Christ as Lord, with others in Jesus's kingdom community, and with the entire Trinity.

Making disciples of all nations also includes "teaching them to observe all that I have commanded you" (28:19 ESV). The disciples do not make their own disciples but point people to become followers of Jesus, the Teacher. As such, the disciples do not put forward their own teachings but faithfully pass on the teachings of the Teacher. Both believing and practicing Jesus's teachings are required by the disciplers and by the new disciples.

Thus, Jesus declares that the mission of his kingdom community is disciple making, and as such is reproductive spirituality. His people are to be focused on the intentional "multiplication of other faithful followers of the King among the nations."[42]

In the very first snapshot of the church in Acts 2, we see that this is exactly what the early church does. Peter preaches the gospel, and 3,000 people believe and are baptized. What is next for these new believers? "They devoted themselves to the apostles' teaching, to the fellowship, to the breaking of bread, and to prayer" (v. 42). From the beginning, the church is devoted to what Jesus taught: making disciples through going, baptizing, and teaching.

As a result, the church is involved in evangelism (2:38–41), sharing the gospel with those who do not know Christ as the means of seeing them trust Christ for salvation. The church is committed to discipleship (v. 42), teaching believers how to follow Jesus as a way of life. The church is devoted to fellowship (vv. 42–47), sharing life together, knowing one another, loving one another. The church is also involved in ministry (vv. 42–46), praying for one another, giving to one another, meeting each other's needs. The church is active in worship (v. 46), praising God, publicly

---

[42] Jeff Lewis, "God's Great Commissions for the Nations," in *Discovering the Mission of God: Best Missional Practices for the Twenty-First Century*, ed. Mike Barnett and Robin Martin (Downers Grove, IL: InterVarsity, 2012), 104.

meeting together, and privately teaching, praying, giving, and partaking together.[43] As such, we are both recipients and agents of God's mission.

KEY TERMS

apostle

apostolicity of the church

baptism

body of Christ

bride of Christ

catholicity

church/churches

church, attributes

church, believers'

church, government

church, marks

congregational government

cornerstone

deacons

discipleship

discipline

elders

episcopal government

evangelism

excommunication

family of God

fellowship

Great Commission

head of the church

heresy

holiness of the church

immersion

invisible church

kingdom of God

Lord's Supper

means of grace

mission

new humanity

ordinances or sacraments

pastors

Pentecost

people of God

prayer

preaching

presbyterian government

Roman Catholic government

sacerdotalism

temple of the Spirit

unity of the church

universality of the church

visible church

Word of God

worship

---

[43] In corporate worship, churches participate together in several activities: reading Scripture, preaching and teaching, praying, singing, confessing faith, baptizing, and participating in the Lord's Supper (Acts 2:40–47; 1 Cor 11:2–16; Eph 5:21; 1 Tim 4:11).

▓ RESOURCES FOR FURTHER STUDY

Allison, Gregg R. *Historical Theology: An Introduction to Christian Doctrine*. Grand Rapids: Zondervan, 2011, 565–680.

———. *Sojourners and Strangers: The Doctrine of the Church*. Foundations of Evangelical Theology. Wheaton, IL: Crossway, 2012.

Beale, G. K. *The Temple and the Church's Mission: A Biblical Theology of the Dwelling Place of God*. New Studies in Biblical Theology. D. A. Carson, ed. Downers Grove, IL: InterVarsity, 2004.

Carson, D. A., ed. *The Church in the Bible and the World: An International Study*. Grand Rapids: Baker, 1987.

Chute, Anthony L., Christopher W. Morgan, and Robert A. Peterson, eds. *Why We Belong: Evangelical Unity and Denominational Diversity*. Wheaton, IL: Crossway, 2013.

Clowney, Edmund P. *The Church*. Contours of Christian Theology. Downers Grove, IL: InterVarsity, 1995.

Dever, Mark. *The Church: The Gospel Made Visible*. 9Marks. Nashville: B&H Academic, 2012.

Easley, Kendell H., and Christopher W. Morgan, eds. *The Community of Jesus: A Theology of the Church*. Nashville: B&H Academic, 2013.

Hammett, John. *Biblical Foundations for Baptist Churches: A Contemporary Ecclesiology*. Grand Rapids: Kregel, 2005.

Morgan, Christopher W., and Robert A. Peterson, eds. *The Kingdom of God*. Vol. 4 of Theology in Community. Wheaton, IL: Crossway, 2012.

Schreiner, Thomas R., and Matthew R. Crawford, eds. *The Lord's Supper: Remembering and Proclaiming Christ Until He Comes*. NAC Studies in Bible & Theology 10. Nashville: B&H Academic, 2011.

Schreiner, Thomas R., and Shawn D. Wright, eds. *Believer's Baptism: Sign of the New Covenant in Christ*. NAC Studies in Bible & Theology 2. Nashville: B&H Academic, 2006.

Whitney, Donald S. *Spiritual Disciplines within the Church*. Chicago; Moody Press, 1996.

11

THE FUTURE

At times in church history, Christians have speculated concerning scriptural teaching of things to come (eschatology). We live in one of those times. There have been two inadequate responses to such speculation. Some have overemphasized particular aspects of last things, even breaking fellowship with other Christians over views of the timing of Christ's return, the millennium, and so on. In reaction to this, others have turned away from a study of the future, neglecting important biblical teaching. In this chapter we will seek to avoid both tendencies and give attention to the Bible's teaching on things to come, emphasizing what is clear and presenting the major Christian views on things not as clear.

After treating the place of last things in the biblical story, we will survey passages from both Testaments that speak of the future. Then we will engage biblical topics, including fulfilled and unfilled prophecy, death and the intermediate state, the return and reign of Christ, the resurrection, the last judgment, and eternal destinies (the new heavens and the new earth and hell). We will highlight clear biblical truths held by Christians from the early centuries until today. We will fairly present views on matters disputed by Christians, urging readers to hold fast to clear truths while showing brotherly love toward those who arrive at different conclusions on things not as clear.

▨ OBJECTIVES

- To lay a biblical foundation for understanding last things
- To motivate us to love, anticipate, and be prepared for Christ's return
- To motivate us to evangelism and holiness in light of heaven and hell
- To urge us to hold core truths firmly and to maintain the unity of the church on debatable matters
- To establish our identity as those who will reign with Christ on the new earth forever

▨ OUTLINE

The Future in the Biblical Story
The Future in Selected Passages
     Daniel 12:1–3
     Matthew 25:31–46
     Philippians 3:20–21
     Revelation 21:1–8
The Kingdom: We Live in God's Kingdom
     The Two Ages
     The Kingdom of God
     The "Already" and the "Not Yet"
The Intermediate State: We Die and Enter It
     Death
     The Intermediate State
     Immortality
The Second Coming: Our Lord Returns
     The Manner of Our Lord's Return
     The Timing of Our Lord's Return
Signs of the Times
The Millennium: Our Lord Reigns
     Amillennialism
     Postmillennialism
     Historic Premillennialism

The Future in the Biblical Story

The biblical story begins, "In the beginning God created the heavens and the earth" (Gen 1:1). It culminates with "Then I saw a new heaven and a new earth" (Rev 21:1), and it closes with Jesus's words "Yes, I am coming soon," to which the church replies, "Amen! Come, Lord Jesus!" (22:20–21). From its beginning Scripture points to the end, the grand finale of God's plan for history. The story line moves from creation, to disruption in the fall, to salvation in Christ, to the consummation of history.

Eschatology, the study of last things, focuses on the destiny of humanity and the world.

Although eschatology focuses on the future, it is rooted in the past and unites the whole biblical story. God creates for his glory and people's good. He creates human beings in his image to love and serve him and to rule his creation (Gen 1:26–31). In the fall, Adam and Eve rebel against God's goals, bringing in the rule of sin and death (Genesis 3). In mercy, God enters into a formal relationship (a covenant) with Abraham, promising him a land and a people, through whom God would bless all families of the earth (12:1–3).

God expands his promises to Abraham in a covenant with David, to whom God promises a dynasty and an eternal kingdom (2 Sam 7:12–16). Isaiah foretells the coming of one who will be both God and man and will, by God's might, reign on David's throne forever (Isa 9:6–7). Finally, God promises a new covenant characterized by obedience to his Word, widespread knowledge of God, forgiveness, and newness of life (Jer 31:31–34).

In the New Testament, the promised Messiah comes as "Jesus Christ, the Son of David, the Son of Abraham" (Matt 1:1). Through his incarnation, sinless life, crucifixion, and resurrection, Jesus fulfills the messianic promises, accomplishes the messianic mission, and brings redemption to a lost world.

The New Testament also proclaims that Jesus will return to reign as King, bringing justice, peace, delight, and victory. The kingdom is not chiefly a locality but God's reign over a people through King Jesus. The kingdom is both a present reality and a future promise tied to Christ's second coming. Jesus brings it in phases. It is inaugurated in his public ministry as he teaches, performs miracles, and casts out demons (Matt 13:1–50; 12:28). When Jesus ascends to God's right hand, the place of greatest power, the kingdom expands (Eph 1:20–21), and thousands enter the kingdom through the apostles' preaching (Acts 2:41, 47). The fullness of the kingdom awaits Christ's return, when he will sit on his glorious throne (Matt 25:31). Jesus will judge the world, inviting believers into the final stage of the kingdom while banishing unbelievers to hell (vv. 34, 41).

The Future in Selected Passages

In these passages Daniel predicts a time of terrible distress, which Jesus later connects with his second coming. Daniel teaches that God will raise the dead to contrasting destinies, the righteous to everlasting life and the lost to everlasting disgrace.

Christ's second coming, unlike his first, will be glorious. As King, he will sit on his glorious throne and judge the nations. The works of believers are evidence of salvation, and those of unbelievers, evidence of lack of the same. God's people will enjoy endless happiness, while the lost will suffer endless punishment. Paul teaches that though believers are citizens of earthly countries, their true home is heavenly. Because Christ purchases us with his death, our primary allegiance is to him, at the Father's right hand in heaven. Our ultimate hope focuses on the return of Christ, for whom we wait zealously. The returning Christ will equip us for everlasting life on the new earth. By his almighty power he will glorify us, transforming our weak mortal bodies into resurrection bodies like his glorious one.

As the Bible's story begins with God creating the heaven and earth, it ends with a new heaven and a new earth. God will not annihilate the present earth but will cleanse and renew it. When we die, our spirits, separated from our bodies, join the Lord in heaven. But in the end, God will unite our souls with our resurrected bodies, and we will live forever as whole beings on a redeemed earth. God's presence with us on the new earth will eliminate death, grief, crying, and pain. Sadly, though, many never trust Christ and will be punished accordingly in hell.

Daniel 12:1–3[1]

Daniel speaks of an unequaled "time of distress" (12:1) and of the resurrection of the dead (v. 2). Jesus refers to this distress and connects it with

---

[1] We acknowledge help from Robert Peterson's material in Edward William Fudge and Robert A. Peterson, *Two Views of Hell: A Biblical and Theological Dialogue* (Downers Grove, IL: InterVarsity, 2000), 133–37.

his second coming "on the clouds of heaven with power and great glory" (Matt 24:21, 30). In spite of this coming adversity, God promises that his people will escape. Michael, a powerful angel who appears earlier battling on God's side (Dan 10:13, 21), will arise to fight for all "found written in the book" (12:1). This is the image of the citizen list of the true Jerusalem (see Ps 69:28; Mal 3:16), reassuring its inhabitants that in the last days God will deliver his people.

Though God will deliver his own, both the wicked and the righteous will suffer casualties. Because God is Lord over death, however, his conquest extends beyond the grave. He will raise his martyrs to glory and his enemies to shame. Daniel does not contradict the fact that God will raise everyone from the dead, but his focus lies elsewhere: on the resurrection of the martyrs. The prophet uses language of awakening people who are asleep to depict the bodily resurrection of the last day: "Many of those who sleep . . . will awake" (Dan 12:2).

When Daniel speaks of the dead sleeping "in the dust of the earth" (v. 2), he alludes to God's creation and animation of Adam: "The LORD God formed the man out of the dust from the ground and breathed the breath of life into his nostrils, and the man became a living being" (Gen 2:7). God created Adam from dust, and after the fall he promised, "You will return to dust" (3:19). It is not surprising, then, that the Creator will resurrect bodies from the dust.

Daniel teaches the resurrection of the dead and contrasts the destinies of the righteous and the wicked. The resurrected form two groups that are headed for opposite fates: some will awake "to eternal life," others "to disgrace and eternal contempt" (Dan 12:2).

The phrase "eternal life" appears only here in the Old Testament, but the concept appears elsewhere without the same words (Job 19:26; Ps 73:23–24; Isa 26:19). In Dan 12:2 the word "everlasting" (ESV; Heb. *olam*) is used to describe the fates of the just and the unjust. This word is an adjective signifying long duration with limits set by the context. For example, it describes the period of time a willing bond slave could choose to serve his master: "he will serve his master *for life*" (Exod 21:6). When used of God, it means "eternal": "from *eternity* to *eternity*, you are God" (Ps 90:2). In this case the limits of the long duration indicated by *olam* are set by God's eternal life. The Old Testament uses this word to speak of the eternal God (Gen 21:33), his eternal name (Exod 3:15), his eternal attributes ("love": 1 Kgs 10:9), eternal salvation (Isa 51:6, 8), and the eternal word (40:8).

In Dan 12:2 this word describes the destinies of both the righteous and the wicked. Both are "eternal." The godly will be raised to "eternal life." The wicked are raised not to eternal life but to "disgrace and eternal contempt." The first word means "humiliation" or "disgrace" (2 Sam 13:13; Lam 5:1). The second appears only twice in the Old Testament, here and in Isa 66:24, where it also describes the fate of the unsaved: they "will be *a horror* to all mankind."

God will not forsake his people, even when they die. Instead, he will resurrect them from the grave and reward them, even as he promises Daniel: "But as for you, go on your way to the end; you will rest, and then you will stand to receive your allotted inheritance at the end of the days" (Dan 12:13). The righteous and wicked will experience opposite destinies: God will raise his people to eternal life but will raise the lost to eternal disgrace.

Matthew 25:31–46

Jesus's message about the sheep and the goats is the Bible's most famous passage on heaven and hell. It begins with Christ's second coming, which, like his first coming, will be accompanied by angels. Unlike his first coming in humility, his second coming will be full of glory (Matt 25:31). As King, he will sit on his glorious throne and judge the nations. He will separate the people into sheep on his right hand and goats on his left (vv. 32–33).

King Jesus will say to those on his right hand, "Come, you who are blessed by my Father; inherit the kingdom prepared for you from the foundation of the world" (v. 34). Jesus explains that they have served him by performing acts of kindness for the least of his brothers and sisters (vv. 35–40). By "brothers and sisters" Jesus refers to his disciples (see 12:46–50). These good works are not the cause of their salvation but its evidence.

King Jesus also speaks to those on his left: "Depart from me, you who are cursed, into the eternal fire prepared for the devil and his angels!"

(Matt 25:41). Although Jesus blesses the sheep, he curses the goats. In contrast to the sheep's destiny in God's kingdom, the goats go to "the eternal fire," that is, hell. God originally prepared hell for the devil and demons, but he will also send unsaved human beings there. Scripture leaves no doubt as to what this fate is, for near the end of the Bible's story we read, "The devil who deceived them was thrown into the lake of fire and sulfur where the beast and the false prophet are, and they will be tormented day and night forever and ever" (Rev 20:10). The fate of the unsaved is never-ending conscious suffering, away from the joyous presence of God. Even as the saved give evidence of knowing Jesus by the way they treat his disciples, so the unsaved give evidence of not knowing him by their deeds: they fail to love Jesus's followers.

Jesus's last words concerning the sheep and goats are Scripture's most quoted words on eternal destinies: "And they will go away into eternal punishment, but the righteous into eternal life" (Matt 25:46). The fates of the lost and saved are "punishment" and "life," respectively. And because the same adjective, "eternal," describes both fates, they both will know no end. God's people will enjoy endless bliss while the lost will suffer endless punishment.

Philippians 3:20–21

After urging the Philippians to follow his example and that of other godly believers, Paul alerts them to bad examples. As previously, he warns of many first-century opponents of Christianity. By their behavior they oppose Christ's atonement for sin, the heart of the Christian message (Phil 3:18). Paul criticizes the foes' lifestyle as shameful, worldly, and preoccupied with matters of the flesh. He is frank: the opponents are headed for future destruction at the hands of God.

In contrast to the opponents' focus on earthly things, "our citizenship is in heaven, and we eagerly wait for a Savior from there, the Lord Jesus Christ" (v. 20). It was unusual for a city removed from Italy to be granted Roman citizenship, but that is what happened to Philippi, and it brought the Philippians special privileges. Paul says believers' "citizenship is in heaven," which brings special privileges too. We are citizens of a country on earth, but our chief identity is heavenly because Christ has purchased us with his death. As a result, we belong to him, and he belongs to us (1 Cor 6:19–20). Therefore, our primary allegiance is to King Jesus, who is at the Father's right hand in heaven.

Our ultimate hope has to do with the return of Christ, and we wait eagerly for him (Phil 3:20). Christ will return from heaven to bless his people. His return leads to the resurrection of the dead—the last judgment, at which God will justify believers—and the eternal state. Contrary to popular opinion, our final state of bliss is not an out-of-body existence in a spiritual heaven but a resurrected, holistic existence on the new earth, with God and all the saints of all the ages. Our hope centers on Christ and the eternal salvation he will bring. Such a focus greatly affects our present life.

The returning Christ will equip us for everlasting life on the new earth. Our present bodies are mortal, subject to decay, weak, dishonored in death and burial, and natural (humble). Our humble bodies will be transformed into resurrection bodies that are immortal, incorruptible, powerful, glorious, and spiritual—dominated by the Holy Spirit (1 Cor 15:42–44, 53). Who will perform such a supernatural feat? Although other Scriptures ascribe this work to the Father and the Spirit (Rom 8:11), here Paul ascribes it to Christ (Phil 3:21). Christ will renovate our present bodies "into the likeness of his glorious body" (v. 21). Christ will glorify us, including our bodies. He will share his glory with us, and as a result, although we will always remain creatures, our bodies will be like his glorified resurrection body. Christ will do this "by the power that enables him to subject everything to himself" (v. 21b). The resurrected, ascended Christ is omnipotent, and his almighty power will enable him to raise and transform our bodies.

The Christian view of the future, then, is entirely wrapped up in Jesus Christ. His return will begin the sequence of events—Second Coming, resurrection, judgment, eternal state—that will bring about the final state of affairs. The lost will suffer forever in hell, but all God's people will love, serve, and enjoy him forever on the new earth. We are to be preoccupied with Jesus and his return. Such a preoccupation will promote God's glory and the good of others.

Voices from Church History: *Epistle of Mathetes to Diognetus*

An anonymous Christian in the second century wrote the *Epistle of Mathetes* (Greek for "disciple") *to Diognetus* (who is unknown). It is a defense of the Christian faith and an account of Christians living in a hostile world. The following quotation is from a chapter depicting "the manner of the Christians":

> For the Christians are distinguished from other men neither by country, nor language, nor the customs which they observe. But, inhabiting Greek as well as barbarian cities . . . they display to us their wonderful and confessedly striking method of life. . . . They pass their days on earth, but they are citizens of heaven. They obey the prescribed laws, and at the same time surpass the laws by their lives. They love all men, and are persecuted by all. . . . They are evil spoken of, and yet are justified; they are reviled, and bless; they are insulted, and repay the insult with honour; they do good, yet are punished as evil-doers. When punished, they rejoice as if quickened into life; they are assailed by the Jews as foreigners, and are persecuted by the Greeks; yet those who hate them are unable to assign any reason for their hatred.[2]

Revelation 21:1–8[3]

Corresponding to the Bible's first verse (Gen 1:1), its next-to-last chapter begins, "Then I saw a new heaven and a new earth; for the first heaven and the first earth had passed away" (Rev 21:1; see also Isa 65:17). As the story begins with God's creating the heaven and earth, it ends with a new heaven and a new earth. God will not destroy the present earth but will cleanse and renew it (Rom 8:20–22; 2 Pet 3:10–13). When believers die, our spirits, separated from our bodies, join the Lord in heaven. But in the

---

[2] *The Epistle of Diognetus*, chap. 5, in Philip Schaff, ed., *Ante-Nicene Fathers*, vol 1, *The Apostolic Fathers with Justin Martyr and Irenaeus* (1885), Christian Classics Ethereal Library, http://www.ccel.org/ccel/schaff/anf01/Page_26.html.

[3] We acknowledge help from Beale, *The Book of Revelation*, 1039–62 (see chap. 9, n. 2).

end, God will unite our souls with our resurrected bodies, and we will live forever as whole beings on a purified earth.

With various pictures John portrays God moving from heaven to earth to dwell with his people forever. John sees the city of God descending from heaven to earth (Rev 21:2). This is a picture of the intermediate state giving way to the final state. Believers will no longer die and go to heaven because there will be no more death, and God and heaven will come down to earth. The church is a bride adorned for marriage to her husband, Christ, after which they will be united forever. God announces that his dwelling is with his people on earth, fulfilling the covenant promises in Scripture: "They will be his peoples, and God himself will be with them and will be their God" (v. 3). The plural "peoples" shows that the redeemed will include human beings from "every tribe and language and people and nation" (5:9).

God's presence with us on the new earth will eliminate death, grief, crying, and pain (21:4). Although now these things greatly affect our lives, then they will be no more. Instead, we will live in perfect happiness, loving and serving the Lord. It does not surprise us, then, when God declares, "Look, I am making everything new" (v. 5).

God is "the Alpha and the Omega [the A and the Z], the beginning and the end" of history (v. 6) and governs everything that happens in between. This eternal and sovereign God offers an invitation: drink "from the spring of the water of life" (v. 6b). This is a gracious offer of eternal life to any who trust in the Lamb's atoning death. Eternal life, knowing the Father and the Son (John 17:3), begins now and lasts forever. Saving faith also perseveres and receives God's promise: "I will be his God, and he will be my son" (Rev 21:7).

Unfortunately, many never trust Christ and will be punished accordingly in hell (v. 8). The Bible's last two chapters focus on God's people and salvation. But they also speak of those who refuse to repent and of the judgment awaiting them (v. 27; 22:15). Although 21:8 pertains to all unbelievers, it includes so-called Christians, those who profess Christ but whose lives contradict their confession. Unlike those who conquer (v. 7), the "cowards" of v. 8 are those who lack the courage to reject the world system, revealing their unbelieving hearts when persecution hits.

The Kingdom: We Live in God's Kingdom

We introduce the study of last things by exploring three themes: the two ages, the kingdom of God, and the "already" and the "not yet."

The Two Ages

The New Testament contrasts two ages: the present age and the age to come. Sometimes they are called *this* age and *that* age. For example,

> "Whoever speaks a word against the Son of Man, it will be for-given him; but whoever speaks against the Holy Spirit, it will not be forgiven him, either in this age or in the one to come." (Matt 12:32; see also Luke 20:34–35)

> He exercised this power in Christ by raising him from the dead and seating him at his right hand in the heavens—far above every ruler and authority, power and dominion, and every title given, not only in this age but also in the one to come. (Eph 1:20–21)

The New Testament contrasts the two ages. Paul speaks of "this present evil age" (Gal 1:4) and says it is characterized by spiritual blindness (Eph 2:2)[4] and spiritual death (2 Cor 4:4). Jesus says the age to come is characterized by "the resurrection from the dead" (Luke 20:35–36) and "eternal life" (Luke 18:30). Paul portrays it as greatly demonstrating God's grace (Eph 2:7).

There is a sense in which the consummation of the ages has come. This current age is the fulfillment of the Old Testament hope:

> Long ago God spoke to the fathers by the prophets at different times and in different ways. In these last days, he has spoken to us by his Son. God has appointed him heir of all things and made the universe through him. (Heb 1:1–2)

---

[4] The same word (*aiōn*) is sometimes translated "age" and sometimes "world," depending on whether time or location is in view.

These things happened to them as examples, and they were written for our instruction, on whom the ends of the ages have come. (1 Cor 10:11)

But now he has appeared one time, at the end of the ages, for the removal of sin by the sacrifice of himself. (Heb 9:26)

The New Testament also teaches that people in this age experience the age to come:

It is impossible to renew to repentance those who were once enlightened, who tasted the heavenly gift, who shared in the Holy Spirit, who tasted God's good word and the powers of *the coming age,* and who have fallen away. This is because, to their own harm, they are recrucifying the Son of God and holding him up to contempt. (Heb 6:4–6)

How do we as God's people experience the age to come in the present? George Ladd suggests that the age to come overlaps the present age, so that we experience the future in the present.[5] Another way to see it is that we who live in the present age experience a foretaste of the one to come. The Holy Spirit enables us to enjoy salvation now in anticipation of a fuller enjoyment at the end of the age.

The Kingdom of God

The kingdom of God primarily refers to his reign over his people. It is "the King's power over the King's people in the King's place."[6] In the beginning, God is Lord of Adam and Eve and of the garden of Eden. As the Old Testament unfolds, he reigns over his people Israel and the Promised Land. In the end, God is "the one seated on the throne" (Rev 4:9), and he rules over the new heavens and new earth (20:11; 21:1).

---

[5] George E. Ladd, *The Presence of the Future* (Grand Rapids: Eerdmans, 1973, 1996).

[6] Patrick Schreiner, *The Kingdom of God and the Glory of the Cross*, Short Studies in Biblical Theology (Wheaton, IL: Crossway, 2018), 18.

God's kingdom is present and future; it is "already" and "not yet." He reigns in the present age and will reign more fully in the age to come. God's reign is present and future, encompassing his invasion of history now and his final establishment of the kingdom at the end of the age.

Before we consider the kingdom of God in Jesus's ministry, it is good to look at Old Testament background.[7] In its broadest sense, the kingdom is God's *universal* rule (Ps 103:17–22): "The Lord has established his throne in heaven, and his kingdom rules over all" (v. 19). God's kingdom extends beyond Israel to all nations, as a pagan king of an idolatrous nation confesses: "His dominion is an everlasting dominion, and his kingdom is from generation to generation. All the inhabitants of the earth are counted as nothing, and he does what he wants with the army of heaven and the inhabitants of the earth" (Dan 4:34–35; see also 7:13–14).

The kingdom of God is also his *particular* rule over his people. God reigns over his people Israel in a special sense, and he makes promises of an eternal kingdom to David and his descendants, including the Messiah (2 Sam 7:12–16; Isa 9:6–7).

Although the kingdom of God appears in the Old Testament, it comes with newness and power in the New Testament. It is inaugurated by Jesus, the Messiah (the Christ), expands in his exaltation, and will be consummated at his return.

The Kingdom Is Inaugurated in Jesus's Ministry

Jesus is the King, whose words and deeds bring the spiritual kingdom of God. He preaches the parables of the kingdom (Matt 13:1–50). His deeds, especially his casting out demons by the Spirit, usher in the kingdom: "If I drive out demons by the Spirit of God, then the kingdom of God has come upon you" (12:28; see also Luke 11:20).

---

[7] See Bruce K. Waltke, "The Kingdom of God in the Old Testament: Definitions and Story," in *The Kingdom of God*, ed. Christopher W. Morgan and Robert A. Peterson (Wheaton, IL: Crossway, 2012), 49–71.

THE KINGDOM IS EXPANDED IN JESUS'S EXALTATION

In his ascension Jesus moves from the limited earthly sphere to the transcendent heavenly one. He sits at God's right hand "in the heavens—far above every ruler and authority, power and dominion" (Eph 1:20–21) now and forever. When Jesus pours out the Spirit on the church at Pentecost, God's kingdom expands mightily as thousands come to Christ (Acts 2:41, 47; 4:4). Peter explains: "God exalted this man to his right hand as ruler and Savior, to give repentance to Israel and forgiveness of sins" (Acts 5:31). God rescues sinners "from the domain of darkness" and transfers them "into the kingdom of the Son he loves" (Col 1:13–14).

Voices from the Global Church: René Padilla

Padilla, (1932–), Ecuadorian evangelical missiologist, opposed liberation theology and promoted "integral mission"—Christians' duty to preach the gospel and engage in social activism. At the Lausanne Conference (1974), his ideas globally influenced evangelical mission strategy. He said (*Mission between the Times: Essays on the Kingdom of God* [1985]):

> The kingdom of God is God's dynamic power made visible through concrete signs pointing to Jesus as the Messiah. It is a new reality that has entered into the flow of history and affects human life not only morally and spiritually but physically and psychologically, materially and socially. In anticipation of the eschatological consummation at the end time, it has been inaugurated in the person and work of Christ. . . . The completion of God's purpose still lies in the future, but a foretaste of the eschaton is already possible. . . . The New Testament presents the church as the community of the kingdom in which Jesus is acknowledged as Lord of the universe and through which, in anticipation of the end, the kingdom is concretely manifested in history.[8]

---

[8] René Padilla, *Mission between the Times: Essays on the Kingdom of God* (Grand Rapids: Eerdmans, 1985), 189–90.

The Kingdom Will Be Consummated at Jesus's Return

Although Jesus in his earthly ministry brings the kingdom, and it expands exponentially at Pentecost, the fullness of the kingdom awaits until "the Son of Man comes in his glory" and sits "on his glorious throne" (Matt 25:31). Then the angels will proclaim, "The kingdom of the world has become the kingdom of our Lord and of his Christ, and he will reign forever and ever" (Rev 11:15). Jesus will judge the world, inviting believers to "inherit the kingdom" while consigning the lost to eternal punishment (Matt 25:31–46). At "the end" Jesus will hand "over the kingdom to God the Father" (1 Cor 15:24).

The "Already" and the "Not Yet"

An essential aspect of the doctrine of last things is the "already" and the "not yet." Major aspects of last things are fulfilled in part, yet await a greater fulfillment at the end of the age.

Antichrist is "already": "Children, it is the last hour. And as you have heard that antichrist is coming, even now many antichrists have come" (1 John 2:18). Antichrist is also "not yet": "For that day will not come unless . . . the man of lawlessness is revealed, the man doomed to destruction. He opposes and exalts himself above every so-called god" (2 Thess 2:3–4).

Jesus's second coming is "already": Jesus said, "If anyone loves me, he will keep my word. My Father will love him, and we will come to him and make our home with him" (John 14:23). But Jesus's return is also "not yet," as he taught: "If I go away and prepare a place for you, I will come again and take you to myself, so that where I am you may be also" (v. 3).

Salvation and condemnation are also "already" and "not yet." They are realities now:

> God did not send his Son into the world to condemn the world,
> but to save the world through him. Anyone who believes in him
> is not condemned, but anyone who does not believe is already

condemned, because he has not believed in the name of the one and only Son of God. (John 3:17–18)

In addition, salvation and condemnation are still future. Jesus, foretelling his return, says concerning unsaved and saved, respectively: "They will go away into eternal punishment, but the righteous into eternal life" (Matt 25:46).

The resurrection of the dead also exhibits both features. Jesus teaches that the resurrection is "already" realized in our spiritual resurrection or new birth:

I tell you: Anyone who hears my word and believes him who sent me has eternal life and will not come under judgment but has passed from death to life. Truly I tell you: An hour is coming, and is now here, when the dead will hear the voice of the Son of God, and those who hear will live. (John 5:24–25)

Jesus also declares that the resurrection is "not yet," meaning the resurrection of the body: "A time is coming when all who are in the graves will hear his voice and come out—those who have done good things, to the resurrection of life, but those who have done wicked things, to the resurrection of condemnation" (John 5:28–29).

We live, then, in the tension between the "already" and the "not yet." The great events of Christ's death and resurrection have occurred. Their effects have begun, but their full effects await his return.

The Intermediate State: We Die and Enter It

Death

Our Death Is Unnatural and the Result of Sin

Contrary to modern opinion, human death is not natural. God creates us to live, not to die. Death is a consequence of the fall of Adam and Eve into sin.[9] First, God warns our shared parents of the penalty of disobedience—death: "You must not eat from the tree of the knowledge of good and evil, for on the day you eat from it, you will certainly die" (Gen 2:17). Second, God declares the death sentence: "You will eat bread by the sweat of your brow until you return to the ground, since you were taken from it. For you are dust, and you will return to dust" (3:19). Third, God executes the death sentence spiritually, as our first parents' actions reveal: "Then the man and his wife . . . hid from the LORD God among the trees of the garden" (v. 8). The death sentence's physical execution comes next: Abel dies, Adam dies, and the list goes on (4:8; 5:5, 8, 11, 14, 17).

OUR DEATH IS BOTH SPIRITUAL AND PHYSICAL

Here we highlight an important point previously mentioned. Death in Scripture focuses on separation, not cessation of existence. Adam and Eve do not cease to exist when they die spiritually, but they are separated from God's fellowship and hide from him. When they die physically, their souls or spirits are separated from their bodies. Unsaved people are physically alive but spiritually dead (Eph 2:1). Those who die without knowing Christ will suffer the second death, which is eternal separation from God's love in hell (Rev 20:14–15).

When God gives us the new birth, he makes us alive spiritually (Eph 2:5). And when God raises us from the dead to eternal life in immortal bodies, he will overcome spiritual and physical death forever.

OUR DEATH IS NOT THE END

A result of the fall, death is both spiritual and physical. Death is our foe, but it is not the end. Christ at his return will put "all his enemies under his feet. The last enemy to be abolished is death" (1 Cor 15:25–26). On that day, death will be "swallowed up in victory," so routed that it will be mocked: "Where, death, is your victory? Where, death, is your sting?" (vv. 54–55). Although the complete results of his victory are still future, Christ in his death and resurrection conquers death. As a result, we have reason

---

[9] For more on how sin entered history, and death through sin, see chapter 5, "Humanity and Sin."

for hope, as John announces: "Blessed are the dead who die in the Lord from now on" (Rev 14:13).

The Intermediate State

The normal state of affairs is for human beings to be whole, with body and soul connected together.[10] That is how God created us, that is how we live now, and that is how we will live forever after the resurrection of the dead. Death is separation, and physical death temporarily and abnormally separates what is otherwise joined—our material and immaterial parts. God will reunite our bodies and souls in the resurrection.

For Believers

At death a believer's body is put in a grave, but his immaterial part goes immediately into Christ's presence, as the following passages show:[11]

> Jesus assured the dying thief: "Today you will be with me in paradise." (Luke 23:43)

> Paul expresses his desire: "For me, to live is Christ and to die is gain. Now if I live on in the flesh, this means fruitful work for me; and I don't know which one I should choose. I am torn between the two. I long to depart and be with Christ—which is far better—but to remain in the flesh is more necessary for your sake." (Phil 1:21–24)

> Paul explains, "So we are always confident and know that while we are at home in the body we are away from the Lord. For we walk by faith, not by sight. In fact, we are confident, and we would

---

[10] For more on the holistic nature of humanity, see chapter 5, "Humanity and Sin."

[11] Scripture does not teach "soul sleep" for the saved or lost. Soul sleep is the false view that at death souls "sleep," living but unconscious, until the resurrection of the body. To the contrary, both believers and unbelievers are conscious at death, as their immaterial parts go into the presence of Christ or hell, respectively.

prefer to be away from the body and at home with the Lord." (2 Cor 5:6–8; see also Heb 12:22–23)

FOR UNBELIEVERS

Although Scripture says much more about the final state of the wicked—hell—in at least two places it teaches that the unsaved will experience an intermediate hell, where the soul goes after separation from the body at death. In a parable, Jesus points to this as he contrasts the fates of Lazarus, a godly poor man, and that of a wicked rich man (Luke 16:19–31). Peter also states, "The Lord knows how to rescue the godly from trials and to keep the unrighteous under punishment for the day of judgment, especially those who follow the polluting desires of the flesh and despise authority" (2 Pet 2:9–10).

Immortality

ONLY GOD IS INHERENTLY IMMORTAL

The only intrinsically immortal being is God himself. God is eternal, without beginning or end. Paul praises him as "the blessed and only Sovereign, the King of kings, and the Lord of lords, who alone is immortal and who lives in unapproachable light, whom no one has seen or can see, to him be honor and eternal power" (1 Tim 6:15–16).

GOD GIVES IMMORTALITY TO US

Graciously God gives immortality to us as his human creatures, and although we have a beginning, we have no end. Scripture implies this when it teaches the eternity of punishment for the wicked and of life for the righteous: "They will go away into eternal punishment, but the righteous into eternal life" (Matt 25:46).

Although "the immortality of the soul" is a popular expression, Scripture does not speak in those terms. Rather, it ascribes immortality to resurrected human beings' bodies: "For this corruptible body must be clothed with incorruptibility, and this mortal body must be clothed with immortality" (1 Cor 15:53).

The Second Coming: Our Lord Returns

The return of Christ is central to the Christian faith. Its essence is quite clear, but the details quickly become complex. To lay a foundation for understanding Jesus's return and to clear up misunderstandings, we begin with the basics. Each point will include an affirmation and a denial.

The Manner of Our Lord's Return

IT WILL BE PERSONAL

Jesus *himself* will return, as he predicts in his famous discourse on last things: "Then they will see the Son of Man coming in clouds with great power and glory" (Mark 13:26). After Jesus's ascension in the presence of his apostles, angels affirm, "Men of Galilee, why do you stand looking up into heaven? This same Jesus, who has been taken from you into heaven, will come in the same way that you have seen him going into heaven" (Acts 1:11). That is, his return will be personal and visible. Jesus's promise even concludes the New Testament: "Yes, I am coming soon," to which John responds for the church: "Amen! Come, Lord Jesus!" (Rev 22:20).

Although Jesus's sending of the Holy Spirit at Pentecost could be understood as the "already" fulfillment of his promise to return, it is not the "not yet" or ultimate fulfillment. Instead, he will personally return to bless his own and to judge the wicked: "It is just for God to repay with affliction those who afflict you and to give relief to you who are afflicted, along with us. This will take place at the revelation of the Lord Jesus from heaven with his powerful angels, when he takes vengeance with flaming fire on those who don't know God" (2 Thess 1:6–8).

IT WILL BE VISIBLE

The second coming of Christ will be visible and unmistakable. Jesus warns of reports of false messiahs and false prophets, who will perform miracles. We are not to be fooled by reports that Christ has returned secretly, because his coming will be as evident as great lightning bolts illuminating the sky:

If anyone tells you then, "See, here is the Messiah!" or, "Over here!" do not believe it. For false messiahs and false prophets will arise and perform great signs and wonders to lead astray, if possible, even the elect. Take note: I have told you in advance. So if they tell you, "See, he's in the wilderness!" don't go out; or, "See, he's in the storerooms!" do not believe it. For as the lightning comes from the east and flashes as far as the west, so will be the coming of the Son of Man. (Matt 24:23–27)

John also assures us that Christ's return will be evident: "Look, he is coming with the clouds, and every eye will see him. . . . And all the tribes of the earth will mourn over him" (Rev 1:7). Some claim that the second coming of Christ is the invisible coming of God at death to take believers to heaven. This is incorrect, for Jesus will return visibly with great glory.

It Will Be Glorious

The New Testament broadcasts the fact that Christ will return with glory:

When the Son of Man comes in his glory, and all the angels with him, then he will sit on his glorious throne. (Matt 25:31)

Then they will see the Son of Man coming in a cloud with power and great glory. (Luke 21:27)

The grace of God has appeared . . . while we wait for the blessed hope, the appearing of the glory of our great God and Savior, Jesus Christ. (Titus 2:11, 13)

Rejoice as you share in the sufferings of Christ, so that you may also rejoice with great joy when his glory is revealed. (1 Pet 4:13)

Christ's glorious second advent contrasts with his first advent in humiliation (Matt 8:20; 2 Cor 8:9; Phil 2:6–8). The second time he will come not to suffer and die but to judge and reign.

The Timing of Our Lord's Return

Many errors pepper church history and continue to occur because of a failure to take into account Scripture's full witness concerning the timing of the Second Coming. Despite biblical prohibitions, some continue to predict the date of Christ's return. Others live with little thought of the Second Coming, which they relegate to the distant future. Still others overemphasize its nearness and refuse to plan for the future. None of these approaches does justice to biblical teaching. To correct such tendencies, we suggest holding together three kinds of passages:

- imminence passages, which teach Christians to live in light of Christ's return
- interval passages, which teach that certain things must occur before Christ returns
- ignorance passages, which teach that no human being knows when Christ will return

IMMINENCE PASSAGES

Some passages teach believers to look for Christ to return and to live accordingly:

> [Jesus said,] "Watch! Be alert! For you don't know when the time is coming. . . . Therefore be alert, since you don't know when the master of the house is coming. . . . And what I say to you, I say to everyone: Be alert!" (Mark 13:33, 35, 37)

> You need endurance, so that after you have done God's will, you may receive what was promised. "For yet in a very little while, the Coming One will come and not delay." (Heb 10:36–37)

> He who testifies about these things says, "Yes, I am coming soon." Amen! Come, Lord Jesus! The grace of the Lord Jesus be with everyone. Amen. (Rev 22:20–21)

Such passages stress this: *Be alert, for Jesus is coming quickly.*

INTERVAL PASSAGES

Some passages teach that certain events will precede the Second Coming:

> I don't want you to be ignorant of this mystery, brothers and sisters, so that you will not be conceited: A partial hardening has come upon Israel until the fullness of the Gentiles has come

in. And in this way all Israel will be saved, as it is written, "The Deliverer will come from Zion; he will turn godlessness away from Jacob." (Rom 11:25–26)

Such passages stress this: *Be patient, for Jesus's coming follows after certain signs.*

IGNORANCE PASSAGES

Some passages teach that no human being knows when Jesus will return:

"Be alert, because you don't know either the day or the hour." (Matt 25:13)

So when they had come together, they asked him, "Lord, are you restoring the kingdom to Israel at this time?" He said to them, "It is not for you to know times or periods that the Father has set by his own authority." (Acts 1:6–7)

You yourselves know very well that the day of the Lord will come just like a thief in the night. When they say, "Peace and security," then sudden destruction will come upon them, like labor pains on a pregnant woman, and they will not escape. But you, brothers and sisters, are not in the dark, for this day to surprise you like a thief. (1 Thess 5:2–4)

Such passages stress this: *Be wise, for no one knows the exact time of Jesus's coming.*

THE THREE TYPES OF TEXTS COMBINED

Jesus combines the three types of texts treating his return in his famous discourse on last things in Matthew 24:

Imminence: "This is why you are also to be ready, because the Son of Man is coming at an hour you do not expect." (v. 44)

Interval: "This good news of the kingdom will be proclaimed in all the world as a testimony to all nations, and then the end will come." (v. 14)

Ignorance: "Now concerning that day and hour no one knows—neither the angels of heaven, nor the Son[12]—except the Father alone. As the days of Noah were, so the coming of the Son of Man will be. For in those days before the flood they were eating and drinking, marrying and giving in marriage, until the day Noah boarded the ark. They didn't know until the flood came and swept them all away." (vv. 36–39)

Here Jesus teaches us to coordinate the three types of texts. In imminence texts Jesus and his apostles want us to know that he is coming again and to live accordingly. We are to love his appearing (2 Tim 4:8). It is to be a source of encouragement, godliness, and joy for us (1 Thess 4:18; Titus 2:12–13). This was God's will for first-century Christians too. Although he did not return then, their hope kept them on their spiritual toes, as God intended. It is the same for us, and any theology that extinguishes this hope fails at that point.

Interval passages teach us that we are to plan for the future while praying for Christ's return. Because each aspect of last things is fulfilled now while awaiting greater fulfillment ("already" and "not yet"), we do not know if a particular sign of the times is the final one; importantly, the signs are characteristic of the whole period between Christ's first and second comings.

Most important, ignorance passages humble us because they prohibit our predicting the date of the Second Coming. Some have erroneously supposed that they have calculated the date for Christ's return, and they have failed and will fail time and time again.[13] Plainly, God does not want

---

[12] Although the incarnate Son retained all of his divine powers, he gave up the independent use of them. He only exercised divine powers when it was the Father's will. During Christ's state of humiliation, it was not the Father's will for the Son to know the time of his return. Now, in his state of exaltation, the Son knows when he will return.

[13] Examples of failed predictions of the Second Coming include Adventist William Miller's prediction that Jesus would return in 1844 ("the great disappointment"); the Jehovah's Witnesses' prediction of 1914; and more recently, Harold Camping's prediction of May 21, 2011.

us to know the date of Jesus's coming, and we need to trust him and accept that fact.

ITS FUNCTION: TO PROMOTE SPIRITUAL READINESS

The motto of both the Girl Scouts and the Boy Scouts is "Be prepared." This charge is a major function of Second Coming texts, as Jesus's words indicate:

> This is why you are also to be ready, because the Son of Man is coming at an hour you do not expect. (Matt 24:44)

> Watch! Be alert! For you don't know when the time is coming. It is like a man on a journey, who left his house, gave authority to his servants, gave each one his work, and commanded the doorkeeper to be alert. Therefore be alert, since you don't know when the master of the house is coming—whether in the evening or at midnight or at the crowing of the rooster or early in the morning. Otherwise, when he comes suddenly he might find you sleeping. And what I say to you, I say to everyone: Be alert! (Mark 13:33–37)

> Be alert at all times, praying that you may have strength to escape all these things that are going to take place and to stand before the Son of Man. (Luke 21:36)

Signs of the Times

What Are "Signs of the Times"?

The "signs of the times" are people or events, predicted by Jesus or the apostles, that are precursors of the Second Coming. Such signs are characteristic of the whole inter-adventual period (the time between Jesus's first and second comings). Therefore, appearance of any sign of the times is not a sure indicator that the Second Coming will occur soon. Rather, each sign is both "already" and "not yet," both fulfilled in part and awaiting greater fulfillment at the end of the age. Although the signs of the times could be categorized in various ways, here is one way to distinguish them:

- signs showing the grace of God
- signs showing opposition to God
- signs showing divine judgment

Will Christ's Return Be Expected?

Christ's return will be unexpected by the careless and indifferent, for as Peter writes, "Scoffers will come in the last days scoffing and following their own evil desires, saying, 'Where is his "coming" that he promised? Ever since our ancestors fell asleep, all things continue as they have been since the beginning of creation'" (2 Pet 3:3–4). But Christ's return will be expected, although not predicted, by the watchful.[14] They will love their Lord's appearing (2 Tim 4:8) but in obedience to him will not yield to the temptation to calculate the time of his return.

What Does Jesus Mean When He Says, "Watch"?

Jesus, in telling believers to "watch," is instructing them to "be alert" (Mark 13:37). They are to be spiritually ready, living in light of his return. They are to be morally prepared (vv. 33–37).

What Signs Show the Grace of God?

The proclamation of the gospel to the nations. Jesus says, "This good news of the kingdom will be proclaimed in all the world as a testimony to all nations, and then the end will come" (Matt 24:14). The proclamation of the gospel to all nations is "the outstanding and most characteristic sign

---

[14] We learned this way of putting things from David Clyde Jones, late professor of systematic theology and ethics at Covenant Theological Seminary.

of the times."[15] How gracious of the Savior to make the foremost sign of the times a grand incentive for missions!

The salvation of the fullness of Israel. Another sign that shows God's grace is Paul's declaration, "In this way all Israel will be saved, as it is written: 'The Deliverer will come from Zion; he will turn godlessness away from Jacob'" (Rom 11:26). There are two main views concerning the meaning of "all Israel will be saved" here. Some hold that "Israel" refers to spiritual Israel, all of God's chosen people, Jews and Gentiles.[16] Others hold that Paul refers to ethnic Israel, the physical descendants of Abraham. Because Paul consistently refers to ethnic Israel in Romans 9–11, we favor the second view.

The second view has four subsets. First, some maintain that "all Israel will be saved" refers to the sum total of believing Jews between Christ's first and second comings. Second, some understand it as referring to the conversion of many Jews before Jesus's second coming. Third is the dispensational view that "all Israel" refers to a political entity following the rapture of the church, the nation of Israel. Fourth, some think "all Israel" refers to a combination of the first two views above. Paul speaks of the sum total of saved Jews between Christ's advents *and* a conversion of many Jews before the Second Coming. We prefer this fourth view, in part because it repeats a familiar pattern concerning last things, that of the "already" and the "not yet."[17]

What Signs Show Opposition to God?

Some signs show opposition to God. These include tribulation, apostasy, and the Antichrist.

---

[15] Anthony A. Hoekema, *The Bible and the Future* (Grand Rapids: Eerdmans, 1979), 138.

[16] O. Palmer Robertson, *The Israel of God: Yesterday, Today, and Tomorrow* (Phillipsburg, NJ: P&R, 2000).

[17] See Hoekema, *The Bible and the Future*, 139–47, for discussion of the first three views. We credit David Clyde Jones for the fourth view.

Tribulation. Jesus, in harmony with the Old Testament (Dan 12:1), predicts that God will visit the earth with terrible wrath because of human rebellion: "At that time there will be great distress, the kind that hasn't taken place from the beginning of the world until now and never will again. Unless those days were cut short, no one would be saved. But those days will be cut short because of the elect" (Matt 24:21–22).

In context Jesus seems to be referring to both the destruction of Jerusalem in AD 70 and the future great tribulation. Once more, then, we find an appearance of the "already" and the "not yet" of eschatology. Jesus's words are fulfilled in the terrible Roman destruction of Jerusalem and its temple. But still future is the great time of distress and misery for a world that hates God.

Apostasy. Another sign that shows opposition to God is apostasy, the renouncing of a faith once professed. Jesus warns that many professed believers will "fall away, betray one another and hate one another" (Matt 24:10). He predicts this to prepare believers for such offense and betrayal. Jesus also goes to the root of the problem: "False messiahs and false prophets will arise and perform great signs and wonders to lead astray, if possible, even the elect" (v. 24). Because of God's grace, it is impossible to lead astray the elect, but Jesus's words attest to the power of the false miracles of the impostors.

Jesus's words warn of apostasy throughout the period between his advents. Paul warns of an apostasy near the return of Christ:

> Now concerning the coming of our Lord Jesus Christ and our being gathered to him: We ask you, brothers and sisters, not to be easily upset or troubled, either by a prophecy or by a message or by a letter supposedly from us, alleging that the day of the Lord has come. Don't let anyone deceive you in any way. For that day will not come unless the apostasy comes first and the man of lawlessness is revealed, the man doomed to destruction. (2 Thess 2:1–3)

Like so many features of last things, this sign of the times is fulfilled in the time between Christ's first and second comings. There is apostasy "already" and a bigger fulfillment at the end still to come ("not yet").

The Antichrist. Antichrists are people who deny the incarnation (2 John 7) and that Jesus is God's Messiah (Christ, 1 John 2:22); *the* Antichrist is the final pseudo-messiah. John speaks of both: "Children, it is the last hour. And as you have heard that antichrist is coming, even now many antichrists have come. By this we know that it is the last hour" (1 John 2:18; see also v. 22; 2 John 7). John says that many antichrists appeared in the first century, and this is how he knows it is the last days. So, importantly, even the last days are "already" and "not yet."

John implies that the final Antichrist is still to come. Paul plainly speaks of him when he says that Jesus will destroy him when he returns:

> That day [the day of the Lord] will not come unless the apostasy comes first and the man of lawlessness is revealed, the man doomed to destruction. He opposes and exalts himself above every so-called god or object of worship, so that he sits in God's temple, proclaiming that he himself is God. . . . And then the lawless one will be revealed. The Lord Jesus will destroy him with the breath of his mouth and will bring him to nothing at the appearance of his coming. The coming of the lawless one is based on Satan's working, with all kinds of false miracles, signs, and wonders, and with every wicked deception among those who are perishing. (2 Thess 2:3–4, 8–10)

The signs of opposition to God are connected because the false prophets and antichrists will deceive people, leading them to apostasy. Lost people will find the "false miracles, signs, and wonders" convincing and will turn away from the truth of the gospel and will suffer condemnation (2 Thess 2:11–12). As a result of such rebellion, God will visit the earth with great tribulation.

What Signs Show Divine Judgment?

Jesus told of signs indicative of God's displeasure with obstinate people and his subsequent judgment of them. These include wars and natural phenomena.

Wars. In his famous discourse on last things, Jesus warns, "You are going to hear of wars and rumors of wars. See that you are not alarmed, because these things must take place, but the end is not yet. For nation will rise up against nation, and kingdom against kingdom" (Matt 24:6–7).

Natural phenomena. Jesus includes natural phenomena in signs of divine judgment: "There will be famines and earthquakes in various places" (Matt 24:7). Because wars and famines, earthquakes, and other natural disasters are signs of the times characterizing the whole inter-adventual period, this is evidence once again that God gives the signs to keep the church ready and watchful.

The Millennium: Our Lord Reigns

The famous passage mentioning the millennium, or thousand years, appears in Rev 20:1–6:

> Then I saw an angel coming down from heaven holding the key to the abyss and a great chain in his hand. He seized the dragon, that ancient serpent who is the devil and Satan, and bound him for a thousand years. He threw him into the abyss, closed it, and put a seal on it so that he would no longer deceive the nations until the thousand years were completed. After that, he must be released for a short time.

> Then I saw thrones, and people seated on them who were given authority to judge. I also saw the souls of those who had been beheaded because of their testimony about Jesus and because of the word of God, who had not worshiped the beast or his image, and who had not accepted the mark on their foreheads or their hands. They came to life and reigned with Christ for a thousand years. The rest of the dead did not come to life until the thousand years were completed.

> This is the first resurrection. Blessed and holy is the one who shares in the first resurrection! The second death has no power over them, but they will be priests of God and of Christ, and they will reign with him for a thousand years.

We will overview how each of the four millennial positions answers five key questions that emerge from this passage:[18]

- What do the thousand years describe (vv. 4–6)?
- To what does the binding of Satan refer (v. 2)?
- When will Christ return in relation to the millennium?
- How many phases are there to the Second Coming?
- How many resurrections of the dead are there?

Amillennialism

Proponents include Anthony Hoekema and Sam Storms.[19]

WHAT DO THE THOUSAND YEARS DESCRIBE (VV. 4–6)?

The thousand years, the millennium, describe the souls of dead believers reigning now with Jesus in heaven. The millennium is thus present rather than future. It is another way of describing the intermediate state, as deceased believers actively reign with Christ. Amillennialists do believe that Christ will reign on earth—forever in the eternal state.

TO WHAT DOES THE BINDING OF SATAN REFER (V. 2)?

The binding of Satan means he cannot prevent the spread of the gospel during the present age. Some protest that the binding John describes is more extensive than this, involving seizure, tying up, and throwing into the prison of the abyss, which is then closed and sealed. Amillennialists reply that John's description of the purpose of the extensive binding is "so that he would no longer deceive the nations until the thousand years were completed" (v. 2). Satan's binding thus allows the worldwide spread of the

---

[18] For helpful discussion of the millennial views, see Stanley J. Grenz, *The Millennial Maze: Sorting Out Evangelical Options* (Downers Grove, IL: InterVarsity, 1992). For the millennial views in dialogue, see Darrell L. Bock, ed., *Three Views on the Millennium and Beyond* (Grand Rapids: Zondervan, 1999); Robert G. Clouse, ed., *The Meaning of the Millennium: Four Views* (Downers Grove, IL: InterVarsity, 1977).

[19] Hoekema, *The Bible and the Future*, 173–238; Sam Storms, *Kingdom Come: The Amillennial Alternative* (Fearn, UK: Mentor, 2015).

gospel to the Gentiles after Christ's death, resurrection, and pouring out of the Spirit in power at Pentecost.

WHEN WILL CHRIST RETURN IN RELATION TO THE MILLENNIUM?

Because they equate the millennium with the intermediate state, amillennialists hold that Christ will return *after* the millennium.

HOW MANY PHASES ARE THERE TO THE SECOND COMING?

Amillennialists hold that Christ's second coming is a single event, at which time he will bless his people and judge the lost. They argue that this is the historic position of the church[20] and cite many passages, including 1 Thess 4:13–5:11, in which the returning Christ blesses and curses (see also Matt 25:46; 2 Thess 1:5–10).

HOW MANY RESURRECTIONS OF THE DEAD ARE THERE?

Amillennialists hold that there will be one general resurrection of the dead, involving both the righteous and the unrighteous. They appeal to Dan 12:2; John 5:28–29; Acts 24:15; and Rev 20:11–15.[21]

Postmillennialism

Proponents include John Jefferson Davis and Keith Mathison.[22]

WHAT DO THE THOUSAND YEARS DESCRIBE (VV. 4–6)?

The current age gradually merges into the millennium because a majority of the world will come to Christ as they believe the gospel. Postmillennialists cite passages to support their view, including Ps 22:27–28; Isa 2:2–4; Hab 2:14; and Matt 13:31–33.

---

[20] Proponents include Augustine, Aquinas, Luther, and Calvin.

[21] They hold to one *physical* resurrection and interpret "the first resurrection" of Rev 20:4–5 as a *spiritual* resurrection (regeneration). See also John 5:25–29.

[22] Keith A. Mathison, *Postmillennialism: An Eschatology of Hope* (Phillipsburg, NJ: P&R, 1999); John Jefferson Davis, *Christ's Victorious Kingdom: Postmillennialism Reconsidered*, 5th ed. (Laurel, MS: Audubon Press, 2006).

It is incorrect to assume that postmillennialists look for the millennium to be brought in through economic and political means. Instead, most hold that it will come through successful worldwide gospel preaching. Postmillennialists agree with amillennialists and all Christians that Christ will reign on the new earth forever.

To What Does the Binding of Satan Refer (v. 2)?

The binding of Satan means the same as it does for amillennialists: the evil one cannot prevent the spread of the gospel during the present age.

When Will Christ Return in Relation to the Millennium?

As its name *post*millennialism implies, Christ will return *after* the millennium.

How Many Phases Are There to the Second Coming?

Like amillennialists, postmillennialists hold that Christ's return is a single event at which he will bless his people and curse the lost.

How Many Resurrections of the Dead Are There?

Once more, like amillennialists, postmillennialists maintain that there will be one general resurrection of believers and unbelievers.

Historic Premillennialism

Proponents include George Ladd, Craig Blomberg, and Sung Wook Chung.[23]

What Do the Thousand Years Describe (vv. 4–6)?

The millennium is Christ's reign on earth for a thousand years after his return and before the eternal state. In contrast to postmillennialism, premillennialism does not believe that the world will be gradually

---

[23] Craig Blomberg and Sung Wook Chung, eds., *A Case for Historic Premillennialism* (Grand Rapids: Baker, 2009); George Eldon Ladd, *The Blessed Hope: A Biblical Study of the Second Advent and the Rapture* (Grand Rapids: Eerdmans, 1956, 1990).

Christianized as a majority of people believe the gospel; rather, Christ's coming will usher in the millennium powerfully and immediately.

To What Does the Binding of Satan Refer (v. 2)?

The binding of Satan means he will be unable to deceive the nations during the future millennium. Because premillennialists hold to a future millennium, the binding of the devil pertains to that time period. His extensive binding does not describe the current rebellious age but partially accounts for righteousness and peace of Christ's universal reign during the thousand years following the Second Coming.

When Will Christ Return in Relation to the Millennium?

As its name implies, *pre*millennialism maintains that Christ will come back *before* the thousand years. In fact, he will bring about the millennium at his coming.

How Many Phases Are There to the Second Coming?

Like amillennialism and postmillennialism, historic premillennialism asserts that the Second Coming will be a single event.

How Many Resurrections of the Dead Are There?

Unlike amillennialism and postmillennialism, which hold to one resurrection, historic premillennialism interprets Rev 20:4–5 as teaching that there will be two resurrections, one before and one after the millennium. Before the millennium, deceased saints will be raised to participate in the thousand years. After the millennium, believers who die during the thousand years will be raised along with all the wicked.

Dispensational Premillennialism

Proponents include Charles Ryrie, Craig Blaising, and Darrell Bock.[24]

---

[24] Charles C. Ryrie, *Dispensationalism Today* (Chicago: Moody, 1965); Craig A. Blaising and Darrell L. Bock, *Progressive Dispensationalism* (Grand Rapids: Baker, 2000).

What Do the Thousand Years Describe (vv. 4–6)?

Dispensational premillennialists (dispensationalists) stand in agreement with historic premillennialists that the millennium refers to Christ's thousand-year reign on earth after his return and before the new heavens and the new earth. Traditionally, dispensationalists teach a Jewish character to the millennium, often including a restored temple and blood sacrifices.

To What Does the Binding of Satan Refer (v. 2)?

Dispensational premillennialists agree with historic premillennialists that the binding of Satan means he will be unable to deceive the nations during the future millennium.

When Will Christ Return in Relation to the Millennium?

Like other premillennialists, dispensational *pre*millennialists teach that Christ's return will occur *before* the millennium.

How Many Phases Are There to the Second Coming?

Unique to dispensational premillennialism is the view that the Second Coming will occur in two stages: the rapture of the church before the tribulation and the Second Coming to earth after the tribulation and before the millennium.

How Many Resurrections of the Dead Are There?

Historic premillennialism holds to two future resurrections, one before and one after the millennium. Dispensational premillennialism adds a third resurrection at the rapture. Accordingly, church saints, including resurrected deceased ones, will be raptured to heaven before the great tribulation on earth. Jewish believers will be raised from the dead to participate in the Jewish millennium on earth. People who have come to Christ during the millennium and all the wicked will be raised after the millennium to appear before God at the last judgment.

Summary of the Millennial Views

Mill = Millennium, SC = Second Coming, Amil = Amillennialism, Post = Postmillennialism, H-Pre = Historic Premillennialism, D-Pre = Dispensational Premillennialism

	Mill	Satan's Binding	Christ Returns	Phases of SC	Resurrection(s)
Amil	Church age	Evangelism	After Mill	One	One
Post	Church age	Evangelism	After Mill	One	One
H-Pre	Future	Future	Before Mill	One	Two
D-Pre	Future	Future	Before Mill	Two	Three

Learning from Each Millennial View

Although contradictory understandings of Rev 20:1–6 cannot be correct, the various millennial views underscore vital truths, regardless of the correctness of their expositions of Revelation 20.[25]

Amillennialism may or may not be correct in understanding the millennium as Jesus's reigning now in heaven along with the spirits of deceased believers. But Scripture clearly teaches that Christ reigns now: Eph 1:20–23; Heb 1:3–4, 8–9, 13; and Rev 1:5. And amillennialists do not deny that Christ will reign on the earth but affirm with all Christians that he will reign forever over the new earth in the eternal state.

Whether amillennial and postmillennial understandings of the binding of Satan are correct, they rightly affirm that the gospel succeeds as

---

[25] Grenz, *The Millennial Maze*, 175–95.

never before between the comings of Christ (Matt 13:31–33; 16:17–18; John 4:34–38; Col 1:5–6; Rev 7:9–10).

Premillennialism has increased the emphasis on readiness and watch-fulness, two major biblical themes. The imminence passages above (see page 513) teach us to look for Jesus to return, and usually premillennial-ists do just that.

The interpretive issues are complex here, requiring ample time and patience to work through related passages and biblical themes. This should lead not to our preoccupation with the differences between the millennial views but to a focus on core beliefs. Christians from the first to the twenty-first century have held at least four eschatological truths in common:

- the return of Christ
- the resurrection of the dead
- the last judgment
- eternal destinies (heaven and hell)

The Resurrection: We Are Raised

Unlike the Platonic view that the final destiny of human beings is to live forever as immortal souls, both Old and New Testaments teach God's resurrection of the body.

Timing of the Resurrection

When will the resurrection of the body occur?

AT THE END OF THE AGE

Jesus teaches that he will raise the dead at the end of the age. He says concerning each believer, "I will raise him up on the last day" (John 6:40, 44, 54).

AFTER THE SECOND COMING

Paul teaches that after Christ's resurrection the resurrection of his people will occur: "but each in his own order: Christ, the firstfruits; afterward, at his coming, those who belong to Christ" (1 Cor 15:23). Paul explains that at the return of Christ the dead will be resurrected: "For the Lord himself will descend from heaven with a shout, with the archangel's voice, and with the trumpet of God, and the dead in Christ will rise first" (1 Thess 4:16).

Scope of the Resurrection

Both Testaments present a universal resurrection.

> Daniel looks to the future: "Many who sleep in the dust of the earth will awake, some to eternal life, and some to shame and eternal contempt." (Dan 12:2)

> Jesus announces that he will raise the dead: "Do not be amazed at this, because a time is coming when all who are in the graves will hear his voice and come out—those who have done good things, to the resurrection of life, but those who have done wicked things, to the resurrection of condemnation." (John 5:28–29)

> Paul confesses to Governor Felix concerning his fellow Jews: "I have a hope in God, which these men themselves also accept, that there will be a resurrection, both of the righteous and the unrighteous." (Acts 24:15)

Stages of the Resurrection

Evangelicals agree that God will resurrect all human beings, but they disagree as to how many stages are involved. Amillennialism and postmillennialism hold to a one-stage general resurrection at the end of the age. Historic premillennialism asserts that the resurrection will take place in two stages. Before the millennium God will raise dead saints to take part in the thousand years. After the millennium he will raise believers who die during the thousand years, as well as all the unsaved. Dispensational premillennialism affirms three stages to the resurrection. To historic premillennialism they add a third resurrection of church saints at the rapture.

Nature of Our Resurrection Bodies

Although Scripture does not answer all of our questions concerning our resurrection bodies, it teaches that there will be continuity and discontinuity between our current bodies and our resurrection bodies.

Continuity with Our Current Bodies

This is usually the emphasis of Scripture. Paul affirms that God will bring to life our "mortal bodies" by the Holy Spirit: "And if the Spirit of him who raised Jesus from the dead lives in you, then he who raised Christ from the dead will also bring your mortal bodies to life through his Spirit who lives in you" (Rom 8:11). Paul explains that when Jesus returns from heaven, "he will transform the body of our humble condition into the likeness of his glorious body, by the power that enables him to subject everything to himself" (Phil 3:21).

The experience of Christ, our forerunner and the prototype of resurrected human beings, also argues for continuity between our present bodies and our resurrection bodies. After contemplating the disastrous results that would follow if Jesus were not raised, Paul affirms, "But as it is, Christ has been raised from the dead, the firstfruits of those who have fallen asleep" (1 Cor 15:20).

Is Jesus raised in his earthly body or in a different body? He is raised in his earthly body, as his words reveal. Speaking of the temple of his body, Jesus tells the Jewish leaders, "Destroy this temple, and I will raise it up in three days" (John 2:19). Later in John's Gospel, Jesus says, "This is why the Father loves me, because I lay down my life so that I may take it up again. No one takes it from me, but I lay it down on my own. I have the right to lay it down, and I have the right to take it up again. I have received this command from my Father" (10:17–18). Since Jesus, the firstfruits of God's eschatological harvest, is raised in his earthly body, it is the same for all those constituting the rest of the harvest: our current bodies will be raised.

Transformation of Our Current Bodies

Having given priority to continuity between our present bodies and our resurrection bodies, we now describe the discontinuity between the two.

Paul contrasts the "humble condition" of our present bodies with their future state when Christ's omnipotence transforms them to "the likeness of his glorious body" in the resurrection (Phil 3:20–21). In 1 Corinthians 15 Paul describes our current bodies as perishable, dishonored, weak, and mortal and our resurrection bodies as imperishable, glorious, powerful, immortal, and spiritual (vv. 42–44, 53–54). Our present bodies are perishable: we get sick and grow old and die. They are dishonored, as they are put in the grave at death or burned up. They are weak, as even world-class athletes realize if they live to be ninety. They are mortal, not by creation but because of the fall, and eventually die.

By contrast, our perfected bodies will be imperishable and immortal, incapable of getting sick or dying. They will be powerful and glorious. They will not grow tired or weak but will be beautiful or handsome as they reflect "the image of the man of heaven," Christ (v. 49). Our bodies will be also "spiritual" (v. 44). This has sometimes been misunderstood: it does not mean that our resurrection bodies will be incorporeal but teaches that they will be dominated by the Spirit and thereby fitted for everlasting life on the new earth.

Paul captures the attitude that should permeate the lives of those who have such a hope: "This corruptible body must be clothed with incorruptibility, and this mortal body must be clothed with immortality. When this corruptible body is clothed with incorruptibility, and this mortal body is clothed with immortality, then the saying that is written will take place: 'Death has been swallowed up in victory'" (1 Cor 15:53–54).

The Judgment: We Face God

Timing

The Last Judgment will occur at the end of the age, as Jesus teaches in the parable of the weeds:

> Just as the weeds are gathered and burned in the fire, so it will be
> at the end of the age. The Son of Man will send out his angels, and
> they will gather from his kingdom all who cause sin and those

guilty of lawlessness. They will throw them into the blazing furnace where there will be weeping and gnashing of teeth. Then the righteous will shine like the sun in their Father's kingdom. Let anyone who has ears listen. (Matt 13:40–43)

More specifically, the Last Judgment will take place after Jesus returns (Matt 25:31–32, 34, 41, 46), after the resurrection of the dead (Rev 20:12–13), and before the new heavens and new earth (2 Pet 3:7, 13).

Purposes

To Display the Glory of God

The chief purpose of the Last Judgment concerns God, not human beings. The chief purpose of everything in the universe is the glory of God, and so it will be with the Last Judgment. Specifically, there God will display his glory in manifesting his attributes, as the book of Revelation shows. Such attributes include his sovereignty (11:17–18), righteousness (16:5–6), power (11:17–18), truth (15:3), and holiness (15:4).

To Assign, Not to Determine, Eternal Destinies

God does not determine eternal destinies at the Last Judgment, for they are determined before death. All who trust Christ as Savior can know in this life that they are "not condemned." And all who do not trust Christ in this life can know that they are "already condemned" (John 3:18; see also v. 36).

God does not determine destinies at the judgment, but he does assign them, as Jesus explains, referring to his own voice: "Do not be amazed at this, because a time is coming when all who are in the graves will hear his voice and come out—those who have done good things, to the resurrection of life, but those who have done wicked things, to the resurrection of condemnation" (John 5:28–29; see also Matt 25:34, 41).

To Reveal Degrees of Reward and Punishment

Believers agree that, as befits God's justice, there will be degrees of punishment for the lost at the Last Judgment. Jesus warns the Galilean cites in which he performs the most miracles:

> Woe to you, Chorazin! Woe to you, Bethsaida! For if the miracles
> that were done in you had been done in Tyre and Sidon, they would
> have repented in sackcloth and ashes long ago. But I tell you, it will
> be more tolerable for Tyre and Sidon on the day of judgment than
> for you. And you, Capernaum, will you be exalted to heaven? No,
> you will go down to Hades. For if the miracles that were done in
> you had been done in Sodom, it would have remained until today.
> But I tell you, it will be more tolerable for the land of Sodom on the
> day of judgment than for you. (Matt 11:21–24)

Moreover, Jesus speaks of unfaithful servants, who know better, as being
"severely beaten" (Luke 12:47) and of unfaithful servants, who do not
know better, as receiving a "light beating" (v. 48). Paul warns hypocrites
that when they resist repentance, they are increasing their punishment:
"Because of your hardened and unrepentant heart you are storing up
wrath for yourself in the day of wrath, when God's righteous judgment is
revealed" (Rom 2:5).

Believers disagree concerning whether there will be degrees of
reward for God's people. After all, what could be better than heaven?
Thinking of the final state of the righteous as life on the new earth helps
us conceive of the possibility of different responsibilities based on degree
of faithfulness in this life. In the parable of the ten minas, the master gives
different rewards to his servants: "authority over ten towns" (Luke 19:17)
and authority "over five towns" (v. 19). Paul the apostle, in a famous
reward passage, promises the faithful church leader that "he will receive
a reward" (1 Cor 3:14) whereas the unfaithful "will experience loss, but he
himself will be saved—but only as through fire" (v. 15).

Circumstances

The scene of the Last Judgment includes the Judge, those who are judged,
and the judgment itself.

THE JUDGE: GOD

Scripture presents the Father as the Judge at the Last Judgment:

If you appeal to the Father who judges impartially according to each one's work, you are to conduct yourselves in reverence during your time living as strangers. (1 Pet 1:17)

But you, why do you judge your brother or sister? Or you, why do you despise your brother or sister? For we will all stand before the judgment seat of God. (Rom 14:10)

Then I saw a great white throne and one seated on it. Earth and heaven fled from his presence, and no place was found for them. (Rev 20:11)

Scripture also presents the Son as the Judge at the Last Judgment:

When the Son of Man comes in his glory, and all the angels with him, then he will sit on his glorious throne. All the nations will be gathered before him, and he will separate them one from another, just as a shepherd separates the sheep from the goats. (Matt 25:31–32)

The Father, in fact, judges no one but has given all judgment to the Son. (John 5:22)

He commanded us to preach to the people and to testify that he is the one appointed by God to be the judge of the living and the dead. (Acts 10:42; see also 17:31)

Scripture never names the Holy Spirit as the Judge, but because God is one and inseparable, it is best to say that the Trinity will be the Judge—especially the Father and the Son.

THE JUDGED: ANGELS AND ALL HUMAN BEINGS

Those who will be judged include angels and all human beings. God will judge evil angels:

[Jesus said,] "Then he will also say to those on the left, 'Depart from me, you who are cursed, into the eternal fire prepared for the devil and his angels!'" (Matt 25:41)

And the angels who did not keep their own position but abandoned their proper dwelling, [God] has kept in eternal chains in deep darkness for the judgment on the great day. (Jude v. 6)

The devil who deceived them was thrown into the lake of fire and sulfur where the beast and the false prophet are, and they will be tormented day and night forever and ever. (Rev 20:10)

God will judge human beings:

If our unrighteousness highlights God's righteousness, what are we to say? I am using a human argument: Is God unrighteous to inflict wrath? Absolutely not! Otherwise, how will God judge the world? (Rom 3:5–6)

The dead were judged according to their works by what was written in the books. Then the sea gave up the dead that were in it, and death and Hades gave up the dead that were in them; each one was judged according to their works. Death and Hades were thrown into the lake of fire. This is the second death, the lake of fire. And anyone whose name was not found written in the book of life was thrown into the lake of fire. (Rev 20:12–15)

THE JUDGMENT: BASED ON OUR THOUGHTS, WORDS, AND DEEDS

God will justly judge human beings based on what they think, say, and do.

Thoughts: "Don't judge anything prematurely, before the Lord comes, who will both bring to light what is hidden in darkness and reveal the intentions of the hearts. And then praise will come to each one from God." (1 Cor 4:5)

Words: [Jesus said,] "I tell you that on the day of judgment people will have to account for every careless word they speak." (Matt 12:36)

Deeds: "We must all appear before the judgment seat of Christ, so that each may be repaid for what he has done in the body, whether good or evil." (2 Cor 5:10)

"Then the sea gave up the dead that were in it, and death and
Hades gave up the dead that were in them; each one was judged
according to their works." (Rev 20:13)

Does judgment based on works threaten salvation by grace? No, for
four reasons. First, initial salvation occurs during one's lifetime, while the
Last Judgment occurs at the end. Second, judgment is different from salvation. Judgment occurs in order to test if salvation is present. Those who
are saved pass the judgment; those who are lost do not.

Third, it is not difficult to see God's justice in judging the lost based
on what they have done. They have done nothing to the glory of God.
They will justly receive what they deserve for their rebellion against
their Maker. The difficulty comes because God's declaring the righteous
saved based on their good works sounds like salvation by works, which
Scripture rejects. Salvation is by grace alone through faith alone in Christ
alone. But true saving faith is never alone; it works. Paul, who in many
passages denies that salvation is based on works (Eph 2:8–9; Titus 3:4–5),
often affirms that true salvation produces fruit, sometimes in the same
passages (Eph 2:10; Titus 3:8). Paul concludes, "In Christ Jesus neither
circumcision nor uncircumcision accomplishes anything; what matters
is faith working through love" (Gal 5:6). James teaches similarly: "Show
me your faith without works, and I will show you faith by my works"
(Jas 2:18). It is impossible to show faith without deeds, for faith is invisible. Faith becomes visible precisely in deeds. Believers' faith in Christ for
salvation shows up in deeds, which are noted at the Last Judgment.

Fourth, salvation is not only an initial, once-for-all-time event; it is
also a lifelong process and a final confirmation in holiness and glory. It
is the lifelong process that is revealed at the Last Judgment. Viewed from
this perspective, the good works that inevitably come are the work of the
Trinity in believers. They are the deeds of the Father "who works in" us
"both to will and to work for his good pleasure" (Phil 2:13 ESV). They are
the work of Christ, the vine, apart from whom we "can do nothing" (John
15:5). And they are the "fruit of the Spirit" (Gal 5:22).[26]

---

[26] For more discussion of the judgment, see Robert A. Peterson, "The Great
White Throne," *Tabletalk*, December 2000: 14–15, 56–57.

Hell: Unbelievers Are Punished Forever

The Bible teaches much about hell, but five truths predominate.[27]

Hell as Punishment

Hell is a place where people suffer the just penalty for their sin. Punishment is the Bible's primary picture of hell. That hell is punishment is clearly communicated by every New Testament author: Matthew (5:20–30; 24–25); Mark (9:42–48); Luke (16:19–31); Paul (2 Thess 1:5–10); the author of Hebrews (10:27–31); James (4:12; 5:1–5); Peter (2 Pet 2:4–17); Jude (vv. 13–23); and John (Rev 20:10–15). Three passages are most striking.

First are Jesus's words in Matt 25:31–46, famous for their emphasis on Jesus's solidarity with his people and the necessity to display faith through works of love. It also teaches the eternal destinies of heaven and hell, for returning King Jesus will say to the righteous and the lost, respectively, "Come, you who are blessed by my Father, inherit the kingdom prepared for you from the foundation of the world" (v. 34), and "Depart from me, you who are cursed, into the eternal fire prepared for the devil and his angels!" (v. 41). Jesus exercises his divine prerogative as Judge to determine eternal destinies. People's destinies are linked to their relationship to him, revealed in their treatment of his followers. He sums up matters for the lost and the saved: "And they will go away into eternal punishment, but the righteous into eternal life" (v. 46).

The second passage is from the apostle Paul, who encourages believers suffering at the hands of persecutors by emphasizing "God's righteous judgment . . . since it is just for God to repay with affliction those who afflict you . . . when he takes vengeance with flaming fire on those who don't know God and on those who don't obey the gospel of our Lord Jesus. They will pay the penalty" (2 Thess 1:5–6, 8–9). God is the just Judge, who declares sinners guilty and punishes accordingly. Hell is appropriate retributive punishment on unbelievers.

---

[27] For more discussion on hell, see Christopher W. Morgan and Robert A. Peterson, ed. *Hell under Fire: Modern Scholarship Reinvents Eternal Punishment* (Grand Rapids: Zondervan, 2004).

Third, like Jesus and Paul, John also teaches that hell is just punishment. In Revelation he recounts the final judgment and the eternal punishment of the devil and wicked human beings:

> The devil who had deceived them was thrown into the lake of fire and sulfur where the beast and the false prophet are, and they will be tormented day and night forever and ever. (20:10)

> Then I saw a great white throne and one seated on it. Earth and heaven fled from his presence, and no place was found for them. I also saw the dead, the great and the small, standing before the throne. . . . Death and Hades were thrown into the lake of fire. This is the second death, the lake of fire. And anyone whose name was not found written in the book of life was thrown into the lake of fire. (vv. 11–12, 14–15)

These three passages emphasize that in the end, God's justice will prevail. The wicked are cast into hell while the righteous experience the glorious presence of God on the new earth. The punishment of hell is deserved. It is just. The justice of the future punishment of the wicked is for the most part assumed by the biblical writers—a just God judges justly. Yet for clarity and emphasis, the biblical writers sometimes stress the justice of this retributive punishment.

The biblical writers also underscore the justice of hell to comfort persecuted believers. Indeed, we could speak of the "comfort of hell." This is ironic, for the doctrine of hell leads many today to question God's justice. In the early church, however, hell reassured God's people that ultimately evil and evildoers would be defeated. God will one day conquer everything opposed to him and bring total victory, justice, and peace. Everyone on God's side will share in his victory; everyone opposing him and his people will be defeated (see also Luke 16:19–31; 2 Thess 1:5–10; Jas 1:9–11; Rev 6:10; 11:15–18; 14:14–15:4; 19:1–8; 20–22). When God's people are oppressed in the current evil age, these truths should not disturb but give hope. They enable believers to endure suffering, confident that God will win and that they will reign with him.

Hell as Destruction

Second, hell as destruction or death also plays a central role in Scripture. This theme occurs in the writings of most New Testament authors. The only exception is Mark, who addresses hell in just one passage, so it is not surprising that he does not allude to hell as the destruction of human beings. Destruction is clearly used to depict hell (Matt 7:13–14, 24–27; 24:51; Luke 13:3–5; John 3:16; Rom 9:22; Gal 6:8; Phil 1:28; 3:19; 1 Thess 5:3; 2 Thess 1:5–10; 1 Tim 6:9; Heb 10:27; Jas 1:11, 15; 4:12; 5:3–5, 20; 2 Pet 2:6; Rev 21:8).

Jesus speaks of destruction as unbelievers' future: "Enter through the narrow gate. For the gate is wide and the road broad that leads to destruction, and there are many who go through it. How narrow is the gate and difficult the road that leads to life, and few find it" (Matt 7:13–14).

John also contrasts the final states as life and death: "God loved the world in this way: He gave his one and only Son, so that everyone who believes in him will not perish but have eternal life" (John 3:16). Those who trust Christ have eternal life; those who do not, perish. Later, John speaks of future punishment as "the second death" (Rev 20:14; 21:8).

Paul teaches about hell, not only as punishment but also as destruction, calling it "eternal destruction" (2 Thess 1:9). He also speaks of unbelievers' future punishment as death: "The wages of sin is death, but the gift of God is eternal life in Christ Jesus our Lord" (Rom 6:23).

What does hell as destruction and death mean? Douglas Moo answers: "Destruction" and related words in the New Testament "refer to the situation of a person or object that has lost the essence of its nature or function." Citing many examples, Moo concludes, "In none of these cases do the objects cease to exist; they cease to be useful or to exist in their original, intended state."[28]

Hell, then, is destruction in the sense that it is final and utter loss, ruin, or waste. This picture graphically illustrates that those in hell have failed to embrace the meaning of life but instead have wasted it.

---

[28] Douglas J. Moo, "Paul on Hell," in *Hell Under Fire*, 105.

Trying to find life in themselves and sin, they have forfeited true life. Only ruin remains.

Hell as Banishment

A third key New Testament picture of hell is one of banishment. The idea of hell as banishment, separation, or exclusion occurs in every New Testament author except James and the author of Hebrews. Hell as banishment is prominent in Jesus's teachings, particularly in Matthew. This makes sense, for kingdom themes are prominent in Jesus's teaching in Matthew. He contrasts two future destinies: God welcomes believers into the kingdom but banishes unbelievers from it.

John the Baptist preaches the final separation of the righteous from the wicked (Matt 3:1–12). Later, Jesus proclaims what he will declare to unbelievers: "Depart from me" (7:21–23), excluding them from his kingdom. He regularly portrays hell as being outside the kingdom (in outer darkness), where the wicked are shut out (8:12; 13:41–42, 49–50; 25:10–12, 30). In his end-time sermon, Jesus says that he will personally banish the wicked: "Depart from me, you who are cursed, into the eternal fire prepared for the devil and his angels!" (25:41).

In Revelation 21–22, John contrasts hell with heaven. In heaven, the saints experience the glorious presence of God. But the wicked are left outside, unable to enter the heavenly city, forever excluded from wondrous fellowship with God (22:14–15).

Whereas punishment stresses the justice of hell, banishment highlights what those in hell miss. Evangelicals often hint at this idea of banishment when they say that hell is eternal "separation from God." While the idea of separation is certainly correct and included in this New Testament concept of banishment, separation alone does not do justice to the force of this picture of hell. It is akin to using the phrase "passing away" as a euphemism for death. *Separation* from God could imply divine passivity, but *banishment* suggests God's active judgment. *Banishment* underscores the dreadfulness of exclusion from God's grace and stresses the desolation and finality of the predicament. Through this picture of hell, Scripture reveals that Christ eternally excludes the unrighteous from his kingdom. The wicked never experience fellowship with God. They are forever banished from his majestic presence and completely miss the reason for their existence: "to glorify God and to enjoy him forever" (Westminster Shorter Catechism #1).

Hell as a Place of Suffering

Fourth, Scripture teaches that those in hell experience suffering. This is a frequent emphasis in the New Testament.

John the Baptist teaches that God will burn the wicked "with unquenchable fire" (Matt 3:12 ESV). Jesus teaches that hell is a fate worse than being drowned in the sea (Mark 9:42). Indeed, it is worse than any earthly suffering—even maiming (Mark 9:43; Matt 5:29–30). Still worse, the suffering never ends (Mark 9:48; Matt 25:41). Being cast into hell is likened to being thrown into a fiery furnace and means suffering unimaginable sorrow, remorse, and pain. The pain is described as producing "weeping and gnashing of teeth" (Matt 8:12; 13:42, 50; 22:13; 24:51; 25:30). Moreover, it seems likely that this suffering is both emotional/spiritual and physical (involving bodily resurrection) (see John 5:28–29).

The author of Hebrews warns that hell is utterly fearful and dreadful (10:27–31). James depicts graphically the suffering linked to future punishment as "miseries that are coming" upon the wicked, eating their "flesh like fire" in "a day of slaughter" (5:1–5).

John's portraits in Revelation are hard to forget. Those in hell will feel the full force of God's fury (14:10). They will be "tormented with fire" (vv. 10–11). This suffering is best understood as endless: the "smoke of their torment will go up forever and ever" (v. 11). Even worse, the suffering is constant. Those in hell will "have no rest, day or night" (v. 11 ESV) but "will be tormented day and night forever" (20:10).

This suffering is conscious. If hell did not consist of conscious suffering, it is hard to see how it could in any meaningful sense be worse than death, worse than earthly suffering, filled with weeping and gnashing of teeth, or a place of misery. These images communicate that people in hell will be aware that they are suffering just punishment.

Hell as Eternal

The biblical teaching is straightforward: hell is eternal. The historic church confesses that the suffering of the lost in hell will have no end.[29] This is contrary to *universalism* and *annihilationism*. Universalism is the view that in the end everyone will be gathered into the love of God and be saved. Annihilationism, also known as *conditional immortality*, or *conditionalism* for short, holds that the wicked will be cast into hell to suffer for their sins. When they have paid the debt for their sins, God will exterminate them so that they will exist no more.

We distinguish universalism and annihilationism but oppose both of them because of Scripture's clear teaching that hell exists and that the punishment of hell is never-ending. We can only summarize here what we have explained in more detail previously.[30]

Daniel contrasts "everlasting life" with "shame and everlasting contempt" as the fates of the resurrected righteous and unrighteous, respectively (Dan 12:2 ESV). Along with "the new heavens and the new earth" for the righteous, Isaiah foresees this fate for "the dead bodies of those who have rebelled against" God (Isa 66:22, 24): "Their worm shall not die, their fire shall not be quenched" (v. 24 ESV). In fact, Jesus appeals to this passage in Isaiah when he warns his hearers that going to hell involves "unquenchable fire" in a place "where their worm does not die, and the fire is not quenched" (Mark 9:43, 48).

In the most famous passage on hell, Jesus equates the final fate of unsaved human beings with that of "the devil and his angels": "eternal fire" (Matt 25:41). Revelation 20:10 leaves no doubt as to that fate: "They will be tormented day and night forever and ever." Furthermore, in Matt 25:46, where Jesus contrasts the destinies of the figurative goats and the sheep—the unrighteous "will go away into eternal punishment, but the

---

[29] Examples include Tertullian, Augustine, Aquinas, Luther, Calvin, and Edwards. See Peterson, *Hell on Trial*, 97–138 (see chap. 5, n. 46).

[30] Peterson, *Hell on Trial*, 21–96, 139–202; Christopher W. Morgan "Annihilationism: Will the Unsaved Be Punished Forever?" in Morgan and Peterson, eds., *Hell Under Fire*, 195–218; Morgan, *Jonathan Edwards and Hell* (Fearn, UK: Mentor, 2004); see also Peterson's material in Fudge and Peterson, *Two Views of Hell*, 129–69.

righteous into eternal life"—he describes both destinies in a single sentence as "eternal."[31] Unless one is prepared to limit the bliss of the righteous, it is difficult to escape the conclusion that the punishment of the lost is also without end.

Jude speaks of a "punishment of eternal fire" and warns that false teachers are "wandering stars, for whom the gloom of utter darkness has been reserved forever" (Jude vv. 7, 13 ESV).

Revelation 14 powerfully testifies to the eternity of hell. The idolater "will drink the wine of God's wrath, which is poured full strength into the cup of his anger. He will be tormented with fire and sulfur . . . and the smoke of [his] torment will go up forever" (vv. 10–11). Far from being annihilated, the lost "have no rest, day or night" (v. 11 ESV).

The endlessness of this punishment is also confirmed by the forceful pronouncement in Rev 20:10, where it is said of Satan, among others, "The devil . . . was thrown into the lake of fire and sulfur . . . and they will be tormented day and night forever and ever." Five verses later John teaches, in agreement with Matt 25:41, that unsaved human beings will share the devil's fate: "And if anyone's name was not found written in the book of life, he was thrown into the lake of fire" (Rev 20:15 ESV).

Regardless of what we might like to be true, Scripture's witness is clear: the suffering of unbelievers in body and soul in hell will never end. There will never come a time when people in hell find relief. They have rebelled against God and missed out on true life forever. They are punished by God and banished from his kingdom, and they suffer endlessly. In rejecting God, they will never experience his glorious presence or the ultimate covenant blessing—eternal life.

Heaven: We Are Blessed Forever on the New Earth

Scripture depicts heaven and hell as parallel final destinies.

---

[31] The adjective *eternal* means "age-long," with the context determining the length of the "age." The age to come is determined by the life of God himself and thus is never-ending. See Peterson, *Hell on Trial*, 34–36.

Many who sleep in the dust of the earth will awake, some to eternal life, and some to disgrace and eternal contempt. (Dan 12:2)

"[The unrighteous] will go away into eternal punishment, but the righteous into eternal life." (Matt 25:46)

"Do not be amazed at this, because a time is coming when all who are in the graves will hear his voice and come out—those who have done good things, to the resurrection of life, but those who have done wicked things, to the resurrection of condemnation." (John 5:28–29)

Scripture puts heaven and hell side by side. We all will exist forever in one place or the other. There does not exist a "third place" called purgatory.[32] Heaven and hell are alternative destinies. This means that the joys of heaven shed light on the torments of hell. And heaven's glories are properly appreciated only against hell's agonies. The Bible paints at least six chief pictures of heaven.[33]

We Will Delight in the New Creation

Heaven will be the renewal of creation. God will deliver his good creation from sin, for a time is coming "when there will no longer be any curse" (Rev 22:3). Then the longings of the personified creation will be fulfilled: "The creation eagerly waits with anticipation for God's sons to be revealed . . . in the hope that the creation itself will also be set free from the bondage to decay into the glorious freedom of God's children" (Rom 8:19–21). As resurrected believers, we will live forever under the

---

[32] Roman Catholic doctrine views purgatory as a place where the venial (not mortal) sins of faithful Catholics are cleansed (purged) after death until they are ready for heaven. To the contrary, Christ's death purchased salvation for all believers (Heb 10:10; 13:12). Believers' sins do not need purging at death. Rather, because of Christ's work God will "sanctify" us "completely . . . at the coming of our Lord Jesus Christ" (1 Thess 5:23).

[33] For more discussion on heaven, see Morgan and Peterson, ed., *Heaven*, vol. 6 (see chap. 8, n. 1).

new heavens on the new earth. By contrast, lost human beings will be banished from the city of God and will suffer forever in the lake of fire (Rev 20:15; 21:8; 22:15).

This is our Christian hope: eternal life with God and all the saints on the new earth. This hope means that our work for God now "is not in vain" (1 Cor 15:58), because he will transform this present world into the new heaven and new earth. It also means that we will enjoy the best of this world's culture forever, for "the glory and honor of the nations" will enter the new earth (Rev 21:26). Although some hold that the present earth will be destroyed and that God will create a totally new earth, we hold that the present earth will be renewed to become the new earth (Isa 66:22; see also 65:17; Rom 8:18–28; 2 Pet 3:10–13; Rev 21:1–5).

We Will Flourish in the Kingdom of God

Second, heaven will be the final stage of the kingdom of God. The kingdom of God will be at peace only in the end. Though Jesus's victory has been won, the battle rages until his second coming (1 Pet 5:8). As God's people, we conquer through Christ, who loves us and gave himself for us (Gal 2:20). "The Lion from the tribe of Judah," who "has conquered," is the slain Lamb (Rev 5:5–6). When the final installment of the kingdom arrives, the struggles of the present life will be past. By God's grace, as believers we will exercise dominion with Christ. Human life will flourish and human culture will thrive in the city of God (Heb 2:5–10; Rev 21:24–26). Jesus will return, deliver his people, and bring the final installment of his kingdom (11:15). But the wicked will not inherit the kingdom of God. Instead, King Jesus will condemn them to "eternal punishment" (Matt 25:46), even "the eternal fire prepared for the devil and his angels" (v. 41; see also Rev 20:10, 15).

Heaven involves serving our great King as subjects of his kingdom now and forever: "they are before the throne of God, and they serve him day and night" (Rev 7:15). The evil one is a defeated foe who will one day be thrown into the lake of fire (20:10). Through Christ we overcome death, so that at death we go to be with him (Phil 1:23), and in the resurrection, death will be banished (1 Cor 15:26; Rev 21:4).

We Will Enjoy Everlasting Rest

Third, heaven will be our everlasting rest. It is true that Jesus brings real rest now: "Come to me, all of you who are weary and burdened, and I will give you rest" (Matt 11:28). He gives us rest from war, wearisome labor, and wandering from God.

When Jesus returns, however, there will be no more sin or strife in the lives of individuals, families, or nations. We will find fulfillment, eagerly serving Jesus in the perpetual Sabbath rest of the new creation (Heb 4:9–11; Rev 14:13). And the wicked? "The smoke of their torment will go up forever and ever. There is no rest day or night" (14:11).

There will be only perfect rest when Christ returns and we are raised to enjoy the new earth. In contrast to the temptations, struggles, and failures that God's people have endured for so long, God our Father will provide us with everlasting hospitality in his house (John 14:1–3). This is our eternal Sabbath rest as God dwells forever in his people's midst (Rev 21:1–3).

We Will Live in God's Presence Forever

Fourth, in heaven we will be in the gracious presence of God forever. In Old Testament times God dwells with his people in tabernacle and temple. Since the resurrection of Christ, the Holy Spirit dwells in believers individually and the church corporately (1 Cor 6:19; 3:16). But in that day we will experience God's presence as never before. In ourselves we would fear to stand before our Maker. But because of the perfect work of Christ, when he returns, we will delight in God's presence. Heaven and earth will be one in that day, as God himself will dwell in the midst of his people: "Look, God's dwelling is with humanity, and he will live with them. They will be his peoples, and God himself will be with them and will be their God" (Rev 21:3). But the unbelieving "will suffer the punishment of eternal destruction, away from the presence of the Lord and from the glory of his might" (2 Thess 1:9 ESV). By contrast, believers will experience great joy in God's presence: "Then the King [Jesus] will say to those on his right, 'Come, you who are blessed by my Father; inherit the kingdom prepared for you from the foundation of the world'" (Matt 25:34; see also Rev 21:4).

We Will See God Face-to-Face

Fifth, heaven will be the final seeing of God. God warns Moses, the man with whom he speaks as to a friend (Exod 33:11), "You cannot see my face, for humans cannot see me and live" (v. 20). God gives his people glimpses of him in the Old Testament (Exod 24:10–11; 34:5–8). But amazingly, in Scripture's last book, speaking of himself, God says of his people, "They will see his face" (Rev 22:4). How do we explain the difference?

The answer lies in who Jesus is and what he accomplishes for us. He is God the Son, who becomes a human, lives a perfect life, dies in our place, and rises victorious over all our foes. When Jesus comes again, as he promises, we will see God: "Blessed are the pure in heart, for they will see God" (Matt 5:8). In the meantime, we live by faith in Jesus, not by sight: "Though you have not seen him, you love him; though not seeing him now, you believe in him, and you rejoice with inexpressible and glorious joy" (1 Pet 1:8). Therefore, "we hope for what we do not see," and "we eagerly wait for it with patience" (Rom 8:25).

At present, we know the Father's great love, but the world knows neither him nor us. Now we are the children of God, and our future destiny is so great as to be incomprehensible. We do not know its details, but we do know this: "When [Jesus] appears, we will be like him because we will see him as he is" (1 John 3:2). While redeemed human beings will rejoice to see their gracious God, the unsaved will be in outer darkness, where "there will be weeping and gnashing of teeth" (Matt 8:12; 13:42, 50; 22:13; 24:51; 25:30; Luke 13:28).

We Will Partake of God's Glory

Sixth, heaven will involve our shining in glory forever. Paul contrasts the new covenant with the old: the Ten Commandments came with glory, so that Moses had to veil his face, but since Christ has come and ratified the new covenant in his death, the new covenant "overflows with even more glory" (2 Cor 3:9). The prophet Daniel foretold the glory that would be ours in the new earth: "Those who have insight will shine like the bright expanse of the heavens, and those who lead many to righteousness, like the stars forever and ever" (Dan 12:3).

When Christ came, the apostles "observed his glory, the glory as the one and only Son from the Father" (John 1:14). Because of the excellence of Christ's person and work, Scripture describes both our present and our final salvation in terms of glory. Astonishingly, Paul describes Christians' lives like this: "We all, with unveiled faces, are looking as in a mirror at the glory of the Lord and are being transformed into the same image from glory to glory" (2 Cor 3:18). When Paul considers our present troubles in light of our future glory, they become "momentary light affliction" compared to "an absolutely incomparable eternal weight of glory" (4:17). Peter puts believers' suffering in eternal perspective: "The God of all grace, who called you to his eternal glory in Christ, will himself restore, establish, strengthen, and support you after you have suffered a little while" (1 Pet 5:10).

Our salvation is so bound up with Christ that Paul can say, "When Christ who is your life appears, then you also will appear with him in glory" (Col 3:4). Our bodies will be raised in glory and our whole beings will be glorified. We will not only behold God's glory; we will be transformed by it so that we actually partake of his glory. The glory of the Trinity will flood the new heavens and new earth forever (1 Cor 15:43; 1 Pet 5:1; Rev 21:10–11, 19–26). By contrast, the wicked will be raised and fitted for "disgrace and eternal contempt" (Dan 12:2), the suffering of everlasting destruction in body and soul (Matt 10:28).

Conclusion

Contemplating heaven and hell takes us to the end of the biblical story of creation, fall, redemption (of Israel and the church), and now the consummation. John's vision in Revelation 21–22 includes the new heavens and new earth (mainly) and also hell (to a lesser extent). When viewed as alternatives, heaven looks more glorious and hell more dreadful. But heaven and hell are not the main subjects of the Bible's last two chapters—God and his victory are.

The whole Bible, culminating in the end of the story, exalts God himself, the Creator, sustainer, Redeemer, and now the consummator. In the grand finale, God wins! He will punish evil and magnify the righteousness of his Son in his people. And in all of this he will glorify himself. The scriptural story line thus ends wonderfully with God on the throne, evil banished from his eternal kingdom, and all of us who are his children reigning with him in resurrected bodies on the new earth.

▨ KEY TERMS

age to come

ages, the two

"already" and "not yet"

amillennialism

annihilationism

Antichrist

apostasy

banishment, hell as

binding of Satan

city of God

conditionalism

consummation

day of the Lord

death

destinies, eternal

destruction

devil

dispensationalism

eschatology

eternal punishment

glorification

heaven

hell

historic premillennialism

hope

immortality

inheritance

intermediate state

Israel

Jerusalem, destruction of

judgment

kingdom of God

last days

last things

millennium

new heavens and new earth

new Jerusalem

paradise

postmillennialism

premillennialism

presence of God

present age

punishment, eternal

purgatory

rapture

reign of Christ

rest, everlasting

resurrection

resurrection bodies

return of Christ

rewards

Second Coming

second death

seeing God

separation from God

signs of the times

suffering

tribulation

victory

RESOURCES FOR FURTHER STUDY

Allison, Gregg R. *Historical Theology: An Introduction to Christian Doctrine*. Grand Rapids: Zondervan, 2011, 683–733.

Barber, Dan C., and Robert A. Peterson. *Life Everlasting: The Unfolding Story of Heaven*. Phillipsburg, NJ: P&R, 2012.

Bock, Darrell L., ed. *Three Views on the Millennium and Beyond*. Grand Rapids: Zondervan, 1999.

Grenz, Stanley J. *The Millennial Maze: Sorting Out Evangelical Options*. Downers Grove, IL: InterVarsity, 1992.

Hoekema, Anthony A. *The Bible and the Future*. Grand Rapids: Eerdmans, 1979.

Ladd, George E. *The Presence of the Future: The Eschatology of Biblical Realism*. Grand Rapids: Eerdmans, 1974.

Milne, Bruce. *The Message of Heaven and Hell: Grace and Destiny*. The Bible Speaks Today. Downers Grove, IL: InterVarsity, 2002.

Morgan, Christopher W., and Robert A. Peterson. *Heaven*. Vol. 6 of Theology in Community. Wheaton, IL: Crossway, 2014.

———. *Hell Under Fire: Modern Scholarship Reinvents Eternal Punishment*. Grand Rapids: Zondervan, 2004.

———. *The Kingdom of God*. Vol. 4 of Theology in Community. Wheaton, IL: Crossway, 2012.

———. *What Is Hell?* Basics of the Faith. Phillipsburg, NJ: P&R, 2000.

Peterson, Robert A. *Hell on Trial*. Phillipsburg, NJ: P&R, 1995.

Poythress, Vern. *The Returning King: A Guide to the Book of Revelation*. Phillipsburg, NJ: P&R, 2000.

Schnabel, Eckhard. *40 Questions about the End Times*. Grand Rapids: Kregel, 2012.

12

THE
CHRISTIAN
LIFE

G od is not only the subject of our theology; he is the goal of it.[1] God's
Word communicates truth about God so that we know God, walk in
his ways, and in doing so, glorify God. The Bible portrays the Christian
life in various ways, referring to it as walking with God, holiness, obedience, discipleship, following Christ, life in the Spirit, worship, maturity,
and sanctification, to name a few. The biblical material is massive and
hard even to begin to summarize. J. I. Packer puts forward this vision for
the Christian life:

> I want to see a focused vision of spiritual maturity—the expan-
> sion of the soul is the best phrase I can use for it. That is, a
> renewed sense of the momentousness of being alive, the sheer
> bigness and awesomeness of being a human being alive in God's
> world with light, with grace, with wisdom, with responsibility,
> with biblical truth.[2]

D. A. Carson similarly calls for an "all-of-life approach" to the Christian
life—"every aspect of human existence, personal and corporate, brought

---

[1] See Packer, *Knowing God*, 13–19 (see chap. 4, n. 18).

[2] Wendy Murray Zoba, "Knowing Packer: The Lonely Journey of a Passionate
Puritan," *Christianity Today*, April 6, 1998: 40.

under the discipline of the Word of God, brought under the consciousness that we live in the presence of God, by his grace and for his glory."[3]

So, God calls us to walk with him, to live with "a renewed sense of the momentousness of being alive in God's world" as God's people led by God's Spirit through God's Word to godly, Christlike character—all for God's mission by God's grace and for God's glory.[4] To get a closer look at this, we briefly consider the Christian life in the biblical story, selected passages, and theology.

OUTLINE

---

[3] D. A. Carson, "When Is Spirituality Spiritual? Reflections on Some Problems of Definition," *Journal of the Evangelical Theological Society* 37, no. 3 (September 1994): 394.

[4] We rely on, condense, and rework here the more thorough treatment of Morgan and McLendon, "A Trajectory of Spirituality," in Morgan, *Biblical Spirituality*, 19–54 (see chap. 10, n. 11).

The Christian Life in the Biblical Story

We find our stories within the biblical story. Already in existence before matter, space, and time, God creates a good universe for the good of his creatures. God "creates, says, sees, separates, names, makes, appoints, blesses, finishes, makes holy, and rests."[5] The personal God creates humans in his image to know him, live in community with one other, and serve creation. God provides the garden of Eden as a place for them to live and work (Gen 2:4–25). God walks among them, establishes the terms for living in his presence, and sets only one prohibition: they shall not eat from the tree of the knowledge of good and evil.

Against this unspoiled backdrop, Genesis 3 recounts a tempter who calls into question God's truthfulness, sovereignty, and goodness. Sadly, Eve sees, takes, eats, and gives, and then Adam eats. The forbidden fruit does not deliver what the tempter promised but brings divine justice. The couple feels shame and senses their estrangement from God and one another. Even the blessings of fertility and work are now connected with pain and toil. Marked by death and banished from God's glorious presence, the couple no longer walks rightly with God.

Thankfully, sin is no match for God's grace, showcased in God's covenants, forming a people, giving the law, and ultimately in providing Christ's redeeming work. In the fullness of time, God the Son enters human history "to redeem those under the law, so that we might receive adoption as sons" (Gal 4:5). Jesus defeats sin through his substitutionary death and triumphs over death through his victorious resurrection. Christ's accomplishment is applied by the Spirit. In Christ, believers are blessed with new life, a right relationship with God, adoption into God's family, holiness before God, and an enduring hope.

This future hope becomes history when Christ returns. Believers will be resurrected, vindicated in the final judgment, and will live forever on the new earth. They will flourish in the kingdom of God, live in God's presence, and partake of God's glory—for all eternity.

---

[5] Collins, *Genesis 1–4*, 71 (see chap. 1, n. 8).

The Christian Life in Selected Passages

In the following passages Jesus brings the kingdom of God (his reign over his people), and even greater kingdom blessings await his return. In the Sermon on the Mount, Jesus outlines the ethic that is to characterize his kingdom's citizens. The Beatitudes focus on kingdom values, insisting that Jesus's people exhibit godly character qualities, not worldly ones. Jesus pronounces joy now and ultimate salvation to believers who know their spiritual poverty, repent, humble themselves, long for righteousness, show mercy, are inwardly pure, make peace, and suffer for his name. Jesus demands genuine, internal holiness and genuine worship, contrasts heavenly and earthly treasures, and promotes overflowing love. He tells his disciples that they are salt for a decaying world and light for a world shadowed by sin. After his resurrection, Jesus, Lord over all, issues the Great Commission, which centers on his command to makes disciples of all nations, including Gentiles. His disciples live in fellowship with Jesus and one another. He instructs them to baptize new disciples in the name of the Father, Son, and Holy Spirit. Making disciples also means faithfully passing on Jesus's teachings.

Paul teaches that love is more important than all the spiritual gifts and is the central focus of the Christian life. Paul describes love by its response to others in the church. Love is patient, enduring difficult people. It is kind and not jealous, wanting the best for others. Love is not self-promoting, but humble. It does not insist on its own way but focuses on blessing others. Love is neither irritable nor resentful but is long-suffering and forgiving. It endorses justice and truth. And love keeps on loving because people matter. James portrays God's Word as vital to the Christian life. God uses his Word in the lives of his people at the beginning, middle, and end of their faith (which becomes sight at death). The Christian life studies the Word, receives guidance from it, acts according to it, and perseveres in it. James warns that God's people must hear and integrate the Word into their lives. Therefore, people of the Word bridle their tongues, love the poor and the oppressed, and are committed to personal holiness.

Matthew 5:3–16

From the beginning of his public ministry, Jesus stresses the kingdom, God's reign over his people (Matt 4:17).[6] The kingdom comes into history in the person of Jesus and will ultimately "come at the end of the age in a mighty irruption into history inaugurating the perfect order of the age to come."[7] As the bearer of this kingdom, Jesus demands repentance, which involves rejecting the way of the world and embracing God's rule and way of life. Jesus also calls disciples, who follow him, walk alongside him, believe his teachings, embrace his way of life, and participate in his mission (4:17–19).

In the next chapter of Matthew's Gospel, Jesus begins the Sermon on the Mount, where he outlines the ethic that is to characterize his kingdom's citizens. The Beatitudes introduce the Sermon by focusing on kingdom values. Jesus's people must exhibit godly character qualities, not those of the world. Indeed, Jesus pronounces believers who are aware of their spiritual poverty, repent, humble themselves, long for righteousness, show mercy, are inwardly pure, make peace, and willingly suffer for his name as "blessed."

Jesus promises final salvation to all those whose lives are so characterized. He expresses final salvation in seven different ways:

- The kingdom of heaven belongs to them.
- God will comfort them.
- They will inherit the new earth.
- God will sanctify them fully.
- God will show them mercy.
- They will see God.
- God will call them his children.
- The kingdom of heaven belongs to them.

---

[6] For more on how spirituality, the church, and mission interrelate, see Chute and Morgan, "Missional Spirituality as Congregational," 75–95 (see chap. 10, n. 11).

[7] George Eldon Ladd, *The Presence of the Future*, rev. ed. (Grand Rapids: Eerdmans, 1974), 144–49.

These are not seven different things, but the same thing—ultimate salvation—epitomized by ownership of the kingdom (put first and last). In fact, although these blessings focus on the ultimate manifestation of the kingdom, they already have begun to bear fruit in believers' lives.

The remainder of the Sermon on the Mount develops the character of the citizens of the kingdom. Jesus calls for genuine, internal holiness, nurtured by the Word of God (Matt 5:17–48). He demands genuine worship, directed to our heavenly Father rather than to earthly audiences (6:1–18). Jesus insists on kingdom values, contrasting heavenly and earthly treasures (6:19–34). He promotes overflowing love, which rejects a judgmental spirit and follows the golden rule (Matthew 7). All of this shows Jesus's unflinching demands for discipleship.

Jesus is aware of two temptations that can easily befall his disciples—either contamination by or isolation from a sinful world that opposes his kingdom. Such errors misunderstand his sermon, for his way is that of infiltration, being in the world but not of it. Jesus teaches that character fuels mission, and he tells his disciples that they are the "salt of the earth" (5:13) and the "light of the world" (v. 14). The godly disciples are salt for a decaying world. And they are light for a world dark in sin.

Matthew 28:18–20

After his crucifixion and resurrection, Jesus issues the Great Commission. Jesus is the exalted Son, who is the Lord over all, both in heaven and on earth, including all nations (Matt 28:18; see also Dan 7:14). The universality of the commission is striking: Jesus has all authority, directs his people to make disciples of all nations, instructs them to teach all that he has commanded, and charges them to do so until the end of the age. The particularity of the commission is also striking: Jesus uniquely is Lord, he alone is worthy of worship by all nations, his teachings have binding authority, and his presence fortifies his followers for mission.

Jesus's command to makes disciples of all nations is the center of his Great Commission. Jesus calls his disciples to make other disciples, who also follow him and reflect his ways. His disciples live in community, in fellowship with Jesus and one another.[8] Making disciples of all nations expands the mission beyond Israel to all Gentiles (Gen 12:3; Rev 5:9–10).

Jesus's command to make disciples is expanded by three participles: going, baptizing, and teaching. Disciples must go, since they can only make other disciples of all nations if they go to people who do not yet know Jesus. Jesus's community baptizes these new disciples in the name of the Father, Son, and Holy Spirit (Matt 28:19). Through baptism, they publicly identify with Christ as Lord, with one another in Jesus's kingdom community, and—amazingly—even with the entire Trinity. Making disciples of all nations also includes "teaching them to observe everything I have commanded you" (v. 20). Jesus's disciples do not make their own disciples but faithfully pass on the teachings of Jesus the Teacher. Both disciplers and new disciples must believe and practice Jesus's teachings.

1 Corinthians 13:1–7

In treating spiritual gifts, Paul points to his readers' highest spiritual aspirations and then turns the tables on them. To experience spiritual gifts beyond measure, to have faith that leads to miracles, to know truth as exhaustively as it can be known, to give everything to the poor, or to be willing to die as a martyr—to reach all of these without "hav[ing] love" is worthless: "I am nothing" (1 Cor 13:2); "I gain nothing" (v. 3). Radical devotion without love is worthless.

Paul then points to the central focus of the Christian life: love. He does not so much define love as describe and personify it as someone who thinks and acts. Addressing real-life problems in the Corinthian church, Paul warns that their approach to religion is warped, and he portrays love as what is "central, characteristic, and irreplaceable in biblical Christianity."[9]

---

[8] Schnabel, *Early Christian Mission*, 1:353–56 (see chap. 10, n. 13).

[9] D. A. Carson, *Showing the Spirit: A Theological Exposition of 1 Corinthians 12–14* (Grand Rapids: Baker, 1987), 66.

Paul describes love by its response to others in the church. Love is patient, enduring difficult people. Love is kind and not jealous, since it wants the best for others. Love is not self-promoting or proud, but humble and servant-oriented. Love is pure, clean, and holy. Love does not insist on its own way but focuses on how to generously bless others. Love is neither irritable nor resentful but is long-suffering and forgiving. Love advocates for justice and endorses truth. Love bears, believes, and hopes, refusing to be suspicious, cynical, or pessimistic about others. And love keeps on loving, persevering in relationships because people matter.

In the context of frustrating circumstances and people, love appears as patience. In the context of the successes of others, love does not allow envy but rejoices with those who rejoice. In the context of one's own successes, love refrains from self-promotion and practices humility. In the context of the sin of another, love appears as forgiveness and not keeping track of wrongs. In each case, love genuinely desires the good of others and serves them for their good.

James 1:18–27

Voices from the Global Church: René Padilla

Padilla from Ecuador wrote, "A church without social ethics rooted in the moral vision of the Scripture with its emphasis on justice, mercy, and humility before God is in no condition to avoid irrelevance in relation to the great problems that affect humankind. At best it will concentrate on empty ritualism and private morality, but will remain indifferent to the plight of the poor and the rape of God's creation. At worst it will fail to recognize its own captivity to the culture-ideology of consumerism."[10]

James highlights God's Word as central to the Christian life (1:18–25). Just as God's word is his agency throughout the story of creation, redemption,

---

[10] René Padilla, "The Biblical Basis for Social Ethics," *Transforming the World? The Gospel and Social Responsibility*, ed. Jamie A. Grant and Dewi A. Hughes (Nottingham: InterVarsity Press, 2009), 191.

and the new creation, God uses his written Word holistically in the lives of his people at the beginning, middle, and end of their faith (that is, just before it becomes sight). Through his authoritative and powerful Word, God births believers into a new creation and brings about their final salvation. Because of this, they are to be quick to "listen" to the Word (v. 19), to lay aside sin to receive it with meekness, and to hear and do it. Those who do the Word will be blessed in their doing. The Christian life is thus Word-driven, Word-saturated, and Word-centric, as the committed Christian studies the Word, receives guidance from the Word, acts according to the Word, and perseveres in the Word, and is blessed by God accordingly.

James warns that the Christian life is more than hearing the Word. God's people must also integrate the Word into their daily lives (vv. 22–27). Indeed, people of the Word bridle their tongues (v. 26 ESV). They love those whom God loves—the poor and the oppressed (v. 27). People of the Word are committed to personal holiness. Such religion is "pure," "undefiled," and acceptable to God. Some in the churches to which James writes are more concerned with ritual purity than with moral purity, and utter empty words without active compassion for the oppressed. By stressing that God accepts true worship, James implies that God rejects their false approaches, even calling their worship "worthless." Such worship is worthless because it does not show love for God or others. Indeed, it is worthless because it does not show love for God *through* love for others.

True religion is "to look after orphans and widows in their distress" (v. 27). James reflects Exod 22:22: "You must not mistreat any widow or fatherless child," as well as Isa 1:17: "Defend the rights of the fatherless. Plead the widow's cause." He also clarifies God's requirements for acceptable religion and worship (see Deut 10:16–19). Together, widows and orphans represent those without protection or provision. Daniel Doriani notes, "Kindness to the needy is God-like. *We* sustain aliens, widows, and orphans because *he* sustains aliens, widows, and orphans (Ps. 146:9)."[11] The Christian life is integrated, receiving the Word and obeying

---

[11] Daniel M. Doriani, *James*, REC (Phillipsburg, NJ: P&R, 2007), 59, italics in original.

the Word, and it reflects God's holiness and love by ministering to the poor and oppressed.

"Already" and "Not Yet": Our Tensions in the Christian Life

Voices from the Global Church: Dieumeme Noelliste

Noelliste from Jamaica wrote, "Biblically, ethics is shaped and motivated by what God has done in Christ and what he promises to do in the future. The new age longed for in the Old Testament has dawned in Jesus, but it has not yet been brought to full completion. Biblical ethics, then, is really an interim ethics: it is for those who live between the times (Titus 2:11–14; 2 Pet. 3:13–14)."[12]

All journeys have a beginning, and the Christian life begins with the new birth (John 3:1–7). To be born again means to receive new life in Christ and "is a work of God's grace whereby believers become new creatures in Christ Jesus. It is a change of heart wrought by the Holy Spirit through conviction of sin, to which the sinner responds in repentance toward God and faith in the Lord Jesus Christ. Repentance and faith are inseparable experiences of grace."[13]

With repentance from sin and faith in Christ come our justification, in which God, through the sinless life, substitutionary death, and bodily resurrection of Christ, forgives us of our sin, grants Christ's righteousness to us, judicially declares us righteous, and adopts us into his family. Our new life also leads us to a new way of life: sanctification. In our initial sanctification, the Spirit has already set us apart from sin for holiness as saints. Final sanctification is not yet realized, and we are currently experiencing progressive sanctification. We live in between the "already" and the "not yet" of our salvation, and this causes us to experience the tensions of

---

[12] Dieumeme Noelliste, "Biblical Ethics: An Introduction," in *ESV Global Study Bible*, 1893 (see chap. 2, n. 35).

[13] See "Salvation," in the Baptist Faith and Message 2000 at http://www.sbc.net/bfm2000/bfm2000.asp.

living in the meantime. We are works in progress, still under construction, on the path to spiritual maturity.

The Holy Spirit: Our Power for the Christian Life

The Holy Spirit not only joins us to Christ, he also empowers us to live for God. The New Testament portrays the power for Christian living in three ways, and all are related to our union with Christ and the work of the Spirit. First, it simply calls it "power." Paul prays for the Ephesians to know the "immeasurable greatness of his power toward us who believe" (Eph 1:19). He extols this power as that which raised Christ from the dead and that he now exercises at God's right hand, above all things and with everything under his feet (vv. 19–23). A second way is to speak of enabling grace, which we will treat later.

A third way is to speak of the power of the Holy Spirit. The New Testament often associates the Spirit with God's power. The same Spirit who empowers Jesus in his earthly ministry (Acts 10:38) also works as he makes atonement (Heb 9:14). The same Spirit who raises Jesus from the dead (Rom 1:4) strengthens us to live for him. The empowering Spirit works within to grant spiritual gifts to us (1 Cor 12:11), enabling us to grow in holiness (Rom 8:13), to "overflow with hope" (15:13), and to gain strength and encouragement (Eph 3:16). The Spirit also works outside of us to deliver us from difficult circumstances (Phil 1:19), empower us for witness (Acts 1:8), and produce fruit from our evangelism (Rom 15:18–19).

The Spirit empowers us to walk with God. Each of us can say with Paul, "I labor . . . , striving with his strength that works powerfully in me" (Col 1:29).

Christlikeness: Our Goal for the Christian Life

The Spirit is at work in and through us to form us into people who reflect God's character and ways. Christlikeness, or godliness, is the goal: "Train yourself in godliness" (1 Tim 4:7). Romans 8:29 stresses that God's purpose is to conform us to the image of his Son. Second Corinthians 3:18

elaborates that as we behold the glory of the Lord, we "are being transformed into the same image from glory to glory."

Such Christlikeness is practical. God's grace teaches us to "deny godlessness and worldly lusts" and to pursue life "in a sensible, righteous, and godly way" as we await the "appearing of the glory of our great God and Savior, Jesus Christ" (Titus 2:11–13).

Christlikeness is also personal. "The fruit of the Spirit is love, joy, peace, patience, kindness, goodness, faithfulness, gentleness, and self-control" (Gal 5:22–23). In Christ each of our lives is increasingly characterized by his character and life.

Christlikeness is also communal. As the church, we are the community of God's kingdom living in the "already" and "not yet." We display God and the realities of the new creation. We are currently marked by godliness—goodness, unity, holiness, truth, and love—and we increasingly pursue godliness.

Love: Our Focus in the Christian Life

Voices from Church History: Jonathan Edwards

Edwards (1703–1758), an American preacher, philosopher, and theologian, was vital to the First Great Awakening. He penned many books, including *The End For Which God Created the World*; *The Life of David Brainerd*, which inspired thousands of missionaries; and *Religious Affections*, still read today. He wrote,

> Selfishness is a principle that contracts the heart and confines it to the self, while love enlarges it and extends it to others. By love, a man's self is so extended and enlarged that others, so far as they are beloved, do, as it were, become parts of himself so that, wherein their interest is promoted, he believes his own is promoted; and wherein theirs is injured, his is also injured. . . . [Christian love] does not spring out of self, so neither does it tend to self. It delights in the honor and glory of God for His own sake, and not merely for the sake of self; and it seeks and delights in the good of men for their sake and for God's sake. . . . But if you do not selfishly seek your own, but do seek the things that are

Jesus Christ's, and the things of your own fellow-beings, then God will make your interest and happiness His own charge; and He is infinitely more able to provide for and promote it than you are.[14]

Quoting the Old Testament, Jesus crystallizes the focus of the Christian life: "Love the Lord your God with all your heart, with all your soul, and with all your mind. This is the greatest and most important command. The second is like it: Love your neighbor as yourself. All the Law and the Prophets depend on these two commands" (Matt 22:37–40). Love for God and others are the highest commands and shape the biblical revelation.

Paul also exalts love as the pinnacle of true spirituality in 1 Corinthians 13, a passage we previously treated. Love desires the good of others and gives for their sake. Love is integrated with and at the core of other Christian virtues: patience, mercy, humility, holiness, justice, and truth. Jonathan Edwards synthesizes: "[Love] is the root and spring and, as it were, a comprehension of all virtues. It is a principle that, if implanted in the heart, is alone sufficient to produce all good practice; and every right disposition toward God and man is summed up in it and comes from it, as the fruit from the tree or stream from the fountain."[15] Edwards elaborates:

> The graces of Christianity are all connected together, and are mutually dependent on each other. . . .
>
> They so go together that where there is one, there are all. . . . Where there is faith, there are love, hope, and humility; and where there is love, there is trust; and where there is a holy trust in God, there is love for God. . . . Where there is love for God, there is a gracious love for man; and where there is a Christian love for man, there is love for God. . . .

---

[14] Jonathan Edwards, *Charity and Its Fruits* (repr., Orlando: Soli Deo Gloria, 2005), 149, 151, 159.

[15] Edwards, 9.

> [T]he graces of Christianity depend on one another. . . . [T]here is also a mutual dependence between them, so that one cannot be without the other. . . . Faith promotes love. . . . Then again, love enlarges and promotes faith. . . . So love promotes humility. . . . Humility promotes love. . . . Love tends to repentance. . . . And repentance tends to humility. . . . A true love for God tends to love for men who bear the image of God.[16]

Therefore, our focus on love does not divert our attention from other Christian virtues but actually fosters them.

The Church: Our Community for the Christian Life

God loves us and transforms us into people of love. His love extends to us and leads us to love him and others (1 John 4:7–12). God's love has ripple effects, as our love extends to others, through them to still others, and back to us as well. On and on it goes, as the God-glorifying process of his self-giving love spirals in and through his church.

As such, the church is our community of love, our community for the Christian life. Ephesians helps us see that as the church, we are one new people, called to display God to the world.[17] We are the new creation in the image of God, called to reflect Christ and embody God's character (2:14–16). As the church, we are composed of believers who were alienated from God and, through the saving work of Christ, have been united to Christ and reconciled to one another (vv. 4–22). As the church, we showcase God's eternal purpose of cosmic unity to the world; we demonstrate that the kingdom of God has already broken into history (3:9–12; 1:9–11). God will bring about a new creation, and he is already doing so in the church. As the firstfruits of the ultimate new creation, the church is both the genuine reality of the new creation and the foretaste of more to come.

---

[16] Edwards, 237–40. For more on love, see Christopher W. Morgan, ed., *The Love of God*, vol. 7 of Theology in Community (Wheaton, IL: Crossway, 2016).

[17] For more on the church, see Morgan, "The Church and God's Glory," in *The Community of Jesus*, 213–35 (see chap. 4, n. 4).

As the church, we are the new humanity, new society, new temple—a new creation. We are a foretaste of heaven on earth, a genuine embodiment of the kingdom, a glimpse of the way things are supposed to be, and a glimpse of the way the cosmos will be. In sum, we are a showcase of God's eternal plan of cosmic unity.

Our unity is grounded in God's unity: there is one God, one Lord, one Spirit, one body, one faith, and one baptism (Eph 4:4–6). Unity is also a goal we pursue. As the one body of Christ, we are to be eager to maintain unity amid real diversity (vv. 3–7). God has given the church apostles, prophets, evangelists, pastors, and teachers (v. 11). He gives people to the church, and he gives the church to people. We are given gifts to serve others, and others are given gifts to serve others, including us. As we serve, others grow and we grow. And as others serve, we all grow.

Our life together as the church is guided by our union with Christ: "We are members of one another" (Eph 4:25). Because we are linked together as the community of Jesus, we refuse to nurse anger but speak and live truthfully with each other (vv. 25–27). We refuse to steal but instead work hard so that we can share with others in the body who have need (v. 28). We choose our words carefully because we realize that God gives grace to others through our words (v. 29). We put away bitterness, anger, and slander, and put on kindness, tenderness, forgiveness, and love (vv. 31–32). Life together is maintained by our love for Christ and one another, in which we embrace Jesus's people as our own (4:32–5:2). By the grace of God, he gives us a community for the Christian life: the church.[18]

Ordinary Life: Our Context for the Christian Life

While the church is our community for the Christian life, our context for walking with God is ordinary life. Our Christian walk is normally cultivated in and manifests itself in our physical bodies, our rhythms of sleep and rest, our work, our roles as wives and husbands, our roles as children

---

[18] See Bonhoeffer, *Life Together and Prayerbook of the Bible*, 30–38 (see chap. 10, n. 23).

and parents, and more (Eph 4:1–6:9). The context is seldom a spiritual retreat center. More often, it includes loving our families, working hard to serve others, paying the bills with integrity, and forgiving our neighbors.

Such matters seem too ordinary to be significant, too commonplace to be the context of our faith. But ordinary life is where we live out our faith. Combating the tendency to sequester Jesus into Sunday mornings, quiet times, and mission trips requires a robust commitment to the lordship of Christ in all of life. As Vern Poythress states, "If he is Lord of all, he is Lord over business and work and education and science and home life."[19]

The Christian life is an embodied one. We are on-the-ground expressions of God's ongoing work in us, and ordinary life provides the context and opportunities to show our faith (Rom 12:1–2; Col 3:1–4:6). Martin Luther frequently stressed this point. Luther complained that believers should not live in monasteries to serve God, for there they are largely serving themselves. Instead, we follow Christ and love and serve our neighbors through our vocations in the world, where our neighbors encounter and need us. Luther argued, "God does not need our good works, but our neighbor does."[20] The ordinary is spiritual, and it serves as the primary context of our Christian faith.

Indwelling Sin/Temptation:
Our Obstacles in the Christian Life

Ordinary life, as the context of our faith, is filled with blessings. God's goodness shines in the beauty of sunsets, snowcapped mountains, and a daughter's smile. But ordinary life is also filled with more danger than we think, as David Calhoun cautions: "The world entices us to fit in with, to adjust to, to experiment with, its values."[21]

---

[19] Vern Poythress, *The Lordship of Christ* (Wheaton, IL: Crossway, 2016), 31.

[20] Gustav Wingren, *Luther on Vocation*, trans. Carl C. Rasmussen (Philadelphia: Muhlenberg, 1957; repr., Evansville, IN: Ballast, 2004), 2. We were helped in this section by Michael S. Horton, *People and Place: A Covenant Ecclesiology* (Louisville: Westminster John Knox, 2008), 304.

[21] David B. Calhoun, "Sin and Temptation," in *Fallen*, 253 (see chap. 5, n. 26).

Ephesians relates three opponent forces at work (2:2–3). Prior to salvation we were under the domain of two external forces: the course of the world and Satan. And we were under an internal force working with these external forces: our dark hearts. Thankfully, God intervened and saved us by his grace for holiness; thus, we are "created in Christ Jesus for good works, which God prepared ahead of time for us to do" (v. 10). This call to holiness requires that we battle against those forces that held our former allegiance (6:10–18). We know who we once were, and we now fight against indwelling sin that still entangles us (Rom 6:1–14; Heb 12:1–2). We long to put off the old self and put on the new (Eph 4:17–24), desiring holiness, knowing that it is God's will for us (1 Thess 4:3).

This process of putting off sin/putting on godliness is continual. Because of this, James urges perseverance and cautions us about the nature of temptation: God does not tempt us, but external temptation stirs our internal desire, and this lust leads to sin, which leads to death (Jas 1:13–18; see also Proverbs 5; 7). Sin deceives, entices, conceives, develops, and kills.[22] Temptation is effective because it masks sin's danger. To discover temptation's source, we should look within—at our evil desires.[23] God is holy and never the source of temptations. God is for us. He is the source of "every good and perfect gift," including our holiness (Jas 1:17). God enables us to fight sin, confess it, repent of it, and walk in holiness.

"Victory over temptation is not gained in the moment of temptation," Calhoun advises. "It is won in the daily living of our redeemed lives. It is won as we 'make every effort to supplement [our] faith with virtue, and virtue with knowledge, and knowledge with self-control, and self-control with steadfastness, and steadfastness with godliness, and godliness with brotherly affection, and brotherly affection with love' (2 Pet. 1:5–7)."[24]

---

[22] John Owen, "Indwelling Sin," in *Overcoming Sin and Temptation*, 295–96 (see chap. 9, n. 16).

[23] For more on Jas 1:12–18 and temptation, see Christopher W. Morgan and B. Dale Ellenburg, *James: Wisdom for the Community*, Focus on the Bible Commentaries (Fearn, UK: Christian Focus, 2008), 59–73.

[24] Calhoun, "Sin and Temptation," 258.

Word, Prayer, and Church:
Our Means for the Christian Life

Paul's language of putting off and putting on suggests actions we must take to fight against the lure of sin. The Bible offers no shortcuts to holiness. Instead, we are encouraged repeatedly to give ourselves to the time-honored means of Bible reading and meditation (Ps 1:2), prayer (Phil 4:6), worship (Eph 5:18–20), witnessing (Matt 28:19–20), fellowship (Heb 10:24–25), and self-control (Gal 5:23). Cruise control is a wonderful technology in our cars, but there is no such option in the journey of the Christian life. We will not coast into godliness; our exertion is required. "Train yourself in godliness" (1 Tim 4:7), writes Paul.

In his *Spiritual Disciplines for the Christian Life,* Donald Whitney appropriately begins his analysis with two chapters on Bible intake, stating, "No spiritual discipline is more important than the intake of God's Word. Nothing can substitute for it. There simply is no healthy Christian life apart from a diet of the milk and meat of Scripture."[25] Biblical intake includes reading, meditating on, and carefully studying God's Word.

Scripture also teaches us the importance of prayer for our growth in godliness. We offer prayers of praise, thanks, confession, intercession, petition, and more. Our praying is a practice that encompasses all seasons, and it is a pursuit that requires our commitment and concentration.

God also uses the church to mature us, as we previously discussed. In sum, God is not only the source, power, and goal of our holiness; he also gives us the means by which we grow and help others to grow.

Reproducing Disciples:
Our Mission in the Christian Life

Our lives are not about us but others. Jesus clarifies the Christian life, which includes being a disciple and making disciples. Jesus's call, "Follow

---

[25] We were helped in this section by Donald S. Whitney, *Spiritual Disciplines for the Christian Life* (Colorado Springs: NavPress, 1991), 24. See also his *Praying the Bible* (Wheaton, IL: Crossway, 2015).

me, and I will make you fish for people" (Matt 4:19), reveals that part of being his disciple is following him. And inherent in following Jesus is becoming "fishers for people" and thus participants in his own mission. From the beginning of Jesus's ministry, "discipleship and mission are inseparably linked."[26] As his disciples, we are called and sent—called to follow the way of the kingdom and sent to call others to do the same.

Jesus also describes us as the "salt of the earth" (5:13) and the "light of the world" (5:14). These images build on the Beatitudes, in which Jesus associates God's kingdom not with human strength and honor but with our spiritual poverty, crying, meekness, hunger, mercy, peace, and persecution. Such distinctive living undergirds our mission as salt and light.

What Jesus teaches in Matt 4:17 and 5:3–16, he spells out more directly in 28:18–20: our mission is reproducing disciples. As previously said, in Jesus's Great Commission he commands us to make disciples of all nations. He calls his disciples to make other disciples, who are also expected to follow Jesus, listen to his teaching, and reflect his ways. This is our mission: the intentional "multiplication of other faithful followers of the King among the nations."[27]

The Grace Of God: Our Encouragement in the Christian Life

The grace of God begins our salvation (Eph 2:1–10; Titus 3:4–7), and the grace of God will complete our salvation (Phil 1:6; Rom 8:18–39; 1 Pet 1:3–5). In the meantime, the grace of God provides encouragement for our journeys. Charles Spurgeon says it well: "Between here and heaven, every minute that the Christian lives will be a minute of grace."[28]

When we are in need, God's grace gives us boldness: "Therefore, let us approach the throne of grace with boldness, so that we may receive

---

[26] Schnabel, *Early Christian Mission*, 1:272–79.

[27] Lewis, "God's Great Commissions for the Nations," in Barnett and Martin, eds., *Discovering the Mission of God*, 104 (see chap. 10, n. 42).

[28] Charles Haddon Spurgeon, "The Tenses" (no. 2718), sermon preached May 13, 1880, accessed November 27, 2017, https://www.ccel.org/ccel/spurgeon /sermons47.xi.html.

mercy and find grace to help us in time of need" (Heb 4:16). When we are in sin, God's grace fosters our repentance and promotes our holiness: "The grace of God has appeared, bringing salvation for all people, instructing us to deny godlessness and worldly lusts, and to live in a sensible, righteous, and godly way in the present age" (Titus 2:11–12).

When we need strength to keep on serving God, God's grace enables us, as Paul testifies: "I worked harder than any of them, yet not I, but the grace of God that was with me" (1 Cor 15:10). When we are tired and weak, God's grace fortifies us, as Paul attests: "[God's] grace is sufficient for you, for [his] power is perfected in weakness" (2 Cor 12:9). When we forget our security in Christ, God's grace reminds us that we will "persevere in holiness because God perseveres in grace."[29]

The Glory of God:
Our Ultimate End of the Christian Life

What is the ultimate end of the Christian life? Since God is the source, power, goal, means, and encouragement for the Christian life, it is no surprise that God's glory is its ultimate end.

Ephesians is helpful here. From the outset, Paul establishes that God's ultimate end is his glory, and he praises God for his comprehensive blessings of salvation. In his praise, Paul highlights the work of the Trinity in salvation (1:3–14) and explicitly incorporates a refrain: "to the praise of his glorious grace" (v. 6), and to the "praise" of "his glory" (vv. 12, 14). Paul's point is unmistakable: the ultimate end of our salvation is not our salvation, as important as that is. God chooses, redeems, adopts, unites, and seals us to the praise of his glory.

Paul continues this emphasis in Ephesians 2. Because of his love and grace, God makes us alive in Christ "so that in the coming ages he might display the immeasurable riches of his grace through his kindness to us in Christ Jesus" (v. 7). That God's glory is his ultimate end is also clear in Ephesians 3, where Paul stresses that his salvation, apostolic calling, and

---

[29] Charles Haddon Spurgeon, *All of Grace*, Read and Reflect with the Classics (repr., Nashville: B&H, 2017), 162.

mission to the Gentiles have as their ultimate end the glorious display of God and his wisdom. The doxology continues this theme: "Now to him who is able to do above and beyond all that we ask or think according to the power that works in us—to him be glory in the church and in Christ Jesus to all generations, forever and ever. Amen" (vv. 20–21). The prayer and praise of the church focuses on God receiving glory for all eternity.

God's glory is his ultimate end.[30] But what does this mean? Two aspects stand out in Ephesians. First, God acts to further the praise of his glory (1:6, 12, 14). Second, God acts to display himself throughout creation, revealing his love, mercy, grace, kindness, and wisdom (2:4–10; 3:8–10). That in and of itself glorifies him. So, according to Ephesians, God's glory as his ultimate end means that he acts to receive worship and acts to show himself and communicate his greatness.

Remarkably, both aspects of God's glory as ultimate end relate directly to our identity and purpose as human beings created in the image of God. Sinclair Ferguson explains:

> In Scripture, image and glory are interrelated ideas. As the image of God, man was created to reflect, express and participate in the glory of God, in miniature, creaturely form. Restoration to this is effected through the Spirit's work of sanctification, in which he takes those who have distorted God's image in the shame of sin, and transforms them into those who bear that image in glory. . . .
>
> The mark we were created to reach, but have missed, was glory. We have sinned and failed to attain that destiny. Against this background, the task of the Spirit may be stated simply: to bring us to glory, to create glory within us, and to glorify us together with Christ. The startling significance of this might be plainer if we expressed it thus: the Spirit is given to glorify us; not just to "add" glory as a crown to what we are, but actually to transform the very constitution of our being so that we become glorious.

---

[30] See Edwards, "The End for Which God Created the World," 125–36 (see chap. 4, n. 27). See also Morgan, "Toward a Theology of the Glory of God," 153–87 (see chap. 4, n. 23).

In the New Testament, this glorification is seen to begin already in the present order, in believers. Through the Spirit they are already being changed from glory to glory, as they gaze on/reflect the face of the Lord (2 Cor. 3:17–18). But the consummation of this glorification awaits the eschaton and the Spirit's ministry in the resurrection. Here, too, the pattern of his working is: as in Christ, so in believers and, by implication, in the universe. . . .

The image and image-bearers are one in Spirit to the end, so that when Christ appears in glory image-bearers are one with him in that glory (Col. 3:4). We are raised in Christ, with Christ, by Christ, to be like Christ.[31]

In other words, we were created to be worshippers of God and the display people of God, but we all refused to acknowledge God's glory and instead sought our own glory. Through this we forfeited the glory God intended for us as his image bearers. By his grace and through union with Christ, the perfect image, however, God restores us as full image bearers to participate in and reflect the glory we longed for the whole time. Thus, we are recipients of glory, are undergoing transformation in glory, and will be sharers of glory. Our salvation is not merely from sin but is also to glory. We who exchanged the glory of God for idols, we who rebelled against God's glory, have been, are being, and will be completely transformed by the very glory we despised and rejected (Rom 1:18–31; 3:23; 8:28–30; 2 Cor 3:18). And through union with Christ, together we are the church, the new humanity, bearing God's image, displaying how life ought to be, and making known the manifold wisdom of God.

Even more, we are a part of something far bigger than ourselves. We are a part of the story of the glorious God who graciously and joyfully communicates his fullness, chiefly through his creation, image bearers, providence, and redemptive acts. As his people we respond by glorifying him, and in this God receives glory. Further, through uniting us to the glorious Christ, the perfect image of God, God transforms us and shares his glory with us. All of this redounds to his glory, as God in his

---

[31] Ferguson, *The Holy Spirit*, 139–40, 249, 251 (see chap. 8, n. 37).

manifold perfections is exhibited, known, rejoiced in, and prized. Our entire salvation is from God, through God, and to God. He is the beginning, middle, and end of the Christian life. No wonder Paul exclaims, "From him and through him and to him are all things. To him be the glory forever" (Rom 11:36).

◼ KEY TERMS

"already" and "not yet"

Christ's example

Christlikeness

church and churches

devil, the

discipleship

evil desires

faith

faithfulness

flesh, the

forgiveness of sins

gentleness

glory of God

godliness

golden rule, the

goodness

grace of God

Great Commission, the

holiness

Holy Spirit

humility

indwelling sin

joy

kingdom of God

lordship of Christ

love

meditation

mission

obedience

patience

peace

persecution

perseverance

poor, the

praise

prayer

reconciliation with others

repentance

righteousness

sanctification

Satan

social justice

spiritual disciplines

spirituality

temptation

truth

virtues, Christian

walking in the Spirit

Word of God

world, the

worship

RESOURCES FOR FURTHER STUDY

Chapell, Bryan. *Holiness by Grace: Delighting in the Joy That Is Our Strength*. Wheaton, IL: Crossway, 2001.

Edwards, Jonathan. *Charity and Its Fruits*. Carlisle, PA: Banner of Truth, 1969.

Finn, Nathan A., and Keith Whitfield, eds. *Spirituality for the Sent: Casting a New Vision for the Missional Church*. Downers Grove, IL: IVP Academic, 2017.

Keller, Timothy, with Katherine Leary Alsdorf. *Every Good Endeavor: Connecting Your Work to God's Work*. New York: Riverhead, 2012.

Morgan, Christopher W., ed. *Biblical Spirituality*. Vol. 8 of Theology in Community. Wheaton, IL: Crossway, 2019.

Owen, John. *Overcoming Sin and Temptation*. Kelly M. Kapic and Justin Taylor, eds. Wheaton, IL: Crossway, 2006.

Packer, J. I. *A Quest for Godliness: The Puritan Vision of the Christian Life*. Wheaton, IL: Crossway, 1990.

———. *Rediscovering Holiness: Know the Fullness of Life with God*. Ventura, CA: Regal, 2009.

Peterson, David. *Possessed by God: A New Testament Theology of Sanctification and Holiness*. New Studies in Biblical Theology. Downers Grove, IL: InterVarsity, 1995.

Piper, John. *Desiring God: Meditations of a Christian Hedonist*. Revised edition. Colorado Springs, CO: Multnomah, 2004.

Poythress, Vern. *The Lordship of Christ: Serving Our Savior All of the Time, in All of Life, with All of Our Heart*. Wheaton, IL: Crossway, 2016.

Tidball, Derek. *The Message of Holiness*. The Bible Speaks Today. Downers Grove, IL: InterVarsity, 2010.

Whitney, Donald S. *Praying the Bible*. Wheaton, IL: Crossway, 2015.

———. *Spiritual Disciplines for the Christian Life*. Colorado Springs, CO: NavPress, 1991.

Wright, Christopher J. H. *Old Testament Ethics for the People of God*. Downers Grove, IL: InterVarsity, 2004.

NAME INDEX

SUBJECT INDEX

SCRIPTURE INDEX

587